Get the eBook FREE!

(PDF, ePub, Kindle, and liveBook all included)

We believe that once you buy a book from us, you should be able to read it in any format we have available. To get electronic versions of this book at no additional cost to you, purchase and then register this book at the Manning website.

Go to https://www.manning.com/freebook and follow the instructions to complete your pBook registration.

That's it!
Thanks from Manning!

Praise for the Third Edition

Naomi's book epitomizes what it is to be Pythonic: beautiful is better than ugly, simple is better than complex, and readability counts.

—From the Foreword by Nicholas Tollervey, Python Software Foundation

Leads you from a basic knowledge of Python to its most interesting features, always using accessible language.

— Eros Pedrini, everis

Unleash your Pythonic powers with this book and start coding real-world applications fast.

— Carlos Fernandez Manzano, Aguas de Murcia

The complete and definitive book to start learning Python.

— Christos Paisios, e-Travel

Excellent starter for beginners in Python.

—Ruslan Vidert, Yandex

When time is precious, this is THE book to learn Python quickly and efficiently.

— Aaron Jensen, Shoot the Moon Products

This book is concise yet comprehensive and provides the tools to quickly solve real-world problems using Python!

—Negmat Mullodzhanov, Wavemaker

The definitive place to start introducing you to code on Python!

—Felipe E. Vildoso-Castillo, University of Chile

The Quick Python Book, Fourth Edition

NAOMI CEDER

FOREWORD BY LUCIANO RAMALHO

MANNING
SHELTER ISLAND

For online information and ordering of this and other Manning books, please visit www.manning.com. The publisher offers discounts on this book when ordered in quantity.

For more information, please contact

    Special Sales Department
    Manning Publications Co.
    20 Baldwin Road
    PO Box 761
    Shelter Island, NY 11964
    Email: orders@manning.com

Manning Publications Co.	Development editor:	Doug Rudder
20 Baldwin Road	Technical editor:	Kenneth W. Alger
PO Box 761	Review editor:	Dunja Nikitović
Shelter Island, NY 11964	Production editor:	Kathy Rossland
	Copy editor:	Kari Lucke
	Proofreader:	Katie Tennant
	Typesetter:	Tamara Švelić Sabljić
	Cover designer:	Marija Tudor

ISBN 9781633436336
Printed in the United States of America

To my friends past, present, and future in the global Python community,
with gratitude for your love, acceptance, and support

contents

foreword

I read the first edition of *The Quick Python Book* by Daryl Harms and Kenneth McDonald in late 1999. At the time there were only a handful of books about Python, and I believe I had them all. *The Quick Python Book* was the best book-length Python tutorial in the market. It offered a gentle learning curve and lots of practical advice, and it went beyond small snippets to discuss how to organize complete Python modules and programs.

All the qualities I mentioned remain, enhanced by new examples and insights by Naomi Ceder, who took over as the main author in the second edition.

The most important quality of *The Quick Python Book* has always been the practical context around the technical details. The labs at the end of the chapters and the chapter-length case study are about the creation and evolution of complete, useful programs.

In this fourth edition, Naomi complemented coverage of new Python features with two major changes. The first is using interactive notebooks on Google's Colaboratory. That allows readers to jump right into coding and experimenting without installing anything on their computers. It also helps them get comfortable with the most popular coding environment for data science and AI: Jupyter notebooks.

The second major change is in the labs. Naomi now compares her solutions with AI-generated code by the Colaboratory and GitHub Copilot. She shows the pros and cons of using those AI assistants, discusses their effects on the coding workflow, and advises on how to write prompts to get the best results.

Updating and improving this excellent book over the last 15 years is only one of Naomi's many contributions to Python. She has devoted countless hours of volunteer time to the Python Software Foundation and the wider Python international community.

Thousands of Python books later, this is still the best book-length Python tutorial that I know about. Thank you, Naomi, for keeping it fresh and ever more relevant in the 21st century!

—LUCIANO RAMALHO
PYTHONISTA SINCE 1998 AND AUTHOR OF *FLUENT PYTHON*

preface

Since I wrote the third edition of this book, more than five years have passed, and in that time we've been through some changes—including a pandemic and various crises but also the continued growth of data science and machine learning, the rise of AI-assisted code (AI everything, it seems), and of course the continued growth of Python, which is now one of the most used coding languages on the planet.

I've been coding in Python for almost 25 years now, far longer than in any other language I've ever used. I've used Python for system administration, web applications, database management, and data analysis over those years, but most important, I've come to use Python just to help myself think about a problem more clearly.

Based on my earlier experience, I would have expected that by now I would have been lured away by some other language that was faster, cooler, sexier, whatever. I think there are two reasons that didn't happen. First, while other languages have come along, none has helped me do what I needed to do quite as effectively as Python. Even after all these years, the more I use Python and the more I understand it, the more I feel the quality of my programming improves and matures.

The second reason I'm still around is the Python community. It's one of the most welcoming, inclusive, active, and friendly communities I've seen, embracing scientists, quants, web developers, systems people, and data scientists on every continent. It's been a joy and honor to work with members of this community, and I encourage everyone to join in.

Writing this book has shown me again how time passes and things change. While we're still on Python 3, today's Python 3 has evolved considerably even from the Python 3.6 of the last edition of this book. Things that were never dreamed of are now features of the language, and even the old nemesis of multicore processing, the GIL, is on the verge of workable solutions.

As the language has changed, so too have the ways people use Python. Although my goal has always been to keep the best bits of the previous edition, there have been a fair number of additions, deletions, and reorganizations that I hope make this edition both useful and timely. I've tried to keep the style clear, low-key, and also accessible to the many Python coders around the world whose first language is not English.

For me, the aim of this book is to share the positive experiences I've gotten from coding in Python by introducing people to Python 3, the latest and, in my opinion, greatest version of Python to date. May your journey be as satisfying as mine has been.

acknowledgments

I want to thank David Fugate of LaunchBooks for getting me into this book in the first place and for all of the support and advice he has provided over the years. I can't imagine having a better agent and friend. I also need to thank Jonathan Gennick of Manning for pushing the idea of doing a fourth edition of this book and supporting me in my efforts to make it as good as the first three. I also thank every person at Manning who worked on this project, with special thanks to Marjan Bace for his support, Doug Rudder for guidance in the development phases, Kathy Rossland for getting the book (and me) through the production process, Kari Lucke for her patience in copy editing, and Katie Tennant for proofreading. Likewise, hearty thanks go to the many reviewers whose insights and feedback were of immense help, especially Ken Alger, the technical editor for this edition of the book. Ken has taught, written about, and presented on various Python topics. In 2017, he served on the board of directors of the Django Software Foundation. Ken has worked with Python off and on since the mid-1990s, helping several industries automate tasks using Python.

Thanks as well go to the many others who provided valuable feedback, including all the reviewers: Aaron S. Bush, Advait Patel, Alfonso Harding, Anders Persson, Anuj Tyagi, Arian Ahmdinejad, Asaad Saad, Cay Horstmann, Chalamayya Batchu, Christian Sutton, Daivid Morgan, Dane Hillard, Darrin Bishop, Felipe Provezano Coutinho, Gajendra Babu Thokala, Ganesh Harke, Glen Mules, Greg Wagner, Harshita Asnani, Heather Ward, Ian Brierley, James Bishop, James Brett, James McCorrie, Jim Mason, Jose Apablaza, Juan Gomez, Justin Reiser, Ken Youens-Clark, Kiran Kumar Gunturu, Laurence Baldwin, Lav Kumar, Lev Veyde, Monisha Athi Kesavan Premalatha, Nicolas Chartier, Peter Van Caeneghem, Raghunath Mysore, Raz Pavel, Rich Hilliar, Robert F. Scheyder, Steve Grey-Wilson, Tanvir Kaur, Vatche Jabagchourian, Venkatesh Rajagopal, and William Jamir. Your suggestions helped make this a better book.

I have to thank the authors of the first edition, Daryl Harms and Kenneth MacDonald, for writing a book so sound that it has remained in print well beyond the average lifespan of most tech books, giving me a chance to do the second, third, and now fourth edition, as well as everyone who bought and gave positive reviews to the previous editions. I hope this version carries on the successful and long-lived tradition of the first three editions.

Thanks also go to Luciano Ramalho for the kindness with which he wrote the foreword to this edition, as well as for our years of friendship and the many years he has spent sharing his vast Python knowledge with communities in Brazil and throughout the world. Muito obrigada, meu amigo. I also owe thanks to the global Python community, an unfailing source of support, wisdom, friendship, and joy over the years. To borrow the quote one more time from Brett Cannon, "I came for the language, but I stayed for the community." Thank you all, my friends.

Most important, as always, I thank my wife, Becky, who both encouraged me to take on this project and supported me through the entire process. I really couldn't have done it without her.

about this book

The Quick Python Book, Fourth Edition, is intended for people who already have experience in one or more programming languages and want to learn the basics of Python 3 as quickly and directly as possible. Although some basic concepts are covered, there's no attempt to teach fundamental programming skills in this book, and the basic concepts of flow control, object-oriented programming (OOP), file access, exception handling, and the like are assumed. This book may also be of service to users of earlier versions of Python who want a concise reference for Python 3.

Who should read this book

This book is intended for readers who know how to write some code and understand basic programming concepts. They might be coming from another programming language, they might still be learning Python and wanting to level up their knowledge, or they might be looking to update and refresh their knowledge. This book provides a compact and accessible view of the Python landscape at the level of the features that are used to get 90% of the work done.

How this book is organized: A road map

Part 1 introduces Python and explains how to use Python via Google's Colaboratory and how to obtain the source code Jupyter notebooks from the book's GitHub repository. It also includes a very general survey of the language, which will be most useful for experienced programmers looking for a high-level view of Python:

- Chapter 1 discusses the strengths and weaknesses of Python and shows why Python is a good choice of programming language for many situations.

- Chapter 2 covers how to use Python via Google's Colaboratory and how to obtain the source code as Jupyter notebooks from the book's GitHub repository.
- Chapter 3 is a short overview of the Python language. It provides a basic idea of the philosophy, syntax, semantics, and capabilities of the language.

Part 2 is the heart of the book. It covers the ingredients necessary for obtaining a working knowledge of Python as a general-purpose programming language. The chapters are designed to allow readers who are beginning to learn Python to work their way through sequentially, picking up knowledge of the key points of the language. These chapters also contain some more advanced sections, allowing you to return to find in one place all the necessary information about a construct or topic:

- Chapter 4 starts with the basics of Python. It introduces Python variables, expressions, strings, and numbers. It also introduces Python's block-structured syntax.
- Chapters 5, 6, and 7 describe the five powerful built-in Python data types: lists, tuples, sets, strings, and dictionaries.
- Chapter 8 introduces Python's control flow syntax and use (loops, `if-else` statements, and the new match-case statement).
- Chapter 9 describes function definition in Python along with its flexible parameter-passing capabilities.
- Chapter 10 describes Python modules, which provide an easy mechanism for segmenting the program namespace.
- Chapter 11 covers creating standalone Python programs, or scripts, and running them on Windows, macOS, and Linux platforms. The chapter also covers the support available for command-line options, arguments, and I/O redirection.
- Chapter 12 describes how to work with and navigate through the files and directories of the filesystem. It shows how to write code that's as independent as possible of the actual operating system you're working on.
- Chapter 13 introduces the mechanisms for reading and writing files in Python, including the basic capability to read and write strings (or byte streams), the mechanism available for reading binary records, and the ability to read and write arbitrary Python objects.
- Chapter 14 discusses the use of exceptions, the error-handling mechanism used by Python. It doesn't assume that you have any previous knowledge of exceptions, although if you've previously used them in C++ or Java, you'll find them familiar.

Part 3 introduces advanced language features of Python—elements of the language that aren't essential to its use but that can certainly be a great help to a serious Python programmer:

- Chapter 15 introduces Python's support for writing object-oriented programs.
- Chapter 16 discusses the regular expression capabilities available for Python.

- Chapter 17 introduces more advanced OOP techniques, including the use of Python's special method attributes mechanism, metaclasses, and abstract base classes.
- Chapter 18 introduces the package concept in Python for structuring the code of large projects.
- Chapter 19 is a brief survey of the standard library. It also includes a discussion of where to find other modules and how to install them.

Part 4 describes more advanced or specialized topics that are beyond the strict syntax of the language. You may read these chapters or not, depending on your needs.

- Chapter 20 dives deeper into manipulating files in Python.
- Chapter 21 covers strategies for reading, cleaning, and writing various types of data files.
- Chapter 22 surveys the process, issues, and tools involved in fetching data over the network.
- Chapter 23 discusses how Python accesses relational and NoSQL databases.
- Chapter 24 is a brief introduction to using Python, Jupyter notebooks, and pandas to explore datasets.
- The case study walks you through using Python to fetch data, clean it, and then graph it. The project combines several features of the language discussed in the chapters, and it gives you a chance to see a project worked through from beginning to end.
- The appendix contains a guide to obtaining and accessing Python's full documentation, the Pythonic style guide, PEP 8, and "The Zen of Python," a slightly wry summary of the philosophy behind Python.

A suggested plan if you're new to Python programming and want to skip straight to the language is to start by reading chapter 3 to obtain an overall perspective and then work through the chapters in part 2 that are applicable. Enter in the interactive examples as they are introduced to immediately reinforce the concepts. You can also easily go beyond the examples in the text to answer questions about anything that may be unclear. This has the potential to amplify the speed of your learning and the level of your comprehension. If you aren't familiar with OOP or don't need it for your application, skip most of chapter 15.

Those who are familiar with Python should also start with chapter 3. It's a good review and introduces differences between Python and what may be more familiar. It's also a reasonable test of whether you're ready to move on to the advanced chapters in parts 3 and 4 of this book.

It's possible that some readers, although new to Python, will have enough experience with other programming languages to be able to pick up the bulk of what they need to get going by reading chapter 3 and by browsing the Python standard library modules listed in chapter 19 and the documentation for the Python standard library.

About the code

The code samples in this book are deliberately kept as simple as possible, because they aren't intended to be reusable parts that can be plugged into your code. Instead, the code samples are stripped down so that you can focus on the principle being illustrated.

This book is based on Python 3.13, including some features not yet supported on Colaboratory (which is on Python 3.11 at the time of writing), and all examples should work on any subsequent version of Python 3. Other than the newest features, the examples also work on Python 3.9 and later, but I strongly recommend using the most current version you can; there are no advantages to using the earlier versions, and each version has several subtle improvements over the earlier ones.

In keeping with the idea of ease of use, the code examples are presented as Jupyter notebook cells that you can run in Google Colaboratory or with any other Jupyter server. Where possible, you should enter and experiment with these samples as much as you can.

The Jupyter notebooks with the code for the examples and the answers to most of the Quick Check and Try This exercises in this book are available from the publisher's website at www.manning.com/books/the-quick-python-book-fourth-edition. You can also find all of the code in a GitHub repository at https://github.com/nceder/qpb4e.

You can get executable snippets of code from the liveBook (online) version of this book at https://livebook.manning.com/book/the-quick-python-book-fourth-edition.

This book contains many examples of source code both in numbered listings and in line with normal text. In both cases, source code is formatted in a `fixed-width font` like this to separate it from ordinary text. The output of the code when run is also **in bold**.

In many cases, the original source code has been reformatted; we've added line breaks and reworked indentation to accommodate the available page space in the book. In some cases, even this was not enough, and listings include line-continuation markers (➥). Additionally, comments in the source code have often been removed from the listings when the code is described in the text. Code annotations accompany many of the listings, highlighting important concepts.

In some cases, a longer code sample is needed, and these cases are identified in the text as file listings. You can download these files from the source code repository or save the listings as files with names matching those used in the text and run them as stand-alone scripts.

liveBook discussion forum

Purchase of *The Quick Python Book, Fourth Edition*, includes free access to liveBook, Manning's online reading platform. Using liveBook's exclusive discussion features, you can attach comments to the book globally or to specific sections or paragraphs. It's a snap to make notes for yourself, ask and answer technical questions, and receive help from the author and other users. To access the forum, go to https://livebook.manning .com/book/the-quick-python-book-fourth-edition/discussion. You can also learn

more about Manning's forums and the rules of conduct at https://livebook.manning
.com/book/discussion.

Manning's commitment to our readers is to provide a venue where a meaningful dia-
logue between individual readers and between readers and the author can take place. It
is not a commitment to any specific amount of participation on the part of the author,
whose contribution to the forum remains voluntary (and unpaid). We suggest you try
asking the author some challenging questions lest their interest stray! The forum and
the archives of previous discussions will be accessible from the publisher's website as
long as the book is in print.

about the author

NAOMI CEDER has been programming in various languages for over 30 years and has been a Linux system administrator, programming teacher, developer, and system architect. She started using Python in 2001 and since then has taught Python to users at all levels, from 12-year-olds to professionals. She gives talks on Python and the benefits of an inclusive community to whomever will listen. A past chair of the Python Software Foundation and recipient of the PSF Distinguished Service Award, Naomi is now retired, which leaves her more free time to play the classical guitar.

about the cover illustration

The figure on the cover of *The Quick Python Book, Fourth Edition,* is "Bavaroise" or "Woman from Bavaria," taken from a 19th-century edition of Sylvain Maréchal's four-volume compendium, *Costumes Civils Actuels de Tous les Peuples Connus.* Each illustration is finely drawn and colored by hand.

In those days, it was easy to identify where people lived and what their trade or station in life was just by their dress. Manning celebrates the inventiveness and initiative of the computer business with book covers based on the rich diversity of regional culture centuries ago, brought back to life by pictures from collections such as this one.

Part 1

Starting out

These first three chapters tell you a little bit about Python, its strengths and weaknesses, and why you should consider learning Python. In chapter 2 you see how to run Python using Google Colaboratory, how to access the book's example code repository on GitHub, and how to write a simple program. Chapter 3 is a quick, high-level survey of Python's syntax and features. If you're looking for the quickest possible introduction to Python, start with chapter 3.

About Python 1

This chapter covers

- Why use Python?
- What Python does well
- What Python is improving

This book is intended to help people get a solid general understanding of Python as quickly as possible, avoiding getting bogged down in advanced topics but covering the essentials to write and read Python code. In particular, this book is intended for people who are coming to Python from other languages and for those who know a bit of Python but are looking to level up their skills as Python continues to gain popularity, particularly in areas like data science, machine learning, and the sciences. While no prior knowledge of Python is needed, some knowledge and experience with programming is necessary to get the most out of this book.

After introducing Python and offering some advice on getting started with a Python environment, the book provides a quick summary of Python's syntax, followed by chapters that build from the built-in data types up through creating functions, classes, and packages, as well as some more advanced features and a case study in handling data.

With the rise of AI tools based on large language models (LLMs), it is now possible to generate increasing amounts of usable code if (and that's a big "if") one has enough knowledge of coding to guide the process intelligently. While this book is *not* a tutorial on AI and its use in code generation, the coding problems posed at the end of each chapter, starting with chapter 5, provide examples of AI responses to the same questions along with a brief discussion of what the AI got right (and wrong). This will help build an understanding of how to use AI tools to generate code that actually works.

1.1   Why should I use Python?

Hundreds of programming languages are available today, from mature languages like C and C++, to newer entries like Rust, Go, and C#, to enterprise juggernauts like Java, to the more web-oriented JavaScript and Typescript. This abundance of choice makes deciding on a programming language difficult. Although no one language is the right choice for every possible situation, I think that Python is a good choice for a large number of programming problems, and it's also a good choice if you're learning to program. Millions of programmers around the world use Python, and the number grows every year.

Python continues to attract new users for a variety of reasons. It's a true cross-platform language, running equally well on Windows, Linux/UNIX, and iOS platforms, as well as others, ranging from supercomputers to mobile devices. It can be used to develop small applications and rapid prototypes, but it scales well to permit the development of large programs. It comes with a powerful and easy-to-use graphical user interface (GUI) toolkit, web programming libraries, and more. Python has also become a vital tool for scientific computing and for data science, machine learning, and work with AI. *And* it's free.

1.2   What Python does well

Python is a modern programming language developed by Guido van Rossum in the 1990s (and named after a famous comedic troupe). Although Python isn't perfect for every application, its strengths make it a good choice for many situations.

1.2.1   Python is easy to use

Programmers familiar with traditional languages will find it easy to learn Python. All of the familiar constructs—loops, conditional statements, arrays, and so forth—are included, but many are easier to use in Python. Here are a few of the reasons why:

- *Types are associated with objects, not variables.* A variable can be assigned a value of any type, and a list can contain objects of many types. This also means that type casting usually isn't necessary and that your code isn't locked into the straitjacket of predeclared types. But while types are not *required* for variables, Python does allow *type hints* that allow developers to check that their code is consistent in the type of object used for parameters, return values, etc.; we'll talk a little bit about type hints later in the book.

- *Python typically operates at a much higher level of abstraction.* This is partly the result of the way the language is built and partly the result of an extensive standard code library that comes with the Python distribution. A program to download a web page can be written in two or three lines!

- *Syntax rules are very simple.* Although becoming an expert Pythonista takes time and effort, even beginners can absorb enough Python syntax to write useful code quickly.

Python is well suited for rapid application development. It isn't unusual for coding an application in Python to take one-fifth the time it would in C or Java and to take as little as one-fifth the number of lines of the equivalent C program. This depends on the particular application, of course; for a numerical algorithm performing mostly integer arithmetic in `for` loops, there would be much less of a productivity gain. For the average application, the productivity gain can be significant.

1.2.2 Python is expressive

Python is a very expressive language. *Expressive* in this context means that a single line of Python code can do more than a single line of code in most other languages. The advantages of a more expressive language are obvious: the fewer lines of code you have to write, the faster you can complete the project. The fewer lines of code there are, the easier the program will be to maintain and debug.

To get an idea of how Python's expressiveness can simplify code, consider swapping the values of two variables, `var1` and `var2`. In a language like Java, this requires three lines of code and an extra variable:

```
int temp = var1;
var1 = var2;
var2 = temp;
```

The variable `temp` is needed to save the value of `var1` when `var2` is put into it, and then that saved value is put into `var2`. The process isn't terribly complex, but reading those three lines and understanding that a swap has taken place takes a certain amount of overhead, even for experienced coders.

By contrast, Python lets you make the same swap in one line and in a way that makes it obvious that a swap of values has occurred:

```
var2, var1 = var1, var2
```

Of course, this is a very simple example, but you can find the same advantages throughout the language.

1.2.3 Python is readable

Another advantage of Python is that it's easy to read. You might think that a programming language needs to be read only by a computer, but humans have to read your code as well: whoever debugs your code (quite possibly you), whoever maintains your code (could be you again), and whoever might want to modify your code in the future. In all of those situations, the easier the code is to read and understand, the better it is.

The easier code is to understand, the easier it is to debug, maintain, and modify. Python's main advantage in this department is its use of indentation. Unlike most languages, Python *insists* that blocks of code be indented. Although this strikes some people as odd, it has the benefit that your code is always formatted in a very easy-to-read style.

The following are two short programs, one written in Perl and one in Python. Both take two equal-size lists of numbers and return the pairwise sum of those lists. I think the Python code is more readable than the Perl code; it's visually cleaner and contains fewer inscrutable symbols:

```
# Perl version.
sub pairwise_sum {
    my($arg1, $arg2) = @_;
    my @result;
    for(0 .. $#$arg1) {
        push(@result, $arg1->[$_] + $arg2->[$_]);
    }
    return(\@result);
}

# Python version.
def pairwise_sum(list1, list2):
    result = []
    for i in range(len(list1)):
        result.append(list1[i] + list2[i])
    return result
```

Both pieces of code do the same thing, but the Python code wins in terms of readability. (There are other ways to do this in Perl, of course, some of which are much more concise—but, in my opinion, are harder to read than the one shown.)

1.2.4   *Python is complete: "Batteries included"*

Another advantage of Python is its "batteries included" philosophy when it comes to libraries. The idea is that when you install Python, you should have everything you need to do real work without the need to install additional libraries. This is why the Python standard library comes with modules for handling email, web pages, databases, operating-system calls, GUI development, and more.

For example, with Python, you can write a web server to share the files in a directory with just two lines of code:

```
import http.server
http.server.test(HandlerClass=http.server.SimpleHTTPRequestHandler)
```

There's no need to install libraries to handle network connections and HTTP; it's already in Python, right out of the box.

1.2.5 *Python has a rich ecosystem of third-party libraries*

While Python is "batteries included," there are still many situations where one needs to go beyond even a well-stocked standard library—a specialized task, a new data format, more complex applications, and so on. Here Python has really come to the forefront over the past decade. In many areas, from web applications and APIs to data handling and visualization, to machine learning and data science and more, Python has one of the richest ecosystems of packages, libraries, and frameworks of any current language. It's very unlikely that you'll find yourself in a situation where there are no Python packages to meet your needs.

1.2.6 *Python is cross-platform*

Python is also an excellent cross-platform language. Python runs on many platforms, including Windows, Mac, Linux, UNIX, and others. Because it's interpreted, the same code can run on any platform that has a Python interpreter, and almost all current platforms have one. There are even versions of Python that run on Java (Jython), .NET (IronPython), and microcontrollers (MicroPython and CircuitPython), giving you even more possible platforms that run Python.

1.2.7 *Python is free*

Python is also free. Python was originally, and continues to be, developed under the open source model, and it's freely available. You can download and install practically any version of Python and use it to develop software for commercial or personal applications, and you don't need to pay a dime.

Although attitudes are changing, some people are still leery of free software because of concerns about a lack of support, fearing such software lacks the clout of paying customers. But Python is used by many established companies as a key part of their business; Google, Bloomberg, NVIDIA, and Capital One are just a few examples. These companies and many others know Python for what it is: a very stable, reliable, and well-supported product with an active and knowledgeable user community. You'll get an answer to even the most difficult Python question more quickly in various Python internet forums than you will on most tech-support phone lines, and the Python answer will be free and correct.

> **Python and open source software**
>
> Not only is Python free but its source code is also freely available, and you're free to modify, improve, and extend it if you want. Because the source code is freely available, you have the ability to go in yourself and change it (or to hire someone to go in and do so for you). You rarely have this option at any reasonable cost with proprietary software.
>
> If this is your first foray into the world of open source software, you should understand that you're not only free to use and modify Python but also able (and encouraged) to contribute to it and improve it. Depending on your circumstances, interests, and

> **(continued)**
>
> skills, those contributions might be financial, as in a donation to the Python Software Foundation, or they may involve participating in one of the special interest groups, testing and giving feedback on releases of the Python core or one of the auxiliary modules, or contributing some of what you or your company develops back to the community. The level of contribution (if any) is, of course, up to you; but if you're able to give back, definitely consider doing so. Something of significant value is being created here, and you have an opportunity to add to it.

Python has a lot going for it: expressiveness, readability, rich included libraries, and cross-platform capabilities. Also, it's open source. What's the catch?

1.3   *What Python is improving*

Although Python has many advantages, no language can do everything, so Python isn't the perfect solution for all your needs. While Python is improving in all of the following areas, to decide whether it is the right language for your situation, you also need to consider these areas where Python doesn't do as well.

1.3.1   *Python is getting faster*

A possible drawback with Python is its speed of execution. It isn't a fully compiled language. Instead, it's first compiled to an internal bytecode form, which is then executed by a Python interpreter. There are some tasks, such as string parsing using regular expressions, for which Python has efficient implementations and is as fast as, or faster than, any C program you're likely to write. Nevertheless, most of the time, using Python results in slower programs than in a language like C. But you should keep this in perspective. Modern computers have so much computing power that, for the vast majority of applications, the speed of the program isn't as important as the speed of development, and Python programs can typically be written much more quickly than others. In addition, it's easy to extend Python with modules written in C or C++, which can be used to run the CPU-intensive portions of a program.

Python's core developers are also hard at work creating new versions of Python that are more efficient, load and run faster, and take better advantage of multiple processor cores. This work has already yielded significant improvements in performance, and the work will continue in the future, so if you have a performance-critical application, you may want to consider carefully if Python will do the job—but don't write it off immediately.

1.3.2   *Python doesn't enforce variable types at compile time*

Unlike in some languages, Python's variables don't work like containers; instead, they're more like labels that refer to various objects: integers, strings, class instances, whatever. That means that although those objects themselves have types, the variables referring to them aren't bound to those particular types. It's possible (if not necessarily desirable) to use the variable x to refer to a string in one line and an integer in another (note: output of the code is in **bold**):

```
x = "2"
x
```

'2' ◄———⌐ **Output of x is the string '2'.**

```
x = int(x)
x
```

2 ◄———⌐ **Output of x is now the integer 2.**

The fact that Python associates types with objects and not with variables means that the interpreter doesn't help you catch variable type mismatches. If you intend a variable count to hold an integer, Python won't complain if you assign the string "two" to it. Traditional coders count this as a disadvantage, because you lose an additional free check on your code.

In response to this concern, Python has added syntax and tools to allow coders to specify the desired type of the object a variable refers to, as well as function parameters, return values, and the like. With these *type hints*, as they are called, various tools can flag any inconsistencies in the types of objects before runtime. In smaller programs, type errors usually aren't hard to find and fix even without type hints, and in any case, Python's testing features makes avoiding type errors manageable. Many Python programmers feel that the flexibility of dynamic typing more than outweighs any advantage mandatory variable typing might offer.

1.3.3 *Python is improving mobile support*

In the past decade, the numbers and types of mobile devices have exploded, and smartphones, tablets, phablets, Chromebooks, and more are everywhere, running on a variety of operating systems. Python isn't a strong player in this space, but various projects are working on the problem, developing toolkits and frameworks that allow writing apps for both iOS and Android platforms. This situation is improving, but as of this writing, using Python to write and distribute commercial mobile apps is a bit of a pain.

1.3.4 *Python is improving support for multiple processors*

Multiple-core processors are everywhere now, producing significant increases in performance in many situations. However, the standard implementation of Python isn't designed to use multiple cores, due to a feature called the *global interpreter lock*. As mentioned in the context of speed, Python's development team is currently working on ways to make Python work more seamlessly and efficiently with multiple processor cores, and the development of multicore Python will continue over the next several years.

Summary

- Python is a modern, high-level language with dynamic typing and simple, consistent syntax and semantics.
- Python is multiplatform, highly modular, and suited for both rapid development and large-scale programming.
- It's reasonably fast and can be easily extended with C or C++ modules for higher speeds.
- Python has built-in advanced features, such as persistent object storage, advanced hash tables, expandable class syntax, and universal comparison functions.
- Python includes a wide range of libraries, such as numeric processing, image manipulation, user interfaces, and web scripting.
- It's supported by a dynamic community.

Getting started

This chapter covers

- Available Python options
- Getting started with Colaboratory
- Accessing the GitHub repository for this book
- Writing a simple program and handling errors
- Using the `help()` and `dir()` functions
- AI tools for generating Python code

This chapter gives you a quick survey of the many options for installing and using Python and guides you through getting up and running with Google Colaboratory, a web-hosted Python environment. Combined with the code for each chapter, available in a GitHub repository at https://github.com/nceder/qpb4e, Colaboratory is one of the quickest and easiest ways to get up and running with Python so that you can test out the code examples in the text and work through the lab exercises throughout the book.

2.1   *Paradox of choice: Which Python?*

As Python has matured, particularly over the past 10 years, the number of options for running Python has exploded. After a brief survey of the versions, sources, devices, environments, and tools in the Python ecosystem, we'll look at our recommended solution, Google Colaboratory, and how to use it to run the sample code snippets in this book and write the code for the lab exercises in most of the chapters.

2.1.1   *Python versions*

For many years, Python had a somewhat variable release cycle, with new versions being released when the core developers felt there were enough new features to be worth it. From Python 3.1 in 2009 to 3.8 in 2018, new versions were released roughly every 18 months. As Python's popularity continued to grow, a quicker and more regular cadence for new releases became the goal. So, beginning with version 3.9, the decision was made (recorded in PEP 602: Annual Release Cycle for Python) to move to an annual release cycle, with a release every October.

The current release schedule for Python means that after the October 2024 release of version 3.13, version 3.14 will come out in October 2025, and so on. As of this writing, Python 3.13 is the most current version, having been released in October 2024. Since the features of 3.13 have already been frozen, I have included the new features of 3.13 and I have tested the code on both 3.12 and 3.13.

> **Choosing a Python version**
>
> Having a new version of Python come out every year is a good thing for releasing new features, but it's not always the most convenient thing for anyone who needs to test and deploy a new version of the language. Because of this, versions of Python are officially supported for a total of five years: the first two years with full releases and then three years with source code only with releases of security fixes.
>
> While it's usually preferable to have the latest version, any supported version (3.9 or later as of this writing) should be fine to use with this book. If you have an earlier version, there will be a few new features that you won't have, but you can still do a lot of work without upgrading.

2.1.2   *Sources of Python*

The classic way to get Python is by downloading and installing a version from the Python Sofware Foundation's website at https://www.python.org/downloads/. There you can find installers for several operating systems and platforms and versions going back to the very beginnings of Python, over 30 years ago. It's possible, however, that the exact version you need or want isn't on python.org. You can also get a data science–oriented distribution of Python from Anaconda at https://www.anaconda.com/download/, or you may be able to use the app store or package manager of your operating system to install Python. If you are into the technical details, you can also fork the source code repository on GitHub and download and compile the source yourself. The choice depends on your preferences and your situation, and since the solution I recommend doesn't require a local install, you can wait to make that decision until you know Python a bit better.

2.1.3 Devices, platforms, and operating systems

You can run Python on a wide variety of devices and on many operating systems. While in the early days, a server or desktop computer was the norm, today Python runs on many processors, from embedded devices and single board computers to phones and tablets, to Chromebooks, laptops, and desktops, to virtual machines and containers, to server clusters, and so on. While the most common implementation of Python is based on the C language, there are versions that are written in and run on Java, in the browser based on WASM, or even in applications like Excel.

2.1.4 Environments and tools

There are also a number of ways that you can run and develop code in Python. It's possible to run the Python interpreter from a command line and interact using either the built-in shell or an enhanced shell like IPython and to write code in the text editor of your choice. You can also use education-oriented IDEs like IDLE (provided with Python), Mu, or Thonny, or you can opt for more advanced Python IDEs like VSCode, Wingware, or PyCharm. Of course, in all of those categories there are too many other fine options to list.

Another option for using and writing Python combines features of the IPython shell with a web interface and is called Jupyter. Jupyter runs on a server and is accessed via browser, and its web interface allows you to combine text (formatted using Markdown) with cells for executing code in a "notebook." The combination has proven to be so useful that Jupyter notebooks are increasingly popular for teaching, data exploration and data science, AI experimentation, and many other uses. While you can run your own Jupyter server locally, it's even more convenient to use a server hosted in the cloud, which brings us to my recommendation for this book.

2.2 Colaboratory: Jupyter notebooks in the cloud

As mentioned at the beginning of this chapter, for this book I recommend using Jupyter notebooks, specifically, the hosted version of Jupyter from Google, Colaboratory. Using Colaboratory means that you don't need to worry about installing (or updating) Python, and you can take advantage of Jupyter's friendly interface, which is becoming increasingly popular, particularly for data science.

Another advantage of Colaboratory is that you can launch a session with one of the code notebooks from this book's source repository on GitHub with a single click, and you can access it on virtually any device that has a modern web browser.

For that reason, in this book, I'll present sample code and problem solutions in Jupyter notebooks. Of course, the code will still work in other environments, and I'll provide text files of the code as well, but unless stated otherwise, you can assume that the code presented is in notebook form.

2.2.1   Getting the source notebooks

The simplest way to get started with Colaboratory and this book is by accessing a notebook in the GitHub repository. If you are not familiar with GitHub, it's a very popular online version control service based on the version control tool Git. To access the notebooks in the repository, you don't need to know how to use Git, nor do you need to have an account on GitHub—just following the links given here will get you started.

You can find the GitHub repository at https://github.com/nceder/qpb4e/tree/main; the notebooks for each chapter are in separate directories inside the `code` directory. To get started, let's find and open the notebook for chapter 2 (this chapter). If you look in the `Chapter 02` directory, you will find a notebook file called Chapter_02.ipynb (direct link at https://mng.bz/gaDG). You should see a page similar to the one shown in figure 2.1.

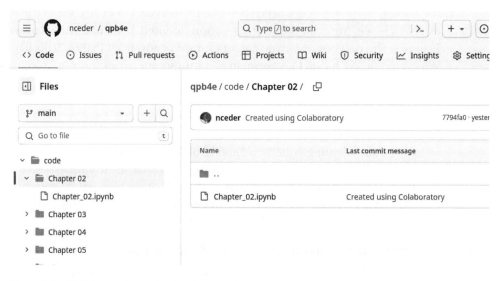

Figure 2.1   GitHub repository, showing Chapter_02 notebook

2.2.2   Getting started with Colaboratory

If you click the Chapter_02.ipynb file, you can view its contents using GitHub's viewer (as shown in figure 2.2), and at the top of the code window (right above 2.2 Getting Started with Python and Colaboratory), you should also see a blue button link Open in Colab.

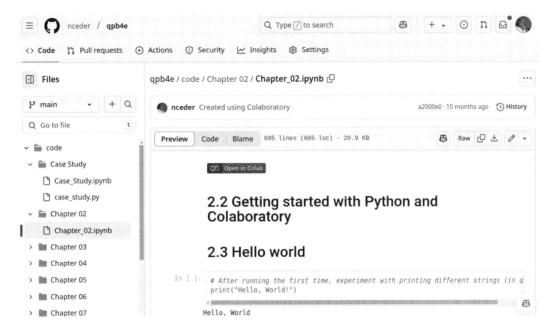

Figure 2.2   Chapter_02.ipynb notebook viewed in GitHub

If you click that link, it will open that notebook in a Colaboratory session where you can edit, run, and experiment with the code, as shown in figure 2.3.

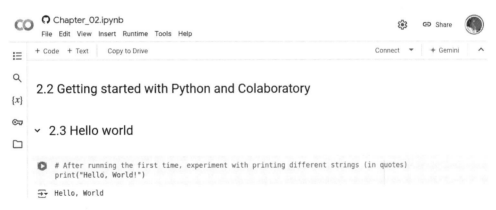

Figure 2.3   Chapter_02.ipynb notebook open in Colaboratory

As with GitHub, you don't need a Google account to access Colaboratory, but to run code and use all of the features, including the ability to save sessions and files, logging in with a Google account is required.

You can also access Colaboratory directly by using your browser to open https://colab
.research.google.com/. This will open Colaboratory with a "Welcome to Colab" notebook (as shown in figure 2.4) that explains some of the platform's features. If you are
unfamiliar with Jupyter notebooks, there are some links at the bottom of this notebook to other notebooks that explain how Colaboratory's version of Jupyter notebooks
works. If you find yourself a bit confused at first, those resources can help.

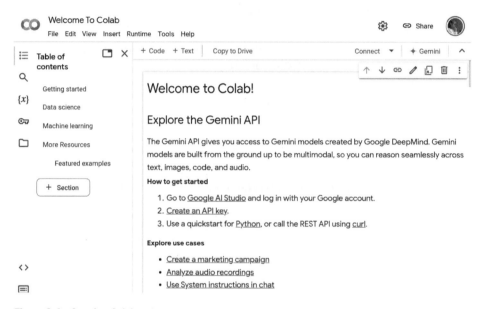

Figure 2.4   Opening Colaboratory

To open a file for this book, you would select the File menu under Welcome to Colab at
the upper left of the window and select the Open notebook option. To illustrate how it
works, again let's look at the notebook for this chapter.

   Enter https://github.com/nceder/qpb4e where it asks for a GitHub URL, and click
the search icon at the end of the line, as shown in figure 2.5. The paths to all of the
notebooks will appear below, and you should then click code/Chapter 02/Chapter_02
.ipynb to open the notebook for chapter 2.

2.2.3   *Colaboratory's Python version*

The good news about using Colaboratory is that you don't have to worry about installing and maintaining a Python environment, and the Jupyter notebooks are accessible
from almost any device with a standard web browser. One minor downside of using
Colaboratory is that the version of Python that it runs may be a few months behind the
latest version, which means that a few of the very newest features of Python may not

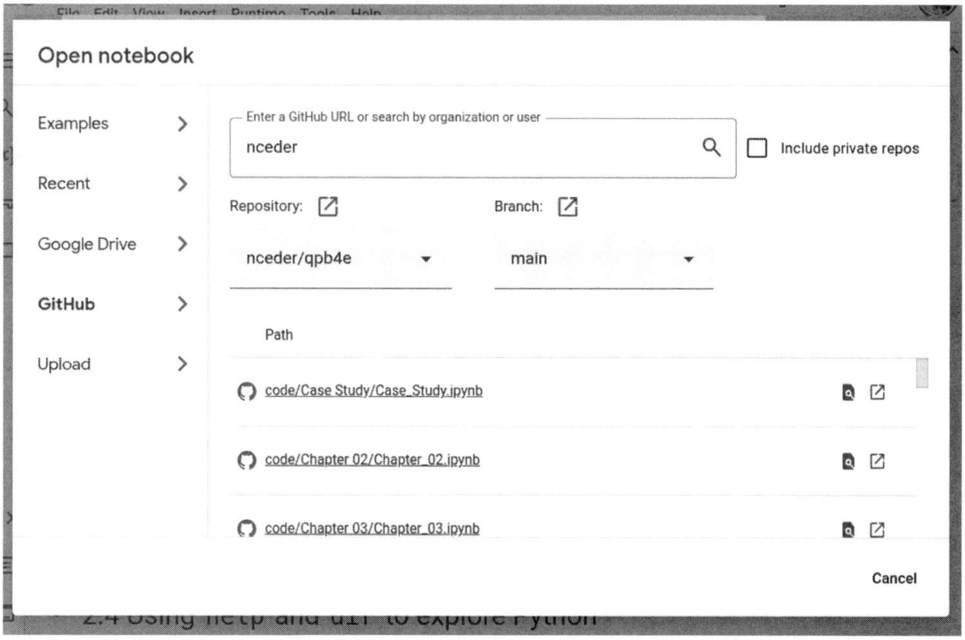

Figure 2.5 Opening a notebook from the GitHub repository

be available. However, Colaboratory's ease of access and use far outweighs this slight drawback.

2.3 *Writing and running code in Colaboratory*

A Jupyter notebook consists of two types of cells: text cells and code cells. The text cells are meant to contain text, which can be formatted using the Markdown text formatting language (there's a guide to Colaboratory's flavor of Markdown at https://mng .bz/eyjq). If you double-click a text cell or right-click and select Edit, the cell will be opened in edit mode, and the text and formatting can be changed. To save the changes and go back to text mode, you can use either Ctrl-Enter or you can right-click the cell and choose Select. Any changes you make to the source notebooks will not be changed in the GitHub repository, nor will they be saved in Colaboratory unless you are logged in with a Google account.

The code cells are for code that can be executed and are always in edit mode. To execute the code, you can either use Ctrl-Enter or you can right-click the cell and click Run the Focused Cell. You can also click the little triangle in a circle that appears to the left of the cell when you hover your mouse over the cell. The first time you run code from a notebook loaded from GitHub, you may see a warning that the code is being loaded from GitHub. This is normal, and it's fine to click the Run Anyway choice to execute the code. If there is any output from the execution of the code, it will appear in the area immediately below the cell. We'll see how all of this works as we run our first bit of code next.

2.3.1 Hello, World

Let's start with the traditional Hello, World program, which is a one-liner in Python:

```
print("Hello, World")
```
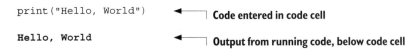

```
Hello, World
```

Here, the code for the `print()` function, along with the string `"Hello, World"` as its parameter, has already been entered into the first code cell of the chapter 2 notebook. To run it, as mentioned earlier, you can use Ctrl-Enter and the output, `"Hello, World"` will be printed below the cell. If you are new to Jupyter notebooks (or to Python), feel free to experiment a bit with the `print` function or other commands in this code cell.

Note that throughout this book, I will show the code that is entered into a code cell in Jupyter (or a Python shell prompt in some other environment) using a normal-weight monospace font and the output as a **monospace bold** font. For comparison, the previous code and output should look something like figure 2.6 in Colaboratory.

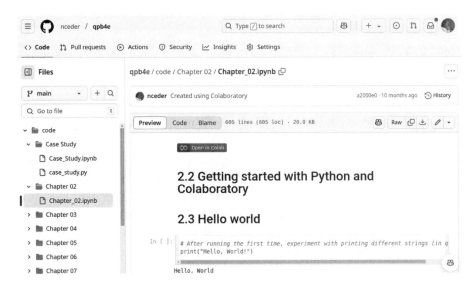

Figure 2.6 Text cells, code cell, and output

2.3.2 Dealing with errors in Jupyter

Errors are something all coders have to deal with in virtually every piece of code we write. If there is an error while running code in a code cell, Jupyter prints Python's error message below the cell where the output would go. Code error messages have been famously difficult to understand, but the latest versions of Python have improved the clarity and usefulness of error messages:

```
# this cell will raise a syntax error
print("Hello, World!"

  File "<ipython-input-3-0d1705def0fc>", line 2
    print("Hello, World!"
                         ^
SyntaxError: incomplete input
```

Code missing closing parenthesis ⟵

Message indicating the line where the error occurs ⟵

Caret indicating location in line ⟵

Name or explanation of error

In this case, the code deliberately has a syntax error—the closing parenthesis has been omitted. Python reports the message and the line where it occurs, puts a caret (^) under the error's location in the line, and finally names the problem "incomplete input."

A nice feature of Colaboratory is that below the Python error message it may offer an option to attempt to fix the error automatically, with a Next Steps: section and a Fix Error button, as shown in figure 2.7. In this case, clicking the Fix Error button will enter the fix in the previous code cell and allow the user to either accept or reject it.

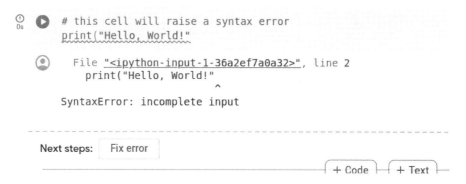

Figure 2.7 **Error with Fix error option**

It's a good idea to examine the suggested fix carefully. While for a simple error like this the suggestion is sound, the more complex the code, the more chance there is that the fix won't be reliable.

2.4 *Using help and dir to explore Python*

There are a couple of handy tools that can help you explore Python. The first is the `help()` function, which has two modes. You can execute `help()` in a code cell to enter the help system, where you can get help on modules, keywords, or topics. When you're in the help system, you see a `help>` prompt, and you can enter a module name, such as `print` or some other topic, to read Python's documentation on that topic. When you want to leave the help system, just press Enter, with no other input. Figure 2.8 shows the result of entering `help()` and then entering `print` into the input box. The help for the `print` function is displayed, and a new `help>` prompt and input box appear below it.

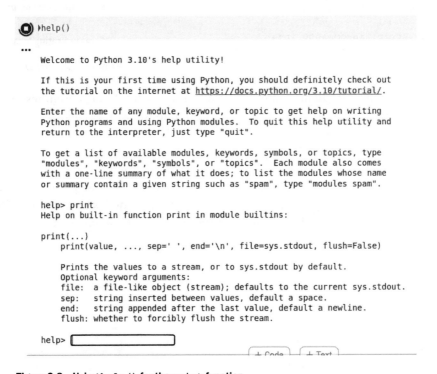

```
▶help()

...
    Welcome to Python 3.10's help utility!

    If this is your first time using Python, you should definitely check out
    the tutorial on the internet at https://docs.python.org/3.10/tutorial/.

    Enter the name of any module, keyword, or topic to get help on writing
    Python programs and using Python modules.  To quit this help utility and
    return to the interpreter, just type "quit".

    To get a list of available modules, keywords, symbols, or topics, type
    "modules", "keywords", "symbols", or "topics".  Each module also comes
    with a one-line summary of what it does; to list the modules whose name
    or summary contain a given string such as "spam", type "modules spam".

    help> print
    Help on built-in function print in module builtins:

    print(...)
        print(value, ..., sep=' ', end='\n', file=sys.stdout, flush=False)

        Prints the values to a stream, or to sys.stdout by default.
        Optional keyword arguments:
        file:  a file-like object (stream); defaults to the current sys.stdout.
        sep:   string inserted between values, default a space.
        end:   string appended after the last value, default a newline.
        flush: whether to forcibly flush the stream.

    help> [                    ]
                                              + Code      + Text
```

Figure 2.8   Using `help()` for the `print` function

Usually, it's more convenient to use `help()` in a more targeted way. Entering a type or variable name as a parameter for `help()` gives you an immediate display of that object's documentation and exits:

```
x = 2
help(x)

Help on int object:

class int(object)
 |  int(x=0) -> integer
 |  int(x, base=10) -> integer
 |
 |  Convert a number or string to an integer, or return 0 if no arguments
```

```
|   are given.  If x is a number, return x.__int__().  For floating point
|   numbers, this truncates towards zero.
|
|   If x is not a number or if base is given, then x must be a string,
|   bytes, or bytearray instance representing an integer literal in the...
(continues with the documentation for an int...)
```

Using `help()` in this way is handy for checking the exact syntax of a method or the behavior of an object.

The `help()` function is part of the `pydoc` library, which has several options for accessing the documentation built into Python libraries. Because every Python installation comes with complete documentation, you can have all the official documentation at your fingertips, even if you aren't online. See the appendix for more information on accessing Python's documentation.

The other useful function is `dir()`, which lists the objects in a particular namespace. Used with no parameters, it lists the current global namespace, but it can also list objects for a module or even a type:

```
dir()

['In',
 'Out',
 '_',
 '__',
 '___',
 '__builtin__',
 '__builtins__',
 '__doc__',
 '__loader__',
 '__name__',
 '__package__',
 '__spec__',
 '_dh',
 '_i',
 '_i1',
 '_i2',
 '_ih',
 '_ii',
 '_iii',
 '_oh',
 'exit',
 'get_ipython',
 'quit',
 'x']

dir(int)

['__abs__',
 '__add__',
 '__and__',
 '__bool__',
 '__ceil__',
```

```
'__class__',
'__delattr__',
'__dir__',
'__divmod__',
'__doc__',
'__eq__',
'__float__',
'__floor__',
'__floordiv__',
'__format__',
'__ge__',
'__getattribute__',
... (continues with more items... ]
```

`dir()` is useful for finding out what methods and data are defined, for reminding yourself at a glance of all the members that belong to an object or module, and for debugging, because you can see what is defined where.

2.5   *Using AI tools to write Python code*

The rise of large language model–based tools, such as ChatGPT, CoPilot, and many others, is beginning to revolutionize how we write software. It is now possible to have these tools generate working code in response to a text prompt. Note, however, that while it is *possible*, it is not yet always *reliable*. I am one of many who believe that human understanding is the vital ingredient for good code but that experience using AI tools to generate code will be increasingly helpful in the future.

With that in mind, we will use some of these tools to generate code for the solutions for the lab exercises in this book, and we will discuss and evaluate the AI-generated solutions. This will give you a feel for what is possible, how to create prompts, and what the potential drawbacks are.

2.5.1   *Benefits of AI tools*

It's undeniable that AI code generation has developed to the point that it has several advantages. First, it's fast. Even fairly large chunks of code can be generated in less than a minute, so even if you spend some time crafting and entering a good prompt for the chatbot to work from, the overall amount of time you need to spend to get a fair bit of code is definitely less than what even a lightning-fast human can achieve.

Second, the code tends to be free of all of the little glitches we humans have in typing in code—a chatbot will probably spell things correctly, use punctuation correctly, etc.

But—and this is a significant "but"—there are some drawbacks to consider.

2.5.2   *Negatives of using AI tools*

One thing to consider is that AI bots use a lot of resources. In this age of concern for the climate and environment, many will be worried about the resource (particularly energy and water) consumption of machines behind these coding tools. One can only hope that future developments will reduce that consumption to sustainable levels.

Second, using an AI bot for coding means that you are by definition sharing your code and using other's code, and the most common mechanisms for that sharing are weak in terms of protecting privacy and intellectual property.

Third, not all of the AI code generators are free, and as companies decide to recover the costs of the resources consumed by their machines, it's likely that fewer will remain free of charge for basic users.

Finally, while the code produced is surprisingly good, it's far from perfect. The bugs and inefficiencies in AI-generated code are not always obvious and can take a trained eye to spot. Putting AI-generated code into production without careful review and testing is at least as dangerous as uncritically using a junior developer's code.

While none of these drawbacks are dealbreakers, they are all things that responsible organizations and developers need to consider before deciding to use generated code.

2.5.3   *AI options*

The most convenient AI code generator is the one offered in Colaboratory, which is currently free of charge for most users. For comparison, we will also discuss solutions generated by GitHub Copilot, which works best with Microsoft's VSCode IDE and a local version of Python. Copilot also requires a $10 monthly subscription fee as of this writing. Given that you need to install Python and VSCode on your machine and pay the subscription, it may not be worth the trouble for the code examples and problems in this book. There are also other options, such as Codeium, that offer a free tier and work better with VSCode than with Colaboratory. Personally, if I were writing production code, I would prefer Copilot, but any of them can work for experimentation, and using an AI tool is purely optional—the results I obtained are all shared in the text and in the source notebooks.

Summary

- Python is available across a wide variety of operating systems, hardware platforms, and user interfaces.
- For ease of use and maintenance, Google Colaboratory is recommended for use with the Jupyter notebooks of example code for this book.
- You can access both the GitHub repository and Colaboratory without an account, but more features may be available with an account.
- Jupyter notebooks consist of two types of cells: formattable text cells and cells for executable code.
- Errors are usually reported in the same area as output below code cells.
- The `help()` and `dir()` functions can be useful in learning more about Python.
- AI tools can be used to generate Python code, and we will use and critique a couple of those tools when we discuss the solutions to the lab exercises later.

The quick
Python overview

This chapter covers

- Surveying Python
- Using built-in data types
- Controlling program flow
- Creating modules
- Using object-oriented programming

The purpose of this chapter is to give you a basic feeling for the syntax, semantics, capabilities, and philosophy of the Python language. It has been designed to provide an initial perspective or conceptual framework to which you'll be able to add details as you encounter them in the rest of the book.

On an initial read, you needn't be concerned about working through and understanding the details of the code segments. You'll be doing fine if you pick up a bit of an idea about what's being done. The subsequent chapters walk you through the specifics of these features and don't assume previous knowledge. You can always return to this chapter and work through the examples in the appropriate sections as a review after you've read the later chapters.

3.1 Python synopsis

Python has several built-in data types, such as integers, floats, complex numbers, strings, lists, tuples, dictionaries, and file objects. These data types can be manipulated using language operators, built-in functions, library functions, or a data type's own methods.

Programmers can also define their own classes and instantiate their own class instances. These class instances can be manipulated by programmer-defined methods, as well as by the language operators and built-in functions for which the programmer has defined the appropriate special method attributes.

> **NOTE** The Python documentation and this book use the term "object" to refer to instances of any Python data type, not just what many other languages would call "class instances." This is because all Python objects are instances of one class or another.

Python provides conditional and iterative control flow through an `if-elif-else` construct along with `while` and `for` loops and a new structural pattern-matching `match-case` feature. It allows function definition with flexible argument-passing options. Exceptions (errors) can be raised by using the `raise` statement, and they can be caught and handled by using the `try-except-else-finally` construct.

Variables (or identifiers) don't have to be declared and can refer to any built-in data type, user-defined object, function, or module.

3.2 Built-in data types

Python has several built-in data types, from scalars, such as numbers and Booleans, to more complex structures, such as lists, dictionaries, and files.

> **NOTE** In the examples, `code` is in `normal monospace` and **`output`** is in **`bold monospace type`**.

3.2.1 Numbers

Python's four number types are integers, floats, complex numbers, and Booleans:

- *Integers*—1, –3, 42, 355, 888888888888888, –7777777777 (integers aren't limited in size except by available memory)
- *Floats*—3.0, 31e12, –6e-4
- *Complex numbers*—3 + 2j, –4 – 2j, 4.2 + 6.3j
- *Booleans*—True, False

You can manipulate them by using the arithmetic operators: + (addition), - (subtraction), * (multiplication), / (division), // (division with truncation to integer), ** (exponentiation), and % (modulus).

The following examples use integers:

```
x = 5 + 2 - 3 * 2
x
```

```
1
```

```
5 / 2
```

```
2.5
```
◄─── **Float result using /**

```
5 // 2
```

```
2
```
◄─── **Result forced to integer using //**

```
5 % 2
```

```
1
```

```
2 ** 8
```

```
256
```

```
1000000001 ** 3
```

```
1000000003000000003000000001
```
◄─── **Integer size limited only by available memory**

Division of integers with / results in a float, and division of integers with // results in truncation to an integer. Note that integers are of unlimited size; they grow as large as you need them to, limited only by the memory available. The following examples work with floats, which are based on the doubles in C:

```
x = 4.3 ** 2.4
x
```

```
33.13784737771648
```

```
3.5e30 * 2.77e45
```

```
9.695e+75
```

```
1000000001.0 ** 3
```

```
1.000000003e+27
```

These examples use complex numbers:

```
(3+2j) ** (2+3j)
```

```
(0.6817665190890336-2.1207457766159625j)
```

```
x = (3+2j) * (4+9j)
x
```
◄─── **x assigned to a complex number**

```
(-6+35j)
```

```
x.real
```

```
-6.0
```

Complex numbers consist of both a real element and an imaginary element, suffixed with `j`. In the preceding code, variable `x` is assigned to a complex number. You can obtain its "real" part by using the attribute notation `x.real` and obtain the "imaginary" part with `x.imag`.

Several built-in functions can operate on numbers. In addition, the library module `cmath` contains functions for complex numbers, and the library module `math` contains functions for the other three types:

```
round(3.49)
```
◄─── **round called with 3.49**

```
3
```

```
import math
math.ceil(3.49)
```
◄─── **The math library module is imported, and its ceil function is called.**

```
4
```

Built-in functions are always available and are called by using a standard function-calling syntax. In the preceding code, `round` is called with a float as its input argument.

The functions in library modules are made available via the `import` statement. In the previous code, the `math` library module is imported, and its `ceil` function is called using attribute notation: *module.function(arguments)*.

The following examples use Booleans:

```
x = False
x
```

```
False
```

```
not x
```

```
True
```

```
y = True * 2
y
```
◄─── **Boolean treated as integer 1**

```
2
```

Other than their representation as `True` and `False`, Booleans behave like the numbers 1 (True) and 0 (False).

3.2.2 Lists

Python has a powerful built-in list type:

```
[]
[1]
```

```
[1, 2, 3, 4, 5, 6, 7, 8, 12]                          A list ist contains ints, float,
[1, "two", 3, 4.0, ["a", "b"], (5,6)]   ◄─────┘       string, list, and tuple.
```

A list can contain a mixture of other types as its elements, including strings, tuples, lists, dictionaries, functions, file objects, and any type of number. A list can be indexed from its beginning or end. You can also refer to a subsegment, or *slice*, of a list by using slice notation:

```
x = ["first", "second", "third", "fourth"]
x[0]
```

                                                      Index from the front
'first'   **using positive index**
                                                      starting from 0
```
x[2]
```

'third'

```
x[-1]
```

'fourth'

                                                      Index from the back
```
x[-2]                                                 using negative index
```                                                   **(–1 is the last element)**

'third'

```
x[1:-1]
```

['second', 'third']

```
x[0:3]
```

['first', 'second', 'third']   **A slice[m:n], where m is**
                                                      the starting point and n is
```
x[-2:-1]                                              the exclusive ending point
```

['third']

```
x[:3]
```

['first', 'second', 'third']

                                                      The slice starts at its
```
x[-2:]                                                beginning (m) and goes
```                                                   **to list's end.**

['third', 'fourth']

Lists can be accessed by index from the front using positive indices (starting with 0 as the first element). Index from the back using negative indices (starting with –1 as the last element). Obtain a slice using `[m:n]`, where m is the inclusive starting point and n is the exclusive ending point (see table 3.1). An `[:n]` slice starts at a list's beginning, and an `[m:]` slice goes to its end.

Table 3.1 List indices

x=	[	"first" ,	"second" ,	"third" ,	"fourth"	]
Positive indices		0	1	2	3	
Negative indices		−4	−3	−2	−1	

You can use this notation to add, remove, and replace elements in a list or to obtain an element or a new list that's a slice from it:

```
x = [1, 2, 3, 4, 5, 6, 7, 8, 9]
x[1] = "two"
x[8:9] = []
x

[1, 'two', 3, 4, 5, 6, 7, 8]

x[5:7] = [6.0, 6.5, 7.0]          ◄──── The size of x increases by 1.
x

[1, 'two', 3, 4, 5, 6.0, 6.5, 7.0, 8]

x[5:]

[6.0, 6.5, 7.0, 8]
```

The size of the list increases or decreases if the new slice is bigger or smaller than the slice it's replacing.

Some built-in functions (`len`, `max`, and `min`), some operators (`in`, `+`, and `*`), the `del` statement, and the list methods (`append`, `count`, `extend`, `index`, `insert`, `pop`, `remove`, `reverse`, and `sort`) operate on lists:

```
x = [1, 2, 3, 4, 5, 6, 7, 8, 9]
len(x)

9

[-1, 0] + x            ◄──── + and * each create a new list.

[-1, 0, 1, 2, 3, 4, 5, 6, 7, 8, 9]

x.reverse()            ◄──── reverse() method called
x                            by using x.reverse()

[9, 8, 7, 6, 5, 4, 3, 2, 1]
```

The operators + and * each create a new list, leaving the original unchanged. A list's methods are called by using attribute notation on the list itself: `x.method(`*arguments*`)`.

Some of these operations repeat functionality that can be performed with slice notation, but they improve code readability.

3.2.3   *Tuples*

Tuples are similar to lists but are *immutable*—that is, they can't be modified after they've been created. The operators (in, +, and *) and built-in functions (len, max, and min) operate on them the same way as they do on lists because none of them modify the original. Index and slice notation work the same way for obtaining elements or slices but can't be used to add, remove, or replace elements. Also, there are only two tuple methods: count and index. An important purpose of tuples is for use as keys for dictionaries. They're also more efficient to use when you don't need modifiability:

```
()
(1,)                                          ◄──────┘ One-element tuple with comma
(1, 2, 3, 4, 5, 6, 7, 8, 12)
(1, "two", 3, 4.0, ["a", "b"], (5, 6))        ◄──────┘ Different types in one list
```

A one-element tuple needs a comma. A tuple, like a list, can contain a mixture of other types as its elements, including strings, tuples, lists, dictionaries, functions, file objects, and any type of number.

A list can be converted to a tuple by using the built-in function tuple:

```
x = [1, 2, 3, 4]
tuple(x)
```

```
(1, 2, 3, 4)
```

Conversely, a tuple can be converted to a list by using the built-in function list:

```
x = (1, 2, 3, 4)
list(x)
```

```
[1, 2, 3, 4]
```

3.2.4   *Strings*

String processing is one of Python's strengths. There are many options for delimiting strings:

```
"A string in double quotes can contain 'single quote' characters."
'A string in single quotes can contain "double quote" characters.'
'''\tA string which starts with a tab; ends with a newline character.\n'''
"""This is a triple double quoted string - triple quoted strings (single
    or double quoted) are only kind that can contain real newlines."""
```

Strings can be delimited by single (' '), double (" "), triple single (''' '''), or triple double (""" """) quotations and can contain tab (\t) and newline (\n) characters.

Strings are also immutable. The operators and functions that work with them return new strings derived from the original. The operators (in, +, and *) and built-in functions (len, max, and min) operate on strings as they do on lists and tuples. Index and slice notation works the same way for obtaining elements or slices but can't be used to add, remove, or replace elements.

Strings have several methods to work with their contents, and the `re` library module also contains functions for working with strings:

```
x = "live and    let \t   \tlive"
x.split()
```

```
['live', 'and', 'let', 'live']
```

```
x.replace("    let \t   \tlive", "enjoy life")
```

```
'live and enjoy life'
```

```
import re                          ◄─────┘  re module used to replace all spaces
regexpr = re.compile(r»[\t ]+»)
regexpr.sub(" ", x)
```

```
'live and let live'
```

The `re` module provides regular expression functionality. It provides more sophisticated pattern extraction and replacement capabilities than the `string` module.

The `print` function outputs strings. Other Python data types can be easily converted to strings and formatted:

```
e = 2.718
x = [1, "two", 3, 4.0, ["a", "b"], (5, 6)]
print("The constant e is:", e,              ◄─────┘  list is automatically converted
      "and the list x is:", x)                        to string by print().
```

```
The constant e is: 2.718 and the list x is:
[1, 'two', 3, 4.0,['a', 'b'], (5, 6)]
```

```
print(f"the value of e is: {e}")    ◄─────┘  f in front of a string creates an
                                              "f-string" with values in { }.
```

```
the value of e is: 2.718
```

Objects are automatically converted to string representations for printing. The `%` operator provides formatting capability similar to that of C's `sprintf`.

3.2.5 *Dictionaries*

Python's built-in dictionary data type provides associative array functionality implemented by using hash tables. The built-in `len` function returns the number of key-value pairs in a dictionary. The `del` statement can be used to delete a key-value pair. As is the case for lists, several dictionary methods (`clear`, `copy`, `get`, `items`, `keys`, `update`, and `values`) are available:

```
x = {1: "one", 2: "two"}        ◄─────┘  Sets the value of a new
x["first"] = "one"                        key, "first", to "one"
```

```
x[("Delorme", "Ryan", 1995)] = (1, 2, 3)
list(x.keys())
```
Keys can be numbers, strings, tuples, or other immutable types.

```
[1, 2, 'first', ('Delorme', 'Ryan', 1995)]
```

```
x[1]
```

```
'one'
```

```
x.get(1, "not available")
```

```
'one'
```

```
x.get(4, "not available")
```
get returns "not available" when a key isn't in a dictionary.

```
'not available'
```

Keys must be of an immutable type, including numbers, strings, and tuples. Values can be any kind of object, including mutable types, such as lists and dictionaries. If you try to access the value of a key that isn't in the dictionary, a KeyError exception is raised. To avoid this error, the dictionary method get optionally returns a user-definable value when a key isn't in a dictionary.

3.2.6   *Sets, frozensets*

A *set* in Python is an unordered collection of objects, used in situations where membership and uniqueness in the set are the main things you need to know about that object. Sets behave as collections of dictionary keys without any associated values:

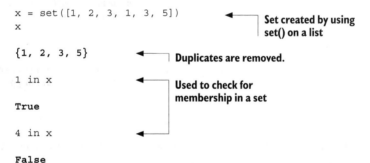

```
x = set([1, 2, 3, 1, 3, 5])
x
```
Set created by using set() on a list

```
{1, 2, 3, 5}
```
Duplicates are removed.

```
1 in x
```
Used to check for membership in a set

```
True
```

```
4 in x
```

```
False
```

You can create a set by using set on a sequence, like a list. When a sequence is made into a set, duplicates are removed. The in keyword is used to check for membership of an object in a set.

A *frozenset* is a set that is immutable. That means that after the set has been created with code like x = frozenset([1, 2, 3, 1, 3, 5]), it cannot be changed, so no elements can be added removed.

3.2.7   *File objects*

A file is accessed through a Python file object:

```
f = open("myfile", "w")
f.write("First line with necessary newline character\n")
```

44

```
f.write("Second line to write to the file\n")
```

33

```
f.close()
f = open("myfile", "r")
line1 = f.readline()
line2 = f.readline()
f.close()
print(line1, line2)
```

The open statement creates a file object, in write ("w") mode.

Opens the same file again, this time in read ("r") mode

First line with necessary newline character
Second line to write to the file

```
import os
directory = os.getcwd()
print(directory)
```

The os module provides functions for working with files and paths.

The directory shown will depend on your environment.

/content

```
filename = os.path.join(directory, "myfile")
print(filename)
```

The join() method combines the directory and filenames into an absolute pathname.

/content/myfile

```
f = open(filename, "r")
print(f.readline())
```

First line with necessary newline character

```
f.close()
```

The open statement creates a file object. Here, the file myfile in the current working directory is being opened in write ("w") mode. After writing two lines to it and closing it, you open the same file again—this time in read ("r") mode. The os module provides several functions for moving around the filesystem and working with the pathnames of files and directories. Here, you move to another directory. But by referring to the file by an absolute pathname, you're still able to access it.

Several other input/output capabilities are available. As we'll see later, you can use the built-in input function to prompt and obtain a string from the user. The sys library module allows access to stdin, stdout, and stderr. The struct library module provides support for reading and writing files that were generated by, or are to be used by, C programs. The Pickle library module delivers data persistence through the ability to easily read and write the Python data types to and from files.

3.3   *Type hints in Python*

Unlike many programming languages, Python by design does not use typed variables and return values. While this makes the language more flexible and readable, it means that in many cases the type of an object referred to by a variable, or needed as a parameter, or returned by a function or method is not always immediately obvious. While inadvertently mixing incompatible types of objects will cause a runtime exception in Python, it will not raise an error at compile time. Particularly for large projects, there are many times when having the types of objects more explicitly available would be useful. For this, Python has added *type hints*.

The type hinting notation can be read by type-checking tools like mypy, pyright, pyre, or pytype, as well as several common IDEs, to flag the use of an incompatible or unexpected type. While these tools can report the error, Python itself does *not* raise a runtime error if the type hints are not followed.

For examples of type hints and a fuller discussion of their use, refer to section 4.4 in the next chapter.

3.4   *Control flow structures*

Python has a full range of structures to control code execution and program flow, including common branching and looping structures.

3.4.1   *Boolean values and expressions*

Python has several ways of expressing Boolean values. The Boolean constant False, 0, the Python nil value None, and empty values (for example, the empty list [] or empty string "") are all taken as False. The Boolean constant True and everything else is considered True.

You can create comparison expressions by using the comparison operators (<, <=, ==, >, >=, !=, is, is not, in, not in) and the logical operators (and, not, or), which all return True or False.

3.4.2   *The if-elif-else statement*

The block of code after the first True condition (of an if or an elif) is executed. If none of the conditions is True, the block of code after the else is executed:

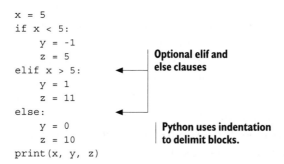

```
x = 5
if x < 5:
    y = -1
    z = 5                    Optional elif and
elif x > 5:                  else clauses
    y = 1
    z = 11
else:                        Python uses indentation
    y = 0                    to delimit blocks.
    z = 10
print(x, y, z)
```

The `elif` and `else` clauses are optional, and there can be any number of `elif` clauses. Python uses indentation to delimit blocks. No explicit delimiters, such as brackets or braces, are necessary. Each block consists of one or more statements separated by new-lines. All these statements must be at the same level of indentation. The output in the example would be 5 0 10.

3.4.3 Structural pattern matching with match

Versions of Python from 3.10 have the `match` statement, which allows for flexible and powerful pattern matching, superficially similar to the `switch` statements familiar to C++ and Java programmers but with more complex and subtle options:

```python
# point is an (x, y) tuple
match point:
    case (0, 0):
        print("Origin")
    case (0, y):
        print(f»Y={y}»)
    case (x, 0):
        print(f"X={x}")
    case (x, y):
        print(f»X={x}, Y={y}»)
    case _:
        raise ValueError("Not a point")
```

We will discuss the many possible options for `match` in the chapters to come.

3.4.4 The while loop

The `while` loop is executed as long as the condition (which here is x > y) is True:

```python
u, v, x, y = 0, 0, 100, 30
while x > y:
    u = u + y
    x = x - y
    if x < y + 2:
        v = v + x
        x = 0
    else:
        v = v + y + 2
        x = x - y - 2
    print(f"{u=} {v=}")
print(u, v)
```

u and v are both assigned a value of 0, x is set to 100, and y to 30.

This is the loop block.

Prints values of u and v each time through the loop

The first line is a shorthand notation. Here, u and v are assigned a value of 0, x is set to 100, and y obtains a value of 30. In this example, the output would be 60 40.

It's also possible for a loop to contain a `break` statement, which ends the loop and jumps to an `else` block if it exists. There can also be a `continue` statement, which aborts the current iteration of the loop and returns to the start of the loop block.

3.4.5   *The for loop*

The for loop is simple but powerful because it's possible to iterate over any iterable type, such as a list or tuple. Unlike in many languages, Python's for loop iterates over each of the items in a sequence, making it more of a foreach loop. The following loop finds the first occurrence of an integer that's divisible by 7:

```
item_list = [3, "string1", 23, 14.0, "string2", 49, 64, 70]     ◁──── x is assigned each
for x in item_list:                                                     value in the list.
    if not isinstance(x, int):
        continue          ◁─────── If x isn't an integer, iteration is aborted by the continue.
    if not x % 7:                                              ◁───┐
        print(f"found an integer divisible by seven: {x}")         │ If x is divisible by 7,
        break             ◁────────┐                                 this will be 0 and
                          break ends the loop.                       therefore False.
```

x is sequentially assigned each value in the list. If x isn't an integer, the rest of this iteration is aborted by the continue statement. Flow control continues with x set to the next item from the list. After the first appropriate integer is found, the loop is ended by the break statement. The output would be

```
found an integer divisible by seven: 49
```

Just as in while loops, a break will cause the loop to end, and the execution will jump to an else block if it exists or to the next line after the loop.

3.4.6   *Function definition*

Python provides flexible mechanisms for passing arguments to functions:

```
def funct1(x, y, z):              ◁───── Functions are defined by using the def
    value = x + 2*y + z**2                statement, parameters by position.
    if value > 0:
        return x + 2*y + z**2     ◁───── The return statement evaluates the
    else:                                 expression and returns its value.
        return 0

u, v = 3, 4
funct1(u, v, 2)
```

```
15
```

```
funct1(u, z=v, y=2)     ◁─────── Here, z and y are entered by name.
```

```
23
```

```
def funct2(x, y=1, z=1):     ◁─────── Function parameter with defaults
    return x + 2 * y + z ** 2

funct2(3, z=4)
```

```
21

def funct3(x, y=1, z=1, *tup):
    print((x, y, z) + tup)
```
◄──── **With a *, this collects all extra positional arguments into a tuple.**

```
funct3(2)
```

(2, 1, 1)

```
funct3(1, 2, 3, 4, 5, 6, 7, 8, 9)
```

(1, 2, 3, 4, 5, 6, 7, 8, 9)

```
def funct4(x, y=1, z=1, **kwargs):
    print(x, y, z, kwargs)
funct4(1, 2, m=5, n=9, z=3)
```
◄──── **With **, this collects all extra keyword arguments into a dictionary.**

1 2 3 {'m': 5, 'n': 9}

Functions are defined by using the `def` statement, with the `return` statement being used to return a value. This value can be of any type, and if no `return` statement is encountered, Python's `None` value is returned.

Function arguments can be entered either by position or by name (keyword). A special parameter with `*` can be defined that collects all extra positional arguments in a function call into a tuple. Likewise, a special parameter can be defined with `**` that collects all extra keyword arguments in a function call into a dictionary.

3.4.7   *Exceptions*

Exceptions (errors) can be caught and handled by using the `try-except-else-finally` compound statement. This statement can also catch and handle exceptions you define and raise yourself. Any exception that isn't caught causes the program to exit. The following code snippet shows basic exception handling; we will discuss more complex examples in our chapter dealing with exceptions:

```
class EmptyFileError(Exception):
    pass
file_names = ["myfile1.txt", "non_existent", "empty_file", "myfile2.txt"]
for file_name in file_names:
    try:
        file = open(file_name, 'r')
        line = file.readline()
        if line == "":
            file.close()
            raise EmptyFileError("{file_name}: is empty")
    except IOError as error:
        print(f"{file_name}: could not be opened: {error.strerror}")
    except EmptyFileError as error:
        print(error)
    else:
```

◄──── **Exception type defined from the base Exception type**

◄──── **Block checked for IOError or EmptyFileError**

◄──── **An IOError might occur.**

◄──── **EmptyFileError raised**

◄──── **An optional else clause is executed if no exception occurs.**

```
        print(f"{file_name}: {line}")
    finally:
        print("Done processing", file_name)
```

An optional finally clause is always executed at the end of the block.

Here, you define your own exception type inheriting from the base `Exception` type. If an `IOError` or `EmptyFileError` occurs during the execution of the statements in the `try` block, the associated `except` block is executed. This is where an `IOError` might be raised. Here, you raise the `EmptyFileError`. The `else` clause is optional; it's executed if no exception occurs in the `try` block. (Note that in this example, `continue` statements in the `except` blocks could have been used instead.) The `finally` clause is optional; it's executed at the end of the block whether an exception was raised or not.

3.4.8   *Context handling using the with keyword*

A more streamlined way of encapsulating the `try-except-finally` pattern is to use the `with` keyword and a context manager. Python defines context managers for things like file access, and it's possible for the developer to define custom context managers. One benefit of context managers is that they may (and usually do) have default cleanup actions defined, which always execute whether or not an exception occurs.

The following example shows opening and reading a file by using `with` and a context manager:

```
filename = "myfile1.txt"
with open(filename, "r") as file:
    for line in file:
        print(line)
```

Here, `with` establishes a context manager that wraps the `open` function and the block that follows. In this case, the context manager's predefined cleanup action closes the file, even if an exception occurs; so, as long as the expression in the first line executes without raising an exception, the file is always closed. That code is equivalent to the following code:

```
filename = "myfile1.txt"
try:
    file = open(filename, "r")
    for line in file:
        print(line)
except Exception as e:
    raise e
finally:
    file.close()
```

3.5   *Module creation*

It's easy to create your own modules, which can be imported and used in the same way as Python's built-in library modules. The example in the following listing is a deliberately oversimplified module with one function that prompts the user to enter a filename and determines the number of times that words occur in this file.

Listing 3.1   File wo.py

Docstring to
document module

Comment to
explain code

```
"""wo module. Contains function: words_occur()"""
# interface functions
def words_occur():
    """words_occur() - count the occurrences of words in a file."""
    # Prompt user for the name of the file to use.
    file_name = input("Enter the name of the file: ")
    # Open the file, read it and store its words in a list.
    file = open(file_name, 'r')
    word_list = file.read().split()
    file.close()
    # Count the number of occurrences of each word in the file.
    occurs_dict = {}
    for word in word_list:
        # increment the occurrences count for this word
        occurs_dict[word] = occurs_dict.get(word, 0) + 1
    # Print out the results.
    print(f"File {file_name} has {len(word_list)} words
      {CA}({len(occurs_dict)} are unique)")
    print(occurs_dict)
if __name__ == '__main__':
    words_occur()
```

read returns all the
characters in a file;
split splits the string
on whitespace.

Common form for
running module as
command with python
wo.py at a command line

Documentation strings, or *docstrings*, are standard ways of documenting modules, functions, methods, and classes. Comments are anything beginning with a # character and should be used to explain something specific about the code. read returns a string containing all the characters in a file, and split returns a list of the words of a string "split out" based on whitespace. The final if statement allows the program to be run as a script by typing python wo.py at a command line.

If a file is in the current directory or in one of the directories on the module search path, which can be found in sys.path, it can be imported like any of the built-in library modules by using the import statement:

```
import wo
wo.words_occur()
```

Function called by using
the module.function

This function is called by using the same attribute syntax used for library module functions.

Note that if you change the file wo.py on disk, import won't bring your changes into the same interactive session. You use the reload function from the imp library in this situation:

```
import imp
imp.reload(wo)
```

<module 'wo'>

For larger projects, there is a generalization of the module concept called *packages*, which allows you to easily group modules in a directory or directory subtree and then import and hierarchically refer to them by using a `package.subpackage.module` syntax. This entails little more than creating a possibly empty initialization file for each package or subpackage.

3.6   *Object-oriented programming*

Python provides full support for object-oriented programming (OOP). Listing 3.2 is an example that might be the start of a simple shapes module for a drawing program. It's intended mainly to serve as a reference if you're already familiar with OOP. The callout notes relate Python's syntax and semantics to the standard features found in other languages.

Listing 3.2   File shape.py

```
"""shape module. Contains classes Shape, Square and Circle"""
class Shape:
    """Shape class: has method move"""
    def __init__(self, x, y):
        self.x = x
        self.y = y
    def move(self, deltaX, deltaY):
        self.x = self.x + deltaX
        self.y = self.y + deltaY
class Square(Shape):
    """Square Class:inherits from Shape"""
    def __init__(self, side=1, x=0, y=0):
        Shape.__init__(self, x, y)
        self.side = side
class Circle(Shape):
    """Circle Class: inherits from Shape and has method area"""
    pi = 3.14159
    def __init__(self, r=1, x=0, y=0):
        Shape.__init__(self, x, y)
        self.radius = r
    def area(self):
        """Circle area method: returns the area of the circle."""
        return self.radius * self.radius * self.pi
    def __str__(self):
        return f"Circle of radius {self.radius} at ({self.x}, {self.y})"
```

Callouts:
- Class defined by class keyword
- The instance initializer __init__
- x and y are created and initialized here.
- Methods defined by using the def keyword
- Class Circle inherits from class Shape.
- pi is a class variable, readable by all instances of the class.
- Subclass calls the initializer of its base class.
- The __str__ method (used by the print function)

Classes are defined by using the `class` keyword. The instance initializer method (constructor) for a class is always called `__init__`, and instance variables x and y are created and initialized here. Methods, like functions, are defined by using the `def` keyword. The first argument of any method is by convention called `self`. When the method is invoked, `self` is set to the instance that invoked the method. Class `Circle` inherits from class `Shape` and is similar to, but not exactly like, a standard class variable. A subclass must, in its initializer, explicitly call the initializer of its base class. The `__str__` method returns a string version of the class and is used by the `print` function. Other special method attributes permit operator overloading or are employed by built-in methods such as the length (`len`) function.

Importing this file makes these classes available:

```
import shape
c1 = shape.Circle()
c2 = shape.Circle(5, 15, 20)
print(c1)
```

The initializer is called when an instance is created.

```
Circle of radius 1 at coordinates (0, 0)

print(c2)
```

The print function implicitly uses __str__.

```
Circle of radius 5 at coordinates (15, 20)

c2.area()

78.539749999999998
```

Circle uses the move method of parent class Shape.

```
c2.move(5,6)
print(c2)

Circle of radius 5 at coordinates (20, 26)
```

The initializer is implicitly called, and a circle instance is created. The `print` function implicitly uses the special `__str__` method. Here, you see that the `move` method of `Circle`'s parent class `Shape` is available. A method is called by using attribute syntax on the object instance: `object.method()`. The first (`self`) parameter is set implicitly.

Summary

- Python has a number of built-in data types, including integers, floating points, and complex numbers; lists and tuples; strings; dictionaries; sets and frozensets; and file objects.
- Python also allows the programmer to make optional non-enforced notations of the type expected for variables and function/method parameters and return values.
- Python has a rich set of control flow structures including `for` and `while` loops, `if-elif-else` structures, structural pattern matching, functions, exceptions, and context handlers.

- Modules are just files of Python code that can be used by loading them with the `import` command.
- Python is an object-oriented language—not only are the built-in data types objects, it's also easy to create custom classes and inherit from other classes.

Part 2

The essentials

In the chapters that follow, I show you the essentials of Python. I start from the absolute basics of what makes a Python program and move through Python's built-in data types and control structures, as well as defining functions and using modules. The last chapter of this part moves on to show you how to write stand-alone Python programs, manipulate files, handle errors, and use classes.

The absolute basics

This chapter covers

- Indenting and block structuring
- Differentiating comments
- Assigning variables
- Optional type hints
- Evaluating expressions
- Using common data types
- Getting user input
- Using correct Pythonic style

This chapter describes the absolute basics in Python: how to use assignments and expressions, how to use numbers and strings, how to indicate comments in code, and so forth. It starts with a discussion of how Python block structures its code, which differs from every other major language.

4.1 Indentation and block structuring

Python differs from most other programming languages because it uses whitespace and indentation to determine block structure (that is, to determine what constitutes the body of a loop, the `else` clause of a conditional, and so on). Most languages use braces of some sort to do this. The following is C code that calculates the factorial of 9, leaving the result in the variable `r`:

```
/* This is C code  */
int n, r;
n = 9;
r = 1;
while (n > 0) {
    r *= n;
    n--;
}
```

The braces delimit the body of the `while` loop, the code that is executed with each repetition of the loop. The code is usually indented more or less as shown, to make clear what's going on, but it could also be written as follows:

```
/* And this is C code with arbitrary indentation */
    int n, r;
        n = 9;
        r = 1;
    while (n > 0) {
r *=  n;
n--;
}
```

The code still would execute correctly, even though it's rather difficult to read.

The Python equivalent is

```
# This is Python code.
n = 9
r = 1
while n > 0:
    r = r * n
    n = n - 1
```

Python also supports C-style r *= n.

Python also supports n –= 1.

Python doesn't use braces to indicate code structure; instead, the indentation itself is used. The last two lines of the previous code are the body of the `while` loop because they come immediately after the `while` statement and are indented one level further than the `while` statement. If those lines weren't indented, they wouldn't be part of the body of the `while`.

Note that while it's more explicit and clearer to say r = r * n, it's also possible and good Pythonic style to use the shorter r *= n form—both are fine in Python.

Using indentation to structure code rather than braces may take some getting used to, but there are significant benefits:

- It's impossible to have missing or extra braces. You never need to hunt through your code for the brace near the bottom that matches the one a few lines from the top.

- The visual structure of the code reflects its real structure, which makes it easy to grasp the skeleton of the code just by looking at it.
- Python coding styles are mostly uniform. In other words, you're unlikely to go crazy from dealing with someone's idea of aesthetically pleasing code. Everyone's code will look pretty much like yours.

You probably use consistent indentation in your code already, so this won't be a big step. If you're using IDLE or one of the most common coding editors or IDEs—Emacs, VIM, VS Code, or PyCharm, to name a few—it will automatically indent lines. You just need to backspace out of levels of indentation when that block is finished. One thing that may trip you up once or twice until you get used to it is the fact that the Python interpreter returns an error message if you have a space (or spaces) preceding the commands you enter in a Jupyter notebook cell or at a Python shell's `>>>` prompt.

4.2 Differentiating comments

For the most part, anything following a # symbol in a Python file is a comment and is disregarded by the interpreter. The obvious exception is a # in a string, which is just a character of that string:

```
# Assign 5 to x
x = 5
x = 3                     # Now x is 3
x = "# This is not a comment"
```

You'll put comments in Python code frequently.

4.3 Variables and assignments

The most commonly used command in Python is assignment, which looks pretty close to what you might've used in other languages. Python code to create a variable called x and assign that variable to the value 5 is

```
x = 5
```

In Python, unlike in many other computer languages, neither a variable type declaration nor an end-of-line delimiter (like a ;) is necessary. The line is ended by the end of the line. Variables are created automatically when they're first assigned.

Variable names are case sensitive and can include any alphanumeric character as well as underscores but must start with a letter or underscore. See section 4.11 for more guidance on the Pythonic style for creating variable names.

Variables in Python: Buckets or labels?

The name *variable* is somewhat misleading in Python; *name* or *label* would be more accurate. However, it seems that pretty much everyone calls variables *variables* at

(continued)

some time or another. Whatever you call them, you should know how they really work in Python.

A common, but inaccurate, explanation is that a variable is a container that stores a value, somewhat like a bucket. This would be reasonable for many programming languages (C, for example).

However, in Python variables aren't buckets. Instead, they're labels or tags that refer to objects in the Python interpreter's namespace. Any number of labels (or variables) can refer to the same object, and when that object changes, the value referred to by *all* of those variables also changes.

To see what this means, look at the following simple code:

```
a = [1, 2, 3]
b = a
c = b
b[1] = 5
print(a, b, c)
[1, 5, 3] [1, 5, 3] [1, 5, 3]
```

If you're thinking of variables as containers, this result makes no sense. How could changing the contents of one container simultaneously change the other two? However, if variables are just labels referring to objects, it makes sense that changing the object that all three labels refer to would be reflected everywhere.

If the variables are referring to constants or immutable values, this distinction isn't quite as clear:

```
a = 1
b = a
c = b
b = 5
print(a, b, c)
1 5 1
```

Because the objects they refer to can't change, the behavior of the variables in this case is consistent with either explanation. In fact, in this case, after the third line, a, b, and c all refer to the same unchangeable integer object with the value 1. The next line, b = 5, makes b refer to the integer object 5 but doesn't change the references of a or c.

Python variables can be set to any object, whereas in C and many other languages, variables can store only the type of value they're declared as. The following is perfectly legal Python code:

```
x = "Hello"
print(x)
```

```
Hello
```

```
x = 5
print(x)
```

```
5
```

x starts out referring to the string object `"Hello"` and then refers to the integer object 5. Of course, this feature can be abused, because arbitrarily assigning the same variable name to refer successively to different data types can make code confusing.

A new assignment overrides any previous assignments. The `del` statement deletes the variable (but not necessarily the object it was attached to). Trying to print the variable's object after deleting it results in an error, as though the variable had never been created in the first place:

```
x = 5
print(x)
```

```
5
```

```
del x
print(x)
------------------------------------------------------------------------
NameError                                     Traceback (most recent call last)
<ipython-input-2-260d38800877> in <cell line: 5>()
      3
      4 del x
----> 5 print(x)                  ◀──────┘ Line where error occurs

NameError: name 'x' is not defined      ◀──────┘ Name of exception that occurred
```

Here, you have your first look at a *traceback*, which is printed when an error, called an *exception*, has been detected. Notice that when we try to access a variable *after* we've deleted it, there is a line of dashes followed by the name of the exception, a `NameError`. The traceback has a little arrow `---->` pointing to the line with the error. The last line explains the exception that was detected, which in this case is a `NameError` exception because x is no longer defined or valid after its deletion.

In general, the full dynamic call structure of the existing function at the time of the error's occurrence is returned. If you're using another Python environment, you might obtain the same information with some small differences. The traceback could look something like the following:

```
Traceback (most recent call last):
  File "/home/naomi/Dropbox/QPB4/code/vscode/ch04.py", line 5, in <module>
    print(x)
        ^                      ◀──────┘ Error location indicated with
                                         a ^ under the problem
NameError: name 'x' is not defined
```

This format is a bit simpler, with just a ^ under the error on the next line, but the same information is there.

Chapter 14 describes this mechanism in more detail. A full list of the possible exceptions and what causes them is in the Python standard library documentation. Use the index to find any specific exception (such as `NameError`) you receive.

4.4   *Optional type hints in Python*

While Python does not *require* that you specify types for variables (and function parameters and return values, etc.), current versions of Python do *allow* you to do so. As mentioned in the previous chapter, in Python many times the type of an object referred to by a variable, or needed as a parameter, or returned by a function or method is not always immediately obvious.

Mixing incompatible types of objects will cause a runtime exception in Python, but it will not raise an error at compile time. Particularly for large projects, there are many times when having the types of objects more explicitly available would be useful. For this, Python has added *type hints*.

The type hinting notation can be read by type-checking tools like mypy, pyright, pyre, or pytype, as well as several common IDEs, to flag the use of an incompatible or unexpected type. While these tools can report the error, Python itself will *not* raise a runtime error if the type hints are not followed.

For example, we can create a simple function to add two numbers and use type hinting to indicate that it should only receive and return objects of type `int`:

```
def add_ints(x: int, y: int) -> int:          ◄──────┐  Parameters and return
    return x + y                                      │  value noted as ints

p: int = 2.3                          ◄──────┐  Variable p marked as
z = add_ints(1, 2)                           │  int but set to float
w = add_ints(1.5, 2.5)                ◄──────┘
                                      └  Function called with floats
```

The function definition specifies that both of the parameters and the return value will be of type `int`. In the first line of code after the function, we specify that the variable p should be of type `int` but then try to set it to a `float`. Then the function `add_ints` is called first with two integers and then with two `floats`.

If we run this code, Python will execute it without any warning or complaint. However, if we save this code in a file test_types.py and run the mypy checker on that file, three errors will be flagged:

**Flags setting int
variable p to a float**

```
naomi@naomi-NUC:~$ mypy test_types.py
test_types.py:4: error: Incompatible types in assignment (expression has
  type "float", variable has type "int")  [assignment]          ◄──────
```

```
test_types.py:8: error: Argument 1 to "add_ints" has incompatible type
  "float"; expected "int"  [arg-type]
test_types.py:8: error: Argument 2 to "add_ints" has incompatible type
  "float"; expected "int"  [arg-type]
Found 3 errors in 1 file (checked 1 source file)
```

Flags calling function with two floats instead of ints

When you run the mypy type checker on this code, it reports an error with setting the variable p to 2.3, not because 2.3 is a bad value for p but because the annotation indicated that it should be an int. It also flags two errors in the second call to add_ints, since both of the parameters are floats, but the function is marked as taking two ints. In both cases, Python will run the code without complaint, but the things marked by mypy indicate some confusion between intention and actual use, and that confusion is likely to lead to bugs later on.

4.4.1 Why use type hints?

One reason that type hints are increasingly used is that they help reduce confusion as to what type is expected, in many situations. In a large codebase, it can be particularly frustrating to hunt a bug where an unexpected type of object is returned. Type hints allow many such situations to be caught and fixed before runtime. Type information also allows many editors and IDEs to warn about such errors and suggest appropriate alternatives during the coding process.

4.4.2 Why not use type hints?

While type hints can be useful in many situations, there are situations where they may not be worth the trouble:

- In smaller, more informal scripts, it may not be worth the extra time and effort to add type hints.
- Trying to fully and explicitly type hint *everything* in a program may make function or method definitions harder to read. In that case, a decision needs to be made on the tradeoff between human readability and completeness of typing.
- Beware of going too far down the type-hinting rabbit hole. Spending too much time obsessed with detailed type hints may not be productive.
- Going back and changing working code solely to add type hints also may not be the best use of your time. It's usually wiser to leave working code alone unless you have a good reason to change it. Adding type hints can be done in the course of other maintenance or refactoring.

4.4.3 Progressive typing

Fortunately, since type hints are optional, you don't have to add type hints for everything all at once. If you have decided it's a good idea to use type hints, you can add them progressively, starting with the places where having the type information handy will do the most good.

In this text, we will not routinely use type hints in the short code examples, but we will use them in some of the longer examples and answers to the lab exercises.

4.5   *Expressions*

Python supports arithmetic and similar expressions; these expressions will be familiar to most readers. The following code calculates the average of 3 and 5, leaving the result in the variable z:

```
x = 3
y = 5
z = (x + y) / 2
```

Note that arithmetic operators involving only integers do *not* always return an integer. Even though all the values are integers, division (starting with Python 3) returns a floating-point number, so the fractional part isn't truncated. If you want traditional integer division returning an integer, you can use // instead.

Standard rules of arithmetic precedence apply. If you'd left out the parentheses in the last line, the code would've been calculated as x + (y / 2).

Expressions don't have to involve just numerical values; strings, Boolean values, and many other types of objects can be used in expressions in various ways. I discuss these objects in more detail as they're used.

> **Try this: Variables and expressions**
>
> In a Jupyter notebook, create some variables. What happens when you try to put spaces, dashes, or other nonalphanumeric characters in the variable name? Play around with a few complex expressions, such as x = 2 + 4 * 5 – 6 / 3. Use parentheses to group the numbers in different ways and see how the result changes compared with the original ungrouped expression.

4.6   *Strings*

You've already seen that Python, like most other programming languages, indicates strings through the use of double quotes. This line leaves the string "Hello, World" in the variable x:

```
x = "Hello, World"
```

Backslashes can be used to escape characters—to give them special meanings. \n means the newline character, \t means the tab character, \\ means a single normal backslash character, and \" is a plain double-quote character. It doesn't end the string:

```
x = "\tThis string starts with a \"tab\"."
x = "This string contains a single backslash(\\)."
```

You can use single quotes instead of double quotes. The following two lines do the same thing:

```
x = "Hello, World"
x = 'Hello, World'
```

The only difference is that you don't need to backslash " characters in single-quoted strings or ' characters in double-quoted strings:

```
x = "Don't need a backslash"
x = 'Can\'t get by without a backslash'
x = "Backslash your \" character!"
x = 'You can leave the " alone'
```

You can't split a normal string across lines. This code won't work:

```
# This Python code will cause an ERROR -- you can't
# split the string across two lines.
x = "This is a misguided attempt to
put a newline into a string without using backslash-n"
File "<ipython-input-3-dc07520d5086>", line 2
    x = "This is a misguided attempt to
         ^
SyntaxError: unterminated string literal (detected at line 2)
```

But Python offers triple-quoted strings, which let you have multiline strings and include single and double quotes without backslashes:

```
x = """Starting and ending a string with triple " or ' characters
permits embedded newlines, and the use of " and ' without
backslashes"""
```

Now x is the entire sentence between the """ delimiters. [You can use triple single quotes (''') instead of triple double quotes to do the same thing.]

Python offers enough string-related functionality that chapter 6 is devoted to the topic.

4.7 Numbers

Because you're probably familiar with standard numeric operations from other languages, this book doesn't contain a separate chapter describing Python's numeric abilities. This section describes the unique features of Python numbers, and the Python documentation lists the available functions.

Python offers four kinds of numbers: *integers, floats, complex numbers,* and *Booleans.* An integer constant is written as an integer—0, –11, +33, 123456—and has unlimited range, restricted only by the resources of your machine. A float can be written with a decimal point or in scientific notation: 3.14, –2E-8, 2.718281828. The precision of these values is governed by the underlying machine but is typically equal to double (64-bit) types in C. Complex numbers are probably of limited interest and are discussed separately later in the section. Booleans are either `True` or `False` and behave identically to 1 and 0 except for their string representations.

Arithmetic is much like it is in C. Operations involving two integers produce an integer, except for division (/), which results in a float. If the // division symbol is used, the result is an integer, rounding down. Operations involving a float always produce a float. Here are a few examples:

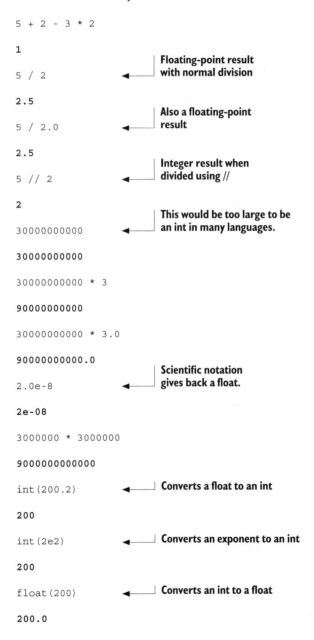

```
5 + 2 - 3 * 2

1
5 / 2
```
Floating-point result with normal division
```
2.5
5 / 2.0
```
Also a floating-point result
```
2.5
5 // 2
```
Integer result when divided using //
```
2
30000000000
```
This would be too large to be an int in many languages.
```
30000000000

30000000000 * 3

90000000000

30000000000 * 3.0

90000000000.0
2.0e-8
```
Scientific notation gives back a float.
```
2e-08

3000000 * 3000000

9000000000000

int(200.2)
```
Converts a float to an int
```
200
int(2e2)
```
Converts an exponent to an int
```
200
float(200)
```
Converts an int to a float
```
200.0
```

The last three commands are explicit conversions between types. Note that converting from a float to an int will truncate the value and discard the decimal portion. On the other hand, converting an int to a float will always add a `.0`.

Numbers in Python have two advantages over C or Java: integers can be arbitrarily large, and the division of two integers results in a float.

4.7.1 *Built-in numeric functions*

Python provides the following number-related functions as part of its core:

```
abs, divmod, float, hex, int, max, min, oct,
pow, round
```

See the documentation for the details of how each works.

4.7.2 *Advanced numeric functions*

More advanced numeric functions, such as the trig and hyperbolic trig functions, as well as a few useful constants, aren't built into Python but are provided in a standard module called `math`. I explain modules in detail later. For now, it's sufficient to know that you must make the math functions in this section available by starting your Python program or interactive session with the statement

```
from math import *
```

The `math` module provides the following functions and constants:

```
acos, asin, atan, atan2, ceil, cos, cosh, e, exp, fabs, floor, fmod,
frexp, hypot, ldexp, log, log10, mod, pi, pow, sin, sinh, sqrt, tan,
tanh
```

See the documentation for details.

4.7.3 *Numeric computation*

The core Python installation isn't well suited to intensive numeric computation because of speed constraints. But the powerful Python extension `NumPy` provides highly efficient implementations of many advanced numeric operations. The emphasis is on array operations, including multidimensional matrices and more advanced functions such as the fast Fourier transform. You should be able to find `NumPy` (or links to it) at www.scipy.org.

4.7.4 *Complex numbers*

Complex numbers are created automatically whenever an expression of the form `nj` is encountered, with `n` having the same form as a Python integer or float. `j` is, of course, standard notation for the imaginary number equal to the square root of −1, for example:

```
(3+2j)
```

```
(3+2j)
```

Note that Python expresses the resulting complex number in parentheses as a way of indicating that what's printed to the screen represents the value of a single object:

```
3 + 2j - (4+4j)
```

```
(-1-2j)
```

```
(1+2j) * (3+4j)
```

```
(-5+10j)
```

```
1j * 1j
```

```
(-1+0j)
```

Calculating j * j gives the expected answer of -1, but the result remains a Python complex-number object. Complex numbers are never converted automatically to equivalent real or integer objects. But you can easily access their real and imaginary parts with real and imag:

```
z = (3+5j)
z.real
```

```
3.0
```

```
z.imag
```

```
5.0
```

Note that real and imaginary parts of a complex number are always returned as floating-point numbers.

4.7.5   *Advanced complex-number functions*

The functions in the math module don't apply to complex numbers; the rationale is that most users want the square root of –1 to generate an error, not an answer! Instead, similar functions, which can operate on complex numbers, are provided in the cmath module:

```
acos, acosh, asin, asinh, atan, atanh, cos, cosh, e, exp, log, log10,
pi, sin, sinh, sqrt, tan, tanh.
```

To make clear in the code that these functions are special-purpose complex-number functions and to avoid name conflicts with the more normal equivalents, it's best to import the cmath module with

```
import cmath
```

and then to explicitly refer to the `cmath` package when using the function:

```
import cmath
cmath.sqrt(-1)
```

```
1j
```

> **Minimizing from <module> import ***
>
> This is a good example of why it's best to minimize the use of the `from <module> import *` form of the `import` statement. If you used it to import first the `math` module and then the `cmath` module, the commonly named functions in `cmath` would override those of `math`. It's also more work for someone reading your code to figure out the source of the specific functions you use. Some modules are explicitly designed to use this form of import.
>
> See chapter 10 for more details on how to use modules and module names.

The important thing to keep in mind is that by importing the `cmath` module, you can do almost anything with complex numbers that you can do with other numbers.

> **Try this: Manipulating strings and numbers**
>
> In a Jupyter notebook, create some string and number variables (integers, floats, *and* complex numbers). Experiment a bit with what happens when you do operations with them, including across types. Can you multiply a string by an integer, for example, or can you multiply it by a float or complex number? Also load the `math` module and try a few of the functions; then load the `cmath` module and do the same. What happens if you try to use one of those functions on an integer or float after loading the `cmath` module? How might you get the `math` module functions back?

4.8   *The None value*

In addition to standard types such as strings and numbers, Python has a special basic data type that defines a single special data object called `None`. As the name suggests, `None` is used to represent an empty value. It appears in various guises throughout Python. For example, a procedure in Python is just a function that doesn't explicitly return a value, which means that, by default, it returns `None`.

`None` is often useful in day-to-day Python programming as a placeholder to indicate a point in a data structure where meaningful data will eventually be found, even though that data hasn't yet been calculated. You can easily test for the presence of `None` because there's only one instance of `None` in the entire Python system (all references to `None` point to the same object), and `None` is equivalent only to itself.

4.9   Getting input from the user

You can use the `input()` function to get input from the user. Use the prompt string you want to display to the user as `input`'s parameter:

```
name = input("Name? ")

Name? Jane

print(name)

Jane

age = int(input("Age? "))     ◄────┐ Converts input from
                                    │ a string to an int

Age? 28

print(age)

28
```

This is a fairly simple way to get user input. The one catch is that the input comes in as a string, so if you want to use it as a number, you have to use the `int()` or `float()` function to convert it to an int or float.

> **Try this: Getting input**
>
> Experiment with the `input()` function to get string and integer input. Using code similar to the previous code, what is the effect of not using `int()` around the call to `input()` for integer input? Can you modify that code to accept a float—say, 28.5? What happens if you deliberately enter the wrong type of value? Examples include a float in which an integer is expected and a string in which a number is expected—and vice versa.

4.10   Built-in operators

Python provides various built-in operators, from the standard (`+`, `*`, and so on) to the more esoteric, such as operators for performing bit shifting, bitwise logical functions, and so forth. Most of these operators are no more unique to Python than to any other language; hence, I won't explain them in the main text. You can find a complete list of the Python built-in operators in the documentation.

4.11   Basic Python style

Python has relatively few limitations on coding style with the obvious exception of the requirement to use indentation to organize code into blocks. Even in that case, the amount of indentation and type of indentation (tabs versus spaces) isn't mandated. However, there are preferred stylistic conventions for Python, contained in Python

Enhancement Proposal (PEP) 8, which is summarized in appendix A and available online at www.python.org/dev/peps/pep-0008/. A selection of Pythonic conventions is provided in table 4.1, but to fully absorb Pythonic style, periodically reread PEP 8.

Table 4.1   Pythonic coding conventions

Situation	Suggestion	Example
Module/package names	Short, all lowercase, underscores only if needed	`imp, sys`
Function names	All lowercase, underscores_for_readablitiy	`foo(), my_func()`
Variable names	All lowercase, underscores_for_readablitiy	`my_var`
Class names	CapitalizeEachWord	`MyClass`
Constant names	ALL_CAPS_WITH_UNDERSCORES	`PI, TAX_RATE`
Indentation	Four spaces per level, no tabs	
Comparisons	Don't compare explicitly to `True` or `False`.	`if my_var:` `if not my_var:`

I strongly urge you to follow the conventions of PEP 8. They're wisely chosen and time tested, and they'll make your code easier for you and other Python programmers to understand.

> ### Quick check: Pythonic style
>
> Which of the following variable and function names do you think are not good Pythonic style? Why?
>
> ```
> bar(), varName, VERYLONGVARNAME, foobar, longvarname,
> foo_bar(), really_very_long_var_name
> ```

Summary

- Python code is organized by using levels of indentation.
- Python comments can be marked with an initial # character.
- Strings in triple quotes at the beginning of a module, function, or method are "docstrings," which explain what the object does and/or how it behaves.
- The intended types of variables, parameters, and function return values can optionally be marked using Python's type hints.
- Python has the usual data types for strings and numbers, as well as data structures like lists, tuples, sets, and dictionaries.

- The `input()` function can be used to get input from the user as a string.
- Python has several built-in operators, including +, -, /, //, %, *, etc.
- The preferred Python style can be found in PEP 8 in the online Python documentation.

Lists, tuples, and sets

5

In this chapter, I discuss the two major Python sequence types: lists and tuples. At first, lists may remind you of arrays in many other languages, but don't be fooled: lists are a good deal more flexible and powerful than plain arrays.

Tuples are like lists that can't be modified; you can think of them as a restricted type of list or as a basic record type. I discuss the need for such a restricted data type later in the chapter. This chapter also discusses another Python collection type: sets. Sets are useful when an object's membership in the collection, as opposed to its position, is important.

Most of the chapter is devoted to lists, because if you understand lists, you pretty much understand tuples. The last part of the chapter discusses the differences between lists and tuples in both functional and design terms.

5.1 *Lists are like arrays*

A list in Python is similar to an array in Java or C or any other language; it's an ordered collection of objects. You create a list by enclosing a comma-separated list of elements in square brackets, as follows:

```
# This assigns a three-element list to x
x = [1, 2, 3]
```

Note that you don't have to worry about declaring the list or fixing its size ahead of time. This line creates the list as well as assigns it, and a list automatically grows or shrinks as needed.

Arrays in Python

A typed `array` module available in Python provides arrays based on C data types. Information on its use can be found in the documentation for the Python standard library. I suggest that you look into it only if you really need performance improvement. If a situation calls for numerical computations, you should consider using `NumPy`, mentioned in chapter 4 and available at www.scipy.org/.

Unlike lists in many other languages, Python lists can contain different types of elements; a list element can be any Python object. The following is a list that contains a variety of elements:

```
# First element is a number, second is a string, third is another list.
x = [2, "two", [1, 2, 3]]
```

Probably the most basic built-in list function is the `len` function, which returns the number of elements in a list:

```
x = [2, "two", [1, 2, 3]]
len(x)
```

```
3
```

Note that the `len` function doesn't count the items in the inner, nested list.

Quick check: len()

What would `len()` return for each of the following? `[0]`; `[]`; `[[1, 3, [4, 5], 6], 7]`

5.2 List indices

Understanding how list indices work will make Python much more useful to you. Please read the whole section!

Elements can be extracted from a Python list by using a notation like C's array indexing. Like C and many other languages, Python starts counting from 0; asking for element 0 returns the first element of the list, asking for element 1 returns the second element, and so forth. The following are a few examples:

```
x = ["first", "second", "third", "fourth"]
x[0]
```

```
'first'
```

```
x[2]
```

```
'third'
```

But Python indexing is more flexible than C indexing. If indices are negative numbers, they indicate positions counting from the end of the list, with –1 being the last position in the list, –2 being the second-to-last position, and so forth. Continuing with the same list x, you can do the following:

```
a = x[-1]
a
```

```
'fourth'
```

```
x[-2]
```

```
'third'
```

For operations involving a single list index, it's generally satisfactory to think of the index as pointing at a particular element in the list. For more advanced operations, it's more correct to think of list indices as indicating positions *between* elements. In the list `["first", "second", "third", "fourth"]`, you can think of the indices as pointing as follows.

x =[		"first",		"second",		"third",		"fourth"		]
Positive indices	0		1		2		3			
Negative indices	-4		-3		-2		-1			

This is irrelevant when you're extracting a single element, but Python can extract or assign to an entire sublist at once—an operation known as *slicing*. Instead of entering `list[index]` to extract the item just after `index`, enter `list[index1:index2]` to extract all items, including `index1` and up to (but not including) `index2`, into a new list. The following are some examples:

```
x = ["first", "second", "third", "fourth"]
x[1:-1]
```

```
['second', 'third']
```

```
x[0:3]
```

```
['first', 'second', 'third']
```

```
x[-2:-1]
```

```
['third']
```

It may seem reasonable that if the second index indicates a position in the list *before* the first index, this code would return the elements between those indices in reverse order, but this isn't what happens. Instead, this code returns an empty list:

```
x[-1:2]
[]
```

When slicing a list, it's also possible to leave out `index1` or `index2`. Leaving out `index1` means "Go from the beginning of the list," and leaving out `index2` means "Go to the end of the list":

```
x[:3]
```

```
['first', 'second', 'third']
```

```
x[2:]
```

```
['third', 'fourth']
```

Omitting both indices makes a new list that goes from the beginning to the end of the original list—that is, copies the list. This technique is useful when you want to make a copy that you can modify without affecting the original list:

```
y = x[:]
y[0] = '1 st'
y
```

```
['1 st', 'second', 'third', 'fourth']
```

```
x
```

```
['first', 'second', 'third', 'fourth']
```

> **Try this: List slices and indexes**
>
> Using what you know about the `len()` function and list slices, how would you combine the two to get the second half of a list when you don't know what size it is? Experiment in the Python shell to confirm that your solution works.

5.3 Modifying lists

You can use list index notation to modify a list as well as to extract an element from it. Put the index on the left side of the assignment operator:

```
x = [1, 2, 3, 4]
x[1] = "two"
x

[1, 'two', 3, 4]
```

Slice notation can be used here too. Saying something like `lista[index1:index2] = listb` causes all elements of `lista` between `index1` and `index2` to be replaced by the elements in `listb`. `listb` can have more or fewer elements than are removed from `lista`, in which case the length of `lista` is altered. You can use slice assignment to do several things, as shown in the following:

```
x = [1, 2, 3, 4]
x[len(x):] = [5, 6, 7]          ◄——— Appends a list to end of a list
x

[1, 2, 3, 4, 5, 6, 7]

x[:0] = [-1, 0]                 ◄——— Appends a list to front of a list
x

[-1, 0, 1, 2, 3, 4, 5, 6, 7]

x[1:-1] = []                    ◄——— Removes elements from a list
x

[-1, 7]
```

Appending a single element to a list is such a common operation that there's a special `append` method for it:

```
x = [1, 2, 3]
x.append("four")
x

[1, 2, 3, 'four']
```

One problem can occur if you try to append one list to another. The list gets appended as a single element of the main list:

```
x = [1, 2, 3, 4]
y = [5, 6, 7]
x.append(y)
x
```

```
[1, 2, 3, 4, [5, 6, 7]]
```

The `extend` method is like the `append` method except that it allows you to add one list to another:

```
x = [1, 2, 3, 4]
y = [5, 6, 7]
x.extend(y)
x
```

```
[1, 2, 3, 4, 5, 6, 7]
```

There's also a special `insert` method to insert new list elements between two existing elements or at the front of the list. `insert` is used as a method of a list object and takes two additional arguments. The first additional argument is the index position in the list where the new element should be inserted, and the second is the new element itself:

```
x = [1, 2, 3]
x.insert(2, "hello")
x
```

```
[1, 2, 'hello', 3]
```

```
x.insert(0, "start")
x
```

```
['start', 1, 2, 'hello', 3]
```

`insert` understands list indices as discussed in section 5.2, but for most uses, it's easiest to think of `list.insert(n, elem)` as meaning insert elem just before the *n*th element of the list. `insert` is just a convenience method. Anything that can be done with `insert` can also be done with slice assignment. That is, `list.insert(n, elem)` is the same thing as `list[n:n] = [elem]` when n is nonnegative. Using `insert` makes for somewhat more readable code, and `insert` even handles negative indices:

```
x = [1, 2, 3]
x.insert(-1, "hello")
print(x)
```

```
[1, 2, 'hello', 3]
```

The `del` statement is the preferred method of deleting list items or slices. It doesn't do anything that can't be done with slice assignment, but it's usually easier to remember and easier to read:

```
x = ['a', 2, 'c', 7, 9, 11]
del x[1]
x
```

```
['a', 'c', 7, 9, 11]
```

```
del x[:2]
x
```

```
[7, 9, 11]
```

In general, `del list[n]` does the same thing as `list[n:n+1] = []`, whereas `del list[m:n]` does the same thing as `list[m:n] = []`.

The `remove` method isn't the inverse of `insert`. Whereas `insert` inserts an element at a specified location, `remove` looks for the first instance of a given value in a list and removes that value from the list:

```
x = [1, 2, 3, 4, 3, 5]
x.remove(3)
x
```

```
[1, 2, 4, 3, 5]
```

```
x.remove(3)
x
```

```
[1, 2, 4, 5]
```

```
x.remove(3)
```

```
-----------------------------------------------------------------------
ValueError                                Traceback (most recent call last)
<ipython-input-9-be7b9eddb459> in <cell line: 1>()
----> 1 x.remove(3)

ValueError: list.remove(x): x not in list
```

If `remove` can't find anything to remove, it raises an error. You can catch this error by using the exception-handling abilities of Python, or you can avoid the problem by using `in` to check for the presence of something in a list before attempting to remove it (see section 5.5.1 for examples of `in`).

The `reverse` method is a more specialized list modification method. It efficiently reverses a list in place:

```
x = [1, 3, 5, 6, 7]
x.reverse()
```

```
x
```

```
[7, 6, 5, 3, 1]
```

> **Try this: Modifying lists**
>
> Suppose that you have a list of 10 items. How might you move the last three items from the end of the list to the beginning, keeping them in the same order?

5.4   *Sorting lists*

Lists can be sorted by using the built-in Python `sort` method:

```
x = [3, 8, 4, 0, 2, 1]
x.sort()
x
```

```
[0, 1, 2, 3, 4, 8]
```

This method does an in-place sort—that is, changes the list being sorted. To sort a list without changing the original list, you have two options. You can use the `sorted()` built-in function, discussed in section 5.4.2, or you can make a copy of the list and sort the copy:

```
x = [2, 4, 1, 3]
y = x[:]            ◄─────────────┐  A full list slice makes
y.sort()            ◄──────────┐  │  a copy of the list.
y                              │  │
                               │  │
[1, 2, 3, 4]                   │  Sorts method on
                               └  copy, not original
x
```

```
[2, 4, 1, 3]
```

Note that here we used the `[:]` notation to make a slice of the entire list. Since slicing creates a new list, this in effect creates a copy of the entire list, which we can then sort using the `sort()` method.

Sorting works with strings too:

```
x = ["Life", "Is", "Enchanting"]
x.sort()
x
```

```
['Enchanting', 'Is', 'Life']
```

The `sort` method can sort just about anything because Python can compare just about anything. But there's one caveat in sorting: the default key method used by `sort` requires all items in the list to be of comparable types. That means that using the `sort` method on a list containing both numbers and strings raises an exception:

```
x = [1, 2, 'hello', 3]
x.sort()
```

```
--------------------------------------------------------------------------
TypeError                                 Traceback (most recent call last)
<ipython-input-8-9c6228d80c69> in <cell line: 2>()
      1 x = [1, 2, 'hello', 3]
----> 2 x.sort()
      3

TypeError: '<' not supported between instances of 'str' and 'int'
```

Conversely, you can sort a list of lists:

```
x = [[3, 5], [2, 9], [2, 3], [4, 1], [3, 2]]
x.sort()
x
```

```
[[2, 3], [2, 9], [3, 2], [3, 5], [4, 1]]
```

According to the built-in Python rules for comparing complex objects, the sublists are sorted first by the ascending first element and then by the ascending second element.

`sort` is even more flexible; it has an optional `reverse` parameter that causes the sort to be in reverse order when `reverse=True`, and it's possible to use your own key function to determine how elements of a list are sorted.

5.4.1 Custom sorting

To use custom sorting, you need to be able to define functions—something I haven't talked about yet. In this section, I also discuss the fact that `len(string)` returns the number of characters in a string. String operations are discussed more fully in chapter 6.

By default, `sort` uses built-in Python comparison functions to determine ordering, which is satisfactory for most purposes. At times, though, you want to sort a list in a way that doesn't correspond to this default ordering. Suppose you want to sort a list of words by the number of characters in each word, as opposed to the lexicographic sort that Python normally carries out.

To do this, write a function that returns the value, or key, that you want to sort on and use it with the `sort` method. That function in the context of `sort` is a function that takes one argument and returns the key or value that the `sort` function is to use.

For number-of-characters ordering, a suitable key function could be

```
def num_of_chars(string1):
    return len(string1)
```

This key function is trivial. It passes the length of each string back to the `sort` method, rather than the strings themselves.

After you define the key function, using it is a matter of passing it to the `sort` method by using the `key` keyword. Because functions are Python objects, they can be passed around like any other Python objects. Here's a small program that illustrates the difference between a default sort and your custom sort:

```
def comp_num_of_chars(string1):
    return len(string1)
word_list = ['Python', 'is', 'better', 'than', 'C']
word_list.sort()
print(word_list)
```

`['C', 'Python', 'better', 'is', 'than']`

```
word_list = ['Python', 'is', 'better', 'than', 'C']
word_list.sort(key=comp_num_of_chars)
print(word_list)
```

`['C', 'is', 'than', 'Python', 'better']`

The first list is in lexicographical order (with uppercase coming before lowercase), and the second list is ordered by ascending number of characters.

It's also possible to use an anonymous `lambda` function in the `sort()` call itself. This can be handy if the sort function is very short (which it usually is) and only used for sorting (again, as it should be). The code using the function `comp_num_of_chars` could also be written with a lambda function as

```
word_list.sort(key=lambda x: len(x))
```

The lambda is defined with three elements: a variable for the parameter, in this case `x`; a colon; and the return value, in this example `len(x)`. For simple functions with only a simple return value, a lambda function saves having to create more function names, and you can see how the sort key works without having to look at the function elsewhere.

Custom sorting is very useful, but if performance is critical, it may be slower than the default. Usually, this effect is minimal, but if the key function is particularly complex, the effect may be more than desired, especially for sorts involving hundreds of thousands or millions of elements.

One particular place to avoid custom sorts is where you want to sort a list in descending, rather than ascending, order. In this case, use the `sort` method's `reverse` parameter set to `True`. If for some reason you don't want to do that, it's still better to sort the list normally and then use the `reverse` method to invert the order of the resulting list. These two operations together—the standard sort and the reverse—will still be much faster than a custom sort.

5.4.2   *The sorted () function*

Lists have a built-in method to sort themselves, but other iterables in Python, such as the keys of a dictionary, don't have a `sort` method. Python also has the built-in function sorted(), which returns a sorted list from any iterable. sorted() uses the same `key` and `reverse` parameters as the `sort` method:

```
x = (4, 3, 1, 2)
y = sorted(x)
y
```

```
[1, 2, 3, 4]
```

```
z = sorted(x, reverse=True)
z
```

```
[4, 3, 2, 1]
```

> **Try this: Sorting lists**
>
> Suppose that you have a list in which each element is in turn a list: `[[1, 2, 3], [2, 1, 3], [4, 0, 1]]`. If you wanted to sort this list by the second element in each list so that the result would be `[[4, 0, 1], [2, 1, 3], [1, 2, 3]]`, what function would you write to pass as the `key` value to the `sort()` method?

5.5 Other common list operations

Several other list methods are frequently useful, but they don't fall into any specific category.

5.5.1 List membership with the in operator

It's easy to test whether a value is in a list by using the `in` operator, which returns a Boolean value. You can also use the inverse: the `not in` operator:

```
3 in [1, 3, 4, 5]
```

True

```
3 not in [1, 3, 4, 5]
```

False

```
3 in ["one", "two", "three"]
```

False

```
3 not in ["one", "two", "three"]
```

True

5.5.2   *List concatenation with the + operator*

To create a list by concatenating two existing lists, use the + (list concatenation) operator, which leaves the argument lists unchanged:

```
z = [1, 2, 3] + [4, 5]
z
```

```
[1, 2, 3, 4, 5]
```

5.5.3   *List initialization with the * operator*

Use the * operator to produce a list of a given size, which is initialized to a given value. This operation is a common one for working with large lists whose size is known ahead of time. Although you can use `append` to add elements and automatically expand the list as needed, you obtain greater efficiency by using * to correctly size the list at the start of the program. A list that doesn't change in size doesn't incur any memory reallocation overhead:

```
z = [None] * 4
z
```

```
[None, None, None, None]
```

When used with lists in this manner, * (which in this context is called the *list multiplication operator*) replicates the given list the indicated number of times and joins all the copies to form a new list. This is the standard Python method for defining a list of a given size ahead of time. A list containing a single instance of `None` is commonly used in list multiplication, but the list can be anything:

```
z = [3, 1] * 2
z
```

```
[3, 1, 3, 1]
```

5.5.4   *List minimum or maximum with min and max*

You can use `min` and `max` to find the smallest and largest elements in a list. You'll probably use `min` and `max` mostly with numerical lists, but you can use them with lists containing any type of element. Trying to find the maximum or minimum object in a set of objects of different types causes an error if comparing those types doesn't make sense:

```
min([3, 7, 0, -2, 11])
```

```
-2
```

```
max([4, "Hello", [1, 2]])
```

```
----------------------------------------------------------------------
TypeError                              Traceback (most recent call last)
<ipython-input-7-15ab1869d5d5> in <cell line: 1>()
----> 1 max([4, "Hello", [1, 2]])

TypeError: '>' not supported between instances of 'str' and 'int'
```

5.5.5 List search with index

If you want to find where in a list a value can be found (rather than wanting to know only whether the value is in the list), use the `index` method. This method searches through a list looking for a list element equivalent to a given value and returns the position of that list element:

```
x = [1, 3, "five", 7, -2]
x.index(7)
```

```
3
```

```
x.index(5)
```

```
----------------------------------------------------------------------
ValueError                             Traceback (most recent call last)
<ipython-input-6-96ad5df81983> in <cell line: 1>()
----> 1 x.index(5)

ValueError: 5 is not in list
```

Attempting to find the position of an element that doesn't exist in the list raises an error, as shown here. This error can be handled in the same manner as the analogous error that can occur with the `remove` method (that is, by testing the list with `in` before using `index`).

5.5.6 List matches with count

`count` also searches through a list, looking for a given value, but it returns the number of times that the value is found in the list rather than positional information:

```
x = [1, 2, 2, 3, 5, 2, 5]
x.count(2)
```

```
3
```

```
x.count(5)
```

```
2
```

```
x.count(4)
```

```
0
```

5.5.7   *Summary of list operations*

You can see that lists are very powerful data structures, with possibilities that go far beyond those of plain old arrays. List operations are so important in Python programming that it's worth laying them out for easy reference, as shown in table 5.1.

Table 5.1   List operations

List operation	Explanation	Example
[]	Creates an empty list	x = []
len	Returns the length of a list	len(x)
append	Adds a single element to the end of a list	x.append('y')
extend	Adds another list to the end of the list	x.extend(['a', 'b'])
insert	Inserts a new element at a given position in the list	x.insert(0, 'y')
del	Removes a list element or slice	del(x[0])
remove	Searches for and removes a given value from a list	x.remove('y')
reverse	Reverses a list in place	x.reverse()
sort	Sorts a list in place	x.sort()
+	Adds two lists together	x1 + x2
*	Replicates a list	x = ['y'] * 3
min	Returns the smallest element in a list	min(x)
max	Returns the largest element in a list	max(x)
index	Returns the position of a value in a list	x.index['y']
count	Counts the number of times a value occurs in a list	x.count('y')
Sum	Sums the items (if they can be summed)	sum(x)
In	Returns whether an item is in a list	'y' in x

Being familiar with these list operations will make your life as a Python coder much easier.

> **Quick check: List operations**
>
> What would be the result of `len([[1,2]] * 3)`? What are two differences between using the `in` operator and a list's `index()` method? Which of the following will raise an exception? `min(["a", "b", "c"])`; `max([1, 2, "three"])`; `[1, 2, 3].count("one")`

> **Try this: List operations**
>
> If you have a list x, write the code to safely remove an item if—and only if—that value is in the list. Modify that code to remove the element only if the item occurs in the list more than once.

5.6 Nested lists and deep copies

This section covers another advanced topic that you may want to skip if you're just learning the language.

Lists can be nested. One application of nesting is to represent two-dimensional matrices. The members of these matrices can be referred to by using two-dimensional indices. Indices for these matrices work as follows:

```
m = [[0, 1, 2], [10, 11, 12], [20, 21, 22]]
m[0]

[0, 1, 2]

m[0][1]

1

m[2]

[20, 21, 22]

m[2][2]

22
```

This mechanism scales to higher dimensions in the manner you'd expect.

Most of the time, this is all you need to concern yourself with. But you may run into a problem with nested lists—specifically, the way that variables refer to objects and how some objects (such as lists) can be modified (are mutable). An example is the best way to illustrate:

```
nested = [0]
original = [nested, 1]
original

[[0], 1]
```

Figure 5.1 shows what this example looks like.

Now the value in the nested list can be changed by using either the nested or the original variables:

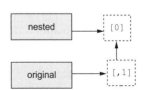

Figure 5.1   A list with its first item referring to a nested list

```
nested[0] = 'zero'
original
```

[['zero'], 1]

```
original[0][0] = 0
nested
```

[0]

```
original
```

[[0], 1]

But if nested is set to another list, the connection between them is broken:

```
nested = [2]
original
```

[[0], 1]

Figure 5.2 illustrates this condition.

You've seen that you can obtain a copy of a list by taking a full slice (that is, x[:]). You can also obtain a copy of a list by using the + or * operators (for example, x + [] or x * 1). These techniques are slightly less efficient than the slice method. All three create what is called a *shallow* copy of the list, which is probably what you want most of the time. But if your list has other lists nested in it, you may want to make a *deep* copy. You can do this with the deepcopy function of the copy module:

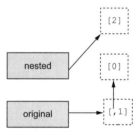

Figure 5.2   The first item of the original list is still a nested list, but the nested variable refers to a different list.

```
original = [[0], 1]
shallow = original[:]
import copy
deep = copy.deepcopy(original)
```

See figure 5.3 for an illustration.

The lists pointed at by the original or shallow variables are connected. Changing the value in the nested list through either one of them affects the other:

```
shallow[1] = 2
shallow
```

[[0], 2]

```
original
```

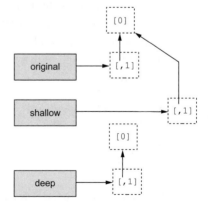

Figure 5.3   A deep copy copies nested lists.

```
[[0], 1]
```

```
shallow[0][0] = 'zero'
original
```

```
[['zero'], 1]
```

The deep copy is independent of the original, and no change to it has any effect on the original list:

```
deep[0][0] = 5
deep
```

```
[[5], 1]
```

```
original
```

```
[['zero'], 1]
```

This behavior is the same for any other nested objects in a list that are modifiable (such as dictionaries).

Now that you've seen what lists can do, it's time to look at tuples.

> **Try this: List copies**
>
> Suppose that you have the following list: x = [[1, 2, 3], [4, 5, 6], [7, 8, 9]] What code could you use to get a copy y of that list in which you could change the elements *without* the side effect of changing the contents of x?

5.7 Tuples

Tuples are data structures that are very similar to lists, but they can't be modified; they can only be created. Tuples are so much like lists that you may wonder why Python bothers to include them. The reason is that tuples have important roles that can't be efficiently filled by lists, such as keys for dictionaries.

5.7.1 Tuple basics

Creating a tuple is similar to creating a list: assign a sequence of values to a variable. A list is a sequence that's enclosed by [and]; a tuple is a sequence that's enclosed by (and):

```
x = ('a', 'b', 'c')
```

This line creates a three-element tuple.

After a tuple is created, using it is so much like using a list that it's easy to forget that tuples and lists are different data types:

```
x[2]
```

```
'c'
```

```
x[1:]
```

```
('b', 'c')
```

```
len(x)
```

```
3
```

```
max(x)
```

```
'c'
```

```
min(x)
```

```
'a'
```

```
5 in x
```

```
False
```

```
5 not in x
```

```
True
```

The main difference between tuples and lists is that tuples are immutable. An attempt to modify a tuple results in a confusing error message, which is Python's way of saying that it doesn't know how to set an item in a tuple:

```
x[2] = 'd'
-------------------------------------------------------------------------
TypeError                                 Traceback (most recent call last)
<ipython-input-2-dcc4b983047e> in <cell line: 1>()
----> 1 x[2] = 'd'

TypeError: 'tuple' object does not support item assignment
```

You can create tuples from existing ones by using the + and * operators:

```
x + x
```

```
('a', 'b', 'c', 'a', 'b', 'c')
```

```
2 * x
```

```
('a', 'b', 'c', 'a', 'b', 'c')
```

A "copy" (actually an alias pointing to the original object) of a tuple can be made in any of the same ways as for lists:

```
x[:]
```

```
('a', 'b', 'c')
```

```
x * 1
```

```
('a', 'b', 'c')
```

```
x + ()
```

```
('a', 'b', 'c')
```

Tuples themselves can't be modified. But if a tuple contains any mutable objects (for example, lists or dictionaries), these objects may be changed if they're still assigned to their own variables. Tuples that contain mutable objects aren't allowed as keys for dictionaries.

Copying tuples

Because tuples can't be modified, the shallow copy methods shown here don't return new objects but aliases pointing to the same object. This is true not only for tuples but also for string and byte objects, which are covered in the next chapter. In practice you can still think of these aliases as "copies" since there is nothing you could do with a true copy that you can't also do with an alias (and aliases are much faster and more memory efficient).

5.7.2   *One-element tuples need a comma*

A small syntactical point is associated with using tuples. Because the square brackets used to enclose a list aren't used elsewhere in Python, it's clear that `[]` means an empty list and that `[1]` means a list with one element. The same thing isn't true of the parentheses used to enclose tuples. Parentheses can also be used to group items in expressions to force a certain evaluation order. If you say `(x + y)` in a Python program, do you mean that x and y should be added and then put into a one-element tuple, or do you mean that the parentheses should be used to force x and y to be added before any expressions to either side come into play?

This situation is a problem only for tuples with one element because tuples with more than one element always include commas to separate the elements, and the commas tell Python that the parentheses indicate a tuple, not a grouping. In the case of one-element tuples, Python requires that the element in the tuple be followed by a comma to disambiguate the situation. In the case of zero-element (empty) tuples, there's no problem. An empty set of parentheses must be a tuple because it's meaningless otherwise:

```
x = 3
y = 4
(x + y)    # This line adds x and y.
```

```
7
```

```
(x + y,)  # Including a comma indicates that the parentheses denote a tuple.
```

(7,)

```
()          # To create an empty tuple, use an empty pair of parentheses.
```

()

5.7.3   *Packing and unpacking tuples*

As a convenience, Python permits tuples of variables to appear on the left side of an assignment operator, in which case variables in the tuple receive the corresponding values from the tuple on the right side of the assignment operator. The following is a simple example:

```
(one, two, three, four) =  (1, 2, 3, 4)
one
```

```
1
```

```
two
```

```
2
```

This example can be written even more simply because Python recognizes tuples in an assignment context even without the enclosing parentheses. The values on the right side are packed into a tuple and then unpacked into the variables on the left side:

```
one, two, three, four = 1, 2, 3, 4
```

One line of code has replaced the following four lines of code:

```
one = 1
two = 2
three = 3
four = 4
```

This technique is a convenient way to swap values between variables. Instead of saying

```
temp = var1
var1 = var2
var2 = temp
```

simply say

```
var1, var2 = var2, var1
```

To make things even more convenient, Python 3 has an extended unpacking feature, allowing an element marked with * to absorb any number of elements not matching the other elements. Again, some examples make this feature clearer:

```
x = (1, 2, 3, 4)
a, b, *c = x
a, b, c

(1, 2, [3, 4])

a, *b, c = x
a, b, c

(1, [2, 3], 4)

*a, b, c = x
a, b, c

([1, 2], 3, 4)

a, b, c, d, *e = x
a, b, c, d, e

(1, 2, 3, 4, [])
```

Note that the starred element receives all the surplus items as a list and that if there are no surplus elements, the starred element receives an empty list.

Packing and unpacking can also be performed with lists:

```
[a, b] = [1, 2]
[c, d] = 3, 4
[e, f] = (5, 6)
(g, h) = 7, 8
i, j = [9, 10]
k, l = (11, 12)
a

1

[b, c, d]

[2, 3, 4]

(e, f, g)

(5, 6, 7)

h, i, j, k, l

(8, 9, 10, 11, 12)
```

5.7.4   *Converting between lists and tuples*

Tuples can be easily converted to lists with the `list` function, which takes any sequence as an argument and produces a new list with the same elements as the original sequence. Similarly, lists can be converted to tuples with the `tuple` function, which does the same thing but produces a new tuple instead of a new list:

```
list((1, 2, 3, 4))

[1, 2, 3, 4]

tuple([1, 2, 3, 4])

(1, 2, 3, 4)
```

As an interesting side note, `list` is a convenient way to break a string into characters:

```
list("Hello")
['H', 'e', 'l', 'l', 'o']
```

This technique works because `list` (and `tuple`) apply to any Python sequence, and a string is just a sequence of characters. (Strings are discussed fully in chapter 6.)

> #### Quick check: Tuples
>
> Explain why the following operations aren't legal for the tuple `x = (1, 2, 3, 4)`:
>
> ```
> x.append(1)
> x[1] = "hello"
> del x[2]
> ```
>
> If you had a tuple `x = (3, 1, 4, 2)`, how might you end up with `x` sorted?

5.8   Sets

A *set* in Python is an unordered collection of objects used when membership and uniqueness in the set are the main things you need to know about that object. Like dictionary keys (discussed in chapter 7), the items in a set must be immutable and hashable. This means that ints, floats, strings, and tuples can be members of a set, but lists, dictionaries, and sets themselves can't.

5.8.1   *Set operations*

In addition to the operations that apply to collections in general, such as `in`, `len`, and iteration in `for` loops, sets have several set-specific operations:

```
x = set([1, 2, 3, 1, 3, 5])          ◄──── Creates a set by using set on a list
x
```

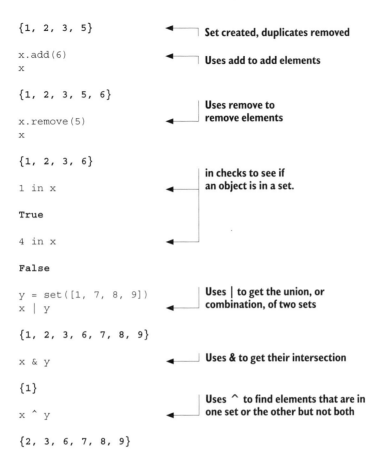

```
{1, 2, 3, 5}                    Set created, duplicates removed

x.add(6)                        Uses add to add elements
x

{1, 2, 3, 5, 6}                 Uses remove to
                                remove elements
x.remove(5)
x

{1, 2, 3, 6}                    in checks to see if
                                an object is in a set.
1 in x

True

4 in x

False

y = set([1, 7, 8, 9])          Uses | to get the union, or
x | y                          combination, of two sets

{1, 2, 3, 6, 7, 8, 9}

x & y                           Uses & to get their intersection

{1}                             Uses ^ to find elements that are in
                                one set or the other but not both
x ^ y

{2, 3, 6, 7, 8, 9}
```

You can create a set by using `set` on a sequence, such as a list. When a sequence is made into a set, duplicates are removed. After creating a set by using the `set` function, you can use `add` and `remove` to change the elements in the set. The `in` keyword is used to check for membership of an object in a set. You can also use | to get the union, or combination, of two sets, `&` to get their intersection, and ^ to find their symmetric difference—that is, elements that are in one set or the other but not both.

These examples aren't a complete listing of set operations, but they are enough to give you a good idea of how sets work. For more information, refer to the official Python documentation.

5.8.2   *Frozen sets*

Because sets aren't immutable and hashable, they can't belong to other sets. To remedy that situation, Python has another set type, `frozenset`, which is just like a set but can't be changed after creation. Because frozen sets are immutable and hashable, they can be members of other sets:

```
x = set([1, 2, 3, 1, 3, 5])
z = frozenset(x)
```

```
z

frozenset({1, 2, 3, 5})

z.add(6)

------------------------------------------------------------------
AttributeError                              Traceback (most recent call last)
<ipython-input-4-60917eecf5a3> in <cell line: 1>()
----> 1 z.add(6)

AttributeError: 'frozenset' object has no attribute 'add'

x.add(z)
x

{1, 2, 3, 5, frozenset({1, 2, 3, 5})}
```

> ### Quick check: Sets
>
> If you were to construct a set from the following list, how many elements would the
> set have? `[1, 2, 5, 1, 0, 2, 3, 1, 1, (1, 2, 3)]`

5.9   *Lab: Examining a list*

In this lab, the task is to read a set of temperature data (the monthly high temperatures at Heathrow Airport for 1948 through 2016) from a file and then find some basic
information: the highest and lowest temperatures, the mean (average) temperature,
and the median temperature (the temperature in the middle if all the temperatures
are sorted).

The temperature data is in the file lab_05.txt in the source code directory for this
chapter. Because I haven't yet discussed reading files, here's the code to read the files
into a list:

```
temperatures = []
with open('lab_05.txt') as infile:
    for row in infile:
        temperatures.append(float(row.strip()))
```

You should find the highest and lowest temperature, the average, and the median.
You'll probably want to use the min(), max(), sum(), len(), and sort() functions/
methods. As a bonus, determine how many unique temperatures are in the list.

5.9.1   *Why solve it the old-fashioned way?*

You should have a try at creating a solution to this problem using your knowledge and
the material presented in this chapter. The preceding code will open a file and read

its contents in as a list of floats. You can then use the functions mentioned to get the answers required. And for a bonus, the key is to think of how to convert a list so that only unique values remain.

You may be thinking, "Why should I write this code? Can't I use AI to generate a solution?" And the answer is yes, you can, but trying to create a solution on your own first helps you both understand the problem better and learn how Python works. Both of those are vital for using an AI code generator—you need a solid understanding of the problem to create an effective prompt for the AI, and a solid understanding of how Python works is essential for evaluating the generated code.

If you are using the Jupyter notebook for this chapter, there is a cell with the code to load the file where you can put in your code to find the mean, median, etc. temperatures. Next, we'll discuss a sample solution created by a human (me) and compare it to the AI solution.

5.9.2 *Solving the problem with AI code generation*

As mentioned in chapter 2, there are several AI code generation tools, and the landscape is rapidly evolving, so it's quite possible you will be using something different from the options available as I write this. For the sake of illustration, I will use the code generator available in Google Colaboratory, which is currently available for free, and GitHub Copilot, which is available by subscription with a free trial and runs in Microsoft's VS Code IDE. I'll discuss one of the solutions and note if the other system produces something dramatically different.

Prompt creation

To generate code in Colaboratory, we need to click the `generate` link shown in an empty cell, "`Start coding or generate with AI`." Once we do that, we get a code generation dialog waiting for a prompt telling the code generator what we want to do. Once we enter the prompt in the field after the Using… button (as shown in the following figure), we can click the Generate button to generate our code.

The code generation prompt in Colaboratory

Creating a prompt is an evolving art, but since the prompt field is limited, we can't simply copy and paste the whole problem statement. Since we already have the code

(continued)

to read the file into a list as a series of floats, our prompt should focus only on what we need the code to do.

With this guidance, you can go ahead and try creating a prompt and generating some code. Try to evaluate the generated code and, if necessary, refine your prompt.

5.9.3 *Solutions and discussion*

To create our prompt, we focused on what we needed the code to do. The following is the list of things we needed done:

1 Use the list temperatures.
2 Find the high and low temperature.
3 Find the mean and median.
4 State how many unique temperatures there are (yes, let's do the bonus).

We might combine this into a prompt as

```
Using the list temperatures, find the high, low, mean, and median
temperatures, and show how many unique temperatures are in the list.
```

This prompt is complete and concise and covers exactly what we need. Remember that we already had the code to load the file, so we don't need to ask for that, but of course we do need to add that code to the generated code:

```
temperatures = []
with open('lab_05.txt') as infile:
    for row in infile:
        temperatures.append(float(row.strip()))
```

THE HUMAN CODED SOLUTION

The solution I came up with follows.

```
max_temp = max(temperatures)
min_temp = min(temperatures)
mean_temp = sum(temperatures)/len(temperatures)
# we'll need to sort to get the median temp
temperatures.sort()                                    ← Sorts the temperatures
                                                         list in place
median_temp = temperatures[len(temperatures)//2]       ← Gets value from midpoint
print(f"max = {max_temp}")                               of list or one above
print(f"min = {min_temp}")                               midpoint if an even
print(f"mean = {mean_temp}")                             number of elements
print(f"median = {median_temp}")
# Bonus
unique_temps = len(set(temperatures))

print(f"number of uniquie temps - {unique_temps}")
```

This solution does the job and reflects my bias to keep things simple and to keep comments to a minimum.

THE AI-GENERATED SOLUTION

The code generated by AI is remarkably similar—probably because the problem is not complex. Using Copilot (the Colaboratory code was nearly identical) we get

```
# High temperature
high_temp = max(temperatures)

# Low temperature
low_temp = min(temperatures)

# Mean temperature
mean_temp = sum(temperatures) / len(temperatures)

# Median temperature
sorted_temps = sorted(temperatures)          ◄──── Creates sorted copy of list
mid = len(sorted_temps) // 2
if len(sorted_temps) % 2 == 0:               ◄──── Checks for even
    median_temp = (sorted_temps[mid - 1]            number of elements
+ sorted_temps[mid]) / 2                      ◄──── Extrapolates median
else:                                                from two values
    median_temp = sorted_temps[mid]

# Unique temperatures
unique_temps = len(set(temperatures))

print("High temperature:", high_temp)
print("Low temperature:", low_temp)
print("Mean temperature:", mean_temp)
print("Median temperature:", median_temp)
print("Unique temperatures:", unique_temps)
```

This code also does the job, with what is arguably nicer formatting and more comments.

The AI version uses more whitespace, which makes the code easier to read. It also uses more comments—to my mind maybe more than needed. It's good style in Python to use comments only where needed to explain why something is as it is, and in my opinion a comment `# High temperature` right before the `high_temp` is not needed. On the other hand, the comment in the human version, `# we'll need to sort to get the median temp`, explains why we're sorting, which is lacking in the AI version. But you could argue that it's a question of preferences.

Besides some difference in printing the results, the main difference between the two is in finding the median. Again, the median is the value exactly in the middle of a series of sorted values, and the human version sorts the list in place and just picks the value in slot `len(temperatures) // 2`. The AI version makes a sorted copy of the list using the `sorted` function, and then, if the list has an even number of elements, meaning that there is no exact middle of the list, it extrapolates a value.

You might think that the AI version is superior: it has more code, and it preserves the original list and takes a more sophisticated view of the median. In real-world programming, however, things are not so clear. If the list of temperatures were several million lines long, then creating a sorted copy may not be an efficient use of memory, and it may well be that there is no need to preserve a version in the original order. It may also be the case that we don't want an extrapolated median but an actual value in the list, or that we don't care if the median value is actually from a slot one higher than the midpoint of the list. In that case, the simpler code would be preferable.

The main takeaway from this example is that while AI tools can generate working code that looks nice, it is important to keep in mind when analyzing the code both the problem to be solved and how the code functions to solve it.

Summary

- Lists and tuples are structures that embody the idea of a sequence of elements, as are strings.
- Lists are like arrays in other languages but with automatic resizing, slice notation, and many convenience functions.
- Tuples are like lists but can't be modified, so they use less memory and can be dictionary keys (see chapter 7).
- Sets are iterable collections, but they're unordered and can't have duplicate elements. Frozen sets are sets that can't be modified.
- AI tools can generate useful code, but it's important to evaluate that code in light of both the problem and how Python works.

Strings

## 6

This chapter covers

- Understanding strings as sequences of characters
- Using basic string operations
- Inserting special characters and escape sequences
- Converting from objects to strings
- Formatting strings
- Using the `bytes` type

Handling text—from user input to filenames to chunks of text to be processed—is a common chore in programming. Python comes with powerful tools to handle and format text. This chapter discusses the standard string and string-related operations in Python.

6.1 Strings as sequences of characters

For the purposes of extracting characters and substrings, strings can be considered to contain sequences of characters, which means that you can use index or slice notation:

```
x = "Hello"
x[0]
```

```
'H'
```

```
x[-1]
```

```
'o'
```

```
x[1:]
```

```
'ello'
```

One use for slice notation with strings is to chop the newline off the end of a string (usually, a line that's just been read from a file):

```
x = "Goodbye\n"
x = x[:-1]
x
```

```
'Goodbye'
```

This code is just an example. You should know that Python strings have other, better methods to strip unwanted characters, but this example illustrates the usefulness of slicing.

It's also worth noting that there is no separate character type in Python. Whether you use an index, slicing, or some other method, when you extract a single "character" from a Python string, it's still a one-character string, with the same methods and behavior as the original string. The same is true for the empty string `""`.

You can also determine how many characters are in the string by using the `len` function, which is used to find the number of elements in a list:

```
len("Goodbye")
```

```
7
```

But strings aren't lists of characters. The most noticeable difference between strings and lists is that, unlike lists, *strings can't be modified*. Attempting to say something like `string.append('c')` or `string[0] = 'H'` results in an error. You'll notice in the previous example that I stripped off the newline from the string by creating a string that was a slice of the previous one, not by modifying the previous string directly. This is a basic Python restriction, imposed for efficiency reasons.

6.2   *Basic string operations*

The simplest (and probably most common) way to combine Python strings is to use the string concatenation operator +:

```
x = "Hello " + "World"
x
```

```
'Hello World'
```

Python also has an analogous string multiplication operator that I've found to be useful sometimes but not often:

```
8 * "x"
```

```
'xxxxxxxx'
```

6.3 *Special characters and escape sequences*

You've already seen a few of the character sequences that Python regards as special when used within strings: \n represents the newline character, and \t represents the tab character. Sequences of characters that start with a backslash and that are used to represent other characters are called *escape sequences*. Escape sequences are generally used to represent *special characters*—that is, characters (such as tab and newline) that don't have a standard one-character printable representation. This section covers escape sequences, special characters, and related topics in more detail.

6.3.1 *Basic escape sequences*

Python provides a brief list of two-character escape sequences to use in strings (see table 6.1). The same sequences also apply to bytes objects, which will be introduced at the end of this chapter.

Table 6.1   Escape sequences for string and byte literals

Escape sequence	Character represented
\'	Single-quote character
\"	Double-quote character
\\	Backslash character
\a	Bell character
\b	Backspace character
\f	Form-feed character
\n	Newline character
\r	Carriage-return character (not the same as \n)
\t	Tab character
\v	Vertical tab character

The ASCII character set defines quite a few more special characters. These characters are accessed by the numeric escape sequences, described in the next section.

6.3.2   *Numeric (octal and hexadecimal) and Unicode escape sequences*

You can include any ASCII character in a string by using an octal (base 8) or hexadecimal (base 16) escape sequence corresponding to that character. An octal escape sequence is a backslash followed by three digits defining an octal number; the ASCII character corresponding to this octal number is substituted for the octal escape sequence. A hexadecimal escape sequence begins with \x rather than just \ and can consist of any number of hexadecimal digits. The escape sequence is terminated when a character is found that's not a hexadecimal digit. For example, in the ASCII character table, the character *m* happens to have decimal value 109. The value of decimal 109 is octal value 155 and hexadecimal value 6D, so

```
'm'
```

'm'

```
'\155'
```

'm'

```
'\x6D'
```

'm'

All three expressions represent a string containing the single character *m*. But these forms can also be used to represent characters that have no printable representation. The newline character \n, for example, has octal value 012 and hexadecimal value 0A:

```
'\n'
```

'\n'

```
'\012'
```

'\n'

```
'\x0A'
```

'\n'

Because all strings in Python 3 are Unicode strings, they can also contain almost every character from every language available. Although a discussion of the Unicode system is far beyond the scope of this book, the following examples illustrate that you can also escape any Unicode character, either by number (as shown earlier) or by Unicode name:

```
unicode_a ='\N{LATIN SMALL LETTER A}'          ◄──────┐ Escapes by Unicode name
unicode_a
```

```
'a'                    ◄────┤ ASCII characters are
                            └ Unicode characters.
```

```
unicode_a_with_acute = '\N{LATIN SMALL LETTER A WITH ACUTE}'
unicode_a_with_acute
```

```
'á'
```

```
"\u00E1"               ◄──────┐ Escapes by number, using \u
```

```
'á'
```

This code shows how you can access characters, including common ASCII characters, by using their Unicode names with \N(*Unicode name*) or by using their number with \u.

6.3.3 *Printing vs. evaluating strings with special characters*

I talked earlier about the difference between evaluating a Python expression interactively and printing the result of the same expression by using the `print` function. Although the same string is involved, the two operations can produce screen outputs that look different. A string that's evaluated at the top level of an interactive Python session is shown with all of its special characters as octal escape sequences, which makes clear what's in the string. Meanwhile, the `print` function passes the string directly to the terminal program, which may interpret special characters in special ways. The following is what happens with a string consisting of an a followed by a newline, a tab, and a b:

```
'a\n\tb'
```

```
'a\n\tb'
```

```
print('a\n\tb')
```

```
a
    b
```

In the first case, the newline and tab are shown explicitly in the string; in the second, they're used as newline and tab characters.

A normal `print` function also adds a newline to the end of the string. Sometimes (that is, when you have lines from files that already end with newlines), you may not want this behavior. Giving the `print` function an `end` parameter of `""` causes the `print` function to suppress the final newline:

```
print("abc\n")
```

```
abc
```

```
print("abc\n", end="")
```

abc

6.4   *String methods*

Most of the Python string methods are built into the standard Python string class, so all string objects have them automatically. The standard `string` module also contains some useful constants. Modules are discussed in detail in chapter 10.

For the purposes of this section, you need only remember that most string methods are attached to the string object they operate on by a dot (.), as in `x.upper()`. That is, they're prepended with the string object followed by a dot. Because strings are immutable, the string methods are used only to obtain their return value and don't modify the string object they're attached to in any way.

I begin with those string operations that are the most useful and most commonly used; then I discuss some less commonly used but still useful operations. At the end of this section, I discuss a few miscellaneous points related to strings. Not all the string methods are documented here. See the documentation for a complete list of string methods.

6.4.1   *The split and join string methods*

Anyone who works with strings is almost certain to find the `split` and `join` methods invaluable. They're the inverse of one another: `split` returns a list of substrings in the string, and `join` takes a list of strings and puts them together to form a single string with the original string between each element. Typically, `split` uses whitespace as the delimiter of the strings it's splitting, but you can change that behavior via an optional argument.

String concatenation using + is useful but not efficient for joining large numbers of strings into a single string, because each time + is applied, a new string object is created. The previous Hello, World example produces three string objects, two of which are immediately discarded. A better option is to use the `join` function, which creates only one new string object:

```
" ".join(["join", "puts", "spaces", "between", "elements"])
```

'join puts spaces between elements'

By changing the string used to `join`, you can put anything you want between the joined strings:

```
"::".join(["Separated", "with", "colons"])
```

'Separated::with::colons'

You can even use an empty string, `""`, to join elements in a list:

```
"".join(["Separated", "by", "nothing"])
```

'Separatedbynothing'

The most common use of `split` is probably as a simple parsing mechanism for string-delimited records stored in text files. By default, `split` splits on any whitespace, not just a single space character, but you can also tell it to split on a particular sequence by passing it an optional argument:

```
x = "You\t\t can have tabs\t\n \t and newlines \n\n " \
            "mixed in"
x.split()
```

['You', 'can', 'have', 'tabs', 'and', 'newlines', 'mixed', 'in']

```
x = "Mississippi"
x.split("ss")
```

['Mi', 'i', 'ippi']

Sometimes it's useful to permit the last field in a joined string to contain arbitrary text, perhaps including substrings that may match what `split` splits on when reading in that data. You can do this by specifying how many splits `split` should perform when it's generating its result, via an optional second argument. If you specify n splits, `split` goes along the input string until it has performed n splits (generating a list with $n + 1$ substrings as elements) or until it runs out of string. The following are some examples:

```
x = 'a b c d'
x.split(' ', 1)
```

['a', 'b c d']

```
x.split(' ', 2)
```

['a', 'b', 'c d']

```
x.split(' ', 9)
```

['a', 'b', 'c', 'd']

When using `split` with its optional second argument, you must supply a first argument. To get it to split on runs of whitespace while using the second argument, use `None` as the first argument.

I use `split` and `join` extensively, usually when working with text files generated by other programs. If you want to create more standard output files from your programs, good choices are the `csv` and `json` modules in the Python standard library.

> ### Quick check: split and join
> How could you use `split` and `join` to change all the whitespace in string x to dashes, such as changing `"this is a test"` to `"this-is-a-test"`?

6.4.2   *Converting strings to numbers*

You can use the functions `int` and `float` to convert strings to integer or floating-point numbers, respectively. If they're passed a string that can't be interpreted as a number of the given type, these functions raise a `ValueError` exception. Exceptions are explained in chapter 14.

In addition, you may pass `int` an optional second argument, specifying the numeric base to use when interpreting the input string:

```
float('123.456')
```

```
123.456
```

```
float('xxyy')
```

```
------------------------------------------------------------------------
ValueError                                  Traceback (most recent call last)
<ipython-input-30-14b25c5b2052> in <cell line: 1>()
----> 1 float('xxyy')

ValueError: could not convert string to float: 'xxyy'
```

```
int('3333')
```

```
3333
```

```
int('123.456')
```
◀── **Can't have decimal point in integer**

```
------------------------------------------------------------------------
ValueError                                  Traceback (most recent call last)
<ipython-input-32-ed4c46a302ea> in <cell line: 1>()
----> 1 int('123.456')

ValueError: invalid literal for int() with base 10: '123.456'
```

```
int('10000', 8)
```
◀── **Interprets 10,000 as octal number**

```
4096
```

```
int('101', 2)
```
◀── **Binary number**

```
5
```

```
int('ff', 16)
```
◀── **Hexadecimal number**

```
255
```

```
int('123456', 6)
```
◀────┐ **Can't interpret 123,456 as base 6 number**

```
-------------------------------------------------------------------------
ValueError                                Traceback (most recent call last)
<ipython-input-36-bdc1281d81c5> in <cell line: 1>()
----> 1 int('123456', 6)

ValueError: invalid literal for int() with base 6: '123456'
```

Did you catch the reason for that last error? I requested that the string be interpreted as a base 6 number, but the digit 6 can never appear in a base 6 number. Sneaky!

> ### Quick check: Strings to numbers
> Which of the following will not be converted to numbers, and why?
>
> ```
> int('a1')
> int('12G', 16)
> float("12345678901234567890")
> int("12*2")
> ```

6.4.3 *Getting rid of extra whitespace*

A trio of surprisingly useful simple methods are the `strip`, `lstrip`, and `rstrip` functions. `strip` returns a new string that's the same as the original string, except that any whitespace at the *beginning or end* of the string has been removed. `lstrip` and `rstrip` work similarly, except that they remove whitespace only at the left or right end of the original string, respectively:

```
x = "  Hello,    World\t\t "
x.strip()
```

```
'Hello,    World'
```

```
x.lstrip()
```

```
'Hello,    World\t\t '
```

```
x.rstrip()
```

```
'  Hello,    World'
```

In this example, tab characters are considered to be whitespace. The exact meaning may differ across operating systems, but you can always find out what Python considers to be whitespace by accessing the `string.whitespace` constant. On my Windows system, Python returns the following:

```
import string
string.whitespace
```

```
' \t\n\r\x0b\x0c'
```

```
" \t\n\r\v\f"
```

```
' \t\n\r\x0b\x0c'
```

The characters given in backslashed hex (\xnn) format represent the vertical tab and form-feed characters. The space character is in there as itself. It may be tempting to change the value of this variable, to attempt to affect how `strip` and so forth work, but don't do it. Such an action isn't guaranteed to give you the results you're looking for.

You can, however, change which characters `strip`, `rstrip`, and `lstrip` remove by passing a string containing the characters to be removed as an extra parameter:

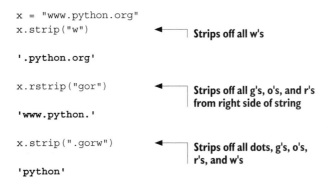

```
x = "www.python.org"
x.strip("w")                        Strips off all w's
```

```
'.python.org'
```

```
x.rstrip("gor")                     Strips off all g's, o's, and r's
                                    from right side of string
'www.python.'
```

```
x.strip(".gorw")                    Strips off all dots, g's, o's,
                                    r's, and w's
'python'
```

Note that `strip` removes any and all of the characters in the extra parameter string, no matter in which order they occur.

The most common use for these functions is as a quick way to clean up strings that have just been read in. This technique is particularly helpful when you're reading lines from files because Python always reads in an entire line, including the trailing newline, if one exists. When you get around to processing the line read in, you typically don't want the trailing newline. `rstrip` is a convenient way to get rid of it.

There are also two new string methods to strip prefixes and suffixes:

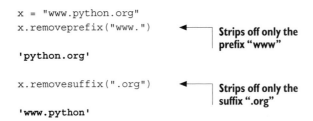

```
x = "www.python.org"
x.removeprefix("www.")              Strips off only the
                                    prefix "www"
'python.org'
```

```
x.removesuffix(".org")              Strips off only the
                                    suffix ".org"
'www.python'
```

Unlike `strip`, `removesuffix` and `removeprefix` will only remove suffixes and prefixes that are exact matches for their parameters, which makes their behavior more predictable.

> ### Quick check: strip
>
> If the string x equals `"(name, date),\n"`, which of the following would return a string containing `"name, date"`?
>
> ```
> x.rstrip("),")
> x.strip("),\n")
> x.strip("\n)(,")
> ```

6.4.4 String searching

The string objects provide several methods to perform simple string searches. Before I describe them, though, I'll talk about another module in Python: `re`. (This module is discussed in depth in chapter 16.)

> ### Another method for searching strings: The re module
>
> The `re` module also does string searching but in a far more flexible manner, using *regular expressions*. Rather than search for a single specified substring, a `re` search can look for a string pattern. You could look for substrings that consist entirely of digits, for example.
>
> Why am I mentioning this when `re` is discussed fully later? In my experience, many uses of basic string searches are inappropriate. You'd benefit from a more powerful searching mechanism but aren't aware that one exists, so you don't even look for something better. Perhaps you have an urgent project involving strings and don't have time to read this entire book. If basic string searching does the job for you, that's great. But be aware that you have a more powerful alternative.

The four basic string-searching methods are similar: `find`, `rfind`, `index`, and `rindex`. A related method, `count`, counts how many times a substring can be found in another string. I describe `find` in detail and then examine how the other methods differ from it.

`find` takes one required argument: the substring being searched for. `find` returns the position of the first character of the first instance of `substring` in the `string` object, or `-1` if `substring` doesn't occur in the string:

```
x = "Mississippi"
x.find("ss")
```

```
2
```

```
x.find("zz")
```

```
-1
```

`find` can also take one or two additional, optional arguments. The first of these arguments, if present, is an integer `start`; it causes `find` to ignore all characters before position start in string when searching for substring. The second optional argument, if present, is an integer end; it causes find to ignore characters at or after position end in string:

```
x = "Mississippi"
x.find("ss", 3)
```

5

```
x.find("ss", 0, 3)
```

-1

rfind is almost the same as find, except that it starts its search at the end of string and so returns the position of the first character of the last occurrence of substring in string:

```
x = "Mississippi"
x.rfind("ss")
```

5

rfind can also take one or two optional arguments, with the same meanings as those for find.

index and rindex are identical to find and rfind, respectively, except for one difference: if index or rindex fails to find an occurrence of substring in string, it doesn't return –1 but raises a ValueError exception. Exactly what this means will be clear after you read chapter 14.

count is used identically to any of the previous four functions but returns the number of nonoverlapping times the given substring occurs in the given string:

```
x = "Mississippi"
x.count("ss")
```

2

You can use two other string methods to search strings: startswith and endswith. These methods return a True or False result, depending on whether the string they're used on starts or ends with one of the strings given as parameters:

```
x = "Mississippi"
x.startswith("Miss")
```

True

```
x.startswith("Mist")
```

False

```
x.endswith("pi")
```

True

```
x.endswith("p")
```

False

Both `startswith` and `endswith` can look for more than one string at a time. If the parameter is a tuple of strings, both methods check for all the strings in the tuple and return `True` if any one of them is found:

```
x.endswith(("i", "u"))
```

True

`startswith` and `endswith` are useful for simple searches where you're sure that what you're checking for is at the beginning or end of a line.

> ### Quick check: String searching
> If you wanted to check whether a line ends with the string `"rejected"`, what string method would you use? Would there be any other ways to get the same result?

6.4.5   *Modifying strings*

Strings are immutable, but string objects have several methods that can operate on a string and return a new string that's a modified version of the original string. This provides much the same effect as direct modification, for most purposes. You can find a more complete description of these methods in the documentation.

You can use the `replace` method to replace occurrences of `substring` (its first argument) in the string with `newstring` (its second argument). This method also takes an optional third argument (see the documentation for details):

```
x = "Mississippi"
x.replace("ss", "+++")
```

'Mi+++i+++ippi'

Like the string search functions, the `re` module is a much more powerful method of substring replacement.

The functions `string.maketrans` and `string.translate` may be used together to translate characters in strings into different characters. Although rarely used, these functions can simplify your life when they're needed.

Suppose that you're working on a program that translates string expressions from one computer language into another. The first language uses ~ to mean logical not, whereas the second language uses !; the first language uses ^ to mean logical, and the second language uses &; the first language uses (and), whereas the second language uses [and]. In a given string expression, you need to change all instances of ~ to !, all instances of ^ to &, and all instances of (to [, and all instances of) to]. You could do this by using multiple invocations of replace, but an easier and more efficient way is

```
x = "~x ^ (y % z)"
table = x.maketrans("~^()", "!&[]")
x.translate(table)
```

'!x & [y % z]'

The second line uses maketrans to make up a translation table from its two string arguments. The two arguments must each contain the same number of characters, and a table is made such that looking up the *n*th character of the first argument in that table gives back the *n*th character of the second argument.

　　Next, the table produced by maketrans is passed to translate. Then translate goes over each of the characters in its string object and checks to see whether they can be found in the table given as the second argument. If a character can be found in the translation table, translate replaces that character with the corresponding character looked up in the table to produce the translated string.

　　You can also use translate with an optional argument to specify characters that should be removed from the string. To remove characters, you would use empty strings for the first and second arguments and include a third string of characters to remove:

```
x = "~x ^ (y % z)"
table = x.maketrans("", "", "()~^%")
x.translate(table)
```

'x y z'

Here all of the punctuation marks in the original string are in the third parameter, a string containing the characters to remove.

　　Other functions in the string module perform more specialized tasks. string .lower converts all alphabetic characters in a string to lowercase, and upper does the opposite. capitalize capitalizes the first character of a string, and title capitalizes all words in a string. swapcase converts lowercase characters to uppercase and uppercase to lowercase in the same string. expandtabs gets rid of tab characters in a string by replacing each tab with a specified number of spaces. ljust, rjust, and center pad a string with spaces to justify it in a certain field width. zfill left-pads a numeric string with zeros. Refer to the documentation for details on these methods.

6.4.6　*Modifying strings with list manipulations*

Because strings are immutable objects, you have no way to manipulate them directly in the same way that you can manipulate lists. Although the operations that produce new strings (leaving the original strings unchanged) can be useful, sometimes you want to be able to manipulate a string as though it were a list of characters. In that case, turn the string into a list of characters, do whatever you want, and then turn the resulting list back into a string:

```
text = "Hello, World"
wordList = list(text)
wordList[6:] = []                    Removes everything
wordList.reverse()                   after comma
text = "".join(wordList)
print(text)                          Joins with no space between
```

,olleH

You can also turn a string into a tuple of characters by using the built-in `tuple` function. To turn the list back into a string, use `"".join()`.

You shouldn't go overboard with this method because it causes the creation and destruction of new `string` objects, which is relatively expensive. Processing hundreds or thousands of strings in this manner probably won't have much of an impact on your program; processing millions of strings probably will.

> **Quick check: Modifying strings**
>
> What would be a quick way to change all punctuation in a string to spaces?

6.4.7   Useful methods and constants

`string` objects also have several useful methods to report various characteristics of the string, such as whether it consists of digits or alphabetic characters or is all uppercase or lowercase:

```
x = "123"
x.isdigit()
```

True

```
x.isalpha()
```

False

```
x = "M"
x.islower()
```

False

```
x.isupper()
```

True

For a list of all the possible string methods, refer to the string section of the official Python documentation.

Finally, the `string` module defines some useful constants. You've already seen `string.whitespace`, which is a string made up of the characters Python thinks of as whitespace on your system. `string.digits` is the string `'0123456789'`. `string.hexdigits` includes all the characters in `string.digits`, as well as `'abcdefABCDEF'`, the extra characters used in hexadecimal numbers. `string.octdigits` contains `'01234567'`—only those digits used in octal numbers. `string.ascii_lowercase` contains all lowercase ASCII alphabetic characters; `string.ascii_uppercase` contains all ASCII uppercase alphabetic characters; `string.ascii_letters` contains all the characters in `string.ascii_lowercase` and `string.ascii_uppercase`. You might be tempted to try assigning to these constants to change the behavior of the language. Python would let you get away with this action, but it probably would be a bad idea.

Remember that strings are sequences of characters, so you can use the convenient Python `in` operator to test for a character's membership in any of these strings, although usually the existing string methods are simpler and easier. The most common string operations are shown in table 6.2.

Table 6.2   Common string operations

String operation	Explanation	Example
`+`	Adds two strings together	`x = "hello " + "world"`
`*`	Replicates a string	`x = " " * 20`
`upper`	Converts a string to uppercase	`x.upper()`
`lower`	Converts a string to lowercase	`x.lower()`
`title`	Capitalizes the first letter of each word in a string	`x.title()`
`find, index`	Searches for the target in a string	`x.find(y)` `x.index(y)`
`rfind, rindex`	Searches for the target in a string from the end of the string	`x.rfind(y)` `x.rindex(y)`
`startswith, endswith`	Checks the beginning or end of a string for a match	`x.startswith(y)` `x.endswith(y)`
`replace`	Replaces the target with a new string	`x.replace(y, z)`
`strip, rstrip, lstrip`	Removes whitespace or other characters from the ends of a string	`x.strip()`
`encode`	Converts a Unicode string to a `bytes` object	`x.encode("utf_8")`

Note that these methods don't change the string itself; they return either a location in the string or a string.

> ### Try this: String operations
>
> Suppose that you have a list of strings in which some (but not necessarily all) of the strings begin and end with the double-quote character:
>
> ```
> x = ['"abc"', 'def', '"ghi"', '"klm"', 'nop']
> ```
>
> What code would you use on each element to remove just the double quotes?
>
> What code could you use to find the position of the last `p` in `Mississippi`? When you've found that position, what code would you use to remove just that letter?

6.5 Converting objects to strings

In Python, almost anything can be converted to some sort of a string representation by using the built-in `repr` function. Lists are the only complex Python data types you're familiar with so far, so here, I turn some lists into their representations:

```
repr([1, 2, 3])
```

```
'[1, 2, 3]'
```

```
x = [1]
x.append(2)
x.append([3, 4])
'the list x is ' + repr(x)
```

```
'the list x is [1, 2, [3, 4]]'
```

The example uses `repr` to convert the list x to a string representation, which is then concatenated with the other string to form the final string. Without the use of `repr`, this code wouldn't work. In an expression like `"string" + [1, 2] + 3`, are you trying to add strings, add lists, or just add numbers? Python doesn't know what you want in such a circumstance, so it does the safe thing (raises an error) rather than make any assumptions. In the previous example, all the elements had to be converted to string representations before the string concatenation would work.

Lists are the only complex Python objects that I've described to this point, but `repr` can be used to obtain some sort of string representation for almost any Python object. To see this, try `repr` around a built-in complex object, which is an actual Python function:

```
repr(len)
```

```
'<built-in function len>'
```

Python hasn't produced a string containing the code that implements the `len` function, but it has at least returned a string—`<built-in function len>`—that describes what that function is. If you keep the `repr` function in mind and try it on each Python data type (dictionaries, tuples, classes, and the like) in the book, you'll see that no matter what type of Python object you have, you can get a string that describes something about that object.

This is great for debugging programs. If you're in doubt about what's held in a variable at a certain point in your program, use `repr` and print out the contents of that variable.

I've covered how Python can convert any object to a string that describes that object. The truth is, Python can do this in either of two ways. The `repr` function always returns what might be loosely called the *formal string representation* of a Python object. More specifically, for simpler objects `repr` returns a string representation of a Python object from which the original object can be rebuilt. For large, complex objects, this may not be the sort of thing you want to see, so `repr` returns some descriptive text.

Python also provides the built-in `str` function. In contrast to `repr`, `str` is intended to produce *printable* string representations, and it can be applied to any Python object. `str` returns what might be called the *informal string representation* of the object. A string returned by `str` need not define an object fully and is intended to be read by humans, not by Python code.

You won't notice any difference between `repr` and `str` when you start using them, because until you begin using the object-oriented features of Python, there's no difference. `str` applied to any built-in Python object always calls `repr` to calculate its result. Only when you start defining your own classes does the difference between `str` and `repr` become important, as discussed in chapter 15.

So why talk about this now? I want you to be aware that there's more going on behind the scenes with `repr` than just being able to easily write `print` functions for debugging. As a matter of good style, you may want to get into the habit of using `str` rather than `repr` when creating strings for displaying information.

6.6   *Using the format method*

You can format strings in Python 3 in three ways. One way is to use the string class's `format` method. The `format` method combines a format string containing replacement fields marked with { }, with replacement values taken from the parameters given to the `format` command. If you need to include a literal { or } in the string, you double it to {{ or }}. The `format` command is a powerful string-formatting mini-language that offers almost endless possibilities for manipulating string formatting. Conversely, it's fairly simple to use for the most common use cases, so I look at a few basic patterns in this section. Then, if you need to use the more advanced options, you can refer to the string-formatting section of the standard library documentation.

6.6.1   *The format method and positional parameters*

A simple way to use the string `format` method is with numbered replacement fields that correspond to the parameters passed to the `format` function:

The format method is applied to the format
string, which can also be a string variable.

```
"{0} is the {1} of {2}".format("Ambrosia", "food", "the gods")
```

```
'Ambrosia is the food of the gods'
```

```
"{{Ambrosia}} is the {0} of {1}".format("food", "the gods")
```

```
'{Ambrosia} is the food of the gods'
```

Doubling the { } characters
escapes them so that they don't
mark a replacement field.

Note that the `format` method is applied to the format string, which can also be a string variable. Doubling the { } characters escapes them so that they don't mark a replacement field.

This example has three replacement fields, {0}, {1}, and {2}, which are in turn filled by the first, second, and third parameters. No matter where in the format string you place {0}, it's always replaced by the first parameter, and so on.

You can also use named parameters.

6.6.2 *The format method and named parameters*

The `format` method also recognizes named parameters and replacement fields:

```
"{food} is the food of {user}".format(food="Ambrosia",
    user="the gods")
```

```
'Ambrosia is the food of the gods'
```

In this case, the replacement parameter is chosen by matching the name of the replacement field with the name of the parameter given to the `format` command.

You can also use both positional and named parameters, and you can even access attributes and elements within those parameters:

```
"{0} is the food of {user[1]}".format("Ambrosia",
    user=["men", "the gods", "others"])
```

```
'Ambrosia is the food of the gods'
```

In this case, the first parameter is positional, and the second, `user[1]`, refers to the second element of the named parameter `user`.

6.6.3 *Format specifiers*

Format specifiers let you specify the result of the formatting with even more power and control than the formatting sequences of the older style of string formatting. The format specifier lets you control the fill character, alignment, sign, width, precision, and type of the data when it's substituted for the replacement field. As noted earlier, the syntax of format specifiers is a mini-language in its own right and too complex to cover completely here, but the following examples give you an idea of its usefulness:

```
"{0:10} is the food of gods".format("Ambrosia")          ◄──┐ :10 makes the field 10 spaces
                                                             │ wide, padded with spaces.
'Ambrosia   is the food of gods'

"{0:{1}} is the food of gods".format("Ambrosia", 10)     ◄──┐ :{1} width is from the
                                                             │ second parameter.
'Ambrosia   is the food of gods'

"{food:{width}} is the food of gods".format(food="Ambrosia", width=10)

'Ambrosia   is the food of gods'

"{0:>10} is the food of gods".format("Ambrosia")         ◄──┐ :>10 forces
                                                             │ right justification.
'   Ambrosia is the food of gods'

"{0:&>10} is the food of gods".format("Ambrosia")        ◄──┐ :&>10 forces right justification
                                                             │ padded with & character.
'&&Ambrosia is the food of gods'
```

:10 is a format specifier that makes the field 10 spaces wide and pads with spaces. :{1} takes the width from the second parameter. :>10 forces right justification of the field and pads with spaces. :&>10 forces right justification and pads with & instead of spaces.

Quick check: The format() method

What will be in x when the following snippets of code are executed?

```
x = "{1:{0}}".format(3, 4)
x = "{0:$>5}".format(3)
x = "{a:{b}}".format(a=1, b=5)
x = "{a:{b}}:{0:$>5}".format(3, 4, a=1, b=5, c=10)
```

6.7   *String interpolation with f-strings*

Starting in Python 3.6, the newest way to create strings is called *f-strings*. F-strings, as they're commonly called because they are prefixed with f, are a way to include the values of arbitrary Python expressions inside literal strings. They use curly braces ("{ }") to include and evaluate Python expressions. The syntax of f-strings is almost identical to that of the format method, but without an explicit call to format() they are more compact and easier to read. Thanks to their simplicity, they have become very common.

To use an f-string, you simply put an "f" right before the first quote and then include the Python expressions you want interpolated into the string in curly braces. The following examples give you a basic idea of how f-strings work:

```
value = 42
message = f"The answer is {value}"
print(message)
```

The answer is 42

```
primes = [1, 2, 3, 5]
f"sum of first 4 primes is {sum(primes)}"
```

'sum of first 4 primes is 11'

Just as with the format method, format specifiers may be added:

```
PI = 3.1415
print(f"PI is {PI:{10}.{2}}")
```

PI is   3.1

Another useful feature of f-strings is that adding an "=" after an expression in curly braces will give you "debugging" output by showing both the expression and its value:

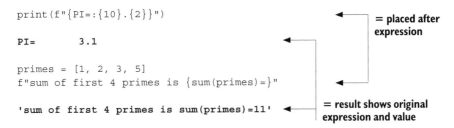

```
print(f"{PI=:{10}.{2}}")
```

PI=   3.1

= placed after expression

```
primes = [1, 2, 3, 5]
f"sum of first 4 primes is {sum(primes)=}"
```

'sum of first 4 primes is sum(primes)=11'

= result shows original expression and value

All of the format specifiers that work for the format method described here should also work for f-strings. While f-strings were a bit limited in their early versions, they have proved so useful as a concise and readable way of creating strings with the values of variables and expressions that they have been extended and are currently used extensively.

6.8 *Formatting strings with %*

This section covers formatting strings with the *string modulus* (%) operator. This operator is used to combine Python values into formatted strings for printing or other use. C users will notice a strange similarity to the `printf` family of functions. The use of % for string formatting is the old style of string formatting, and I cover it here because it was the standard in earlier versions of Python, and you're likely to see it in code that's been ported from earlier versions of Python or was written by coders who are familiar with those versions. This style of formatting shouldn't be used in new code, however, because it's slated to be deprecated and then removed from the language in the future.

The following is an example:

```
"%s is the %s of %s" % ("Ambrosia", "food", "the gods")
```

'Ambrosia is the food of the gods'

The string modulus operator (the last % that occurs in the line, not the three instances of %s that come before it in the example) takes two parts: the left side, which is a string, and the right side, which is a tuple. The string modulus operator scans the left string for special *formatting sequences* and produces a new string by substituting the values on the right side for those formatting sequences, in order. In this example, the only formatting sequences on the left side are the three instances of %s, which stands for "Stick a string in here."

Passing in different values on the right side produces different strings:

```
"%s is the %s of %s" % ("Nectar", "drink", "gods")
```

'Nectar is the drink of gods'

```
"%s is the %s of the %s" % ("Brussels Sprouts", "food",
        "foolish")
```

'Brussels Sprouts is the food of the foolish'

The members of the tuple on the right have str applied to them automatically by %s, so they don't have to already be strings:

```
x = [1, 2, "three"]
"The %s contains: %s" % ("list", x)
```

"The list contains: [1, 2, 'three']"

6.8.1   *Using formatting sequences*

All formatting sequences are substrings contained in the string on the left side of the central %. Each formatting sequence begins with a percent sign and is followed by one or more characters that specify what is to be substituted for the formatting sequence and how the substitution is to be accomplished. The %s formatting sequence used previously is the simplest formatting sequence; it indicates that the corresponding string from the tuple on the right side of the central % should be substituted in place of the %s.

Other formatting sequences can be more complex. The following sequence specifies the field width (total number of characters) of a printed number to be 6, specifies the number of characters after the decimal point to be 2, and left-justifies the number in its field. I've put this formatting sequence in angle brackets so you can see where extra spaces are inserted into the formatted string:

```
"Pi is <%-6.2f>" % 3.14159 # use of the formatting sequence: %-6.2f
```

'Pi is <3.14 >'

All the options for characters that are allowable in formatting sequences are given in the documentation. There are quite a few options, but none is particularly difficult to use. Remember that you can always try a formatting sequence interactively in Python to see whether it does what you expect it to do.

6.8.2 Named parameters and formatting sequences

Finally, one additional feature available with the % operator can be useful in certain circumstances. Unfortunately, to describe it, I have to employ a Python feature that I haven't yet discussed in detail: *dictionaries*, commonly called *hash tables* or *associative arrays* in other languages. You can skip ahead to chapter 7 to learn about dictionaries; skip this section for now and come back to it later; or read straight through, trusting the examples to make things clear.

Formatting sequences can specify what should be substituted for them by name rather than by position. When you do this, each formatting sequence has a name in parentheses immediately following the initial % of the formatting sequence, like so:

```
"%(pi).2f"                        ◄─────┐  Note the name in parentheses.
```

In addition, the argument to the right of the % operator is no longer given as a single value or tuple of values to be printed but as a dictionary of values to be printed, with each named formatting sequence having a correspondingly named key in the dictionary. Using the previous formatting sequence with the string modulus operator, you might produce code like the following:

```
num_dict = {'e': 2.718, 'PI': 3.14159}
print("%(PI).2f - %(PI).4f - %(e).2f" % num_dict)
```

```
3.14 - 3.1416 - 2.72
```

This code is particularly useful when you're using format strings that perform a large number of substitutions, because you no longer have to keep track of the positional correspondences of the right-side tuple of elements with the formatting sequences in the format string. The order in which elements are defined in the dict argument is irrelevant, and the template string may use values from dict more than once (as it does with the pi entry).

Controlling output with the print function

Python's built-in print function also has some options that can make handling simple string output easier. When used with one parameter, print prints the value and a newline character, so that a series of calls to print prints each value on a separate line:

```
print("a")
print("b")
```

(continued)
```
a
b
```

But `print` can do more. You can also give the `print` function several arguments, and those arguments are printed on the same line, separated by spaces and ending with a newline:

```
print("a", "b", "c")
a b c
```

If that's not quite what you need, you can give the `print` function additional parameters to control what separates each item and what ends the line:

```
print("a", "b", "c", sep="|")
a|b|c
print("a", "b", "c", end="\n\n")
a b c
```

Finally, the `print` function can be used to print to files as well as console output:

```
print("a", "b", "c", file=open("testfile.txt", "w"))
```

Using the `print` function's options gives you enough control for simple text output, but more complex situations are best served by using the `format` method.

Quick check: Formatting strings with %

What would be in the variable `x` after the following snippets of code have executed?

```
x = "%.2f" % 1.1111
x = "%(a).2f" % {'a':1.1111}
x = "%(a).08f" % {'a':1.1111}
```

6.9   *Bytes*

A `bytes` object is similar to a `string` object but with an important difference: A `string` is an immutable sequence of Unicode characters, whereas a `bytes` object is a sequence of integers with values from 0 to 256. Bytes can be necessary when you're dealing with binary data, such as reading from a binary data file.

The key thing to remember is that `bytes` objects may look like strings, but they can't be used exactly like strings or combined with strings:

```
unicode_a_with_acute = '\N{LATIN SMALL LETTER A WITH ACUTE}'
unicode_a_with_acute
```

```
'á'
```

```
xb = unicode_a_with_acute.encode()
xb
```

**The encode method converts
string to bytes.**

```
b'\xc3\xa1'
```

**The encoded bytes object is 2 bytes;
it doesn't print as a character.**

```
xb += 'A'
```

bytes string objects are different types.

```
--------------------------------------------------------------------
TypeError                                Traceback (most recent call last)
<ipython-input-93-2c4ecee004ef> in <cell line: 1>()
----> 1 xb += 'A'

TypeError: can't concat str to bytes
```

```
xb.decode()
```

**The object's decode method will
convert it back to a string.**

```
'á'
```

The first thing you can see is that to convert from a regular (Unicode) string to bytes, you need to call the string's encode method. After it's encoded to a bytes object, the character is 2 bytes and no longer prints the same way that the string did. Further, if you attempt to add a bytes object and a string object together, you get a type error because the two types are incompatible. Finally, to convert a bytes object back to a string, you need to call that object's decode method.

Most of the time, you shouldn't need to think about Unicode or bytes at all. But when you need to deal with international character sets (an increasingly common problem), you must understand the difference between regular strings and bytes.

Quick check: Bytes

For which of the following kinds of data would you want to use a string? For which could you use bytes?

Data file storing binary data

Text in a language with accented characters

Text with only uppercase and lowercase roman characters

A series of integers no larger than 255

6.10 *Preprocessing text*

In processing raw text, it's quite often necessary to clean and normalize the text before doing anything else. If you want to find the frequency of words in text, for example, you can make the job easier if, before you start counting, you make sure that everything is lowercase (or uppercase, if you prefer) and that all punctuation has been removed. You can also make things easier by breaking the text into a series of words. In this lab, the task is to read the first part of the first chapter of *Moby Dick*, make sure that everything is one case, remove all punctuation, and write the words one per line to a second file. As mentioned in the previous chapter, you should attempt to create a solution on your own before using AI to generate one.

To solve the problem, your code will need to open the source file, moby_01.txt. If you are using the Jupyter notebook, you can just execute the cell right before the lab. You can also download the file from the GitHub repository's folder for this chapter and save it in the directory you are working in.

You will also need to perform the operations to clean the text: making everything lowercase, removing punctuation, splitting the text into words, and writing the cleaned output to a file. My suggestion is that you process the file line by line since that will save memory, and it's easy to read and write line by line in Python.

Because I haven't yet covered reading and writing files, I provide the code for those operations—just put your code in place of the comments in the `for` loop:

```
with open("moby_01.txt") as infile:
  with open("moby_01_clean.txt", "w") as outfile:
    for line in infile:
        # make all one (lower) case
        # remove punctuation
        # split into words
        # write all words for line
        outfile.write(cleaned_words)
```

Hint: You can work on one cleaning step at a time. First, create the code to make everything lowercase, and check to see that the text in the output file is lowercase. Then, work on removing the punctuation, and make sure that works, and so on.

6.10.1   *Solving the problem with AI-generated code*

Using AI to generate code for this problem is fairly simple. In this case, it's probably easier to let the AI tool take care of opening, reading, and writing the files. To create a prompt, we need to be sure to include requirements:

1   Open the file moby_01.txt.
2   Read the lines of text.
3   Make all the text lowercase.
4   Remove any punctuation.
5   Split the line into words.
6   Write the words of the line to a file moby_01_clean.text.

If you want to try generating a solution using AI, go ahead and create a prompt and see what you get, and test to see if that code works correctly.

6.10.2   *Solutions and discussion*

Unsurprisingly, my solution and the AI solution were very similar. As we will see, however, the AI version misses a couple of tricks that would slightly improve efficiency.

THE HUMAN SOLUTION

Solving this problem using the framework provided here is fairly straightforward—just take it one step at a time:

```python
import string
punct = str.maketrans("",  "", string.punctuation)

with open("moby_01.txt") as infile:
    with open("moby_01_clean.txt", "w") as outfile:
        for line in infile:
            # make all one case
            cleaned_line = line.lower()

            # remove punctuation
            cleaned_line = cleaned_line.translate(punct)

            # split into words
            words = cleaned_line.split()
            cleaned_words = "\n".join(words)
            # write all words for line
            outfile.write(cleaned_words)
```

Imports Python's string library

Creates translation table from string library's list of punctuation

Uses translation table to remove punctuation

Joins current line's words using a newline, so one word per line

This solution is concise and reasonably efficient. In it we import the string library so that we can create a translation table to remove punctuation using Python's list of punctuation rather than creating our own. In processing a line of text, we first use the `lower()` method on the entire line, and then use the `translate` method on the entire line. We then split the line into words, which will return a list of the words without any whitespace, and finally rejoin the words with a newline, which means that when written to the file, there will be one word per line.

THE AI VERSION

Creating the AI version is a bit simpler in that we don't need to keep the scaffolding for opening, reading, and writing files, since the code generator should know how to do that. A reasonably concise prompt for what we need would be

```
For every line the file moby_01.txt, make everything lower case, remove
punctuation, and split into words. Write the words one per line to the file
moby_01_clean.txt.
```

For this problem, the solutions generated in Colaboratory and in Copilot were very similar. A good representative is the following solution generated by Copilot:

```python
import string

# Open the input file
with open('moby_01.txt', 'r') as input_file:
    # Open the output file
    with open('moby_01_clean.txt', 'w') as output_file:
        # Iterate over each line in the input file
```

```
for line in input_file:
    # Convert the line to lowercase
    line = line.lower()

    # Remove punctuation from the line
    line = line.translate(str.maketrans('', '', string.punctuation))

    # Split the line into words
    words = line.split()

    # Write each word to the output file
    for word in words:
        output_file.write(word + '\n')
```

Creates a new translation table for every line

The solution is nicely formatted and well commented, although I might say that a comment like # Iterate over each line in the input file is obvious and redundant coming right before the line for line in input_file:, but that's not important.

A more serious problem is the way that the code uses the translate method. Note that instead of creating a translation table for punctuation once at the beginning of the program (as the human-created version does), it creates a new translation table on the fly for every line. Experienced coders will cringe—repeating an operation inside a loop unnecessarily can make your code run much, much slower and is the sort of rookie mistake most coders want to avoid.

One solution offered by Colaboratory makes this problem even worse. Instead of using the translate method, it suggests looping over every character in string .punctuation using the replace method to remove it from the string:

```
# Remove punctuation
for char in string.punctuation:
    line = line.replace(char, '')
```

Here again we have a loop where translate is a single operation, and in this case, we are looping over all of the punctuation characters in every line and creating a new string object every time a punctuation character is found and removed. While this isn't a problem with a relatively small file, it can quickly become a big problem if we have to process a dataset with millions of lines.

A similar problem occurs in the last section, which writes the words to the output file. While not as much of a potential performance problem as the first one, it's still a problem, for two reasons. First, it loops over the list of words in the line, and second, it uses string concatenation (+) to add the newlines. While Python for loops are heavily optimized, using a loop when one isn't needed will still make things slower than they have to be, and using the + to add two strings together forces the creation of a new string, which also takes a bit of time.

The human version gets around this by using the join method with a newline character. Instead of a loop, this is a single operation, and instead of creating a new string object for every word, it creates just one for the entire line.

In this lab, the code generated by AI tools does the job, but if you tried to put that code into production under any sort of load, the slow performance might well become a problem.

Summary

- Python strings have powerful text-processing features, including searching and replacing, trimming characters, and changing case.
- Strings are immutable; they can't be changed in place.
- Operations that appear to change strings actually return a copy with the changes.
- There are three ways to combine strings and the values of Python expressions: the format method, f-strings, and the legacy method using %.
- The format method has an extensive formatting language to control its output.
- F-strings are a very convenient way to create strings containing the values of variables and expressions and are now used widely.
- Python has a `bytes` data type that contains ints in the range 0 to 255; they look similar to strings but need to be decoded to be converted to strings.

Dictionaries

7

This chapter covers

- Defining a dictionary
- Using dictionary operations
- Determining what can be used as a key
- Creating sparse matrices
- Using dictionaries as caches
- Trusting the efficiency of dictionaries

This chapter discusses dictionaries, Python's name for associative arrays or maps, which it implements by using hash tables. Dictionaries are amazingly useful, even in simple programs.

Because dictionaries are less familiar to many programmers than other basic data structures such as lists and strings, some of the examples illustrating dictionary use are slightly more complex than the corresponding examples for other built-in data structures. It may be necessary to read parts of chapter 8 to fully understand some of the examples in this chapter.

7.1 *What is a dictionary?*

If you've never used associative arrays or hash tables in other languages, a good way to start understanding the use of dictionaries is to compare them with lists:

- Values in lists are accessed by means of integers called *indices*, which indicate where in the list a given value is found.
- Dictionaries access values by means of integers, strings, or other Python objects called *keys*, which indicate where in the dictionary a given value is found. In other words, both lists and dictionaries provide indexed access to arbitrary values, but the set of items that can be used as dictionary indices is much larger than, and contains, the set of items that can be used as list indices. Also, the mechanism that dictionaries use to provide indexed access is quite different from that used by lists.
- Both lists and dictionaries can store objects of any type.
- Values stored in a list are implicitly *ordered* by their positions in the list, because the indices that access these values are consecutive integers. You may or may not care about this ordering, but you can use it if desired. Values stored in a dictionary are *not* implicitly ordered relative to one another because dictionary keys aren't just numbers.
- If you're using a dictionary but also care about the order of the items (the order in which they were added, that is), since Python 3.6 dictionaries store their items in the order they were added. There is also an *ordered dictionary*, which is a dictionary subclass that can be imported from the `collections` module and which offers a few extra features, such as a `move_to_end` method and the ability to access items in reverse order. You can also define an order on the items in a dictionary by using another data structure (often a list) to store such an ordering explicitly.

In spite of the differences between them, the use of dictionaries and lists often appears to be the same. As a start, an empty dictionary is created much like an empty list but with curly braces instead of square brackets:

```
x_list = []          A list
y_dic = {}
                     A dictionary
```

Here, the first line creates a new, empty list and assigns the variable x to it. The second line creates a new, empty dictionary and assigns the variable y to it.

After you create a dictionary, you may store values in it as though it were a list:

```
y_dic[0] = 'Hello'
y_dic[1] = 'Goodbye'
```

Even in these assignments, there's already a significant operational difference between the dictionary and list usage. Trying to do the same thing with a list would result in an error, because in Python, it's illegal to assign to a position in a list that doesn't exist. For example, if you try to assign to the *0*th element of the list x, you receive an error:

```
x_list[0] = 'Hello'
--------------------------------------------------------------------------
IndexError                              Traceback (most recent call last)
<ipython-input-1-ba4ef4c8f6ab> in <cell line: 3>()
      1 x_list = []
      2 y_dic = {}
----> 3 x_list[0] = 'Hello'

IndexError: list assignment index out of range
```

This isn't a problem with dictionaries; new positions in dictionaries are created as necessary.

Having stored some values in the dictionary, now you can access and use them:

```
print(y_dic[0])
print(y_dic[1] + ", Friend.")
```

Hello
Goodbye, Friend.

Overall, this makes a dictionary look pretty much like a list. Now for the big difference: you can store (and use) values under keys that aren't integers:

```
y_dic['greeting'] = "Bon jour"
y_dic['farewell'] = "Adios"
print(y_dic['greeting'])
print(y_dic['farewell'] + ", Friend.")
```

Bon jour
Adios, Friend.

This is definitely something that can't be done with lists! Whereas list indices must be integers, dictionary keys are much less restricted; they may be numbers, strings, or one of a wide range of other Python objects. This makes dictionaries a natural for jobs that lists can't do. For example, it makes more sense to implement a telephone directory application with dictionaries than with lists because the phone number for a person can be stored and indexed by that person's last name.

A dictionary is a way of mapping from one set of arbitrary objects to an associated but equally arbitrary set of objects. Actual dictionaries, thesauri, or translation books are good analogies in the real world. To see how natural this correspondence is, here's the start of an English-to-French color translator:

```
english_to_french = {}                    ◄──────────┐ Creates empty dictionary
english_to_french['red'] = 'rouge'         ◄──────┐
english_to_french['blue'] = 'bleu'                │  Stores three words in it
english_to_french['green'] = 'vert'
```

```
print("red is", english_to_french['red'])
```
←————┐ **Obtains value for "red"**

```
red is rouge
```

> ### Try this: Create a dictionary
> Write the code to ask a user for three names and three ages. After the names and ages are entered, ask the user for one of the names, and print the correct age.

7.2 *Other dictionary operations*

Besides basic element assignment and access, dictionaries support several operations. You can define a dictionary explicitly as a series of key-value pairs separated by commas:

```
english_to_french = {'red': 'rouge', 'blue': 'bleu', 'green': 'vert'}len
returns the number of entries in a dictionary:
len(english_to_french)
```

```
3
```

You can obtain all the keys in the dictionary with the `keys` method. This method is often used to iterate over the contents of a dictionary using Python's `for` loop, described in chapter 8:

```
list(english_to_french.keys())
```

```
['green', 'blue', 'red']
```

In Python 3.5 and earlier, the order of the keys in a list returned by `keys` has no meaning; the keys aren't necessarily sorted, and they don't necessarily occur in the order in which they were created. Your Python code may print out the keys in a different order than my Python code did. If you need keys sorted, you can store them in a list variable and then sort that list. However, as mentioned earlier, starting with Python 3.6, dictionaries preserve the order that the keys were created and return them in that order.

It's also possible to obtain all the values stored in a dictionary by using `values`:

```
list(english_to_french.values())
```

```
['vert', 'bleu', 'rouge']
```

This method isn't used nearly as often as `keys`.

You can use the `items` method to return all keys and their associated values as a sequence of tuples:

```
list(english_to_french.items())
```

```
[('green', 'vert'), ('blue', 'bleu'), ('red', 'rouge')]
```

Like `keys`, this method is often used in conjunction with a `for` loop to iterate over the contents of a dictionary.

The `del` statement can be used to remove an entry (key-value pair) from a dictionary:

```
list(english_to_french.items())
```

```
[('green', 'vert'), ('blue', 'bleu'), ('red', 'rouge')]
```

```
del english_to_french['green']
list(english_to_french.items())
```

```
[('blue', 'bleu'), ('red', 'rouge')]
```

Dictionary view objects

The `keys`, `values`, and `items` methods return not lists but *views* that behave like sequences but are dynamically updated whenever the dictionary changes. That's why you need to use the `list` function to make them appear as a list in these examples. Otherwise, they behave like sequences, allowing code to iterate over them in a `for` loop, using `in` to check membership in them, and so on.

The view returned by `keys` (and in some cases the view returned by `items`) also behaves like a set, with union, difference, and intersection operations.

Attempting to access a key that isn't in a dictionary is an error in Python. To handle this error, you can test the dictionary for the presence of a key with the `in` keyword, which returns `True` if a dictionary has a value stored under the given key and `False` otherwise:

```
'red' in english_to_french
```

```
True
```

```
'orange' in english_to_french
```

```
False
```

Alternatively, you can use the `get` function. This function returns the value associated with a key if the dictionary contains that key but returns its second argument if the dictionary doesn't contain the key:

```
print(english_to_french.get('blue', 'No translation'))
```

```
bleu
```
Chartreuse not found, "No translation" is returned.

```
print(english_to_french.get('chartreuse', 'No translation'))
```

```
No translation
```

The second argument is optional. If that argument isn't included, `get` returns `None` if the dictionary doesn't contain the key.

Similarly, if you want to safely get a key's value *and* make sure that it's set to a default in the dictionary, you can use the `setdefault` method:

```
print(english_to_french.setdefault('chartreuse', 'No translation'))
```

`No translation`   **Chartreuse not found and is added as key, and "No translation" is returned and added as its value.**

The difference between `get` and `setdefault` is that after the `setdefault` call, there's a key in the dictionary `'chartreuse'` with the value `'No translation'`.

There is also a `defaultdict` subclass of `dict` that you can import from the `collections` module, and instances of `defaultdict` can be given a default value and will automatically work the same was as `setdefault`.

You can obtain a copy of a dictionary by using the `copy` method:

```
x = {0: 'zero', 1: 'one'}
y = x.copy()
y
```

```
{0: 'zero', 1: 'one'}
```

This method makes a shallow copy of the dictionary, which is likely to be all you need in most situations. For dictionaries that contain any modifiable objects as values (for example, lists or other dictionaries), you may want to make a deep copy by using the `copy.deepcopy` function. See chapter 5 for an introduction to the concept of shallow and deep copies.

The `update` method updates the dictionary it is a member of with all the key-value pairs of a second dictionary. For keys that are common to both dictionaries, the values from the second dictionary override those of the first:

```
z = {1: 'ONE', 2: 'Two'}
x = {0: 'zero', 1: 'one'}
x.update(z)
x
```

```
{0: 'zero', 1: 'ONE', 2: 'Two'}
```

Dictionary methods give you a full set of tools to manipulate and use dictionaries. For quick reference, table 7.1 lists some of the main dictionary functions.

Table 7.1   Dictionary operations

Dictionary operation	Explanation	Example
`{}`	Creates an empty dictionary	`x = {}`
`len`	Returns the number of entries in a dictionary	`len(x)`
`keys`	Returns a view of all keys in a dictionary	`x.keys()`

Table 7.1 Dictionary operations (*continued*)

Dictionary operation	Explanation	Example
values	Returns a view of all values in a dictionary	`x.values()`
items	Returns a view of all items in a dictionary	`x.items()`
del	Removes an entry from a dictionary	`del(x[key])`
in	Tests whether a key exists in a dictionary	`'y' in x`
get	Returns the value of a key or a configurable default	`x.get('y', None)`
setdefault	Returns the value if the key is in the dictionary; otherwise, sets the value for the key to the default and returns the value	`x.setdefault('y', None)`
copy	Makes a shallow copy of a dictionary	`y = x.copy()`
update	Combines the entries of two dictionaries	`x.update(z)`

This table isn't a complete list of all dictionary operations. For a complete list, refer to the Python standard library documentation.

> **Quick check: Dictionary operations**
>
> Assume that you have a dictionary x = { 'a':1, 'b':2, 'c':3, 'd':4 } and a dictionary y = { 'a':6, 'e':5, 'f':6 }. What would be the contents of x after the following snippets of code have executed?
>
> ```
> del x['d']
> z = x.setdefault('g', 7)
> x.update(y)
> ```

7.3   *Word counting*

Assume that you have a file that contains a list of words, one word per line. You want to know how many times each word occurs in the file. You can use dictionaries to perform this task easily:

```
sample_string = "To be or not to be"
occurrences = {}
for word in sample_string.split():
    occurrences[word] = occurrences.get(word, 0) + 1     ◄─── Increments the
                                                              occurrences count
for word in occurrences:                                      for the word
    print("The word", word, "occurs", occurrences[word],
            "times in the string")

The word To occurs 1 times in the string
The word be occurs 2 times in the string
The word or occurs 1 times in the string
```

```
The word not occurs 1 times in the string
The word to occurs 1 times in the string
```

This is a good example of the power of dictionaries, using each word as a dictionary key and the `get()` method to increment the count for that word if found. The code is simple, but because dictionary operations are highly optimized in Python, it's also quite fast. This pattern is so handy, in fact, that it's been standardized as the `Counter` class in the `collections` module of the standard library.

7.4   What can be used as a key?

The previous examples use strings as keys, but Python permits more than just strings to be used in this manner. Any Python object that is immutable and hashable can be used as a key to a dictionary.

In Python, as discussed earlier, any object that can be modified is called *mutable*. Lists are mutable because list elements can be added, changed, or removed. Dictionaries are also mutable for the same reason. Numbers are immutable. If a variable x is referring to the number 3 and you assign 4 to x, you've made x refer to a different number (4) but you haven't changed the number 3 itself; 3 still has to be 3. Strings are also immutable. `list[n]` returns the *n*th element of `list`, `string[n]` returns the *n*th character of `string`, and `list[n] = value` changes the *n*th element of `list`, but `string[n] = character` is illegal in Python and causes an error, because strings in Python are immutable.

Unfortunately, the requirement that keys be immutable and hashable means that lists can't be used as dictionary keys, but in many instances, it would be convenient to have a listlike key. For example, it's convenient to store information about a person under a key consisting of the person's first and last names, which you could easily do if you could use a two-element list as a key.

Python solves this difficulty by providing tuples, which are basically immutable lists; they're created and used similarly to lists, except that, once created, they can't be modified. There's one further restriction: keys must also be hashable, which takes things a step further than just immutable. To be hashable, an object must have a hash value (provided by a __hash__ method) that never changes throughout the life of the value. That means that tuples containing mutable objects are *not* hashable, although the tuples themselves are technically immutable. Only tuples that don't contain any mutable objects nested within them are hashable and valid to use as keys for dictionaries. Table 7.2 illustrates which of Python's built-in types are immutable, hashable, and eligible to be dictionary keys.

Table 7.2   Python values eligible to be used as dictionary keys

Python type	Immutable?	Hashable?	Dictionary key?
int	Yes	Yes	Yes
float	Yes	Yes	Yes

Table 7.2   Python values eligible to be used as dictionary keys (*continued*)

Python type	Immutable?	Hashable?	Dictionary key?
boolean	Yes	Yes	Yes
complex	Yes	Yes	Yes
str	Yes	Yes	Yes
bytes	Yes	Yes	Yes
bytearray	No	No	No
list	No	No	No
tuple	Yes	Sometimes	Sometimes
set	No	No	No
frozenset	Yes	Yes	Yes
dictionary	No	No	No

The next sections give examples illustrating how tuples and dictionaries can work together.

> **Quick check: What can be a key?**
>
> Decide which of the following expressions can be a dictionary key: 1; 'bob'; ('tom', [1, 2, 3]); ["filename"]; "filename"; ("filename", "extension").

7.5   *Sparse matrices*

In mathematical terms, a *matrix* is a two-dimensional grid of numbers, usually written in textbooks as a grid with square brackets on each side, as shown here:

$$
\begin{bmatrix}
3 & 0 & -2 & 11 \\
0 & 9 & 0 & 0 \\
0 & 7 & 0 & 0 \\
0 & 0 & 0 & -5
\end{bmatrix}
$$

A fairly standard way to represent such a matrix is by means of a list of lists. In Python, a matrix is presented like this:

```
matrix = [[3, 0, -2, 11], [0, 9, 0, 0], [0, 7, 0, 0], [0, 0, 0, -5]]
```

Elements in the matrix can be accessed by row and column number:

```
element = matrix[rownum][colnum]
```

But in some applications, such as weather forecasting, it's common for matrices to be very large—thousands of elements to a side, meaning millions of elements in total. It's also common for such matrices to contain many zero elements. In some applications, all but a small percentage of the matrix elements may be set to zero. To conserve memory, it's common for such matrices to be stored in a form in which only the nonzero elements are actually stored. Such representations are called *sparse matrices*.

It's simple to implement sparse matrices by using dictionaries with tuple indices. For example, the previous sparse matrix can be represented as follows, with each key being the row and column of a value:

```
matrix = {(0, 0): 3, (0, 2): -2, (0, 3): 11,
          (1, 1): 9, (2, 1): 7, (3, 3): -5}
```

Now you can access an individual matrix element at a given row and column number by this bit of code:

```
if (rownum, colnum) in matrix:
    element = matrix[(rownum, colnum)]
else:
    element = 0
```

A slightly less clear (but more efficient) way of doing this is to use the dictionary `get` method, which you can tell to return `0` if it can't find a key in the dictionary and, otherwise, return the value associated with that key, preventing one of the dictionary lookups:

```
element = matrix.get((rownum, colnum), 0)
```

If you're considering doing extensive work with matrices, you may want to look into `NumPy`, the numeric computation package.

7.6 Dictionaries as caches

This section shows how dictionaries can be used as *caches*, data structures that store results to avoid recalculating those results over and over. Suppose that you need a function called `sole`, which takes three integers as arguments and returns a result. The function might look something like the following:

```
def sole(m, n, t):
    # . . . do some time-consuming calculations . . .
    return(result)
```

But if this function is very time consuming, and if it's called tens of thousands of times, the program might run too slowly.

Now suppose that `sole` might be called with about 200 different combinations of arguments during any program run. That is, you might call `sole(12, 20, 6)` 50 or more times during the execution of your program and similarly for many other combinations of arguments. By eliminating the recalculation of sole on identical arguments, you'd save a huge amount of time. You could use a dictionary with tuples as keys, like so:

```
sole_cache = {}
def sole(m, n, t):
    if (m, n, t) in sole_cache:
        return sole_cache[(m, n, t)]
    else:
        # . . . do some time-consuming calculations . . .
        sole_cache[(m, n, t)] = result
        return result
```

The rewritten sole function uses a global variable to store previous results. The global variable is a dictionary, and the keys of the dictionary are tuples corresponding to argument combinations that have been given to sole in the past. Then, anytime sole passes an argument combination for which a result has already been calculated, it returns that stored result rather than recalculating it.

> **Try this: Using dictionaries**
>
> Suppose that you're writing a program that works like a spreadsheet. How might you use a dictionary to store the contents of a sheet? Write some sample code to both store a value in and retrieve a value from a particular cell. What might be some drawbacks to this approach?

7.7   *Efficiency of dictionaries*

If you come from a traditional compiled-language background, you may hesitate to use dictionaries, worrying that they're less efficient than lists (arrays). The truth is that the Python dictionary implementation is quite fast. Many of the internal language features rely on dictionaries, and a lot of work has gone into making them efficient. Because all of Python's data structures are heavily optimized, you shouldn't spend much time worrying about which is faster or more efficient. If the problem can be solved more easily and cleanly by using a dictionary than by using a list, do it that way, and consider alternatives only if it's clear that dictionaries are causing an unacceptable slowdown.

7.8   *Word counting*

In the previous lab, you took the text of the first chapter of *Moby Dick*, normalized the case, removed punctuation, and wrote the separated words to a file. In this lab, we will use the file created in chapter 6 to count the number of times each word occurs.

To do this, we will read the file and use a dictionary as described previously to count the occurrences, using the words as the keys and the number of occurrences as the values. Once we have processed the file, we'll print out the five most common and five least common words and the number of times they occur.

To open and read the file, we can use code that's similar to what we used the last time, but we won't need an output file:

```
with open("moby_01_clean.txt", "r") as infile:
    for word in infile:
        # use stip() method to remove any extra whitespace
        # increase the count for current word
```

In addition to using a dictionary to count occurrences, you'll need to use the `items()` method to get the keys and values as a series of tuples that you can sort. For this you may need to refer to chapter 5 on lists.

Hint: You will also need to create an empty dictionary to hold the word counts *before* you start processing the words.

7.8.1 Solving the problem with AI-generated code

Again, the main factor in using AI to generate the code will be in creating the prompt. As in the previous chapter, we don't need to worry about telling the AI chatbot how to read a file, but in this case if we want to be sure it uses a dictionary and not the `Counter` class, we will need to specify that. So our prompt should mention the following:

1. Open the file moby_01_clean.txt.
2. Use a dictionary to count the number of occurrences of each word.
3. Print the five most common words and their number of occurrences.
4. Print the five least common words and their number of occurrences.

If you are using an AI chatbot, create a prompt and see what solution you get.

7.8.2 Solutions and discussion

While this problem is a little more complex than the last lab, it is still straightforward enough that my solution and the AI solutions are similar. The AI solutions, however, still suggest doing things in slightly less efficient ways.

THE HUMAN SOLUTION

The solution to this problem requires a bit more thought than the one in the previous chapter, since more processing has to occur after the file is read, and you need to remember to create a dictionary to hold the word counts before processing the words:

```
word_count = {}
with open("moby_01_clean.txt", "r") as infile:
    for word in infile:
        # use stip() method to remove any extra whitespace
        word = word.strip()

        # increase the count for current word
        word_count.setdefault(word, 0)      ← If word not present, adds and sets count to zero
        word_count[word] += 1                ← Adds 1 to count

word_list = list(word_count.items())         ← Gets items as list of tuples
```

```
word_list.sort(key=lambda x: x[1])
print("Most common words:")
for word in reversed(word_list[-5:]):
    print(word)
print("\nLeast common words:")
for word in word_list[:5]:
    print(word)
```

◄────┐ **Sorts the items by frequency**

◄──── **Reverses order so higher
frequency is first**

The key to this solution is using the dictionary's `setdefault()` method to set the word's entry in the dictionary to zero if it doesn't already exist in the dictionary. Then we add 1 to the word's value in the dictionary.

Once all of the words have been counted, we use the dictionary's `items()` method to get a list of word-frequency tuples we can sort by frequency. We can then reverse that list to get the most frequent and use the original order to get the least frequent.

THE AI VERSION

Just as with the previous problem, the AI generators provide code that works and is nicely commented.

As mentioned earlier, the prompt should be explicit that the `Counter` class should not be used, so the prompt that I used was

```
Open the file moby_01_clean.txt and use a dictionary to count the
occurrences of each word. Do not use a Counter. Print the five most common
words and their number of occurrences. Print the five least common words
and their number of occurrences.
```

Both Colaboratory and Copilot came up with very similar approaches. In this case, let's look at Colaboratory's solution:

```
# Open the file and read the text into a variable.
with open('moby_01_clean.txt', 'r') as f:
  text = f.read()
```

◄────┐ **Reads entire file**

```
# Split the text into words.
words = text.split()
```

◄────┘ **Splits entire file into list of words**

```
# Create a dictionary to count the occurrences of each word.
word_counts = {}
for word in words:
  if word not in word_counts:
    word_counts[word] = 0
  word_counts[word] += 1
```

◄────┐ **Uses if to check if
word is in dictionary**

```
# Find the five most common words and their number of occurrences.
most_common = sorted(word_counts.items(), key=lambda item: item[1],
                     reverse=True)[:5]
```

◄────┐ **Creates reversed sorted list
to get most frequent**

```
# Find the five least common words and
  {CA}their number of occurrences.
```

◄────┐ **Creates normal sorted list
to get least frequent**

```
least_common = sorted(word_counts.items(), key=lambda item: item[1])[:5]

# Print the results.
print("Most common words:")
for word, count in most_common:
  print(f"{word}: {count}")

print("\nLeast common words:")
for word, count in least_common:
  print(f"{word}: {count}")
```

The Copilot version is similar, and both solutions read the entire file into memory and then split it into one big list of words. This might be a problem if the size of the file is quite large. The human version takes advantage of there being one word per line to process the file line by line, which would avoid this problem. Interestingly, even if the AI chatbots were told in the prompt that there was only one word per line, they wouldn't take advantage of that fact.

There are a couple of interesting differences between the two. The Copilot version uses a slightly more verbose way of checking the list:

```
for word in words:
    if word in word_counts:
        word_counts[word] += 1
    else:
        word_counts[word] = 1
```

Note that, in this case, if the word isn't already in the dictionary, it adds it with a value of 1, since it wouldn't have checked if it hadn't hit an occurrence of the word. Otherwise, it increments the value for the word in place. Theoretically this might be a tiny bit faster, but neither solution will be quite as good as using setdefault (or get), which the human version does.

The second difference is in getting the most- and least-common words. To do this, the list of items needs to be sorted at least once. The problem with the Colaboratory solution is that it does *two* sorts: one in reverse order and one in normal order. Obviously, doing twice the work could be a problem with larger datasets. The Copilot version only does one sort, in reverse order, and then gets the first five elements as the most frequent and the last five as the least frequent:

```
# Sort the word counts in descending order
sorted_word_counts = sorted(word_counts.items(), key=lambda x: x[1],
                            reverse=True)
```

The human version also does only one sort, in normal order, and then, to get the most frequent, it uses the reversed function on a slice of the last five items, so that they are printed from most frequent to least frequent. reversed returns an iterator so in fact no new list is created, even with those five items. In fact, a reverse slice would also have worked just as efficiently.

Just as in the previous labs, in this lab both AI chatbots produced code that works but with variations that could be problematic in production environments with large datasets.

Summary

- Dictionaries are powerful data structures, used for many purposes, even within Python itself.
- Items in a dictionary are accessed by keys, not by their order in the dictionary.
- Dictionary keys must be immutable, but any immutable object can be a dictionary key.
- All dictionaries maintain items in the order in which they were added, but ordered dictionaries (found in the collections library) offer some extra features.
- By using the keys as part of the data, dictionaries can be used for tasks like counting elements, caching values, or creating sparse matrices.
- Using keys means accessing collections of data more efficiently and with less code than many other solutions.

Control flow

This chapter covers

- Making decisions: the `if-elif-else` statement
- Structural pattern matching
- Repeating code with a `while` loop
- Iterating over a list with a `for` loop
- Using list and dictionary comprehensions
- Delimiting statements and blocks with indentation
- Evaluating Boolean values and expressions

Python provides a complete set of control flow elements, with loops and conditionals. This chapter examines each element in detail.

8.1 The if-elif-else statement

One of the most important control flow features in most programming languages is the one for branching—that is, for making decisions on whether or not to execute or skip a piece of code based on some conditional. In Python, as in many languages, there are three parts to this: an `if` section, optionally one or more `elif` sections that are only checked if the `if` condition (and any previous `elif`s) is false, and a final optional `else` section that is only executed if neither the `if` or `elif` sections were executed.

The general form of the `if-elif-else` construct in Python is

```
if condition1:
    body1
elif condition2:
    body2
elif condition3:
    body3
.
.
.
elif condition(n-1):
    body(n-1)
else:
    body(n)
```

It says: if `condition1` is `True`, execute `body1`; otherwise, if `condition2` is `True`, execute `body2`; otherwise—and so on until it either finds a condition that evaluates to `True` or hits the `else` clause, in which case it executes `body(n)`. The `body` sections are again sequences of one or more Python statements that are separated by newlines and are at the same level of indentation.

For example, if you wanted to see if a guess in a guessing game was low, correct, or high, you might do this:

```
guess = 4
target = 7

if guess < target:
  print("Low")
elif guess == target:
  print("Correct!")              If the guess is not low and
else:                            not equal, it must be high.
  print("High")
```

Low

You don't need all that baggage for every conditional, of course. Both the `elif` and the `else` parts are optional. If a conditional can't find any body to execute (no conditions evaluate to `True`, and there's no `else` part), it does nothing.

The `body` after the `if` statement is required. But you can use the `pass` statement here (as you can anywhere in Python where a statement is required). The `pass` statement serves as a placeholder where a statement is needed, but it performs no action:

```
if x < 5:
    pass
else:
    x = 5
```

8.2 *Structural pattern matching with match*

Starting with Python 3.11, Python has the match-case statement, which can select between multiple conditions. It is similar but more powerful than the `case` and `switch` statements of other languages. The official name for what the match statement does is *structural pattern matching* and the "structural" part is important—unlike some other languages, the match-case statement can make matches not only on the basis of equal values but also in terms of matching *types*.

The structure of a match-case statement is

```
match expression:
    case test_expression:
        code block for match
    case _:
        code block if no match (optional)
```

Usually, the `expression` will be a variable or object, and the `test_expression` can either be a specific value or object or it can be a type function or a class constructor. It's also possible to match more than one option by using the "or" operator `|`. Optionally, you may include a case for `"_"`, which will be matched if nothing else is. If none of the cases is matched, no code is executed.

For example, the following code will check both for matches to the string `"A"` or the integer 0, one of the values 1, 2, or 3, or any other string or integer:

```
x = 5
match x:
    case "A":                          ◄——— Matches exactly "A"
        print("A")
    case str():                        ◄——— Matches any other string
        print("some other string")
    case 0:                            ◄——— Matches exactly 0
        print("Zero")
    case 1 | 2 | 3:                    ◄——— Matches any of 1, 2, or 3
        print(f"value {x} in range")
    case int():                        ◄——— Matches any other int
        print(f"The integer {x}")
    case _:                            ◄——— Executed if no match (optional)
        print("Neither string nor int")
```

Pattern matching is quite powerful, but it is also deceptively complex. Given all of the ways that expressions can be matched, it's quite possible to get code that behaves unexpectedly. Before using `match` in your code, it would be a good idea to carefully read the documentation (the Python tutorial online at https://docs.python.org is a good place to start) and to think carefully about possible edge cases and ways to test for them.

8.3 *The while loop*

You've come across the basic `while` loop several times already. The full `while` loop looks like the following:

```
while condition:
    body
else:
    post-code
```

condition is a Boolean expression—that is, one that evaluates to a True or False value. As long as it's True, the body is executed repeatedly. When the condition evaluates to False, the while loop executes the post-code section and then terminates. If the condition starts out by being False, the body won't be executed at all—just the post-code section. The body and post-code are each sequences of one or more Python statements that are separated by newlines and are at the same level of indentation. The Python interpreter uses this level to delimit them. No other delimiters, such as braces or brackets, are necessary.

Note that the else part of the while loop is optional and not often used. That's because as long as there's no break in the body, this loop

```
while condition:
    body
else:
    post-code
```

and this loop

```
while condition:
    body
post-code
```

do the same things—and the second is simpler to understand. On the other hand, if a break is used in the body of the loop, then the else block is *not* executed. This can be useful since it eliminates the need to set a flag before the break and check it after the loop completes.

For example, a while loop that repeats until the user enters a "Q" could be

```
response = ""
while response != "Q":
    response = input("Q to quit, B to break")
    if response == "B":
        break                                    The break will force the while loop
else:                                            to end and skip the else block.
    print("no break")
                         The else block will only be
                         executed if there is no break.
```

The two special statements break and continue can be used in the body of a while loop. If break is executed, it immediately terminates the while loop, and as just mentioned, not even the post-code (if there is an else clause) is executed. If continue is executed, it causes the remainder of the body to be skipped over; the condition is evaluated again, and the loop proceeds as normal.

8.4 *The for loop*

A for loop in Python is different from for loops in some other languages. The traditional pattern is to increment and test a variable on each iteration, which is what C for loops usually do. In Python, a for loop iterates over the values returned by any iterable object—that is, any object that can yield a sequence of values. For example, a for loop can iterate over every element in a list, a tuple, or a string. But an iterable object can also be a special function called range or a special type of function called a *generator or a generator expression*, which can be quite powerful. The general form is

```
for item in sequence:
    body
else:
    post-code
```

body is executed once for each element of sequence. item is set to be the first element of sequence, and body is executed; then item is set to be the second element of sequence, and body is executed; and so on for each remaining element of the sequence.

The else part is optional. Like the else part of a while loop, it's rarely used, but just as in a while loop, the post-code block following the else is not executed if a break occurs. The break and continue statements do the same thing in a for loop as they do in a while loop. If break is executed, it immediately terminates the for loop, and not even the post-code (if there is an else clause) is executed. If continue is executed in a for loop, it causes the code to skip the remainder of the body, and the loop proceeds from the top as normal with the next item.

This small loop prints out the reciprocal of each number in x, skipping zeroes and stopping if it hits a negative number:

```
x = [1.0, 2.0, 3.0, 0.0, -1.0]
for n in x:
    if n == 0.0:
        print("skipping 0.0")          The loop skips back to the top of
        continue             ◀          the loop with the next item n.
    elif n < 0.0:
        print("no negative numbers!")   The loop exits immediately;
        break                ◀          the else block is skipped.
    print(1 / n)                        Only executed if no
else:                                   break is executed
  print("Loop completed normally")  ◀
```

```
1.0
0.5
0.3333333333333333
skipping 0.0
no negative numbers!
```

8.4.1 *The range function*

Sometimes you need to loop with explicit indices (such as the positions at which values occur in a list). You can use the range command together with the len command on a list to generate a sequence of indices for use by the `for` loop. This code prints out all the positions in a list where it finds negative numbers:

```
x = [1, 3, -7, 4, 9, -5, 4]
for i in range(len(x)):
    if x[i] < 0:
        print("Found a negative number at index ", i)
```

Given a number *n*, `range(n)` returns a sequence 0, 1, 2, ..., *n* − 2, *n* − 1. So passing it the length of a list (found using `len`) produces a sequence of the indices for that list's elements. The `range` function doesn't build a Python list of integers; it just appears to. Instead, it creates a `range` object that produces integers on demand. This is useful when you're using explicit loops to iterate over really large lists. Instead of building a list with 10 million elements in it, for example, which would take up quite a bit of memory, you can use `range(10000000)`, which takes up only a small amount of memory and generates a sequence of integers from 0 up to (but *not* including) 10,000,000 as needed by the `for` loop.

8.5   *Controlling range with starting and stepping values*

You can use two variants on the `range` function to gain more control over the sequence it produces. If you use `range` with two numeric arguments, the first argument is the starting number for the resulting sequence, and the second number is the number the resulting sequence goes up to (but doesn't include). Here are a few examples:

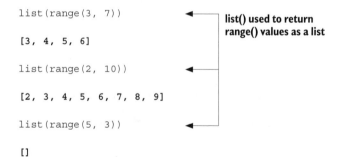

```
list(range(3, 7))
```

**list() used to return
range() values as a list**

```
[3, 4, 5, 6]

list(range(2, 10))

[2, 3, 4, 5, 6, 7, 8, 9]

list(range(5, 3))

[]
```

In the preceding code, `list()` is used only to force the items `range` to appear as a list and may not be used often in production code.

Using a starting point after the end point doesn't allow you to count backward, which is why the value of `list(range(5, 3))` is an empty list. To count backward, or to count by any amount other than 1, you need to use the optional third argument to `range`, which gives a step value by which counting proceeds:

```
list(range(0, 10, 2))

[0, 2, 4, 6, 8]
```

```
list(range(5, 0, -1))
```

```
[5, 4, 3, 2, 1]
```

Sequences returned by `range` always include the starting value given as an argument to `range` and never include the ending value given as an argument.

8.6 *The for loop and tuple unpacking*

You can use tuple unpacking to make some `for` loops cleaner. The following code takes a list of two-element tuples and calculates the value of the sum of the products of the two numbers in each tuple (a moderately common mathematical operation in some fields):

```
somelist = [(1, 2), (3, 7), (9, 5)]
result = 0
for t in somelist:
    result = result + (t[0] * t[1])
```

Here's the same thing but cleaner:

```
somelist = [(1, 2), (3, 7), (9, 5)]
result = 0

for x, y in somelist:
    result = result + (x * y)
```

This code uses a tuple `x, y` immediately after the `for` keyword instead of the usual single variable. On each iteration of the `for` loop, `x` contains element 0 of the current tuple from `list`, and `y` contains element 1 of the current tuple from `list`. Using a tuple in this manner is a convenience of Python, and doing this indicates to Python that each element of the list is expected to be a tuple of appropriate size to unpack into the variable names mentioned in the tuple after the `for`.

8.7 *The enumerate function*

You can combine tuple unpacking with the `enumerate` function to loop over both the items and their index. This is similar to using `range` but has the advantage that the code is clearer and easier to understand. Like the previous example, the following code prints out all the positions in a list where it finds negative numbers:

```
x = [1, 3, -7, 4, 9, -5, 4]
for i, n in enumerate(x):
    if n < 0:
        print("Found a negative number at index ", i)
```

enumerate() returns tuples of (index, item).

Accesses item without the index

The index is also available.

The `enumerate` function returns tuples of (`index`, `item`) for each item in the list. You can access either value without looking at the other.

8.8   *The zip function*

Sometimes it's useful to combine two or more iterables before looping over them. The `zip` function takes the corresponding elements from one or more iterables and combines them into tuples until it reaches the end of the shortest iterable:

```
x = [1, 2, 3, 4]
y = ['a', 'b', 'c']          ◄───────┐ y is three elements;
z = zip(x, y)                        │ x is four elements.
list(z)

[(1, 'a'), (2, 'b'), (3, 'c')]     ◄───────┘ z has only three elements.
```

Try this: Looping and if statements

Suppose that you have a list `x = [1, 3, 5, 0, -1, 3, -2]`, and you need to remove all negative numbers from that list. Write the code to do this.

How would you count the total number of negative numbers in the following list?

```
y = [[1, -1, 0], [2, 5, -9], [-2, -3, 0]]?
```

What code would you use to print `very low` if the value of `x` is below –5, `low` if it's from –5 up to 0, `neutral` if it's equal to 0, `high` if it's greater than 0 up to 5, and `very high` if it's greater than 5?

8.9   *List, set, and dictionary comprehensions*

The pattern of using a `for` loop to iterate through a list, modify or select individual elements, and create a new list or dictionary is very common. Such loops often look a lot like the following:

```
x = [1, 2, 3, 4]
x_squared = []
for item in x:
    x_squared.append(item * item)

x_squared

[1, 4, 9, 16]
```

This sort of situation is so common that Python has a special shortcut for such operations, called a *comprehension.* You can think of a list, set, or dictionary comprehension as a one-line `for` loop that creates a new list, set, or dictionary from a sequence. The pattern of a list comprehension is as follows:

```
new_list = [expression1 for variable in old_list if expression2]
```

Note that any sequence can be used in place of `old_list`, and what makes the value of the comprehension a list is the use of square brackets `[]` around the comprehension. A set comprehension would be similar but would use `{}` around the comprehension, and the value returned would be a set:

```
new_set = {expression1 for variable in old_list if expression2}
```

Finally, a dictionary comprehension looks like a set comprehension but needs both a key and value expression (e.g., `list` might contain two element tuples):

```
new_dict = {expression1:expression2 for variable in old_list if expression3}
```

In both cases, the heart of the expression is similar to the beginning of a `for` loop—`for variable in list`—with some expression using that variable to create a new key or value and an optional conditional expression using the value of the variable to select whether it's included in the new list or dictionary. The following code does exactly the same thing as the previous code but is a list comprehension:

```
x = [1, 2, 3, 4]
x_squared = [item * item for item in x]
x_squared
```

```
[1, 4, 9, 16]
```

You can even use `if` statements to select items from the list:

```
x = [1, 2, 3, 4]
x_squared = [item * item for item in x if item > 2]
x_squared
```

```
[9, 16]
```

Dictionary comprehensions are similar, but you need to supply both a key and a value. If you want to do something similar to the previous example but have the number be the key and the number's square be the value in a dictionary, you can use a dictionary comprehension, like so:

```
x = [1, 2, 3, 4]
x_squared_dict = {item: item * item for item in x}
x_squared_dict
```

```
{1: 1, 2: 4, 3: 9, 4: 16}
```

List, set, and dictionary comprehensions are very flexible and powerful, and when you get used to them, they make list-processing operations much simpler. I recommend that you experiment with them and try them anytime you find yourself writing a `for` loop to process a list of items.

8.9.1   *Generator expressions*

Generator expressions don't use square brackets or curly braces (as list or dictionary comprehnesions do); they use parentheses instead. The following example is the generator-expression version of the list comprehension already discussed:

```
x = [1, 2, 3, 4]
x_squared = (item * item for item in x)
x_squared

<generator object <genexpr> at 0x102176708>

for square in x_squared:
    print(square,)

1 4 9 16
```

As well as the change from square brackets, notice that this expression doesn't return a list. Instead, it returns a generator object that could be used as the iterator in a `for` loop, as shown, which is very similar to what the `range()` function does. The advantage of using a generator expression is that the entire list isn't generated in memory, so arbitrarily large sequences can be generated with little memory overhead.

> **Try this: Comprehensions**
>
> What list comprehension would you use to process the list x so that all negative values are removed?
>
> Create a generator that returns only odd numbers from 1 to 100. (Hint: A number is odd if there is a remainder if divided by 2; use % 2 to get the remainder of division by 2.)
>
> Write the code to create a dictionary of the numbers and their cubes from 11 through 15.

8.10   *Statements, blocks, and indentation*

Because the control flow constructs you've encountered in this chapter are the first to make use of blocks and indentation, this is a good time to revisit the subject.

Python uses the indentation of the statements to determine the delimitation of the different blocks (or bodies) of the control flow constructs. A block consists of one or more statements, which are usually separated by newlines. Examples of Python statements are the assignment statement, function calls, the `print` function, the placeholder `pass` statement, and the `del` statement. The control flow constructs (if-elif-else, while, and for loops) are compound statements:

```
compound statement clause:
    block
compound statement clause:
    block
```

A compound statement contains one or more clauses that are each followed by indented blocks. Compound statements can appear in blocks just like any other statements. When they do, they create nested blocks.

You may also encounter a couple of special cases. While it's usually not good Python style, multiple statements may be placed on the same line if they're separated by semicolons. A block containing a single line may be placed on the same line after the colon of a clause of a compound statement:

```
x = 1; y = 0; z = 0
if x > 0: y = 1; z = 10
else: y = -1

print(x, y, z)
```

```
1 1 10
```

Improperly indented code results in an exception being raised. You may encounter two forms of this exception. The first is

```
x = 1
 x = 2
```

```
  File "<ipython-input-21-c75cba843d9b>", line 2
    x = 2
    ^
IndentationError: unexpected indent
```

This code indented a line that shouldn't have been indented. In the basic mode, the carat (^) indicates the spot where the problem occurred.

One situation where this can occur can be confusing. If you're using an editor that displays tabs in four-space increments (or Windows interactive mode, which indents the first tab only four spaces from the prompt) and indent one line with four spaces and then the next line with a tab, the two lines may appear to be at the same level of indentation. But you receive this exception because Python maps the tab to eight spaces. The best way to avoid this problem is to use only spaces in Python code. If you must use tabs for indentation, or if you're dealing with code that uses tabs, be sure never to mix them with spaces.

If you are using the basic interactive shell mode or the IDLE Python shell, you've likely noticed that you need an extra line after the outermost level of indentation:

```
>>> x = 1
... if x == 1:
...     y = 2
```

```
...      if y > 0:
...          z = 2
...          v = 0
...
>>> x = 2
```

No line is necessary after the line z = 2, but in a basic shell one is needed after the line
v = 0. This line is unnecessary if you're using Jupyter notebooks or placing your code
in a module in a file.

The second form of exception occurs if you indent a statement in a block less than
the legal amount:

```
x = 1
if x == 1:
    y = 2
  z = 2
  File "<tokenize>", line 4
    z = 2
    ^
IndentationError: unindent does not match any outer indentation level
```

In this example, the line containing z = 2 isn't lined up properly below the line containing y = 2. This form is rare, but I mention it again because in a similar situation, it
may be confusing.

Python allows you to indent any amount and won't complain regardless of how much
you vary indentation as long as you're consistent within a single block. Please don't take
improper advantage of this flexibility. The recommended standard is to use four spaces
for each level of indentation.

Before leaving indentation, I'll cover breaking up statements across multiple lines,
which of course is necessary more often as the level of indentation increases. You can
explicitly break up a line by using the backslash character. You can also implicitly break
any statement between tokens when within a set of (), {}, or [] delimiters (that is, when
typing a set of values in a list, a tuple, or a dictionary; a set of arguments in a function
call; or any expression within a set of brackets). You can indent the continuation line of
a statement to any level you desire:

```
print('string1', 'string2', 'string3' \
    , 'string4', 'string5')
```

string1 string2 string3 string4 string5

```
x = 100 + 200 + 300 \
    + 400 + 500
x
```

1500

```
v = [100, 300, 500, 700, 900,
    1100, 1300]
```

```
v

[100, 300, 500, 700, 900, 1100, 1300]

max(1000, 300, 500,
       800, 1200)

1200

x = (100 + 200 + 300
         + 400 + 500)
x

1500
```

You can break a string with a \ as well. But any indentation tabs or spaces become part of the string, and the line *must* end with the \. To avoid this situation, be sure to use quotes around the segments you are breaking up. Remember that any string literals separated by whitespace are automatically concatenated by the Python interpreter:

```
"strings separated by whitespace "    \
   '''are automatically'''  ' concatenated'
```

'strings separated by whitespace are automatically concatenated'

```
x = 1
if x > 0:
       string1 = "this string broken by a backslash will end up \
               with the indentation tabs in it"

string1
```

'this string broken by a backslash will end up   with the
indentation tabs in it'

```
if x > 0:
       string1 = "this can be easily avoided by splitting the " \
              "string in this way"

string1
```

'this can be easily avoided by splitting the string in this way'

8.11 Boolean values and expressions

The previous examples of control flow use conditional tests in a fairly obvious manner but never really explain what constitutes true or false in Python or what expressions can be used where a conditional test is needed. This section describes these aspects of Python.

Python has a Boolean object type that can be set to either True or False. Any expression with a Boolean operation returns True or False.

8.11.1 *Most Python objects can be used as Booleans*

In addition, Python is similar to C with respect to Boolean values, in that C uses the integer 0 to mean false and any other integer to mean true. Python generalizes this idea: 0 or empty values are `False`, and any other values are `True`. In practical terms, this means the following:

- The numbers 0, 0.0, and 0+0j are all `False`; any other number is `True`.
- The empty string "" is `False`; any other string is `True`.
- The empty list [] is `False`; any other list is `True`.
- The empty dictionary { } is `False`; any other dictionary is `True`.
- The empty set set () is `False`; any other set is `True`.
- The special Python value None is always `False`.

We haven't looked at some Python data structures yet, but generally, the same rule applies. If the data structure is empty or 0, it's taken to mean false in a Boolean context; otherwise, it's taken to mean true. Some objects, such as file objects and code objects, don't have a sensible definition of a 0 or empty element, and these objects shouldn't be used in a Boolean context.

8.11.2 *Comparison and Boolean operators*

You can compare objects by using normal operators: <, <=, >, >=, and so forth. == is the equality test operator, and != is the "not equal to" test. There are also in and not in operators to test membership in sequences (lists, tuples, strings, and dictionaries), as well as is and is not operators to test whether two objects are the same.

Expressions that return a Boolean value may be combined into more complex expressions using the and, or, and not operators. The following code snippet checks to see whether a variable is within a certain range:

```
if 0 < x and x < 10:
   . . .
```

Python offers a nice shorthand for this particular type of compound statement. You can write it as you would in a math paper:

```
if 0 < x < 10:
   . . .
```

Various rules of precedence apply; when in doubt, use parentheses to make sure that Python interprets an expression the way you want it to. Using parentheses is probably a good idea for complex expressions, regardless of whether it's necessary, because it makes clear to future maintainers of the code exactly what's happening. See the Python documentation for more details on precedence.

The rest of this section provides more advanced information. If you're reading this book as you're learning the language, you may want to skip that material for now.

The and and or operators return objects. The and operator returns either the first false object (that an expression evaluates to) or the last object. Similarly, the or operator returns either the first true object or the last object. This may seem a little confusing, but it works correctly; if an expression with and has even one false element, that element makes the entire expression evaluate as False, and that False value is returned. If all of the elements are True, the expression is True, and the last value, which must also be True, is returned. The converse is true for or; only one True element makes the statement logically True, and the first True value found is returned. If no True values are found, the last (False) value is returned. In other words, as with many other languages, evaluation stops as soon as a true expression is found for the or operator or as soon as a false expression is found for the and operator:

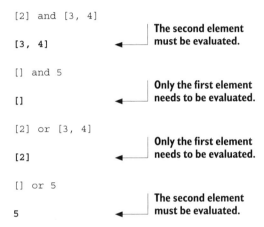

```
[2] and [3, 4]

[3, 4]
```
The second element must be evaluated.

```
[] and 5

[]
```
Only the first element needs to be evaluated.

```
[2] or [3, 4]

[2]
```
Only the first element needs to be evaluated.

```
[] or 5

5
```
The second element must be evaluated.

The == and != operators test to see whether their operands contain the same values. == and != are used in most situations, as opposed to is and is not operators, which test to see whether their operands are the same object:

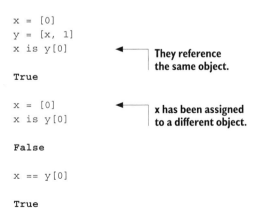

```
x = [0]
y = [x, 1]
x is y[0]

True
```
They reference the same object.

```
x = [0]
x is y[0]

False
```
x has been assigned to a different object.

```
x == y[0]

True
```

Revisit section 5.6 if this example isn't clear.

Quick check: Booleans and truthiness

Decide whether the following statements are true or false: `1`, `0`, `-1`, `[0]`, `1 and 0`, `1 > 0 or []`.

8.12 *Writing a simple program to analyze a text file*

To give you a better sense of how a Python program works, this section looks at a small example that roughly replicates the UNIX wc utility and reports the number of lines, words, and characters in a file. The sample in this listing is deliberately written to be clear to programmers who are new to Python and to be as simple as possible.

Listing 8.1   word_count.py

```
#!/usr/bin/env python3

""" Reads a file and returns the number of lines, words,
    and characters - similar to the UNIX wc utility
"""

infile = open('word_count.tst')           ◄──── Opens file

lines = infile.read().split("\n")          ◄──── Reads file; splits into lines

line_count = len(lines)                    ◄──── Gets number of lines with len()

word_count = 0
char_count = 0         │ Initializes other counts

for line in lines:                         ◄──── Iterates through lines

    words = line.split()                   ◄──── Splits into words
    word_count += len(words)

    char_count += len(line)                ◄──── Returns number of characters

print("File has {0} lines, {1} words, {2} characters".format(
        line_count, word_count, char_count))        ◄──── Prints answers
```

To test, you can run this sample against a sample file containing the first paragraph of this chapter's summary, as shown in the following listing.

Listing 8.2   word_count.tst

```
Python provides a complete set of control flow elements,
including while and for loops, and conditionals.
Python uses the level of indentation to group blocks
of code with control elements.
```

If you are running the preceding code in a notebook, be sure to also execute the cell that creates the file word_count.tst. If you have saved the code in a file named word_count.py, you could also run the code from a command line:

```
naomi@mac:~/quickpythonbook/code $ python3 word_count.py
```

Either way, as long as the file word_count.tst was in the same directory, you would get the following output:

```
File has 4 lines, 30 words, 186 characters
```

This code can give you an idea of a Python program. There isn't much code, and most of the work gets done in three lines of code in the `for` loop. In fact, this program could be made even shorter and more idiomatic, as we'll see in this chapter's lab. Most Pythonistas see this conciseness as one of Python's great strengths.

8.13 Refactoring word_count

Rewrite the word-count program from section 8.1.2 to make it shorter. You may want to look at the string and list operations already discussed, as well as think about different ways to organize the code. You may also want to make the program smarter so that only alphabetic strings (not symbols or punctuation) count as words.

8.13.1 Solving the problem with AI-generated code

In this lab we're *refactoring* some existing code—that is, rewriting it to improve it. The goal is to make the code shorter and optionally to count only words that don't contain symbols or numbers.

To refactor the code, we need to give the AI chatbot the existing code and some guidance as to how we want it refactored:

1 Indicate what code we want refactored.

2 Give our goal in refactoring: shorter code.

3 (Optional) Ask for a change so that only alphabetic strings are counted.

8.13.2 Solutions and discussion

Since both my solution and the AI solutions start from the same program, they will tend to be quite similar. Again, however, the AI versions are less cautious with resources, choosing to read the entire file into memory.

THE HUMAN SOLUTION

The human solution is a bit longer, since again I chose to read the file line by line:

```
""" Reads a file and returns the number of lines, words,
    and characters - similar to the UNIX wc utility
"""
```

```
# initialize counts
line_count = 0
word_count = 0                    Initializes counts to zero
char_count = 0

# open the file
with  open('word_count.tst') as infile:
    for line in infile:                    ◄───┐ Processes file line by line
        line_count += 1
        char_count += len(line)
        word_count += len(line.split())

# print the answers using the format() method
print("File has {0} lines, {1} words, {2} characters".format(line_count,
                                    word_count, char_count))
```

That means that the count variables all need to be initialized to zero. The other consequence of going line by line is that all of the counts need to be incremented with the values for each line. This approach would be able to handle files of almost any size, but, as we'll see, it does result in code that's a tiny bit longer than AI versions. Put it down to the instincts of an old data wrangler, but in most cases this caution would probably be unnecessary.

THE AI VERSION

In Colaboratory, we can just refactor the code of the preceding word counter program, so the prompt is

```
Refactor the word-count program above to make it shorter. You may want to
look at the string and list, as well as think about different ways to
organize the code.
```

For Copilot, we give it the existing code in the chat window and add the instructions, including the optional task of counting only all-letter words:

```
Refactor this code to make it shorter. You may want to look at the string
and list, as well as think about different ways to organize the code. You
may also want to make the program smarter so that only alphabetic strings
(not symbols or punctuation) count as words.
```

The two versions are similar, so let's start from the Copilot version:

```
""" Reads a file and returns the number of lines, words,
    and characters - similar to the UNIX wc utility
"""
                                              The readlines method returns
with open('word_count.tst') as infile:        a list of lines (with newlines).
    lines = infile.readlines()          ◄───┘

                                              Generator expression
line_count = len(lines)                        to get number of
word_count = sum(len(line.split()) for line in lines)  ◄──┘  words in each line
```

```
char_count = sum(len(line) for line in lines)

print(f"{line_count} lines, {word_count} words, {char_count} characters")
```

**Generator expression to
get length of each line**

This version reads all of the file in at once but uses the `readlines()` method, which returns a list of lines. This means that it doesn't need to break up the lines, but it might be a problem with a very large file. Once the lines have been read, the number of lines is the line count, and the word and character counts are determined using the `sum` function over generator expressions iterating over the list of lines.

If we want to count only strictly alphabetic strings as words, the `word_count` line is a little more complex: Copilot suggests a list comprehension inside the generator expression to filter on the `isalpha` string method:

```
word_count = sum(len([word for word in line.split() if word.isalpha()])
                    for line in lines)
```

Either way, the code Copilot suggests is concise and works fine, as long as the data size is not too much for memory.

The Colaboratory code has an important difference in the body of the code:

```
with open('word_count.tst') as infile:
    lines = infile.read().split("\n")
```
Splits entire file on newline

This version reads the entire file into memory and then splits it into lines by using the split method on the newline character (`"\n"`). This means that it has to perform a split operation on the entire file, which neither the human nor the Copilot version has to do. In fact, this is what the original program does as well, and both programs share a subtle bug. When you split a string, you get a list of substrings broken by the specified string (or whitespace if no string is specified). What is *not* included is the separator string (`"\n"`). Since there are four lines in our sample, separated by three newlines, both the original version and the Colaboratory refactor give character counts that are 3 less than they should be:186 instead of the correct 189 returned by both the human and Copilot refactors.

In the end, the AI versions performed quite well on this refactoring problem. While neither version was quite as cautious about saving memory as I was, the Copilot version managed to improve performance over the original by removing a `split` function, and it also fixed the bug in the original's character count.

Summary

- Python uses indentation to group blocks of code.
- Python has loops using `while` and `for`, conditionals using `if-elif-else`, and a `match` statement that selects from multiple options.

- Some common `for` loop patterns can be replaced by list, dictionary, or set comprehensions.
- Generator expressions are similar to comprehensions but usually use less memory.
- Python has the Boolean values `True` and `False`, which can be referenced by variables.
- Most Python objects can also be evaluated as Booleans, with zero or empty values being `False` and all other values being `True`.

Functions

9

This chapter covers

- Defining functions
- Using function parameters
- Passing mutable objects as parameters
- Understanding local and global variables
- Creating and using generator functions
- Creating and using lambda expressions
- Using decorators

This chapter assumes that you're familiar with function definitions in at least one other computer language and with the concepts that correspond to function definitions, arguments, parameters, and so forth.

9.1 Basic function definitions

The basic syntax for a Python function definition is

```
def name(parameter1, parameter2, . . .):
    body
```

As it does with control structures, Python uses indentation to delimit the body of the function definition. The following simple example puts the code to calculate a factorial into a function body, so you can call a `fact` function to obtain the factorial of a number:

```
def fact(n):
    '''Return the factorial of the given number.'''    ◄───────  Optional documentation
    r = 1                                                         string, or docstring
    while n > 0:
        r = r * n
        n = n - 1                    ┌─ Value sent back to the
    return r              ◄──────────┘  code calling the function
```

If the function has a `return` statement, like the preceding one, that value will be returned to the code calling the function and can be assigned to a variable. If no `return` is used, the function will return a `None` value.

You can obtain the value of the docstring (the second line of the preceding function) by printing `fact.__doc__`. The intention of docstrings is to describe the external behavior of a function and the parameters it takes, whereas comments should document internal information about how the code works. Docstrings are strings that immediately follow the first line of a function definition and are usually triple-quoted to allow for multiline descriptions. Browsing tools are available that extract the first line of document strings. It's standard practice for multiline documentation strings to give a synopsis of the function in the first line, follow this synopsis with a blank second line, and end with the rest of the information.

Procedure or function?

In some languages, a function that doesn't return a value is called a *procedure*. Although you can (and will) write functions that don't have a `return` statement, they aren't really procedures. All Python procedures are functions; if no explicit `return` is executed in the procedure body, the special Python value `None` is returned, and if `return result` is executed, the value `result` is immediately returned. Nothing else in the function body is executed after a `return` has been executed. Because Python doesn't have true procedures, I'll refer to both types as *functions*.

Although all Python functions return values, it's up to you whether a function's return value is used:

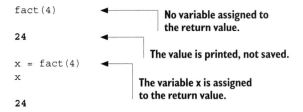

```
fact(4)          ◄────────┐   No variable assigned to
                          │   the return value.
24               ◄────────┤
                          │   The value is printed, not saved.
x = fact(4)      ◄────────┤
x                         │   The variable x is assigned
                          │   to the return value.
24
```

Even if a function returns a value, it's not required to capture and use that value. If no variable is assigned to the return value of a function, it will be discarded, although if the function call is the last statement in a cell, its value will be displayed. If a variable is assigned, that variable and its value can be used like any other variable.

9.2 *Function parameter options*

Most functions need parameters, and each language has its own specifications for how function parameters are defined. Python is flexible and provides three options for defining function parameters. These options are outlined in this section.

9.2.1 *Positional parameters*

The simplest way to pass parameters to a function in Python is by position. In the first line of the function, you specify variable names for each parameter; when the function is called, the parameters used in the calling code are matched to the function's parameter variables based on their order. The following function computes x to the power of y:

```
def power(x, y):
    r = 1
    while y > 0:
        r = r * x
        y = y - 1
    return r

power(3, 3)
```

```
27
```

This method requires that the number of parameters used by the calling code exactly matches the number of parameters in the function definition; otherwise, a `Type-Error` exception is raised:

```
power(3)
```

```
---------------------------------------------------------------------------
TypeError                                 Traceback (most recent call last)
<ipython-input-5-1bbb88d7a603> in <cell line: 1>()
----> 1 power(3)

TypeError: power() missing 1 required positional argument: 'y'
```

Default values

Function parameters can have default values, which you declare by assigning a default value in the first line of the function definition, like so:

```
def fun(arg1, arg2=default2, arg3=default3, . . .)
```

> **(continued)**
>
> Any number of parameters can be given default values. Parameters with default values must be defined as the last ones in the parameter list because Python, like most languages, pairs arguments with parameters on a positional basis. There must be enough arguments to a function that the last parameter in that function's parameter list without a default value gets an argument. See section 9.2.2 for a more flexible mechanism.

The following function also computes x to the power of y. But if y isn't given in a call to the function, the default value of 2 is used, and the function is just the square function:

```
def power(x, y=2):
    r = 1
    while y > 0:
        r = r * x
        y = y - 1
    return r
```

You can see the effect of the default argument in the following interactive session:

```
power(3, 3)
```

27

```
power(3)
```

9

9.2.2 *Passing arguments by parameter name*

You can also pass arguments into a function by using the name of the corresponding function parameter rather than its position. Continuing with the previous interactive example, you can type

```
power(y=2, x=3)
```

9

Because the arguments to power in the final invocation are named, their order is irrelevant; the arguments are associated with the parameters of the same name in the definition of power, and you get back 3^2. This type of argument passing is called *keyword passing*.

Keyword passing, in combination with the default argument capability of Python functions, can be highly useful when you're defining functions with large numbers of possible arguments, most of which have common defaults. Consider a function that's intended to produce a list with information about files in the current directory and that uses Boolean arguments to indicate whether that list should include information such as file size, last modified date, and so forth for each file. You can define such a function along these lines:

```
def list_file_info(size=False, create_date=False, mod_date=False, ...):
    ...get file names...
    if size:
        # code to get file sizes goes here
    if create_date:
        # code to get create dates goes here
    # do any other stuff desired

    return fileinfostructure
```

and then call it from other code using keyword argument passing to indicate that you want only certain information (in this example, the file size and modification date but *not* the creation date):

```
fileinfo = list_file_info(size=True, mod_date=True)
```

This type of argument handling is particularly suited for functions with very complex behavior, and one place where such functions occur is in a GUI. If you ever use the `tkinter` package to build GUIs in Python, you'll find that the use of optional, keyword-named arguments like this is invaluable.

9.2.3 *Variable numbers of arguments*

Python functions can also be defined to handle variable numbers of arguments, which you can do in two ways. One way handles the relatively familiar case in which you want to collect an unknown number of arguments at the end of the argument list into a list, which is commonly called `*args` in the argument list. The other method can collect an arbitrary number of keyword-passed arguments, which have no correspondingly named parameter in the function parameter list, into a dictionary, usually named `**kwargs` in the parameter list. These two mechanisms are discussed next.

DEALING WITH AN INDEFINITE NUMBER OF POSITIONAL ARGUMENTS

Prefixing the final parameter name of the function with a `*` causes all excess non-keyword arguments in a call of a function (that is, those positional arguments not assigned to another parameter) to be collected together and assigned as a tuple to the given parameter. The following is a simple way to implement a function to find the maximum in a list of numbers.

First, implement the function:

```
def maximum(*numbers):
    if len(numbers) == 0:          ◄─────  * means capture any
        return None                        number of parameters.
    else:
        maxnum = numbers[0]        ◄─────┘ numbers is a list of all parameters.
```

```
    for n in numbers[1:]:
        if n > maxnum:
            maxnum = n
    return maxnum
```

Putting the * in front of `numbers` makes it capture all positional parameters as a list. Now test the behavior of the function:

```
maximum(3, 2, 8)
```

8

```
maximum(1, 5, 9, -2, 2)
```

9

DEALING WITH AN INDEFINITE NUMBER OF ARGUMENTS PASSED BY KEYWORD

An arbitrary number of keyword arguments can also be handled. If the final parameter in the parameter list is prefixed with `**`, it collects all excess keyword-passed arguments into a dictionary. The key for each entry in the dictionary is the keyword (parameter name) for the excess argument. The value of that entry is the value of the argument. An argument passed by keyword is excess in this context if the keyword by which it was passed doesn't match one of the parameter names in the function definition—for example:

`**` indicates capture all named parameters.

```
def example_fun(x, y, **other):
    print(f"x: {x}, y: {y}, keys in 'other': {list(other.keys())}".
    other_total = 0
    for k in other.keys():
        other_total = other_total + other[k]
    print(f"The total of values in 'other' is {other_total}"
```

Named parameters collected in dictionary other

Using `**` will result in all unmatched keyword parameters being collected into a dictionary, with the keys being the names and values being the parameter values.

Trying out this function in an interactive session reveals that it can handle arguments passed in under the keywords `foo` and `bar`, even though `foo` and `bar` aren't parameter names in the function definition:

```
example_fun(2, y="1", foo=3, bar=4)
```

x: 2, y: 1, keys in 'other': ['foo', 'bar']
The total of values in 'other' is 7

9.2.4   *Mixing argument-passing techniques*

It's possible to use all of the argument-passing features of Python functions at the same time, although it can be confusing if not done with care. The general rule for using mixed-argument passing is that positional arguments come first, then named arguments, followed by the indefinite positional argument with a single *, and last of all the indefinite keyword argument with **. See the documentation for full details.

> **Quick check: Functions and parameters**
>
> How would you write a function that could take any number of unnamed arguments and print their values out in reverse order?
>
> What do you need to do to create a procedure or void function—that is, a function with no return value?
>
> What happens if you capture the return value of a function with a variable?

9.3 *Mutable objects as arguments*

Arguments are passed in by object reference. The parameter becomes a new reference to the object. For immutable objects (such as tuples, strings, and numbers), what is done with a parameter has no effect outside the function. But if you pass in a mutable object (such as a list, dictionary, or class instance), any change made to the object changes what the argument is referencing outside the function. Reassigning the parameter doesn't affect the argument, as shown in figures 9.1 and 9.2:

```
def f(n, list1, list2):
    list1.append(3)          ◄──────┘ One item added to list1
    list2 = [4, 5, 6]        ◄──
    n = n + 1
                                     list2 is replaced locally
x = 5                                with a new list.
y = [1, 2]
z = [4, 5]
f(x, y, z)
x, y, z
```

```
(5, [1, 2, 3], [4, 5])
```

Figure 9.1 shows the state of the variables before the code is executed. Note that both n and x are referring to the constant 5, both y and list1 refer to the list [1, 2], and both z and list2 refer to the list [4,5]. When we execute the function, we get the result illustrated in figure 9.2.

Figures 9.2 illustrates what happens when function f is called. The variable x isn't changed because it's immutable. Instead, the function parameter n is set to refer to the new value of 6. Likewise, variable z is unchanged because inside function f, its corresponding parameter list2 was set to refer to a new object, [4, 5, 6]. Only y sees a change because the actual list it points to was changed.

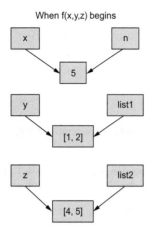

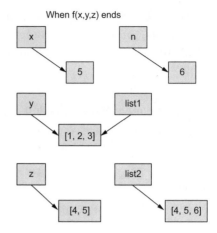

Figure 9.1   At the beginning of function f(), both the initial variables and the function parameters refer to the same objects.

Figure 9.2   At the end of function f(), y (list1 inside the function) has been changed internally, whereas n and list2 refer to different objects.

9.3.1   *Mutable objects as default values*

Passing mutable objects as parameter values can cause bugs but is quite often the most convenient and efficient way to do things. It does mean that you need to be aware that changing that object might have a side effect outside the function.

It's much worse to use a mutable object as a default parameter value and then mutate that object. For example, suppose I'm going to check a list for odd numbers and add them to a list of odd numbers I pass in as a parameter:

```
def odd_numbers(test_list, odds):
  for number in test_list:
    if number % 2:
      odds.append(number)
  return odds

odds = []
odds = odd_numbers([1, 5, 7, 9, 10], odds)
odds

[1, 5, 7, 9]
```

This works, but say you decide you don't want to have to bother with creating an empty list for the odd numbers, so you make an empty list to be the default value of the odds parameter. Now you don't need to explicitly create or pass that list, right?

```
def odd_numbers(test_list, odds=[]):
  for number in test_list:
    if number % 2:
```
◄———┐ **Empty list as default**
     parameter value

```
        odds.append(number)
    return odds

odds = odd_numbers([1, 5, 7, 9, 10])
odds
```

```
[1, 5, 7, 9]
```

It looks like this works just fine, but if you run the same function a second time, the result changes:

```
odds = odd_numbers([1, 5, 7, 9, 10])
odds
```

```
[1, 5, 7, 9, 1, 5, 7, 9]
```

When a default parameter value is used, Python assigns the object to be used as the default when the function is first compiled, and it does not change for the life of the program. So, if you have a mutable object as the default and mutate, as we did by appending items to our list of odd numbers, every time that default value is used it will be the same object, and that object will reflect all of the times the function has been called with it.

> ### Quick check: Mutable function parameters
> What would be the result of changing a list or dictionary that was passed into a function as a parameter value? Which operations would be likely to create changes that would be visible outside the function? What steps might you take to minimize that risk?

9.4 Local, nonlocal, and global variables

Let's return to the definition of `fact` from the beginning of this chapter:

```
def fact(n):
    """Return the factorial of the given number."""
    r = 1
    while n > 0:
        r = r * n
        n = n - 1
    return r
```

Both the variables `r` and `n` are *local* to any particular call of the factorial function; changes to them made when the function is executing have no effect on any variables outside the function. Any variables in the parameter list of a function, and any variables created within a function by an assignment (like `r = 1` in `fact`) are local to the function.

You can explicitly make a variable global by declaring it so before the variable is used, using the `global` statement. Global variables can be accessed and changed by the function. They exist outside the function and can also be accessed and changed by other functions that declare them global or by code that's not within a function. The following is an example that shows the difference between local and global variables:

```
def fun():
    global a
    a = 1
    b = 2
```

This example defines a function that treats a as a global variable and b as a local variable and attempts to modify both a and b.

Now test this function:

```
a = "one"
b = "two"

fun()
a

1

b

'two'
```

The assignment to a within `fun` is an assignment to the global variable a also existing outside `fun`. Because a is designated `global` in `fun`, the assignment modifies that global variable to hold the value 1 instead of the value `"one"`. The same isn't true for b; the local variable called b inside `fun` starts out referring to the same value as the variable b outside `fun`, but the assignment causes b to point to a new value that's local to the function `fun`.

Similar to the `global` statement is the `nonlocal` statement, which causes an identifier to refer to a previously bound variable in the closest enclosing scope. I discuss scopes and namespaces in more detail in chapter 10, but the point is that `global` is used for a top-level variable, whereas `nonlocal` can refer to any variable in an enclosing scope, as the example in the following listing illustrates.

Listing 9.1   File nonlocal.py

g_var in global scope

```
g_var = 0
nl_var = 0
print("top level-> g_var: {0} nl_var: {1}".format(g_var, nl_var))
def test():
    nl_var = 2
    print("in test-> g_var: {0} nl_var: {1}".format(g_var, nl_var))
```

nl_var in global scope

nl_var in test (not global)

```
def inner_test():

    global g_var
    nonlocal nl_var
    g_var = 1
    nl_var = 4
    print("in inner_test-> g_var: {0} nl_var: {1}".format(g_var,
                                                           nl_var))


inner_test()
print("in test-> g_var: {0} nl_var: {1}".format(g_var, nl_var))

test()
print("top level-> g_var: {0} nl_var: {1}".format(g_var, nl_var))
```

> The use of **global** makes g_var in inner_test bind to top-level g_var.
>
> The use of **nonlocal** makes nl_var bind to nl_var in test.

The preceding code shows how using the global and nonlocal keywords can make variables in one scope refer either to a variable at the top level of the module or to the closest variable of the same name in an enclosing scope.

When run, this code prints the following:

```
top level-> g_var: 0 nl_var: 0
in test-> g_var: 0 nl_var: 2
in inner_test-> g_var: 1 nl_var: 4
in test-> g_var: 1 nl_var: 4
top level-> g_var: 1 nl_var: 0
```

Note that the value of the top-level `nl_var` hasn't been affected, which would happen if `inner_test` contained the line `global nl_var`.

The bottom line is that if you want to *assign* to a variable existing outside a function, you must explicitly declare that variable to be nonlocal or global. But if you're just *reading* a variable that exists outside the function, you don't need to declare it nonlocal or global. If Python can't find a variable name in the local function scope, it attempts to look up the name in the enclosing scopes and the global scope. Hence, accesses to global variables are automatically sent through to the correct global variable. Personally, I don't recommend using this shortcut. It's much clearer to a reader if all global variables are explicitly declared as global. Further, you probably want to limit the use of global variables within functions to rare occasions.

Try this: Global vs. local variables

Assuming that x = 5, what will be the value of x after `funct_1()` below executes? After `funct_2()` executes?

```
def funct_1():
    x = 3
def funct_2():
    global x
    x = 2
```

9.5   *Assigning functions to variables*

Functions can be assigned, like other Python objects, to variables, as shown in the following example:

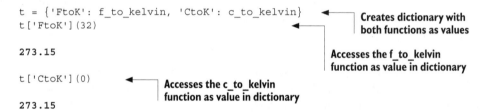

```
def f_to_kelvin(degrees_f):
    return 273.15 + (degrees_f - 32) * 5 / 9
```
      Defines the f_to_kelvin kelvin function

```
def c_to_kelvin(degrees_c):
    return 273.15 + degrees_c
```
      Defines the c_to_kelvin function

```
abs_temperature = f_to_kelvin
abs_temperature(32)
```
      Assigns function to variable

```
273.15
```

```
abs_temperature = c_to_kelvin
abs_temperature(0)
```

```
273.15
```

In the preceding code, we define two different functions: one for converting Fahrenheit temperatures to Kelvin and the other for converting Celsius. We can then assign either one of the functions to the variable `abs_temperature` and use that as function, which will call whichever function it is currently assigned to.

    You can place functions in lists, tuples, or dictionaries:

```
t = {'FtoK': f_to_kelvin, 'CtoK': c_to_kelvin}
t['FtoK'](32)
```
      Creates dictionary with both functions as values

      Accesses the f_to_kelvin function as value in dictionary

```
273.15
```

```
t['CtoK'](0)
```
      Accesses the c_to_kelvin function as value in dictionary

```
273.15
```

A variable that refers to a function can be used in exactly the same way as the function itself. This last example shows how you can use a dictionary to call different functions by the value of the strings used as keys. This pattern is common in situations in which different functions need to be selected based on a string value, and in many cases, it takes the place of the `switch` structure found in languages such as C and Java.

9.6   *lambda expressions*

Short functions like those you just saw can also be defined by using `lambda` expressions of the form

```
lambda parameter1, parameter2, . . .: expression
```

`lambda` expressions are anonymous little functions that you can quickly define inline. Often, a small function needs to be passed to another function, like the key function used by a list's `sort` method. In such cases, a large function is usually unnecessary, and it would be awkward to have to define the function in a separate place from where it's used. The dictionary in the previous subsection can be defined all in one place with

```
t2 = {'FtoK': lambda deg_f: 273.15 + (deg_f - 32) * 5 / 9,
      'CtoK': lambda deg_c: 273.15 + deg_c}
t2['FtoK'](32)
```
⟵ **lambda functions as dictionary values**

```
273.15
```

This example defines `lambda` expressions as values of the dictionary, rather than using the formally defined functions.

Note that `lambda` expressions don't have a `return` statement because the value of the expression is automatically returned.

9.7 Generator functions

A *generator* function is a special kind of function that you can use to define your own iterators. When you define a generator function, you return each iteration's value using the `yield` keyword. When the generator function is called, it returns a *generator object*, which can be used as an iterator. Each time the generator is called, it runs the code up to `yield`, uses the `yield` to return a value, and then will resume right after the `yield` the next time it's called. The generator will stop returning values when there are no more iterations or it encounters either an empty `return` statement or the end of the function. Local variables in a generator function are saved from one call to the next, unlike in normal functions:

```
def four():
    x = 0                                    ⟵ Sets initial value of x to 0
    while x < 4:
        print("in generator, x =", x)
        yield x                              ⟵ Returns current value of x
        x += 1                               ⟵ Increments value of x
for i in four():                             ⟵
    print(f"Value from generator {i}")
```
A call to the generator function creates a generator (iterator) for use in a for loop.

```
in generator, x = 0
Value from generator 0
in generator, x = 1
Value from generator 1
in generator, x = 2
Value from generator 2
in generator, x = 3
Value from generator 3
```

When the function `four` is called in the `for` loop, a generator object is returned, and that generator is the iterator that controls the `for` loop.

Note that this generator function has a `while` loop that limits the number of times the generator executes. Depending on how it's used, a generator that doesn't have some condition to halt it could cause an endless loop when called.

yield vs. yield from

Starting with Python 3.3, a new key word for generators, `yield from`, joins `yield`. Basically, `yield from` makes it possible to string generators together. `yield from` behaves the same way as `yield`, except that it delegates the generator machinery to a subgenerator. So in a simple case, you could do this:

```
def subgen(x):
    for i in range(x):
        yield i

def gen(y):
    yield from subgen(y)

for q in gen(6):
    print(q)

0
1
2
3
4
5
```

This example allows the `yield` expression to be moved out of the main generator, making refactoring easier.

You can also use generator functions with `in` to see whether a value is in the series that the generator produces:

```
2 in four()

in generator, x = 0
in generator, x = 1
in generator, x = 2
True

5 in four()

in generator, x = 0
in generator, x = 1
in generator, x = 2
in generator, x = 3
False
```

Quick check: Generator functions

What would you need to modify in the previous code for the function `four()` to make it work for any number? What would you need to add to allow the starting point to also be set?

9.8   *Decorators*

Because functions are first-class objects in Python, they can be assigned to variables, as you've seen. Functions can also be passed as arguments to other functions and passed back as return values from other functions.

It's possible, for example, to write a Python function that takes another function as its parameter, wraps it in another function that does something related, and then returns the new function. This new combination can be used instead of the original function:

```
def decorate(func):
    print("in decorate function, decorating", func.__name__)
    def wrapper_func(*args):
        print("Executing", func.__name__)
        return func(*args)
    return wrapper_func

def myfunction(parameter):
    print(parameter)

myfunction = decorate(myfunction)

in decorate function, decorating myfunction

myfunction("hello")

Executing myfunction
hello
```

A decorator is syntactic sugar for this process and lets you wrap one function inside another with a one-line addition. It still gives you exactly the same effect as the previous code, but the resulting code is much cleaner and easier to read.

Very simply, using a decorator involves two parts: defining the function that will be wrapping or "decorating" other functions and then using an @ followed by the decorator immediately before the wrapped function is defined. The decorator function should take a function as a parameter and return a function, as follows:

```
def decorate(func):
    print("in decorate function, decorating",
            func.__name__)                          ◄─── Prints the name of
    def wrapper_func(*args):                             function being wrapped
        print("Executing", func.__name__)
        return func(*args)
    return wrapper_func                       ◄───┘ Returns the wrapped function

@decorate                           ◄───┐ myfunction is decorated
def myfunction(parameter):                │ using @decorate.
    print(parameter)

in decorate function, decorating myfunction    ◄───┘ The wrapped function is called.
```

```
myfunction("hello")
```

```
Executing myfunction
hello
```

The `decorate` function prints the name of the function it's wrapping when the function is defined, and when it's finished, the decorator returns the wrapped function. This is exactly the same process as in our first example, but instead of the explicit code, `myfunction` is decorated using `@decorate`. Then the wrapped function is called using the function's original name.

Using a decorator to wrap one function in another can be handy for several purposes. In web frameworks such as Django, decorators are used to make sure that a user is logged in before executing a function, and in graphics libraries, decorators can be used to register a function with the graphics framework.

> **Try this: Decorators**
>
> How would you modify the code for the decorator function to remove unneeded messages and enclose the return value of the wrapped function in `"<html>"` and `"</html>"` so that `myfunction ("hello")` would return `"<html>hello<html>"`?

9.9   *Useful functions*

Looking back at the labs in chapters 6 and 7, refactor the code to clean and count the words in a text file into functions for cleaning and processing the data. The goal should be that most of the logic is moved into functions. Use your own judgment as to the types of functions and parameters, but keep in mind that functions should do just one thing, and they shouldn't have any side effects that carry over outside the function.

9.9.1   *Solving the problem with AI-generated code*

This problem is similar to the one in the previous chapter, except that instead of asking the AI generators to refine our code on a line level, we will want to improve the structure of the code. One factor that makes things simpler, both in terms of creating a prompt and in actually producing the code, is that we are starting from existing, working code, which of course we need to give to the current sessions of the AI bots.

In deciding what we want to ask for in the prompt, we want to be clear that we want the code to be rewritten using functions and that we want the bulk of the data processing to be done in those functions.

9.9.2   *Solutions and discussion*

The solutions to this problem involve understanding and modifying existing code. As we'll see, this is not necessarily easier for AI models.

THE HUMAN SOLUTION

The human version works and breaks things down acceptably, if not brilliantly. This was a simple exercise in taking the human solution from the last chapter and moving the individual parts into functions. The trick with making the functions was to create reasonable function names and to make sure that the functions returned values and that the main code used those returned values.

One danger in doing this sort of refactoring is that instead of the function returning a value, the old variables will end up being used as global variables. For example, since the variable `cleaned_line` is used in both the function and the calling code, if we didn't make sure that `cleaned_line` in the calling code was set to the return of the function, it might have ended up being used as a global variable, which could make debugging deceptive:

```python
import string
punct = str.maketrans('', '', string.punctuation)

def clean_line(line):
    """changes case and removes punctuation"""
    # make all one case
    cleaned_line = line.lower()

    # remove punctuation
    cleaned_line = cleaned_line.translate(punct)
    return cleaned_line


def get_words(line):
    """splits line into words, and rejoins with newlines"""
    words = line.split()
    return "\n".join(words) + "\n"


def count_words(words):
    """takes list of cleaned words, returns count dictionary"""
    word_count = {}
    for word in words:
        count = word_count.setdefault(word, 0)
        word_count[word] += 1
    return word_count


def word_stats(word_count):
    """Takes word count dictionary and returns top
       and bottom five entries"""
    word_list = list(word_count.items())
    word_list.sort(key=lambda x: x[1])
    least_common = word_list[:5]
    most_common = word_list[-1:-6:-1]
    return most_common, least_common

with open("moby_01.txt") as infile, open("moby_01_clean.txt", "w") as
    outfile:
```

```
    for line in infile:
        cleaned_line = clean_line(line)

        cleaned_words = get_words(cleaned_line)

        # write all words for line
        outfile.write(cleaned_words)
moby_words = []
with open('moby_01_clean.txt') as infile:
    for word in infile:
        if word.strip():
            moby_words.append(word.strip())


word_count = count_words(moby_words)

most, least = word_stats(word_count)
print("Most common words:")
for word in most:
    print(word)
print("\nLeast common words:")
for word in least:
    print(word)
```

THE AI SOLUTIONS

For Colaboratory, I put the old code into two cells right above the active cell, and the prompt instructed the chatbot to refactor that code:

```
Refactor the code in the previous 2 cells into functions for cleaning and
processing the data.  The goal should be that most of the logic is moved
into functions.
```

The following was generated in Colaboratory:

```
# Function to clean a line of text by converting it to lowercase and
removing punctuation
def clean_line(line):
  line = line.lower()
  line = line.translate(str.maketrans('', '', string.punctuation))
  return line

# Function to split a line of text into words and write each word to a new
line in a file
def write_words_to_file(line, output_file):
  words = line.split()
  for word in words:
    output_file.write(word + '\n')

# Function to count the occurrences of each word in a list of words
def count_word_occurrences(words):
  word_counts = {}
  for word in words:
```

```
    if word not in word_counts:
      word_counts[word] = 0
    word_counts[word] += 1
  return word_counts

# Function to find the most/least common words in a dictionary
def find_most_and_least_common_words(word_counts):
  most_common = sorted(word_counts.items(), key=lambda item: item[1],
reverse=True)[:5]
  least_common = sorted(word_counts.items(), key=lambda item: item[1])[:5]
  return most_common, least_common

# Open the input file for reading
with open('moby_01.txt', 'r') as input_file:
  # Open the output file for writing
  with open('moby_01_clean.txt', 'w') as output_file:
    # Iterate over each line in the input file
    for line in input_file:
      # Clean the line of text
      clean_line = clean_line(line)

      # Write each word in the clean line to the output file
      write_words_to_file(clean_line, output_file)

# Open the file and read the text into a variable.
with open('moby_01_clean.txt', 'r') as f:
  text = f.read()

# Split the text into words.
words = text.split()

# Count the occurrences of each word.
word_counts = count_word_occurrences(words)

# Find the most and least common words.
most_common, least_common = find_most_and_least_common_words(word_counts)

# Print the results.
print("Most common words:")
for word, count in most_common:
  print(f"{word}: {count}")

print("\nLeast common words:")
for word, count in least_common:
  print(f"{word}: {count}")
```

When we run the Colaboratory version, we get a pair of surprises:

```
---------------------------------------------------------------------------
NameError                                 Traceback (most recent call last)
<ipython-input-4-dd9d43b3f3c2> in <cell line: 34>()
     38       for line in input_file:
     39         # Clean the line of text
---> 40         clean_line = clean_line(line)
     41
```

```
   42              # Write each word in the clean line to the output file

<ipython-input-4-dd9d43b3f3c2> in clean_line(line)
        7 def clean_line(line):
        8   line = line.lower()
----> 9   line = line.translate(str.maketrans('', '', string.punctuation))
       10   return line
       11

NameError: name 'string' is not defined
```

The error here is that the string library hasn't been imported. Adding the line

```
import string
```

at the top of the cell or file will fix that one. But after that, we still get an error:

```
---------------------------------------------------------------------------
TypeError                                 Traceback (most recent call last)
<ipython-input-5-dd9d43b3f3c2> in <cell line: 34>()
       38        for line in input_file:                    ◄──────│ Loops over all lines of input
       39            # Clean the line of text
----> 40            clean_line = clean_line(line)          ◄──────────┐
       41                                                            │
       42            # Write each word in the clean line to the output file │

TypeError: 'str' object is not callable        clean_line name assigned to
                                               result of clean_line function
```

That's right, the version that Colaboratory created from its own original code has an error. The traceback shows that in line 40 the return value of the `clean_line` function, which will be a string cleaned of punctuation characters, is assigned the name `clean_line`, the same name as the function. That is legal in Python, but since we are in a loop, the next iteration of that loop will try to use the name `clean_line` as a function; since it now refers to a string, it can't be executed. The code will work if we use a different name to refer to the return value of the function, say, `cleaned_line`:

```
for line in input_file:
  # Clean the line of text
  cleaned_line = clean_line(line)

  # Write each word in the clean line to the output file
  write_words_to_file(cleaned_line, output_file)
```

But note that we must change the name both where the function is called and where we use its return value three lines later. Otherwise, the Colaboratory refactor is fine, even iterating over the file line by line, where the original read the entire file at once.

For Copilot, the process was similar but easier. I pasted the two programs into the same file; then selected all of the code, right-clicked, and opened Copilot; and finally started an inline chat with a similar prompt:

Refactor the selected code into functions for cleaning and processing the data. The goal should be that most of the logic is moved into functions.

Copilot then produced a split screen diff-style listing of the old code and its proposed refactor, which was accepted without changes.

The following solution was offered by Copilot:

```python
# Generated by Copilot
import string

def clean_line(line):
    # Convert the line to lowercase
    line = line.lower()

    # Remove punctuation from the line
    line = line.translate(str.maketrans('', '', string.punctuation))

    return line

def write_words_to_file(words, output_file):
    # Write each word to the output file
    for word in words:
        output_file.write(word + '\n')

def count_word_occurrences(words):
    # Count the occurrences of each word using a dictionary
    word_counts = {}
    for word in words:
        if word in word_counts:
            word_counts[word] += 1
        else:
            word_counts[word] = 1

    return word_counts

def print_common_words(word_counts, n):
    # Sort the word counts in descending order
    sorted_word_counts = sorted(word_counts.items(),
                                key=lambda x: x[1], reverse=True)

    # Print the n most common words and their occurrences
    print(f"{n} most common words:")
    for word, count in sorted_word_counts[:n]:
        print(f"{word}: {count}")

def print_least_common_words(word_counts, n):
    # Sort the word counts in descending order
    sorted_word_counts = sorted(word_counts.items(),
                                key=lambda x: x[1], reverse=True)

    # Print the n least common words and their occurrences
    print(f"{n} least common words:")
    for word, count in sorted_word_counts[-n:]:
        print(f"{word}: {count}")
```

```
def process_file(input_file_path, output_file_path):
    # Open the input file for reading
    with open(input_file_path, 'r') as input_file:
        # Open the output file for writing
        with open(output_file_path, 'w') as output_file:
            # Iterate over each line in the input file
            for line in input_file:
                # Clean the line
                cleaned_line = clean_line(line)

                # Split the line into words
                words = cleaned_line.split()

                # Write the words to the output file
                write_words_to_file(words, output_file)

def main():
    input_file_path = 'moby_01.txt'
    output_file_path = 'moby_01_clean.txt'

    # Process the file
    process_file(input_file_path, output_file_path)

    # Open the file
    with open(output_file_path, 'r') as file:
        # Read the file content
        content = file.read()

    # Split the content into words
    words = content.split()

    # Count word occurrences
    word_counts = count_word_occurrences(words)

    # Print the five most common words and their occurrences
    print_common_words(word_counts, 5)

    # Print the five least common words and their occurrences
    print_least_common_words(word_counts, 5)

if __name__ == "__main__":
    main()
```

The Copilot refactored version doesn't have any errors and in general is nicely done, but it still reads in the entire file at once rather than line by line, just as it did in the original code.

One problem with both of the refactors is that the functions created are documented with comments beginning with #. For the Colaboratory version, those comments are before the function definition, while for the Copilot version they are after the definition:

```
# Function to count the occurrences of each word in a list of words
def count_word_occurrences(words):
```

```
def clean_line(line):
    # Convert the line to lowercase
```

Of course, having documentation is better than not having it, but for functions, the preferred Python style would be to use a docstring, a triple-quoted string, right after the definition, as is done in the human version:

```
ef clean_line(line):
    """changes case and removes punctuation"""          ◄━━━━┛ Docstring
```

This isn't purely an esthetic thing—the comments will be totally ignored when the code is loaded, while a docstring will become the value of the function object's __doc__ property available for use by documentation tools and Python's `help()` function.

Overall, both AI tools were able to handle changing the structure of our previous code so that the main functionality was in functions. Even with the minor error made by Colaboratory, the ability to refactor structure, not just lines of code, is quite helpful.

Summary

- The basic function is defined using the `def` keyword, a name, parenthesis, and colon followed by a code block with an optional `return` statement at the end.
- Arguments may be passed by position or by parameter name.
- Default values may be provided for function parameters.
- Functions can collect arguments into tuples, giving you the ability to define functions that take an indefinite number of arguments.
- Functions can collect arguments into dictionaries, giving you the ability to define functions that take an indefinite number of arguments passed by parameter name.
- External variables can easily be accessed within a function by using the `global` or `nonlocal` keywords.
- The `lambda` keyword is used to create anonymous inline functions.
- Generator objects are created by functions that use `yield` or `yield from` instead of `return`.
- Functions are first-class objects in Python, which means that they can be assigned to variables, accessed by way of variables, and decorated.

Modules and scoping rules

This chapter covers

- Defining a module
- Writing a first module
- Using the `import` statement
- Modifying the module search path
- Making names private in modules
- Importing standard library and third-party modules
- Understanding Python scoping rules and namespaces

Modules are used to organize larger Python projects. The Python standard library is split into modules to make it more manageable. You don't need to organize your own code into modules, but if you're writing any programs that are more than a few pages long or any code that you want to reuse, you should probably do so.

10.1 *What is a module?*

A *module* is a file containing code. It defines a group of Python functions or other objects, and the name of the module is derived from the name of the file.

Modules most often contain Python source code, but they can also be compiled C or C++ object files. Compiled modules and Python source modules are used the same way.

As well as grouping related Python objects, modules help avert name-clash problems. You might write a module for your program called `mymodule`, which defines a function called `reverse`. In the same program, you might also want to use somebody else's module called `othermodule`, which also defines a function called `reverse` that does something different from your `reverse` function. In a language without modules, it would be impossible to use two different functions named `reverse`. In Python, the process is trivial; you refer to the functions in your main program as `mymodule.reverse` and `othermodule.reverse`.

Using the module names keeps the two `reverse` functions straight because Python uses namespaces. A *namespace* is essentially a dictionary of the identifiers available to a block, function, class, module, and so on. I will discuss namespaces a bit more at the end of this chapter, but be aware that each module has its own namespace, which helps prevent naming conflicts.

Modules are also used to make Python itself more manageable. Most standard Python functions aren't built into the core of the language but are provided via specific modules, which you can load as needed.

> **Using modules with Colaboratory**
>
> Since we are using Colaboratory as our preferred Python environment, we need to say a bit about using modules with it. To use a module with Colaboratory, that module needs to be uploaded to your current notebook's session, which you can do by clicking the Files icon at the left, and then the upload icon at the top.
>
> In the notebooks that go with this book, there is code to either create a module or fetch it from the code repository so that it's available when you need it. In the notebook for this chapter, for example, the first code cell contains code to write the first module, and you should execute that code before trying to access the module in the following cells.
>
> If you are using a Python interpreter installed on your local machine instead, then you will need to manually copy any modules to the current directory where you are using the Python interpreter.

10.2 *A first module*

The best way to learn about modules is probably to make one, which we start in this section.

Colaboratory doesn't easily support creating or editing a simple Python module, but there are some workarounds. For the examples we discuss in the text, there will be code to write the contents of the module to disk so that you can import the resulting module. Be sure to execute the cell that contains such code.

The following is what the cell in the notebook uses to create that module file on disk. Note that it puts the entire file's contents in triple single quotes and then uses the `open` function to open a file for writing and the `write` method to write to the file:

```
open("mymath.py", "w").write(
'''"""mymath - our example math module"""
pi = 3.14159
def area(r):
    """area(r): return the area of a circle with radius r."""
    return(pi * r * r)
''')
```

Listing 10.1 is the plain listing of mymath.py. Going forward, we'll use this style for file listings, even if in the associated notebooks the code will either write the file or fetch it from the repository.

Listing 10.1   File mymath.py

```
"""mymath - our example math module"""
pi = 3.14159
def area(r):
    """area(r): return the area of a circle with radius r."""
    return(pi * r * r)
```

The code for this module merely assigns `pi` a value and defines a function `area`. The .py filename suffix is *strongly* suggested for all Python code files; it identifies that file to the Python interpreter as consisting of Python source code. As with functions, you have the option of putting in a document string as the first line of your module.

Now try out the following:

```
pi
```

```
---------------------------------------------------------------------------
NameError                                 Traceback (most recent call last)
<ipython-input-1-f84ab820532c> in <cell line: 1>()
----> 1 pi

NameError: name 'pi' is not defined
```

```
area(2)
```

```
---------------------------------------------------------------------------
NameError                                 Traceback (most recent call last)
<ipython-input-2-8be925061d22> in <cell line: 1>()
----> 1 area(2)

NameError: name 'area' is not defined
```

Those errors mean that Python doesn't have the constant `pi` or the function `area` built in.

Now we can try importing the module:

```
import mymath          ◄────────┐ Loads module from mymath.py
pi
```

```
- - - - - - - - - - - - - - - - - - - - - - - - - - - - - - - - - - - - - - - - - - - - - - - - - - -
NameError                                    Traceback (most recent call last)
<ipython-input-2-85b32257cf04> in <cell line: 2>()
      1 import mymath
----> 2 pi

NameError: name 'pi' is not defined
```

You've brought in the definitions for `pi` and `area` from the mymath.py file, using the `import` statement (which automatically adds the .py suffix when it searches for the file defining the module named `mymath`). But the new definitions aren't directly accessible; typing `pi` by itself gave an error, and typing `area(2)` by itself would also give an error.

Instead, you access `pi` and `area` by *prepending* them with the name of the module that contains them:

```
mymath.pi
```

```
3.14159
```

```
mymath.area(2)
```

```
12.56636
```

```
mymath.__doc__          ◄────────┘ Contains module's docstring
```

```
'mymath - our example math module'
```

```
mymath.area.__doc__                    ◄────────┘ area function's docstring
```

```
'area(r): return the area of a circle with radius r.'
```

Accessing a module's attributes by *prepending* them with the name of the module that contains them guarantees name safety. Another module out there may also define `pi` (maybe the author of that module thinks that pi is 3.14 or 3.14159265), but that module is of no concern. Even if that other module is imported, its version of `pi` will be accessed by *othermodulename*`.pi`, which is different from `mymath.pi`. This form of access is often referred to as *qualification* (that is, the variable `pi` is being qualified by the module `mymath`). You may also refer to `pi` as an *attribute* of `mymath`.

Definitions within a module can access other definitions within that module without prepending the module name. The `mymath.area` function accesses the `mymath.pi` constant as just `pi`.

If you want to, you can also specifically ask for names from a module to be imported in such a manner that you don't have to prepend them with the module name by using the format `from modulename import attribute`:

```
from mymath import pi
pi
```

3.14159

```
area(2)
```

```
--------------------------------------------------------------------------
NameError                                    Traceback (most recent call last)
<ipython-input-10-8be925061d22> in <cell line: 1>()
----> 1 area(2)

NameError: name 'area' is not defined
```

The name `pi` is now directly accessible because you specifically requested it by using `from mymath import pi`. The function `area` still needs to be called as `mymath.area`, though, because it wasn't explicitly imported.

Reloading a module

While developing and testing a module interactively, you make changes to a module and then reimport it into the current session to test it. But if you change your module on disk or upload a new version to Colaboratory, retyping the `import` command won't cause it to load again, because Python tracks the loaded modules and won't load the same module twice.

To load a fresh version of the module from disk you have two options: you can go to the Runtime menu in Colaboratory and select Restart Session, which gives you a clean, new session of the Python interpreter; or you can use the `reload` function from the `importlib` module for this purpose. The `importlib` module provides an interface to the mechanisms behind importing modules:

```
import mymath, importlib
importlib.reload(mymath)
```

<module 'mymath' from '/content/mymath.py'>

When a module is reloaded (or imported for the first time), all of its code is parsed. A syntax exception is raised if an error is found. On the other hand, if everything is okay, a .pyc file (for example, mymath.pyc) containing Python byte code is created.

Reloading a module doesn't put you back into exactly the same situation as when you start a new session and import it for the first time. But the differences won't normally cause you any problems. If you're interested, you can look up `reload` in the section on the `importlib` module in the Python language reference, found at https://docs.python.org/3/reference/import.html in this page's `importlib` section, to find the details.

Modules don't need to be used only from the interactive Python shell, of course. You can also import them into scripts (or other modules, for that matter); enter suitable `import` statements at the beginning of your program file. Internally to Python, the interactive session and a script are considered to be modules as well.

To summarize:

- A module is a file defining one or more Python objects.
- If the name of the module file is modulename.py, the Python name of the module is `modulename`.
- You can bring a module named `modulename` into use with the `import modulename` statement. After this statement is executed, objects defined in the module can be accessed as `modulename.objectname`.
- Specific names from a module can be brought directly into your program by using the `from modulename import objectname` statement. This statement makes `objectname` accessible to your program without your needing to prepend it with `modulename`, and it's useful for bringing in names that are often used.

10.3 *The import statement*

The `import` statement takes three different forms. The most basic is

```
import modulename
```

which searches for a Python module of the given name, parses its contents, and makes it available. The importing code can use the contents of the module, but any references by that code to names within the module must still be prepended with the module name. If the named module isn't found, an error is generated. I will discuss exactly where Python looks for modules in section 10.4.

The second form permits specific names from a module to be explicitly imported into the code:

```
from modulename import name1, name2, name3, . . .
```

Each of `name1`, `name2`, and so forth from within `modulename` is made available to the importing code; code after the `import` statement can use any of `name1`, `name2`, `name3`, and so on without your prepending the module name.

Finally, there's a general form of the `from . . . import . . .` statement:

```
from modulename import *
```

The `*` stands for all the exported names in `modulename`. `from modulename import *` imports all public names from `modulename`—that is, those that don't begin with an underscore—and makes them available to the importing code without the necessity of prepending the module name. But if a list of names called `__all__` exists in the module (or the package's __init__.py), the names are the ones imported, whether or not they begin with an underscore.

For example, if we used this style with mymath.py:

```
from mymath import *
```

We would be able to directly access both `py` and `area()` without using the module name.

You should take care when using this particular form of importing. If two modules define the same name, and you import both modules using this form of importing, you'll end up with a name clash, and the name from the second module will replace the name from the first. This technique also makes it more difficult for readers of your code to determine where the names you're using originate. When you use either of the two previous forms of the import statement, you give your reader explicit information about where they're from.

But some modules (such as `tkinter`) name their functions to make it obvious where they originate and to make it unlikely that name clashes will occur. It's also common to use the general import to save keystrokes when using an interactive shell.

10.4   *The module search path*

Exactly where Python looks for modules is defined in a variable called `path`, which you can access through a module called `sys`. Enter the following:

```
import sys
sys.path
```

```
import sys
sys.path
['/content',
 '/env/python',
 '/usr/lib/python310.zip',
 '/usr/lib/python3.10',
 '/usr/lib/python3.10/lib-dynload',
 '',
 '/usr/local/lib/python3.10/dist-packages',     This listing will depend
 '/usr/lib/python3/dist-packages',              on your Python setup.
 '/usr/local/lib/python3.10/dist-packages/IPython/extensions',
 '/root/.ipython']
```

The value shown depends on the configuration of your system. Regardless of the details, the `sys.path` indicates a list of directories that Python searches (in order) when attempting to execute an `import` statement. The first module found that satisfies the `import` request is used. If there's no satisfactory module in the module search path, an `ImportError` exception is raised.

The `sys.path` variable is initialized from the value of the environment (operating system) variable PYTHONPATH, if it exists, or from a default value that's dependent on your installation. In addition, whenever you run a Python script, the `sys.path` variable for that script has the directory containing the script inserted as its first element, which provides a convenient way of determining where the executing Python program is located. In an interactive session such as the previous one, the first element of `sys.path` is set to the empty string, which Python takes as meaning that it should first look for modules in the current directory.

10.4.1 *Where to place your own modules*

In the example that starts this chapter, the `mymath` module is accessible to Python because (1) when you execute Python interactively, the first element of `sys.path` is `""`, telling Python to look for modules in the current directory, and (2) you uploaded the mymath.py file to Colaboratory's current directory. In a production environment, neither of these conditions would necessarily be true. You won't be running Python interactively, and Python code files won't be located in your current directory. To ensure that your programs can use the modules you coded, you need to

- Place your modules in one of the directories that Python normally searches for modules.
- Place all the modules used by a Python program in the same directory as the program.
- Create a directory (or directories) to hold your modules and modify the `sys.path` variable so that it includes this new directory (or directories).

Of these three options, the first is apparently the easiest and is also an option that you should *never* choose unless your version of Python includes local code directories in its default module search path. Such directories are specifically intended for site-specific code (that is, code specific to your machine) and aren't in danger of being overwritten by a new Python install because they're not part of the Python installation. If your `sys.path` refers to such directories, you can put your modules there.

The second option is a good choice for modules that are associated with a particular program. Just keep them with the program.

The third option is the right choice for site-specific modules that will be used in more than one program at that site. You can modify `sys.path` in various ways. You can assign to it in your code, which is easy, but doing so hardcodes directory locations into your program code. You can set the `PYTHONPATH` environment variable, which is relatively easy, but it may not apply to all users at your site; or you can add it to the default search path by using a .pth file.

Examples of how to set `PYTHONPATH` are in the Python documentation in the Python Setup and Usage section (under Command Line and Environment). The directory or directories you set it to are prepended to the `sys.path` variable. If you use `PYTHONPATH`, be careful that you don't define a module with the same name as one of the existing library modules that you're using. If you do that, your module will be found before the library module. In some cases, this may be what you want, but probably not often.

You can avoid this problem by using a .pth file. In this case, the directory or directories you added will be appended to `sys.path`. The last of these mechanisms is best illustrated by an example. On Windows, you can place a .pth file in the directory pointed to by `sys.prefix`. Assume your `sys.prefix` is `c:\program files\python` and place the file in the following listing in that directory.

Listing 10.2   File mymodules.pth

```
mymodules
c:\Users\naomi\My Documents\python\modules
```

The next time a Python interpreter is started, `sys.path` will have `c:\program files\python\mymodules` and `c:\Users\naomi\My Documents\python\modules` added to it, if they exist. Now you can place your modules in these directories. Note that the `mymodules` directory still runs the danger of being overwritten with a new installation. The `modules` directory is safer. You also may have to move or create a mymodules.pth file when you upgrade Python. See the description of the `site` module in the documentation for the Python standard library if you want more details on using .pth files.

10.5   *Private names in modules*

I mentioned earlier in the chapter that you can enter `from module import *` to import *almost* all names from a module. The exception is that identifiers in the module beginning with an underscore can't be imported with `from module import *`. People can write modules that are intended for importation with `from module import *` but still keep certain functions or variables from being imported. By starting all internal names (that is, names that shouldn't be accessed outside the module) with an underscore, you can ensure that `from module import *` brings in only those names that the user will want to access.

To see this technique in action, assume that you have a file called modtest.py containing the code in the following listing.

Listing 10.3   File modtest.py

```
"""modtest: our test module"""
def f(x):
    return x
def _g(x):          ◄———┘ Private function name
    return x
a = 4
_b = 2              ◄———┘ Private variable name
```

Now start up an interactive session and enter the following:

```
from modtest import *
f(3)
```

3

```
_g(3)
```

```
------------------------------------------------------------------------
NameError                                  Traceback (most recent call last)
<ipython-input-15-787abdf7161a> in <cell line: 1>()
----> 1 _g(3)

NameError: name '_g' is not defined
```

```
a
```

```
4
```

```
_b
```

```
------------------------------------------------------------------------
NameError                                  Traceback (most recent call last)
<ipython-input-17-8352e74fe22a> in <cell line: 1>()
----> 1 _b

NameError: name '_b' is not defined
```

As you can see, the names f and a are imported, but the names _g and _b remain hidden outside modtest. Note that this behavior occurs only with from ... import *. You can do the following to access _g or _b:

```
import modtest
modtest._b
```

```
2
```

```
from modtest import _g
_g(5)
```

```
5
```

The convention of leading underscores to indicate private names is used throughout Python, not just in modules.

10.6   *Library and third-party modules*

At the beginning of this chapter, I mentioned that the standard Python distribution is split into modules to make it more manageable. After you've installed Python, all the functionality in these library modules is available to you. All that's needed is to import the appropriate modules, functions, classes, and so forth explicitly, before you use them.

Many of the most common and useful standard modules are discussed throughout this book. But the standard Python distribution includes far more than what this book describes. At the very least, you should browse the table of contents of the documentation for the Python standard library.

Available third-party modules and links to them are identified in the Python Package Index, which I discuss in chapter 19. You need to download these modules and install them in a directory in your module search path to make them available for import into your programs.

> **Quick check: Modules**
>
> Suppose that you have a module called `new_math` that contains a function called `new_divide`. What are the ways that you might import and then use that function? What are the pros and cons of each method?
>
> Suppose that the `new_math` module contains a function called `_helper_mat-h()`. How will the underscore character affect the way that `_helper_math()` is imported?

10.7   *Python scoping rules and namespaces*

Python's scoping rules and namespaces will become more interesting as your experience as a Python programmer grows. If you're new to Python, you probably don't need to do anything more than quickly read through this section to get the basic ideas. For more details, look up *namespaces* in the documentation for the Python standard library.

The core concept here is that of a namespace. A *namespace* in Python is a mapping from identifiers to objects—that is, how Python keeps track of what variables and identifiers are active and what they point to. So a statement like x = 1 adds x to a namespace (assuming that it isn't already there) and associates it with the value 1. When a block of code is executed in Python, it has three namespaces: *local, global,* and *built-in* (see figure 10.1).

When an identifier is encountered during execution, Python first looks in the *local namespace* for it. If the identifier isn't found, the *global namespace* is checked. If the identifier still hasn't been found, the *built-in namespace* is checked. If it doesn't exist there, this situation is considered to be an error, and a `NameError` exception occurs.

For a module, a command executed in an interactive session, or a script running from a file, the global and local namespaces are the same. Creating any variable or function or importing anything from another module results in a new entry, or *binding*, being made in this namespace.

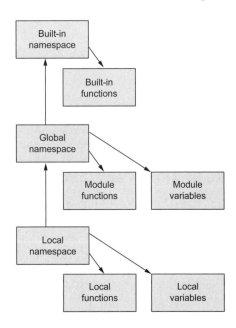

Figure 10.1   **The order in which namespaces are checked to locate identifiers**

But when a function call is made, a local namespace is created, and a binding is entered in it for each parameter of the call. Then a new binding is entered into this local namespace whenever a variable is created within the function. The global namespace of a function is the global namespace of the containing block of the function (that of the module, script file, or interactive session). It's independent of the dynamic context from which it's called.

In all of these situations, the built-in namespace is that of the __builtins__ module. This module contains, among other things, all the built-in functions you've encountered (such as len, min, max, int, float, list, tuple, range, str, and repr) and the other built-in classes in Python, such as the exceptions (like NameError).

One thing that sometimes trips up new Python programmers is the fact that you can override items in the built-in module. If, for example, you create a list in your program and put it in a variable called list, you can't subsequently use the built-in list function. The entry for your list is found first. There's no differentiation between names for functions and modules and other objects. The most recent occurrence of a binding for a given identifier is used.

Enough talk—it's time to explore some examples. The examples use two built-in functions: locals and globals. These functions return dictionaries containing the bindings in the local and global namespaces, respectively.

Let's see what those two namespaces are in our current session:

```
locals()
```

```
{'__name__': '__main__',
 '__doc__': 'Automatically created module for IPython interactive
 environment',
 '__package__': None,
 '__loader__': None,
 '__spec__': None,
 '__builtin__': <module 'builtins' (built-in)>,
 '__builtins__': <module 'builtins' (built-in)>,
 '_ih': ['',
... (Many other entries}
```

```
globals()
```

```
{'__name__': '__main__',
 '__doc__': 'Automatically created module for IPython interactive
 environment',
 '__package__': None,
 '__loader__': None,
 '__spec__': None,
 '__builtin__': <module 'builtins' (built-in)>,
 '__builtins__': <module 'builtins' (built-in)>,
 '_ih': ['',
... (Many other entries}
```

The local and global namespaces for this notebook session are the same. They have three initial key-value pairs that are for internal use: (1) a documentation string __doc__, (2) the main module name __name__ (which, for interactive sessions and scripts run from files is always __main__), and (3) the module used for the built-in namespace __builtins__ (the module __builtins__).

If you continue by creating a variable and importing from modules, you see several bindings created (all the way at the bottom of the long list):

```
z = 2
import math
from cmath import cos
globals()

 'z': 2,
 'math': <module 'math' (built-in)>,
 'cos': <function cmath.cos(z, /)>}

locals()

 'z': 2,
 'math': <module 'math' (built-in)>,
 'cos': <function cmath.cos(z, /)>}

math.ceil(3.4)

4
```

As expected, the local and global namespaces continue to be equivalent. Entries have been added for z as a number, math as a module, and cos from the cmath module as a function.

You can use the del statement to remove these new bindings from the namespace (including the module bindings created with the import statements):

```
del z, math, cos
locals()

{'__builtins__': <module 'builtins' (built-in)>, '__package__': None,
'__name__': '__main__', '__doc__': None}

math.ceil(3.4)

---------------------------------------------------------------
NameError                                 Traceback (most recent call last)
<ipython-input-26-307799385d47> in <cell line: 1>()
----> 1 math.ceil(3.4)

NameError: name 'math' is not defined

import math
math.ceil(3.4)

4
```

The result isn't drastic, because you're able to import the `math` module and use it again. Using `del` in this manner can be handy when you're in the interactive mode.

> **NOTE** Using `del` and then `import` again won't pick up changes made to a module on disk. It isn't removed from memory and then loaded from disk again. The binding is taken out of and then put back into your namespace. You still need to use `importlib.reload` if you want to pick up changes made to a file.

For the trigger-happy, yes, it's also possible to use `del` to remove the __doc__, __main__, and __builtins__ entries. But resist doing this, because it wouldn't be good for the health of your session!

Now look at a function created in an interactive session:

```
def f(x):\
    print("Entry local: ", locals())
    y = x
    print("Exit local: ", locals())

z = 2

f(z)

Entry local:  {'x': 2}
Exit local:  {'x': 2, 'y': 2}
```

When you look at the locals from inside the function, you see that, as expected, upon entry the parameter x is the original entry in f's local namespace, but by the time the function ends, y has been added.

In a production environment, you normally call functions that are defined in modules. Their global namespace is that of the module in which the functions are defined. Assume that you've created the file in the following listing.

Listing 10.4 File scopetest.py

```
"""scopetest: our scope test module"""
v = 6
def f(x):
    """f: scope test function"""
    print("global: ", list(globals().keys()))
    print("entry local:", locals())
    y = x
    w = v
    print("exit local:", locals().keys())
```

Note that you'll be printing only the keys (identifiers) of the dictionary returned by `globals` to reduce clutter in the results. You print only the keys because modules are optimized to store the whole __builtins__ dictionary as the value field for the __builtins__ key:

```
import scopetest
z = 2
scopetest.f(z)

global:  ['__name__', '__doc__', '__package__', '__loader__', '__spec__',
          '__file__', '__cached__', '__builtins__', 'v', 'f']
entry local: {'x': 2}
exit local: dict_keys(['x', 'w', 'y'])
```

Now the global namespace is that of the scopetest module and includes the function f and integer v (but not z from your interactive session). Thus, when creating a module, you have complete control over the namespaces of its functions.

10.7.1 The built-in namespace

I've covered local and global namespaces. Next, I move on to the built-in namespace. This example introduces another built-in function, dir, which, given a module, returns a list of the names defined in it:

```
dir(__builtins__)
```

```
['ArithmeticError', 'AssertionError', 'AttributeError', 'BaseException',
'BlockingIOError', 'BrokenPipeError', 'BufferError', 'BytesWarning',
'ChildProcessError', 'ConnectionAbortedError', 'ConnectionError',
'ConnectionRefusedError', 'ConnectionResetError', 'DeprecationWarning',
'EOFError', 'Ellipsis', 'EncodingWarning', 'EnvironmentError', 'Exception',
'False', 'FileExistsError', 'FileNotFoundError', 'FloatingPointError',
'FutureWarning', 'GeneratorExit', 'IOError', 'ImportError',
'ImportWarning', 'IndentationError', 'IndexError', 'InterruptedError',
'IsADirectoryError', 'KeyError', 'KeyboardInterrupt', 'LookupError',
'MemoryError', 'ModuleNotFoundError', 'NameError', 'None',
'NotADirectoryError', 'NotImplemented', 'NotImplementedError', 'OSError',
'OverflowError', 'PendingDeprecationWarning', 'PermissionError',
'ProcessLookupError', 'RecursionError', 'ReferenceError',
'ResourceWarning', 'RuntimeError', 'RuntimeWarning', 'StopAsyncIteration',
'StopIteration', 'SyntaxError', 'SyntaxWarning', 'SystemError',
'SystemExit', 'TabError', 'TimeoutError', 'True', 'TypeError',
'UnboundLocalError', 'UnicodeDecodeError', 'UnicodeEncodeError',
'UnicodeError', 'UnicodeTranslateError', 'UnicodeWarning', 'UserWarning',
'ValueError', 'Warning', 'ZeroDivisionError', '__IPYTHON__',
'__build_class__', '__debug__', '__doc__', '__import__', '__loader__',
'__name__', '__package__', '__spec__', 'abs', 'aiter', 'all', 'anext',
'any', 'ascii', 'bin', 'bool', 'breakpoint', 'bytearray', 'bytes',
'callable', 'chr', 'classmethod', 'compile', 'complex', 'copyright',
'credits', 'delattr', 'dict', 'dir', 'display', 'divmod', 'enumerate',
'eval', 'exec', 'execfile', 'filter', 'float', 'format', 'frozenset',
'get_ipython', 'getattr', 'globals', 'hasattr', 'hash', 'help', 'hex',
'id', 'input', 'int', 'isinstance', 'issubclass', 'iter', 'len', 'license',
'list', 'locals', 'map', 'max', 'memoryview', 'min', 'next', 'object',
'oct', 'open', 'ord', 'pow', 'print', 'property', 'range', 'repr',
'reversed', 'round', 'runfile', 'set', 'setattr', 'slice', 'sorted',
'staticmethod', 'str', 'sum', 'super', 'tuple', 'type', 'vars', 'zip']
```

There are a lot of entries here. Those entries ending in `Error` and `Exit` are the names of the exceptions built into Python, which I discuss in chapter 14.

The last group (from `abs` to `zip`) is built-in functions of Python. You've already seen many of these functions in this book and will see more, but I don't cover all of them here. If you're interested, you can find details on the rest in the documentation for the Python standard library. You can also easily obtain the documentation string for any of them by using the `help()` function or by printing the docstring directly:

```
print(max.__doc__)

max(iterable, *[, default=obj, key=func]) -> value
max(arg1, arg2, *args, *[, key=func]) -> value

With a single iterable argument, return its biggest item. The
default keyword-only argument specifies an object to return if
the provided iterable is empty.
With two or more arguments, return the largest argument.
```

As I mentioned earlier, it's not unheard of for a new Python programmer to inadvertently override a built-in function:

```
list("Peyto Lake")

['P', 'e', 'y', 't', 'o', ' ', 'L', 'a', 'k', 'e']

list = [1, 3, 5, 7]          ◄───┐ Makes list refer to [1, 3, 5, 7]
list("Peyto Lake")
```

```
-------------------------------------------------------------------------
TypeError                                Traceback (most recent call last)
<ipython-input-39-7845f2807d9f> in <cell line: 2>()
      1 list = [1, 3, 5, 7]
----> 2 list("Peyto Lake")

TypeError: 'list' object is not callable
```

The Python interpreter won't look beyond the new binding for `list` as a list, even though you're using the built-in `list` function syntax.

The same thing happens, of course, if you try to use the same identifier twice in a single namespace. The previous value is overwritten, regardless of its type:

```
import mymath
mymath = mymath.area
mymath.pi
```

```
AttributeError                           Traceback (most recent call last)
<ipython-input-40-4e7325de62ae> in <cell line: 3>()
      1 import mymath
      2 mymath = mymath.area
----> 3 mymath.pi

AttributeError: 'function' object has no attribute 'pi'
```

When you're aware of this situation, it isn't a significant problem. Reusing identifiers, even for different types of objects, wouldn't make for the most readable code anyway. If you do inadvertently make one of these mistakes when in interactive mode, it's easy to recover. You can use `del` to remove your binding, to regain access to an overridden built-in, or to import your module again to regain access:

```
del list
list("Peyto Lake")

['P', 'e', 'y', 't', 'o', ' ', 'L', 'a', 'k', 'e']

import mymath
mymath.pi

3.14159
```

The `locals` and `globals` functions can be useful as simple debugging tools. The `dir` function doesn't give the current settings, but if you call it without parameters, it returns a sorted list of the identifiers in the local namespace. This practice helps you catch the mistyped variable error that compilers usually catch for you in languages that require declarations:

```
xl = 6
xl = xl - 2    ◀─────  The lowercase letter "L" is
xl                     not the same as number "1."

6

dir()

...                ◀─────  Jupyter notebook variables
  'mymath',
  'quit',
  'xl',
  'xl',
  'z']
```

The variables tool in Colaboratory, accessed via the {*x*} icon at the left, also allows you to view the variable values currently active in your notebook session.

Quick check: Namespaces and scope

Consider a variable `width` that's in the module make_window.py. In which of the following contexts is `width` in scope?

(A) Within the module itself

(B) Inside the `resize()` function in the module

(C) Within the script that imported the make_window.py module

10.8   Creating a module

Package the functions created at the end of chapter 9 as a standalone module. Although you can include code to run the module as the main program, the goal should be for the functions to be completely usable from another script. To test, create a new Jupyter notebook and write the code to load and use the module to get the same results as the code in chapter 9.

Uploading a module to Colaboratory

If you create your own module using a code editor or IDE, you will need to upload it to Colaboratory. To do that, you should select the file folder icon at the right and then upload the document icon (as shown in figure 10.2), which will open a file upload dialog.

Figure 10.2   The file and upload icons in Colaboratory

10.8.1   Solving the problem with AI-generated code

This lab isn't about writing new code but again involves repackaging existing code using a new structure. The functions we created in the previous chapter now need to be packaged into a separate file or module, and the remaining code that uses the functions needs to be modified to import the module and correctly call the functions from that module.

To be sure we're separating things properly, our prompt will need to be explicit about the separation of the function code into one file and the client code into another.

Finally, we'll need to be sure that the bots have access to the code we refactored in the previous chapter, either in specific cells in our current notebook or in the current file if we are using VS Code and Copilot.

10.8.2 Solutions and discussion

This problem doesn't require much actual coding, just the reorganization and tweaking of existing code. The functions can be simply copied and pasted into a new module file, while the new main file needs to be changed so that the module functions are imported and then called correctly, depending on how they were imported.

For example, it would be legal code (but questionable Python style) to import everything into the active namespace:

```
from clean_string_module import *
```

In this case, the bare function names could still be used in the main program. If, on the other hand, the `import clean_string_module` style of import is used, the module name would need to be attached to every function call.

THE HUMAN SOLUTION

The human solution is pretty straightforward; it just moves the functions to module file text_processing_author.py and then imports the module and adds the module name in front of all calls to functions from the module:

```
with open("text_processing_author.py", "w") as f:
    f.write(r'''
# Author's version
import string
punct = str.maketrans('', '', string.punctuation)

def clean_line(line):
    """changes case and removes punctuation"""
    # make all one case
    cleaned_line = line.lower()

    # remove punctuation
    cleaned_line = cleaned_line.translate(punct)
    return cleaned_line


def get_words(line):
    """splits line into words, and rejoins with newlines"""
    words = line.split()
    return "\n".join(words) + "\n"


def count_words(words):
    """takes list of cleaned words, returns count dictionary"""
    word_count = {}
    for word in words:
        count = word_count.setdefault(word, 0)
```

```
                word_count[word] += 1
        return word_count


def word_stats(word_count):
    """Takes word count dictionary and returns top
        and bottom five entries"""
    word_list = list(word_count.items())
    word_list.sort(key=lambda x: x[1])
    least_common = word_list[:5]
    most_common = word_list[-1:-6:-1]
    return most_common, least_common
'''
    )


import text_processing_author


with open("moby_01.txt") as infile, open("moby_01_clean.txt",
        "w") as outfile:
    for line in infile:
        cleaned_line = text_processing_author.clean_line(line)

        cleaned_words = text_processing_author.get_words(cleaned_line)

        # write all words for line
        outfile.write(cleaned_words)

moby_words = []
with open('moby_01_clean.txt') as infile:
    for word in infile:
        if word.strip():
            moby_words.append(word.strip())


word_count = text_processing_author.count_words(moby_words)

most, least = text_processing_author.word_stats(word_count)
print("Most common words:")
for word in most:
    print(word)
print("\nLeast common words:")
for word in least:
    print(word)
```

THE AI SOLUTIONS

For Colaboratory, the process is straightforward. Since the code we developed in the lab for the previous chapter is our starting point, we need to add that code (the code that created functions for the text cleaning/processing functionality) to a cell in our current notebook.

Once we have the code in a cell, we can tell the bot to reference that cell to create our module and client code, which we do using this prompt:

Package the functions in the cell above as a standalone module so that the module can be used by other code. Then write the code to use the module to achieve the same result as the cell above.

The results from Colaboratory look promising, and we can see that the bot's suggestion is even clever enough to write the module to a file, enclosing the actual module code in a long triple-quoted string, just as we did in the human version. As we'll see in a moment, however, the bot wasn't *quite* clever enough. In any case, Colaboratory suggests

```
# Generated by colaboratory
# prompt: Package the functions in the cell above as a standalone module
#         so that the module can be used by other code. Then write the
#         code to use the module to achieve the same result as the cell
#         above.

# Save the functions as a module named "text_processing.py"
with open("text_processing.py", "w") as f:
    f.write("""
def clean_line(line):
    # Convert the line to lowercase
    line = line.lower()

    # Remove punctuation from the line
    line = line.translate(str.maketrans('', '', string.punctuation))

    return line

def write_words_to_file(words, output_file):
    # Write each word to the output file
    for word in words:
        output_file.write(word + '\n')

def count_word_occurrences(words):
    # Count the occurrences of each word using a dictionary
    word_counts = {}
    for word in words:
        if word in word_counts:
            word_counts[word] += 1
        else:
            word_counts[word] = 1

    return word_counts

def print_common_words(word_counts, n):
    # Sort the word counts in descending order
    sorted_word_counts = sorted(word_counts.items(),
                                key=lambda x: x[1], reverse=True)

    # Print the n most common words and their occurrences
    print(f"{n} most common words:")
    for word, count in sorted_word_counts[:n]:
        print(f"{word}: {count}")
```

```python
def print_least_common_words(word_counts, n):
    # Sort the word counts in descending order
    sorted_word_counts = sorted(word_counts.items(),
                                key=lambda x: x[1], reverse=True)

    # Print the n least common words and their occurrences
    print(f"{n} least common words:")
    for word, count in sorted_word_counts[-n:]:
        print(f"{word}: {count}")

def process_file(input_file_path, output_file_path):
    # Open the input file for reading
    with open(input_file_path, 'r') as input_file:
        # Open the output file for writing
        with open(output_file_path, 'w') as output_file:
            # Iterate over each line in the input file
            for line in input_file:
                # Clean the line
                cleaned_line = clean_line(line)

                # Split the line into words
                words = cleaned_line.split()

                # Write the words to the output file
                write_words_to_file(words, output_file)
""")

# Use the module
import text_processing

input_file_path = 'moby_01.txt'
output_file_path = 'moby_01_clean.txt'

# Process the file
text_processing.process_file(input_file_path, output_file_path)

# Open the file
with open(output_file_path, 'r') as file:
    # Read the file content
    content = file.read()

# Split the content into words
words = content.split()

# Count word occurrences
word_counts = text_processing.count_word_occurrences(words)

# Print the five most common words and their occurrences
text_processing.print_common_words(word_counts, 5)

# Print the five least common words and their occurrences
text_processing.print_least_common_words(word_counts, 5)
```

The problem comes with the way that Python writes the big string containing the module code to a file. When we try to execute this cell, we get a puzzling error:

```
File "/usr/local/lib/python3.10/dist-packages/IPython/core/
    interactiveshell.py", line 3553, in run_code
    exec(code_obj, self.user_global_ns, self.user_ns)

File "<ipython-input-1-b6ebc2b78dfe>", line 70, in <cell line: 70>
    import text_processing

File "/content/text_processing.py", line 14
    output_file.write(word + '
                              ^
SyntaxError: unterminated string literal (detected at line 14)
```

If we download the generated text_processing.py module, we see that at line 14 we have

```
        output_file.write(word + '
')
```

instead of the

```
        output_file.write(word + '\n')
```

that the AI bot intended. In other words, in writing the module file to disk, the `'\n'` that we want the module to add to lines of text it processes is instead written as a line break *in the code*, which causes the error. The fix for this is easy, but only if you know it— to keep that `'\n'` from being translated into an actual newline too early, we need to tell Python to treat that entire string as "raw" text that shouldn't be interpreted normally. We can do that by adding the "raw" operator r immediately before the triple quotes, as in the previous human solution:

```
with open("text_processing.py", "w") as f:
    f.write(r"""
```

When we do that and retry the code, we get yet another exception:

```
--------------------------------------------------------------------------
NameError                                 Traceback (most recent call last)
<ipython-input-2-472b2a5e47db> in <cell line: 76>()
     74
     75 # Process the file
---> 76 text_processing.process_file(input_file_path, output_file_path)
     77
     78 # Open the file

1 frames
/content/text_processing.py in clean_line(line)
      5
      6       # Remove punctuation from the line
----> 7       line = line.translate(str.maketrans('', '',
                                  string.punctuation))
```

```
8
9        return line
```

NameError: name 'string' is not defined

If we look at the module code, we can see that it does not import the string library needed to provide the punctuation characters in `string.punctuation`.

To fix that, we can add `import string` at the top of our module code:

```
with open("text_processing.py", "w") as f:
    f.write(r"""
import string
def clean_line(line):
```

If we do that and execute the cell to regenerate our module, the error seems to persist. That's because the original flawed module is still loaded in our current Python session, as mentioned back in section 10.2's sidebar on reloading a module. Again, we can either restart the session (under the Runtime menu in Colaboratory) or we can import the `reload` function from `importlib`:

```
import importlib
importlib.reload(text_processing)
```

Once that fix is made, the newly created module works just fine.

For Copilot, we can simply open the file we created in chapter 9 in VS Code, select the functions, and give the chatbot the following prompt:

```
Package the selected functions and write them to a standalone module file
so that the module can be used by other code. Then write the code to use
the module to achieve the same result as the cell above.
```

For this, it's important to use a full Copilot chat session (accessed via the speech balloon icon at the left). Copilot then first outlines the steps it intends to follow:

```
Here's the plan:
1. Create a new Python file named text_processing.py.
2. Copy all the functions from the active selection into this new file.
3. At the end of the file, add a conditional if __name__ == "__main__": to
allow or prevent parts of code from being run when the modules are
imported.
4. Inside this conditional, write the code to use the functions to achieve
the same result as the original code. This will involve calling
process_file with an input file path and an output file path.
5. In the user's current Python file, import the new module and use its
functions.
```

Copilot then generates both a module file and a main file that uses the module, but both of the files must be manually saved under the correct names, which are specified in comment lines at the top of each file:

```python
# FILENAME: word_processing.py

import string

def clean_line(line):
    line = line.lower()
    line = line.translate(str.maketrans('', '', string.punctuation))
    return line

def write_words_to_file(words, output_file):
    for word in words:
        output_file.write(word + '\n')

def count_word_occurrences(words):
    word_counts = {}
    for word in words:
        if word in word_counts:
            word_counts[word] += 1
        else:
            word_counts[word] = 1
    return word_counts

def print_common_words(word_counts, n):
    sorted_word_counts = sorted(word_counts.items(),
                                key=lambda x: x[1], reverse=True)
    print(f"{n} most common words:")
    for word, count in sorted_word_counts[:n]:
        print(f"{word}: {count}")

def print_least_common_words(word_counts, n):
    sorted_word_counts = sorted(word_counts.items(),
                                key=lambda x: x[1], reverse=True)
    print(f"{n} least common words:")
    for word, count in sorted_word_counts[-n:]:
        print(f"{word}: {count}")

def process_file(input_file_path, output_file_path):
    with open(input_file_path, 'r') as input_file:
        with open(output_file_path, 'w') as output_file:
            for line in input_file:
                cleaned_line = clean_line(line)
                words = cleaned_line.split()
                write_words_to_file(words, output_file)
```

Copilot handles the task of creating the module file nicely, producing a working file with the correct import of the string library. The only complaint that I have about this module is that it removed the comments that documented each function. I noted in the last chapter that using comments to document functions wasn't ideal Python style, but in this case, removing even that documentation is a negative:

```python
# FILENAME: main.py

import word_processing
```

```
input_file_path = "path_to_input_file"
output_file_path = "path_to_output_file"

# Process the file
word_processing.process_file(input_file_path, output_file_path)

# Count word occurrences
with open(output_file_path, 'r') as output_file:
    words = output_file.read().split()
    word_counts = word_processing.count_word_occurrences(words)

# Print common and least common words
word_processing.print_common_words(word_counts, 10)
word_processing.print_least_common_words(word_counts, 10)

10 most common words:
the: 14
and: 9
i: 9
of: 8
is: 7
a: 6
it: 6
me: 5
to: 5
in: 4
10 least common words:
hours: 1
previous: 1
were: 1
out: 1
sight: 1
land: 1
look: 1
at: 1
crowds: 1
watergazers: 1
```

The file main.py only needed to load and use the module, which it did correctly. There was only one aspect that needed a change—it used `path_to_input_file` and `path_to_output_file` as the filenames of the data files. The bot did display a reminder under the generated code to "Please replace "`path_to_your_input_file`" and "`path_to_your_output_file`" with the actual paths to your input and output files," and once the filenames were adjusted to moby_01.txt and moby_01_clean.txt, the code ran correctly.

This exercise was a step up in terms of abstraction—we have now moved from creating code to organizing that code into functions to organizing those functions into a module and calling it correctly. As we've seen at each step along the way, versions generated by AI are both impressive in their ability to generate a possible solution and susceptible to subtle bugs and simple errors.

Summary

- Python modules allow you to put related code and objects into a file.
- Using modules also helps prevent conflicting variable names, because imported objects are normally named in association with their module.
- `import` can be used to import an entire module or to access specific elements in a module.
- Elements whose names begin with an underscore are not imported by `from module import *`.
- A namespace is the dictionary that connects objects and their names for a particular scope.
- Something in global scope is accessible everywhere in the module.
- Something in local scope is only accessible in the immediately enclosing namespace.
- Objects in the built-in namespace are always accessible.

Python programs

11

This chapter covers

- Creating a very basic program
- Making a program directly executable on Linux/ UNIX
- Writing programs on macOS
- Selecting execution options in Windows
- Combining programs and modules
- Distributing Python applications

Up until now, you've been using the Python interpreter mainly in interactive mode in Colaboratory. For production use, you may need to create Python programs or scripts. Several of the sections in this chapter focus on command-line programs. If you come from a Linux/UNIX background, you may be familiar with scripts that can be started from a command line and given arguments and options that can be used to pass in information and possibly redirect their input and output. If you're from a Windows or Mac background, these things may be new to you, and you may be more inclined to question their value. While you certainly can use Python from the command line in any of those environments, it becomes a bit trickier if you are using an Android or iOS device. Since we have been using Colaboratory as our reference environment, we'll discuss how to run command-line scripts from within a notebook.

It's true that command-line scripts are sometimes less convenient to use in a GUI environment, but the Mac has the option of a UNIX command-line shell, and Windows also offers enhanced command-line options. It will be well worth your time to read the bulk of this chapter at some point. You may find occasions when these techniques are useful, or you may run across code you need to understand that uses some of them. In particular, command-line techniques are very useful when you need to process large numbers of files.

11.1 Creating a very basic program

Any group of Python statements placed sequentially in a file can be used as a program, or *script*. But it's more standard and useful to introduce additional structure. In its most basic form, this task is a simple matter of creating a controlling a function in a file and calling that function.

Listing 11.1   File script1.py

```
def main():
    print("this is our first test script file")     ◄──┐  Controlling function main
main()                                               ◄──┐  Calls main
```

In this script, `main` is the controlling—and only—function. First, it's defined, and then it's called. Although it doesn't make much difference in a small program, this structure can give you more options and control when you create larger applications, so it's a good idea to make using it a habit from the beginning.

11.1.1 Starting a script from a command line

If we enter the contents of script1.py into a cell in Colaboratory, it works just fine. But we can also use a special syntax in a code cell to run commands in Colaboratory's host environment, which is a version of Ubuntu Linux. To run a command from the "command line" in Colaboratory, we can use the same commands as would be used in Linux but with the ! character as a prefix. The one catch is that you need to have the file saved in that Colaboratory session. The code notebooks for this book include cells that have code that will either fetch the script files from the GitHub repository or write the code to a file, and to be sure that the same code behaves as expected, you need to be sure to either execute those cells or upload the files manually.

In Colaboratory, using the ! prefix, you would use the following to start the script:

```
! python script1.py
```

this is our first test script file

If you're using Linux/UNIX, make sure that Python is on your path and you're in the same directory as your script. Then you would use the following:

```
python script1.py
```

If you're using a Mac running macOS, the procedure is the same as for other UNIX systems. You need to open a terminal program, which is in the Utilities folder of the Applications folder. You have several other options for running scripts on macOS, which I will discuss shortly.

If you're using Windows, open the Terminal (Windows 11—you can find it by right-clicking the Start Menu button) or Command Prompt (this can be found in different menu locations depending on the version of Windows; in Windows 10, it's in the Windows System menu) or PowerShell. Either of these opens in your home folder, and if necessary, you can use the cd command to change to a subdirectory. Running script1.py if it was saved on your desktop would look like the following:

```
C:\Users\naomi> cd Desktop                          ◄─────┐ Changes to Desktop folder

C:\Users\naomi\Desktop> python script1.py           ◄─────┐ Runs script1.py
this is our first test script file                  ◄─────┤
                                                          └ Output of script1.py
C:\Users\naomi\Desktop>
```

We'll look at other options for calling scripts later in this chapter, but we'll stick with using the ! prefix in Colaboratory for our examples.

11.1.2 Command-line arguments

With command-line scripts, it's often useful to get parameters or arguments from the command line that runs the script. A simple mechanism is available for passing in command-line arguments. All of the arguments on the command line are in a list that can be accessed via sys.argv. Note that to access this list, you first need to import the sys module.

Listing 11.2 File script2.py

```
import sys                                           ◄─────┐ Imports sys module
def main():
    print("this is our second test script file")
    print(sys.argv)                                  ◄─────┐ Accesses list in sys.argv
main()
```

If you call this with the line (leave out the ! if you are not in a notebook)

```
! python script2.py arg1 arg2 3
```

you get

```
this is our second test script file
['script2.py', 'arg1', 'arg2', '3']
```

You can see that the command-line arguments have been stored in `sys.argv` as a list of strings. You can also see that the first item in that list is the command itself. You should also note that any numbers entered on the command line will come in as string representations of those numbers and may need to be converted to the right type before being used.

11.1.3 *Executing code only as main script*

The most commonly used Python script structure has one more element, which is an `if` statement that surrounds the main code that we want executed when the file is run as the `main` script. This is useful because it protects code from being executed when a file is imported as a module, as we'll see later in this chapter. This safeguard is essential when we want a script to be usable both as a standalone script and as a module.

Adding this feature to a script is a matter of putting the following conditional test around the code that we want executed if the file is run as a script:

```
if __name__ == '__main__':
    main()
else:                                    ◄──┘ The else section is optional.
    # module-specific initialization code if any
```

If a file with this structure is called as a script, the variable `__name__` is set to `__main__`, which means that the controlling function, `main`, will be called. If the script has been imported into a module by some other script, its name will be its filename, and the code won't be executed. On the other hand, if we include the totally optional and less often used `else` block, that will only be executed if the file has been imported as a module.

When creating a script, I try to use this structure right from the start. This practice allows me to import the file into a session and interactively test and debug my functions as I create them or run the module as a script. This doesn't add much functionality to a tiny script, but if the script grows (as they often do), it can give more flexibility in how it's used.

11.1.4 *Redirecting the input and output of a script*

Particularly on Unix/Linux systems, it is common to redirect the contents of a file or the output of another process into a script instead of using keyboard output or to redirect the output of your script to the input of yet another process. Redirecting input and output this way allows you to chain small, specialized programs together to achieve an infinite variety of more complex tasks.

To redirect a file into input instead of having the user enter input, you need to specify that you want to read from standard input, which in the Python world is accessed by using the `stdin` object in the `sys` library. You can also specify writing to the standard output by using `sys.stdout`, although in fact the `print` function also writes to `stdout` by default. To redirect from a file to input, you would use < on the command line, and for sending output to a file you would use >.

It's easier to understand what's going on with an example like the short script in the following listing.

Listing 11.3 File replace.py

```
import sys                                                    Reads from sys.stdin
def main():                                                   into contents
    contents = sys.stdin.read()
    sys.stdout.write(contents.replace(sys.argv[1], sys.argv[2]))
if __name__ == "__main__":
    main()                                       Replaces first argument with
                                                 second; writes to sys.stdout
```

This script gets its input by reading standard input (`sys.stdin`) as a file. Unlike the input function, it will keep reading (or waiting to read) data until it encounters an end-of-file indicator. If this script is run without redirecting standard input, it will read from the terminal and will keep reading and waiting until the user enters a Ctrl-D character to signal the end of the "file." Once it's done reading, it writes to its standard output whatever it has read, with all occurrences of its first argument replaced with its second argument.

Called as follows, with redirection of both input and output, the script places in `outfile` a copy of `infile`, with all occurrences of `zero` replaced by `0`:

```
python replace.py zero 0 < infile > outfile        Redirects input (<) to read
                                                   from infile and output (>)
                                                   to write to outfile
```

Note that this sort of redirection usually only makes sense from a command prompt.

In general, the line

```
python script.py arg1 arg2 arg3 arg4 < infile > outfile
```

has the effect of having any `input` or `sys.stdin` operations directed out of `infile` and any `print` or `sys.stdout` operations directed into `outfile`. The effect is as though you set `sys.stdin` to `infile` with `'r'` (read) mode and `sys.stdout` to `outfile` with `'w'` (write). It's also possible to use >> to indicate appending to a file rather than overwriting:

```
python replace.py a A < infile >> outfile
```

This line causes the output to be appended to `outfile` rather than to overwrite it, as happened in the previous example.

You can also use the | to *pipe* in the output of one command as the input of another command:

```
python replace.py 0 zero < infile | python replace.py 1 one > outfile
```

This code first runs replace.py with the parameters `0 zero` reading the contents of `infile` and replacing all `0`s with `zero`. The output of that process is directed to the input of a second run of replace.py, which replaces any `1`s in that stream with `one` and writes the results to `outfile`, which will finally have the contents of `infile`, with all occurrences of `0` changed to `zero` and all occurrences of `1` changed to `one`.

This technique may seem strange if you are used to thinking in terms of larger programs, particularly on Window or iOS, but combining small, specialized programs in this way is very powerful and at the heart of the Unix coding tradition.

11.1.5 *The argparse module*

You can configure a script to accept command-line options as well as arguments. The `argparse` module provides support for parsing different types of arguments and can even generate usage messages.

To use the `argparse` module, you create an instance of `ArgumentParser`, populate it with arguments, and then read both the optional and positional arguments. The following listing illustrates the module's use.

Listing 11.4   File opts.py

```
from argparse import ArgumentParser

def main():                                          Adds indent and
    parser = ArgumentParser()                        input file arguments
    parser.add_argument("indent", type=int, help="indent for report")
    parser.add_argument("input_file",
                help="read data from this file")
    parser.add_argument("-f", "--file",
                dest="filename",                     Adds optional -f
                help="write report to FILE", metavar="FILE")    or --file followed
    parser.add_argument("-x", "--xray",              by filename
                help="specify xray strength factor")
    parser.add_argument("-q", "--quiet",
                action="store_false", dest="verbose",
                default=True,
                help="don't print status messages to stdout")

    args = parser.parse_args()                       Adds -q or --quiet
                                                     argument; defaults to True
    print("arguments:", args)
if __name__ == "__main__":
    main()
```

This code creates an instance of `ArgumentParser` and then adds two positional arguments, `indent` and `input_file`, which are the arguments entered after all of the optional arguments have been parsed. *Positional arguments* are those without a prefix character (usually (`"-"`) and are required, and in this case, the `indent` argument must also be parsable as an `int`.

The next line adds an optional filename argument with either `"-f"` or `"--file"`. The final option added, the `"quiet"` option, also adds the ability to turn off the verbose option, which is `True` by default (`action="store_false"`). The fact that these options begin with the prefix character `"-"` tells the parser that they're optional.

The final argument, `"-q"`, also has a default value (`True`, in this case) that will be set if the option isn't specified. The `action="store_false"` parameter specifies that if the argument *is* specified, a value of `False` will be stored in the destination.

The `argparse` module returns a namespace object containing the arguments as attributes. You can get the values of the arguments by using dot notation. If there's no argument for an option, its value is `None`. Thus, if you call the previous script with the line

```
! python opts.py -x100 -q -f outfile 2 arg2
```

Options come after the script name.

the following output results:

```
arguments: Namespace(indent=2, input_file='arg2', filename='outfile',
xray='100', verbose=False)
```

If an invalid argument is found, or if a required argument isn't given, `parse_args` raises an error:

```
! python opts.py -x100 -r
```

This line results in the following response:

```
usage: opts.py [-h] [-f FILE] [-x XRAY] [-q] indent input_file
opts.py: error: the following arguments are required: indent, input_file
```

11.1.6 *Using the fileinput module*

The `fileinput` module is sometimes useful for scripts. It provides support for processing lines of input from one or more files. It automatically reads the command-line arguments (out of `sys.argv`) and takes them as its list of input files. Then it allows you to sequentially iterate through these lines. The simple example script in the following listing (which strips out any lines starting with ##) illustrates the module's basic use.

> **Listing 11.5   File script4.py**

```
import fileinput
def main():
    for line in fileinput.input():
        if not line.startswith('##'):
            print(line, end="")
if __name__ == "__main__":
    main()
```

Now assume that you have the data files shown in the next two listings.

Listing 11.6   File sole1.tst

```
## sole1.tst: test data for the sole function
0 0 0
0 100 0
##
```

Listing 11.7   File sole2.tst

```
## sole2.tst: more test data for the sole function
12 15 0
##
100 100 0
```

Also assume that you make this call:

```
! python script4.py sole1.tst sole2.tst
```

You obtain the following result with the comment lines stripped out and the data from the two files combined:

```
0 0 0
0 100 0
12 15 0
100 100 0
```

If no command-line arguments are present, the standard input is all that is read. If one of the arguments is a hyphen (-), the standard input is read at that point.

The `fileinput` module provides several other functions. These functions allow you at any point to determine the total number of lines that have been read (`lineno`), the number of lines that have been read out of the current file (`filelineno`), the name of the current file (`filename`), whether this is the first line of a file (`isfirstline`), and/or whether standard input is currently being read (`isstdin`). You can at any point skip to the next file (`nextfile`) or close the whole stream (`close`). The short script in the following listing (which combines the lines in its input files and adds file-start delimiters) illustrates how you can use these functions.

Listing 11.8   File script5.py

```python
import fileinput
def main():
    for line in fileinput.input():
        if fileinput.isfirstline():
            print("<start of file {0}>".format(fileinput.filename()))
        print(line, end="")
if __name__ == "__main__":
    main()
```

Using the call

```
python script5.py file1 file2
```

results in the following (where the dotted lines indicate the lines in the original files):

```
<start of file file1>
.....................
.....................
<start of file file2>
.....................
.....................
```

Finally, if you call `fileinput.input` with an argument of a single filename or a list of filenames, they're used as its input files rather than the arguments in `sys.argv`. `fileinput.input` also has an `inplace` option that leaves its output in the same file as its input while optionally leaving the original around as a backup file. See the documentation for a description of this option.

Quick check: Scripts and arguments

Match the following ways of interacting with the command line and the correct use case for each.

Multiple arguments and options	`sys.argv`
No arguments or just one argument	Use `fileinput` module
Processing multiple files	Redirect standard input and output
Using the script as a filter	Use `argparse` module

11.2 Running scripts in different operating systems

Running Python scripts from a command line or shell varies depending on one's operating system. In this section, we'll look briefly at running scripts in Windows, macOS, and Linux.

11.2.1 Making a script directly executable on UNIX

If you're on Colaboratory, as mentioned earlier, or a UNIX-type system, you can easily make a script directly executable, with two steps. First, add the following line at the top of the file:

```
#! /usr/bin/env python3
```

Next, you need to use the `chmod` command to change its mode so that it can be executed directly, with the following command:

```
! chmod +x replace.py
```

Then if you place your script somewhere on your path (for example, in your bin directory), you can execute it regardless of the directory you're in by typing its name and
the desired arguments. In Colaboratory, we're fine putting our files in the default
/content directory. For example, we could execute replace.py with

```
! replace.py zero 0 < infile > outfile
```

The < and > characters cause the input and output to be redirected to and from the
file, which works fine on Linux and Mac systems (and in Colaboratory) but may not
work on Windows.

   If you're writing administrative scripts on UNIX, several library modules are available
that you may find useful. These modules include grp for accessing the group database,
pwd for accessing the password database, resource for accessing resource usage information, syslog for working with the syslog facility, and stat for working with information about a file or directory obtained from an os.stat call. You can find information
on these modules in the documentation for the Python standard library.

11.2.2 *Scripts on macOS*

In many ways, Python scripts on macOS behave the same way as they do on Linux/
UNIX. You can run Python scripts from a terminal window exactly the same way as on
any UNIX box. But on the Mac, you can also run Python programs from the Finder,
either by dragging the script file to the Python Launcher app or by configuring Python
Launcher as the default application for opening your script (or, optionally, all files with
a .py extension.)

   You have several options for using Python on a Mac. The specifics of all the options
are beyond the scope of this book, but you can get a full explanation by going to the
www.python.org website and checking out the "Using Python on a Mac" section of the
"Python Setup and Usage" section of the documentation for your version of Python
(https://docs.python.org/3.10/using/mac.html).

   If you're interested in writing administrative scripts for macOS, you should look at
packages that bridge the gap between Apple's Open Scripting Architecture and Python.

11.2.3 *Script execution options in Windows*

If you're on Windows, you have several options for starting a script that vary in their
capability and ease of use. Unfortunately, exactly what those options might be and how
they are configured can vary considerably across the various versions of Windows currently in use.

   One option is installing the Linux subsystem for Windows, which gives you a Linux
environment you can run as an application in Windows. This environment is based
on Ubuntu Linux and gives you all of the options for Linux systems discussed earlier.
For information on the other options for running Python on your system, consult the

online Python documentation for your version of Python and look for "Using Python on Windows."

STARTING A SCRIPT FROM A COMMAND WINDOW OR POWERSHELL

To run a script from a command window or PowerShell window, open a command prompt or PowerShell window. When you're at the command prompt and have navigated to the folder where your scripts are located, you can use Python to run your scripts in much the same way as on UNIX/Linux/macOS systems:

```
> python replace.py zero 0 < infile > outfile
```

Python doesn't run?

If Python doesn't run when you enter `python3` at the Windows command prompt, it probably means that the location of the Python executable isn't on your command path. You either need to add the Python executable to your system's PATH environment variable manually or rerun the installer to have it do the job. To get more help setting up Python on Windows, refer to the Python Setup and Usage section of the online Python documentation. There you'll find a section on using Python on Windows, with instructions for installing Python. In general, installing Python from the Microsoft Store should get you up and running without problems.

This is the most flexible of the ways to run a script on Windows because it allows you to use input and output redirection.

On Windows, you can edit the environment variables (see the previous section) to add .py as a magic extension, making your scripts automatically executable:

```
PATHEXT=.COM;.EXE;.BAT;.CMD;.VBS;.JS;.PY
```

Try this: Making a script executable

Experiment with executing scripts on your platform. Also, try to redirect input and output into and out of your scripts.

11.3 *Programs and modules*

For small scripts that contain only a few lines of code, a single function works well. But if the script grows beyond this size, separating your controlling function from the rest of the code is a good option to take. The rest of this section illustrates this technique and some of its benefits. I start with an example using a simple controlling function. The script in the following listing returns the English-language name for a given number between 0 and 99.

Listing 11.9 File script6.py

```
#! /usr/bin/env python3
import sys
# conversion mappings
_1to9dict = {'0': '', '1': 'one', '2': 'two', '3': 'three', '4': 'four',
             '5': 'five', '6': 'six', '7': 'seven', '8': 'eight',
             '9': 'nine'}
_10to19dict = {'0': 'ten', '1': 'eleven', '2': 'twelve',
               '3': 'thirteen', '4': 'fourteen', '5': 'fifteen',
               '6': 'sixteen', '7': 'seventeen', '8': 'eighteen',
               '9': 'nineteen'}
_20to90dict = {'2': 'twenty', '3': 'thirty', '4': 'forty', '5': 'fifty',
               '6': 'sixty', '7': 'seventy', '8': 'eighty', '9': 'ninety'}
def num2words(num_string):
    if num_string == '0':
        return'zero'
    if len(num_string) > 2:
        return "Sorry can only handle 1 or 2 digit numbers"
    num_string = '0' + num_string                         ◀─┐ Pads on left in case it's
    tens, ones = num_string[-2], num_string[-1]             │ a single-digit number
    if tens == '0':
        return _1to9dict[ones]
    elif tens == '1':
        return _10to19dict[ones]
    else:
        return _20to90dict[tens] + ' ' + _1to9dict[ones]
def main():
    print(num2words(sys.argv[1]))                         ◀─┐ Calls num2words with
if __name__ == "__main__":                                  │ first argument
    main()
```

If you call it with

```
! python script6.py 59
```

you get the following result:

```
fifty nine
```

The controlling function here calls the function num2words with the appropriate argument and prints the result. It's standard to have the call at the bottom, but sometimes you'll see the controlling function's definition at the top of the file. I prefer this function at the bottom, just above the call, so that I don't have to scroll back up to find it after going to the bottom to find out its name. This practice also cleanly separates the scripting plumbing from the rest of the file, which is useful when combining scripts and modules.

People combine scripts with modules when they want to make functions they've created in a script available to other modules or scripts. Also, a module may be instrumented so it can run as a script either to provide a quick interface to it for users or to provide hooks for automated module testing.

As mentioned earlier, combining a script and a module is a simple matter of putting the following conditional test around the call to the controlling function:

```
if __name__ == '__main__':
    main()
else:
    # module-specific initialization code if any
```

Again, I recommend using this structure from the start when creating a script. This practice allows me to import it into a session and interactively test and debug my functions as I create them, and only the controlling function needs to be debugged externally. If the script grows and I find myself writing functions I might be able to use elsewhere, I can go ahead and use those functions by importing the script as a module, with the option of moving those functions into their own module later.

The script in listing 11.10 is an extension of the previous script but modified to be safe to be used as a module. The functionality has also been expanded to allow the entry of a number from 0 to 999,999,999,999,999 rather than just from 0 to 99. The controlling function (main) does the checking of the validity of its argument and also strips out any commas in it, allowing more user-readable input, like 1,234,567.

Listing 11.10 File n2w.py

```
#! /usr/bin/env python3
"""n2w: number to words conversion module: contains function
    num2words. Can also be run as a script                          ◄─── Usage message;
usage as a script: n2w num                                               includes example
           (Convert a number to its English word description)
           num: whole integer from 0 and 999,999,999,999,999 (commas are
           optional)
example: n2w 10,003,103
           for 10,003,103 say: ten million three thousand
one hundred three
"""
import sys, string, argparse
_1to9dict = {'0': '', '1': 'one', '2': 'two', '3': 'three',         ◄─── Conversion
             '4': 'four',                                                mappings, for
             '5': 'five', '6': 'six', '7': 'seven', '8': 'eight',        internal module
             '9': 'nine'}                                                use only
_10to19dict = {'0': 'ten', '1': 'eleven', '2': 'twelve',
               '3': 'thirteen', '4': 'fourteen', '5': 'fifteen',
               '6': 'sixteen', '7': 'seventeen', '8': 'eighteen',
               '9': 'nineteen'}
_20to90dict = {'2': 'twenty', '3': 'thirty', '4': 'forty', '5': 'fifty',
               '6': 'sixty', '7': 'seventy', '8': 'eighty', '9': 'ninety'}
_magnitude_list = [(0, ''), (3, ' thousand '), (6, ' million '),
                  (9, ' billion '), (12, ' trillion '),(15, '')]      ◄─── Handles special
def num2words(num_string):                                                conditions
    """num2words(num_string): convert number to English words"""          (number is zero
    if num_string == '0':                                                 or too large)
        return 'zero'
    num_string = num_string.replace(",", "")     ◄─── Removes commas from number
```

```
        num_length = len(num_string)
        max_digits = _magnitude_list[-1][0]
        if num_length > max_digits:

            return "Sorry, can't handle numbers with more than  " \
                   "{0} digits".format(max_digits)

        num_string = '00' + num_string          ◄──────  Pads number on left
        word_string = ''                         ◄──────┘  Initiates string for number
        for mag, name in _magnitude_list:
            if mag >= num_length:
                return word_string
            else:
                hundreds, tens, ones = (num_string[-mag-3],
                        num_string[-mag-2], num_string[-mag-1])
                if not (hundreds == tens == ones == '0'):
                    word_string = _handle1to999(hundreds, tens, ones) + \
                                  name + word_string              ◄──────
def _handle1to999(hundreds, tens, ones):         ◄──────          Creates string
    if hundreds == '0':                                            containing number
        return _handle1to99(tens, ones)
    else:                                         For internal module use only
        return _1to9dict[hundreds] + ' hundred ' + _handle1to99(tens, ones)
def _handle1to99(tens, ones):
    if tens == '0':
        return _1to9dict[ones]
    elif tens == '1':
        return _10to19dict[ones]
    else:
        return _20to90dict[tens] + ' ' + _1to9dict[ones]
def test():                                      ◄──────  Function for module test mode
    values = sys.stdin.read().split()
    for val in values:
        print("{0} = {1}".format(val, num2words(val)))
def main():
    parser = argparse.ArgumentParser(usage=__doc__)          Gathers all values for
    parser.add_argument("num", nargs='*')       ◄──────      that argument into a list
    parser.add_argument("-t", "--test", dest="test",
                        action='store_true', default=False,
                        help="Test mode: reads from stdin")
    args = parser.parse_args()
    if args.test:                                ◄──────  Runs in test mode if
        test()                                            test variable is set
    else:
        try:                                              Catches KeyErrors due to
            result = num2words(args.num[0])      ◄──────  argument containing nondigits
        except KeyError:
            parser.error('argument contains non-digits')
        else:
            print("For {0}, say: {1}".format(args.num[0], result))
if __name__ == '__main__':
    main()                                       ◄──────  Calls main function
else:                                                     if run as script
    print("n2w  loaded as a module")
```

If this file is called as a script, the __name__ will be __main__. If it's imported as a module, it will be named n2w. Remember that the variables and functions with names starting with an underscore ("_") are intended to be only used internally by the module itself and should not be used by client code.

This main function illustrates the purpose of a controlling function for a command-line script, which in effect is to create a simple UI for the user. It may handle the following tasks:

- Ensure that there's the right number of command-line arguments and that they're of the right types. Inform the user, giving usage information if not. Here, the function ensures that there is a single argument, but it doesn't explicitly test to ensure that the argument contains only digits.

- Possibly handle a special mode. Here, a "--test" argument puts you in a test mode.

- Map the command-line arguments to those required by the functions and call them in the appropriate manner. Here, commas are stripped out, and the single function num2words is called.

- Possibly catch and print a more user-friendly message for exceptions that may be expected. Here, KeyErrors are caught, which occurs if the argument contains nondigits. (A better way to do this would be to explicitly check for nondigits in the argument using the regular expression module that will be introduced later. This would ensure that we don't hide KeyErrors that occur due to other reasons.)

- Map the output if necessary to a more user-friendly form, which is done here in the print statement. If this were a script to run on Windows, you'd probably want to let the user open it with the double-click method—that is, to use the input to query for the parameter, rather than have it as a command-line option and keep the screen up to display the output by ending the script with the line

```
input("Press the Enter key to exit")
```

But you may still want to leave the test mode as a command-line option.

The test mode in the following listing provides a regression test capability for the module and its num2words function. In this case, you use it by placing a set of numbers in a file.

Listing 11.11 File n2w.tst

```
0 1 2 3 4 5 6 7 8 9 10 11 12 13 14 15 16 17 18 19 20 21 98 99 100
101 102 900 901 999
999,999,999,999,999
1,000,000,000,000,000
```

Then type

```
! python n2w.py --test < n2w.tst

0  = zero
1  = one
2  = two
3  = three
4  = four
5  = five
6  = six
7  = seven
8  = eight
9  = nine
10 = ten
11 = eleven
12 = twelve
13 = thirteen
14 = fourteen
15 = fifteen
16 = sixteen
17 = seventeen
18 = eighteen
19 = nineteen
20 = twenty
21 = twenty one
98 = ninety eight
99 = ninety nine
100 = one hundred
101 = one hundred one
102 = one hundred two
900 = nine hundred
901 = nine hundred one
999 = nine hundred ninety nine
999,999,999,999,999 = nine hundred ninety nine trillion nine hundred ninety
nine billion nine hundred ninety nine million nine hundred ninety nine
thousand nine hundred ninety nine
1,000,000,000,000,000 = Sorry, can't handle numbers with more than 15 digits
```

You could also save the output to a file using redirection—for example, `> test_output`
`.txt`. The output can then easily be checked for correctness. This example was run several times during its creation and can be rerun any time `num2words` or any of the functions it calls are modified. And yes, I'm aware that full exhaustive testing certainly didn't
occur and that well over 999 trillion valid inputs for this program haven't been checked!

Often, the provision of a test mode for the module is the only reason for having a `main`
function in that module. I know of at least one company in which part of the development policy is to always create at least one such test for every Python module developed.
Python's built-in data object types and methods usually make this process easy, and those
who practice this technique seem to be unanimously convinced that it's well worth the
effort. See chapter 19, section 19.1.5, for more about testing your Python code.

In this example, it would be easy to create a separate file with only the portion of the
`main` function that handles the argument and import `n2w` into this file. Then only the
test mode would be left in the `main` function of `n2w.py`.

> **Quick check: Programs and modules**
>
> What problem is the use of `if __name__ == "__main__":` meant to prevent, and how does it do that? Can you think of any other way to prevent this problem?

11.4 *Distributing Python applications*

You can distribute your Python scripts and applications in several ways. You can share the source files, of course, probably bundled in a zip or tar file, which leaves a lot to be desired, particularly if the eventual user isn't comfortable in Python. Assuming that the applications were written portably *and* that the user had the correct version of Python installed, you could theoretically ship only the bytecode as .pyc files, but that is not recommended.

In fact, how best to distribute Python applications and manage their dependencies has been discussed a lot and various solutions have been (and continue to be) proposed. It's beyond our scope to even scratch the surface of the available options, so we'll stick with the basics.

11.4.1 *Wheels packages*

The current standard way of packaging and distributing Python modules and applications is to use packages called *wheels*. Wheels are designed to make installing Python code more reliable and to help manage dependencies. The details of how to create wheels are beyond the scope of this chapter, but full details about the requirements and the process for creating wheels are in the Python Packaging User Guide at https://packaging.python.org.

11.4.2 *zipapp and pex*

If you have an application that's in multiple modules, you can also distribute it as an executable zip file. This format relies on two facts about Python.

First, if a zip file contains a file named __main__.py, Python can use that file as the entry point to the archive and execute the __main__.py file directly. In addition, the zip file's contents are added to sys.path, so they're available to be imported and executed by __main__.py.

Second, zip files allow arbitrary contents to be added to the beginning of the archive. If you add a shebang line pointing to a Python interpreter, such as `#!/usr/bin/env python3`, and give the file the needed permissions, the file can become a self-contained executable.

In fact, it's not that difficult to manually create an executable `zipapp`. Create a zip file containing a __main__.py, add the shebang line to the beginning, and set the permissions.

Starting with Python 3.5, the `zipapp` module is included in the standard library; it can create `zipapps` either from the command line or via the library's API.

A more powerful tool, pex, isn't in the standard library but is available from the package index via pip. Pex does the same basic job but offers many more features and options, and it's available for Python 2.7, if needed. Either way, zip file apps are convenient ways to package and distribute multifile Python apps ready to run.

11.4.3 py2exe and py2app

Although it's not the purpose of this book to dwell on platform-specific tools, it's worth mentioning that py2exe creates standalone Windows programs and that py2app does the same on the macOS platform. By *standalone*, I mean that they're single executables that can run on machines that don't have Python installed. In many ways, standalone executables aren't ideal, because they tend to be larger and less flexible than native Python applications. But in some situations, they're the best—and sometimes the only—solution.

11.4.4 Creating executable programs with freeze

It's also possible to create an executable Python program that runs on machines that don't have Python installed by using the freeze tool. You'll find the instructions for this in the Readme file inside the freeze directory in the Tools subdirectory of the Python source directory. If you're planning to use freeze, you'll probably need to download the Python source distribution.

In the process of "freezing" a Python program, you create C files, which are then compiled and linked using a C compiler, which you need to have installed on your system. The frozen application will run only on the platform for which the C compiler you use provides its executables.

Several other tools try in one way or another to convert and package a Python interpreter/environment with an application in a standalone application. In general, however, this path is still difficult and complex, and you probably want to avoid it unless you have a strong need and the time and resources to make the process work.

11.5 Creating a program

In chapter 8, you created a version of the UNIX wc utility to count the lines, words, and characters in a file. Now that you have more tools at your disposal, refactor that program to make it work more like the original. In particular, the program should have options to show only lines (-l), only words (-w), and only characters (-c). If none of those options are given, all three stats are displayed. But if any of these options are present, only the specified stats are shown.

For an extra challenge, add the -L option to show the length of the longest line. You can test your version against the system's wc command on Colaboratory or a Linux/UNIX system. For help with wc and its options, use ! wc --help in Colaboratory,

11.5.1 Solving the problem with AI-generated code

We are refactoring our previous code in this lab, so we need to be sure that the chatbot session has access to that code. For Colaboratory, we can copy the code from chapter 8's lab into a cell in our current notebook. The Colaboratory and Copilot versions then were very similar, but there was a minor bug in the Colaboratory code, so we'll use the Copilot version as our starting point for both in this lab.

In addition to providing the code, we'll also need to make sure that the chatbot is told to mimic the Unix wc utility with the options -l, -w, -c, and -L. We can assume that the chatbot has access to an accurate description of the options for wc.

The prompt used for Colaboratory is

```
Refactor the code in the previous cell into a commandline program that
works like the Unix wc utility, and supports the -l, -w, and -c options,
and the -L option. Output should be similar to output of wc.
```

The Copilot prompt is put forth after selecting the same code, and then once the code is generated, it is saved to a new file:

```
efactor the selected code into a commandline program that works like the
Unix wc utility, and supports the -l, -w, and -c options, and the -L
option. Output should be similar to output of wc.
```

As we want the bot to create a new file, this prompt has to be entered into the full chat interface.

11.5.2 *Solutions and discussion*

The actual code for counting lines, words, and characters is the same as what we did before in chapter 8, but handling the options can get a bit tricky. In particular, for wc, if none of -l, -w, or -c are present, that means that all of the options should be selected, while -L must be explicitly selected whether the other options are there or not. Making this work will take some experimentation.

The other bit of new code that must be written is a way to find the length of the longest line. It's simplest to do this by checking and updating a variable as each line is read.

THE HUMAN SOLUTION

The biggest chunk of code in the human solution is spent in setting up the argparse parser object and then processing the options, while the actual processing of the file is fairly brief. In the course of making the code behave like wc, there are some Python idioms used in the following code that are worth noting:

```python
#!/usr/bin/env python3
# File: word_count_program.py
""" Reads a file and returns the number of lines, words,
    and characters - similar to the UNIX wc utility
"""
import sys
import argparse


def main():
    # initialze counts
```

```
        line_count = 0
        word_count = 0
        char_count = 0
        longest_line = 0

        parser = argparse.ArgumentParser(usage=__doc__)
        parser.add_argument("-c", "--characters",
                    action="store_true", dest="chars", default=False,
                    help="display number of characers")
        parser.add_argument("-w", "--words",
                    action="store_true", dest="words", default=False,
                    help="display number of words")
        parser.add_argument("-l", "--lines",
                    action="store_true", dest="lines", default=False,
                    help="display number of lines")
        parser.add_argument("-L", "--longest",
                    action="store_true", dest="longest", default=False,
                    help="display longest line length")
        parser.add_argument("filename", help="read data from this file")
        args = parser.parse_args()

        filename = args.filename      # open the file
        with open(filename) as infile:
            for line in infile:
                line_count += 1
                char_count += len(line)
                words = line.split()
                word_count += len(words)
                if len(line) > longest_line:          ◄─┐  longest_line updated if
                    longest_line = len(line)               current line is longer

        default_args = any([getattr(args, _) for _ in ('chars', 'words',
                            'lines', 'longest')])       ◄─┐
                                                           List comprehension to
                                                           get option values; any()
        if not default_args:                               sees if any are set.
            args.chars = args.lines = args.words = True  ◄─  Setting values
                                                             can be chained
        if args.lines:
            print(f"{line_count:3}", end=" ")      ◄─┐
        if args.words:
            print(f"{word_count:4}", end=" ")          Specifying widths for fields in
        if args.chars:                                 f-strings with : and specifying
            print(f"{char_count:4}", end=" ")          end to keep things on one line
        if args.longest:
            print(f'{longest_line}', end=" ")
        print(f'{filename}')
if __name__ == '__main__':
    main()
```

The first thing to touch upon is the setup of the `ArgumentParser`, `parser`. Note that all of the option arguments default to `False`, meaning that if nothing is specified for an option, nothing will be stored in the parser. This is important as we try to decide what gets printed. If there is an option specified, its value is printed, so that if one, two, three, or all of the options are specified on the command line, the corresponding values will be displayed.

The trick is in detecting the case where no options are given, meaning that the standard set of line count, word count, and character count should be displayed. This solution handles it in a Pythonic, way, but it may seem a bit tricky to people (and AI bots) new to Python—we use a list comprehension that includes calling the `getattr` function on the parser with each of the possible options: `'chars'`, `'words'`, `'lines'`, and `'longest'`. If nothing has been set on the command line, this will be a list of `False` values, so calling the `any` function on that list will also be `False`. On the other hand, if even one of those values is `True`, then `any` will also return `True`. The same result could also be achieved with a long `if` statement check using `or` several times but would be more cumbersome to read.

The second part of this feature is what the code does if the value in `default_args` is `False`. Note that all three of the variables are set on the same line, chaining three `=` operators. We can do that (and in fact it's reasonable Python style) because using the `=` operator gives a return value: it returns the value the variable is being set to. So each `=` operation returns `True` to set the variable to the left of the expression until they all are set.

Finally, as in the solution in chapter 8, this solution iterates through the file it's processing line by line, updating the values for all the stats each time. This is an approach I take almost automatically, since it's rarely noticeably slower and it handles files of any size. I've had to go back and switch to this approach enough times in the past that it's now second nature to me.

THE AI SOLUTIONS

This Colaboratory solution was one of four very similar options offered. This one was chosen because its output was closest to that of wc. It is worth noting, however, that "closest to" doesn't mean "correct," as we'll see:

```
# prompt: Refactor the code in the previous cell into a commandline program
#   that works like the Unix wc utility, and supports the -l, -w, and
#   -c options, and the -L option. Output should be similar to
output of wc.

#!/usr/bin/env python3

""" Reads a file and returns the number of lines, words,
    and characters - similar to the UNIX wc utility
"""

import argparse

def main():
    parser = argparse.ArgumentParser(usage=__doc__)
    parser.add_argument("filename", nargs='*')
    parser.add_argument("-l", "--lines", dest="lines",
                    action='store_true', default=False,
                    help="Show only line count")
```

```
parser.add_argument("-w", "--words", dest="words",
                    action='store_true', default=False,
                    help="Show only word count")
parser.add_argument("-c", "--chars", dest="chars",
                    action='store_true', default=False,
                    help="Show only character count")
parser.add_argument("-L", "--longest", dest="longest",
                    action='store_true', default=False,
                    help="Show length of longest line")
args = parser.parse_args()

for filename in args.filename:
    with open(filename) as infile:
        lines = infile.readlines()

    line_count = len(lines)
    word_count = sum(len(line.split()) for line in lines)
    char_count = sum(len(line) for line in lines)
    longest_line_length = max(len(line) for line in lines)

    if args.lines:
        print(f"{line_count} {filename}")
    elif args.words:
        print(f"{word_count} {filename}")
    elif args.chars:
        print(f"{char_count} {filename}")
    elif args.longest:
        print(f"{longest_line_length} {filename}")
    else:
        print(f"{line_count} {word_count} {char_count} {filename}")

if __name__ == '__main__':
    main()
```

This solution correctly creates an `ArgumentParser` and adds the needed options. It also maintains the choice in the original code (as discussed in the lab for chapter 8) to read the entire file into memory and then split the lines on the \n newline character. It can then use the length of the resulting list as the line count and use generator expressions to iterate through the list of lines to find the number of words and the longest line.

The drawback, as mentioned in chapter 8, is that the entire file must be read into memory, and during the life of the generator expression, a separate list of all the words also must exist in memory. This could be a problem if processing a very large file. The wc utility, on the other hand, doesn't have this limitation, nor does my solution.

The other flaw with this solution is that its output doesn't quite work the way the wc utility's does. The solution does add the filename after the numeric output, which is correct, and it also can handle any single option being selected, as well as no options being selected. But look at the if-elif-else setup. What happens if, say, both the -l and -w options are selected? That's right: only the line count is displayed, while for the wc utility, it would mean that both the line and word count would be shown.

The Copilot solution initially was less like the wc utility than Colaboratory version, but after giving it an extra prompt it ended up being the most faithful to the original.

To create a standalone file, rather than just rewrite some code in an existing file, we needed to use full chat interface in VS Code, as we did in the last chapter.

Before it started generating code, Copilot created the following plan and then generated the following code:

1 Import the `argparse` module to handle command-line arguments.
2 Define a function `count_stats` that takes a file path as input and returns the number of lines, words, and characters.
3 Create an `argparse.ArgumentParser` instance to handle the command-line arguments.
4 Add arguments for `-l`, `-w`, `-c`, and `-L` options. These arguments should be optional and default to `False`.
5 Add an argument for the file path.
6 Parse the arguments using `argparse.ArgumentParser.parse_args()`.
7 Call `count_stats` with the file path from the parsed arguments.
8 Depending on the options provided, print the number of lines, words, and characters.

```python
# wc.py

import argparse

def count_stats(file_path):
    with open(file_path) as infile:
        lines = infile.readlines()

    line_count = len(lines)
    word_count = sum(len(line.split()) for line in lines)
    char_count = sum(len(line) for line in lines)
    max_line_length = max(len(line) for line in lines)

    return line_count, word_count, char_count, max_line_length

def main():
    parser = argparse.ArgumentParser(description=
                        'Count lines, words, and characters in a file.')
    parser.add_argument('file', help='File to count')
    parser.add_argument('-l', '--lines', action='store_true',
                        help='Count lines')
    parser.add_argument('-w', '--words', action='store_true',
                        help='Count words')
    parser.add_argument('-c', '--chars', action='store_true',
                        help='Count characters')
    parser.add_argument('-L', '--max-line-length', action='store_true',
                        help='Print length of the longest line')
    args = parser.parse_args()

    line_count, word_count, char_count, max_line_length = count_stats(args.
     file)
```

```
    if args.lines:
        print(f'Lines: {line_count}')
    if args.words:
        print(f'Words: {word_count}')
    if args.chars:
        print(f'Characters: {char_count}')
    if args.max_line_length:
        print(f'Max line length: {max_line_length}')

if __name__ == '__main__':
    main()
```

The plan seems fine, although creating a separate function to do the processing isn't really necessary. However, there are some problems with this solution. First, the values are output on separate lines, unlike wc, and with labels describing what the values are. Also, a problem is that if no option is specified on the command line, nothing is output. This behavior isn't wrong as far as processing the text goes, but it isn't like wc, which is what we specified in the prompt.

Since it's easy to continue interaction in the chat interface, I asked for a correction with the following prompt:

```
The options and their output should be the same as the wc utility
```

This was specified in the original prompt, but maybe "similar to" gives it some room for variation, so this time "the same" output is specified. In response, Copilot came up with the following comment and a new plan.

The wc utility in Unix outputs the line, word, and byte counts by default, and the output is in a single line. The -l option outputs only the line count, -w outputs only the word count, -c outputs the byte count, and -L outputs the length of the longest line. If no option is provided, all counts are output.

The plan was

1 Modify the count_stats function to return the byte count instead of the character count.

2 Modify the main function to print the counts in a single line in the order: line count, word count, byte count, filename.

3 If the -l, -w, -c, or -L options are provided, print only the corresponding count.

4 If no option is provided, print all counts.

The commentary and the plan are much more correct this time and cover the requested options accurately. Copilot is correct that technically the -c option indicates that bytes, not characters, should be counted (depending on the encoding, some characters might take more than 1 byte), but leaving that aside, the more significant change is in how it handles what to output. In this it gets much closer to the actual output of the wc utility, and as it happens, it comes up with something similar to the human-based solution. Most of the code is unchanged, but here is what it came up with for the actual printing of the results:

```
if args.lines:
    print(line_count, end=' ')
if args.words:
    print(word_count, end=' ')
if args.bytes:
    print(byte_count, end=' ')
if args.max_line_length:
    print(max_line_length, end=' ')
if not any([args.lines, args.words, args.bytes, args.max_line_length]):
    print(f'{line_count} {word_count} {byte_count} {args.file}')
else:
    print(args.file)
```

As we can see, this code checks all of the parser options and prints the default if no option is specified. It also handles any combination of options correctly and prints only the values, with no labels. It also prints the filename correctly for all variations, although that may be a bit confusing to pick out the first time someone reads the code—printing the filename for the specified options is in the `else` statement for no options specified.

The good news is that both AI chatbots did know how the `wc` utility works, so there was no need go into great detail in the prompts. On the other hand, it did require some attention to go detail and specific prompts to get exactly the desired result.

Summary

- Python scripts and modules in their most basic form are just sequences of Python statements placed in a file.

- Modules can be instrumented to run as scripts, and scripts can be set up so that they can be imported as modules.

- Scripts can be made executable on the UNIX, macOS, or Windows command lines. They can be set up to support command-line redirection of their input and output, and with the `argparse` module, it's easy to parse out complex combinations of command-line arguments.

- On macOS, you can use the Python Launcher to run Python programs, either individually or as the default application for opening Python files.

- On Windows, you can call scripts in several ways: by opening them with a double-click, using the Run window, or using a command-prompt window.

- Python scripts can be distributed as scripts, as bytecode, or in special packages called wheels.

- `py2exe`, `py2app`, and the `freeze` tool provide an executable Python program that runs on machines that don't contain a Python interpreter.

Using the filesystem

12

This chapter covers

- Managing paths and pathnames
- Getting information about files
- Performing filesystem operations
- Processing all files in a directory subtree

Working with files involves one of two things: basic I/O (described in chapter 13) and working with the filesystem (for example, naming, creating, moving, or referring to files), which is a bit tricky, because different operating systems have different filesystem conventions.

Since we are assuming Google Colaboratory, which is hosted on Linux, as our default environment, most of the examples in this chapter will be based on Linux. It's quite possible, however, that you will want to write scripts that access files that run on other platforms, so we will include mention of how the same operations work on those platforms, particularly Windows, as needed.

It would be easy enough to learn how to perform basic file I/O without learning all the features Python has provided to simplify cross-platform filesystem interaction—but I wouldn't recommend it. Instead, read at least the first part of this chapter, which gives you the tools you need to refer to files in a manner that doesn't depend on your particular operating system. Then, when you use the basic I/O operations, you can open the relevant files in this manner.

12.1 os and os.path vs. pathlib

The traditional way that file paths and filesystem operations have been handled in Python is by using functions included in the `os` and `os.path` modules. These functions have worked well enough but often resulted in more verbose code than necessary. Since Python 3.5, a new library, `pathlib`, has been added; it offers a more object-oriented and unified way of doing the same operations. Because a lot of code out there still uses the older style, I've retained those examples and their explanations. On the other hand, `pathlib` has a lot going for it and is likely to become the new standard, so after each example of the old method, I include an example (and brief explanation, where necessary) of how the same thing would be done with `pathlib`.

12.2 Paths and pathnames

All operating systems refer to files and directories with strings naming a given file or directory. Strings used in this manner are usually called *pathnames* (or sometimes just *paths*), which is the word I'll use for them. The fact that pathnames are strings introduces possible complications to working with them. Python does a good job of providing functions that help avert these complications; but to use these Python functions effectively, you need to understand the underlying problems. This section discusses these details.

Pathname semantics across operating systems are very similar because the filesystem on almost all operating systems is modeled as a tree structure, with a disk being the root, and folders, subfolders, and so on being branches, subbranches, and so on. This means that most operating systems refer to a specific file in fundamentally the same manner: with a pathname that specifies the path to follow from the root of the filesystem tree (the disk) to the file in question. (This characterization of the root corresponding to a hard disk is an oversimplification, but it's close enough to the truth to serve for this chapter.) This pathname consists of a series of folders to descend into to get to the desired file.

Different operating systems have different conventions regarding the precise syntax of pathnames. The character used to separate sequential file or directory names in a Linux/UNIX pathname is /, whereas the character historically used to separate file or directory names in a Windows pathname is \. In addition, the UNIX filesystem has a single root (which is referred to by having a / character as the first character in a pathname), whereas the Windows filesystem has a separate root for each drive, labeled A:\, B:\, C:\, and so forth (with C: usually being the main drive). Because of these differences, files have different pathname representations on different operating systems. A file called C:\data\myfile in MS Windows might be called /data/myfile on UNIX and on the macOS. Python provides functions and constants that allow you to perform common pathname manipulations without worrying about such syntactic details. There are also differences in the way that the operating system treats upper- versus lowercase strings. In Linux and in some iOS file systems, case matters, so that file_a is not the same filename as File_A. Windows has traditionally ignored case differences. It's a good idea to keep this in mind and follow a convention of, for example, only using lowercase filenames to minimize confusion if your code needs to interact with files on different systems. With a little care, you can write your Python programs in such a manner that they'll run correctly no matter what the underlying filesystem happens to be.

12.2.1 *Absolute and relative paths*

Most operating systems allow two types of pathnames:

- *Absolute* pathnames specify the exact location of a file in a filesystem without any ambiguity; they do this by listing the entire path to that file, starting from the root of the filesystem.
- *Relative* pathnames specify the position of a file relative to some other point in the filesystem, and that other point isn't specified in the relative pathname itself; instead, the absolute starting point for relative pathnames is provided by the context in which they're used.

As examples, here are two Windows absolute pathnames:

```
C:\Program Files\Doom
D:\backup\June
```

Here are two Linux absolute pathnames and a Mac absolute pathname:

```
/bin/Doom
/floppy/backup/June
/Applications/Utilities
```

Here are two Windows relative pathnames:

```
mydata\project1\readme.txt
games\tetris
```

These are Linux/UNIX/Mac relative pathnames:

```
mydata/project1/readme.txt
games/tetris
Utilities/Java
```

Relative paths need context to anchor them. This context is typically provided in one of two ways.

The simpler way is to append the relative path to an existing absolute path, producing a new absolute path. You might have a relative Windows path, Start Menu\Programs\ Startup, and an absolute path, C:\Users\Administrator. By appending the two, you have a new absolute path: C:\Users\Administrator\Start Menu\Programs\Startup, which refers to a specific location in the filesystem. By appending the same relative path to a different absolute path (say, C:\Users\myuser), you produce a path that refers to the Startup folder in a different user's (myuser's) Profiles directory.

The second way in which relative paths may obtain a context is via an implicit reference to the *current working directory*, which is the particular directory where a Python program considers itself to be at any point during its execution. Python commands may implicitly make use of the current working directory when they're given a relative path as an argument. If you use the `os.listdir(path)` command with a relative path argument, for example, the anchor for that relative path is the current working directory, and the result of the command is a list of the filenames in the directory whose path is formed by appending the current working directory with the relative path argument.

12.2.2 *The current working directory*

Whenever you edit a document on a computer, you have a concept of where you are in that computer's file structure because you're in the same directory (folder) as the file you're working on. Similarly, whenever Python is running, it has a concept of where in the directory structure it is at any moment. This fact is important because the program may ask for a list of files stored in the current directory. The directory that a Python program is in is called the *current working directory* for that program. This directory may be different from the directory the program resides in.

To see this in action, start Python and use the `os.getcwd` (get current working directory) command to find Python's initial current working directory:

```
import os
os.getcwd()
```

```
'/content'
```

Note that `os.getcwd` is used as a zero-argument function call, to emphasize the fact that the value it returns isn't a constant but will change as you put forth commands that alter the value of the current working directory. (That directory probably will be `'/content'` in Colaboratory, or the directory the Python program itself resides in, or the directory you were in when you started Python. On Windows machines, you'll see extra backslashes inserted into the path because Windows uses \ as its path separator, and in Python strings (as discussed in section 6.3.1), \ has a special meaning unless it is itself backslashed.

Now type

```
os.listdir(os.curdir)
```

```
['.config', 'sample_data']
```

The constant `os.curdir` returns a string reflecting whatever the current directory is. On both UNIX and Windows, the current directory is represented as a single dot, but to keep your programs portable, you should always use `os.curdir` instead of typing just the dot. This string is a relative path, meaning that `os.listdir` appends it to the path for the current working directory, giving the same path. This command returns a list of all the files or folders inside the current working directory (on Colaboratory, it should be the list shown earlier). To look at the folder `'sample_data'`, type

```
os.chdir('sample_data')        ◄──────┐  "Change directory" function
os.getcwd()
```

As you can see, Python moves into the folder specified as the argument of the `os.chdir` function. Another call to `os.listdir(os.curdir)` would return a list of files in the folder `'sample_data'`, because `os.curdir` would then be taken relative to the new current working directory. Many Python filesystem operations use the current working directory in this manner.

12.2.3 *Accessing directories with pathlib*

To get the current directory with `pathlib`, you could do the following:

```
import pathlib
cur_path = pathlib.Path()
cur_path.cwd()
```

PosixPath('/content/sample_data')

There's no way for `pathlib` to change the current directory in the way that `os.chdir()` does (see the preceding section), since a path is by definition a specific directory location. However, you can work with a new folder by creating a new path object, as discussed in section 12.2.5.

12.2.4 *Manipulating pathnames*

Now that you have the background to understand file and directory pathnames, it's time to look at the facilities Python provides for manipulating these pathnames. These facilities consist of several functions and constants in the `os.path` submodule, which you can use to manipulate paths without explicitly using any operating-system-specific syntax. Paths are still represented as strings, but you need never think of them or manipulate them as such.

To start, construct a few pathnames on different operating systems using the `os` `.path.join` function. Note that importing `os` is sufficient to bring in the `os.path` submodule also; there's no need for an explicit `import os.path` statement.

In our notebook, we can do something like this:

```
import os
print(os.path.join('bin', 'utils', 'disktools'))
```

bin/utils/disktools

The os.path.join function interprets its arguments as a series of directory names or filenames, which are to be joined to form a single string understandable as a relative path by the underlying operating system. In a Windows system, that means path component names would be joined with backslashes. In other words, os.path.join lets you form file paths from a sequence of directory or filenames without any worry about the conventions of the underlying operating system. os.path.join is the fundamental way by which file paths may be built in a manner that doesn't constrain the operating systems on which your program will run.

The arguments to os.path.join need not be a single directory or filename; they may also be subpaths that are then joined to make a longer pathname. The following example illustrates this in the Windows environment and is also a case in which you'd find it necessary to use double backslashes in your strings. Note that you could enter the pathname with forward slashes (/) as well, because Python converts them before accessing the Windows operating system:

```
import os
print(os.path.join('mydir\\bin', 'utils\\disktools\\chkdisk'))
```

mydir\bin\utils\disktools\chkdisk

If you always use os.path.join to build up your paths, of course, you'll rarely need to worry about this situation. To write this example in a portable manner, you could enter

```
path1 = os.path.join('mydir', 'bin')
path2 = os.path.join('utils', 'disktools', 'chkdisk')
print(os.path.join(path1, path2))
```

mydir\bin\utils\disktools\chkdisk ◄————┐ **On a Windows system**

This will work also work correctly on a Linux/Unix-based system:

mydir/bin/utils/disktools/chkdisk ◄————┐ **On a Linux system**

The os.path.join command also has some understanding of absolute versus relative pathnames. In Linux/UNIX, an *absolute* path always begins with a / (because a single slash denotes the topmost directory of the entire system, which contains everything else, including the various other drives that might be available). A *relative* path in UNIX is any legal path that does *not* begin with a slash. Under any of the Windows operating systems, the situation is more complicated because the way in which Windows handles relative and absolute paths is messier. Rather than go into all of the details, I'll just say that the best way to handle this situation is to work with the following simplified rules for Windows paths:

- A pathname beginning with a drive letter followed by a colon and a backslash and then a path is an absolute path: C:\Program Files\Doom. (Note that C: by itself, without a trailing backslash, can't reliably be used to refer to the top-level directory on the C: drive. You must use C:\ to refer to the top-level directory on C:. This requirement is a result of DOS conventions, not Python design.)

- A pathname beginning with neither a drive letter nor a backslash is a relative path: mydirectory\letters\business.

- A pathname beginning with \\ followed by the name of a server is the path to a network resource.

- Anything else can be considered to be an invalid pathname.

Regardless of the operating system used, the os.path.join command doesn't perform sanity checks on the names it's constructing. It's possible to construct pathnames containing characters that, according to your OS, are forbidden in pathnames. If such checks are a requirement, probably the best solution is to write a small path-validity-checker function yourself.

The os.path.split command returns a two-element tuple splitting the basename of a path (the single file or directory name at the end of the path) from the rest of the path. You might use this example on a Windows system:

```
import os
print(os.path.split(os.path.join('some', 'directory', 'path')))
```

```
('some/directory', 'path')
```

The os.path.basename function returns only the basename of the path, and the os .path.dirname function returns the path up to but not including the last name, as in this example:

```
import os
os.path.basename(os.path.join('some', 'directory', 'path.jpg'))
```

```
'path.jpg'
```

```
os.path.dirname(os.path.join('some', 'directory', 'path.jpg'))
```

```
'some/directory'
```

To handle the dotted extension notation used by most filesystems to indicate file type (the Mac is a notable exception), Python provides os.path.splitext:

```
os.path.splitext(os.path.join('some', 'directory', 'path.jpg'))
```

```
('some/directory/path', '.jpg')
```

The last element of the returned tuple contains the dotted extension of the indicated file (if there was a dotted extension). The first element of the returned tuple contains everything from the original argument except the dotted extension.

You can also use more specialized functions to manipulate pathnames. os.path .commonprefix(path1, path2, ...) finds the common prefix (if any) for a set of paths.

This technique is useful if you want to find the lowest-level directory that contains every file in a set of files. `os.path.expanduser` expands username shortcuts in paths, such as for UNIX. Similarly, `os.path.expandvars` does the same for environment variables. Here's an example on a Windows system:

```
import os
os.path.expandvars('$HOME\\temp')
```

'C:\\Users\\administrator\\personal\\temp'

12.2.5 *Manipulating pathnames with pathlib*

Just as you did in the preceding section, let's start by constructing a few pathnames on different operating systems, using the path object's methods.

First, start Python under Windows:

```
from pathlib import Path
cur_path = Path()
print(cur_path.joinpath('bin', 'utils', 'disktools'))
```

bin/utils/disktools

The same result can be achieved by using the slash operator:

```
cur_path / 'bin' / 'utils' / 'disktools'
```

PosixPath('bin/utils/disktools')

Note that in the representation of the path object, forward slashes are always used, but Windows path objects have the forward slashes converted to backslashes as required by the OS. So if you try the same thing in UNIX

```
cur_path = Path()
print(cur_path.joinpath('bin', 'utils', 'disktools'))
```

bin/utils/disktools

the `parts` property returns a tuple of all the components of a path. For example:

```
a_path = Path('bin/utils/disktools')
print(a_path.parts)
```

('bin', 'utils', 'disktools')

The `name` property returns only the basename of the path, the `parent` property returns the path up to but not including the last name, and the `suffix` property handles the dotted extension notation used by most filesystems to indicate file type (but the Mac is a notable exception). Here's an example:

```
a_path = Path('some', 'directory', 'path.jpg')
a_path.name
```

'path.jpg'

```
print(a_path.parent)
```

some/directory

```
a_path.suffix
```

'.jpg'

Several other methods associated with `Path` objects allow flexible manipulation of both pathnames and files themselves, so you should review the documentation of the `pathlib` module. It's likely that the `pathlib` module will make your life easier and your file-handling code more concise.

12.2.6 *Useful constants and functions*

You can access several useful path-related constants and functions to make your Python code more system independent than it otherwise would be. The most basic of these constants are `os.curdir` and `os.pardir`, which respectively define the symbol used by the operating system for the directory and parent directory path indicators. In Windows as well as Linux/UNIX and macOS, these indicators are `.` and `..`, respectively, and they can be used as normal path elements. This example

```
os.path.isabs(os.path.join(os.pardir, path))
```

asks whether the parent of the parent of `path` is a directory. `os.curdir` is particularly useful for requesting commands on the current working directory. This example

```
os.listdir(os.curdir)
```

returns a list of filenames in the current working directory (because `os.curdir` is a relative path, and `os.listdir` always takes relative paths as being relative to the current working directory).

The `os.name` constant returns the name of the Python module imported to handle the operating system–specific details. Here's an example on Colaboratory:

```
import os
os.name
```

'posix'

Colaboratory, being hosted on Linux, returns `'posix'`. Note that on Windows, `os.name` returns `'nt'` even though the actual version of Windows could be Windows 10 or 11. Most versions of Windows are identified as `'nt'`.

On a Mac running macOS and on Linux/UNIX, the response is `posix`. You can use this response to perform special operations, depending on the platform you're working on:

```python
import os
if os.name == 'posix':
    root_dir = "/"
elif os.name == 'nt':
    root_dir = "C:\\"
else:
    print("Don't understand this operating system!")
```

The only other possible value for `os.name` as of this writing is `'java'`, which is returned by Jython (Python running on a Java virtual machine).

You may also see programs use `sys.platform`, which gives more exact information. Even on Windows 11, `sys.platform` is set to `win32`—even though the machine is running the 64-bit version of the operating system. On Linux, you will see `linux`, whereas on macOS it will be `darwin`. There have been changes to the list of possible values as platforms come and go, but you can always find the complete list of possible values in the documentation for `sys.platform`.

All your environment variables and the values associated with them are available in a dictionary called `os.environ`. On most operating systems, this dictionary includes variables related to paths—typically, search paths for binaries and so forth.

At this point, you've received an introduction to the major aspects of working with pathnames in Python. While you now know enough to open files for reading or writing, the rest of the chapter will give you further information about pathnames, testing what they point to, useful constants, and so forth.

> ### Quick check: Manipulating paths
>
> How would you use the `os` module's functions to take a path to a file called test.log and create a new file path in the same directory for a file called test.log.old? How would you do the same thing using the `pathlib` module?
>
> What path would you get if you created a pathlib `Path` object from `os.pardir`? Try it and find out.

12.3 Getting information about files

File paths are supposed to indicate actual files and directories on your hard drive. You're probably passing a path around, of course, because you want to know something about the file or directory it points to. Various Python functions are available for this purpose.

The most commonly used Python path-information functions are `os.path.exists`, `os.path.isfile`, and `os.path.isdir`, all of which take a single path as an argument.

os.path.exists returns True if its argument is a path corresponding to something that exists in the filesystem. os.path.isfile returns True if and only if the path it's given indicates a normal data file of some sort (executables fall under this heading), and it returns False otherwise, including the possibility that the path argument doesn't indicate anything in the filesystem. os.path.isdir returns True if and only if its path argument indicates a directory; it returns False otherwise. These examples are valid on my system. You may need to use different paths on yours to investigate the behavior of these functions:

```
import os
os.path.exists('/content/sample_data/')
```

True

```
os.path.exists('/content/sample_data/README.md')
```

True

```
os.path.exists('/content/sample_data/ljsljkflkjs')
```

False

```
os.path.isdir('/content/sample_data/')
```

True

```
os.path.isdir('/content/sample_data/README.md')
```

False

```
os.path.isfile('/content/sample_data/README.md')
```

True

Several similar functions provide more specialized queries. os.path.islink and os.path.ismount are useful in the context of Linux and other UNIX operating systems that provide file links and mount points; they return True if, respectively, a path indicates a file that's a link or a mount point. os.path.islink does *not* return True on Windows shortcuts files (files ending with .lnk), for the simple reason that such files aren't true links. However, os.path.islink returns True on Windows systems for true symbolic links created with the mklink() command. The OS doesn't assign them a special status, and programs can't transparently use them as though they were the actual file. os.path.samefile(path1, path2) returns True if and only if the two path arguments point to the same file. os.path.isabs(path) returns True if its argument is an absolute path; it returns False otherwise. os.path.getsize(path), os.path.getmtime(path), and os.path.getatime(path) return the size, last modify time, and last access time of a pathname, respectively.

If you want to use Path objects, there are methods that have names and functionality similar to the os functions mentioned earlier.

12.3.1 Getting information about files with scandir

In addition to the `os.path` functions listed, you can get more complete information about the files in a directory by using `os.scandir`, which returns an iterator of `os.DirEntry` objects. `os.DirEntry` objects expose the file attributes of a directory entry, so using `os.scandir` can be faster and more efficient than combining `os.listdir` (discussed in the next section) with the `os.path` operations. If, for example, you need to know whether the entry refers to a file or directory, `os.scandir`'s ability to access more directory information than just the name will be a plus. `os.DirEntry` objects have methods that correspond to the `os.path` functions mentioned in the previous section, including `exists`, `is_dir`, `is_file`, `is_socket`, and `is_symlink`.

`os.scandir` also supports a context manager using `with`, and using one is recommended to ensure resources are properly disposed of. This example code iterates over all of the entries in a directory and prints both the name of the entry and whether it's a file:

```
with os.scandir("..") as my_dir:
    for entry in my_dir:
        print(entry.name, entry.is_file())
```

```
.config False
sample_data False
```

12.4 More filesystem operations

In addition to obtaining information about files, Python lets you perform certain filesystem operations directly through a set of basic but highly useful commands in the `os` module.

I describe only those true cross-platform operations in this section. These commands (and the versions of them that `pathlib` supports, as discussed later) not only work on Windows, iOS, and Linux but also work just fine on the filesystem in Colaboratory (which is Linux). Many operating systems have access to more advanced filesystem functions, and you need to check the main Python library documentation for the details.

You've already seen that, to obtain a list of files in a directory, you use `os.listdir`:

```
os.chdir('/content/sample_data')
os.listdir(os.curdir)
```

```
['anscombe.json',
 'README.md',
 'california_housing_train.csv',
 'california_housing_test.csv',
 'mnist_test.csv',
 'mnist_train_small.csv']
```

Note that unlike the list-directory command in many other languages or shells, Python does *not* include the `os.curdir` and `os.pardir` indicators in the list returned by `os.listdir`.

The glob function from the glob module (named after an old UNIX function that did pattern matching) expands Linux/UNIX shell-style wildcard characters and character sequences in a pathname, returning the files in the current working directory that match. A * matches any sequence of characters. A ? matches any single character. A character sequence ([h,H] or [0-9]) matches any single character in that sequence:

```
import glob
glob.glob("*")

['anscombe.json',
 'README.md',
 'california_housing_train.csv',
 'california_housing_test.csv',
 'mnist_test.csv',
 'mnist_train_small.csv']

glob.glob("*json")

['anscombe.json']

glob.glob("?.tmp")

['1.tmp', '2.tmp', 'a.tmp']

glob.glob("[0-9].tmp")

['1.tmp', '2.tmp']
```

To rename (move) a file or directory, use os.rename:

```
os.rename('README.md', 'README.md.old')
os.listdir(os.curdir)

['anscombe.json',
 'README.md.old',
 '1.tmp',
 '2.tmp',
 'a.tmp',
 'california_housing_train.csv',
 'california_housing_test.csv',
 'mnist_test.csv',
 'mnist_train_small.csv']
```

You can use this command to move files across directories as well as within directories.

Remove or delete a data file with os.remove:

```
os.remove('a.tmp')
os.listdir(os.curdir)

['anscombe.json',
 'README.md.old',
 '1.tmp',
 '2.tmp',
```

```
'california_housing_train.csv',
'california_housing_test.csv',
'mnist_test.csv',
'mnist_train_small.csv']
```

Note that you can't use os.remove to delete directories. This restriction is a safety feature, to ensure that you don't accidentally delete an entire directory substructure.

Files can be created by writing to them, as discussed in chapter 11. To create a directory, use os.makedirs or os.mkdir. The difference between them is that os.mkdir doesn't create any necessary intermediate directories, but os.makedirs does:

```
os.makedirs('mydir')
os.listdir(os.curdir)
```

```
['anscombe.json',
 'README.md.old',
 'mydir',
 '1.tmp',
 '2.tmp',
 'california_housing_train.csv',
 'california_housing_test.csv',
 'mnist_test.csv',
 'mnist_train_small.csv']
```

```
os.path.isdir('mydir')
```

True

To remove a directory, use os.rmdir. This function removes only empty directories. Attempting to use it on a nonempty directory raises an exception:

```
os.rmdir('mydir')
os.listdir(os.curdir)
```

```
['anscombe.json',
 'README.md.old',
 '1.tmp',
 '2.tmp',
 'california_housing_train.csv',
 'california_housing_test.csv',
 'mnist_test.csv',
 'mnist_train_small.csv']
```

To remove nonempty directories, use the shutil.rmtree function. It recursively removes all files in a directory tree. See the Python standard library documentation for details on its use.

12.4.1 *More filesystem operations with pathlib*

Path objects have most of the same methods mentioned earlier. Some differences exist, however. The iterdir method is similar to the os.path.listdir function except that it returns an iterator of paths rather than a list of strings:

```
new_path = cur_path.joinpath('/content', 'sample_data')
list(new_path.iterdir())
```

```
[PosixPath('/content/sample_data/anscombe.json'),
 PosixPath('/content/sample_data/.ipynb_checkpoints'),
 PosixPath('/content/sample_data/README.md.old'),
 PosixPath('/content/sample_data/1.tmp'),
 PosixPath('/content/sample_data/2.tmp'),
 PosixPath('/content/sample_data/california_housing_train.csv'),
 PosixPath('/content/sample_data/california_housing_test.csv'),
 PosixPath('/content/sample_data/mnist_test.csv'),
 PosixPath('/content/sample_data/mnist_train_small.csv')]
```

Note that in a Windows environment, the paths returned are `WindowsPath` objects, whereas on macOS or Linux, they're `PosixPath` objects.

`pathlib` path objects also have a `glob` method built in, which again returns not a list of strings but an iterator of path objects. Otherwise, this function behaves very much like the `glob.glob` function demonstrated previously:

```
list(cur_path.glob("*"))
```

```
[PosixPath('anscombe.json'),
 PosixPath('.ipynb_checkpoints'),
 PosixPath('README.md.old'),
 PosixPath('1.tmp'),
 PosixPath('2.tmp'),
 PosixPath('california_housing_train.csv'),
 PosixPath('california_housing_test.csv'),
 PosixPath('mnist_test.csv'),
 PosixPath('mnist_train_small.csv')]
```

```
list(cur_path.glob("*json"))
```

```
[PosixPath('anscombe.json')]
```

```
list(cur_path.glob("?.tmp"))
```

```
[PosixPath('1.tmp'), PosixPath('2.tmp')]
```

```
list(cur_path.glob("[0-9].tmp"))
```

```
[PosixPath('1.tmp'), PosixPath('2.tmp')]
```

To rename (move) a file or directory, use the path object's `rename` method:

```
old_path = Path('README.md.old')
new_path = Path('README.md')
old_path.rename(new_path)
list(cur_path.iterdir())
```

```
[PosixPath('anscombe.json'),
 PosixPath('README.md'),
 PosixPath('.ipynb_checkpoints'),
```

```
  PosixPath('1.tmp'),
  PosixPath('2.tmp'),
  PosixPath('california_housing_train.csv'),
  PosixPath('california_housing_test.csv'),
  PosixPath('mnist_test.csv'),
  PosixPath('mnist_train_small.csv')]
```

You can use this command to move files across directories as well as within directories.

To remove or delete a data file, you can use `unlink`:

```
new_path = Path('1.tmp')
new_path.unlink()
list(cur_path.iterdir())
```

```
[PosixPath('anscombe.json'),
 PosixPath('README.md'),
 PosixPath('.ipynb_checkpoints'),
 PosixPath('2.tmp'),
 PosixPath('california_housing_train.csv'),
 PosixPath('california_housing_test.csv'),
 PosixPath('mnist_test.csv'),
 PosixPath('mnist_train_small.csv')]
```

Note that, as with `os.remove`, you can't use the `unlink` method to delete directories. This restriction is a safety feature, to ensure that you don't accidentally delete an entire directory substructure.

To create a directory by using a path object, use the path object's `mkdir` method. If you give the `mkdir` method a `parents=True` parameter, it creates any necessary intermediate directories; otherwise, it raises a `FileNotFoundError` if an intermediate directory isn't there:

```
new_path = Path ('mydir')
new_path.mkdir(parents=True)
list(cur_path.iterdir())
```

```
[PosixPath('anscombe.json'),
 PosixPath('README.md'),
 PosixPath('.ipynb_checkpoints'),
 PosixPath('mydir'),
 PosixPath('2.tmp'),
 PosixPath('california_housing_train.csv'),
 PosixPath('california_housing_test.csv'),
 PosixPath('mnist_test.csv'),
 PosixPath('mnist_train_small.csv')]
```

```
new_path.is_dir()
```

```
True
```

To remove a directory, use the `rmdir` method. This method removes only empty directories. Attempting to use it on a nonempty directory raises an exception:

```
new_path = Path('mydir')
new_path.rmdir()
list(cur_path.iterdir())

[PosixPath('anscombe.json'),
 PosixPath('README.md'),
 PosixPath('.ipynb_checkpoints'),
 PosixPath('2.tmp'),
 PosixPath('california_housing_train.csv'),
 PosixPath('california_housing_test.csv'),
 PosixPath('mnist_test.csv'),
 PosixPath('mnist_train_small.csv')]
```

As you can see from the previous examples, `Path` objects are a bit different from the functions offered by the `os` library. It's important to remember that `Path` objects are objects, each of which represents a particular path or location on your system, while the `os` functions are designed to operate on any path or directory location.

12.5   *Processing all files in a directory subtree*

Finally, a highly useful function for traversing recursive directory structures is the `os.walk` function. You can use it to walk through an entire directory tree, returning three things for each directory it traverses: the root, or path, of that directory; a list of its subdirectories; and a list of its files.

`os.walk` is called with the path of the starting, or top, directory and can have three optional arguments: `os.walk(directory, topdown=True, onerror=None, followlinks=False)`. `directory` is a starting directory path; if `topdown` is `True` or not present, the files in each directory are processed *before* its subdirectories, resulting in a listing that starts at the top and goes down; whereas if `topdown` is `False`, the subdirectories of each directory are processed *first*, giving a bottom-up traversal of the tree. The `onerror` parameter can be set to a function to handle any errors that result from calls to `os.listdir`, which are ignored by default. `os.walk` by default doesn't walk down into folders that are symbolic links unless you give it the `followlinks=True` parameter.

When called, `os.walk` creates an iterator that recursively applies itself to all the directories contained in the `top` parameter. In other words, for each subdirectory *subdir* in `names`, `os.walk` recursively invokes a call to itself, of the form `os.walk(subdir, ...)`. Note that if `topdown` is `True` or not given, the list of subdirectories may be modified (using any of the list-modification operators or methods) before its items are used for the next level of recursion; you can use this to control into which—if any— subdirectories `os.walk` will descend.

To get a feel for `os.walk`, I recommend iterating over the tree and printing out the values returned for each directory. As an example of the power of `os.walk`, list the current working directory and all of its subdirectories along with a count of the number of entries in each of them but without listing the contents of any .config directories:

```
import os
for root, dirs, files in os.walk(os.curdir):
```

```
print("{0} has {1} files".format(root, len(files)))
if ".config" in dirs:
    dirs.remove(".config")
```

Checks for directory named .config

Removes .config (only the .config directory) from directory list

This example is complex, and if you want to use os.walk to its fullest extent, you should probably play around with it quite a bit to understand the details of what's going on.

The copytree function of the shutil module recursively makes copies of all the files in a directory and all of its subdirectories, preserving permission mode and stat (that is, access/modify times) information. shutil also has the already mentioned rmtree function for removing a directory and all of its subdirectories, as well as several functions for making copies of individual files. See the standard library documentation for details.

12.6 *More file operations*

How might you calculate the total size of all files ending with .test that aren't symlinks in a directory? If your first answer was using os and os.path, also try it with pathlib, and vice versa.

Write some code that builds off your solution and moves the .test files detected previously to a new subdirectory in the same directory called "backup."

Note that you will need to be sure you have at least some files ending in .test in your starting directory and its subdirectories. In Colaboratory, just be sure to execute the cell right before the answers.

12.6.1 *Solving the problem with AI-generated code*

This exercise calls for a bit more original thinking—while the first part of the problem is not that complex, it requires combining several elements of either the os or the pathlib libraries to achieve a working solution, which is then built upon for the full solution. Since there are two libraries that can be used to accomplish the task, it's good experience to modify your solution to use the other library.

The prompts for Copilot are

```
Write a Python script to calculate the total size of all files with a .test
extension that are not symlinks in the current directory and
subdirectories.
```

To add moving the files to a backup directory:

```
Modify that script to also move the files with a .test extension to a
subdirectory of the current directory called backup
```

And to refactor to use pathlib:

```
Refactor the previous script using the pathlib library instead of os and
shutil
```

The prompts for Colaboratory are the same, with the addition "in the previous cell" for the two refactorings.

12.6.2 Solutions and discussion

While the scripts created in this lab are fairly short, they are also fairly dense in that they require several different elements of the libraries, and those elements must be combined in specific ways.

THE HUMAN SOLUTION

My first solution uses `pathlib`, since treating paths as objects makes for clearer, more coherent code in my opinion. The first part of the task, getting the total size of all .test files, is fairly straightforward, thanks to the various methods of the `Path` class:

```
import pathlib
cur_path = pathlib.Path("sample_data")

size = 0
for text_path in cur_path.rglob("*.test"):
    if not text_path.is_symlink():
        size += text_path.stat().st_size

print(size)
```

Finds all files with names ending in .test

Makes sure they are not symlinks

Gets size and adds total

There are three things that this code needs to do—find the target files, which the `glob` method does; check to see if they are symlinks, which is handled by a specific method; and get the size via the `stat()` method and add it to the total size. Having all of those methods be part of the `Path` object for the current directory makes the code concise and clear.

The next task is to refactor that code so that, in addition to finding the target files and totaling up their size, we move those files to a subdirectory called "backup":

```
import pathlib
cur_path = pathlib.Path("sample_data")
new_path = pathlib.Path("backup")
new_path.mkdir(exist_ok=True)

size = 0
for text_path in cur_path.rglob("*.test"):
    if not text_path.is_symlink():
        size += text_path.stat().st_size
        text_path.rename(new_path / text_path.name)

print(size)
```

Creates backup directory if needed

Moves to new directory by renaming

The first modification is that we need to be sure that the "backup" directory exists. That means that we need a `Path` object for the "backup" directory. We can then use that object to create the actual directory on disk only if it doesn't already exist. The `exist_ok=True` parameter makes sure that a directory is created if it doesn't exist but that no exception is raised if the directory already exists.

The other necessary operation is to actually move the file. In the Unix tradition, we can move a file by changing the name of its location. So, in this case, we can take the current file's path and add our backup directory path to its beginning and tell the file's path to rename itself to the new value. The use of "rename" to move something may seem odd, but keep in mind that the actual location of the bytes on the disk does not move, just the way we refer to its location, which we are in effect giving a new name.

The last part of the exercise is to refactor our solution to use the other library's approach. Since I started with `pathlib`, it's now time to use the `os` library. Normally I would probably just refactor the final answer, but to keep things clear and consistent, I've done it in the same two steps—first just getting the total size and then creating a version to move the files:

```
import os
cur_path = "."

size = 0
for root, dirs, files in os.walk(os.curdir):          ◄──  Visits all directories
    for file in files:                                 ◄──  Checks for files ending in .test and
        test_path = os.path.join(root, file)                makes sure they are not symlinks

        if (not os.path.islink(test_path) and
            os.path.splitext(test_path)[-1] == ''):    ◄──  Gets size and adds total
            print(os.path.join(root, file))
            size += os.path.getsize(test_path)
print(f"{size}")
```

This solution uses `os.walk` to get all of the files in the directory and its subdirectories, and it's clearly a bit more cumbersome and harder to understand. The main loop uses `os.walk` to get each directory and uses that directory recursively as the root directory until we have visited every directory under the current directory. For each directory, we need to check to make sure that the file is not a symlink and that it ends with .test. If so, we can get its size and add that to our total.

The refactor to move the target files requires similar changes to the `pathlib` version, except that we don't have `pathlib`'s / operator to join parts of pathnames:

```
import os

cur_path = "."
new_path = os.path.join(cur_path,"backup")

# create backup directory
os.makedirs(new_path, exist_ok=True)              ◄──  Creates backup
size = 0                                                directory if needed
for root, dirs, files in os.walk(os.curdir):
    for file in files:
        test_path = os.path.join(root, file)
        print(test_path)
```

```
            if (not os.path.islink(test_path)
              and os.path.splitext(test_path)[-1] == ".test"):
                print(os.path.join(root, file))
                size += os.path.getsize(test_path)
                os.rename(test_path, os.path.join(new_path,      ◄──┐ Moves to new
                    os.path.basename(test_path)))  ◄───────────────┘ directory by renaming
print(f"{size}")
```

The changes to move the files are similar to those used with `Path` objects, but the code is a bit longer and to my mind definitely harder to read. Still, if you have a definite preference, it's just fine to use this approach. While the Zen of Python says, "there should be one—and preferably only one—obvious way to do it," in this case, as the language has developed, there are two perfectly fine ways to do file operations of this type.

THE AI SOLUTIONS

Solving the problem with AI proved a little bit more involved. As mentioned earlier, the prompt for the first part of the problem is

```
Write a Python script to calculate the total size of all files with an
extension that are not symlinks in the current directory and
subdirectories.
```

In response, Copilot offered the following plan for the first part:

1. Import the `os` module.
2. Initialize a variable `size` to 0.
3. Use `os.walk` to iterate over all files in the current directory and its subdirectories.
4. For each file, check if it is not a symlink using `os.path.islink`.
5. If it is not a symlink, check if its extension is .test using `os.path.splitext`.
6. If its extension is .test, add its size to `size` using `os.path.getsize`.
7. After the loop, print `size`.

This is a nicely detailed plan of the steps involved in solving the problem, and it's quite handy to see what the bot is going to do:

```
# txt_file_size.py

import os

size = 0
for root, dirs, files in os.walk(os.curdir):
    for file in files:
        file_path = os.path.join(root, file)
        if (not os.path.islink(file_path)
            and os.path.splitext(file)[1] == '.test'):
            size += os.path.getsize(file_path)

print(f"Total size of all  files that are not symlinks: {size} bytes")
```

For the second part, this is the prompt:

```
Modify that script to also move the files with a .test extension to an
subdirectory of the current directory called backup
```

Copilot answered with the following plan:

1 Import the os and shutil modules.

2 Initialize a variable size to 0.

3 Create a directory named backup in the current directory using os.makedirs, if it doesn't already exist.

4 Use os.walk to iterate over all files in the current directory and its subdirectories.

5 For each file, check if it is not a symlink using os.path.islink.

6 If it is not a symlink, check if its extension is .test using os.path.splitext.

7 If its extension is .test, add its size to size using os.path.getsize.

8 Move the file to the backup directory using shutil.move.

9 After the loop, print size.

The code that resulted was straightforward and not that different from my solution:

```python
# txt_file_size_and_move.py

import os
import shutil

size = 0
os.makedirs('backup', exist_ok=True)
for root, dirs, files in os.walk(os.curdir):
    for file in files:
        file_path = os.path.join(root, file)
        if (not os.path.islink(file_path)
                and os.path.splitext(file)[1] == '.test'
                and "backup" not in file_path):
            size += os.path.getsize(file_path)
            shutil.move(file_path, 'backup')

print(f"Total size of all .test files that are not symlinks: {size} bytes")
```

The only thing that is really different from the human solution is the use of the shutil library to move the target files. This is certainly an acceptable way to do it, but it ignores the fact that os.rename can do the same job without importing another library. My personal preference would be to import as few libraries as possible. In this example, it's not hard to keep track of what's going on, but as projects grow, they often end up with more and more imports, which can make things harder to parse. In my opinion, the best way to keep that from happening is to be slow to add imports.

The next and final step is to refactor the code to use the other option—in this case, to use pathlib instead of os and shutil. The prompt used for this is

Refactor the previous script using the pathlib library instead of os and shutil

The plan for converting this to use `pathlib` offered by Copilot was

1 Import the `pathlib` module.
2 Initialize a variable `size` to 0.
3 Create a `pathlib.Path` object for the current directory and a subdirectory named `backup`.
4 Create the backup directory if it doesn't already exist using `Path.mkdir`.
5 Use `Path.rglob` to iterate over all files in the current directory and its subdirectories.
6 For each file, check if it is not a symlink using `Path.is_symlink`.
7 If it is not a symlink, check if its extension is .test using `Path.suffix`.
8 If its extension is `.test`, add its size to `size` using `Path.stat`.
9 Move the file to the backup directory using `Path.rename`.
10 After the loop, print `size`.

The resulting code was quite similar to the human solution:

```python
# txt_file_size_and_move.py

from pathlib import Path

size = 0
backup_dir = Path('backup')
backup_dir.mkdir(exist_ok=True)

for file in Path().rglob('*'):
    if not file.is_symlink() and file.suffix == '.test':
        size += file.stat().st_size
        file.rename(backup_dir / file.name)

print(f"Total size of all .test files that are not symlinks: {size} bytes")
```

In fact, there isn't much to say about this code that we haven't already said in discussing the human solution earlier.

The AI bot for Colaboratory was a little less ideal. While three of the four solutions offered broke putting the main code into a function, we chose the one that didn't, to keep the code more or less similar. In any case, all of Colaboratory's solutions took the same approach to the core functionality.

The prompt used is

Write a Python script to calculate the total size of all files with a .test extension that are not symlinks in the current directory and subdirectories.

And Colaboratory's solution was

```
# prompt: Write a Python script to calculate the total size of all files
#         with a .test extension that are not symlinks in the current
#         directory and subdirectories.

import os

total_size = 0

for root, _, files in os.walk('.'):
    for file in files:
        if (file.endswith('.test') and
            not os.path.islink(os.path.join(root, file))):
            total_size += os.path.getsize(os.path.join(root, file))

print(f"Total size of .test files: {total_size} bytes")
```

This code is perfectly fine, with only a couple of things worth noting. First, the use of "_" in the first `for` loop is a Python idiom. "_" is a legal character for a variable name and is often used by itself to indicate a temporary loop variable whose contents are not important or not used. Second, the way that the `if` statement is constructed, while legal, is rather long and hard to read.

The second part of the assignment, to move the target files to a backup directory, uses the prompt

```
Modify that script in the previous cell to also move the files with a .test
extension to a subdirectory of the current directory called backup
```

The resulting code was reasonable:

```
# prompt: Modify that script in the previous cell to also move the files
#         with a .test extension to a subdirectory of the current directory
#         called backup

import os

total_size = 0
backup_dir = os.path.join(os.getcwd(), 'backup')

# Create the backup directory if it doesn't exist
if not os.path.exists(backup_dir):
    os.makedirs(backup_dir)

for root, _, files in os.walk('.'):
    for file in files:
        if (file.endswith('.test') and
            not os.path.islink(os.path.join(root, file))):
            total_size += os.path.getsize(os.path.join(root, file))
            # Move the file to the backup directory
            os.rename(os.path.join(root, file),
```

```
                       os.path.join(backup_dir, file))

print(f"Total size of .test files: {total_size} bytes")
```

In addition to the previous comments, it's worth noting that, in creating the backup directory, this version explicitly checks for the existence of the directory instead of relying on the exist_ok=True parameter to simplify the code.

The final step, the refactor to use pathlib, is where Colaboratory disappoints. The prompt used is

```
Rewrite the script in the previous cell to use pathlib instead of os and
os.path. Do not use os or os.path modules.
```

In spite of the explicit instructions in the prompt, the solution returned used os and os.path:

```
# prompt: Rewrite the script in the previous cell to use pathlib instead of
#         os and os.path. Do not use os or os.path modules.

from pathlib import Path

total_size = 0
backup_dir = Path.cwd().joinpath('backup')

# Create the backup directory if it doesn't exist
if not backup_dir.exists():
    backup_dir.mkdir(parents=True)

for root, _, files in Path('.').walk():
    for file in files:
        if file.endswith('.test') and not file.is_symlink():
            total_size += file.stat().st_size
            # Move the file to the backup directory
            file.rename(backup_dir.joinpath(file))

print(f"Total size of .test files: {total_size} bytes")
```

This solution has several things worth commenting on. First, this solution uses Path .walk(), which was only introduced in Python 3.12. That's not a problem in itself, but it might be a problem for any environment with an older version of Python. In fact, at the time of writing, Colaboratory itself was only at Python 3.10, so it was unable to run its own suggested solution.

In addition, using walk() when we don't absolutely need to means that there has to be one for loop to get directories and a nested for loop to process the files for each directory. Nesting for loops can quite often cause the code to be much slower, particularly as the number of elements increases, so one advantage of using pathlib is that the rglob method handles recursion into all the directories. The final concern is that if the code uses walk() instead of the recursive rglob, it will need to check explicitly to see if the filename matches the target.

The final conclusion is that, while both Copilot and Colaboratory came up with acceptable solutions, I would prefer Copilot, whose solution was on a par with the human solution.

Summary

- Python provides a group of functions and constants that handle filesystem references (pathnames) and filesystem operations in a manner independent of the underlying operating system.
- For more advanced and specialized filesystem operations that typically are tied to a certain operating system or systems, the two main Python libraries are the `os` and `pathlib` modules.
- Python can handle both relative and absolute paths and pathnames in an operating system agnostic way using both the `os` and `pathlib` libraries.
- Using `os` functions or `pathlib` methods, you can fully access information about files and directories.
- Both file manipulation libraries have functions or methods to move, rename, copy, and delete files and directories.
- All the files in a directory can be processed using either `os.walk` or `Path.rglob` and methods in either the `os` or `pathlib` libraries.
- For convenience, a summary of the functions discussed in this chapter is given in table 12.1 and 12.2.

Table 12.1 Summary of filesystem values and functions

Function	Filesystem value or operation
`os.getcwd()`, `Path.cwd()`	Gets the current directory
`os.name`	Provides generic platform identification
`sys.platform`	Provides specific platform information
`os.environ`	Maps the environment
`os.listdir(path)`	Gets files in a directory
`os.scandir(path)`	Gets an iterator of `os.DirEntry` objects for a directory
`os.chdir(path)`	Changes directory
`os.path.join(elements)`, `Path.joinpath(elements)`	Combines elements into a path
`os.path.split(path)`	Splits the path into a base and tail (the last element of the path)
`Path.parts`	A tuple of the path's elements
`os.path.splitext(path)`	Splits the path into a base and a file extension

Table 12.1   Summary of filesystem values and functions (*continued*)

Function	Filesystem value or operation
`Path.suffix`	The path's file extension
`os.path.basename(path)`	Gets the basename of the path
`Path.name`	The basename of the path
`os.path.commonprefix(list_of_paths)`	Gets the common prefix for all paths on a list
`os.path.expanduser(path)`	Expands ~ or ~user to a full pathname
`os.path.expandvars(path)`	Expands environment variables
`os.path.exists(path)`	Tests to see if a path exists
`os.path.isdir(path)`, `Path.is_dir()`	Tests to see if a path is a directory
`os.path.isfile(path)`, `Path.is_file()`	Tests to see if a path is a file
`os.path.islink(path)`, `Path.is_link()`	Tests to see if a path is a symbolic link (not a Windows shortcut)
`os.path.ismount(path)`	Tests to see if a path is a mount point
`os.path.isabs(path)`, `Path.is_absolute()`	Tests to see if a path is an absolute path
`os.path.samefile(path_1, path_2)`	Tests to see if two paths refer to the same file
`os.path.getsize(path)`	Gets the size of a file
`os.path.getmtime(path)`	Gets the modification time
`os.path.getatime(path)`	Gets the access time
`os.rename(old_path, new_path)`	Renames a file
`os.mkdir(path)`	Creates a directory
`os.makedirs(path)`	Creates a directory and any needed parent directories
`os.rmdir(path)`	Removes a directory
`glob.glob(pattern)`	Gets matches to a wildcard pattern
`os.walk(path)`	Gets all filenames in a directory tree

Table 12.2   Partial list of `pathlib` properties and functions

Method or property	Value or operation
`Path.cwd()`	Gets the current directory
`Path.joinpath(elements)` or `Path / element / element`	Combines elements into a new path
`Path.parts`	A tuple of the path's elements
`Path.suffix`	The path's file extension

Table 12.2   Partial list of `pathlib` properties and functions (*continued*)

Method or property	Value or operation
`Path.name`	The basename of the path
`Path.exists()`	Tests to see if a path exists
`Path.is_dir()`	Tests to see if a path is a directory
`Path.is_file()`	Tests to see if a path is a file
`Path.is_symlink()`	Tests to see if a path is a symbolic link (not a Windows shortcut)
`Path.is_absolute()`	Tests to see if a path is an absolute path
`Path.samefile(Path2)`	Tests to see if two paths refer to the same file
`Path1.rename(Path2)`	Renames a file
`Path.mkdir([parents=True])`	Creates a directory; if `parents` is `True`, also creates needed parent directories
`Path.rmdir()`	Removes a directory
`Path.glob(pattern)`	Gets matches to a wildcard pattern

13

Reading and writing files

File operations are a common feature in the daily routines of many developers. The most common file type is the simple text file, which is used in a wide variety of situations, from raw data files to log files to source code and more. If text files can't do the job, binary files can be used to store almost anything, often by using the `struct` module for specific binary formats or even the `pickle` and `shelve` modules to store and retrieve Python objects. Let's walk through reading and writing data to files with Python.

13.1 *Opening files and file objects*

One truth about computing is that files are everywhere. The data we use is in files; the code we use to process it is files; and much of the time when we process data, we write the results to files. We download them, copy them, search them, attach them, encrypt them, and archive them. But most of all, the single most common thing you'll want to do with files is open and read them.

In Python, you open and read a file by using the built-in `open` function and various built-in reading operations. Instead of worrying about filenames, Python uses that `file` object to keep track of a file and how much of the file has been read or written. All Python file I/O is done using `file` objects. The following short Python program reads in one line from a text file named myfile:

```python
with open('myfile', 'r') as file_object:
    line = file_object.readline()
```

The first argument to the `open` function is a pathname. In the previous example, you're opening what you expect to be an existing file called "myfile" in the current working directory. `open` doesn't read anything from the file; instead, it returns an object called a `file` object that you can use to access the opened file.

Note also that this example uses the `with` keyword, indicating that the file will be opened with a context manager, which I'll explain in more detail in chapter 14. For now, it's enough to note that this style of opening files better manages potential I/O errors and is generally preferred.

File objects have various methods to read and write data, change position in the file, and so on. In the previous example, the first call to `readline` reads and returns the first line in the `file` object, everything up to and including the first newline character (or the entire file if there's no newline character in the file); the next call to `readline` returns the second line, if it exists, and so on.

The following opens a file at an absolute location—c:\My Documents\test\myfile:

```python
import os
file_name = os.path.join("c:", "My Documents", "test", "myfile")
file_object = open(file_name, 'r')
```

This example opens the file directly (but doesn't read anything) and also shows a safe way of creating a path string, the `os.path.join()` function, which will join the elements according to the current operating system's conventions.

13.2 *Closing files*

After all data has been read from or written to a `file` object, it should be closed. Closing a `file` object frees up system resources, allows the underlying file to be read or written to by other code, and in general makes the program more reliable. For small scripts, not closing a `file` object generally doesn't have much of an effect; `file` objects are automatically closed when the script or program terminates. For larger programs, too many open `file` objects may exhaust system resources, causing the program to abort.

You close a `file` object by using the `close` method when the `file` object is no longer needed. The earlier short program then becomes

```
file_object = open("myfile", 'r')
line = file_object.readline()
# . . . any further reading on the file_object . . .
file_object.close()
```

Using the keyword `with` (which automatically invokes a context manager) is also a good way to automatically close files when you're done:

```
with open("myfile", 'r') as file_object:
    line = file_object.readline()
    # . . . any further reading on the file_object . . .
```

In this example, even though there is no explicit call to the `close()` method, the file is closed as part of the context manager, initiated by the `with` keyword.

13.3   *Opening files in write or other modes*

The second argument of the `open` command is a string denoting how the file should be opened. `'r'` means "Open the file for reading," `'w'` means "Open the file for writing" (any data already in the file will be erased), and `'a'` means "Open the file for appending" (new data will be appended to the end of any data already in the file). If you want to open the file for reading, you can leave out the second argument; `'r'` is the default. The following short program writes "Hello, World" to a file:

```
file_object = open("myfile", 'w')
file_object.write("Hello, World\n")
file_object.close()
```

Depending on the operating system, `open` may also have access to additional file modes. These modes aren't necessary for most purposes. As you write more advanced Python programs, you may want to consult the Python reference manuals for details.

`open` can take an optional third argument, which defines how reads or writes for that file are buffered. *Buffering* is the process of holding data in memory until enough data has been requested or written to justify the time cost of doing a disk access. Other parameters to `open` control the encoding for text files and the handling of newline characters in text files. Again, these features aren't things you often need to worry about, but as you become more advanced in your use of Python, you will want to read up on them.

13.4   *Functions to read and write text or binary data*

I've already presented the most common text file–reading function, `readline`. This function reads and returns a single line from a `file` object, including any newline character on the end of the line. If there's nothing more to be read from the file, readline returns an empty string, which makes it easy to (for example) count the number of lines in a file:

```
file_object = open("myfile", 'r')
count = 0
while file_object.readline() != "":
    count = count + 1
print(count)
file_object.close()
```

For this particular problem, an even shorter way to count all the lines is to use the built-in readlines method, which reads *all* the lines in a file and returns them as a list of strings, one string per line (with trailing newlines still included):

```
file_object = open("myfile", 'r')
print(len(file_object.readlines()))
file_object.close()
```

If you happen to be counting all the lines in a huge file, of course, this method may cause your computer to run out of memory because it reads the entire file into memory at once. It's also possible to overflow memory with readline if you have the misfortune to try to read a line from a huge file that contains no newline characters, although this situation is highly unlikely. To handle such circumstances, both readline and readlines can take an optional argument affecting the amount of data they read at any one time. See the Python reference documentation for details.

Another way to iterate over all of the lines in a file is to treat the file object as an iterator in a for loop:

```
file_object = open("myfile", 'r')
count = 0
for line in file_object:
    count = count + 1
print(count)
file_object.close()
```

This method has the advantage that the lines are read into memory and processed one line at a time, so even with large files, running out of memory isn't a concern. The other advantage of this method is that it's simpler and easier to read.

A possible problem with reading text files is that the lines may be terminated by different characters, depending on which OS they were created in. In text mode, on a Mac the default line ending is \r, whereas on Windows "\r\n" pairs are used. By default, a Python file object will read text files in "universal" mode, which translates both endings to "\n". If those strings are written to another text file, they will no longer be using the OS's default line endings, which may be a problem.

You can specify the treatment of newline characters by using the newline parameter when you open the file, specifying newline="\n", "\r", or "\r\n", which forces only that string to be used as a newline:

```
input_file = open("myfile", newline="\n")
```

This example forces only "\n" to be considered to be a newline. If the file has been opened in binary mode, the newline parameter isn't needed, because all bytes are returned exactly as they are in the file.

You can also use `newline=""` with `open`, which will accept all of the various options as line endings but will return whatever was used in the file with no translation.

The write methods that correspond to the `readline` and `readlines` methods are the `write` and `writelines` methods. Note that there's no `writeline` function. `write` writes a single string, which can span multiple lines if newline characters are embedded within the string, as in this example:

```
myfile.write("Hello\nWorld\nHow are you?")
```

`write` doesn't write out a newline after it writes its argument; if you want a newline in the output, you must put it there yourself. If you open a file in text mode (using `w`), any `\n` characters are mapped back to the platform-specific line endings (that is, `'\r\n'` on Windows or `'\r'` on macOS platforms). Again, opening the file with a specified newline prevents this situation.

`writelines` is something of a misnomer because it doesn't necessarily write lines; it takes a list of strings as an argument and writes them, one after the other, to the given `file` object without writing newlines. If the strings in the list end with newlines, they're written as lines; otherwise, they're effectively concatenated in the file. But `writelines` is a precise inverse of `readlines` in that it can be used on the list returned by `readlines` to write a file identical to the file that `readlines` read from. Assuming that myfile .txt exists and is a text file, this bit of code creates an exact copy of myfile.txt called myfile2.txt:

```
input_file = open("myfile.txt", 'r', newline="")
lines = input_file.readlines()
input_file.close()
output = open("myfile2.txt", 'w')
output.writelines(lines)
output.close()
```

While these basic operations to read and write files are simple, in my experience, they are all you need for a wide variety of cases in everyday coding.

13.4.1 *Using binary mode*

On some occasions, you may want to read all the data in a file into a single `bytes` object, especially if the data isn't a string, and you want to get it all into memory so you can treat it as a byte sequence. Or you may want to read data from a file as `bytes` objects of a fixed size. You may be reading data without explicit newlines, for example, where each line is assumed to be a sequence of characters of a fixed size. To do so, open the file for reading in binary mode (`'rb'`) and use the `read` method. Without any argument, this method reads all of a file from the current position and returns that data as a `bytes` object. With a single-integer argument, it reads that number of bytes (or less, if there isn't enough data in the file to satisfy the request) and returns a `bytes` object of the given size:

```
input_file = open("myfile", 'rb')        Reads in binary mode
header = input_file.read(4)
data = input_file.read()                  Reads four bytes into header
input_file.close()
                                          Reads remaining data as bytes
```

The first line opens a file for reading in binary mode, the second line reads the first four bytes as a header in bytes, and the third line reads the rest of the file in bytes as a single piece of data.

Keep in mind that files open in binary mode deal only in bytes, not strings. To use the data as strings, you must decode any `bytes` objects to `string` objects. This point is often important in dealing with network protocols, where data streams often behave as text files but need to be interpreted as bytes, not strings.

> **Quick check: Binary mode**
>
> What is the significance of adding a `"b"` to the file open mode string, as in `open ("file", "wb")`?
>
> Suppose that you want to open a file named myfile.txt and write additional data on the end of it. What command would you use to open myfile.txt? What command would you use to reopen the file to read from the beginning?

13.5 *Reading and writing with pathlib*

In addition to its path-manipulation powers discussed in chapter 12, a `Path` object can be used to read and write text and binary files. This capability can be convenient because no `open` or `close` is required, and separate methods are used for text and binary operations. One limitation, however, is that you have no way to append when using `Path` methods, because writing replaces any existing content:

```
from pathlib import Path
p_text = Path('my_text_file')
p_text.write_text('Text file contents')

18                         Number of bytes written

p_text.read_text()

'Text file contents'

p_binary = Path('my_binary_file')
```

```
p_binary.write_bytes(b'Binary file contents')
```

20   ◄─────┐ **Number of bytes written**

```
p_binary.read_bytes()
```

b'Binary file contents'   ◄─────┘ **Data as bytes**

In these examples, the Path object takes care of reading and writing in binary mode by using its read_bytes and write_bytes methods.

13.6 *Terminal input/output and redirection*

Sometimes you don't want or need to read and write files, but rather you want to interact with a command-line user. This can be handy for simple utilities and for testing, for example. You can use the built-in input method to prompt for and read an input string:

```
x = input("enter file name to use: ")
```

enter file name to use: myfile

```
x
```

'myfile'

The prompt to the user is optional and can be any string (including f-strings). The user's input is terminated by pressing the Enter key, but the newline at the end of the input line is stripped off. input handles everything as a string, so to read in numbers using input, you need to explicitly convert the string that it returns to the correct number type. The following example uses int:

```
x = int(input("enter your number: "))
```

enter your number: 39

```
x
```

39

In this example, the code will try to convert anything entered into an int, which will raise an exception if that isn't possible.

input writes its prompt to the *standard output* and reads from the *standard input*. Lower-level access to standard input and output and to *standard error* can be obtained by using the sys module, which has sys.stdin, sys.stdout, and sys.stderr attributes. These attributes can be treated as specialized file objects.

For sys.stdin, you have the read, readline, and readlines methods. For sys .stdout and sys.stderr, you can use the standard print function as well as the write and writelines methods, which operate as they do for other file objects:

```
import sys
print("Write to the standard output.")
```

```
Write to the standard output.
```

```
sys.stdout.write("Write to the standard output.\n")
```

sys.stdout.write returns the number of characters written in a command window but not in Colaboratory.

```
Write to the standard output.
30
```

The following example shows how you can use `sys.stdin` to get input. *This will not work in Colaboratory,* again, since it takes fuller control of standard input and output. The workaround is to save the code as a Python file and run it directly using the ! prefix, as mentioned in chapter 11 in section 11.1.1:

```
s = sys.stdin.readline()
```

```
An input line
```

```
s
```

```
'An input line\n'
```

Usually there is little need to use standard input and output, but in some specific cases it can be handy, particularly if you want to redirect I/O to or from files.

You can redirect standard input to read from a file. Similarly, standard output or standard error can be set to write to files and then programmatically restored to their original values by using `sys.__stdin__`, `sys.__stdout__`, and `sys.__stderr__`:

Opens file

```
import sys
f = open("outfile.txt", "w")
sys.stdout = f
sys.stdout.writelines(["A first line.\n",
                       "A second line.\n"])
print("A line from the print function")

sys.stdout = sys.__stdout__
f.close()
```

Sets outfile.txt to be new sys.stdout

Writes to outfile.txt (redirected sys.stdout)

Resets sys.stdout to default

Since we changed `sys.stdout` to be the file outfile.txt, after the call to `sys.stdout` `.writelines`, the file outfile.txt will contain two lines: "A first line" and "A second line." Likewise, the `print` function will also write to that file, so at the end of this example, outfile.txt will also contain a third line, "A line from the print function":

```
A first line.
A second line.
A line from the print function
```

Warning about Colaboratory and Jupyter

Since Colaboratory (and Jupyter in general) takes more control of standard input and output, the use of `sys.__stdout__` (and `sys.__stdin__` and `sys.__stderr__`) shown earlier won't work as indicated in a Colaboratory cell; instead, you need to save the old value of `sys.stdout` before changing it and then restore the old value after using the redirected value:

```
import sys
f = open("outfile.txt", 'w')
old_sys_stdout = sys.stdout
sys.stdout = f
sys.stdout.writelines(["A first line.\n", "A second line.\n"])
print("A line from the print function")
sys.stdout = old_sys_stdout
f.close()
! cat outfile.txt
```

Saves old sys.stdout to old_sys_stdout

Changes sys.stdout to point to file f

Restores value of sys.stdout from old_sys_stdout

The `print` function also can be redirected to any file without changing standard output, by using its `file` parameter:

```
import sys
f = open("outfile.txt", 'w')
print("A first line.\n", "A second line.\n", file=f)
f.close()
```

Opens file

Writes to file

This will write two lines to the file:

```
A first line.
A second line.
```

Redirecting the output of `print` can be useful, since `print` has a simpler and more familiar syntax. While the standard output is redirected, you receive prompts and tracebacks from errors but no other output.

You'd normally use this technique when you're running a script or program. But it sometimes happens that, during an interactive session, you will want to temporarily redirect standard output to a file to capture what might otherwise scroll off the screen. The short module shown in the following listing implements a set of functions that provides this capability.

Listing 13.1   File mio.py

```
"""mio: module, (contains functions capture_output, restore_output,
    print_file, and clear_file )"""
import sys
_file_object = None
def capture_output(file="capture_file.txt"):
```

```
    """"capture_output(file='capture_file.txt'): redirect the standard
    output to 'file'."""
    global _file_object
    print("output will be sent to file: {0}".format(file))
    print("restore to normal by calling 'mio.restore_output()'")
    _file_object = open(file, 'w')
    sys.stdout = _file_object

def restore_output():
    """restore_output(): restore the standard output back to the
            default (also closes the capture file)"""
    global _file_object
    sys.stdout = sys.__stdout__
    _file_object.close()
    print("standard output has been restored back to normal")

def print_file(file="capture_file.txt"):
    """print_file(file="capture_file.txt"): print the given file to the
        standard output"""
    f = open(file, 'r')
    print(f.read())
    f.close()

def clear_file(file="capture_file.txt"):
    """clear_file(file="capture_file.txt"): clears the contents of the
        given file"""
    f = open(file, 'w')
    f.close()
```

Here, `capture_output()` redirects standard output to a file that defaults to "capture-_file.txt." The function `restore_output()` restores standard output to the default. Assuming `capture_output` hasn't been executed, `print_file()` prints this file to the standard output, and `clear_file()` clears its current contents.

> **Try this: Redirecting output**
>
> Write some code to use the mio.py module in listing 13.1 to capture all the print output of a script to a file named myfile.txt, reset the standard output to the screen, and print that file to screen.
>
> Note: This will *not* work with Colaboratory or Jupyter notebooks unless you write the code for mio.py and your test code to Python files and then execute your file using the ! prefix. The code notebook has a cell that will write mio.py to a Python file.

13.7 *Handling structured binary data with the struct module*

Generally speaking, when working with your own files, you probably don't want to read or write binary data in Python. For very simple storage needs, it's usually best to use text or `bytes` input and output. For more sophisticated applications, Python provides the ability to easily read or write arbitrary Python objects (*pickling*, described in section

13.8). This ability is much less error prone than directly writing and reading your own binary data and is highly recommended.

But there's at least one situation in which you'll likely need to know how to read or write binary data: when you're dealing with files that are generated or used by other programs. This section describes how to do this by using the struct module. Refer to the Python reference documentation for more details.

As you've seen, Python supports explicit binary input or output by using bytes instead of strings if you open the file in binary mode. But because most binary files rely on a particular structure to help parse the values, writing your own code to read and split them into variables correctly is often more work than it's worth. Instead, you can use the standard struct module to permit you to treat those strings as formatted byte sequences with some specific meaning.

Assume that you want to write and read in a binary file called data, containing a series of records generated by a C program. Each record consists of a C short integer, a C double float, and a sequence of four characters that should be taken as a four-character string. You store this data in a Python list of tuples, with each tuple containing an integer, a floating-point number, and a string.

The first thing to do is define a *format string* understandable to the struct module, which tells the module how the data in one of your records is packed. The format string uses characters meaningful to struct to indicate what type of data is expected where in a record. The character 'h', for example, indicates the presence of a single C short integer, and the character 'd' indicates the presence of a single C double-precision floating-point number. Not surprisingly, 's' indicates the presence of a string. Any of these may be preceded by an integer to indicate the number of values; in this case, '7s' indicates a string consisting of seven characters. For your records, the appropriate format string is therefore 'hd7s'. struct understands a wide range of numeric, character, and string formats. See the documentation for the Python standard library for details.

As you may already have guessed, struct provides the ability to take Python values and convert them to packed byte sequences. This conversion is accomplished through the struct.pack function, which takes a format string as its first argument and then enough additional arguments to satisfy the format string. To produce a binary record and store it to a file "data," you might do something like this:

```
import struct
record_format = 'hd7s'
data_record = struct.pack(record_format, 42, 3.14, b'goodbye')
data_file = open("data", "wb")
data_file.write(data_record)
data_record
```

```
b'*\x00\x00\x00\x00\x00\x00\x1f\x85\xebQ\xb8\x1e\t@goodbye'
```

This will convert and pack the values into the correct binary format.

Before you start reading records from your file, you need to know how many bytes to read at a time. Fortunately, struct includes a calcsize function, which takes your format string as an argument and returns the number of bytes used to contain data in such a format.

To read each record, you use the `read` method described earlier in this chapter. Then the `struct.unpack` function conveniently returns a tuple of values by parsing a read record according to your format string. `struct.unpack` is almost the inverse of `struct.pack`. The *almost* is due to the fact that, while `struct.unpack` returns a tuple of Python values, `struct.pack` takes enough separate arguments to satisfy its format string. The program to read your binary data file is remarkably simple:

```
import struct

record_format = 'hd7s'
record_size = struct.calcsize(record_format)
result_list = []
with open("data", 'rb') as input:
    while True:
        record = input.read(record_size)          ◄──── Reads in a single record
        if not record:                            ◄──── Checks to see if
            break                                        record is empty
        result_list.append(struct.unpack(record_format, record))  ◄──

print(result_list)                    Unpacks record into a
                                      tuple; appends to results
[(42, 3.14, b'goodbye')]]
```

If the record is empty, you're at the end of the file, so you quit the loop. Note that there's no checking for file consistency; if the last record is an odd size, the `struct.unpack` function raises an error.

`struct` gets even better; you can insert other special characters into the format string to indicate that data should be read/written in big-endian, little-endian, or machine-native-endian format (default is machine-native) and to indicate that things like a C short integer should be sized either as native to the machine (the default) or as standard C sizes. If you need these features, it's nice to know that they exist. See the documentation for the Python standard library for details.

> **Quick check: struct**
>
> What use cases can you think of in which the `struct` module would be useful for either reading or writing binary data?

13.8 Pickling objects to files

Python can write any data structure into a file, read that data structure back out of a file, and re-create it with just a few commands. This capability is unusual but can be useful, because it can save you many pages of code that do nothing but dump the state of a program into a file (and can save a similar amount of code that does nothing but read that state back in).

Python provides this capability via the `pickle` module. Pickling is powerful but simple to use. In the words of the Python docs, "'Pickling' is the process whereby a Python object hierarchy is converted into a byte stream, and 'unpickling' is the inverse operation, whereby a byte stream (from a binary file or bytes-like object) is converted back into an object hierarchy." So pickling is a way to convert Python objects in a running Python session into a series of bytes that can be stored and/or moved around.

Assume that the entire state of a program is held in three variables: a, b, and c. You can save this state to a file called "state" as follows:

```python
import pickle
a = 42
b = 3.14
c = "test"
file = open("state", 'wb')
pickle.dump(a, file)
pickle.dump(b, file)
pickle.dump(c, file)
file.close()
```

It doesn't matter what was stored in a, b, and c. The content might be as simple as numbers or as complex as a list of dictionaries containing instances of user-defined classes. `pickle.dump` saves everything.

Now, to read that data back in on a later run of the program, just write

```python
import pickle
file = open("state", 'rb')
a = pickle.load(file)
b = pickle.load(file)
c = pickle.load(file)
file.close()
print(f"{a=} {b=} {c=}")
```

a=42 b=3.14 c='test'

Any data that was previously in the variables a, b, or c is restored to them by `pickle` `.load`.

The `pickle` module can store almost anything in this manner. It can handle lists, tuples, numbers, strings, dictionaries, and just about anything made up of these types of objects, which includes all class instances. It also handles shared objects, cyclic references, and other complex memory structures correctly, storing shared objects only once and restoring them as shared objects, not as identical copies. But code objects (what Python uses to store byte-compiled code) and system resources (like files or sockets) can't be pickled.

More often than not, you won't want to save your entire program state with `pickle`. Most applications can have multiple documents open at one time, for example. If you saved the entire state of the program, you would effectively save all open documents in one file. An easy and effective way of saving and restoring only data of interest is to write a save function that stores all data you want to save into a dictionary and then uses `pickle` to save the dictionary. Then you can use a complementary restore function to read the dictionary back in (again using `pickle`) and to assign the values in the dictionary to the appropriate program variables. This technique also has the advantage that there's no possibility of reading values back in an incorrect order—that is, an order different from the order in which the values were stored. Using this approach with the previous example, you get code looking something like this:

```
import pickle

def save_data(data_dict):
    with open("state", 'wb') as file:
        pickle.dump(data_dict, file)

def restore_data():
    with open("state", 'rb') as file:
        data_dict = pickle.load(file)
    return data_dict

if __name__ == '__main__':
    data_dict = {'a': 42,
                 'b': 3.14,
                 'c': "test"
                 }
    save_data(data_dict)
    restored_data = restore_data()
    print(restored_data)
```

```
{'a': 42, 'b': 3.14, 'c': 'test'}
```

This example is somewhat unrealistic in that you probably won't be saving the state of the top-level variables of your interactive mode very often. However, if you need the values of a few variables or the state of a few objects to persist *and* there are no security concerns, pickling can be a useful technique.

A real-life application is an extension of the cache example given in chapter 7. In that chapter, you called a function that performed a time-intensive calculation based on its three arguments. During the course of a program run, many of your calls to that function ended up using the same set of arguments. You were able to obtain a significant performance improvement by caching the results in a dictionary, keyed by the arguments that produced them. But it was also the case that many sessions of this program were being run many times over the course of days, weeks, and months. Therefore, by pickling the cache, you can avoid having to start over with every session. Listing 13.2 is a pared-down version of the module you might use for this purpose.

The code in listing 13.2 assumes that the cache file already exists. To create a cache file, use the following to initialize the cache file:

```
import pickle
file = open("solecache",'wb')
pickle.dump({}, file)
file.close()
```

Listing 13.2   File sole.py

```
"""sole module: contains functions sole, save, show"""
import pickle
_sole_mem_cache_d = {}
_sole_disk_file_s = "solecache"
file = open(_sole_disk_file_s, 'rb')
_sole_mem_cache_d = pickle.load(file)
file.close()
```

> Initialization code executes when the module loads.

```
def sole(m, n, t):
    """sole(m, n, t): perform the sole calculation using the cache."""
    global _sole_mem_cache_d
    if (m, n, t) in _sole_mem_cache_d:
        return _sole_mem_cache_d[(m, n, t)]
    else:
        # . . . do some time-consuming calculations . . .
        result = f"{m=}, {n=}, {t=}"
        _sole_mem_cache_d[(m, n, t)] = result
        return result
```

> Public functions

> Converts to string for illustration

```
def save():
    """save(): save the updated cache to disk."""
    global _sole_mem_cache_d, _sole_disk_file_s
    file = open(_sole_disk_file_s, 'wb')
    pickle.dump(_sole_mem_cache_d, file)
    file.close()

def show():
    """show(): print the cache"""
    global _sole_mem_cache_d
    print(_sole_mem_cache_d)
```

Experimenting with this code might go something like this:

```
sole(1, 2, 3)
sole(11, 22, 33)
show()
save()
```

```
{(1, 2, 3): 'm=1, n=2, t=3', (11, 22, 33): 'm=11, n=22, t=33'}
```

You also, of course, would need to replace the comment # . . . do some time-consuming calculations with an actual calculation rather than just converting the variables into a string. Note that for production code, this situation is one in which you'd probably use an absolute pathname for your cache file, and that filename would probably not be hardcoded in the file. Also, concurrency isn't being handled here. If two people run overlapping sessions, you end up with only the additions of the last person to save. If this situation was a problem, you could limit the overlap window significantly by using the dictionary update method in the save function.

13.8.1 *Reasons not to pickle*

Although it may make some sense to use a pickled object in the previous scenario, you should also be aware of the drawbacks to pickles:

- Pickling is neither particularly fast nor space efficient as a means of serialization. Even using JSON to store serialized objects is faster and results in smaller files on disk.

- Pickling isn't secure, and loading a pickle with malicious content can result in the execution of arbitrary code on your machine. Therefore, you should avoid pickling if there's *any* chance at all that the pickle file will be accessible to anyone who might alter it.

Quick check: Pickles

Think about why a pickle would or would not be a good solution in the following use cases:

- Saving some state variables from one run to the next
- Keeping a high-score list for a game
- Storing usernames and passwords
- Storing a large dictionary of English terms

13.9 *Shelving objects*

This topic is somewhat advanced but certainly not difficult. You can think of a `shelve` object as being a dictionary that stores its data in a file on disk rather than in memory, which means that you still have the convenience of access with a key, but you don't have the limitations of the amount of available RAM.

This section is likely of most interest to people whose work involves storing or accessing pieces of data in large files, because the Python `shelve` module does exactly that: permits the reading or writing of pieces of data in large files without reading or writing the entire file. For applications that perform many accesses of large files (such as database applications), the savings in time can be spectacular. Like the `pickle` module (which it uses), the `shelve` module is simple.

In this section, we explore this module through an address book. This sort of thing usually is small enough that an entire address file can be read in when the application is started and written out when the application is done. If you're an extremely friendly sort of person and your address book is too big for this example, it would be better to use `shelve` and not worry about it.

Assume that each entry in your address book consists of a tuple of three elements, giving the first name, phone number, and address of a person. Each entry is indexed by the last name of the person the entry refers to. This setup is so simple that your application will be an interactive session with the Python shell.

First, import the `shelve` module and open the address book. `shelve.open` creates the address book file if it doesn't exist:

```
import shelve
book = shelve.open("addresses")
```

Now, add a couple of entries. Notice that you're treating the object returned by `shelve.open` as a dictionary (although it's a dictionary that can use only strings as keys):

```
book['flintstone'] = ('fred', '555-1234', '1233 Bedrock Place')
book['rubble'] = ('barney', '555-4321', '1235 Bedrock Place')
```

Finally, close the file and end the session:

```
book.close()
```

So what? Well, in that same directory, start Python again, and open the same address book:

```
import shelve
book = shelve.open("addresses")
```

But now, instead of entering something, see whether what you put in before is still around:

```
book['flintstone']
```

('fred', '555-1234', '1233 Bedrock Place')

The addresses file created by `shelve.open` in the first interactive session has acted just like a persistent dictionary. The data you entered before was stored to disk, even though you did no explicit disk writes. That's exactly what `shelve` does.

More generally, `shelve.open` returns a `shelf` object that permits basic dictionary operations, key assignment or lookup, `del`, `in`, and the `keys` method. But unlike a normal dictionary, `shelf` objects store their data on disk, not in memory. Unfortunately, `shelf` objects do have one significant restriction compared with dictionaries: they can use only strings as keys, versus the wide range of key types allowable in dictionaries.

It's important to understand the advantage `shelf` objects give you over dictionaries when dealing with large datasets. `shelve.open` makes the file accessible; it doesn't read an entire `shelf` object file into memory. File accesses are done only when needed (typically, when an element is looked up), and the file structure is maintained in such a manner that lookups are very fast. Even if your data file is really large, only a couple of disk accesses will be required to locate the desired object in the file, which can improve your program in several ways. The program may start faster because it doesn't need to read a potentially large file into memory. Also, the program may execute faster because more memory is available to the rest of the program; thus, less code must be swapped out into virtual memory. You can operate on datasets that are otherwise too large to fit in memory.

You have a few restrictions when using the `shelve` module. As previously mentioned, `shelf` object keys can be only strings, but any Python object that can be pickled can be stored under a key in a `shelf` object. While lookups are fast for a file-based solution, be warned that storing new values can be costly, so if you are adding and updating a lot of keys, you may find performance unacceptably slow. Also, `shelf` objects aren't suitable for multiuser databases because they provide no control for concurrent access. Make sure that you close a `shelf` object when you're finished; closing is sometimes required for the changes you've made (entries or deletions) to be written back to disk.

As written, the cache example in listing 13.1 is an excellent candidate to be handled with shelves. You wouldn't, for example, have to rely on the user to explicitly save their work to the disk. The only possible problem is that you wouldn't have the low-level control when you write back to the file.

> **Quick check: shelf**
>
> Using a `shelf` object looks very much like using a dictionary. In what ways is using a `shelf` object different? What disadvantages would you expect in using a `shelf` object?

13.10 *Final fixes to wc*

One thing that the `wc` utility can do that our current Python version can't is handle input redirection, which is common particularly in Linux/Unix command-line environments. Refactor your existing Python version to handle redirection. That is, if a file is given as a command-line argument, the utility should read from and process that file, but if no file argument is given, it should read from and process `stdin`. For example, with a filename:

```
! python wc_redirect.py wc_redirect.py

 62   182 2058 wc_redirect.py
```

The file itself is given as the file argument; process normally.

With redirection (no filename):

```
! python wc_redirect.py < wc_redirect.py

 62   182 2058
```

There is no file argument, but input is redirected via < from file.

TIP If you use the `argparse` library, you need to be able to handle both having and *not* having an argument for the input filename, since, if the input is coming via redirection, `argparse` will not have a filename. To deal with this, look at the `argparse` documentation for `nargs` at https://mng.bz/9YEr and particularly the `'?'` options.

13.10.1 *Solving the problem with AI-generated code*

This is the final refactoring of our version of the wc utility to make it (nearly) identical to the built-in Unix version. As such, we will need to have the AI bot start from our last version, as developed in chapter 11, and ask the bot to add the ability to redirect input to be from standard input and output to be to standard output.

An earlier version of this problem asked to add both input redirection and the ability to count characters in text mode and bytes in binary files differently (with -c being used for bytes and -m for characters), since files containing Unicode characters can actually have more binary mode bytes than text mode characters. Adding both features seemed to make things much harder in human terms, and it turned out to be impossible for the versions of Copilot and Colaboratory that were available in mid-2024. In fact, either the AI-generated code wouldn't run without modification, or it handled the difference between text and binary modes incorrectly, or both.

That level of difficulty led me to modify the problem, but if you want to really test your coding superpowers, you can try to add that feature and to coax one of the AI bots to create a working solution.

13.10.2 *Solutions and discussion*

There are two problems to be solved in updating our former wc utility to handle standard input. As mentioned in the hint for the lab, the first is that the script will need to be able to handle having no filename argument.

The second problem is that the code must read from sys.stdin if there is no filename argument. Doing that while avoiding unnecessarily duplicating code takes a little bit of thought on the design, but some of the default argument options in the argparse library can make this easier.

Finally, if you are using Colaboratory (or some other Jupyter notebook) you need to be aware that to use the wc script with redirection, you must write it to a .py file and run it with python using the ! prefix. If you do that, then redirection will work as expected.

THE HUMAN SOLUTION

My version relies on using argparse's FileType argument type to make sure that if a file is specified on the command line, it will be opened. That way, the part that reads the file doesn't open the file and can treat either the file or sys.stdin in the same way, since sys.stdin can be thought of as a perpetually open file:

```
#!/usr/bin/env python3
# File: word_count_program.py
""" Reads a file and returns the number of lines, words,
    and characters - similar to the UNIX wc utility
"""
import sys
import argparse


def main():
```

```python
    # initialize counts
    line_count = 0
    word_count = 0
    char_count = 0
    byte_count = 0
    longest_line = 0

    parser = argparse.ArgumentParser(usage=__doc__)
    parser.add_argument("-c", "--chars",
                action="store_true", dest="chars", default=False,
                help="display number of characters")
    parser.add_argument("-w", "--words",
                action="store_true", dest="words", default=False,
                help="display number of words")
    parser.add_argument("-l", "--lines",
                action="store_true", dest="lines", default=False,
                help="display number of lines")
    parser.add_argument("-L", "--longest",
                action="store_true", dest="longest", default=False,
                help="display longest line length")
    parser.add_argument("file", nargs='?',
                    type=argparse.FileType('r'),
                    default=sys.stdin,
                    help="read data from this file")
    args = parser.parse_args()

    with args.file as infile:
        for line in infile.readlines():
            line_count += 1
            char_count += len(line)
            words = line.split()
            word_count += len(words)
            if len(line) > longest_line:
                longest_line = len(line)

    default_args = any([getattr(args, _) for _ in ('chars',
                                    'words', 'lines', 'longest')])

    if not default_args:
        args.chars = args.lines = args.words = True

    if args.lines:
        print(f"{line_count:3}", end=" ")
    if args.words:
        print(f"{word_count:4}", end=" ")
    if args.chars:
        print(f"{char_count:4}", end=" ")
    if args.longest:
        print(f'{longest_line}', end=" ")
    if args.file.name != '<stdin>':
        print(f'{args.file.name}', end=" ")
    print()

if __name__ == '__main__':
    main()
```

argparse.FileType('r') will open the file named for reading.

If no file given, uses stdin as file

No need to open file, since file opened by parser

Don't print a filename if using stdin.

The main changes for this version are in adding arguments to the parser. The `argparse` module offers a `FileType` argument type, which can be used to open a file automatically, in this case for reading in text mode with the `'r'` parameter, and the `nargs` option can be used to control the number of arguments required. In this case, the `?` indicates that the parser is looking for zero or one filename arguments. If zero filename arguments are received, the parser will use the default—`sys.stdin`—as the file.

While the parser takes care of most of the work, there are two changes to make to the rest of the code. First, we no longer need to open a file, since the parser will have done that (and `sys.stdin` doesn't need to be opened), so we can just use the file object from the parser as we process the file. Second, if we don't have a file argument, we don't want to print the name of stdin (`'<stdin>'`), so we can check for that before printing the filename.

THE AI SOLUTIONS

Copilot was given the following prompt:

```
Refactor the current file wc_coplilot.py to make the script support
input/output redirection. Output should be similar to that of wc utility.
```

Copilot's plan was

1 Import the `sys` module.
2 Modify the `count_stats` function to accept a file object instead of a file path.
3 Modify the `count_stats` function to read the file as bytes.
4 Modify the `argparse.ArgumentParser` in the `main` function to accept a file object instead of a file path.
5 If no file is provided as an argument, read from standard input using `sys.stdin`.
6 If the output is redirected, it will be handled automatically by the shell.
7 Modify the output format to match the `wc` utility.

Following that plan, Copilot generated the following code, which is very like the human solution, except that it does not print the filename and it doesn't handle the default case where leaving the options unspecified is the same as giving it `-l -w -c` to print lines, words, and characters:

```python
# wc_copilot.py

import argparse
import sys

def count_stats(file):
    lines = file.readlines()

    line_count = len(lines)
    word_count = sum(len(line.split()) for line in lines)
    char_count = sum(len(line) for line in lines)
    max_line_length = max(len(line) for line in lines)
```

```
        return line_count, word_count, char_count, max_line_length

def main():
    parser = argparse.ArgumentParser(description='Count lines,
                                words, and characters in a file.')
    parser.add_argument('file', nargs='?', type=argparse.FileType('r'),
     default=sys.stdin, help='File to count')
    parser.add_argument('-l', '--lines', action='store_true',
                    help='Count lines')
    parser.add_argument('-w', '--words', action='store_true',
                    help='Count words')
    parser.add_argument('-c', '--chars', action='store_true',
                    help='Count characters')
    parser.add_argument('-L', '--max-line-length', action='store_true',
                    help='Print length of the longest line')
    args = parser.parse_args()

    line_count, word_count, char_count, max_line_length =\
 count_stats(args.file)

    output = []
    if args.lines:
        output.append(str(line_count))
    if args.words:
        output.append(str(word_count))
    if args.chars:
        output.append(str(char_count))
    if args.max_line_length:
        output.append(str(max_line_length))

    print(' '.join(output))

if __name__ == '__main__':
    main()
```

As mentioned earlier, this solution is similar to the human solution, except that it reads in the entire file, and it doesn't quite match the requested behavior. That is, it doesn't print the filename if reading a file, and when no options are specified, it prints nothing, unlike the wc utility, which assumes -1 -w -c if no options are specified.

In Colaboratory a very similar prompt was used:

```
Refactor the cell above to make the script support input/output
redirection. Output should be similar to that of wc utility.
```

Colaboratory doesn't report its steps but instead offers four alternative versions for the user to choose from. All of the versions worked about the same, but none of them printed the filename. I selected the first version since it had a couple of interesting differences in how it handled the input files and how it did the redirection:

```
# prompt: Refactor the cell above to make the script support input/output
#         redirection. Output should be similar to that of wc utility.

import argparse
```

```
import sys

""" Reads a file and returns the number of lines, words,
    and characters - similar to the UNIX wc utility
"""


def main():
    parser = argparse.ArgumentParser(usage=__doc__)
    parser.add_aargument("filename", nargs='*')
    parser.add_argument("-l", "--lines", dest="lines",
                        action='store_true', default=False,
                        help="Show only line count")
    parser.add_argument("-w", "--words", dest="words",
                        action='store_true', default=False,
                        help="Show only word count")
    parser.add_argument("-c", "--chars", dest="chars",
                        action='store_true', default=False,
                        help="Show only character count")
    parser.add_argument("-L", "--longest", dest="longest",
                        action='store_true', default=False,
                        help="Show length of longest line")
    args = parser.parse_args()

    if not sys.stdin.isatty():
        # Read from standard input
        lines = sys.stdin.readlines()
    else:
        for filename in args.filename:
            with open(filename) as infile:
                lines = infile.readlines()

    line_count = len(lines)
    word_count = sum(len(line.split()) for line in lines)
    char_count = sum(len(line) for line in lines)
    longest_line_length = max(len(line) for line in lines)

    if args.lines:
        print(f"{line_count}")
    elif args.words:
        print(f"{word_count}")
    elif args.chars:
        print(f"{char_count}")
    elif args.longest:
        print(f"{longest_line_length}")
    else:
        print(f"{line_count} {word_count} {char_count}")

if __name__ == '__main__':
    main()
```

Allows for any number of filename arguments, no default given

If sys.stdin is not the terminal (therefore is a file), uses sys.stdin

Loops through list of filename arguments

The first interesting variation is that this version allows for multiple filename arguments, by using the "*" option for the argument. This means that the filenames will be returned as a list, so processing the files will need to loop through the list of filenames. At first glance, it would seem that this version is more like the `wc` utility than the other solutions, since if you specify multiple files for `wc`, it processes them all correctly:

```
$ wc wc_redirect.py wc_redirect_colab.py
  61   182 2058 wc_redirect.py
  53   162 1853 wc_redirect_colab.py
 114   344 3911 total
```

The problem is that, while this solution reads all of the files, it only actually processes the last file:

```
$ python wc_redirect_colab.py wc_redirect.py wc_redirect_colab.py
53 162 1853
```

To behave correctly, the loop would have to be around all of the processing and printing (which would be a problem for handling redirection), and it would need to calculate overall totals for each category. In other words, beware of suggested code that seems like it works but misunderstands the scope of the process.

The second variation is in how this version decides to use redirection. It checks to see if `stdin` is the terminal with `if not sys.stdin.isatty():`, and if it is not the terminal, it assumes that it must be redirected from a file and reads from `stdin`. This approach works with input redirected from a file and from the output of another program, but unlike the `wc` utility and the human solution, it will not work with direct console input and instead throws an exception. For example, with the human solution, if we enter the command without a filename, it will wait for input to be typed in, followed by `<Enter>` and `Control-D`:

```
$ python wc_redirect.py
this is a line typed in on the terminal
  1    9   40
```

Command entered on command line with no filename

Typed in, followed by `<Enter>` and Control-D

Output

The Colaboratory solution will instead raise an exception:

```
$ python wc_redirect_colab.py
Traceback (most recent call last):
  File "/home/naomi/Dropbox/QPB4/code/samples/wc_redirect_colab.py",
line 53, in <module>
    main()
  File "/home/naomi/Dropbox/QPB4/code/samples/wc_redirect_colab.py",
line 36, in main
    line_count = len(lines)
                     ^^^^^
UnboundLocalError: cannot access local variable 'lines' where it is
not associated with a value
```

That is because it checks for a nonterminal `stdin` to use redirection. This may not make much difference in many applications, but it's still a good idea to be aware that the code generated doesn't do *exactly* what is asked for.

Finally, because it uses an `if-elif-else` structure, this version will print the data for only one option or (if no options are specified) the default of lines, words, and characters. Again, while the code seems to work, you need to wary of exactly how the logic works and if it handles various cases in the expected ways.

Summary

- File input and output in Python uses file objects with methods to open, read, write, and close files.

- While by default Python treats files as text, there is also binary mode, which processes files as bytes.

- Python makes it easy to redirect standard input, output, and error channels to read and write from files.

- Path objects from the `pathlib` library can also be used for reading and writing text or binary objects.

- In addition to reading and writing text, the `struct` module gives you the ability to read or write data packed into structured binary formats.

- The `pickle` module provides a simple, safe, and powerful way of saving and accessing arbitrarily complex Python structures.

- The `shelve` module offers a convenient way to save and load objects, similar to using a dictionary, so long as the keys are strings.

Exceptions

This chapter discusses exceptions, which are language features specifically aimed at handling unusual circumstances during the execution of a program. The most common use for exceptions is to handle errors that arise during the execution of a program, but they can also be used effectively for many other purposes. Python provides a comprehensive set of exceptions, and new ones can be defined by users for their own purposes.

The concept of exceptions as an error-handling mechanism has been around for some time. C and Perl, the most commonly used systems and scripting languages, don't provide any exception capabilities, and even programmers who use languages such as C++, which does include exceptions, are often unfamiliar with them. This chapter doesn't assume familiarity with exceptions on your part but instead provides detailed explanations.

14.1   Introduction to exceptions

The following sections provide an introduction to exceptions and how they're used. If you're already familiar with exceptions, you can skip directly to section 14.2.

14.1.1   General philosophy of errors and exception handling

Any program may encounter errors during its execution. For the purposes of illustrating exceptions, I look at the case of a word processor that writes files to disk and that therefore may run out of disk space before all of its data is written. There are various ways of coming to grips with this problem.

SOLUTION 1: DON'T HANDLE THE PROBLEM

The simplest way to handle this disk-space problem is to assume that there'll always be adequate disk space for whatever files you write and that you needn't worry about it. Unfortunately, this option seems to be the most commonly used. It's usually tolerable for small programs dealing with small amounts of data, but it's completely unsatisfactory for more mission-critical programs.

SOLUTION 2: ALL FUNCTIONS RETURN SUCCESS/FAILURE STATUS

The next level of sophistication in error handling is realizing that errors will occur and defining a methodology using standard language mechanisms for detecting and handling them. There are numerous ways to do this, but a typical method is to have each function or procedure return a status value that indicates whether that function or procedure call executed successfully. Normal results can be passed back in a call-by-reference parameter.

Consider how this solution might work with a hypothetical word-processing program. Assume that the program invokes a single high-level function, `save_to_file`, to save the current document to file. This function calls subfunctions to save different parts of the entire document to the file, such as `save_text_to_file` to save the actual document text, `save_prefs_to_file` to save user preferences for that document, `save_formats_to_file` to save user-defined formats for the document, and so forth. Any of these subfunctions may in turn call its own subfunctions, which save smaller pieces to the file. At the bottom are built-in system functions, which write primitive data to the file and report on the success or failure of the file-writing operations.

You could put error-handling code into every function that might get a disk-space error, but that practice makes little sense. The only thing the error handler will be able to do is put up a dialog box telling the user that there's no more disk space and asking the user to remove some files and save again. It wouldn't make sense to duplicate this code everywhere you do a disk write. Instead, put one piece of error-handling code into the main disk-writing function: `save_to_file`.

Unfortunately, for `save_to_file` to be able to determine when to call this error-handling code, every function it calls that writes to disk must itself check for disk-space errors and return a status value indicating the success or failure of the disk write. In addition, the `save_to_file` function must explicitly check every call to a function that writes to disk, even though it doesn't care about which function fails. The code, using C-like syntax, looks something like this:

```
const ERROR = 1;
const OK = 0;
int save_to_file(filename) {
    int status;
    status = save_prefs_to_file(filename);
    if (status == ERROR) {
        ...handle the error...
    }
    status = save_text_to_file(filename);
    if (status == ERROR) {
        ...handle the error...
    }
    status = save_formats_to_file(filename);
    if (status == ERROR) {
        ...handle the error...
    }
    .
    .
    .
}
int save_text_to_file(filename) {
    int status;
    status = ...lower-level call to write size of text...
    if (status == ERROR) {
        return(ERROR);
    }
    status = ...lower-level call to write actual text data...
    if (status == ERROR) {
        return(ERROR);
    }
    .
    .
    .
}
```

The same applies to `save_prefs_to_file`, `save_formats_to_file`, and all other functions that either write to `filename` directly or (in any way) call functions that write to `filename`.

Under this methodology, code to detect and handle errors can become a significant portion of the entire program, because every function and procedure containing calls that might result in an error needs to contain code to check for an error. Often, programmers don't have the time or the energy to put in this type of complete error checking, and programs end up being unreliable and crash prone.

SOLUTION 3: THE EXCEPTION MECHANISM

It's obvious that most of the error-checking code in the previous type of program is largely repetitive: the code checks for errors on each attempted file write and passes an error status message back up to the calling procedure if an error is detected. The disk-space error is handled in only one place: the top-level `save_to_file`. In other words, most of the error-handling code is plumbing code that connects the place where an error is generated with the place where it's handled. What you really want to do is get rid of this plumbing and write code that looks something like this:

```
def save_to_file(filename)
    try to execute the following block
        save_text_to_file(filename)
        save_formats_to_file(filename)
        save_prefs_to_file(filename)
        .
        .
        .

    except that, if the disk runs out of space while
        executing the above block, do this
        ...handle the error...

def save_text_to_file(filename)
    ...lower-level call to write size of text...
    ...lower-level call to write actual text data...
    .
    .
    .
```

The error-handling code is completely removed from the lower-level functions; an error (if it occurs) is generated by the built-in file-writing routines and propagates directly to the `save_to_file` routine, where your error-handling code will (presumably) take care of it. Although you can't write this code in C, languages that offer exceptions permit exactly this sort of behavior—and of course, Python is one such language. Exceptions let you write clearer code and handle error conditions better.

14.1.2 *A more formal definition of exceptions*

The act of generating an exception is called *raising* or *throwing* an exception. In the previous example, all exceptions are raised by the disk-writing functions, but exceptions can also be raised by any other functions or can be explicitly raised by your own code. In the previous example, the low-level disk-writing functions (not seen in the code) would throw an exception if the disk were to run out of space.

The act of responding to an exception is called *catching* an exception, and the code that handles an exception is called *exception-handling code* or just an *exception handler*. In the example, the `except that...` line catches the disk-write exception, and the code that would be in place of the `...handle the error...` line would be an exception handler for disk-write (out of space) exceptions. There may be other exception handlers for other types of exceptions or even other exception handlers for the same type of exception but at another place in your code.

14.1.3 *Handling different types of exceptions*

Depending on exactly what event causes an exception, a program may need to take different actions. An exception raised when disk space is exhausted needs to be handled quite differently from an exception that's raised if you run out of memory, and both of these exceptions are completely different from an exception that arises when a divide-by-zero error occurs. One way to handle these different types of exceptions is to globally record an error message indicating the cause of the exception and have all exception handlers examine this error message and take appropriate action. In practice, a different method has proved to be much more flexible.

Rather than defining a single kind of exception, Python, like most modern languages that implement exceptions, defines different types of exceptions corresponding to various problems that may occur. Depending on the underlying event, different types of exceptions may be raised. In addition, the code that catches exceptions may be told to catch only certain types. This feature is used in the pseudocode in solution 3 earlier in this chapter that said `except that, if the disk runs out of space . . .`, `do this`; this pseudocode specifies that this particular exception-handling code is interested only in disk-space exceptions. Another type of exception wouldn't be caught by that exception-handling code. That exception would be caught by an exception handler that was looking for numeric exceptions, or (if no such exception handler existed) it would cause the program to exit prematurely with an error.

14.2 *Exceptions in Python*

The remaining sections of this chapter talk specifically about the exception mechanisms built into Python. The entire Python exception mechanism is built around an object-oriented paradigm, which makes it both flexible and expandable. If you aren't familiar with object-oriented programming, you don't need to learn object-oriented techniques to use exceptions.

An exception is an object generated automatically by Python code with a `raise` statement. After the object is generated, the `raise` statement, which raises an exception, causes execution of the Python program to proceed in a manner different from what would normally occur. Instead of proceeding with the next statement after the `raise` or whatever generated the exception, the current call chain is searched for a handler that can handle the generated exception. If such a handler is found, it's invoked and may access the exception object for more information. If no suitable exception handler is found, the program aborts with an error message.

Easier to ask forgiveness than permission

The way that Python thinks about handling error situations in general is different from that common in languages such as Java, for example. Those languages rely on checking for possible errors as much as possible before they occur, since handling exceptions after they occur tends to be costly in various ways. This style is described in the first section of this chapter and is sometimes described as a "look before you leap" (LBYL) approach.

Python, on the other hand, is more likely to rely on exceptions to deal with errors after they occur. Although this reliance may seem to be risky, if exceptions are used well,

(continued)
the code is less cumbersome and easier to read, and errors are dealt with only as they occur. This Pythonic approach to handling errors is often described by the phrase "easier to ask forgiveness than permission" (EAFP).

14.2.1 *Types of Python exceptions*

It's possible to generate different types of exceptions to reflect the actual cause of the error or exceptional circumstance being reported. Python 3.13 provides several exception types:

```
BaseException
    BaseExceptionGroup
    GeneratorExit
    KeyboardInterrupt
    SystemExit
    Exception
        ArithmeticError
            FloatingPointError
            OverflowError
            ZeroDivisionError
        AssertionError
        AttributeError
        BufferError
        EOFError
        ExceptionGroup [BaseExceptionGroup]
        ImportError
            ModuleNotFoundError
        LookupError
            IndexError
            KeyError
        MemoryError
        NameError
            UnboundLocalError
        OSError
            BlockingIOError
            ChildProcessError
            ConnectionError
                BrokenPipeError
                ConnectionAbortedError
                ConnectionRefusedError
                ConnectionResetError
            FileExistsError
            FileNotFoundError
            InterruptedError
            IsADirectoryError
            NotADirectoryError
            PermissionError
            ProcessLookupError
            TimeoutError
        ReferenceError
```

```
RuntimeError
    NotImplementedError
    PythonFinalizationError
    RecursionError
StopAsyncIteration
StopIteration
SyntaxError
    IncompleteInputError
    IndentationError
        TabError
SystemError
TypeError
ValueError
    UnicodeError
        UnicodeDecodeError
        UnicodeEncodeError
        UnicodeTranslateError
Warning
    BytesWarning
    DeprecationWarning
    EncodingWarning
    FutureWarning
    ImportWarning
    PendingDeprecationWarning
    ResourceWarning
    RuntimeWarning
    SyntaxWarning
    UnicodeWarning
    UserWarning
```

The Python exception set is hierarchically structured, as reflected by the indentation in this list of exceptions. As you saw in a previous chapter, you can obtain an alphabetized list from the __builtins__ module.

Each type of exception is a Python class, which inherits from its parent exception type. But if you're not into object-oriented programming yet, don't worry about that. An IndexError, for example, is also an instance of LookupError and (by inheritance) an Exception and also a BaseException.

This hierarchy is deliberate: most exceptions inherit from Exception, and it's strongly recommended that any user-defined exceptions also subclass Exception, not BaseException. The reason is that if you have code set up like the following

```
try:
    # do stuff
except Exception:
    # handle exceptions
```

you could still interrupt the code in the try block with Ctrl-C without triggering the exception-handling code, because the KeyboardInterrupt exception is a subclass of BaseException, *not* a subclass of Exception.

You can find an explanation of the meaning of each type of exception in the documentation, but you'll rapidly become acquainted with the most common types as you program!

14.2.2 Raising exceptions

Exceptions are raised by many of the Python built-in functions:

```
alist = [1, 2, 3]
element = alist[7]
```

```
---------------------------------------------------------------------------
IndexError                                Traceback (most recent call last)
<ipython-input-7-189983935c4d> in <cell line: 2>()
      1 alist = [1, 2, 3]
----> 2 element = alist[7]

IndexError: list index out of range
```

Error-checking code built into Python detects that the second input line requests an element at a list index that doesn't exist and raises an `IndexError` exception. This exception propagates all the way back to the top level (the interactive Python interpreter), which handles it by printing out a message stating that the exception has occurred.

Exceptions may also be raised explicitly in your own code through the use of the `raise` statement. The most basic form of this statement is

```
raise exception(args)
```

The `exception(args)` part of the code creates an exception. The arguments to the new exception are typically values that aid you in determining what happened—something that I discuss next. After the exception has been created, `raise` throws it upward along the stack of Python functions that were invoked in getting to the line containing the `raise` statement. The new exception is thrown up to the nearest (on the stack) exception catcher looking for that type of exception. If no catcher is found on the way to the top level of the program, the program terminates with an error or (in an interactive session) causes an error message to be printed to the console.

Try the following:

```
raise IndexError("Just kidding")
```

```
---------------------------------------------------------------------------
IndexError                                Traceback (most recent call last)
<ipython-input-8-680ffd4ba189> in <cell line: 1>()
----> 1 raise IndexError("Just kidding")

IndexError: Just kidding
```

The use of `raise` here generates what at first glance looks similar to all the Python list-index error messages you've seen so far. Closer inspection reveals this isn't the case. The actual error reported isn't as serious as those other ones.

The use of a string argument when creating exceptions is common. Most of the built-in Python exceptions, if given a first argument, assume that the argument is a message to be shown to you as an explanation of what happened. This isn't always the case, though, because each exception type is its own class, and the arguments expected when a new exception of that class is created are determined entirely by the class definition. Also, programmer-defined exceptions, created by you or by other programmers, are often used for reasons other than error handling; as such, they may not take a text message.

14.2.3 *Catching and handling exceptions*

The important thing about exceptions isn't that they cause a program to halt with an error message. Achieving that function in a program is never much of a problem. What's special about exceptions is that they don't have to cause the program to halt. By defining appropriate exception handlers, you can ensure that commonly encountered exceptional circumstances don't cause the program to fail; perhaps they display an error message to the user or do something else, or perhaps even fix the problem, but they don't crash the program.

The basic Python syntax for exception catching and handling is as follows, using the `try`, `except`, and sometimes `else` keywords:

```
try:
    body
except exception_type1 as var1:
    exception_code1
except exception_type2 as var2:
    exception_code2
except (exception_type3, exception_type4  as var3:
    exception_code3
        .
except:
    default_exception_code
else:
    else_body
finally:
    finally_body
```

A `try` statement is executed by first executing the code in the `body` part of the statement. If this execution is successful (that is, no exceptions are thrown to be caught by the `try` statement), the `else_body` is executed, and the `try` statement is finished. Because there is a `finally` statement, `finally_body` is executed. If an exception is thrown to the `try`, the `except` clauses are searched sequentially for one whose associated exception type matches that which was thrown. If a matching `except` clause is found, the thrown exception is assigned to the variable named after the associated exception type, and the exception code body associated with the matching exception is executed. If the line `except exception_type as var:` matches some thrown exception `exc`, the variable `var` is created, and `exc` is assigned as the value of `var` before the exception-handling code of the `except` statement is executed. You don't need to put in `var`; you can say something like `except exception_type:`, which still catches exceptions of the given type but doesn't assign them to any variable. It is also possible for an `except` clause to have a tuple of exceptions—in that case, it will catch any of those exceptions.

If no matching `except` clause is found, the thrown exception can't be handled by that `try` statement, and the exception is thrown farther up the call chain in the hope that some enclosing `try` will be able to handle it.

The last `except` clause of a `try` statement can optionally refer to no exception types at all, in which case it handles all types of exceptions. This technique can be convenient for some debugging and extremely rapid prototyping but generally isn't a good idea: all errors are hidden by the `except` clause, which can lead to some confusing behavior on the part of your program.

The `else` clause of a `try` statement is optional and rarely used. This clause is executed if and only if the `body` of the `try` statement executes without throwing any errors.

The `finally` clause of a `try` statement is also optional and executes after the `try`, `except`, and `else` sections have executed. If an exception is raised in the `try` block and isn't handled by any of the `except` blocks, that exception is raised again after the `finally` block executes. Because the `finally` block always executes, it gives you a chance to include code to clean up after any exception handling by closing files, resetting variables, and so on.

> **Try this: Catching exceptions**
>
> Write code that gets two numbers from the user and divides the first number by the second. Check for and catch the exception that occurs if the second number is zero (`ZeroDivisionError`).

14.2.4 *Defining new exceptions*

You can easily define your own exception. The following two lines do this for you:

```
class MyError(Exception):
    pass
```

This code creates a class that inherits everything from the base `Exception` class. But you don't have to worry about that if you don't want to.

You can raise, catch, and handle this exception like any other exception. If you give it a single argument (and you don't catch and handle it), it's printed at the end of the traceback:

```
raise MyError("Some information about what went wrong")
```

```
------------------------------------------------------------------------
MyError                                    Traceback (most recent call last)
<ipython-input-10-04991f64f605> in <cell line: 1>()
----> 1 raise MyError("Some information about what went wrong")

MyError: Some information about what went wrong
```

This argument, of course, is available to a handler you write as well:

```
try:
    raise MyError("Some information about what went wrong")
except MyError as error:
    print("Situation:", error)
```

The result is

```
Situation: Some information about what went wrong
```

If you raise your exception with multiple arguments, these arguments are delivered to your handler as a tuple, which you can access through the `args` variable of the error:

```
try:
    raise MyError("Some information", "my_filename", 3)
except MyError as error:
    print("Situation: {0} with file {1}\n error code: {2}".format(
        error.args[0],
 error.args[1], error.args[2]))
```

The result is

```
Situation: Some information with file my_filename
error code: 3
```

Because an exception type is a regular class in Python and happens to inherit from the root `Exception` class, it's a simple matter to create your own subhierarchy of exception types for use by your own code. You don't have to worry about this process on a first read of this book. You can always come back to it after you've read chapter 15. Exactly how you create your own exceptions depends on your particular needs. If you're writing a small program that may generate only a few unique errors or exceptions, subclass the main `Exception` class as you've done here. If you're writing a large, multifile code library with a special goal in mind—say, weather forecasting—you may decide to define a unique class called `WeatherLibraryException` and then define all the unique exceptions of the library as subclasses of `WeatherLibraryException`.

> ### Quick check: Exceptions as classes
>
> If `MyError` inherits from `Exception`, what is the difference between `except Exception as e` and `except MyError as e`?

14.2.5 *Exception groups*

In Python 3.11 two new exceptions were added: `BaseExceptionGroup`, which inherits from `BaseException`, and `ExceptionGroup`, which inherits from `Exception`. The purpose of exception groups is to bundle exceptions together to make it possible to handle more than one exception at a time. While the most common case is that exceptions occur one at a time, in concurrent programming, multiple exceptions can be raised at practically the same time.

To handle multiple exceptions, the `ExceptionGroup` was added to wrap multiple exceptions in a special exception. The way that exception groups are handled is that they are caught by using `except*` instead of `except`, and each `except*` will handle any exceptions in the group that match its type. Consider the following example:

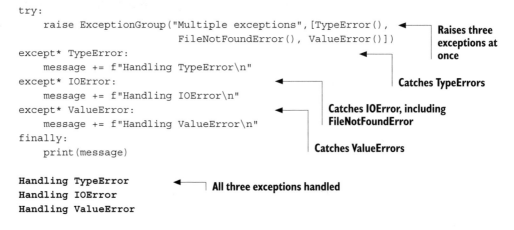

```
try:
    raise ExceptionGroup("Multiple exceptions", [TypeError(),
                         FileNotFoundError(), ValueError()])
except* TypeError:
    message += f"Handling TypeError\n"
except* IOError:
    message += f"Handling IOError\n"
except* ValueError:
    message += f"Handling ValueError\n"
finally:
    print(message)
```

Raises three exceptions at once

Catches TypeErrors

Catches IOError, including FileNotFoundError

Catches ValueErrors

```
Handling TypeError
Handling IOError
Handling ValueError
```

All three exceptions handled

The preceding code raises an exception of type `ExceptionGroup` that wraps three different exceptions—`TypeError`, `FileNotFoundError`, and `ValueError`. The `except*` clauses in turn check for those exceptions, with the second one checking for IOError, which will match all of its subclasses, including `FileNotFoundError`. The output shows that, rather than handling just the first exception, all three were caught.

14.2.6 *Debugging programs with the assert statement*

The `assert` statement is a specialized form of the `raise` statement:

```
assert expression, argument
```

The `AssertionError` exception with the optional `argument` is raised if the `expression` evaluates to `False` and the system variable `__debug__` is `True`. The `__debug__` variable defaults to `True` and is turned off by starting the Python interpreter with the `-O` or `-OO` option or by setting the system variable `PYTHONOPTIMIZE` to `True`. The optional argument can be used to include an explanation of the assertion.

The code generator creates no code for assertion statements if `__debug__` is `False`. You can use `assert` statements to instrument your code with debug statements during development and leave them in the code for possible future use with no runtime cost during regular use:

```
x = (1, 2, 3)
assert len(x) > 5, "len(x) not > 5"
```

```
--------------------------------------------------------------------
AssertionError                          Traceback (most recent call last)
<ipython-input-13-52a42f33655e> in <cell line: 2>()
      1 x = (1, 2, 3)
----> 2 assert len(x) > 5, "len(x) not > 5"

AssertionError: len(x) not > 5
```

> ### Try this: The assert statement
>
> Write a simple program that gets a number from the user and then uses the `assert` statement to raise an exception if the number is zero. Test to make sure that the `assert` statement fires; then turn it off, using one of the methods mentioned in this section.

14.2.7 *The exception inheritance hierarchy*

In this section, I expand on an earlier notion that Python exceptions are hierarchically structured and on what that structure means in terms of how `except` clauses catch exceptions.

The following code

```
try:
    body
except LookupError as error:
    exception code
except IndexError as error:
    exception code
```

catches two types of exceptions: `IndexError` and `LookupError`. It just so happens that `IndexError` is a subclass of `LookupError`. If `body` throws an `IndexError`, that error is first examined by the `except LookupError as error:` line, and because an `IndexError` is a `LookupError` by inheritance, the first `except` succeeds. The second `except` clause is never used because it's subsumed by the first `except` clause.

Conversely, flipping the order of the two `except` clauses could potentially be useful; then the first clause would handle `IndexError` exceptions, and the second clause would handle any `LookupError` exceptions that aren't `IndexError` errors.

14.2.8 *Example: A disk-writing program in Python*

In this section, I revisit the example of a word-processing program that needs to check for disk out-of-space conditions as it writes a document to disk:

```
def save_to_file(filename) :
    try:
        save_text_to_file(filename)
        save_formats_to_file(filename)
        save_prefs_to_file(filename)
        .

        .

        .

    except IOError:
        ...handle the error...
def save_text_to_file(filename):
    ...lower-level call to write size of text...
    ...lower-level call to write actual text data...
    .

    .

    .
```

Notice how unobtrusive the error-handling code is; it's wrapped around the main sequence of disk-writing calls in the `save_to_file` function. None of the subsidiary disk-writing functions needs any error-handling code. It would be easy to develop the program first and add error-handling code later. That's often what programmers do, although this practice isn't the optimal ordering of events.

As another note of interest, this code doesn't respond specifically to disk-full errors; rather, it responds to `IOError` exceptions, which Python's built-in functions raise automatically whenever they can't complete an I/O request, for whatever reason. That's probably satisfactory for your needs, but if you need to identify disk-full conditions, you can do a couple of things. The `except` body can check to see how much room is available on disk. If the disk is out of space, clearly, the problem is a disk-full problem and should be handled in this `except` body; otherwise, the code in the `except` body can throw the `IOError` farther up the call chain to be handled by some other `except`. If that solution isn't sufficient, you can do something more extreme, such as going into the C source for the Python disk-writing functions and raising your own `DiskFull` exceptions as necessary. I don't recommend the latter option, but it's nice to know that this possibility exists if you need it.

14.2.9 *Example: Exceptions in normal evaluation*

Exceptions are most often used in error handling but can also be remarkably useful in certain situations involving what you'd think of as normal evaluation. Consider the problems in implementing something that works like a spreadsheet. Like most spreadsheets, it would have to permit arithmetic operations involving cells, and it would also permit cells to contain values other than numbers. In such an application, blank cells used in a numerical calculation might be considered to contain the value 0, and cells containing any other nonnumeric string might be considered invalid and represented as the Python value None. Any calculation involving an invalid value should return an invalid value.

The first step is to write a function that evaluates a string from a cell of the spreadsheet and returns an appropriate value:

```
def cell_value(string):
    try:
        return float(string)
    except ValueError:
        if string == "":
            return 0
        else:
            return None
```

Python's exception-handling ability makes this function a simple one to write. The code tries to convert the string from the cell to a number and return it in a try block using the float built-in function. float raises the ValueError exception if it can't convert its string argument to a number, so the code catches that exception and returns either 0 or None, depending on whether the argument string is empty or nonempty.

The next step is handling the fact that some of the arithmetic might have to deal with a value of None. In a language without exceptions, the normal way to do this is to define a custom set of arithmetic functions, which check their arguments for None and then use those functions rather than the built-in arithmetic functions to perform all of the spreadsheet arithmetic. This process is time consuming and error prone, however, and it leads to slow execution because you're effectively building an interpreter in your spreadsheet. This project takes a different approach. All the spreadsheet formulas can actually be Python functions that take as arguments the x and y coordinates of the cell being evaluated and the spreadsheet itself and calculate the result for the given cell by using standard Python arithmetic operators, using cell_value to extract the necessary values from the spreadsheet. You can define a function called safe_apply that applies one of these formulas to the appropriate arguments in a try block and returns either the formula's result or None, depending on whether the formula evaluated successfully:

```
def safe_apply(function, x, y, spreadsheet):
    try:
        return function(x, y, spreadsheet)
    except TypeError:
        return None
```

These two changes are enough to integrate the idea of an empty (None) value into the semantics of the spreadsheet. Trying to develop this ability without the use of exceptions is a highly educational exercise.

14.2.10 *Where to use exceptions*

Exceptions are natural choices for handling almost any error condition. It's an unfortunate fact that error handling is often added when the rest of the program is largely complete, but exceptions are particularly good at intelligibly managing this sort of after-the-fact error-handling code (or, stated more optimistically, when you're adding more error handling after the fact).

Exceptions are also highly useful in circumstances where a large amount of processing may need to be discarded after it becomes obvious that a computational branch in your program has become untenable. The spreadsheet example is one such case; others are branch-and-bound algorithms and parsing algorithms.

Quick check: Exceptions

Do Python exceptions force a program to halt?

Suppose that you want accessing a dictionary x to always return None if a key doesn't exist in the dictionary (that is, if a KeyError exception is raised). What code would you use?

Try this: Exceptions

What code would you use to create a custom ValueTooLarge exception and raise that exception if the variable x is over 1000?

14.3   *Context managers using the with keyword*

Some situations, such as reading files, follow a predictable pattern with a set beginning and end. In the case of reading from a file, quite often the file needs to be open only one time: while data is being read. Then the file can be closed. In terms of exceptions, you can code this kind of file access like this:

```
try:
    infile = open(filename)
    data = infile.read()
finally:
    infile.close()
```

Python 3 offers a more generic way of handling situations like this: context managers. Context managers wrap a block and manage requirements on entry and departure from the block and are marked by the `with` keyword. File objects are context managers, and you can use that capability to read files:

```
with open(filename) as infile:
    data = infile.read()
```

These two lines of code are equivalent to the five previous lines. In both cases, you know that the file will be closed immediately after the last read, whether or not the operation was successful. In the second case, closure of the file is also assured because it's part of the file object's context management, so you don't need to write the code. In other words, by using `with` combined with a context manager (in this case, a file object), you don't need to worry about the routine cleanup.

After Python 3.10, `with` statements no longer need to be a single line. `with` statements may now use parentheses to split the statement across several lines, improving readability, so that the following code, which nests calls to read and write files using the same `with`

```
with open("empty.txt") as infile, open("other.txt", "w") as outfile:
    data = infile.read()
    outfile.write(data)
```

can be written more readably as

```
with (
    open("empty.txt") as infile,
    open("other.txt", "w") as outfile
):
    data = infile.read()
    outfile.write(data)
```

As you might expect, it's also possible to create your own context managers if you need them. You can learn a bit more about how to create context managers and the various ways they can be manipulated by checking out the documentation for the `contextlib` module of the standard library.

Context managers are great for things like locking and unlocking resources, closing files, committing database transactions, and so on. Since their introduction, context managers have become standard best practice for such use cases.

Quick check: Context managers

Assume that you're using a context manager in a script that reads and/or writes several files. Which of the following approaches do you think would be best?

- Put the entire script in a block managed by a `with` statement.
- Use one `with` statement for all file reads and another for all file writes.

(continued)

- Use a `with` statement each time you read a file or write a file (for each line, for example).
- Use a `with` statement for each file that you read or write.

14.4   Adding exceptions

Think about the module you wrote in chapter 9 to count word frequencies. What errors might reasonably occur in those functions? Refactor those functions to handle those exception conditions appropriately.

14.4.1   Solving the problem with AI-generated code

This problem is easy to put into a prompt. As long as the previous version of the code is available, you can simply point to the old code and tell the AI tool to refractor to add exceptions appropriately.

14.4.2   Solutions and discussion

The trick with this problem lies in the word "appropriately." It's pretty simple to tell the bot to add exceptions, but they may not be the right exceptions. As we'll see, that is more of a problem for Colaboratory than Copilot.

THE HUMAN SOLUTION

My solution modifies the functions that deal with processing the text and also adds some I/O exception handling to the functions that read and write files:

```python
# Author's version
import string
punct = str.maketrans('', '', string.punctuation)

class EmptyStringError(Exception):          # Defines custom exception
    pass
def clean_line(line):
    """changes case and removes punctuation"""

    # raise exception if line is empty
    if not line.strip():
        raise EmptyStringError()          # Raises custom exception
    # make all one case
    cleaned_line = line.lower()

    # remove punctuation
    cleaned_line = cleaned_line.translate(punct)
    return cleaned_line


def count_words(words):
    """takes list of cleaned words, returns count dictionary"""
    word_count = {}
```

```
        for word in words:
            try:
                count = word_count.setdefault(word, 0)
            except TypeError:
                #if 'word' is not hashable, skip to next word.
                pass
            word_count[word] += 1
        return word_count

def word_stats(word_count):
    """Takes word count dictionary and returns top, bottom five entries"""
    word_list = list(word_count.items())
    try:
        word_list.sort(key=lambda x: x[1])
    except TypeError as e:
        print(f"Error sorting word list: {e}")
```

◄─── **Catches TypeError**

```
    least_common = word_list[:5]
    most_common = word_list[-1:-6:-1]

    return most_common, least_common


def get_words(line):
    """splits line into words, and rejoins with newlines"""
    words = line.split()
    return "\n".join(words) + "\n"

def clean_file(filename, outfilename):
    try:
        with open(filename) as infile, open(outfilename, "w") as outfile:
            for line in infile:
                if line.strip():
                    cleaned_line = clean_line(line)
                    cleaned_words = get_words(cleaned_line)

                    # write all words for line
                    outfile.write(cleaned_words)
    except IOError as e:
        print(f"Error reading or writing to file: {e}")
```

◄─── **Catches file I/O errors**

```
def load_words(cleaned_filename):
    words = []
    print(cleaned_filename)
    try:
        with open(cleaned_filename) as infile:
            for word in infile:
                if word.strip():
                    words.append(word.strip())
    except IOError as e:
        print(f"Error reading or writing to file: {e}")
    return words

clean_file("moby_01.txt", "moby_clean.txt")
moby_words = load_words("moby_clean.txt")
```

```
word_count = count_words(moby_words)

most, least = word_stats(word_count)
print("Most common words:")
for word in most:
    print(word)
print("\nLeast common words:")
for word in least:
    print(word)
```

This solution adds a custom exception, `EmptyStringError`, as an illustration of how one would do that. In fact, there really isn't much need for a custom exception here, and I probably wouldn't bother with it normally unless I had some particular reason to worry about empty strings being passed around.

Otherwise, the other exception explicitly checked is `TypeError` to handle what would probably be rare cases of unhashable keys or lists that would be unsortable, probably because not all of the elements were strings, as well as any problems reading or writing files.

THE AI SOLUTIONS

The AI solutions show more variation than we've seen before, which is probably not surprising, considering the somewhat fuzzy nature of the problem.

The Copilot solution was not bad. The prompt used was

```
Refactor the code in the current file word_count_copilot.py to handle
errors that might reasonably occur in those functions appropriately.
```

The results were interesting and quite usable. The plan Copilot came up with was

1 In the `write_words_to_file` function, handle the `IOError` that might occur when writing to the file.

2 In the `count_word_occurrences` function, check if the input is iterable. If not, raise a `TypeError`.

3 In the `print_common_words` and `print_least_common_words` functions, check if n is a positive integer. If not, raise a `ValueError`.

4 In the `print_common_words` and `print_least_common_words` functions, handle the `IndexError` that might occur when there are less than n words.

The resulting code only covered the functions that need refactoring, which I've added into the following full file, using comments to mark the start and end of the refactored section:

```
# Generated by Copilot
import string
def clean_line(line):
    # Convert the line to lowercase
    line = line.lower()

    # Remove punctuation from the line
    line = line.translate(str.maketrans('', '', string.punctuation))
```

```
        return line

#=== Refactored code to add exception handling===========
def write_words_to_file(words, output_file):
    try:
        for word in words:
            output_file.write(word + '\n')
    except IOError as e:                          ◄────┐  Handles file I/O error
        print(f"Error writing to file: {e}")

def count_word_occurrences(words):
    if not hasattr(words, '__iter__'):
        raise TypeError("Input must be iterable")  ◄────   Raises TypeError if
                                                           word list is not iterable
    word_counts = {}
    for word in words:
        if word in word_counts:
            word_counts[word] += 1
        else:
            word_counts[word] = 1

    return word_counts
```

Raises exeption if a negative number of positions requested

```
def print_common_words(word_counts, n):
    if not isinstance(n, int) or n <= 0:
        raise ValueError("n must be a positive integer")  ◄───────

    sorted_word_counts = sorted(word_counts.items(), key=lambda x: x[1],
                                reverse=True)

    print(f"{n} most common words:")
    try:                                    **Raises IndexError (will
        for word, count in sorted_word_counts[:n]:   not occur with this code)**
            print(f"{word}: {count}")
    except IndexError as e:                  ◄───────
        print(f"Less than {n} words in input: {e}")

def print_least_common_words(word_counts, n):
    if not isinstance(n, int) or n <= 0:
        raise ValueError("n must be a positive integer")  ◄───

    sorted_word_counts = sorted(word_counts.items(), key=lambda x: x[1])

    print(f"{n} least common words:")
    try:
        for word, count in sorted_word_counts[:n]:
            print(f"{word}: {count}")
    except IndexError as e:                  ◄───────
        print(f"Less than {n} words in input: {e}")

#=== End of refactored code to add exception handling===========

def process_file(input_file_path, output_file_path):
    # Open the input file for reading
    with open(input_file_path, 'r') as input_file:
```

```
        # Open the output file for writing
        with open(output_file_path, 'w') as output_file:
            # Iterate over each line in the input file
            for line in input_file:
                # Clean the line
                cleaned_line = clean_line(line)

                # Split the line into words
                words = cleaned_line.split()

                # Write the words to the output file
                write_words_to_file(words, output_file)

def main():
    input_file_path = 'moby_01.txt'
    output_file_path = 'moby_01_clean.txt'

    # Process the file
    process_file(input_file_path, output_file_path)

    # Open the file
    with open(output_file_path, 'r') as file:
        # Read the file content
        content = file.read()

    # Split the content into words
    words = content.split()

    # Count word occurrences
    word_counts = count_word_occurrences(words)

    # Print the five most common words and their occurrences
    print_common_words(word_counts, 5)

    # Print the five least common words and their occurrences
    print_least_common_words(word_counts, 5)

if __name__ == "__main__":
    main()
```

This looks convincing but is not quite right. Handling potential file I/O errors makes perfect sense and is correctly implemented. It also makes some sense to ensure that the word list is iterable, although I would argue that it's unnecessarily paranoid. It's true that if the words parameter is not iterable, the code will fail, but lists, tuples, files, etc. are all iterable by definition, so in practice the likelihood that words will not be iterable is so tiny that it would make more sense to leave that condition unhandled.

The other two exception conditions that the code is concerned with are the check for the n parameter (number of places to return) being negative and if the number of places is greater than the number of words.

In the first case, having n be negative will cause the code to raise a ValueError warning that the value is negative. This makes some sense, since if a negative number of places is requested, no values will be returned, although no error will occur. The second case, where an `IndexError` is caught, is actually completely pointless. Given the way that the code is written, no error will be raised even if the value of n is greater than the number of items in the list `sorted_word_counts`. Even if `sorted_word_counts` is empty, `sorted_word_counts[:100]` will not be an error but will return an empty list. So that particular exception condition can never occur, and that code will only serve to confuse people in the future.

Colaboratory came up with rather different code. Again, the prompt was in reference to a cell containing the previous code, immediately above the target cell:

```
Refactor the code in the cell above to handle errors that might reasonably
occur in those functions appropriately.
```

The result was somewhat disappointing, as we'll see:

```
# prompt: Refactor the code in the cell above to handle errors that might
# reasonably occur in those functions appropriately.
import string
# Function to clean a line of text by converting it to lowercase and
# removing punctuation
def clean_line(line):
  try:
    line = line.lower()
    line = line.translate(str.maketrans('', '', string.punctuation))
  except Exception as e:
    raise Exception("Error cleaning line: {}".format(e))
  return line


# Function to split a line of text into words and
# write each word to a new line in a file
def write_words_to_file(line, output_file):
  try:
    words = line.split()
    for word in words:
      output_file.write(word + '\n')
  except Exception as e:
    raise Exception("Error writing words to file: {}".format(e))


# Function to count the occurrences of each word in a list of words
def count_word_occurrences(words):
  word_counts = {}
  for word in words:
    try:
      if word not in word_counts:
        word_counts[word] = 0
      word_counts[word] += 1
    except Exception as e:
      raise Exception("Error counting word occurrences: {}".format(e))
  return word_counts


# Function to find the most and least common words in a
# dictionary of word counts
```

```
def find_most_and_least_common_words(word_counts):
  try:
    most_common = sorted(word_counts.items(), key=lambda item: item[1],
                         reverse=True)[:5]
    least_common = sorted(word_counts.items(),
                          key=lambda item: item[1])[:5]
  except Exception as e:
    raise Exception("Error finding most and least common words:
➡ {}".format(e))
  return most_common, least_common

# Open the input file for reading
with open('moby_01.txt', 'r') as input_file:
  # Open the output file for writing
  with open('moby_01_clean.txt', 'w') as output_file:
    # Iterate over each line in the input file
    for line in input_file:
      # Clean the line of text
      try:
        cleaned_line = clean_line(line)
      except Exception as e:
        print("Error cleaning line: {}".format(e))
        continue

      # Write each word in the clean line to the output file
      try:
        write_words_to_file(cleaned_line, output_file)
      except Exception as e:
        print("Error writing words to file: {}".format(e))
        continue

# Open the file and read the text into a variable.
try:
  with open('moby_01_clean.txt', 'r') as f:
    text = f.read()
except Exception as e:
  raise Exception("Error opening file: {}".format(e))

# Split the text into words.
try:
  words = text.split()
except Exception as e:
  raise Exception("Error splitting text into words: {}".format(e))

# Count the occurrences of each word.
try:
  word_counts = count_word_occurrences(words)
except Exception as e:
  raise Exception("Error counting word occurrences: {}".format(e))

# Find the most and least common words.
try:
  most_common, least_common = find_most_and_least_common_words(word_counts)
except Exception as e:
  raise Exception("Error finding most and least common words:
```

```
➡ {}".format(e))

# Print the results.
print("Most common words:")
for word, count in most_common:
  print(f"{word}: {count}")

print("\nLeast common words:")
for word, count in least_common:
  print(f"{word}: {count}")
```

First, this code has a lot of `try-except` blocks—almost a dozen—which might lead you to believe that the error handling is good. Unfortunately, there are some problems with this approach to exception handling. First, nearly everything is wrapped in a `try-except` structure, including string operations that are very unlikely to have an error. In fact, the call to the `clean_line` function is checked for exceptions, and then inside that function, the string code is checked again. While this may seem to be a good thing—being extra conscientious in checking for errors—it's not really a great idea. For one thing, so many `try-except` structures make the code harder to read; having to parse those structures makes seeing and understanding the logic of the code more difficult.

The second problem is the way those `try-except` structures are implemented. In every case, they check for `Exception`, which is the most general exception, which will catch every Python exception other than the handful that are inherited directly from `BaseException`. Even worse, when an exception is caught, the code simply raises a new exception, with a message that vaguely indicates where the problem occurred and with the name of the exception. This is bad because while it behaves pretty much the same way as having no `try-except` at all, in fact, there is less information since this way of handling exceptions hides the traceback.

While Copilot's suggestion has one completely useless exception check, Colaboratory's is worse—even when the exception checks are not totally useless, they return less information than doing nothing and letting Python's default exception handling take over.

Summary

- Python's philosophy is that errors shouldn't pass silently unless they're explicitly silenced.
- Python's exception-handling mechanism and exception classes provide a rich system to handle runtime errors in your code.
- Python exception types are organized in a hierarchy because exceptions, like all objects in Python, are classes.
- By using `try`, `except`, `else`, and `finally` blocks, and by selecting and even creating the types of exceptions caught, you can have very fine-grained control over how exceptions are handled and ignored.

- You can define a new exception by inheriting (preferably) from `Exception`.
- Exceptions can be conditionally raised by using an `assert` statement.
- Invoking a context manager by using the `with` keyword can ensure actions even if an exception occurs, as in reading or writing a file.

Part 3

Advanced language features

The previous chapters have been a survey of the basic features of Python: the features that most programmers will use most of the time. What follows is a look at some more advanced features, such as how classes and objects work in Python, regular expressions, packages, and the standard library. While you may not use these every day (depending on your needs), knowledge of these topics is vital when you need them.

15

Classes and object-oriented programming

In this chapter, I discuss Python classes, which can be used to hold both data and code. Although most programmers are probably familiar with classes or objects in other languages, I make no particular assumptions about knowledge of a specific language or paradigm. In addition, this chapter is a description only of the constructs available in Python; it's not an exposition on object-oriented programming (OOP) itself.

15.1 *Defining classes*

A *class* in Python is effectively a data type. All the data types built into Python are classes, and Python gives you powerful tools to manipulate every aspect of a class's behavior. You define a class with the class statement:

```
class MyClass:
    body
```

body is a list of Python statements—typically, variable assignments and function definitions. No assignments or function definitions are required. The body can be just a single pass statement.

By convention, class identifiers are in CapCase—that is, the first letter of each component word is capitalized, to make the identifiers stand out. After you define the class, you can create a new object of the class type (an instance of the class) by calling the class name as a function:

```
instance = MyClass()
```

15.1.1 *Using a class instance as a structure or record*

Class instances can be used as structures or records. Unlike C structures or Java classes, the data fields of an instance don't need to be declared ahead of time; they can be created on the fly. The following short example defines a class called Circle, creates a Circle instance, assigns a value to the radius field of the circle, and then uses that field to calculate the circumference of the circle:

```
class Circle:
    pass

my_circle = Circle()
my_circle.radius = 5
print(2 * 3.14 * my_circle.radius)
```

```
31.4
```

As in Java and many other languages, the fields of an instance/structure are accessed and assigned to by using dot notation.

You can initialize fields of an instance automatically by including an __init__ initialization method in the class body. This function is run every time an instance of the class is created, with that new instance as its first argument, self. The __init__ method is similar to a constructor in Java, but it doesn't really *construct* anything; it *initializes* fields of the class. Also, unlike those in Java and C++, Python classes may only have one __init__ method. This example creates circles with a radius of 1 by default:

```
class Circle:
    def __init__(self):
```
◄──────┘ **self as parameter for __init__()**

```
        self.radius = 1
my_circle = Circle()
print(2 * 3.14 * my_circle.radius)

my_circle.radius = 5
print(2 * 3.14 * my_circle.radius)

6.28
31.400000000000002
```

Creates instance of Circle

radius field already set

Overwriting radius

Different result with different radius

By convention, `self` is always the name of the first argument of `__init__`. `self` is set to the newly created circle instance when `__init__` is run. Next, the code uses the class definition. You first create a `Circle` instance object. The next line makes use of the fact that the `radius` field is already initialized. You can also overwrite the `radius` field; as a result, the last line prints a different result from the previous `print` statement.

Python also has something more like a constructor: the `__new__` method, which is what is called on object creation and returns an uninitialized object. Unless you're subclassing an immutable type, like `str` or `int`, or using a metaclass to modify the object creation process, it's rare to override the existing `__new__` method.

You can do a great deal more by using true OOP, and if you're not familiar with it, I urge you to read up on it. Python's OOP constructs are the subject of the remainder of this chapter.

15.2 *Instance variables*

Instance variables are the most basic feature of OOP. Take a look at the `Circle` class again:

```
class Circle:
    def __init__(self):
        self.radius = 1
```

`radius` is an *instance variable* of `Circle` instances. That is, each instance of the `Circle` class has its own copy of `radius`, and the value stored in that copy may be different from the values stored in the `radius` variable in other instances. In Python, you can create instance variables as necessary by assigning to a field of a class instance:

```
instance.variable = value
```

If the variable doesn't already exist, it's created automatically, which is how `__init__` creates the `radius` variable.

All uses of instance variables, both assignment and access, require *explicit mention* of the containing instance—that is, `instance.variable`. A reference to `variable` by itself is a reference not to an instance variable but to a local variable in the executing method. This is different from C++ and Java, where instance variables are referred to in the same manner as local method function variables. I rather like Python's requirement for explicit mention of the containing instance because it clearly distinguishes instance variables from local function variables.

> **Try this: Instance variables**
>
> What code would you use to create a `Rectangle` class?

15.3 *Methods*

A *method* is a function associated with a particular class. You've already seen the special `__init__` method, which is called on a new instance when that instance is created. In the following example, you define another method, `area`, for the `Circle` class; this method can be used to calculate and return the area for any `Circle` instance. Like most user-defined methods, `area` is called with a *method invocation syntax* that resembles instance variable access:

```
class Circle:
    def __init__(self):
        self.radius = 1
    def area(self):
        return self.radius * self.radius * 3.14159

c = Circle()
c.radius = 3
print(c.area())
```

28.27431

Method invocation syntax consists of an instance, followed by a period, followed by the method to be invoked on the instance. When a method is called in this way, it's a *bound* method invocation. However, a method can also be invoked as an *unbound* method by accessing it through its containing class. This practice is less convenient and is almost never done, because when a method is invoked in this manner, its first argument must be an instance of the class in which that method is defined and is less clear:

```
print(Circle.area(c))
```

28.27431

Like `__init__`, the area method is defined as a function within the body of the class definition. The first argument of any method is the instance it was invoked by or on, named `self` by convention. In many languages the instance, often called `this`, is implicit and is never explicitly passed, but Python's design philosophy prefers to make things explicit.

Methods can be invoked with arguments if the method definitions accept those arguments. This version of `Circle` adds an argument to the `__init__` method so that you can create circles of a given radius without needing to set the radius after a circle is created:

```
class Circle:
    def __init__(self, radius):
        self.radius = radius
    def area(self):
        return self.radius * self.radius * 3.14159
```

Note the two uses of `radius` here. `self.radius` is the instance variable called `radius`; `radius` by itself is the local function parameter called `radius`. The two aren't the same! In practice, you'd probably call the local function parameter something like `r` or `rad` to avoid any possibility of confusion.

Using this definition of `Circle`, you can create circles of any radius with one call on the `Circle` class. The following creates a `Circle` of radius 5:

```
c = Circle(5)
```

All the standard Python function features—default argument values, extra arguments, keyword arguments, and so forth—can be used with methods. You could have defined the first line of `__init__` to be

```
def __init__(self, radius=1):
```

Then calls to `circle` would work with or without an extra argument; `Circle()` would return a circle of radius 1, and `Circle(3)` would return a circle of radius 3.

There's nothing magical about method invocation in Python, which can be considered shorthand for normal function invocation. Given a method invocation `instance.method(arg1, arg2, . . .)`, Python transforms it into a normal function call by using the following rules:

1 Look for the method name in the instance namespace. If a method has been changed or added for this instance, it's invoked in preference over methods in the class or superclass. This lookup is the same sort of lookup discussed in section 15.4.1 later in this chapter.

2 If the method isn't found in the instance namespace, look up the class type `class` of `instance`, and look for the method there. In the previous examples, `class` is `Circle`—the type of the instance c.

3 If the method still isn't found, look for the method in the superclasses.

4 When the method has been found, make a direct call to it as a normal Python function, using the instance as the first argument of the function and shifting all the other arguments in the method invocation one space over to the right. So `instance.method(arg1, arg2, . . .)` becomes `class.method(instance, arg1, arg2, . . .)`.

> **Try this: Instance variables and methods**
>
> Update the code for a `Rectangle` class so that you can set the dimensions when
> an instance is created, just as for the `Circle` class previously. Also, add an `area()`
> method.

15.4 *Class variables*

A *class variable* is a variable associated with a class, not an instance of a class, and is
accessible by *all* instances of the class. A class variable might be used to keep track of
some class-level information, such as how many instances of the class have been created at any point. Python provides class variables, although using them requires slightly
more effort than in most other languages. Also, you need to watch out for an interaction between class and instance variables.

A class variable is created by an assignment in the class body, not in the __init__
function. After it has been created, it can be seen by all instances of the class. You can
use a class variable to make a value for `pi` accessible to all instances of the `Circle` class:

```
class Circle:
    pi = 3.14159
    def __init__(self, radius):
        self.radius = radius
    def area(self):
        return self.radius * self.radius * Circle.pi
```

With the definition entered, you can type

```
Circle.pi
```

3.14159

```
Circle.pi = 4
Circle.pi
```

4

```
Circle.pi = 3.14159
Circle.pi
```

3.14159

This example is exactly how you'd expect a class variable to act; it's associated with
and contained in the class that defines it. Notice in this example that you're accessing
`Circle.pi` before any circle instances have been created. Obviously, `Circle.pi` exists
independently of any specific instances of the `Circle` class.

You can also access a class variable from a method of a class, through the class name.
You do so in the definition of `Circle.area`, where the `area` function makes specific

reference to `Circle.pi`. In operation, this has the desired effect; the correct value for `pi` is obtained from the class and used in the calculation:

```
c = Circle(3)
c.area()
```

28.27431

You may object to hardcoding the name of a class inside that class's methods. You can avoid doing so through use of the special __class__ attribute, available to all Python class instances. This attribute returns the class of which the instance is a member—for example:

```
Circle
```

<class '__main__.Circle'>

```
c.__class__
```

<class '__main__.Circle'>

The class named `Circle` is represented internally by an abstract data structure, and that data structure is exactly what is obtained from the __class__ attribute of c, an instance of the `Circle` class. This example lets you obtain the value of `Circle.pi` from c without ever explicitly referring to the `Circle` class name:

```
c.__class__.pi
```

3.14159

You could use this code internally in the `area` method to get rid of the explicit reference to the `Circle` class; replace `Circle.pi` with `self.__class__.pi`.

15.4.1 *An oddity with class variables*

There's a bit of an oddity with class variables that can trip you up if you aren't aware of it. When Python is looking up an instance variable, if it can't find an instance variable of that name, it tries to find and return the value in a class variable of the same name. Only if it can't find an appropriate class variable will Python signal an error. Class variables make it efficient to implement default values for instance variables; just create a class variable with the same name and appropriate default value and avoid the time and memory overhead of initializing that instance variable every time a class instance is created. But this also makes it easy to inadvertently refer to an instance variable rather than a class variable without signaling an error. In this section, I look at how class variables operate in conjunction with the previous example.

First, you can refer to the variable `c.pi`, even though c doesn't have an associated instance variable named `pi`. Python first tries to look for such an instance variable;

when it can't find an instance variable, Python looks for and finds a class variable `pi` in `Circle`:

```
c = Circle(3)
c.pi
```

3.14159

This result may or may not be what you want. This technique is convenient but can be prone to error, so be careful.

Now, what happens if you attempt to use `c.pi` as a true class variable by changing it from one instance with the intention that all instances should see the change? Again, you use the earlier definition for `Circle`:

```
c1 = Circle(1)
c2 = Circle(2)
c1.pi = 3.14
c1.pi
```

3.14

```
c2.pi
```

3.14159

```
Circle.pi
```

3.14159

This example doesn't work as it would for a true class variable; `c1` now has its own copy of `pi`, distinct from the `Circle.pi` accessed by `c2`. This happens because the assignment to `c1.pi` *creates* an instance variable in `c1`; it doesn't affect the class variable `Circle.pi` in any way. Subsequent lookups of `c1.pi` return the value in that instance variable, whereas subsequent lookups of `c2.pi` look for an instance variable `pi` in `c2`, fail to find it, and resort to returning the value of the class variable `Circle.pi`. If you want to change the value of a class variable, access it through the class name, not through the instance variable `self`.

15.5 *Static methods and class methods*

Python classes can also have methods that correspond explicitly to static methods in a language such as Java. In addition, Python has *class* methods, which are a bit more advanced.

15.5.1 *Static methods*

Just as in Java, you can invoke static methods even though no instance of that class has been created, although you can call them by using a class instance. To create a static method, use the `@staticmethod` decorator, as shown in the following listing.

Listing 15.1   File circle.py

```
"""circle module: contains the Circle class."""
class Circle:
    """Circle class"""
    all_circles = []
    pi = 3.14159
    def __init__(self, r=1):
        """Create a Circle with the given radius"""
        self.radius = r
        self.__class__.all_circles.append(self)
    def area(self):
        """determine the area of the Circle"""
        return self.__class__.pi * self.radius * self.radius

    @staticmethod
    def total_area():
        """Static method to total the areas of all Circles """
        total = 0
        for c in Circle.all_circles:
            total = total + c.area()
        return total
```

> Class variable containing list of all circles that have been created

> When an instance is initialized, it adds itself to the all_circles list.

Now interactively type the following:

```
import circle
c1 = circle.Circle(1)
c2 = circle.Circle(2)
circle.Circle.total_area()
```

15.70795

```
c2.radius = 3
circle.Circle.total_area()
```

31.415899999999997

Also notice that documentation strings are used. In a real module, you'd probably put in more informative strings, indicating in the class docstring what methods are available and including usage information in the method docstrings:

```
circle.__doc__
```

'circle module: contains the Circle class.'

```
circle.Circle.__doc__
```

'Circle class'

```
circle.Circle.area.__doc__
```

'determine the area of the Circle'

15.5.2 *Class methods*

Class methods are similar to static methods in that they can be invoked before an object of the class has been instantiated or by using an instance of the class. But class methods are implicitly passed the class they belong to as their first parameter, so you can code them more simply.

Listing 15.2 File circle_cm.py

```
'''circle_cm module: contains the Circle class.'''
class Circle:
    '''Circle class'''
    all_circles = []
    pi = 3.14159
    def __init__(self, r=1):
        '''Create a Circle with the given radius'''
        self.radius = r
        self.__class__.all_circles.append(self)
    def area(self):
        '''determine the area of the Circle'''
        return self.__class__.pi * self.radius * self.radius

    @classmethod
    def total_area(cls):
        total = 0
        for c in cls.all_circles:
            total = total + c.area()
        return total
```

Variable containing list of all circles that have been created

@classmethod decorator

cls used instead of self

cls can be used in place of Circle.

```
import circle_cm
c1 = circle_cm.Circle(1)
c2 = circle_cm.Circle(2)
circle_cm.Circle.total_area()

15.70795

c2.radius = 3
circle_cm.Circle.total_area()

31.415899999999997
```

The `@classmethod` decorator is used before the method `def`. The class parameter is traditionally `cls`. You can use `cls` instead of `Circle`.

By using a class method instead of a static method, you don't have to hardcode the class name into `total_area`. As a result, any subclasses of `Circle` can still call `total_area` and refer to their own members, not those in `Circle`.

Try this: Class methods

Write a class method similar to `total_area()` that returns the total circumference of all circles. Remember that the circumference of a circle is 2 times the radius times pi.

15.6 *Inheritance*

Inheritance in Python is easier and more flexible than inheritance in compiled languages such as Java and C++ because the dynamic nature of Python doesn't force as many restrictions on the language.

To see how inheritance is used in Python, start with the `Circle` class discussed earlier in this chapter and generalize. You might want to define an additional class for squares:

```
class Square:
    def __init__(self, side=1):
        self.side = side
```
◄——— **Length of any side of square**

Now, if you want to use these classes in a drawing program, they must define some sense of where on the drawing surface each instance is. You can do so by defining an `x` coordinate and a `y` coordinate in each instance:

```
class Square:
    def __init__(self, side=1, x=0, y=0):
        self.side = side
        self.x = x
        self.y = y
class Circle:
    def __init__(self, radius=1, x=0, y=0):
        self.radius = radius
        self.x = x
        self.y = y
```

This approach works but results in a good deal of repetitive code as you expand the number of shape classes, because you presumably want each shape to have this concept of position. No doubt you know where I'm going here; this situation is a standard one for using inheritance in an object-oriented language. Instead of defining the x and y variables in each shape class, you can abstract them out into a general `Shape` class and have each class define a specific shape inherited from that general class. In Python, that technique looks like the following:

```
class Shape:
    def __init__(self, x, y):
        self.x = x
        self.y = y
class Square(Shape):
    def __init__(self, side=1, x=0, y=0):
        super().__init__(x, y)
        self.side = side
class Circle(Shape):
    def __init__(self, r=1, x=0, y=0):
        super().__init__(x, y)
        self.radius = r
```

◄——— **Says Square inherits from Shape**

◄——— | **Says Circle inherits from Shape**

Must call __init__ method of Shape

There are (generally) two requirements in using an inherited class in Python, both of which you can see in the bolded code in the `Circle` and `Square` classes. The first requirement is defining the inheritance hierarchy, which you do by giving the classes inherited from, in parentheses, immediately after the name of the class being defined with the class keyword. In the previous code, Circle and Square both inherit from Shape. The second and more subtle element is the necessity to explicitly call the __init__ method of inherited classes. Python doesn't automatically do this for you, but you can use the super function to have Python figure out which inherited class to use. This task is accomplished in the example code by the super().__init__(x,y) lines. This code calls the Shape initialization function with the instance being initialized and the appropriate arguments. Otherwise, in the example, instances of Circle and Square wouldn't have their x and y instance variables set.

Instead of using super, you could call Shape's __init__ by explicitly naming the inherited class using Shape.__init__(self, x, y), which would also call the Shape initialization function with the instance being initialized. This technique wouldn't be as flexible in the long run because it hardcodes the inherited class's name, which could be a problem later if the design and the inheritance hierarchy change. On the other hand, the use of super can be tricky in more complex cases. Because the two methods don't exactly mix well, clearly document whichever approach you use in your code.

Inheritance also comes into effect when you attempt to use a method that isn't defined in the subclass or derived class but is defined in the superclass. To see this effect, define another method in the Shape class called move, which moves a shape by a given displacement. This method modifies the x and y coordinates of the shape by an amount determined by arguments to the method. The definition for Shape now becomes

```
class Shape:
    def __init__(self, x, y):
        self.x = x
        self.y = y
    def move(self, delta_x, delta_y):
        self.x = self.x + delta_x
        self.y = self.y + delta_y
```

If you enter this definition for Shape and the previous definitions for Circle and Square, you can engage in the following interactive session:

```
c = Circle(1)
c.move(3, 4)
f"c.x = {c.x}, c.y = {c.y}"

'c.x = 3, c.y = 4'
```

If you try this code in an interactive session, be sure to reenter the Circle class after the redefinition of the Shape class.

The Circle class in the example didn't define a move method immediately within itself, but because it inherits from a class that implements move, all instances of Circle can make use of move. In more traditional OOP terms, you could say that all Python methods are virtual—that is, if a method doesn't exist in the current class, the list of superclasses is searched for the method, and the first one found is used.

> **Try this: Inheritance**
>
> Rewrite the code for a `Rectangle` class to inherit from `Shape`. Because squares and rectangles are related, would it make sense to inherit one from the other? If so, which would be the base class, and which would inherit?
>
> How would you write the code to add an `area()` method for the `Square` class? Should the `area` method be moved into the base `Shape` class and inherited by `Circle`, `Square`, and `Rectangle`? If so, what problems would result?

15.7 *Inheritance with class and instance variables*

Inheritance allows an instance to inherit attributes of a class. Instance variables are associated with object instances, and only one instance variable of a given name exists for a given instance.

Consider the following example. Using these class definitions,

```
class P:
    z = "Hello"
    def set_p(self):
        self.x = "Class P"
    def print_p(self):
        print(self.x)
class C(P):
    def set_c(self):
        self.x = "Class C"
    def print_c(self):
        print(self.x)
```

execute the following code:

```
c = C()
c.set_p()
c.print_p()
```

```
Class P
```

```
c.print_c()
```

```
Class P
```

```
c.set_c()
c.print_c()
```

```
Class C
```

```
c.print_p()
```

```
Class C
```

The object c in this example is an instance of class C. C inherits from P but c doesn't inherit from some invisible instance of class P. It inherits methods and class variables directly from P. Because there is only one instance (c), any reference to the instance variable x in a method invocation on c must refer to c.x. This is true regardless of which class defines the method being invoked on c. As you can see, when they're invoked on c, both set_p and print_p, defined in class P, refer to the same variable, which is referred to by set_c and print_c when they're invoked on c.

In general, this behavior is what is desired for instance variables, because it makes sense that references to instance variables of the same name should refer to the same variable. Occasionally, somewhat different behavior is desired, which you can achieve by using private variables (see section 15.9).

Class variables are inherited, but you should take care to avoid name clashes and be aware of a generalization of the behavior you saw in the subsection on class variables. In the example, a class variable z is defined for the superclass P and can be accessed in three ways: through the instance c, through the derived class C, or directly through the superclass P:

```
f"{c.z=} {C.z=} {P.z=}"
```

```
'c.z='Hello' C.z='Hello' P.z='Hello''
```

But if you try setting the class variable z through the class C, a new class variable is created for the class C. This result has no effect on P's class variable itself (as accessed through P). But future accesses through the class C or its instance c will see this new variable rather than the original:

```
C.z = "Bonjour"
f"{c.z=} {C.z=} {P.z=}"
```

```
'c.z='Bonjour' C.z='Bonjour' P.z='Hello''
```

Similarly, if you try setting z through the instance c, a new instance variable is created, and you end up with three different variables:

```
c.z = "Ciao"
f"{c.z=} {C.z=} {P.z=}"
```

```
'c.z='Ciao' C.z='Bonjour' P.z='Hello''
```

15.8   *Recap: Basics of Python classes*

The points I've discussed so far are the basics of using classes and objects in Python. Before I go any further, I'll bring the basics together in a single example. In this section, you create a couple of classes with the features discussed earlier, and then you see how those features behave.

First, create a base class:

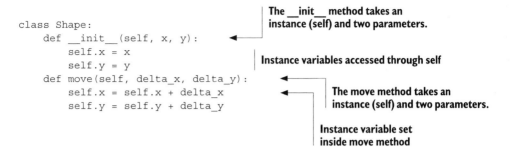

```
class Shape:
    def __init__(self, x, y):
        self.x = x
        self.y = y
    def move(self, delta_x, delta_y):
        self.x = self.x + delta_x
        self.y = self.y + delta_y
```

The __init__ method takes an instance (self) and two parameters.

Instance variables accessed through self

The move method takes an instance (self) and two parameters.

Instance variable set inside move method

Next, create a subclass that inherits from the base class `Shape`:

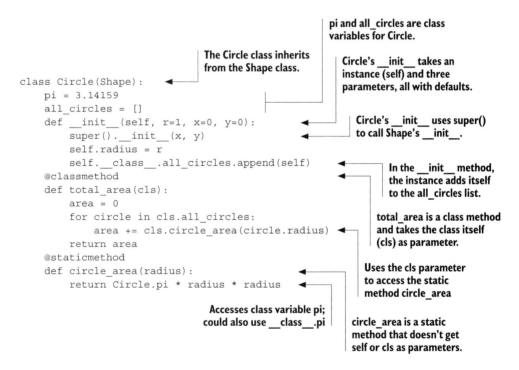

```
class Circle(Shape):
    pi = 3.14159
    all_circles = []
    def __init__(self, r=1, x=0, y=0):
        super().__init__(x, y)
        self.radius = r
        self.__class__.all_circles.append(self)
    @classmethod
    def total_area(cls):
        area = 0
        for circle in cls.all_circles:
            area += cls.circle_area(circle.radius)
        return area
    @staticmethod
    def circle_area(radius):
        return Circle.pi * radius * radius
```

pi and all_circles are class variables for Circle.

The Circle class inherits from the Shape class.

Circle's __init__ takes an instance (self) and three parameters, all with defaults.

Circle's __init__ uses super() to call Shape's __init__.

In the __init__ method, the instance adds itself to the all_circles list.

total_area is a class method and takes the class itself (cls) as parameter.

Uses the cls parameter to access the static method circle_area

Accesses class variable pi; could also use __class__.pi

circle_area is a static method that doesn't get self or cls as parameters.

Now you can create some instances of the `Circle` class and put them through their paces. Because `Circle`'s __init__ method has default parameters, you can create a `Circle` without giving any parameters:

```
c1 = Circle()
c1.radius, c1.x, c1.y
```

```
(1, 0, 0)
```

If you do give parameters, they are used to set the instance's values:

```
c2 = Circle(2, 1, 1)
c2.radius, c2.x, c2.y
```

(2, 1, 1)

If you call the move() method, Python doesn't find a move() in the Circle class, so it moves up the inheritance hierarchy and uses Shape's move() method:

```
c2.move(2, 2)
c2.radius, c2.x, c2.y
```

(2, 3, 3)

Also, because part of what the __init__ method does is add each instance to a list that is a class variable, you get the Circle instances:

```
Circle.all_circles
```

[<__main__.Circle object at 0x7fa88835e9e8>, <__main__.Circle object at ➥0x7fa88835eb00>]

```
[c1, c2]
```

[<__main__.Circle object at 0x7fa88835e9e8>, <__main__.Circle object at ➥0x7fa88835eb00>]

You can also call the Circle class's total_area() class method, either through the class itself or through an instance:

```
Circle.total_area()
```

15.70795

```
c2.total_area()
```

15.70795

Finally, you can call the static method circle_area(), again either via the class itself or an instance. As a static method, circle_area doesn't get passed the instance or the class, and it behaves more like an independent function that's inside the class's namespace. In fact, quite often, static methods are used to bundle utility functions with a class:

```
Circle.circle_area(c1.radius)
```

3.14159

```
c1.circle_area(c1.radius)
```

3.14159

These examples show the basic behavior of classes in Python. Now that you've got the basics of classes down, you can move on to more advanced topics.

15.9 *Private variables and private methods*

A *private variable* or *private method* is one that can't be seen outside the methods of the class in which it's defined. Private variables and methods are useful for two reasons: they enhance security and reliability by selectively denying access to important or delicate parts of an object's implementation, and they prevent name clashes that can arise from the use of inheritance. A class may define a private variable and inherit from a class that defines a private variable of the same name, but this doesn't cause a problem, because the fact that the variables are private ensures that separate copies of them are kept. Private variables make it easier to read code, because they explicitly indicate what's used only internally in a class. Anything else is the class's interface.

Most languages that define private variables do so through the use of the keyword "private" or something similar. The convention in Python is simpler, and it also makes it easier to immediately see what is private and what isn't. Any method or instance variable whose name begins—but doesn't end—with a *double underscore* (__) is private; anything else isn't private.

As an example, consider the following class definition:

```
class Mine:
    def __init__(self):
        self.x = 2
        self.__y = 3
    def print_y(self):
        print(self.__y)
```

Defines __y as private by using leading double underscores

Using this definition, create an instance of the class:

```
m = Mine()
```

x isn't a private variable, so it's directly accessible:

```
print(m.x)
```

```
2
```

__y is a private variable. Trying to access it directly raises an error:

```
print(m.__y)
```

```
---------------------------------------------------------------
AttributeError                          Traceback (most recent call last)
<ipython-input-74-c09dfe1cad43> in <cell line: 1>()
----> 1 print(m.__y)

AttributeError: 'Mine' object has no attribute '__y'
```

The `print_y` method isn't private, and because it's in the `Mine` class, it can access `__y` and print it:

```
m.print_y()
```

```
3
```

Finally, you should note that the mechanism used to provide privacy *mangles* the name of private variables and private methods when the code is compiled to bytecode. What specifically happens is that `_classname` is prepended to the variable name:

```
dir(m)
```

```
['_Mine__y',
 ...
 'print_y',
 'x']
```

The purpose is to prevent any accidental access. If someone wanted to, they could deliberately simulate the mangling and access the value. But performing the mangling in this easily readable form makes debugging easy.

> **Try this: Private instance variables**
>
> Modify the `Rectangle` class's code to make the dimension variables private. What restriction will this modification impose on using the class?

15.10 *Using @property for more flexible instance variables*

Python allows you as the programmer to access instance variables directly, without the extra machinery of the getter and setter methods often used in Java and other object-oriented languages. This lack of getters and setters makes writing Python classes cleaner and easier, but in some situations, using getter and setter methods can be handy. Suppose that you want a value before you put it into an instance variable or where it would be helpful to figure out an attribute's value on the fly. In both cases, getter and setter methods would do the job—but at the cost of losing Python's easy instance variable access.

The solution is to use a property. A *property* combines the ability to pass access to an instance variable through methods like getters and setters and the straightforward access to instance variables through dot notation.

To create a property, you use the property decorator with a method that has the property's name:

```
class Temperature:
    def __init__(self):
```

```
        self._temp_fahr = 0
    @property
    def temp(self):
        return (self._temp_fahr - 32) * 5 / 9
```

Without a setter, such a property is read-only. To change the property, you need to add a setter:

```
    @temp.setter
    def temp(self, new_temp):
        self._temp_fahr = new_temp * 9 / 5 + 32
```

Now you can use standard dot notation to both get and set the property `temp`. Notice that the name of the method remains the same, but the decorator changes to the property name (`temp`, in this case), plus `.setter` indicates that a setter for the `temp` property is being defined:

```
t = Temperature()
t._temp_fahr
```

```
0
```

```
t.temp                    ◄────┐   The getter etter returns centigrade.
```

```
-17.77777777777778
```

```
t.temp = 34               ◄────┐   The setter converts and
t._temp_fahr                   │   stores in _temp_fahr.
```

```
93.2                           │
```

```
t.temp                    ◄────┘
```

```
34.0
```

The `0` in `_temp_fahr` is converted to centigrade by the getter method before it's returned, and the `34` is converted back to Fahrenheit by the setter.

One big advantage of Python's ability to add properties is that you can do initial development with plain-old instance variables and then seamlessly change to properties whenever and wherever you need to without changing any client code. The access is still the same, using dot notation.

> ### Try this: Properties
> Update the dimensions of the `Rectangle` class to be properties with getters and setters that don't allow negative sizes.

15.11 *Scoping rules and namespaces for class instances*

Now you have all the pieces to put together a picture of the scoping rules and namespaces for a class instance.

When you're in a method of a class, you have direct access to the *local namespace* (parameters and variables declared in the method), the *global namespace* (functions and variables declared at the module level), and the *built-in namespace* (built-in functions and built-in exceptions). These three namespaces are searched in the following order: local, global, and built-in (see figure 15.1).

You also have access through the `self` variable to the *instance's namespace* (instance variables, private instance variables, and superclass instance variables), its *class's namespace* (methods, class variables, private methods, and private class variables), and its *superclass's namespace* (superclass methods and superclass class variables). These three namespaces are searched in the order instance, class, and then superclass (see figure 15.2).

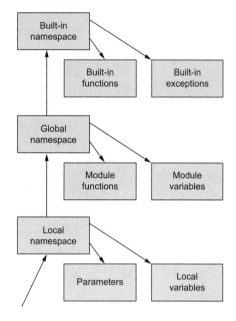

Figure 15.1   Direct namespaces

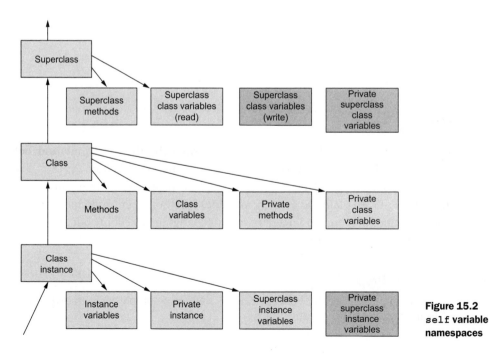

Figure 15.2 `self` variable namespaces

Private superclass instance variables, private superclass methods, and private superclass class variables can't be accessed by using `self`. A class is able to hide these names from its children.

The module in the following listing puts these two examples together to concretely demonstrate what can be accessed from within a method.

Listing 15.3 File cs.py

```python
"""cs module: class scope demonstration module."""
mod_var ="module variable: mod_var"
def mod_func():
    return ("module level function: mod_func()")
class SuperClass:
    super_class_var = "superclass class variable: self.super_class_var"
    __priv_super_class_var = "private superclass class variable: no access"
    def __init__(self):
        self.super_instance_var = "superclass instance variable:
➥self.super_instance_var "
        self.__psiv = "private superclass instance variable: no access"
    def super_class_method(self):
        return "superclass method: self.super_class_method()"
    def superclass_priv_method(self):
        return "superclass private method: no access"
class Class_(SuperClass):
    class_var = "class variable: self.class_var or Class_.class_var
➥(for assignment)"
    __priv_class_var = "class private variable: self.__priv_class_var
➥ Class_.__priv_class_var "
    def __init__(self):
        SuperClass.__init__(self)
        self.__priv_instance_var = "private instance variable:
➥self.__priv_instance_var"
    def method_2(self):
        return "method: self.method_2()"
    def __priv_method(self):
        return "private method: self.__priv_method()"
    def method_1(self, param="parameter: param"):
        local_var = "local variable: local_var"
        self.instance_var = "instance variable: self.instance_var"
        print("Local")
        print("Access local, global and built-in namespaces directly")
        print("local namespace:", list(locals().keys()))
        print(param)                                    ◀──┐ **Parameter**

        print(local_var)              ◀──┐ **Local variable**
        print()
        print("global namespace:", list(globals().keys()))
        print(mod_var)                          ◀──┐ **Module variable**

        print(mod_func())        ◀──┐ **Module function**
        print()
        print("Access instance, class, and superclass namespaces through
➥'self'")
```

```
print("Instance namespace:", self.__dict__)

print(self.instance_var)                              ◄——┘ Instance variable

print(self.__priv_instance_var)                       ◄——┘ Private instance variable

print(self.super_instance_var)                   ◄——┘ Superclass instance variable
print("\nClass_ namespace:", Class_.__dict__)
print(self.class_var)                                 ◄——┘ Class variable

print(self.method_2())                  ◄——┘ Method

print(self.__priv_class_var)            ◄——┘ Private class variable

print(self.__priv_method())                      ◄——┘ Private method
print("\nSuperclass namespace:", SuperClass.__dict__)
print(self.super_class_method())                    ◄——┐ Superclass method

print(self.super_class_var)           ◄——┐ Superclass class variable
                                           │ through instance
```

This output is considerable, so we'll look at it in pieces.

In the first part, class `Class_`'s method `method_1`'s local namespace contains the parameters `self` (which is the instance variable) and `param` along with the local variable `local_var` (all of which can be accessed directly):

```
import cs
c = cs.Class_()
c.method_1()

Access local, global and built-in namespaces directly
local namespace: ['self', 'param', 'local_var']
parameter: param
local variable: local_var
```

Next, method `method_1`'s global namespace contains the module variable `mod_var` and the module function `mod_func` (which, as described in a previous section, you can use to provide a class method functionality). There are also the classes defined in the module (the class `Class_` and the superclass `SuperClass`). All these classes can be directly accessed:

```
global namespace: ['__name__', '__doc__', '__package__', '__loader__',
'__spec__', '__builtin__', '__builtins__', 'mod_var', 'mod_func',
'SuperClass', ]
module variable: mod_var
module level function: mod_func()
```

Instance c's namespace contains instance variable `instance_var` and the superclass's instance variable `super_instance_var` (which, as described in a previous section, is no different from the regular instance variable). It also has the mangled name of private instance variable `__priv_instance_var` (which you can access through `self`) and the mangled name of the superclass's private instance variable `__psiv` (which you can't access):

```
Access instance, class, and superclass namespaces through 'self'
Instance namespace: {'super_instance_var': 'superclass instance variable:
self.super_instance_var ', '_SuperClass__psiv': 'private superclass
instance variable: no access', '_Class___priv_instance_var': 'private
instance variable: self.__priv_instance_var', 'instance_var': 'instance
variable: self.instance_var'}
instance variable: self.instance_var
private instance variable: self.__priv_instance_var
superclass instance variable: self.super_instance_var
```

Class `Class_`'s namespace contains the class variable `class_var` and the mangled name of the private class variable `__priv_class_var`. Both can be accessed through `self`, but to assign to them, you need to use class `Class_`. Class `Class_` also has the class's two methods `method_1` and `method_2`, along with the mangled name of the private method `__priv_method` (which can be accessed through `self`):

```
Class_ namespace: {'__module__': '__main__', 'class_var': 'class variable:
self.class_var or Class_.class_var (for assignment)',
'_Class___priv_class_var': 'class private variable: self.__priv_class_var
or Class_.__priv_class_var ', '__init__': <function Class_.__init__ at
0x7b4b3e3dbeb0>, 'method_2': <function Class_.method_2 at 0x7b4b3e3db640>,
'_Class___priv_method': <function Class_.__priv_method at 0x7b4b3e3da560>,
'method_1': <function Class_.method_1 at 0x7b4b3e3db520>, '__doc__': None}
class variable: self.class_var or Class_.class_var (for assignment)
method: self.method_2()
class private variable: self.__priv_class_var or Class_.__priv_class_var
private method: self.__priv_method()
```

Finally, superclass `SuperClass`'s namespace contains superclass class variable `super_class_var` (which can be accessed through `self`, but to assign to it, you need to use the superclass `SuperClass`) and superclass method `super_class_method`. It also contains the mangled names of private superclass method `superclass_priv_method` and private superclass class variable `__priv_super_class_var`, neither of which can be accessed through `self`:

```
Superclass namespace: {'__module__': '__main__', 'super_class_var':
'superclass class variable: self.super_class_var',
'_SuperClass__priv_super_class_var': 'private superclass class variable: no
access', '__init__': <function SuperClass.__init__ at 0x7b4b3e3d9360>,
'super_class_method': <function SuperClass.super_class_method at
0x7b4b3e3d9480>, 'superclass_priv_method': <function
SuperClass.superclass_priv_method at 0x7b4b3e3d9120>, '__dict__':
<attribute '__dict__' of 'SuperClass' objects>, '__weakref__': <attribute
'__weakref__' of 'SuperClass' objects>, '__doc__': None}
superclass method: self.super_class_method()
superclass class variable: self.super_class_var
```

This example is a rather full one to decipher at first. You can use it as a reference or a base for your own exploration. As with most other concepts in Python, you can build a solid understanding of what's going on by experimenting with a few simplified examples.

15.12 Destructors and memory management

You've already seen class initializers (the __init__ methods). A destructor can be defined for a class as well. But unlike in C++, creating and calling a destructor isn't necessary to ensure that the memory used by your instance is freed. Python provides automatic memory management through a reference-counting mechanism. That is, it keeps track of the number of references to your instance; when this number reaches zero, the memory used by your instance is reclaimed, and any Python objects referenced by your instance have their reference counts decremented by one. *You almost never need to define a destructor.*

You may occasionally encounter a situation in which you need to deallocate an external resource explicitly when an object is removed. In such a situation, the best practice is to use a context manager, as discussed in chapter 14. As mentioned there, you can use the `contextlib` module from the standard library to create a custom context manager for your situation.

15.13 Multiple inheritance

Compiled languages place severe restrictions on the use of *multiple inheritance*—the ability of objects to inherit data and behavior from more than one parent class. The rules for using multiple inheritance in C++, for example, are so complex that many people avoid using it. In Java, multiple inheritance is disallowed, although Java does have an interface mechanism.

Python places no such restrictions on multiple inheritance. A class can inherit from any number of parent classes in the same way that it can inherit from a single parent class. In the simplest case, none of the involved classes, including those inherited indirectly through a parent class, contains instance variables or methods of the same name. In such a case, the inheriting class behaves like a synthesis of its own definitions and all of its ancestors' definitions. Suppose that class A inherits from classes B, C, and D; class B inherits from classes E and F; and class D inherits from class G (see figure 15.3). Also suppose that none of these classes shares method names. In this case, an instance of class A can be used as though it were an instance of any of the classes B–G, as well as A; an instance of class B can be used as though it were an instance of class E or F as well as class B; and an instance of class D can be used as though it were an instance of class G as well as class D. In terms of code, the class definitions look like this:

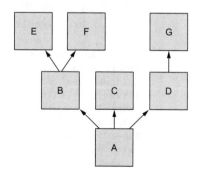

Figure 15.3 Inheritance hierarchy

```
class E:
        . . .
class F:
        . . .
class G:
        . . .
class D(G):
        . . .
class C:
        . . .
class B(E, F):
        . . .
class A(B, C, D):
        . . .
```

The situation is more complex when some of the classes share method names, because Python must decide which of the identical names is the correct one. Suppose that you want to resolve a method invocation a.f() on an instance a of class A, where f isn't defined in A but is defined in all of F, C, and G. Which of the various methods will be invoked?

The answer lies in the order in which Python searches base classes when looking for a method not defined in the original class on which the method was invoked. In the simplest cases, Python looks through the base classes of the original class in left-to-right order, but it always looks through all of the ancestor classes of a base class before looking in the next base class. In attempting to execute a.f(), the search goes something like this:

1 Python first looks in the class of the invoking object, class A.

2 Because A doesn't define a method f, Python starts looking in the base classes of A. The first base class of A is B, so Python starts looking in B.

3 Because B doesn't define a method f, Python continues its search of B by looking in the base classes of B. It starts by looking in the first base class of B, class E.

4 E doesn't define a method f and also has no base classes, so there's no more searching to be done in E. Python goes back to class B and looks in the next base class of B, class F.

Class F does contain a method f, and because it was the first method found with the given name, it's the method used. The methods called f in classes C and G are ignored.

Using internal logic like this isn't likely to lead to the most readable or maintainable of programs, of course. And with more complex hierarchies, other factors come into play to make sure that no class is searched twice and to support cooperative calls to super.

But this hierarchy is probably more complex than you'd expect to see in practice. If you stick to the more standard uses of multiple inheritance, as in the creation of mixin or addin classes, you can easily keep things readable and avoid name clashes.

Some people have a strong conviction that multiple inheritance is a bad thing. It can certainly be misused, and nothing in Python forces you to use it. One of the biggest dangers seems to be creating inheritance hierarchies that are too deep, and multiple inheritance can sometimes be used to help keep this problem from happening. That topic is beyond the scope of this book. The example I use here only illustrates how multiple inheritance works in Python and doesn't attempt to explain the use cases for it (such as in mixin or addin classes).

15.14 HTML classes

In this lab, you create classes to represent an HTML document. To keep things simple, assume that each element can contain only text and one subelement. So the `<html>` element contains only a `<body>` element, and the `<body>` element contains (optional) text and a `<p>` element that contains only text.

The key feature to implement is the `__str__()` method, which in turn calls its subelement's `__str__()` method, so that the entire document is returned when the `str()` function is called on an `<html>` element. You can assume that any text comes before the subelement.

Here's example output from using the classes:

```
para = p(text="this is some body text")
doc_body = body(text="This is the body", subelement=para)
doc = html(subelement=doc_body)
print(doc)

<html>
<body>
This is the body
<p>
this is some body text
</p>
</body>
</html>
```

15.14.1 Solving the problem with AI-generated code

This problem is well suited to an AI solution as phrased, in that it specifies how the problem should be solved and gives some sample code and output. This shows in the results—the AI did a better job on this problem than any of the others so far.

15.14.2 Solutions and discussion

The point of this problem is to use the power of inheritance to avoid repetitive code and to use the ability of objects to model the behavior needed for the problem. That implies much more work on the base class and ideally very little on the subclasses.

THE HUMAN SOLUTION

My solution puts most of the processing into the base class element and then creates subclasses with no new code, which rely totally on the base class for functionality:

```
class element:
    def __init__(self, text=None, subelement=None):
        self.subelement = subelement
        self.text = text

    def __str__(self):
        value = f"<{self.__class__.__name__}>\n"    ◄────┐ Gets the instance's class
        if self.text:                                      and then the class name
            value += f"{self.text}\n"
        if self.subelement:
            value += str(self.subelement)
        value += f"</{self.__class__.__name__}>\n"
        return value

class html(element):
    pass                ◄──────  pass is the minimum needed
                                  for an "empty" class.
class body(element):
    pass

class p(element):
    pass

#test
para = p(text="this is some body text")
doc_body = body(text="This is the body", subelement=para)
doc = html(subelement=doc_body)
print(doc)
```

As mentioned earlier, this solution puts all of the code into the base class `element`, which has the advantage of making future changes quite simple. It also uses the class names as the text of the corresponding HTML tags, which means that adding classes to handle more HTML elements would be trivial. Since I have the habit of using lowercase for HTML tags, the class names are also lowercase, which is a minor violation of standard Python style, which calls for class names to be capitalized. In this case I would invoke the Zen of Python and say, "practicality beats purity," but I'm sure others would disagree.

THE AI SOLUTIONS

For the Copilot solution, the prompt was very similar to the previous problem statement:

```
Create classes to represent an HTML document, and assume that each element
can contain only text and one subelement. So the <html> element contains
only a <body> element, and the <body> element contains (optional) text and
a <p> element that contains only text.

The key feature to implement is the str() method, which in turn calls its
subelement's str() method so that the entire document is returned when the
str() function is called on an element. You can assume that any text comes
before the subelement.

Following is example output from using the classes:
```

```
para = p(text="this is some body text")
doc_body = body(text="This is the body", subelement=para)
doc = html(subelement=doc_body)
print(doc)
```

The plan that Copilot created was

1 Create a base class `Element` with a `__str__` method that returns the text and the string representation of the subelement.

2 Create classes `Html`, `Body`, and `P` that inherit from `Element`.

3 Each class will have a `tag` class attribute that represents the HTML tag.

4 The `__str__` method in the base class will use the `tag` to create the HTML string.

The solution that Copilot suggested was similar to my solution with a couple of stylistic differences:

```
class Element:
    tag = ""

    def __init__(self, text="", subelement=None):
        self.text = text
        self.subelement = subelement

    def __str__(self):
        result = f"<{self.tag}>\n"
        if self.text:
            result += self.text + "\n"
        if self.subelement:
            result += str(self.subelement)
        result += f"</{self.tag}>\n"
        return result

class Html(Element):
    tag = "html"

class Body(Element):
    tag = "body"

class P(Element):
    tag = "p"

# Usage:
para = P(text="this is some body text")
doc_body = Body(text="This is the body", subelement=para)
doc = Html(subelement=doc_body)
print(doc)
```

This code is fine, and I wouldn't make any changes. It is similar to the human solution in that it puts the functionality into the base class. It differs from the human solution in only two aspects. First, it follows the Python convention of capitalizing class names.

Since the example code it was given put the HTML in lowercase, the solution is then to use a class attribute `tag` to hold the lowercase tag name. That approach is fine—there isn't a difference in the size or efficiency of the code, nor, I would argue, is there much difference in readability. So, well done, Copilot!

The Colaboratory solution was disappointing. Since the prompt window for code generation in Colaboratory is limited to 400 characters, and the prompt used for Copilot was nearly twice that size, the problem statement was placed in the cell above and Colaboratory was given this prompt:

```
Generate the code described in the cell above.
```

The result of that prompt was good enough to show that the model did process the prompt, but the solution has a lot of duplicated code that doesn't take advantage of inheritance:

```
class html:
    def __init__(self, subelement):
        self.subelement = subelement
    def __str__(self):
        return f'<html>\n{str(self.subelement)}\n</html>'

class body:
    def __init__(self, text, subelement=None):
        self.text = text
        self.subelement = subelement
    def __str__(self):
        sub = ''
        if self.subelement:
            sub = f'\n{str(self.subelement)}'
        return f'<body>\n{self.text}{sub}\n</body>'

class p:
    def __init__(self, text):
        self.text = text
    def __str__(self):
        return f'<p>\n{self.text}\n</p>'

para = p(text="this is some body text")
doc_body = body(text="This is the body", subelement=para)
doc = html(subelement=doc_body)
print(doc)
```

In fact, this was the only one of four suggested options that used f-strings—the other options used string concatenation with the + operator but took the same general approach. More to the point, this solution creates a new class for every tag, and there is no common base class that the elements inherit from. This means that the processing is duplicated, with only minor differences between the three elements. This code strikes me as something I would expect a junior developer to write, and it would not make it through code review as written.

Summary

- Defining a class in effect creates a new data type.
- `__init__` is used to initialize data when a new instance of a class is created, but it isn't a constructor.
- The `self` parameter refers to the current instance of the class and is passed as the first parameter to methods of a class.
- Static methods can be called without creating an instance of the class, so they don't receive a `self` parameter.
- Class methods are passed a `cls` parameter, which is a reference to the class, instead of `self`.
- All Python methods are virtual. That is, if a method isn't overridden in the subclass or private to the superclass, it's accessible by all subclasses.
- Class variables are inherited from superclasses unless they begin with two underscores (`__`), in which case they're private and can't easily be seen by subclasses. Methods can be made private in the same way.
- Properties let you have attributes with defined getter and setter methods, but they still behave like plain instance attributes.
- Python allows multiple inheritance, which is often used with mixin classes.

Regular expressions *16*

Some might wonder why I'm discussing regular expressions in this book at all. Regular expressions are implemented by a single Python module and are advanced enough that they don't even come as part of the standard library in languages like C or Java. But if you're using Python, you're probably doing text parsing; if you're doing that, regular expressions are too useful to be ignored. If you've used Perl, Tcl, or Linux/UNIX, you may be familiar with regular expressions; if not, this chapter goes into them in some detail.

16.1   *What is a regular expression?*

A *regular expression* (regex) is a way of recognizing and often extracting data from certain patterns of text. A regex that recognizes a piece of text or a string is said to *match* that text or string. A regex is defined by a string in which certain characters (the so-called *metacharacters*) can have a special meaning, which enables a single regex to match many different specific strings.

It's easier to understand this through example than through explanation. The following is a program with a regular expression that counts how many lines in a text file contain the word *hello*. A line that contains *hello* more than once is counted only once:

```
import re
regexp = re.compile("hello")
count = 0
file = open("textfile", 'r')
for line in file.readlines():
    if regexp.search(line):
        count = count + 1
file.close()
print(count)
```

The program starts by importing the Python regular expression module, called `re`. Then it takes the text string `"hello"` as a *textual regular expression* and compiles it into a *compiled regular expression,* using the `re.compile` function. This compilation isn't strictly necessary, but compiled regular expressions can significantly increase a program's speed, so they're almost always used in programs that process large amounts of text.

What can the regex compiled from `"hello"` be used for? You can use it to recognize other instances of the word `"hello"` within another string; in other words, you can use it to determine whether another string contains `"hello"` as a substring. This task is accomplished by the `search` method, which returns `None` if the regular expression isn't found in the string argument; Python interprets `None` as `false` in a Boolean context. If the regular expression is found in the string, Python returns a special object that you can use to determine various things about the match (such as where in the string it occurred). I discuss this topic later.

16.2   *Regular expressions with special characters*

The previous example has a small flaw: it counts how many lines contain `"hello"` but ignores lines that contain `"Hello"` because it doesn't take capitalization into account.

One way to solve this problem would be to use two regular expressions—one for `"hello"` and one for `"Hello"`—and test each against every line. A better way is to use the more advanced features of regular expressions. For the second line in the program, substitute

```
regexp = re.compile("hello|Hello")
```

This regular expression uses the vertical-bar special character |. A *special character* is a character in a regex that isn't interpreted as itself; it has some special meaning. | means *or*, so the regular expression matches `"hello"` *or* `"Hello"`.

Another way of solving this problem is to use

```
regexp = re.compile("(h|H)ello")
```

In addition to using |, this regular expression uses the *parentheses* special characters to group things, which in this case means that the | chooses between a small or capital *H*. The resulting regex matches either an *h* or an *H*, followed by *ello*.

Another way to perform the match is

```
regexp = re.compile("[hH]ello")
```

The special characters [and] take a string of characters between them and match any single character in that string. There's a special shorthand to denote ranges of characters in [and]; [a-z] matches a single character between *a* and *z*, [0-9A-Z] matches any digit or any uppercase character, and so forth. Sometimes you may want to include a real hyphen in the [], in which case you should put it as the first character to avoid defining a range; [-012] matches a hyphen, a *0*, a *1*, or a *2*, and nothing else.

Quite a few special characters are available in Python regular expressions, and describing all of the subtleties of using them in regular expressions is beyond the scope of this book. A complete list of the special characters available in Python regular expressions, as well as descriptions of what they mean, is in the online documentation of the regular expression `re` module in the standard library. For the remainder of this chapter, I describe the special characters I use as they appear.

Quick check: Special characters in regular expressions

What regular expression would you use to match strings that represent the numbers –5 through 5?

What regular expression would you use to match a hexadecimal digit? Assume that allowed hexadecimal digits are 1, 2, 3, 4, 5, 6, 7, 8, 9, 0, A, a, B, b, C, c, D, d, E, e, F, and f.

16.3 *Regular expressions and raw strings*

The functions that compile regular expressions, or search for matches to regular expressions, understand that certain character sequences in strings have special meanings in the context of regular expressions. `regex` functions understand that \n represents a newline character, for example. But if you use normal Python strings as regular expressions, the `regex` functions typically never see such special sequences, because many of these sequences also possess a special meaning in normal strings.

\n, for example, also means newline in the context of a normal Python string, and Python automatically replaces the string sequence \n with a newline character before the `regex` function ever sees that sequence. The `regex` function, as a result, compiles strings with embedded newline characters—not with embedded \n sequences.

In the case of \n, this situation makes no difference because `regex` functions interpret a newline character as exactly that and do the expected thing: attempt to match the character with another newline character in the text being searched.

Now look at another special sequence, \\, which represents a *single* backslash to regular expressions. Assume that you want to search text for an occurrence of the string "\ten". Because you know that you have to represent a backslash as a double backslash, you might try

```
regexp = re.compile("\\ten")
```

This example compiles without complaining, but it's wrong. The problem is that \\ also means a single backslash in Python strings. Before `re.compile` is invoked, Python interprets the string you typed as meaning \ten, which is what is passed to `re.compile`. In the context of regular expressions, \t means *tab*, so your compiled regular expression searches for a tab character followed by the two characters *en*.

To fix this problem while using regular Python strings, you need four backslashes. Python interprets the first two backslashes as a special sequence representing a single backslash, and likewise for the second pair of backslashes, resulting in two *actual* backslashes in the Python string. Then that string is passed in to `re.compile`, which interprets the two actual backslashes as a regex special sequence representing a single backslash. Your code looks like this:

```
regexp = re.compile("\\\\ten")
```

That seems confusing, and it's why Python has a way of defining strings that doesn't apply the normal Python rules to special characters. Strings defined this way are called *raw strings*.

16.3.1 *Raw strings to the rescue*

A raw string looks similar to a normal string except that it has a leading *r* character immediately preceding the initial quotation mark of the string. The following are some raw strings:

```
r"Hello"
r"""\tTo be\n\tor not to be"""
r'Goodbye'
r'''12345'''
```

As you can see, you can use raw strings with either the single or double quotation marks and with the regular or triple-quoting convention. You can also use a leading *R* instead of *r*. No matter how you do it, raw-string notation can be taken as an instruction to Python: "Don't process special sequences in this string." In the previous examples, all the raw strings are equivalent to their normal string counterparts except the second example, in which the `\t` and `\n` sequences aren't interpreted as tabs or newlines but are left as two-string character sequences beginning with a backslash.

Raw strings aren't different types of strings. They represent a different way of *defining* strings. It's easy to see what's happening by running a few examples interactively:

```
r"Hello" == "Hello"
```

True

```
r"\the" == "\\the"
```

True

```
r"\the" == "\the"
```

False

```
print(r"\the")
```

\the

```
print("\the")
```

**   he**

Using raw strings with regular expressions means that you don't need to worry about any funny interactions between string special sequences and regex special sequences. You use the regex special sequences. Then the previous regex example becomes

```
regexp = re.compile(r"\\ten")
```

which works as expected. The compiled regex looks for a single backslash followed by the letters *ten*.

You should get into the habit of using raw strings whenever defining regular expressions, and you'll do so for the remainder of this chapter.

16.4   *Extracting matched text from strings*

One common use of regular expressions is to perform simple pattern-based parsing on text. This task is something you should know how to do, and it's also a good way to learn more regex special characters.

Assume that you have a list of people and phone numbers in a text file. Each line of the file looks like this:

```
surname, firstname middlename: phonenumber
```

You have a surname followed by a comma and space, followed by a first name, followed by a space, followed by a middle name, followed by a colon and a space, followed by a phone number.

But to make things complicated, a middle name may not exist, and a phone number may have different formats depending on the country and the users' preferences. For our purposes, let's assume that the only phone numbers will be in US/Canadian format with a three-digit area code, a three-digit exchange, and a four-digit number, separated by dashes, like 800-123-4567. Even so, a phone number might not have an area code. (It might be 800-123-4567 or 123-4567.) You *could* write code to explicitly parse data out from such a line, but that job would be tedious and error prone. Regular expressions provide a simpler answer.

Start by coming up with a regex that matches lines of the given form. The next few paragraphs throw quite a few special characters at you. Don't worry if you don't get them all on the first read; as long as you understand the gist of things, that's all right.

For simplicity's sake, assume that first names, surnames, and middle names consist of letters and possibly hyphens. You can use the [] special characters discussed in the previous section to define a pattern that defines only name characters:

```
[-a-zA-Z]
```

This pattern matches a single hyphen, a single lowercase letter, or a single uppercase letter.

To match a full name (such as McDonald), you need to repeat this pattern. The + metacharacter repeats whatever comes before it one or more times as necessary to match the string being processed. So the pattern

```
[-a-zA-Z]+
```

matches a single name, such as Kenneth or McDonald or Perkin-Elmer. It also matches some strings that aren't names, such as — or -a-b-c-, but that's all right for the purposes of this example.

Now, what about the phone number? The special sequence \d matches any digit, and a hyphen outside [] is a normal hyphen. A good pattern to match the phone number is

```
\d\d\d-\d\d\d-\d\d\d\d
```

That's three digits followed by a hyphen, followed by three digits, followed by a hyphen, followed by four digits. This pattern matches only phone numbers with an area code, and your list may contain numbers that don't have one. The best solution is to enclose the area-code part of the pattern in (); group it; and follow that group with a ? special character, which says that the thing coming immediately before the ? is optional:

```
(\d\d\d-)?\d\d\d-\d\d\d\d
```

This pattern matches a phone number that may or may not contain an area code. You can use the same sort of trick to account for the fact that some of the people in your list have middle names (or initials) included and others don't. (Make the middle name optional by using grouping and the ? special character.)

You can also use {} to indicate the number of times that a pattern should repeat, so for the preceding phone number examples, you could use:

```
(\d{3}-)?\d{3}-\d{4}
```

This pattern also means an optional group of three digits plus a hyphen, three digits followed by a hyphen, and then four digits.

Commas, colons, and spaces don't have any special meanings in regular expressions; they mean themselves.

Putting everything together, you come up with a pattern that looks like the following:

```
[-a-zA-Z]+, [-a-zA-Z]+( [-a-zA-Z]+)?: (\d{3}-)?\d{3}-\d{4}
```

A real pattern probably would be a bit more complex, because you wouldn't assume that there's exactly one space after the comma, exactly one space after the first and middle names, and exactly one space after the colon. But that's easy to add later.

The problem is that, whereas the preceding pattern lets you check to see whether a line has the anticipated format, you can't extract any data yet. All you can do is write a program like the following:

```
import re
regexp = re.compile(r"[-a-zA-Z]+,"          ◀———  Last name and comma
                    r" [-a-zA-Z]+"          ◀———  First name
                    r"( [-a-zA-Z]+)?"       ◀———
                    r": (\d{3}-)?\d{3}-\d{4}" ◀———  Optional middle name
                    )                             Colon and phone number
file = open("textfile", 'r')
for line in file.readlines():
    if regexp.search(line):
        print("Yeah, I found a line with a name and number. So what?")
        break
file.close()
```

Notice that you've split your regex pattern, using the fact that Python implicitly concatenates any set of strings separated by whitespace. As your pattern grows, this technique can be a great aid in keeping the pattern maintainable and understandable. It also solves the problem with the line length possibly increasing beyond the right edge of the screen.

Fortunately, you can use regular expressions to extract data from patterns, as well as to see whether the patterns exist. The first step is to group each subpattern corresponding to a piece of data you want to extract by using the () special characters. Then give each subpattern a unique name with the special sequence ?P<*name*>, as follows:

```
(?P<last>[-a-zA-Z]+), (?P<first>[-a-zA-Z]+)( (?P<middle>([-a-zA-Z]+)))?:
(?P<phone>(\d{3}-)?\d{3}-\d{4}
```

(Please note that you should enter these lines as a single line, with no line breaks. Due to space constraints, the code can't be represented here in that manner.)

There's an obvious point of confusion here: The question marks in ?P<...> and the question mark special characters indicating that the middle name and area code are optional have nothing to do with one another. It's an unfortunate semicoincidence that they happen to be the same character.

Now that you've named the elements of the pattern, you can extract the matches for those elements by using the group method. You can do so because when the search function returns a successful match, it doesn't return just a truth value; it also returns a data structure that records what was matched. You can write a simple program to extract names and phone numbers from your list and print them out again, as follows:

```
import re
regexp = re.compile(r"(?P<last>[-a-zA-Z]+),"      ◀─────┤ Last name and comma
            r" (?P<first>[-a-zA-Z]+)"             ◀─────
              r"( (?P<middle>([-a-zA-Z]+)))?"     ◀─────┤ First name
          r": (?P<phone>((\d{3}-)?\d{3}-\d{4}))"  ◀─────
            )                                            Optional middle name
file = open("textfile", 'r')                             Colon and phone
for line in file.readlines():                            number
    result = regexp.search(line)
    if result == None:                            ◀─────┤ No match found
        print("Oops, I don't think this is a record")
    else:
        last_name = result.group('last')
        first_name = result.group('first')
        middle_name = result.group('middle')
        if middle_name == None:
                middle_name = ""
        phone_number = result.group('phone')
        print(f"Name: {first_name} {middle_name} {last_name} Number:
{phone_number}")file.close()
```

There are some points of interest here:

- You can find out whether a match succeeded by checking the value returned by search. If the value is None, the match failed; otherwise, the match succeeded, and you can extract information from the object returned by search.

- group is used to extract whatever data matched your named subpatterns. You pass in the name of the subpattern you're interested in.

- Because the middle subpattern is optional, you can't count on it to have a value, even if the match as a whole is successful. If the match succeeds but the match for the middle name doesn't, using group to access the data associated with the middle subpattern returns the value None.

- Part of the phone number is optional, but part isn't. If the match succeeds, the phone subpattern must have some associated text, so you don't have to worry about it having a value of None.

> **Try this: Extracting matched text**
>
> Making international calls usually requires a + and the country code. Assuming that the country code is two digits, how would you modify the preceding code to extract the + and the country code as part of the number? (Again, not all numbers have a country code.) How would you make the code handle country codes of one to three digits?

16.5 *Substituting text with regular expressions*

In addition to extracting strings from text, you can use Python's regex module to find strings in text and substitute other strings in place of those that were found. You accomplish this task by using the regular substitution method sub. The following example replaces instances of "the the" (presumably, a typo) with single instances of "the":

```
import re
string = "If the the problem is textual, use the the re module"
pattern = r"the the"
regexp = re.compile(pattern)
regexp.sub("the", string)
```

```
'If the problem is textual, use the re module'
```

The sub method uses the invoking regex (regexp, in this case) to scan its second argument (string, in the example) and produces a new string by replacing all matching substrings with the value of the first argument ("the", in this example).

16.5.1 *Using a function with sub*

But what if you want to replace the matched substrings with new ones that reflect the value of those that matched? This is where the elegance of Python comes into play. The first argument to sub—the replacement substring, "the" in the example—doesn't have to be a string at all. Instead, it can be a function. If it's a function, Python calls it with the current match object; then it lets that function compute and return a replacement string.

To see this function in action, build an example that takes a string containing integer values (no decimal point or decimal part) and returns a string with the same numerical values but as floating-point numbers (with a trailing decimal point and zero):

```
import re
int_string = "1 2 3 4 5"
def int_match_to_float(match_obj):
```

```
                return(match_obj.group('num') + ".0")

pattern = r"(?P<num>[0-9]+)"
regexp = re.compile(pattern)
regexp.sub(int_match_to_float, int_string)
```

'1.0 2.0 3.0 4.0 5.0'

In this case, the pattern looks for a number consisting of one or more digits (the `[0-9]+` part). But it's also given a name (the `?P<num>...` part) so that the replacement string function can extract any matched substring by referring to that name. Then the `sub` method scans down the argument string `"1 2 3 4 5"`, looking for anything that matches `[0-9]+`. When `sub` finds a substring that matches, it makes a `match` object defining exactly which substring matched the pattern. Then it calls the `int_match_to_float` function with that `match` object as the sole argument. `int_match_to_float` uses `group` to extract the matching substring from the `match` object (by referring to the group name `num`) and produces a new string by concatenating the matched substring with `".0"`. `sub` then returns the new string and incorporates it as a substring into the overall result. Finally, `sub` starts scanning again right after the place where it found the last matching substring, and it keeps going like that until it can't find any more matching substrings. Whatever is *not* matched by `sub` is left alone. For example, if we instead used the string `"1 2 3 4 5 Python"`, then `"1.0 2.0 3.0 4.0 5.0 Python"` would be returned with "Python" (and all of the spaces, of course) left unchanged.

Try this: Replacing text

In the checkpoint in section 16.4, you extended a phone number regular expression to also recognize a country code. How would you use a function to make any numbers that didn't have a country code now have +1 (the country code for the United States and Canada)?

16.6   *Phone number normalizer*

In the United States and Canada, phone numbers consist of 10 digits, usually separated into a three-digit area code, a three-digit exchange code, and a four-digit station code. As mentioned in section 16.4, they may or may not be preceded by +1, the country code. In practice, however, you have many ways to format a phone number, such as (NNN) NNN-NNNN, NNN-NNN-NNNN, NNN NNN-NNNN, NNN.NNN.NNNN, and NNN NNN NNNN, to name a few. Also, the country code may not be present, may not have a +, and usually (not always) is separated from the number by a space or dash. Whew!

In this lab, your task is to create a phone number normalizer that takes any of the formats and returns a normalized phone number 1-NNN-NNN-NNNN.

The following are all possible phone numbers:

| +1 223-456-7890 | 1-223-456-7890 | +1 223 456-7890 |
| (223) 456-7890 | 1 223 456 7890 | 223.456.7890 |

Bonus: The first digit of the area code and the exchange code can only be 2 to 9, and the second digit of an area code can't be 9. Use this information to validate the input and return a `ValueError` exception of `invalid phone number` if the number is invalid.

16.6.1 Solving the problem with AI-generated code

Programmers like to joke that if you have a problem and decide to use a regular expression to solve it, you now have *two* problems. There's some truth to that, since it can be tricky to get a regular expression to do all that you want and only what you want. You need to be very careful testing your code to make sure your tests cover all of your desired positive matches as well as the cases you expect *not* to match. Do not trust the AI to create a perfect solution or to generate the right test cases.

16.6.2 Solutions and discussion

There are a couple of approaches to this problem. You can try to match the most likely phone number patterns, which was my approach, or you can try to strip out everything but the numbers and then add the separators. If in fact you know that the input will be a phone number, the second approach is probably better.

THE HUMAN SOLUTION

My solution uses a function to normalize the numbers as the main regular expression's parameter and two additional regular expressions in that function to check for illegal numbers:

```
def return_number(match_obj):          ◄──── Function passed to
    # adds country if needed                  regexp.sub method
    country = match_obj.group("country")   ◄──┐ Adds country if needed
    if not country:
        country = "1"

    # BONUS: raise ValueError if not valid
    if not re.match(r"[2-9][0-8]\d",                    │ Checks area code
                    match_obj.group("area")):    ◄──────┘
        raise ValueError("invalid phone number area code {}".format(match_
    obj.group("area")))
    if not re.match(r"[2-9]\d\d",                │ Checks exchange
                    match_obj.group("exch") ):  ◄┘
        raise ValueError("invalid phone number exchange {}".format(match_obj.
    group("exch")))

    return(f"{country}-{match_obj.group('area')}-{match_obj.group('exch')}
➡ -{match_obj.group('number')}")
```

```
regexp = re.compile(r"\+?(?P<country>\d{1,3})?[- .]?\(?(?P<area>\d{3})\)
?[- .]?(?P<exch>(\d{3}))[- .](?P<number>\d{4})")
for number in test_numbers:
    print(regexp.sub(return_number, number))
```
◄————┐ **Calls main regexp**

```
# Test
phone_numbers = ["+1 223-456-7890",
                 "1-223-456-7890",
                 "+1 223 456-7890",
                 "(223) 456-7890",
                 "1 223 456 7890",
                 "999.456.7890",
                 "1-989-111-2222",
                 "223.456.7890"]
```

```
regexp = re.compile(r"\+?(?P<country>\d{1,3})?[- .]?\(?(?P<area>\d{3})\)
?[- .]?(?P<exch>(\d{3}))[- .](?P<number>\d{4})")
```

```
for number in test_numbers:
    try:
        normalized_phone_number = regexp.sub(return_number, number)
        print(f'{normalized_phone_number}')
    except ValueError as e:
        print(f'{number} is not a valid phone number: {e}')
```

```
1-223-456-7890
1-223-456-7890
1-223-456-7890
1-223-456-7890
1-223-456-7890
999.456.7890 is invalid: invalid phone number area code 999
1-989-111-2222 is invalid: invalid phone number exchange 111
1-223-456-7890
```

While regular expressions themselves can be tricky, the code that uses them usually isn't. In this case, the work is done by the function return_number, which is passed to the main regular expression sub method as the first parameter.

That function checks to see if there is a country code and adds +1 if there isn't. It then uses two other regular expressions to check the area code and exchange to make sure they are allowed and raises a ValueError with the appropriate message if not. One obvious optimization that this code does not implement would be to precompile the area code and exchange regular expressions.

The main regular expression looks to match the most common separators but will not handle numbers that use different separators, nor different groupings of numbers. On reflection, it might have made more sense to assume that the separator patterns don't matter and just extract the digits.

THE AI SOLUTIONS

Copilot came up with a reasonable solution by first stripping nonnumeric characters and then worrying about the checking and formatting. The prompt used was

```
import re

def normalize_phone_number(phone_number):
    phone_number = re.sub(r'\D', '', phone_number)          ◄─── Removes all nondigit
                                                                 (\D) characters

    if len(phone_number) not in [10, 11]:                   ◄─── The length must be 10 or 11.
        raise ValueError("Invalid phone number length")

                                                                 Checks area code
    if not re.match(r'^[2-9][0-8][0-9][2-9]',                    and exchange at once
                    phone_number[-10:]):                    ◄───
        raise ValueError("Invalid area code or exchange code")

    if len(phone_number) == 10:                  ◄─── Adds country code if needed
        phone_number = '1' + phone_number

    phone_number = re.sub(r'(\d{1})(\d{3})(\d{3})(\d{4})',
                    r'\1-\2-\3-\4', phone_number)           ◄───
                                                                 Adds dashes between
    return phone_number                                          elements

# Test the function.
phone_numbers = ["+1 223-456-7890",
                "1-223-456-7890",
                "+1 223 456-7890",
                "(223) 456-7890",
                "1 223 456 7890",
                "999.456.7890",
                "1-989-111-2222",
                "223.456.7890"]

for number in test_numbers:
    try:
        normalized_phone_number = normalize_phone_number(number)
        print(f'{normalized_phone_number}')
    except ValueError as e:
        print(f'{number} is not a valid phone number: {e}')
```

```
1-223-456-7890
1-223-456-7890
1-223-456-7890
1-223-456-7890
1-223-456-7890
999.456.7890 is invalid: Invalid area code or exchange code
1-989-111-2222 is invalid: Invalid area code or exchange code
1-223-456-7890
```

The first thing this code does is replace all nondigit characters (\D) in the string, leaving only digits. If the length is not 10 or 11 digits, there must be an error, which is raised. The next regular expression looks at the last 10 digits and checks to make sure that the first four digits are correct, with 1 not allowed in the first or fourth position and 9 not allowed in the second position. It also checks the third position but allows all digits there. Then, if the string is only 10 digits long, it adds a 1 at the front. Finally, it uses a sub to group the digits appropriately and insert dashes.

In my opinion this solution is arguably more flexible and robust than my own solution. This solution also does not precompile the regular expressions, which would be a good idea in production. I would have only two other caveats. First, if the input could have letters and other characters in them along with the digits, this solution will accept them without complaint, as long as the number of *digits* is 10 or 11. That might not be a good thing. The other more minor caveat is that the error message returned for illegal digits in the area code or exchange is not very specific and should be a bit friendlier to debugging.

Colaboratory was given a similar prompt (in a separate notebook in a fresh session, to prevent it from "cheating" from the other solutions). Again, to work around the limitation on prompt lengths, the prompt was entered into a text cell and the then the AI generator was directed to that cell:

```
Using regular expressions, write code to normalize phone numbers in formats
(NNN) NNN-NNNN, NNN-NNN-NNNN, NNN NNN-NNNN, NNN.NNN.NNNN, and NNN NNN NNNN
(with or without a country code and a +) to 1-NNN-NNN-NNNN. Also raise a
ValueError if the first digit of the area code and the exchange code is not
2-9, or the second digit of the area code is 9.

Write the code to normalize phone numbers as specified in the cell above.
```

Unfortunately, all four of the options offered by Colaboratory were unsatisfactory, with two being unable to run without errors. Another option incorrectly flagged numbers with a 1 country code as illegal but passed a number with a 999 area code, and removed spaces, dots, hyphens, and parentheses with an ugly chain of string `replace` calls:

```
phone_number.replace(' ', '').replace('.', '').replace('-',
    '').replace('(', '').replace(')', '')
```

The remaining solution took a similar approach Copilot's, but with some problems:

```
# prompt: Write the code to normalize phone numbers as specified
#         in the cell above.

import re

def normalize_phone_number(phone_number):
  """
  Normalizes a phone number to the format 1-NNN-NNN-NNNN.

  Args:
    phone_number: The phone number to normalize.

  Returns:
    The normalized phone number.

  Raises:
    ValueError: If the phone number is not in a valid format.
  """
```

```
# Remove all non-digit characters.
phone_number = re.sub(r'\D', '', phone_number)
```
← **Removes all nondigits (\D)**

```
# Check if the phone number is in a valid format.
if not re.match(r'^(1)?\d{10}$', phone_number):
    raise ValueError('Invalid phone number format.')
```
← **Checks for valid length, prefix (if present)**

```
# Check if the first digit of the area code and the exchange code
# is not 2-9, or the second digit of the area code is 9.
if not re.match(r'^1?[2-9]\d{2}[2-9]\d{6}$', phone_number):
    raise ValueError('Invalid area code or exchange code.')
```
←

```
# Normalize the phone number to the format 1-NNN-NNN-NNNN.
return '-'.join([phone_number[0:1], phone_number[1:4], phone_number[4:7],
                 phone_number[7:]])
```
← **Checks the first digits of exchange and area code**

```
# Test the function.
phone_numbers = ["+1 223-456-7890",
                 "1-223-456-7890",
                 "+1 223 456-7890",
                 "(223) 456-7890",
                 "1 223 456 7890",
                 "999.456.7890",
                 "1-989-111-2222",
                 "223.456.7890"]
```
Joins elements separated by position in string

```
for number in test_numbers:
    try:
        normalized_phone_number = normalize_phone_number(number)
        print(f'{normalized_phone_number}')
    except ValueError as e:
        print(f'{number} is not a valid phone number: {e}')
```

```
1-223-456-7890
1-223-456-7890
1-223-456-7890
2-234-567-890
1-223-456-7890
9-994-567-890
1-989-111-2222 is invalid: Invalid area code or exchange code.
2-234-567-890
```

The two main problems here are that this solution doesn't actually add a 1 as a prefix if it's missing, which fails the main part of the problem. The failure to add a 1 if needed then causes the elements to be off in those cases, returning the odd grouping of N-NNN-NNN-NNN. Yes, the number would still "work," I suppose, but it's not normalized as specified.

Second, this solution misses the bonus because it doesn't check to make sure that the second digit of the area code is not a 9. It's a little bit odd, since the comment placed immediately above that regular expression does explicitly mention that requirement.

In terms of performance, thanks to using a regular expression to insert the dashes, the Copilot version ends up taking about twice as long as my solution, which is the fastest. This isn't surprising—for all their powers, regular expressions are not likely to be particularly fast, which is something to keep in mind if performance is vital.

Summary

- A regular expression (regex) is a way of recognizing and often extracting data from certain patterns of text.

- In Python, regular expressions are handled by the `re` module of the standard library.

- For a complete list and explanation of the regex special characters, refer to the Python documentation.

- Adding an 'r' before a string tells Python to handle it as a "raw" string and not process escape sequences.

- The most common regular expression methods are the `search` and `sub` methods.

- In addition to the `search` and `sub` methods, many other methods can be used to split strings, extract more information from `match` objects, look for the positions of substrings in the main argument string, and precisely control the iteration of a regex search over an argument string.

- Besides the `\d` special sequence, which can be used to indicate a digit character, many other special sequences are listed in the documentation.

- There are also regex flags, which you can use to control some of the more esoteric aspects of how extremely sophisticated matches are carried out.

- Regular expression methods can also be given a function to handle matches, in place of replacement expressions.

Data types as objects
17

This chapter covers

- Treating types as objects
- Using types
- Creating user-defined classes
- Understanding duck typing
- Using special method attributes
- Subclassing built-in types

By now you've learned the basic Python types as well as how to create your own data types using classes. For many languages, that would be pretty much it as far as data types are concerned. But Python is dynamically typed, meaning that types are determined at runtime, not compile time. This fact is one of the reasons Python is so easy to use. It also makes it possible, and sometimes necessary, to compute with the types of objects (not just the objects themselves).

17.1   *Types are objects too*

Fire up a Python session and try out the following:

```
type(5)
```

<class 'int'>

```
type(['hello', 'goodbye'])
```

<class 'list'>

This example is the first time we've seen the built-in `type` function in Python. It can be applied to any Python object and returns the type of that object. In this example, the function tells you that 5 is an `int` (integer) and that `['hello', 'goodbye']` is a `list`—things that you probably already knew.

Of greater interest is the fact that Python returns objects in response to the calls to type; `<class 'int'>` and `<class 'list'>` are the screen representations of the returned objects. What sort of object is returned by a call of `type(5)`? You have an easy way of finding out. Just use `type` on that result:

```
type_result = type(5)
type(type_result)
```

<class 'type'>

The object returned by `type` is an object whose type happens to be `<class 'type'>`; you can call it a *type object*. A type object is what we commonly think of as a class, and while the two terms are used in somewhat different contexts, in fact "type" and "class" in Python refer to the same thing. Apart from the somewhat confusing notion that a type or class has the type `<class 'type'>`, the important thing to understand is that classes (or types) in Python are objects like almost everything else.

17.2   *Using types*

Now that you know that data types can be represented as Python type objects, what can you do with them? You can compare them to see if they are equal, because any two Python objects can be compared:

```
type("Hello") == type("Goodbye")
```

True

```
type("Hello") == type(5)
```

False

The types of `"Hello"` and `"Goodbye"` are the same (they're both strings), but the types of `"Hello"` and 5 are different. Among other things, you could use this technique to provide type checking in your function and method definitions.

17.3   *Types and user-defined classes*

The most common reason to be interested in the types of objects, particularly instances of user-defined classes, is to find out whether a particular object is an instance of a class. After determining that an object is of a particular type, the code can treat it appropriately. An example makes things much clearer. To start, define a couple of empty classes to set up a simple inheritance hierarchy:

```
class A:
    pass

class B(A):
    pass
```

Now create an instance of class B:

```
b = B()
```

As expected, applying the `type` function to b tells you that b is an instance of the class B that's defined in your current __main__ namespace:

```
type(b)
<class '__main__.B'>
```

You can also obtain exactly the same information by accessing the instance's special __class__ attribute:

```
b.__class__
<class '__main__.B'>
```

You'll be working with that class quite a bit to extract further information, so store it somewhere:

```
b_class = b.__class__
```

Now, to emphasize that everything in Python is an object, prove that the class you obtained from b is the class you defined under the name B:

```
b_class == B
True
```

In this example, you didn't need to store the class of b—you already had it—but I want to make clear that a class is just another Python object and can be stored or passed around like any Python object.

Given the class of b, you can find the name of that class by using its __name__ attribute:

```
b_class.__name__
'B'
```

And you can find out what classes a class inherits from by accessing its __bases__ attribute, which contains a tuple of all of its base classes:

```
b_class.__bases__
(<class '__main__.A'>,)
```

Used together, __class__, __bases__, and __name__ allow a full analysis of the class inheritance structure associated with any instance.

But two built-in functions provide a more user-friendly way of obtaining most of the information you usually need: isinstance and issubclass. The isinstance function is what you should use to determine whether, for example, a class passed into a function or method is of the expected type:

```
class C:
    pass

class D:
    pass

class E(D):
    pass

x = 12
c = C()
d = D()
e = E()
isinstance(x, E)

False

isinstance(c, E)          ◀──────  Checks instance against class E

False

isinstance(e, E)

True

isinstance(e, D)          ◀──────  Checks against class D

True

isinstance(d, E)          ◀──────  Checks d against E

False

y = 12
isinstance(y, type(5))          ◀──────  Uses type() plus example of class

True
```

The `issubclass` function is only for class types:

```
issubclass(C, D)
```

False

```
issubclass(E, D)
```

True

```
issubclass(D, D)        ◄──── Class is a subclass of itself.
```

True

```
issubclass(e.__class__, D)
```

True

For class instances, we first check x, c, and e against the class E. Then we see that e is an instance of class D because E inherits from D. But d isn't an instance of class E. If we don't have the class object handy, as with built-in types, we can use an instance of the class with the `type` function. A class is considered to be a subclass of itself.

Quick check: Types

Suppose that you want to make sure that object x is a `list` before you try appending to it. What code would you use? What would be the difference between using `type()` and `isinstance()`? Would this be the "look before you leap" or "easier to ask forgiveness than permission" of programming? What other options might you have besides checking the type explicitly?

17.4 Duck typing

Using `type`, `isinstance`, and `issubclass` makes it fairly easy to make code correctly determine an object's or class's inheritance hierarchy. Although this process is easy, Python also has a feature that makes using objects even easier: duck typing. *Duck typing* (as in "If it walks like a duck and quacks like a duck, it probably *is* a duck") refers to Python's way of determining whether an object is the required type for an operation, focusing on an object's interface rather than its type. If an operation needs an iterator, for example, the object used doesn't need to be a subclass of any particular iterator at all. All that matters is that the object used as an iterator is able to yield a series of objects in the expected way.

By contrast, in a language like Java, stricter rules of inheritance are enforced. In short, duck typing means that, in Python, you don't need to worry about type-checking function or method arguments and the like. Instead, you should rely on readable and documented code combined with thorough testing to make sure that an object "quacks like a duck" as needed.

Duck typing can increase the flexibility of well-written code and, combined with the more advanced object-oriented features, gives you the ability to create classes and objects to cover almost any situation.

Particularly for larger codebases, the flexibility of duck typing can allow bugs to slip by undetected. It is becoming more common to avoid or restrict duck typing in favor of explicit type hints, which can be verified by a type checker.

17.5   *What is a special method attribute?*

A *special method attribute* is an attribute of a Python class with a special meaning to Python. It's defined as a method but isn't intended to be used directly by client code. Special methods aren't usually directly invoked; instead, they're called automatically by Python in response to a demand made on an object of that class.

Special method attributes are marked by double underscore characters at both ends of their names. For this reason, they are often referred to as "dunder" methods, short for "double underscore." They are also sometimes called "magic" methods, since they power much of the "magic" of Python classes.

Perhaps the simplest example is the __str__ special method attribute. If it's defined in a class, any time an instance of that class is used where Python requires a user-readable string representation of that instance, the __str__ method attribute is invoked, and the value it returns is used as the required string. To see this attribute in action, let's define a class representing red, green, and blue (RGB) colors as a triplet of numbers, one each for red, green, and blue intensities. As well as defining the standard __init__ special method to initialize instances of the class, we'll define a __str__ special method to return strings representing instances in a reasonably human-friendly format. The definition would look something like this.

> **Listing 17.1   File color_module.py**

```
class Color:
    def __init__(self, red, green, blue):
        self._red = red
        self._green = green
        self._blue = blue
    def __str__(self):
        return f"Color: R={self._red:d},G={self._green:d},B={self._blue:d}"
```

If you put this definition into a file called color_module.py, you can load it and use it in the normal manner:

```
from color_module import Color
```

Or, in Colaboratory, we could just execute the code in a cell and use it without importing:

```
c = Color(15, 35, 3)
```

You can see the presence of the __str__ special method attribute if you use print to print out c:

```
print(c)
```

```
Color: R=15, G=35, B=3
```

Even though your __str__ special method attribute hasn't been explicitly invoked by any of your code, it has nonetheless been used by Python, which knows that the __str__ attribute (if present) defines a method to convert objects into user-readable strings. This characteristic is the defining one of special method attributes; it allows you to define functionality that hooks into Python in special ways. Among other things, special method attributes can be used to define classes whose objects behave in a fashion that's syntactically and semantically equivalent to lists or dictionaries. You could, for example, use this ability to define objects that are used in exactly the same manner as Python lists but that use balanced trees rather than arrays to store data. To a programmer, such objects would appear to be lists but with faster inserts, slower iterations, and certain other performance differences that presumably would be advantageous in the problem at hand.

The rest of this chapter covers longer examples using special method attributes. The chapter doesn't discuss all of Python's available special method attributes, but it does expose you to the concept in enough detail that you can easily use the other special attribute methods, all of which are defined in the standard library documentation for built-in types.

17.6 *Making an object behave like a list*

This example involves a large text file containing records of people; each record consists of a single line containing the person's name, age, and place of residence, with a double semicolon (::) between the fields. A few lines from such a file might look like the following:

```
.
.
.
John Smith::37::Springfield, Massachusetts
Ellen Nelle::25::Springfield, Connecticut
Dale McGladdery::29::Springfield, Hawaii
.
.
.
```

Suppose that you need to collect information about the distribution of ages of people in the file. There are many ways the lines in this file could be processed. Here's one way:

```
fileobject = open(filename, 'r')
lines = fileobject.readlines()
```

```
fileobject.close()
for line in lines:
    . . . do whatever . . .
```

That technique would work in theory, but it reads the entire file into memory at once. If the file were too large to be held in memory (and these files potentially are that large), the program wouldn't work.

Another way to attack the problem is

```
fileobject = open(filename, 'r')
for line in fileobject:
    . . . do whatever . . .
fileobject.close()
```

This code would get around the problem of having too little memory by reading in only one line at a time. It would work fine, but suppose that you wanted to make opening the file even simpler and that you wanted to get only the first two fields (name and age) of the lines in the file. You'd need something that could, at least for the purposes of a `for` loop, treat a text file as a list of lines but without reading the entire text file in at once.

17.7   *The __getitem__ special method attribute*

A solution is to use the __getitem__ special method attribute, which you can define in any user-defined class, to enable instances of that class to respond to list access syntax and semantics. If `AClass` is a Python class that defines __getitem__, and `obj` is an instance of that class, things like `x = obj[n]` and `for x in obj:` are meaningful; `obj` may be used in much the same way as a list.

The resulting code for the `LineReader` class (explanations follow) is

```
class LineReader:
    def __init__(self, filename):          Opens file for reading
        self.fileobject = open(filename, 'r')
    def __getitem__(self, index):          Tries to read line
        line = self.fileobject.readline()
        if line == "":                     If no more data …
            self.fileobject.close()
            raise IndexError               … closes fileobject …
                                           … and raises IndexError
        else:
            return line.split("::")[:2]    Otherwise, splits line,
                                           returns first two fields
for name, age in LineReader("filename"):
    . . . do whatever . . .
```

By implementing a __getitem__() method, we enable instances of the class to be used as an iterable in the `for` loop, which reads a line of the file with each iteration. This will work as long as we also raise an `IndexError` to indicate that we have reached the end of the iterable's items, which we do when reading from the file returns an empty string at the end of the file.

At first glance, this example may look worse than the previous solution because there's more code, and it's more difficult to understand. But most of that code is in a class, which can be put into its own module, such as the `myutils` module. Then the program becomes

```
import myutils
for name, age in myutils.LineReader("filename"):
    . . . do whatever . . .
```

The `LineReader` class handles all the details of opening the file, reading in lines one at a time, and closing the file. At the cost of somewhat more initial development time, it provides a tool that makes working with one-record-per-line large text files easier and less error prone. Note that Python already has several powerful ways to read files, but this example has the advantage that it's fairly easy to understand. When you get the idea, you can apply the same principle in many situations.

17.7.1 *How it works*

`LineReader` is a class, and the `__init__` method opens the named file for reading and stores the opened `fileobject` for later access. To understand the use of the `__getitem__` method, you need to know the following three points:

- Any object that defines `__getitem__` as an instance method can return elements as though it were a list: all accesses of the form `object[i]` are transformed by Python into a method invocation of the form `object.__getitem__(i)`, which is handled as a normal method invocation. It's ultimately executed as `__getitem__(object, i)`, using the version of `__getitem__` defined in the class. The first argument of each call of `__getitem__` is the object from which data is being extracted, and the second argument is the index of that data.

- Because `for` loops access each piece of data in a list, one at a time, a loop of the form `for arg in sequence:` works by calling `__getitem__` over and over again, with sequentially increasing indexes. The `for` loop first sets `arg` to `sequence.__getitem__(0)`, then to `sequence.__getitem__(1)`, and so on.

- A `for` loop catches `IndexError` exceptions and handles them by exiting the loop. This process is how `for` loops are terminated when used with normal lists or sequences.

The `LineReader` class is intended for use only with and inside a `for` loop, and the `for` loop always generates calls with a uniformly increasing index: `__getitem__(self, 0)`, `__getitem__(self, 1)`, `__getitem__(self, 2)`, and so on. The code at the beginning of section 17.7 takes advantage of this knowledge and returns lines one after the other, ignoring the `index` argument.

With this knowledge, understanding how a `LineReader` object emulates a sequence in a `for` loop is easy. Each iteration of the loop causes the special Python attribute method __getitem__ to be invoked on the object; as a result, the object reads in the next line from its stored `fileobject` and examines that line. If the line is nonempty, it's returned. An empty line means that the end of the file has been reached; the object closes the `fileobject` and raises the `IndexError` exception. `IndexError` is caught by the enclosing `for` loop, which then terminates.

Remember that this example is here for illustrative purposes only. Usually, iterating over the lines of a file by using the `for line in fileobject:` type of loop is sufficient, but this example does show how easy it is in Python to create objects that behave like lists or other types.

> **Quick check: __getitem__**
>
> The example use of __getitem__ is very limited and won't work correctly in many situations. What are some cases in which the previous implementation will fail or work incorrectly?

17.7.2 *Implementing full list functionality*

In the previous example, an object of the `LineReader` class behaves like a list object only to the extent that it correctly responds to sequential accesses of the lines in the file it's reading from. You may wonder how this functionality can be expanded to make `LineReader` (or other) objects behave more like a list.

First, the __getitem__ method should handle its index argument in some way. Because the whole point of the `LineReader` class is to avoid reading a large file into memory, it wouldn't make sense to have the entire file in memory and return the appropriate line. Probably the smartest thing to do would be to check that each index in a __getitem__ call is 1 greater than the index from the previous __getitem__ call (or is 0, for the first call of __getitem__ on a `LineReader` instance) and to raise an error if this isn't the case. This practice would ensure that `LineReader` instances are used only in `for` loops, as was intended.

More generally, Python provides several special method attributes relating to list behavior. __setitem__ provides a way of defining what should be done when an object is used in the syntactic context of a list assignment, `obj[n] = val`. Some other special method attributes provide less-obvious list functionality, such as the __add__ attribute, which enables objects to respond to the + operator and hence to perform their version of list concatenation. Several other special methods also need to be defined before a class fully emulates a list, but you can achieve complete list emulation by defining the appropriate Python special method attributes. The next section gives an example that goes further toward implementing a full list class.

17.8   *Giving an object full list capability*

__getitem__ is one of many Python special function attributes that may be defined in a class to permit instances of that class to display special behavior. To see how special method attributes can be carried further, effectively integrating new abilities into Python in a seamless manner, look at another, more comprehensive example.

When lists are used, it's common for any particular list to contain elements of only one type, such as a list of strings or a list of numbers. Some languages, such as C++, have the ability to enforce this restriction. In large programs, the ability to declare a list as containing a certain type of element can help you track down errors. An attempt to add an element of the wrong type to a typed list results in an error message, potentially identifying a problem at an earlier stage of program development than would otherwise be the case.

Python doesn't have typed lists built in, and most Python coders don't miss them. But if you're concerned about enforcing the homogeneity of a list, special method attributes make it easy to create a class that behaves like a typed list. The following is the beginning of such a class (which makes extensive use of the Python built-in `type` and `isinstance` functions to check the type of objects):

```
class TypedList:
    def __init__(self, example_element, initial_list=[]):
        self.type = type(example_element)          ◄───── An example of the
        if not isinstance(initial_list, list):              type allowed
            raise TypeError("Second argument of TypedList must "
                            "be a list.")
        for element in initial_list:
            if not isinstance(element, self.type):
                raise TypeError("Attempted to add an element of "
                                "incorrect type to a typed list.")
        self.elements = initial_list[:]
```

The `example_element` argument defines the type that this list can contain by providing an example of the type of element.

The `TypedList` class, as defined here, gives you the ability to make a call of the form

```
x = TypedList ('Hello', ["List", "of", "strings"])
```

The first argument, `'Hello'`, isn't incorporated into the resulting data structure at all. It's used as an example of the type of element the list must contain (strings, in this case). The second argument is an optional list that can be used to give an initial list of values. The `__init__` function for the `TypedList` class checks that any list elements, passed in when a `TypedList` instance is created, are of the same type as the example value given. If there are any type mismatches, an exception is raised.

This version of the `TypedList` class can't be used as a list, because it doesn't respond to the standard methods for setting or accessing list elements. To fix this problem, you need to define the `__setitem__` and `__getitem__` special method attributes. The `__setitem__` method is called automatically by Python any time a statement of the form `TypedListInstance[i] = value` is executed, and the `__getitem__` method is called any time the expression `TypedListInstance[i]` is evaluated to return the value in the *i*th slot of `TypedListInstance`. The following is the next version of the `TypedList` class.

Because you'll be type-checking a lot of new elements, this function is abstracted out into the new private method __check:

```
class TypedList:
    def __init__(self, example_element, initial_list=[]):
        self.type = type(example_element)
        if not isinstance(initial_list, list):
            raise TypeError("Second argument of TypedList must "
                            "be a list.")
        for element in initial_list:
            self.__check(element)
        self.elements = initial_list[:]
    def __check(self, element):
        if type(element) != self.type:
            raise TypeError("Attempted to add an element of "
                            "incorrect type to a typed list.")
    def __setitem__(self, i, element):
        self.__check(element)
        self.elements[i] = element
    def __getitem__(self, i):
        return self.elements[i]
```

Now instances of the TypedList class look more like lists. The following code is valid, for example:

```
x = TypedList("", 5 * [""])
x[2] = "Hello"
x[3] = "There"
print(x[2] + ' ' + x[3])

Hello There

a, b, c, d, e = x
a, b, c, d

('', '', 'Hello', 'There')
```

The accesses of elements of x in the print statement are handled by __getitem__, which passes them down to the list instance stored in the TypedList object. The assignments to x[2] and x[3] are handled by __setitem__, which checks that the element being assigned into the list is of the appropriate type and then performs the assignment on the list contained in self.elements. The last line uses __getitem__ to unpack the first five items in x and then pack them into the variables a, b, c, d, and e, respectively. The calls to __getitem__ and __setitem__ are made automatically by Python.

Completion of the TypedList class, so that TypedList objects behave in all respects like list objects, requires more code. The special method attributes __setitem__ and __getitem__ should be defined so that TypedList instances can handle slice notation as well as single item access. __add__ should be defined so that list addition (concatenation) can be performed, and __mul__ should be defined so that list multiplication can be performed. `__len__` should be defined so that calls of `len(TypedListInstance)` are evaluated correctly. `__delitem__` should be defined so that the `TypedList` class can handle `del` statements correctly. Also, an `append` method should be defined so that elements can be appended to `TypedList` instances by means of the standard list-style `append`, as well as `insert` and `extend` methods.

> **Try this: Implementing list special methods**
>
> Try implementing the `__len__` and `__delitem__` special methods for `TypedList`, as well as an `append` method.

17.9 Subclassing from built-in types

The previous example makes for a good exercise in understanding how to implement a list-like class from scratch, but it's also a lot of work. In practice, if you were planning to implement your own list-like structure along the lines demonstrated here, you might instead consider subclassing the `list` type or the `UserList` type.

17.9.1 Subclassing list

Instead of creating a class for a typed list from scratch, as you did in the previous examples, you can subclass the `list` type and override all the methods that need to be aware of the allowed type. One big advantage of this approach is that your class has default versions of all list operations because it's a list already. The main thing to keep in mind is that every type in Python is a class, and if you need a variation on the behavior of a built-in type, you may want to consider subclassing that type:

```
class TypedListList(list):
    def __init__(self, example_element, initial_list=[]):
        self.type = type(example_element)
        if not isinstance(initial_list, list):
            raise TypeError("Second argument of TypedList must "
                            "be a list.")
        for element in initial_list:
            self.__check(element)
        super().__init__(initial_list)

    def __check(self, element):
        if type(element) != self.type:
            raise TypeError("Attempted to add an element of "
                            "incorrect type to a typed list.")

    def __setitem__(self, i, element):
        self.__check(element)
        super().__setitem__(i, element)

x = TypedListList("", 5 * [""])
x[2] = "Hello"
```

```
x[3] = "There"
print(x[2] + ' ' + x[3])
```

Hello There

```
a, b, c, d, e = x
a, b, c, d
```

('', '', 'Hello', 'There')

```
x[:]
```

['', '', 'Hello', 'There', '']

```
del x[2]
x[:]
```

['', '', 'There', '']

```
x.sort()
x[:]
```

['', '', '', 'There']

Note that all that you need to do in this case is implement a method to check the type of items being added and then tweak __setitem__ to make that check before calling list's regular __setitem__ method. Other methods, such as sort and del, work without any further coding. Overloading a built-in type can save a fair amount of time if you need only a few variations in its behavior, because the bulk of the class can be used unchanged.

17.9.2 *Subclassing UserList*

If you need a variation on a list (as in the previous examples), there's a third alternative: you can subclass the UserList class, a list wrapper class found in the collections module. UserList was created for earlier versions of Python when subclassing the list type wasn't possible, but it's still useful, particularly for the current situation, because the underlying list is available as the data attribute:

```
from collections import UserList
class TypedUserList(UserList):
    def __init__(self, example_element, initial_list=[]):
        self.type = type(example_element)
        if not isinstance(initial_list, list):
            raise TypeError("Second argument of TypedList must "
                            "be a list.")
        for element in initial_list:
            self.__check(element)
        super().__init__(initial_list)

    def __check(self, element):
        if type(element) != self.type:
```

```
            raise TypeError("Attempted to add an element of "
                            "incorrect type to a typed list.")
        def __setitem__(self, i, element):
            self.__check(element)
            self.data[i] = element
        def __getitem__(self, i):
            return self.data[i]

x = TypedUserList("", 5 * [""])
x[2] = "Hello"
x[3] = "There"
print(x[2] + ' ' + x[3])
```

Hello There

```
a, b, c, d, e = x
a, b, c, d
```

('', '', 'Hello', 'There')

```
x[:]
```

['', '', 'Hello', 'There', '']

```
del x[2]
x[:]
```

['', '', 'There', '']

```
x.sort()
x[:]
```

['', '', '', 'There']

This example is much the same as subclassing `list`, except that in the implementation of the class, the list of items is available internally as the `data` member. In some situations, having direct access to the underlying data structure can be useful. Also, in addition to `UserList`, there are `UserDict` and `UserString` wrapper classes.

17.10 *When to use special method attributes*

As a rule, it's a good idea to be somewhat cautious with the use of special method attributes. Other programmers who need to work with your code may wonder why one sequence-type object responds correctly to standard indexing notation whereas another doesn't.

My general guidelines are to use special method attributes in either of two situations:

- If I have a frequently used class in my own code that behaves in some respects like a Python built-in type, I'll define such special method attributes as needed. This situation occurs most often with objects that behave like sequences in one way or another.

- If I have a class that behaves identically or almost identically to a built-in class, I may choose to define all of the appropriate special function attributes or subclass the built-in Python type and distribute the class. An example of the latter solution might be lists implemented as balanced trees so that access is slower but insertion is faster than with standard lists.

These rules aren't hard and fast. It's often a good idea to define the __str__ special method attribute for a class, for example, so that you can say print(*instance*) in debugging code and get an informative, nice-looking representation of your object printed to the screen.

> ### Quick check: Special method attributes and subclassing types
>
> Suppose that you want a dictionary-like type that allows only strings as keys (maybe to make it work like a `shelf` object, as described in chapter 13). What options would you have for creating such a class? What would be the advantages and disadvantages of each option?

17.11 *Creating a string-only key-value dictionary*

The preceding quick check mentions creating a dictionary that only allows strings as keys. Let's take that idea a step further and actually implement a dictionary that only allows strings for both keys and values. This sort of dictionary might be useful, for example, to cache URLs and web pages in a web application.

As mentioned in the discussion of lists earlier, you would have three possible approaches: write a class from scratch, inherit from the built-in dictionary, or inherit from UserDict. I would suggest, for the best combination of simplicity and functionality, that you inherit from the built-in dict type and override the __setitem__() method.

You should be warned, however, that dictionaries can also be created from a series of key-value tuples and from other dictionaries, bypassing __setitem__(). To handle this, you would need to override the __init__() method. Checking the type of the initial parameter and then checking both keys and values appropriately would be one way to do this, but it would be simpler to call the parent class's __init__() method first and then write only the code to check self afterward. As a final task, add code to your class to override the __init__() method to enforce both keys and values are only strings.

17.11.1 *Solving the problem with AI-generated code*

The first thing to keep in mind is that the AI should be told which approach to take. Since the recommendation is to subclass dict, that should be specified in the prompt, and in fact asking for a subclass of dict makes the prompt simpler. The AI solution will also need to deal correctly with both the __setitem__() and the __init__() methods.

17.11.2 *Solutions and discussion*

As mentioned earlier, for a full solution you need to override both the __setitem__()
and the __init__() methods to make sure that only strings are allowed as keys and
values. This is very straightforward for __setitem__() but a bit trickier for __init__(),
since there are two types of parameters that can be passed in: a sequence of key-value
tuples and another dictionary.

THE HUMAN SOLUTION

My solution is fairly simple, checking the types of the keys and values in the
__setitem__() method and then checking self's keys and values in __init__():

```
""" Create a dictionary that allows only strings for keys and values"""

class StringDict(dict):
    def __setitem__(self, key, value):
        if not isinstance(key, str):
            raise TypeError('key is not a string')          ◀────┐ Checking type
        if not isinstance(value, str):
            raise TypeError('value is not a string')
        super().__setitem__(key, value)

    def __init__(self, *args, **kwargs):
        super().__init__(*args, **kwargs)
        key_error = any(not isinstance(_, str)
                        for _ in self.keys())
        if key_error:                                        ◀──── Checking types iterating
            raise TypeError('key is not a string')                over keys and values
        value_error = any(not isinstance(_, str)
                          for _ in self.values())
        if value_error:                                      ◀────┘
            raise TypeError('value is not a string')
```

In the __setitem__() method, the isinstance function is used to check the type, and
a TypeError is raised with the appropriate message if either the key or the value is not
a string. If they are both strings, the parent class's method is called to add the item to
self.

The __init__() method has to be a bit more complicated. Since this method might
be passed either a sequence of key-value tuples or a dictionary, it could be a bit complicated to write code to check both types. It's a bit simpler to first call the parent class's
__init__ method, which will add either type of value to the new self object and then
check that object using its keys and values methods. We use a generator expression,
which is similar to a list comprehension but more memory efficient. The any function
will return True if any of the values in the generated series are not instances of str. The
other feature of the generator expressions is the use of "_" as the expression variable,
which is a common Python idiom, suggesting that semianonymous, throw-away nature
of that variable.

It might seem a bit odd to be checking `self`, since that implies that the object is already created. In a way, the object has been created, but in fact, an exception in `__init__` will cause the object to be discarded.

THE AI SOLUTIONS

For Copilot, the prompt was simple:

```
Create a subclass of dictionary that allows only strings as both keys and
values.
```

The plan created by Copilot was

1 Create a subclass of `dict` named `StringDict`.

2 Override the `__setitem__` method to check if both the key and value are instances of `str`. If not, raise a `TypeError`.

3 Override the `__init__` method to call the parent's `__init__` method and then check all keys and values in the dictionary. If any are not instances of `str`, raise a `TypeError`.

The following code was then suggested:

```
class StringDict(dict):
    def __setitem__(self, key, value):
        if not isinstance(key, str):
            raise TypeError('keys must be strings')
        if not isinstance(value, str):
            raise TypeError('values must be strings')
        super().__setitem__(key, value)

    def __init__(self, *args, **kwargs):
        super().__init__(*args, **kwargs)
        for key, value in self.items():
            if not isinstance(key, str):
                raise TypeError('keys must be strings')
            if not isinstance(value, str):
                raise TypeError('values must be strings')
```

The resemblance to the human solution is surprising, although in many spots there isn't much opportunity for variation. The key difference is that in `__init__` the suggested code uses simple `for` loops, raising the exception as soon as a nonstring value is encountered. On reflection, I have to admit that this is preferable to the human solution, which will iterate over the entire `self` object's keys and values, while Copilot's solution will stop at the first error. In most cases, this approach probably wouldn't matter much, but if there were a lot of illegal types passed to `__init__`, it could be significantly more efficient.

Colaboratory required a bit more of a prompt. The first prompt was the same as for Copilot:

Create a subclass of dictionary that allows only strings as both keys and values.

This resulted in a class that only overrode __setitem__, which is not enough:

```
class StringDict(dict):
  def __setitem__(self, key, value):
    if not isinstance(key, str) or not isinstance(value, str):
      raise TypeError("Both keys and values must be strings.")
    super().__setitem__(key, value)
```

The prompt was then expanded to

Create a subclass of dictionary that allows only strings as both keys and values, including when creating the instance.

This worked better, giving the following:

```
class StringDict(dict):
  def __init__(self, *args, **kwargs):
    super().__init__()
    for key, value in dict(*args, **kwargs).items():
      self[key] = value

  def __setitem__(self, key, value):
    if not isinstance(key, str) or not isinstance(value, str):
      raise TypeError("Both keys and values must be strings.")
    super().__setitem__(key, value)
```

Creates anonymous dictionary

Calls __setitem__

This code is compact and works just fine. It's worth noting a couple differences in the approach from the Copilot version. First, the __init__ method creates a separate anonymous dictionary by calling dict with its arguments. This works, but if the initial arguments are quite large, it might be an inefficient use of memory, since that anonymous dictionary won't be deleted until all of the items are added to self, which is the dictionary being initialized. Still, this would only be a problem with an enormous amount of data, since only the dictionary structure, not the items themselves, would be duplicate. This approach also does not check the values in __init__ but instead adds each item in a loop that calls __setitem__ each time, checking the values. The advantage of this is that the checking code is not duplicated.

It's also worth mentioning that this code checks both the key and the value in a compound if statement. This is perfectly legal but wouldn't be my choice, since the exception can't specify whether the problem is with a key or a value and because compound if statements are a little bit harder for humans reading the code to parse. Overall, however, this solution would be fine.

While there were some differences in approach, the simplicity of subclassing an existing data structure means that in many ways the solutions to this problem were similar and would be simpler than either using UserDict or implementing dictionary functionality from scratch.

Summary

- Types/classes are just Python objects.
- Types can be assigned a variable and compared to other objects for equality.
- Python has the tools to check the type of objects as needed in your code.
- Duck typing, which relies on the behavior of objects rather than their type, can let you write more flexible code.
- Special method attributes have names beginning and ending with "__" ("dunder" methods) and can be overridden to change the behavior of user-created classes.
- Subclassing built-in classes can be used to create similar classes with customized behavior.
- Python's use of duck typing, special method attributes, and subclassing makes it possible to construct and combine classes in a variety of ways.

18

Packages

This chapter covers

- Defining a package
- Creating a simple package
- Exploring a concrete example
- Using the `__all__` attribute
- Using packages properly

Modules make reusing small chunks of code easy. The problem comes when the project grows and the code you want to reload outgrows, either physically or logically, what would fit into a single file. If having one giant module file is an unsatisfactory solution, having a host of little unconnected modules isn't much better. The answer to this problem is to combine related modules into a package.

In this chapter, we discuss Python packages as structure of directories and files on disk.

NOTE Quite often people speak of a "package" that combines one or more Python modules or packages into a single distributable file that can be uploaded to a package repository like PyPI, which is mentioned in the next chapter. There is an ever-increasing array of options for creating such packages, and that process is beyond the scope of this book A good starting point for learning how to create distributable Python packages would be the Python Packaging User Guide, which can be found at https://packaging.python.org/en/latest/.

18.1 What is a package?

A *module* is a file containing code. A module defines a group of usually related Python functions or other objects. The name of the module is derived from the name of the file.

When you understand modules, packages are easy, because a package is a directory containing code and possibly further subdirectories. A package contains a group of usually related code files (modules). The name of the package is derived from the name of the main package directory.

Packages are a natural extension of the module concept and are designed to handle very large projects. Just as modules group related functions, classes, and variables, packages group related modules.

18.2 A first example: mathproj

To see how packages might work in practice, consider a design layout for a type of project that by nature is very large: a generalized mathematics package along the lines of Mathematica, Maple, or MATLAB. Maple, for example, consists of thousands of files, and some sort of hierarchical structure is vital to keeping such a project ordered. Let's call this project as a whole `mathproj`.

You can organize such a project in many ways, but a reasonable design splits the project into two parts: `ui`, consisting of the UI elements, and `comp`, the computational elements. Within `comp`, it may make sense to further segment the computational aspect into `symbolic` (real and complex symbolic computation, such as high school algebra) and `numeric` (real and complex numerical computation, such as numerical integration). Then it may make sense to have a constants.py file in both the `symbolic` and `numeric` parts of the project.

The constants.py file in the numeric part of the project defines `pi` as

```
pi = 3.141592
```

whereas the constants.py file in the symbolic part of the project defines `pi` as

```
class PiClass:
    def __str__(self):
        return "PI"
pi = PiClass()
```

This means that a name like `pi` can be used in (and imported from) two different files named constants.py, as shown in figure 18.1.

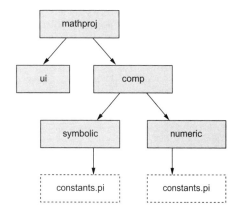

The symbolic constants.py file defines `pi` as an abstract Python object, the sole instance of the `PiClass` class. As the system is developed, various operations can be implemented in this class that return symbolic rather than numeric results.

There's a natural mapping from this design structure to a directory structure. The top-level directory of the project, called `mathproj`, contains subdirectories `ui` and `comp`; `comp` in turn contains subdirectories `symbolic` and `numeric`; and each of `symbolic` and `numeric` contains its own `constants.pi` file.

Figure 18.1   A math package, split into UI and comp components, with symbolic and numberic elements in the components

Given this directory structure, and assuming that the root `mathproj` directory is installed somewhere in the Python search path, Python code both inside and outside the `mathproj` package can access the two variants of `pi` as `mathproj.symbolic.constants.pi` and `mathproj.numeric.constants.pi`. In other words, the Python name for an item in the package is a reflection of the directory pathname to the file containing that item.

That's what packages are all about. They're ways of organizing very large collections of Python code into coherent wholes, by allowing the code to be split among different files and directories and imposing a module/submodule naming scheme based on the directory structure of the package files. Unfortunately, packages aren't this simple in practice because details intrude to make their use more complex than their theory. The practical aspects of packages are the basis for the remainder of this chapter.

18.3 *Implementing the mathproj package*

The rest of this chapter uses the example of the `mathproj` package to illustrate the inner workings of the package mechanism (see figure 18.2). Be careful to distinguish between a *file* that ends in .py and contains module code, and the *module* itself, which does not end in .py, inside the file. The files you'll be using in your example package are shown in listings 18.1 through 18.6.

The file in the following listing is the __init__.py file for the main package, which prints a message to show it was loaded and sets the package's __all__ property.

> **Listing 18.1   File mathproj/__init__.py**

```
print("Hello from mathproj init")
__all__ = ['comp']
version = 1.03
```

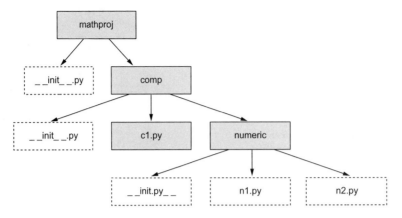

Figure 18.2   Example math package with __init__.py files added

The file in the following listing is the __init__.py file for the comp subpackage, which prints a different message to show it was loaded and sets the subpackage's __all__ property.

Listing 18.2   File mathproj/comp/__init__.py

```
__all__ = ['c1']
print("Hello from mathproj.comp init")
```

The file in the following listing is the c1.py file of the main package, which sets the comp sub-package's x property to 1.0.

Listing 18.3   File mathproj/comp/c1.py

```
x = 1.00
```

The file in the following listing is the __init__.py file for the numeric subpackage, which just prints a message to show it was loaded.

Listing 18.4   File mathproj/comp/numeric/__init__.py

```
print("Hello from numeric init")
```

The file in the following listing is the n1.py file of the numeric subpackage, which imports elements of the main package and the comp subpackage and defines the g() function.

Listing 18.5   File mathproj/comp/numeric/n1.py

```
from mathproj import version
from mathproj.comp import c1
```

```
from mathproj.comp.numeric.n2 import h
def g():
    print("version is", version)
    print(h())
```

Finally, the file in the following listing is the n2.py file of the `numeric` subpackage, which defines the `h()` function.

Listing 18.6 File mathproj/comp/numeric/n2.py

```
def h():
    return "Called function h in module n2"
```

For the purposes of the examples in this chapter, if you are using the Colaboratory notebook, all you need to do is execute the setup cell to create the directories and files. If you are using another Python installation, you will have to create the `mathproj` directories and subdirectories and save the files to them. Then, ensure that the current working directory for Python is the directory containing `mathproj` when executing these examples.

> **NOTE** In most of the examples in this book, it's not necessary to start up a new Python shell for each example. You can usually execute the examples in a Python shell that you've used for previous examples and still get the results shown. *This isn't true for the examples in this chapter*, however, because the Python namespace must be clean (unmodified by previous `import` statements) for the examples to work properly. If you do run the examples that follow, *please ensure that you run each separate example in a new session*. In Colaboratory, this requires using the Runtime menu and selecting Restart Session. In the notebook, there will be comments at the beginning of cells that require a new session.

18.3.1 __init__.py files in packages

You'll have noticed that all the directories in your package—`mathproj`, `mathproj/comp`, and `mathproj/numeric`—contain a file called __init__.py. An __init__.py file serves two purposes:

- Python recognizes a directory containing an __init__.py file as a package. This is optional but prevents directories containing miscellaneous Python code from being accidentally imported as though they defined a package.
- The __init__.py file is automatically executed by Python the first time a package or subpackage is loaded. This execution permits whatever package initialization you desire.

The first point is usually more important. For many packages, you won't need to put anything in the package's __init__.py file; just make sure that an empty __init__.py file is present.

18.3.2 *Basic use of the mathproj package*

Before getting into the details of packages, look at accessing items contained in the `mathproj` package. Start a new Python shell, and do the following:

```
import mathproj

Hello from mathproj init
```

If all goes well, you should get another input prompt and no error messages. Also, the message `"Hello from mathproj init"` should be printed to the screen by code in the mathproj/__init__.py file. I will talk more about __init__.py files soon; for now, all you need to know is that the files run automatically whenever a package is first loaded.

The mathproj/__init__.py file assigns 1.03 to the variable `version`. `version` is in the scope of the `mathproj` package namespace, and after it's created, you can see it via `mathproj`, even from outside the mathproj/__init__.py file:

```
mathproj.version

1.03
```

In use, packages can look a lot like modules; they can provide access to objects defined within them via attributes. This fact isn't surprising, because packages are a generalization of modules.

18.3.3 *Loading subpackages and submodules*

Now start looking at how the various files defined in the `mathproj` package interact with one another. To do so, invoke the function g defined in the file mathproj/comp/numeric/n1.py. The first obvious question is whether this module has been loaded. You've already loaded `mathproj`, but what about its subpackage? To see whether it's known to Python, type

```
mathproj.comp.numeric.n1

Traceback (most recent call last):
  File "<stdin>", line 1, in <module>
AttributeError: module 'mathproj' has no attribute 'n1'
```

In other words, loading the top-level module of a package isn't enough to load all the submodules, which is in keeping with Python's philosophy that it shouldn't do things behind your back. Clarity is more important than conciseness.

This restriction is simple enough to overcome. You import the module of interest and then execute the function g in that module:

```
import mathproj.comp.numeric.n1

Hello from mathproj.comp init
```

```
Hello from numeric init
```

```
mathproj.comp.numeric.n1.g()
```

```
version is 1.03
Called function h in module n2
```

Notice, however, that the lines beginning with `Hello` are printed out as a side effect of loading `mathproj.comp.numeric.n1`. These two lines are printed out by `print` statements in the __init__.py files in `mathproj/comp` and `mathproj/comp/numeric`. In other words, before Python can import `mathproj.comp.numeric.n1`, it has to import `mathproj.comp` and then `mathproj.comp.numeric`. Whenever a package is first imported, its associated __init__.py file is executed, resulting in the `Hello` lines. To confirm that both `mathproj.comp` and `mathproj.comp.numeric` are imported as part of the process of importing `mathproj.comp.numeric.n1`, you can check to see that `mathproj.comp` and `mathproj.comp.numeric` are now known to the Python session:

```
mathproj.comp
```

```
<module 'mathproj.comp' from 'mathproj/comp/__init__.py'>
```

```
mathproj.comp.numeric
```

```
<module 'mathproj.comp.numeric'  from 'mathproj/comp/numeric/__init__.py'>
```

18.3.4 *import statements within packages*

Files within a package don't automatically have access to objects defined in other files in the same package. As in outside modules, you must use `import` statements to explicitly access objects from other package files. To see how this use of `import` works in practice, look back at the `n1` subpackage. The code contained in n1.py is

```
from mathproj import version
from mathproj.comp import c1
from mathproj.comp.numeric.n2 import h
def g():
    print("version is", version)
    print(h())
```

`g` makes use of both `version` from the top-level `mathproj` package and the function `h` from the `n2` module; hence, the module containing `g` must import both `version` and `h` to make them accessible. You import `version` as you would in an `import` statement from outside the `mathproj` package: by saying `from mathproj import version`. In this example, you explicitly import `h` into the code by saying `from mathproj.comp.numeric.n2 import h`, and this technique works in any file; explicit imports of package files are always allowed. But because n2.py is in the same directory as n1.py, you can also use a relative import by prepending a single dot to the submodule name. In other words, you can say

```
from .n2 import h
```

as the third line in n1.py, and it works fine.

You can add more dots to move up more levels in the package hierarchy, and you can add module names. Instead of writing

```
from mathproj import version
from mathproj.comp import c1
from mathproj.comp.numeric.n2 import h
```

you could have written the imports of n1.py as

```
from ... import version
from ..  import c1
from . n2 import h
```

Relative imports can be handy and quick to type, but be aware that they're *relative* to the module's __name__ property. Therefore, any module being executed as the main module and thus having __main__ as its __name__ can't use relative imports.

18.4   *The __all__ attribute*

If you look back at the various __init__.py files defined in mathproj, you'll notice that some of them define an attribute called __all__. This attribute has to do with execution of statements of the form from ... import *, and it requires explanation.

Generally speaking, you'd hope that if outside code executed the statement from mathproj import *, it would import all nonprivate names from mathproj. In practice, life is more difficult. The primary problem is that some operating systems have an ambiguous definition of case when it comes to filenames. Because objects in packages can be defined by files or directories, this situation leads to ambiguity as to the exact name under which a subpackage might be imported. If you say from mathproj import *, will comp be imported as comp, Comp, or COMP? If you were to rely only on the name as reported by the operating system, the results might be unpredictable.

There's no good solution to this problem, which is an inherent one caused by poor OS design. As the best possible fix, the __all__ attribute was introduced. If present in an __init__.py file, __all__ should give a list of strings, defining those names that are to be imported when a from ... import * is executed on that particular package. If __all__ isn't present, from ... import * on the given package does nothing. Because case in a text file is always meaningful, the names under which objects are imported aren't ambiguous, and if the operating system thinks that comp is the same as COMP, that's its problem.

Use the Runtime menu and restart your session again; then try the following:

```
from mathproj import *

Hello from mathproj init
Hello from mathproj.comp init
```

The `__all__` attribute in mathproj/__init__.py contains a single entry, `comp`, and the `import` statement imports only `comp`. It's easy enough to check whether `comp` is now known to the Python session:

```
comp

<module 'mathproj.comp' from 'mathproj/comp/__init__.py'>
```

But note that there's no recursive importing of names with a `from ... import *` statement. The `__all__` attribute for the `comp` package contains `c1`, but `c1` isn't magically loaded by your `from mathproj import *` statement:

```
c1

Traceback (most recent call last):
  File "<stdin>", line 1, in <module>
NameError: name 'c1' is not defined
```

To insert names from `mathproj.comp`, you must again do an explicit import:

```
from mathproj.comp import c1
c1

<module 'mathproj.comp.c1' from 'mathproj/comp/c1.py'>
```

18.5 *Proper use of packages*

Most of your packages shouldn't be as structurally complex as these examples imply. The package mechanism allows wide latitude in the complexity and nesting of your package design. It's obvious that very complex packages *can* be built, but it isn't obvious that they *should* be built.

The following are a couple of suggestions that are appropriate in most circumstances:

- Packages shouldn't use deeply nested directory structures. Except for absolutely huge collections of code, there should be no need for them. For most packages, a single top-level directory is all that's needed. A two-level hierarchy should be able to effectively handle all but a few of the rest. As written in *The Zen of Python* (see the appendix), "Flat is better than nested."
- Although you can use the `__all__` attribute to hide names from `from ... import *` by not listing those names, doing so probably is *not* a good idea, because it's inconsistent. If you want to keep an element from loading when everything is imported, you can do so by prefacing it with an underscore, as mentioned in chapter 10 on modules.

> ### Quick check: Packages
> Suppose that you're writing a package that takes a URL, retrieves all images on the page pointed to by that URL, resizes them to a standard size, and stores them.

> **(continued)**
>
> Leaving aside the exact details of how each of these functions will be coded, how would you organize those features into a package?

18.6   *Creating a package*

In chapter 14, you added error handling to the text-cleaning and word-frequency-counting module that you created in chapter 10. Refactor that code into a package containing at least one module for the cleaning functions, another for the processing functions, and (optionally) one for custom exceptions (if you have any). Then write a simple main function that uses all the modules in the package.

18.6.1   *Solving the problem with AI-generated code*

The main concern in this lab is deciding what to put in each function. This is obviously something where there might be room for different interpretations, so we'll accept any division that is not obviously wrong.

18.6.2   *Solutions and discussion*

As you may recall, back in chapter 10 we created a module of functions to clean a text (part of the first chapter of *Moby Dick*) and count the occurrences of each word. While that module was small enough to be manageable, it wasn't the best design, since there was no separation of different types of functions—functionality for cleaning the data, for counting the words, and for custom exceptions were all in the same module.

Using a package lets us separate those different types of functionality into their own modules (or even subpackages, for something larger). This can make using and maintaining that code easier.

THE HUMAN SOLUTION

I create a package `word_count` by refactoring the module of functions created in chapter 10 into a package with three modules. The first file is __init__.py, which imports the custom exception from exceptions.py, the `clean_line` and `get_words` data cleaning functions from cleaning.py, and the `count_words` and `word_stats` functions from counter.py. Importing those elements into the main package namespace means that the user won't need to worry about specifying the module—they will appear in the top level of the package.

Listing 18.7   __init__.py

```
#__init__.py

from word_count.exceptions import EmptyStringError
from word_count.cleaning import clean_line, get_words
from word_count.counter import count_words, word_stats
```

The second file is exceptions.py, which contains the custom exception. While not always necessary, it's often a good idea to have custom exceptions in a separate file, where they can be imported as needed.

Listing 18.8 exceptions.py

```
# exceptions.py

class EmptyStringError(Exception):
    Pass
```

The third file is cleaning.py, which holds the code concerned with cleaning the data. Note that it imports the custom exception.

Listing 18.9 cleaning.py

```
# cleaning.py

from word_count.exceptions import EmptyStringError

punct = str.maketrans("",   "", "!.,:;-?")

def clean_line(line):
    """changes case and removes punctuation"""

    # raise exception if line is empty
    # uncomment to test EmptyStringError
    #if not line.strip():
    #    raise EmptyStringError()

    # make all one case
    cleaned_line = line.lower()

    # remove punctuation
    cleaned_line = cleaned_line.translate(punct)
    return cleaned_line


def get_words(line):
    """splits line into words, and rejoins with newlines"""
    words = line.split()
    return "\n".join(words) + "\n"
```

The final file is counter.py, which has the code for actually counting the words and compiling the stats. Note that this module now operates independently of the other modules, simply taking a list of words and a dictionary of word counts.

Listing 18.10 counter.py

```
# counter.py

def count_words(words):
```

```
    """"takes list of cleaned words, returns count dictionary"""
    word_count = {}
    for word in words:
        try:
            count = word_count.setdefault(word, 0)
        except TypeError:
            #if 'word' is not hashable, skip to next word.
            pass
        word_count[word] += 1
    return word_count


def word_stats(word_count):
    """Takes word count dictionary, returns top and bottom five entries"""
    word_list = list(word_count.items())
    word_list.sort(key=lambda x: x[1])
    try:
        least_common = word_list[:5]
        most_common = word_list[-1:-6:-1]
    except IndexError as e:
        # if list is empty or too short, just return list
        least_common = word_list
        most_common = list(reversed(word_list))

    return most_common, least_common
```

These functions are the same as those used in the solution to the lab for chapter 10 but now split into three modules, with an __init__.py file to load various functions on import.

The test code is also very similar to that of the solution for the lab in chapter 10 but with the imports changed to use the package. The main difference is now it imports the package and then uses the relevant items from the package to clean the data and create a word count:

```
import word_count

if __name__ == "__main__":
    with (open("moby_01.txt") as infile,
            open("moby_01_clean.txt", "w") as outfile):
        for line in infile:
            cleaned_line = word_count.clean_line(line)

            cleaned_words = word_count.get_words(cleaned_line)

            # write all words for line
            outfile.write(cleaned_words)

    moby_words = []
    with open('moby_01_clean.txt') as infile:
        for word in infile:
            if word.strip():
                moby_words.append(word.strip())

    word_counter = word_count.count_words(moby_words)
```

```
most, least = word_count.word_stats(word_counter)
print("Most common words:")
for word in most:
    print(word)
print("\nLeast common words:")
for word in least:
    print(word)
```

This code will work in a file that is in a directory containing the `word_count` package directory, or in a cell in Colaboratory, or if the `word_count` package directory is otherwise on the Python search path.

THE AI SOLUTIONS

The Copilot solution was disappointing. The prompt given to Copilot, while in the same directory as the files from chapter 10's lab, was

```
Refactor the code in word_processing.py into a package containing at least
one module for the cleaning functions, and another for the processing
functions, and (optionally) one for custom exceptions (if you have any).
The refactor main.py to use the new package.
```

The plan it created was

1 Create a package directory named `word_processing`.
2 Inside `word_processing`, create three modules: `cleaning.py`, `processing.py`, and `exceptions.py`.
3 Move the cleaning functions to `cleaning.py`.
4 Move the processing functions to `processing.py`.
5 If there are any custom exceptions, move them to `exceptions.py`.
6 In `main.py`, import the necessary functions from the `word_processing` package and use them.

While the bot came up with a reasonable structure for a package `word_processing`, it did not copy most of the code, instead just inserting "your implementation goes here" markers. The following listing shows the `clean_line` function.

Listing 18.11   word_processing/cleaning.py

```
def clean_line(line):
    # Your cleaning function implementation here
    pass
```

Note that it does not copy the code—just the function name. The following listing does import from the previous module and contains functions for cleaning the raw file and writing it to another file.

Listing 18.12   word_processing/processing.py

```python
from .cleaning import clean_line

def write_words_to_file(words, output_file):
    # Your write_words_to_file function implementation here
    pass

def print_common_words(word_counts, n):
    # Your print_common_words function implementation here
    pass

def print_least_common_words(word_counts, n):
    # Your print_least_common_words function implementation here
    pass

def process_file(input_file_path, output_file_path):
    with open(input_file_path, 'r') as input_file:
        with open(output_file_path, 'w') as output_file:
            for line in input_file:
                cleaned_line = clean_line(line)
                words = cleaned_line.split()
                write_words_to_file(words, output_file)
```

In this module as well, there is no code for most of the functions, other than the process_file function. Then it creates a file for exceptions.

Listing 18.13   word_processing/exceptions.py

```python
# If you have any custom exceptions, define them here
```

Since custom exceptions were optional, it is fine that none were created. Finally, we have a main file that imports the functions from the processing module.

Listing 18.14   main.py

```python
from word_processing.processing import process_file

# Use the process_file function from the word_processing package
process_file('input.txt', 'output.txt')
```

This module does import from the processing module and calls the process_file function. All that will do is read a raw file and and write it as words to another file. As mentioned earlier, the basic structure of the library meets the requirements of the prompt, although one might argue that the write_words_to_file and process_file functions were more cleaning than processing. The real disappointment is that even though the bot used function names from the original module, it didn't copy the code of the functions, except for the process_file function. In addition, for main.py, it did not use the package as fully as the original did.

Finally, Copilot did not create an __init__.py file until specifically asked to with the following prompt:

```
Also add a init.py that appropriately imports the package's functions.
```

With this prompt, Copilot offered what is shown in the following listing.

Listing 18.15 word_processing/__init__.py

```
from .cleaning import clean_line
from .processing import (write_words_to_file, print_common_words,
                         print_least_common_words, process_file)
```

And it offered the following correct suggestion for importing the package:

```
from word_processing import (clean_line, write_words_to_file,
              print_common_words, print_least_common_words, process_file)
```

Overall, this solution was one of the least helpful offerings from Copilot—and the first one where it was necessary to go back and rework the prompt to specify the output we needed. AI tools sometimes fail to understand what seem to be perfectly clear prompts, and there's no clear way to anticipate when that might happen. The key is to be aware of the possibility and modify the prompt when it happens.

The new prompt explicitly asked Copilot to use the existing code in the functions:

```
Refactor the code in word_processing.py into a package containing at least
one module for the cleaning functions, and another for the processing
functions, and (optionally) one for custom exceptions (if you have any). Be
sure to use the code from the original file to reproduce the functionality
of the original file. Then refactor main.py to use the new package.
```

This time the plan was very similar, but it added a step for creating an __init__.py file, which was created correctly. The result was much better, with most of the functions having code, but the clean_line function (in word_processing/cleaning.py) and the write_words_to_file function (in word_processing/procssing.py) still had only the comment. So another prompt was given to make Copilot complete those:

```
Supply the code for the clean_line and write_words_to_file functions.
```

Copilot supplied the code and then provided the complete files.

First, it created word_processing/cleaning.py for the clean_line function.

Listing 18.16 word_processing/cleaning.py

```
def clean_line(line):
    # Remove punctuation and convert to lowercase
    line = re.sub(r'[^\w\s]', '', line)
```

```
line = line.lower()
return line
```

Following the instruction in the second additional prompt, it copied the correct code to the function but neglected to import the re module. While you could tinker with the prompt more, it's probably easier and faster to just manually add the missing line at the top of the file:

```
import re
```

The second file created is the file for the processing functions.

Listing 18.17   word_processing/processing.py

```
def count_word_occurrences(words):
    word_counts = {}
    for word in words:
        if word in word_counts:
            word_counts[word] += 1
        else:
            word_counts[word] = 1
    return word_counts

def print_common_words(word_counts, n):
    sorted_word_counts = sorted(word_counts.items(),
                                key=lambda x: x[1], reverse=True)
    print(f"{n} most common words:")
    for word, count in sorted_word_counts[:n]:
        print(f"{word}: {count}")

def print_least_common_words(word_counts, n):
    sorted_word_counts = sorted(word_counts.items(),
                                key=lambda x: x[1], reverse=True)
    print(f"{n} least common words:")
    for word, count in sorted_word_counts[-n:]:
        print(f"{word}: {count}")

def write_words_to_file(words, output_file):
    for word in words:
        output_file.write(word + '\n')

def process_file(input_file_path, output_file_path):
    with open(input_file_path, 'r') as input_file:
        with open(output_file_path, 'w') as output_file:
            for line in input_file:
                cleaned_line = clean_line(line)
                words = cleaned_line.split()
                write_words_to_file(words, output_file)
```

Again, this time, with the modified prompt and the second prompt, all of the functions are populated correctly, but again an import is missing. This time it's the import of the clean_line function from cleaning.py. As with the previous file, we could spend more time tweaking the prompt, but it will save time to just manually add it to the top of the file:

```
from text_processor.cleaning import clean_line
```

Copilot next creates a file for exceptions, as requested, but since creating custom exceptions was optional, it quite reasonably doesn't create any.

Listing 18.18   word_processing/exceptions.py

```
# If you have any custom exceptions, define them here
```

In response to the direct request, Copilot now creates an __init__.py module.

Listing 18.19   word_processing/__init__.py

```
from .cleaning import clean_line
from .processing import (
    count_word_occurrences,
    print_common_words,
    print_least_common_words,
    write_words_to_file,
    process_file
)
```

In this module, the imports are all there and are correct and nicely formatted.

The last file it creates is main.py, which has the necessary imports, and then runs the various functions.

Listing 18.20   main.py

```
from word_processing import (
    process_file,
    count_word_occurrences,
    print_common_words,
    print_least_common_words
)

# Example usage
input_file_path = 'input.txt'
output_file_path = 'output.txt'

process_file(input_file_path, output_file_path)

# Assuming you have a list of words from somewhere
words = ["example", "words", "for", "testing", "example", "words"]
word_counts = count_word_occurrences(words)
print_common_words(word_counts, 3)
print_least_common_words(word_counts, 3)
```

This code is less than ideal in that the file names for the raw and cleaned files are hard-coded, but then it ignores the cleaned text file and talks about "a list of words from somewhere" and uses the list `["example", "words", "for", "testing", "example",` `"words"]` to test the program. What it should have done is read the cleaned text file, doing a `split()` to get a list of words.

There would be two ways to fix this. One would be to go back and specify the files and that the cleaned file be used for counting. The problem is that by doing that you are adding another step to your development workflow, and you may need several cycles of tweaking the prompt to get it to generate what you want. The other option is to manually make the fixes, adjusting the filenames and adding code to read and split the correct file to get the list of words to be counted. In coding with AI tools, you need to keep in mind the tradeoffs and decide when more prompt engineering is worth the time and when it's more efficient to make the fixes manually and move on.

The Colaboratory solution had a different set of problems. In a new notebook session with only the solution from chapter 10, it was given the following prompt:

```
Refactor the code in module created in cell above into a package containing
at least one module for the cleaning functions, and another for the
processing functions, and (optionally) one for custom exceptions (if you
have any). Then refactor main() to use the new package.
```

Given the limitations of being in Colaboratory, which is more oriented around cells than files, the solution was promising, but everything was in one cell. To keep things manageable, we'll look at the code in this cell in sections, starting with the prompt and the system command to create the package directory, `text_processor`:

```
# prompt: Refactor the code in module created in cell above into a package
    containing at least one module for the cleaning functions, and another
    for
the processing functions, and (optionally) one for custom exceptions (if
you have any). Then refactor main() to use the new package.
```

```
# Create a directory for the package          Command to create
!mkdir text_processor        ◀──────────      package directory
```

The prompt is fairly straightforward, and the call to the system to create the package directory is necessary before doing anything more.

The next section contains the code for the first file, `text_processor/cleaning.py`, with the cleaning function:

```
# Create a file for the cleaning functions
%%writefile text_processor/cleaning.py
```

```
#### THIS IMPORT WAS ADDED BY AUTHOR          Import of string library
import string        ◀──────────             for punctuation
```

```
def clean_line(line):
```

```
    # Convert the line to lowercase
    line = line.lower()

    # Remove punctuation from the line
    line = line.translate(str.maketrans('', '', string.punctuation))

    return line
```

If this code is in its own cell, it works since the `%%writefile` magic command would be first. As part of all the code suggested, where everything was in one cell, it causes an error. Also missing from the bot's solution was the import of the string library, needed to access the punctuation characters.

The following section contains the processing functions:

```
# Create a file for the processing functions
%%writefile text_processor/processing.py

#### THIS IMPORT WAS ADDED BY AUTHOR                          Needed to call
from text_processor.cleaning import clean_line      ◄───────  clean_line function

def write_words_to_file(words, output_file):
    # Write each word to the output file
    for word in words:
        output_file.write(word + '\n')

def count_word_occurrences(words):
    # Count the occurrences of each word using a dictionary
    word_counts = {}
    for word in words:
        if word in word_counts:
            word_counts[word] += 1
        else:
            word_counts[word] = 1

    return word_counts

def print_common_words(word_counts, n):
    # Sort the word counts in descending order
    sorted_word_counts = sorted(word_counts.items(), key=lambda x: x[1],
                            reverse=True)

    # Print the n most common words and their occurrences
    print(f"{n} most common words:")
    for word, count in sorted_word_counts[:n]:
        print(f"{word}: {count}")

def print_least_common_words(word_counts, n):
    # Sort the word counts in descending order
    sorted_word_counts = sorted(word_counts.items(), key=lambda x: x[1],
                            reverse=True)

    # Print the n least common words and their occurrences
    print(f"{n} least common words:")
```

```
    for word, count in sorted_word_counts[-n:]:
        print(f"{word}: {count}")

def process_file(input_file_path, output_file_path):
    # Open the input file for reading
    with open(input_file_path, 'r') as input_file:
        # Open the output file for writing
        with open(output_file_path, 'w') as output_file:
            # Iterate over each line in the input file
            for line in input_file:
                # Clean the line
                cleaned_line = clean_line(line)

                # Split the line into words
                words = cleaned_line.split()

                # Write the words to the output file
                write_words_to_file(words, output_file)
```

This writes the other code file in the package, `text_processor/processing.py`, and if this section would have been in its own cell, it would have worked. But again, a necessary import was omitted—the import of the `clean_line` function from the cleaning library. Once that import is added, the package will work.

Then we have the code for `text_processor/__init__.py`:

```
# Create an __init__.py file to make the directory a package
%%writefile text_processor/__init__.py
from .cleaning import clean_line
from .processing import process_file, count_word_occurrences,
print_common_words, print_least_common_words
```

This writes the `__init__.py` file in the package and makes importing the package also import the functions from the cleaning and processing modules.

The final section has the code to use the newly created package:

```
# Refactor main() to use the new package
%%writefile main.py
import text_processor

input_file_path = 'moby_01.txt'
output_file_path = 'moby_01_clean.txt'

# Process the file
text_processor.process_file(input_file_path, output_file_path)

# Open the file
with open(output_file_path, 'r') as file:
    # Read the file content
    content = file.read()

# Split the content into words
words = content.split()
```

```
# Count word occurrences
word_counts = text_processor.count_word_occurrences(words)

# Print the five most common words and their occurrences
text_processor.print_common_words(word_counts, 5)

# Print the five least common words and their occurrences
text_processor.print_least_common_words(word_counts, 5)
```

The preceding code creates the `main.py` file, which imports and exercises the package, calling the various functions in the correct order. The names of the raw and cleaned files are hardcoded, but they are correct.

The last bit of code is the command to run the `main.py` script:

```
# Run the main script
!python main.py
```

This command simply calls the system Python interpreter with the `main.py` script.

As mentioned earlier, the main problem with the Colaboratory solution was that, when trying to execute this cell, there was an error at the first `%%writefile` since as a Jupyter cell magic command should be executed as the first command of the cell. If each `%%writefile` section is moved to a separate cell, and the two missing imports noted previously are added, when the cells are executed, all of the files are created correctly.

While Colaboratory's solution does not run as generated, if the corrections discussed previously are made, it does ultimately satisfy the requirements. A corrected version, with everything correctly split into cells and the imports added, is included in the Jupyter notebook for this chapter.

This lab required almost no new code. Instead, the problem demanded a knowledge of the structure of Python packages and the ability to select and move the correct elements of existing code to the appropriate places in the new package. While this would strike most experienced human coders as straightforward, it proved to be quite a challenge for the AI bots. Both bots produced elements that were useful, but neither produced a fully usable solution on their own. While tweaking the prompts can improve this situation, it's also wise to keep in mind the time tradeoff between fiddling with the AI prompt versus writing your code. This is especially worth keeping in mind using AI tools to tackle higher-level problems.

Summary

- Packages let you create libraries of code that span multiple files and directories.
- Using packages allows better organization of large collections of code than single modules would permit.
- An `__init__.py` causes its folder to be recognized by Python as a package and is executed when the package is imported.

- Subpackages need to be explicitly imported, either in your code or in the package __init__.py.
- You should be wary of nesting directories in your packages more than one or two levels deep unless you have a very large and complex library.
- The __all__ attribute can be used to hide elements from a wildcard import, but it's better to explicitly exclude them by beginning their names with a "_".

Using Python libraries

This chapter covers

- Managing various data types—strings, numbers, and more
- Manipulating files and storage
- Accessing operating system services
- Using internet protocols and formats
- Developing and debugging tools
- Accessing the Python Package Index
- Installing Python libraries and virtual environments using `pip` and `venv`

Python has long proclaimed that one of its key advantages is its "batteries included" philosophy. This means that a stock install of Python comes with a rich standard library that lets you handle a wide variety of situations without the need to install additional libraries. This chapter gives you a high-level survey of some of the contents of the standard library, as well as some suggestions on finding and installing

397

external modules. Since the content is purely informational, this chapter doesn't include a lab or other exercises.

19.1 "Batteries included": The standard library

In Python, what's considered to be the *library* consists of several components, including built-in data types and constants that can be used without an `import` statement, such as numbers and lists, as well as some built-in functions and exceptions. The largest part of the library is an extensive collection of modules. If you have Python, you also have libraries to manipulate diverse types of data and files to interact with your operating system, to write servers and clients for many internet protocols, and to develop and debug your code.

What follows is a survey of the high points. Although many of the major modules are mentioned, for the most complete and current information, I recommend that you spend time on your own exploring the library reference that's part of the Python documentation. In particular, before you go in search of an external library, be sure to scan through what Python already offers. You may be surprised by what you find.

19.1.1 Managing various data types

The standard library naturally contains support for Python's built-in types, which I touch on in this section. In addition, three categories in the standard library deal with various data types: string services, data types, and numeric modules.

String services include the modules in table 19.1 that deal with bytes as well as strings. The three main things these modules deal with are strings and text, sequences of bytes, and Unicode operations.

Table 19.1　String services modules

Module	Description and possible uses
string	Compare with string constants, such as `digits` or `whitespace`; format strings (see chapter 6)
re	Search and replace text using regular expressions (see chapter 16)
struct	Interpret bytes as packed binary data and read and write structured data to/from files
difflib	Use helpers for computing deltas, find differences between strings or sequences, and create patches and diff files
textwrap	Wrap and fill text and format text by breaking lines or adding spaces

The data types category is a diverse collection of modules covering various data types, particularly, time, date, and collections, as shown in table 19.2.

Table 19.2 Data types modules

Module	Description and possible uses
datetime, calendar	Date, time, and calendar operations
collections	Container data types
enum	Allows creation of enumerator classes that bind symbolic names to constant values
array	Efficient arrays of numeric values
sched	Event scheduler
queue	Synchronized queue class
copy	Shallow and deep copy operations
pprint	Data pretty printer
typing	Support for annotating code with hints as to the types of objects, particularly of function parameters and return values

As the name indicates, the numeric and mathematical modules deal with numbers and mathematical operations, and the most common of these modules are listed in table 19.3. These modules have everything you need to create your own numeric types and handle a wide range of math operations.

Table 19.3 Numeric and mathematical modules

Module	Description and possible uses
numbers	Numeric abstract base classes
math, cmath	Mathematical functions for real and complex numbers
decimal	Decimal fixed-point and floating-point arithmetic
statistics	Functions for calculating mathematical statistics
fractions	Rational numbers
random	Generate pseudorandom numbers and choices and shuffle sequences
itertools	Functions that create iterators for efficient looping
functools	Higher-order functions and operations on callable objects
operator	Standard operators as functions

19.1.2 *Manipulating files and storage*

Another broad category in the standard library covers files, storage, and data persistence and is summarized in table 19.4. This category ranges from modules for file access to modules for data persistence and compression and handling special file formats.

Table 19.4   **File and storage modules**

Module	Description and possible uses
os.path	Perform common pathname manipulations
pathlib	Deal with pathnames in an object-oriented way
fileinput	Iterate over lines from multiple input streams
filecmp	Compare files and directories
tempfile	Generate temporary files and directories
glob, fnmatch	Use UNIX-style pathname and filename pattern handling
linecache	Gain random access to text lines
shutil	Perform high-level file operations
pickle, shelve	Enable Python object serialization and persistence
sqlite3	Work with a DB-API 2.0 interface for SQLite databases
zlib, gzip, bz2, zipfile, tarfile	Work with archive files and compressions
csv	Read and write CSV files
configparser	Use a configuration file parser; read/write Windows-style configuration .ini files

19.1.3 *Accessing operating system services*

This category is another broad one, containing modules for dealing with your operating system. As shown in table 19.5, this category includes tools for handling command-line parameters, redirecting file and print output and input, writing to log files, running multiple threads or processes, and loading non-Python (usually, C) libraries for use in Python.

Table 19.5   **Operating system modules**

Module	Description
os	Miscellaneous operating system interfaces
io	Core tools for working with streams
time	Time access and conversions

Table 19.5 Operating system modules (*continued*)

Module	Description
optparse	Powerful command-line option parser
logging	Logging facility for Python
getpass	Portable password input
curses	Terminal handling for character-cell displays
platform	Access to underlying platform's identifying data
ctypes	Foreign function library for Python
select	Waiting for I/O completion
threading	Higher-level threading interface
multiprocessing	Process-based threading interface
subprocess	Subprocess management

19.1.4 *Using internet protocols and formats*

The internet protocols and formats category is concerned with encoding and decoding the many standard formats used for data exchange on the internet, from MIME and other encodings to JSON and XML. This category also has modules for writing servers and clients for common services, particularly HTTP, and a generic socket server for writing servers for custom services. The most commonly used modules are listed in table 19.6.

Table 19.6 Modules supporting internet protocols and formats

Module	Description
socket, ssl	Low-level networking interface and SSL wrapper for socket objects
Email	Email and MIME handling package
Json	JSON encoder and decoder
Mailbox	Manipulate mailboxes in various formats
Mimetypes	Map filenames to MIME types
base64, binhex, binascii, quopri, uu	Encode/decode files or streams with various encodings
html.parser, html.entities	Parse HTML and XHTML
xml.parsers.expat, xml.dom, xml.sax, xml.etree.ElementTree	Various parsers and tools for XML

Table 19.6   Modules supporting internet protocols and formats (*continued*)

Module	Description
`cgi, cgitb`	Common Gateway Interface support
`Wsgiref`	WSGI utilities and reference implementation
`urllib.request, urllib.parse`	Open and parse URLs
`ftplib, poplib, imaplib, nntplib, smtplib, telnetlib`	Clients for various internet protocols
`Socketserver`	Framework for network servers
`http.server`	HTTP servers
`xmlrpc.client, xmlrpc.server`	XML-RPC client and server

19.1.5 *Development and debugging tools and runtime services*

Python has several modules to help you debug, test, modify, and otherwise interact with your Python code at runtime. As shown in table 19.7, this category includes two testing tools, profilers, modules to interact with error tracebacks, the interpreter's garbage collection, and so on, as well as modules that let you tweak the importing of other modules.

Table 19.7   Development, debugging, and runtime modules

Module	Description
`Pydoc`	Documentation generator and online help system
`Doctest`	Test interactive Python examples
`Unittest`	Unit testing framework
`test.support`	Utility functions for tests
`Pdb`	Python debugger
`profile, cProfile`	Python profilers
`Timeit`	Measure execution time of small code snippets
`trace`	Trace or track Python statement execution
`sys`	System-specific parameters and functions
`atexit`	Exit handlers
`__future__`	Future statement definitions—features to be added to Python
`gc`	Garbage collector interface
`inspect`	Inspect live objects

Table 19.7   Development, debugging, and runtime modules (*continued*)

Module	Description
`imp`	Access the import internals
`zipimport`	Import modules from zip archives
`modulefinder`	Find modules used by a script

19.2   *Moving beyond the standard library*

Although Python's "batteries included" philosophy and well-stocked standard library mean that you can do a lot with Python out of the box, there will inevitably come a situation in which you need some functionality that doesn't come with Python. This section surveys your options when you need to do something that isn't in the standard library.

19.3   *Adding more Python libraries*

Finding a Python package or module can be as easy as entering the functionality you're looking for (such as `mp3 tags` and `Python`) in a search engine and then sorting through the results. While using this approach casts the widest possible net, keep in mind that not all sources are equally reliable and trustworthy. Ultimately, you are the one responsible for the security and functionality of the software you run on your systems, so be sure to consider the source and quality of the code before trusting it.

In some cases, your search may turn up the module you need packaged for your OS—with an executable Windows or macOS installer or a package for your Linux distribution. This technique can be one of the easiest ways to add a library to your Python installation, because the installer or your package manager takes care of all the dependencies and details of adding the module to your system correctly. It can also be the answer for installing more complex libraries, such as scientific libraries with complex build requirements and dependencies.

On the other hand, except for scientific libraries, such prebuilt packages aren't the rule for Python software. Such packages tend to be a bit older, which may cause version problems with newer packages, and they offer less flexibility in where and how they're installed.

19.4   *The Python Package Index*

Although source packages get the job done, there's one catch: you have to find the correct package, which can be a chore. And when you've found a package, you don't always know if the repository is secure and the package is safe. In short, it would be nice to have a reasonably reliable and easy-to-search source from which to download that package.

To meet this need, various Python package repositories have been made available over the years. Currently, the official (but by no means the only) repository for Python code is the Python Package Index (PyPI) linked from the Python.org website. You can access it from a link on the main page or directly at https://pypi.python.org. PyPI contains packages for various Python versions from over 604,000 projects, listed by date and name but also searchable and broken down by category, Python version, and more.

PyPI is the logical next stop if you can't find the functionality you want with a search of the standard library.

19.5   *Installing Python libraries using pip and venv*

If you need a third-party package that isn't prepackaged for your platform, you'll have to turn to a more native Python package. This fact presents a couple of problems:

- To install the module, you must find and download it.
- Installing even a single Python module correctly can involve a certain amount of hassle in dealing with Python's paths and your system's permissions, which makes a standard installation system helpful.

> **Not needed for Colaboratory**
>
> If you are using Colaboratory, there is some good news—you will probably not have to worry about the processes described in the rest of this section. Colaboratory comes with the most common additional libraries already installed, and since each session is its own temporary environment, you don't need to worry about managing virtual environments.
>
> The rest of this section will be of more use if you are managing your own Python installation and environments.

Python offers `pip` as the current standard solution to both problems. `pip` tries to find the module in the Python Package Index, downloads it and any dependencies, and takes care of the installation. The basic syntax of `pip` is quite simple. To install the popular `requests` library from the command line, for example, all you have to do is type

```
$ python3 -m pip install requests
```

Upgrading to the library's latest version requires only the addition of the `--upgrade` switch:

```
$ python3 -m pip install --upgrade requests
```

Finally, if you need to specify a particular version of a package, you can append it to the name as follows:

```
$ python3 -m pip install requests==2.32.3
$ python3 -m pip install requests>=2.32
```

Note that if you are using Colaboratory, most of the commonly used packages (including `requests`) are already installed, but you can install other packages with the previous commands, prefixed with a !:

```
! python3 -m pip install requests
```

Many distributions of Python include `pip`, but some Linux distributions (e.g., Debian- or Ubuntu-based distros) have split `pip` into its own package that needs to be installed separately.

19.5.1 *Installing with the –user flag*

On many occasions, you can't or don't want to install a Python package in the main system instance of Python. Maybe you need a bleeding-edge version of the library, but some other application (or the system itself) still uses an older version. Or maybe you don't have access privileges to modify the system's default Python. In cases like those, one answer is to install the library with the `--user` flag. This flag installs the library in the user's home directory, where it's not accessible by any other users. To install `requests` for only the local user, type

```
$ python -m pip install --user requests
```

As I mentioned previously, this scheme is particularly useful if you're working on a system on which you don't have sufficient administrator rights to install software or if you want to install a different version of a module. If your needs go beyond the basic installation methods discussed here, a good place to start is "Installing Python Modules," which you can find in the Python documentation.

19.5.2 *Virtual environments*

You have another, better option if you need to avoid installing libraries in the system Python. This option is called a virtual environment (virtualenv). A *virtual environment* is a self-contained directory structure that contains both an installation of Python and its additional packages. Because the entire Python environment is contained in the virtual environment, the libraries and modules installed there can't conflict with those in the main system or in other virtual environments, allowing different applications to use different versions on both Python and its packages.

Creating and using a virtual environment takes two steps. First, you create the environment:

```
myuser@mymachine$ python -m venv test-env
```

This step creates the environment with Python and `pip` installed in a directory called `test-env`. Then, when the environment is created, you activate it. On Windows, you do the following:

```
C:\Users\myuser> test-env\Scripts\activate.bat
```

◀ **The Windows prompt shows the current directory (user's home directory).**

On Unix or macOS systems, you can use `source` or `.` to activate the environment:

```
myuser@mymachine$ source test-env/bin/activate
```

◀ **username@machinename is the common prompt string on linux/Unix systems.**

When you've activated the environment, you can use `pip` to manage packages as earlier, but in the virtual environment, `pip` is a standalone command:

```
(test-env) myuser@mymachine$ pip install requests
```

◀ **Once activated, the environment name is prepended to the prompt.**

In addition, whatever version of Python you used to create the environment will be the default Python for that environment and will be used every time you activate that environment.

Virtual environments are very useful for managing projects and their dependencies and are very much a standard practice, particularly for developers working on multiple projects. For more information, look at the "Virtual Environments and Packages" section of the Python tutorial in the Python online documentation.

19.5.3   *Other options*

For managing both packages and virtual environments, there are a number of other options, and as work continues in this area, I would expect even more choices by the time this book is in print. At the time of writing, I was using Pyenv both to manage virtual environments and for installations of different versions of Python.

Various other systems have come along to do the same tasks that `pip` performs, including poetry, rye, and uv, as well as others. The advantage of `pip` and `venv` is that they are the current standard with Python. As you gain experience and a have a better sense of your requirements, you may want to explore the other tools.

There is another common distribution of Python—Anaconda—which is quite popular for scientific computing and data science. It has its own package management tool, called conda, which is good at handling complex dependencies. The Anaconda ecosystem of packages is not as extensive as the one supported by PyPI, with around 8,000 packages available. The plus side is the focus on packages used by data science and related fields.

Summary

- Python has a rich standard library that covers more common situations than many other languages, and you should check what's in the standard library carefully before looking for external modules.

- Among other things, the standard library has modules for handling different data types, manipulating files and filesystems, accessing operating system services, handing internet protocols, and developing and debugging Python code.
- If you do need an external module, prebuilt packages for your operating system are the easiest option, but they're sometimes older and often hard to find.
- The standard way to install from source is to use `pip`, and the best way to prevent conflicts among multiple projects is to create virtual environments with the venv module.
- Usually, the logical first step in searching for external modules is the PyPI.

Part 4

Working with data

In this part, you get some practice in using Python, and in particular, using it to work with data. Handling data is one of Python's strengths. I start with basic file handling; then I move through reading from and writing to flat files, working with more structured formats such as JSON and Excel, using databases, and using Python to explore data.

These chapters are more project oriented than the rest of the book and are intended to give you the opportunity to get hands-on experience in using Python to handle data. The chapters and projects in this part can be done in any order or combination that suits your needs.

Basic file wrangling

This chapter covers

- Moving and renaming files
- Compressing and encrypting files
- Selectively deleting files

This chapter deals with the basic operations you can use when you have an ever-increasing collection of files to manage. Those files might be log files, or they might be from a regular data feed, but whatever their source, you can't simply discard them immediately. How do you save them, manage them, and ultimately dispose of them according to a plan but without manual intervention?

20.1 The problem: The never-ending flow of data files

Many systems generate a continuous series of data files. These files might be the log files from an e-commerce server or a regular process; they might be a nightly feed of product information from a server; they might be automated feeds of items for online advertising or historical data of stock trades; or they might come from a thousand other sources. They're often flat text files, uncompressed, with raw data that's

411

either an input or a byproduct of other processes. In spite of their humble nature, how-ever, the data they contain has some potential value, so the files can't be discarded at the end of the day—which means that every day, their numbers grow. Over time, files accumulate until dealing with them manually becomes unworkable, and the amount of storage they consume becomes unacceptable.

20.2   *Scenario: The product feed from hell*

A typical situation I've encountered is a daily feed of product data. This data might be coming in from a supplier or going out for online marketing, but the basic aspects are the same.

Consider the example of a product feed coming from a supplier. The feed file comes in once a day, with one row for each item that the business supplies. Each row has fields for the supplier's stock-keeping unit (SKU) number; a brief description of the item; the item's cost, height, length, and width; the item's status (in stock or back-ordered, say); and probably several other things, depending on the business.

In addition to this basic info file, you might well be getting others, possibly of related products, more detailed item attributes, or something else. In that case, you end up with several files with the same filenames arriving every day and landing in the same directory for processing.

Now assume that you get three related files every day: `item_info.txt`, `item_attributes.txt`, and `related_items.txt`. These three files come in every day and get processed. If processing were the only requirement, you wouldn't have to worry much; you could just let each day's set of files replace the last and be done with it. But what if you can't throw the data away? You may want to keep the raw data in case there's a question about the accuracy of the process, and you need to refer to past files. Or you may want to track the changes in the data over time. Whatever the reason, the need to keep the files means that you need to do some processing.

The simplest thing you might do is mark the files with the dates on which they were received and move them to an archive folder. That way, each new set of files can be received, processed, renamed, and moved out of the way so that the process can be repeated with no loss of data.

After a few repetitions, the directory structure might look something like the following:

```
working/                          ◄──┐  Main working folder, with
    item_info.txt                    │  current files for processing
    item_attributes.txt
    related_items.txt
    archive/                      ◄──┐  Subdirectory for
        item_info_2024-09-15.txt     │  archiving processed files
        item_attributes_2024-09-15.txt
        related_items_2024-09-15.txt
        item_info_2024-07-16.txt
        item_attributes_2024-09-16.txt
        related_items_2024-09-16.txt
```

```
item_info_2024-09-17.txt
item_attributes_2024-09-17.txt
related_items_2024-09-17.txt
...
```

Think about the steps needed to make this process happen. First, you need to rename the files so that the current date is added to the filename. To do that, you need to get the names of the files you want to rename; then you need to get the stem of the filenames without the extensions. When you have the stem, you need to add a string based on the current date, add the extension back to the end, and then actually change the filename and move it to the archive directory.

Quick check: Consider the choices

What are your options for handling the tasks I've identified? What modules in the standard library can you think of that will do the job? If you want, you can even stop right now and work out the code to do it. Then compare your solution with the one you develop later.

You can get the names of the files in several ways. If you're sure that the names are always exactly the same and that there aren't many files, you *could* hardcode them into your script. A safer way, however, is to use the `pathlib` module and a path object's `glob` method, as follows:

```python
import pathlib
cur_path = pathlib.Path(".")
FILE_PATTERN = "*.txt"
path_list = cur_path.glob(FILE_PATTERN)
print(list(path_list))
```

```
[PosixPath('item_attributes.txt'), PosixPath('related_items.txt'),
PosixPath('item_info.txt')]
```

Now you can step through the paths that match your `FILE_PATTERN` and apply the needed changes. Remember that you need to add the date as part of the name of each file, as well move the renamed files to the archive directory. When you use `pathlib`, the entire operation might look like the following listing.

Listing 20.1 File files_01.py

```python
import datetime
import pathlib

FILE_PATTERN = "*.txt"        ◀──┐ Sets the pattern
ARCHIVE = "archive"              │ to match files

def main():
```

```
date_string = datetime.date.today().strftime("%Y-%m-%d")

cur_path = pathlib.Path(".")
archive_path = cur_path.joinpath(ARCHIVE)
archive_path.mkdir(exist_ok=True)

paths = cur_path.glob(FILE_PATTERN)

for path in paths:
    new_filename = f"{path.stem}_{date_string}{path.suffix}"
    new_path = archive_path.joinpath(
                            new_filename)
        path.rename(new_path)

if __name__ == '__main__':
    main()
```

Creates a date string
based on today's date

Creates an archive
directory if it doesn't exist

Creates a path from
the archive path and
the new filename

Renames (and moves)
the file as one step

The key elements in this script are finding all files that match *txt; creating a date string to add to the filenames, making sure the archive directory exists; and then moving and renaming the files. It's worth noting here that Path objects make this operation simpler, because no special parsing is needed to separate the filename stem and suffix. This operation is also simpler than you might expect because the rename method can in effect move a file by using a path that includes the new location.

This script is a very simple one and does the job effectively in very few lines of code. In the next sections, you consider how to handle more complex requirements.

Quick check: Potential problems

Because the preceding solution is very simple, there are likely to be many situations that it won't handle well. What are some potential problems that might arise with the example script? How might you remedy these problems?

Consider the naming convention used for the files, which is based on the year, month, and day, in that order. What advantages do you see in that convention? What might be the disadvantages? Can you make any arguments for putting the date string somewhere else in the filename, such as the beginning or the end?

20.3 More organization

The solution to storing files described in the previous section works, but it does have some disadvantages. For one thing, as the files accumulate, managing them might become a bit more trouble, because over the course of a year, you'd have 365 sets of related files in the same directory, and you could find the related files only by inspecting their names. If the files arrive more frequently, of course, or if there are more related files in a set, the hassle would be even greater.

To mitigate this problem, you can change the way you archive the files. Instead of changing the filenames to include the dates on which they were received, you can create a separate subdirectory for each set of files and name that subdirectory after the date received. Your directory structure might look like the following:

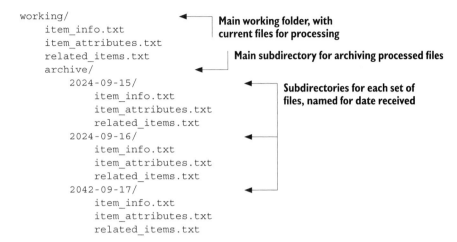

This scheme has the advantage that each set of files is grouped together. No matter how many sets of files you get or how many files you have in a set, it's easy to find all the files of a particular set.

Try this: Implementation of multiple directories

How would you modify the code that you developed to archive each set of files in subdirectories named according to date received? Feel free to take the time to implement the code and test it.

It turns out that archiving the files by subdirectory isn't much more work than the first solution. The only additional step is to create the subdirectory before renaming the file. The following listing shows one way to perform this step.

Listing 20.2 File files_02.py

```python
import datetime
import pathlib

FILE_PATTERN = "*.txt"
ARCHIVE = "archive"

def main():

    date_string = datetime.date.today().strftime("%Y-%m-%d")

    cur_path = pathlib.Path(".")

    archive_path = cur_path.joinpath(ARCHIVE)
```

```
        archive_path.mkdir(exist_ok=True)
        new_path = archive_path.joinpath(date_string)
        new_path.mkdir(exist_ok=True)

        paths = cur_path.glob(FILE_PATTERN)

        for path in paths:
            path.rename(new_path.joinpath(path.name))

if __name__ == '__main__':
    main()
```

This directory needs to be created only the first time the script is run.

This directory needs to be created only once, before the files are moved into it.

The basic elements of this solution are the same as in the previous one but combined slightly differently. In this case, the date string is used to create a subdirectory in the archive directory and is not added to the filename. Then the file is moved to that directory but not renamed. This solution groups related files, which makes managing them as sets somewhat easier.

Quick check: Alternate solutions

How might you create a script that does the same thing without using `pathlib`? What libraries and functions would you use?

20.4 *Saving storage space: Compression and grooming*

So far, you've been concerned mainly with managing the groups of files received. Over time, however, the data files accumulate until the amount of storage they need becomes a concern. When that happens, you have several choices. One option is to get a bigger disk. Particularly if you're on a cloud-based platform, it may be easy and economical to adopt this strategy. Do keep in mind, however, that adding storage doesn't really solve the problem; it merely postpones solving it.

20.4.1 *Compressing files*

If the space that the files are taking up is a problem, the next approach you might consider is compressing them. You have numerous ways to compress a file or set of files, but in general, these methods are similar. In this section, you consider archiving each day's data file to a single zip file. If the files are mainly text files and are fairly large, the savings in storage achieved by compression can be impressive.

For this script, you use the same date string with a .zip extension as the name of each zip file. In listing 20.2, you created a new directory in the archive directory and then moved the files into it, which resulted in a directory structure that looks like the following:

```
working/
    archive/
```

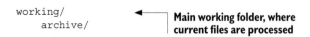

Main working folder, where current files are processed

```
2024-09-15.zip
2024-09-16.zip
2024-09-17.zip
```

Zip files, each one containing that day's files

Obviously, to use zip files, you need to change some of the steps you used previously.

> **Try this: Create the pseudo for archiving to zip files**
>
> Write the pseudocode for a solution that stores data files in zip files. What modules and functions or methods do you intend to use? Try coding your solution to make sure that it works.

One key addition in the new script is an import of the `zipfile` library and, with it, the code to create a new `zipfile` object in the archive directory. After that, you can use the `zipfile` object to write the data files to the new zip file. Finally, because you're no longer actually moving files, you need to remove the original files from the working directory. One solution looks like the following listing.

Listing 20.3   File files_03.py

```python
import datetime
import pathlib
import zipfile                    ◄── Imports zipfile library

FILE_PATTERN = "*.txt"
ARCHIVE = "archive"

def main():

    date_string = datetime.date.today().strftime("%Y-%m-%d")

    cur_path = pathlib.Path(".")
    archive_path = cur_path.joinpath(ARCHIVE)
    archive_path.mkdir(exist_ok=True)

    paths = cur_path.glob(FILE_PATTERN)

    zip_file_path = cur_path.joinpath(ARCHIVE,
                        date_string + ".zip")    ◄── Creates the path to the zip file in the archive directory
    zip_file = zipfile.ZipFile(str(zip_file_path),
                        "w")                      ◄── Opens the new zipfile object for writing

    for path in paths:
        zip_file.write(str(path))      ◄── Writes the current file to the zip file
        path.unlink()                  ◄── Removes the current file from the working directory

if __name__ == '__main__':
    main()
```

This code is a bit more complex because now, instead of creating a subdirectory, we are using the date string to name and create a `zipfile` object. Then the contents of each file in turn are written to the `zipfile` object and that file is unlinked (or deleted). When the `zipfile` object goes out of scope at the end of the script, it is automatically closed.

20.4.2 Grooming files

Compressing data files into zip file archives can save an impressive amount of space and may be all you need. If you have a lot of files, however, or files that don't compress much (such as JPEG image files), you may still find yourself running short of storage space. You may also find that your data doesn't change much, making it unnecessary to keep an archived copy of every dataset in the longer term. That is, although it may be useful to keep every day's data for the past week or month, it may not be worth the storage to keep every dataset for much longer. For data older than a few months, it may be acceptable to keep just one set of files per week or even one set per month.

The process of removing files after they reach a certain age is sometimes called *grooming*. Suppose that after several months of receiving a set of data files every day and archiving them in a zip file, you're told that you should retain only one file a week of the files that are more than one month old.

The simplest grooming script removes any files that you no longer need—in this case, all but one file a week for anything older than a month old. In designing this script, it's helpful to know the answers to two questions:

- Because you need to save one file a week, would it be much easier to simply pick the day of the week you want to save?
- How often should you do this grooming: daily, weekly, or once a month? If you decide that grooming should take place daily, it might make sense to combine the grooming with the archiving script. If, on the other hand, you need to groom only once a week or once a month, the two operations should be in separate scripts.

For this example, to keep things clear, you write a separate grooming script that can be run at any interval and that removes all the unneeded files. Further, assume that you've decided to keep only the files received on Tuesdays that are more than one month old. The following listing shows a sample grooming script.

Listing 20.4   File files_04.py

```
from datetime import datetime, timedelta
import pathlib
import zipfile

FILE_PATTERN = "*.zip"
ARCHIVE = "archive"
ARCHIVE_WEEKDAY = 1
def main():
    cur_path = pathlib.Path(".")
    zip_file_path = cur_path.joinpath(ARCHIVE)

    paths = zip_file_path.glob(FILE_PATTERN)
```

```
    current_date = datetime.today()
```
> Gets a datetime object
> for the current day

```
    for path in paths:
        name = path.stem
```
> Stem = filename
> without any extension

```
        path_date = datetime.strptime(name,
                            "%Y-%m-%d")
        path_timedelta = current_date - path_date
        if (path_timedelta > timedelta(days=30) and
         path_date.weekday() != ARCHIVE_WEEKDAY):
            path.unlink()
```
> **strptime parses a string
> into a datetime object.**

> **Subtracting one date
> from another yields a
> timedelta object.**

```
if __name__ == '__main__':
    main()
```
> **timedelta(days = 30) creates a
> timedelta object of 30 days; the
> weekday() method returns an
> integer for the day of the week,
> with Monday = 0.**

The code shows how Python's `datetime` and `pathlib` libraries can be combined to groom files by date with only a few lines of code. Because your archive files have names derived from the dates on which they were received, you can get those file paths by using the `glob` method, extract the stem, and use `strptime` to parse the stem into a `datetime` object. From there, you can use `datetime`'s `timedelta` objects and the `weekday()` method to find a file's age and the day of the week and then remove (unlink) the files that have passed the time limit.

Quick check: Consider different parameters

Take some time to consider different grooming options. How would you modify the code in listing 20.4 to keep only one file a month? How would you change it so that files from the previous month and older were groomed to save one a week? (Note: This is *not* the same as older than 30 days!)

Summary

- The `pathlib` module can greatly simplify file operations, such as finding the root and extension, moving and renaming, and matching wildcards.

- As the number and complexity of files increases, automated archiving solutions are vital, and Python offers several easy ways to create them.

- Moving data to specific directories is as easy as renaming the files and may make managing them easier.

- You can dramatically save storage space by writing to compressed archives, such as zip files.

- As the amount of data grows, it is often useful to groom data files by deleting files that have a certain age.

21

Processing data files

This chapter covers

- Using extract-transform-load
- Reading text data files (plain text and CSV)
- Reading spreadsheet files
- Normalizing, cleaning, and sorting data
- Writing data files

Much of the data available is contained in text files. This data can range from unstructured text, such as a corpus of tweets or literary texts, to more structured data in which each row is a record and the fields are delimited by a special character, such as a comma, a tab, or a pipe (|). Text files can be huge; a dataset can be spread over tens or even hundreds of files, and the data in it can be incomplete or horribly dirty. With all the variations, it's almost inevitable that you'll need to read and use data from text files. This chapter gives you strategies for using Python to do exactly that.

21.1 Welcome to ETL

The need to get data out of files, parse it, turn it into a useful format, and then do something with it has been around for as long as there have been data files. In fact, there is a standard term for the process: extract-transform-load (ETL). The extraction refers to the process of reading a data source and parsing it, if necessary. The transformation can be cleaning and normalizing the data, as well as combining, breaking up, or reorganizing the records it contains. The loading refers to storing the transformed data in a new place, either a different file or a database. This chapter deals with the basics of ETL in Python, starting with text-based data files and storing the transformed data in other files. I look at more structured data files in chapter 23 and storage in databases in chapter 24.

21.2 Reading text files

The first part of ETL—the "extract" portion—involves opening a file and reading its contents. This process seems like a simple one, but even at this point there can be problems, such as the file's size. If a file is too large to fit into memory and be manipulated, you need to structure your code to handle smaller segments of the file, possibly operating one line at a time.

21.2.1 Text encoding: ASCII, Unicode, and others

Another possible pitfall is in the encoding. This chapter deals with text files, and in fact, much of the data exchanged in the real world is in text files. But the exact nature of *text* can vary from application to application, from person to person, and of course from country to country.

Sometimes, "text" means something in ASCII encoding, which has 128 characters, only 95 of which are printable. The good news about ASCII encoding is that it's the lowest common denominator of most data exchange. The bad news is that it doesn't begin to handle the complexities of the many alphabets and writing systems of the world. Reading files using ASCII encoding is almost certain to cause trouble and throw errors on character values that it doesn't understand, whether it's a German ü, a Portuguese ç, or something from almost any language other than English.

These errors arise because ASCII is based on 7-bit values, whereas the bytes in a typical file are 8 bits, allowing 256 possible values as opposed to the 128 of a 7-bit value. It's routine to use those additional values to store additional characters—anything from extra punctuation (such as the printer's en dash and em dash) to symbols (such as the trademark, copyright, and degree symbols) to accented versions of alphabetical characters. The problem has always been that if, in reading a text file, you encounter a character in the 128 values outside the ASCII range, you have no way of knowing for sure how it was encoded. Is the character value of 214, for example, a division symbol? an Ö? or something else? Short of having the code that created the file, you have no way of knowing.

UNICODE AND UTF-8

One way to mitigate this confusion is Unicode. The Unicode encoding called UTF-8 accepts the basic ASCII characters without any change but also allows an almost unlimited set of other characters and symbols according to the Unicode standard. Because of its flexibility, UTF-8 was used in 98% of web pages served at the time of writing, which means that your best bet for reading text files is to assume UTF-8 encoding. If the files contain only ASCII characters, they'll still be read correctly, but you'll also be covered if other characters are encoded in UTF-8. The good news is that the Python 3 string data type was designed to handle Unicode by default.

Even with Unicode, there'll be occasions when your text contains values that can't be successfully encoded. Fortunately, the open function in Python accepts an optional errors parameter that tells it how to deal with encoding errors when reading or writing files. The default option is 'strict', which causes an error to be raised whenever an encoding error is encountered. Other useful options are 'ignore', which causes the character causing the error to be skipped; 'replace', which causes the character to be replaced by a marker character (often, ?); 'backslashreplace', which replaces the character with a backslash escape sequence; and 'surrogateescape', which translates the offending character to a private Unicode code point on reading and back to the original sequence of bytes on writing. Your particular use case will determine how strict you need to be in handling or resolving encoding problems.

Consider a short example of a file containing an invalid UTF-8 character and see how the different options handle that character. First, write the file, using bytes and binary mode:

```
open('test.txt', 'wb').write(bytes([65, 66, 67, 255, 192,193]))
```

This code results in a file that contains "ABC" followed by three non-ASCII characters, which may be rendered differently depending on the encoding used. If you use an editor like Vim to look at the file, you might see

ABCÿÀÁ

Now that you have the file, try reading it with the default 'strict' errors option:

```
x = open('test.txt').read()
```

```
---------------------------------------------------------------------
UnicodeDecodeError                          Traceback (most recent call last)
<ipython-input-2-2cb3105c1e5f> in <cell line: 1>()
----> 1 x = open('test.txt').read()

/usr/lib/python3.10/codecs.py in decode(self, input, final)
    320         # decode input (taking the buffer into account)
    321         data = self.buffer + input
--> 322         (result, consumed) = self._buffer_decode(data, self.errors,
final)
    323         # keep undecoded input until the next call
    324         self.buffer = data[consumed:]

UnicodeDecodeError: 'utf-8' codec can't decode byte 0xff in position 3:
invalid start byte
```

The fourth byte, which had a value of 255, isn't a valid UTF-8 character in that position, so the `'strict'` errors setting raises an exception. Now see how the other error options handle the same file, keeping in mind that the last three characters raise an error:

```
open('test.txt', errors='ignore').read()
```

'ABC'

```
open('test.txt', errors='replace').read()
```

'ABC   '   ◄─────┐ **Replaced error characters with chr(65533)**

```
open('test.txt', errors='surrogateescape').read()
```

'ABC\udcff\udcc0\udcc1'

```
open('test.txt', errors='backslashreplace').read()
```

'ABC\\xff\\xc0\\xc1'

If you want any problem characters to disappear, `'ignore'` is the option to use. The `'replace'` option only marks the place occupied by the invalid character, and the other options in different ways attempt to preserve the invalid characters without interpretation.

21.2.2 *Unstructured text*

Unstructured text files are the easiest sort of data to read but the hardest to extract information from. Processing unstructured text can vary enormously, depending on both the nature of the text and what you want to do with it, so any comprehensive discussion of text processing is beyond the scope of this book. A short example, however, can illustrate some of the basic topics and set the stage for a discussion of structured text data files.

One of the simplest concerns is deciding what forms a basic logical unit in the file. If you have a corpus of thousands of tweets, the text of *Moby Dick*, or a collection of news stories, you need to be able to break them up into cohesive units. In the case of tweets, each may fit onto a single line, and you can read and process each line of the file fairly simply.

In the case of *Moby Dick* or even a news story, the problem can be trickier. You may not want to treat all of a novel or news item as a single item, in many cases. But if that's the case, you need to decide what sort of unit you do want and then come up with a strategy to divide the file accordingly. Perhaps you want to consider the text paragraph by paragraph. In that case, you need to identify how paragraphs are separated in your file and create your code accordingly. If a paragraph is the same as a line in the text file, the job is easy. Often, however, the line breaks in a text file are shorter, and you need to do a bit more work.

Now look at a couple of examples:

```
Call me Ishmael.  Some years ago--never mind how long precisely--
having little or no money in my purse, and nothing particular
to interest me on shore, I thought I would sail about a little
and see the watery part of the world.  It is a way I have
of driving off the spleen and regulating the circulation.
Whenever I find myself growing grim about the mouth;
whenever it is a damp, drizzly November in my soul; whenever I
find myself involuntarily pausing before coffin warehouses,
and bringing up the rear of every funeral I meet;
and especially whenever my hypos get such an upper hand of me,
that it requires a strong moral principle to prevent me from
deliberately stepping into the street, and methodically knocking
people's hats off--then, I account it high time to get to sea
as soon as I can.  This is my substitute for pistol and ball.
With a philosophical flourish Cato throws himself upon his sword;
I quietly take to the ship.  There is nothing surprising in this.
If they but knew it, almost all men in their degree, some time
or other, cherish very nearly the same feelings towards
the ocean with me.

There now is your insular city of the Manhattoes, belted round by wharves
as Indian isles by coral reefs--commerce surrounds it with her surf.
Right and left, the streets take you waterward.  Its extreme downtown
is the battery, where that noble mole is washed by waves, and cooled
by breezes, which a few hours previous were out of sight of land.
Look at the crowds of water-gazers there.
```

In the sample, which is indeed the beginning of *Moby Dick*, the lines are broken more or less as they might be on the page, and paragraphs are indicated by a single blank line. If you want to deal with each paragraph as a unit, you need to break the text on the blank lines. Fortunately, this task is easy if you use the string split() method. Each newline character in a string can represented by "\n". Naturally, the last line of a paragraph's text ends with a newline, and if the next line is blank, it's immediately followed by a second newline for the blank line:

```
moby_text = open("moby_01.txt").read()          ◀──┐  Reads all of file as a single string
moby_paragraphs = moby_text.split("\n\n")       ◀──┐  Splits on two newlines together
print(moby_paragraphs[1])
```

```
There now is your insular city of the Manhattoes, belted round by wharves
as Indian isles by coral reefs--commerce surrounds it with her surf.
Right and left, the streets take you waterward.  Its extreme downtown
is the battery, where that noble mole is washed by waves, and cooled
by breezes, which a few hours previous were out of sight of land.
Look at the crowds of water-gazers there.
```

Splitting the text into paragraphs can be done by splitting on two newlines— moby_text.split("\n\n"). Such splitting is a very simple first step in handling unstructured text, and you might also need to do more normalization of the text before processing. Suppose that you want to count the rate of occurrence of every word in a text file. If you just split the file on whitespace, you get a list of words in the file. Counting their occurrences accurately will be hard, however, because *This, this, this.,* and *this,* are not the same. The way to make this code work is to normalize the text by removing the punctuation and making everything the same case before processing. For the preceding example text, the code for a normalized list of words might look like this:

```
moby_text = open("moby_01.txt").read()          ◀─────┐ Reads all of the file as a single string
moby_paragraphs = moby_text.split("\n\n")
moby = moby_paragraphs[1].lower()               ◀─────┐ Makes everything lowercase
moby = moby.replace(".", "")                    ◀──┐
moby = moby.replace(",", "")                    ◀──┘   Removes periods
moby_words = moby.split()                            Removes commas
print(moby_words)
```

```
['there', 'now', 'is', 'your', 'insular', 'city', 'of', 'the',
'manhattoes,', 'belted', 'round', 'by', 'wharves', 'as', 'indian', 'isles'
 'by', 'coral', 'reefs--commerce', 'surrounds', 'it', 'with', 'her',
'surf', 'right', 'and', 'left,', 'the', 'streets', 'take', 'you',
'waterward', 'its', 'extreme', 'downtown', 'is', 'the', 'battery,',
'where', 'that', 'noble', 'mole', 'is', 'washed', 'by', 'waves,', 'and',
'cooled', 'by', 'breezes,', 'which', 'a', 'few', 'hours', 'previous',
'were', 'out', 'of', 'sight', 'of', 'land', 'look', 'at', 'the', 'crowds',
'of', 'water-gazers', 'there']
```

Here we use the `.lower` string method first and then use the `.replace` method twice to remove two punctuation characters. Of course, as we saw back in chapter 6, it would probably be more efficient to use the string `.translate` method to replace all of the punctuation in one operation.

> **Quick check: Normalization**
>
> Look closely at the list of words generated. Do you see any problems with the normalization so far? What other problems do you think you might encounter in a longer section of text? How do you think you might deal with those problems?

21.2.3 Delimited flat files

Although reading unstructured text files is easy, the downside is their very lack of structure. It's often much more useful to have some organization in the file to help with picking out individual values. The simplest way is to break the file into lines and have one element of information per line. You may have a list of the names of files to be processed, a list of people's names that need to be printed (on name tags, say), or maybe a series of temperature readings from a remote monitor. In such cases, the data parsing is very simple: you read in the line and convert it to the right type, if necessary. Then the file is ready to use.

Most of the time, however, things aren't quite so simple. Usually, you need to group multiple related bits of information, and you need your code to read them in together. The common way to do this is to put the related pieces of information on the same line, separated by a special character. That way, as you read each line of the file, you can use the special characters to split the file into its different fields and put the values of those fields in variables for later processing.

The following listing shows a simple example of temperature data in delimited format.

Listing 21.1   temp_data_ pipes_00a.txt

```
State|Month Day, Year Code|Avg Daily Max Air Temperature (F)|Record Count
  for Daily Max Air Temp (F)
Illinois|1979/01/01|17.48|994
Illinois|1979/01/02|4.64|994
Illinois|1979/01/03|11.05|994
Illinois|1979/01/04|9.51|994
Illinois|1979/05/15|68.42|994
Illinois|1979/05/16|70.29|994
Illinois|1979/05/17|75.34|994
Illinois|1979/05/18|79.13|994
Illinois|1979/05/19|74.94|994
```

This data is pipe delimited, meaning that each field in the line is separated by the pipe (|) character—in this case, giving you four fields: the state of the observations, the date of the observations, the average high temperature, and the number of stations reporting. Other common delimiters are the tab character and the comma. The comma is perhaps the most common, but the delimiter could be any character you don't expect to occur in the values. (More about that topic next.) Comma delimiters are so common that this format is often called comma-separated values (CSV), and files of this type often have a .csv extension as a hint of their format.

Whatever character is being used as the delimiter, if you know what character it is, you can write your own code in Python to break each line into its fields and return them as a list. In the previous case, you can use the string `split()` method to break a line into a list of values:

```
line = "Illinois|1979/01/01|17.48|994"
print(line.split("|"))
```

```
['Illinois', '1979/01/01', '17.48', '994']
```

Note that this technique is very easy to do but leaves all the values as strings, which might not be convenient for later processing.

> ### Try this: Read a file
>
> Write the code to read a text file (assume the file is temp_data_ pipes_00a.txt, as shown in the example), split each line of the file into a list of values, and add that list to a single list of records.
>
> What concerns or problems did you encounter in implementing this code? How might you go about converting the last three fields to the correct date, real, and int types?

21.2.4 *The csv module*

If you need to do much processing of delimited data files, you should become familiar with the csv module and its options. When I've been asked to name my favorite module in the Python standard library, more than once I've cited the csv module—not because it's glamorous (it isn't) but because it has probably saved me more work and kept me from more self-inflicted bugs over my career than any other module.

The csv module is a perfect case of Python's "batteries included" philosophy. Although it's perfectly possible, and in many cases not even terribly hard, to roll your own code to read delimited files, it's even easier and much more reliable to use the Python module. The csv module has been tested and optimized, and it has features that you probably wouldn't bother to write if you had to do it yourself but that are truly handy and time saving when available.

Look at the previous data and decide how you'd read it by using the csv module. The code to parse the data has to do two things: read each line and strip off the trailing newline character and then break up the line on the pipe character and append that list of values to a list of lines. Your solution to the exercise might look something like the following:

```
results = []
for line in open("temp_data_pipes_00a.txt"):
    fields = line.strip().split("|")
    results.append(fields)

results

[['Notes'],
 ['State',
  'Month Day, Year Code',
  'Avg Daily Max Air Temperature (F)',
  'Record Count for Daily Max Air Temp (F)'],
 ['Illinois', '1979/01/01', '17.48', '994'],
 ['Illinois', '1979/01/02', '4.64', '994'],
 ['Illinois', '1979/01/03', '11.05', '994'],
 ['Illinois', '1979/01/04', '9.51', '994'],
 ['Illinois', '1979/05/15', '68.42', '994'],
 ['Illinois', '1979/05/16', '70.29', '994'],
 ['Illinois', '1979/05/17', '75.34', '994'],
 ['Illinois', '1979/05/18', '79.13', '994'],
 ['Illinois', '1979/05/19', '74.94', '994']]
```

To do the same thing with the `csv` module, the code might be something like

```
import csv
results = [fields for fields in csv.reader(open("temp_data_pipes_00a.txt",
newline=''), delimiter="|")]
results
```

```
[['State', 'Month Day, Year Code', 'Avg Daily Max Air Temperature (F)',
'Record Count for Daily Max Air Temp (F)'], ['Illinois', '1979/01/01',
'17.48', '994'], ['Illinois', '1979/01/02', '4.64', '994'], ['Illinois',
'1979/01/03', '11.05', '994'], ['Illinois', '1979/01/04', '9.51', '994'],
['Illinois', '1979/05/15', '68.42', '994'], ['Illinois', '1979/05/16',
'70.29', '994'], ['Illinois', '1979/05/17', '75.34', '994'], ['Illinois',
'1979/05/18', '79.13', '994'], ['Illinois', '1979/05/19', '74.94', '994']]
```

In this simple case, the gain over rolling your own code doesn't seem so great. Still, the code is two lines shorter and a bit clearer, and there's no need to worry about stripping off newline characters. The real advantages come when you want to deal with more challenging cases.

The data in the example is real, but it's actually been simplified and cleaned. The real data from the source is more complex. The real data has more fields, some fields are in quotes while others are not, and the first field is empty. The original is tab-delimited, but for the sake of illustration, I present it as comma delimited here.

Listing 21.2   temp_data_01.csv

```
"Notes","State","State Code","Month Day, Year","Month Day, Year Code",Avg
Daily Max Air Temperature (F),Record Count for Daily Max Air Temp (F),Min
Temp for Daily Max Air Temp (F),Max Temp for Daily Max Air Temp (F),Avg
Daily Max Heat Index (F),Record Count for Daily Max Heat Index (F),Min for
Daily Max Heat Index (F),Max for Daily Max Heat Index (F),Daily Max Heat
Index (F) % Coverage

,"Illinois","17","Jan 01,
1979","1979/01/01",17.48,994,6.00,30.50,Missing,0,Missing,Missing,0.00%
,"Illinois","17","Jan 02,
1979","1979/01/02",4.64,994,-6.40,15.80,Missing,0,Missing,Missing,0.00%
,"Illinois","17","Jan 03,
1979","1979/01/03",11.05,994,-0.70,24.70,Missing,0,Missing,Missing,0.00%
,"Illinois","17","Jan 04,
1979","1979/01/04",9.51,994,0.20,27.60,Missing,0,Missing,Missing,0.00%
,"Illinois","17","May 15,
1979","1979/05/15",68.42,994,61.00,75.10,Missing,0,Missing,Missing,0.00%
,"Illinois","17","May 16,
1979","1979/05/16",70.29,994,63.40,73.50,Missing,0,Missing,Missing,0.00%
,"Illinois","17","May 17, 1979","1979/05/17",75.34,994,64.00,80.50,82.60,2,82
.40,82.80,0.20%
,"Illinois","17","May 18, 1979","1979/05/18",79.13,994,75.50,82.10,81.42,349,
80.20,83.40,35.11%
,"Illinois","17","May 19, 1979","1979/05/19",74.94,994,66.90,83.10,82.87,78,8
1.60,85.20,7.85%
```

Notice that some fields include commas. The convention in that case is to put quotes around a field to indicate that it's not supposed to be parsed for delimiters. It's quite common, as here, to quote only some fields, especially those in which a value might contain the delimiter character. It also happens, as here, that some fields are quoted even if they're not likely to contain the delimiting character.

In a case like this one, your homegrown code becomes cumbersome. Now you can no longer split the line on the delimiting character; you need to be sure that you look only at delimiters that aren't inside quoted strings. Also, you need to remove the quotes around quoted strings, which might occur in any position or not at all. With the csv module, you don't need to change your code at all. In fact, because the comma is the default delimiter, you don't even need to specify it:

```
results2 = [fields for fields in csv.reader(open("temp_data_01.csv",
newline=''))]
results2
```

```
[[['Notes', 'State', 'State Code', 'Month Day, Year', 'Month Day, Year
Code', 'Avg Daily Max Air Temperature (F)', 'Record Count for Daily Max Air
Temp (F)', 'Min Temp for Daily Max Air Temp (F)', 'Max Temp for Daily Max
Air Temp (F)', 'Avg Daily Max Heat Index (F)', 'Record Count for Daily Max
Heat Index (F)', 'Min for Daily Max Heat Index (F)', 'Max for Daily Max
Heat Index (F)', 'Daily Max Heat Index (F) % Coverage'], [], ['',
'Illinois', '17', 'Jan 01, 1979', '1979/01/01', '17.48', '994', '6.00',
'30.50', 'Missing', '0', 'Missing', 'Missing', '0.00%'], ['', 'Illinois',
'17', 'Jan 02, 1979', '1979/01/02', '4.64', '994', '-6.40', '15.80',
'Missing', '0', 'Missing', 'Missing', '0.00%'], ['', 'Illinois', '17', 'Jan
03, 1979', '1979/01/03', '11.05', '994', '-0.70', '24.70', 'Missing', '0',
'Missing', 'Missing', '0.00%'], ['', 'Illinois', '17', 'Jan 04, 1979',
'1979/01/04', '9.51', '994', '0.20', '27.60', 'Missing', '0', 'Missing',
'Missing', '0.00%'], ['', 'Illinois', '17', 'May 15, 1979', '1979/05/15',
'68.42', '994', '61.00', '75.10', 'Missing', '0', 'Missing', 'Missing',
'0.00%'], ['', 'Illinois', '17', 'May 16, 1979', '1979/05/16', '70.29',
'994', '63.40', '73.50', 'Missing', '0', 'Missing', 'Missing', '0.00%'],
['', 'Illinois', '17', 'May 17, 1979', '1979/05/17', '75.34', '994',
'64.00', '80.50', '82.60', '2', '82.40', '82.80', '0.20%'], ['',
'Illinois', '17', 'May 18, 1979', '1979/05/18', '79.13', '994', '75.50',
'82.10', '81.42', '349', '80.20', '83.40', '35.11%'], ['', 'Illinois',
'17', 'May 19, 1979', '1979/05/19', '74.94', '994', '66.90', '83.10',
\'82.87', '78', '81.60', '85.20', '7.85%']]
```

Notice that the extra quotes have been removed and that any field values with commas have the commas intact inside the fields—all without any more characters in the command.

> ### Quick check: Handling quoting
>
> Consider how you'd approach the problems of handling quoted fields and embedded delimiter characters if you didn't have the csv library. Which would be easier to handle: the quoting or the embedded delimiters?

21.2.5 *Reading a csv file as a list of dictionaries*

In the preceding examples, you got a row of data back as a list of fields. This result works fine in many cases, but sometimes it may be handy to get the rows back as dictionaries where the field name is the key. For this use case, the `csv` library has a `DictReader`, which can take a list of fields as a parameter or can read them from the first line of the data. If you want to open the data with a `DictReader`, the code would look like this:

```
results = [fields for fields in csv.DictReader(open("temp_data_01.csv",
    newline=''))]
results[0]
```

```
{'Notes': '',
 'State': 'Illinois',
 'State Code': '17',
 'Month Day, Year': 'Jan 01, 1979',
 'Month Day, Year Code': '1979/01/01',
 'Avg Daily Max Air Temperature (F)': '17.48',
 'Record Count for Daily Max Air Temp (F)': '994',
 'Min Temp for Daily Max Air Temp (F)': '6.00',
 'Max Temp for Daily Max Air Temp (F)': '30.50',
 'Avg Daily Max Heat Index (F)': 'Missing',
 'Record Count for Daily Max Heat Index (F)': '0',
 'Min for Daily Max Heat Index (F)': 'Missing',
 'Max for Daily Max Heat Index (F)': 'Missing',
 'Daily Max Heat Index (F) % Coverage': '0.00%'}
```

Note that, with a dictionary, the fields stay in their original order:

```
results[0]['State']
```

```
'Illinois'
```

If the data is particularly complex, and specific fields need to be manipulated, a `DictReader` can make it much easier to be sure you're getting the right field; it also makes your code somewhat easier to understand. Conversely, if your dataset is quite large, you need to keep in mind that `DictReader` can take on the order of twice as long to read the same amount of data.

21.3 *Excel files*

The other common file format that I discuss in this chapter is the Excel file, which is the format that Microsoft Excel uses to store spreadsheets. I include Excel files here because the way you end up treating them is very similar to the way you treat delimited files. In fact, because Excel can both read and write CSV files, the quickest and easiest way to extract data from an Excel spreadsheet file often is to open it in Excel and then save it as a CSV file. This procedure doesn't always make sense, however, particularly if you have a lot of files. In that case, even though you could theoretically automate the process of opening and saving each file in CSV format, it's probably faster to deal with the Excel files directly.

It's beyond the scope of this book to have an in-depth discussion of spreadsheet files, with their options for multiple sheets in the same file, macros, and various formatting options. Instead, in this section, I look at an example of reading a simple one-sheet file simply to extract the data from it.

As it happens, Python's standard library doesn't have a module to read or write Excel files. To read that format, you need to install an external module. Fortunately, several modules are available to do the job. For this example, you use one called openpyxl, which is available from the Python package repository. You can install it with the following command from a command line:

```
$pip install openpyxl
```

Figure 21.1 is a view of the previous temperature data, but in a spreadsheet.

	A	B	C	D	E	F	G	H	I	J	K	L	M	N
1	Notes	State	State Co	Month Day, Ye	Month Day, Ye	Avg Daily M	Record C	Min Temp	Max Temp	Avg Daily	Recor	Min for Da	Max for Da	Daily Max He
2		Illinois	17	Jan 01, 1979	1979/01/01	17.48	994	6	30.5	Missing	0	Missing	Missing	0.00%
3		Illinois	17	Jan 02, 1979	1979/01/02	4.64	994	-6.4	15.8	Missing	0	Missing	Missing	0.00%
4		Illinois	17	Jan 03, 1979	1979/01/03	11.05	994	-0.7	24.7	Missing	0	Missing	Missing	0.00%
5		Illinois	17	Jan 04, 1979	1979/01/04	9.51	994	0.2	27.6	Missing	0	Missing	Missing	0.00%
6		Illinois	17	May 15, 1979	1979/05/15	68.42	994	61	75.1	Missing	0	Missing	Missing	0.00%
7		Illinois	17	May 16, 1979	1979/05/16	70.29	994	63.4	73.5	Missing	0	Missing	Missing	0.00%
8		Illinois	17	May 17, 1979	1979/05/17	75.34	994	64	80.5	82.6	2	82.4	82.8	0.20%
9		Illinois	17	May 18, 1979	1979/05/18	79.13	994	75.5	82.1	81.42	349	80.2	83.4	35.11%
10		Illinois	17	May 19, 1979	1979/05/19	74.94	994	66.9	83.1	82.87	78	81.6	85.2	7.85%

Figure 21.1 A view of the previous temperature data, now shown in spreadsheet format

Reading the file is fairly simple, but it's still more work than CSV files require. First, you need to load the workbook; next, you need to get the specific sheet; then, you can iterate over the rows; and from there, you extract the values of the cells. Some sample code to read the spreadsheet looks like the following:

```
from openpyxl import load_workbook
wb = load_workbook('temp_data_01.xlsx')
results = []
ws = wb.worksheets[0]
for row in ws.iter_rows():
    results.append([cell.value for cell in row])

print(results)

[['Notes', 'State', 'State Code', 'Month Day, Year', 'Month Day, Year
Code', 'Avg Daily Max Air Temperature (F)', 'Record Count for Daily Max Air
Temp (F)', 'Min Temp for Daily Max Air Temp (F)', 'Max Temp for Daily Max
Air Temp (F)', 'Avg Daily Max Heat Index (F)', 'Record Count for Daily Max
Heat Index (F)', 'Min for Daily Max Heat Index (F)', 'Max for Daily Max
Heat Index (F)', 'Daily Max Heat Index (F) % Coverage'], [None, 'Illinois',
```

```
17, 'Jan 01, 1979', '1979/01/01', 17.48, 994, 6, 30.5, 'Missing', 0,
'Missing', 'Missing', '0.00%'], [None, 'Illinois', 17, 'Jan 02, 1979',
'1979/01/02', 4.64, 994, -6.4, 15.8, 'Missing', 0, 'Missing', 'Missing',
'0.00%'], [None, 'Illinois', 17, 'Jan 03, 1979', '1979/01/03', 11.05, 994,
-0.7, 24.7, 'Missing', 0, 'Missing', 'Missing', '0.00%'], [None,
'Illinois', 17, 'Jan 04, 1979', '1979/01/04', 9.51, 994, 0.2, 27.6,
'Missing', 0, 'Missing', 'Missing', '0.00%'], [None, 'Illinois', 17, 'May
15, 1979', '1979/05/15', 68.42, 994, 61, 75.1, 'Missing', 0, 'Missing',
'Missing', '0.00%'], [None, 'Illinois', 17, 'May 16, 1979', '1979/05/16',
70.29, 994, 63.4, 73.5, 'Missing', 0, 'Missing', 'Missing', '0.00%'],
[None, 'Illinois', 17, 'May 17, 1979', '1979/05/17', 75.34, 994, 64,
80.5,82.6, 2, 82.4, 82.8, '0.20%'], [None, 'Illinois', 17, 'May 18, 1979',
'1979/05/18', 79.13, 994, 75.5, 82.1, 81.42, 349, 80.2, 83.4,
'35.11%'],[None, 'Illinois', 17, 'May 19, 1979', '1979/05/19', 74.94,
994,66.9, 83.1, 82.87, 78, 81.6, 85.2, '7.85%']]
```

This code gets you the same results as the much simpler code did for a CSV file. It's not surprising that the code to read a spreadsheet is more complex, because spreadsheets are themselves much more complex objects. You should also be sure that you understand the way that data has been stored in the spreadsheet. If the spreadsheet contains formatting that has some significance, if labels need to be disregarded or handled differently, or if formulas and references need to be processed, you need to dig deeper into how those elements should be processed, and you need to write more complex code.

Spreadsheets also often have other possible problems. As of this writing, it's common for spreadsheets to be limited to around a million rows. Although that limit sounds large, more and more often you'll need to handle datasets that are larger. Also, spreadsheets sometimes automatically apply inconvenient formatting. One company I worked for had part numbers that consisted of a digit and at least one letter followed by some combination of digits and letters. It was possible to get a part number such as 1E20. Most spreadsheets automatically interpret 1E20 as scientific notation and save it as $1.00E + 20$ (1×10 to the 20th power) while leaving 1F20 as a string. For some reason, it's rather difficult to keep this from happening, and particularly with a large dataset, the problem won't be detected until farther down the pipeline, if all. For these reasons, I recommend using CSV or delimited files when at all possible. Users usually can save a spreadsheet as CSV, so there's no need to put up with the extra complexity and formatting hassles that spreadsheets involve.

21.4   Data cleaning

One common problem you'll encounter in processing text-based data files is dirty data. By *dirty*, I mean that there are all sorts of surprises in the data, such as null values, values that aren't legal for your encoding, or extra whitespace. The data may also be unsorted or in an order that makes processing difficult. The process of dealing with situations like these is called *data cleaning*.

21.4.1   Cleaning

In a very simple example, you might need to process a file that was exported from a spreadsheet or other financial program, and the columns dealing with money may have percentage and currency symbols (such as %, $, £, and €), as well as extra groupings that use a period or comma. Data from other sources may have other surprises that make processing tricky if they're not caught in advance. Look again at the temperature data you saw previously. The first data line looks like this:

```
[None, 'Illinois', 17, 'Jan 01, 1979', '1979/01/01', 17.48, 994, 6, 30.5,
2.89, 994, -13.6, 15.8, 'Missing', 0, 'Missing', 'Missing', '0.00%']
```

Some columns, such as `'State'` (field 2) and `'Notes'` (field 1), are clearly text, and you wouldn't be likely to do much with them. There are also two date fields in different formats, and you might well want to do calculations with the dates, possibly to change the order of the data and to group rows by month or day or possibly to calculate how far apart in time two rows are.

The rest of the fields seem to be different types of numbers; the temperatures are decimals, and the record counts columns are integers. Notice, however, that the heat index temperatures have a variation: when the value for the `'Max Temp for Daily Max Air Temp (F)'` field is below 80, the values for the heat index fields aren't reported but instead are listed as `'Missing'`, and the record count is 0. Also note that the `'Daily Max Heat Index (F) % Coverage'` field is expressed as a percentage of the number of temperature records that also qualify to have a heat index. Both of these things will be problematic if you want to do any math calculations on the values in those fields, because both `'Missing'` and any number ending with % will be parsed as strings, not numbers.

Cleaning data like this can be done at different steps in the process. Quite often, I prefer to clean the data as it's being read from the file, so I might well replace the `'Missing'` with a `None` value or an empty string as the lines are being processed. You could also leave the `'Missing'` strings in place and write your code so that no math operations are performed on a value if it is `'Missing'`.

> **Try this: Cleaning data**
>
> How would you handle the fields with `'Missing'` as possible values for math calculations? Can you write a snippet of code that averages one of those columns?
>
> What would you do with the Daily Max Heat Index (F) % Coverage column at the end so that you could also report the average coverage? In your opinion, would the solution to this problem be at all linked to the way that the `'Missing'` entries were handled?

21.4.2 *Sorting*

As I mentioned earlier, it's often useful to have data in the text file sorted before processing. Sorting the data makes it easier to spot and handle duplicate values, and it can also help bring together related rows for quicker or easier processing. In one case, I received a 20 million–row file of attributes and values, in which arbitrary numbers of them needed to be matched with items from a master SKU list. Sorting the rows by the item ID made gathering each item's attributes much faster. How you do the sorting depends on the size of the data file relative to your available memory and on the complexity of the sort. If all the lines of the file can fit comfortably into available memory, the easiest thing may be to read all of the lines into a list and use the list's `sort` method. For example, if `datafile` contained the following lines:

```
ZZZZZZ
CCCCCC
QQQQQQ
AAAAAA
```

then we could sort them this way:

```
lines = open("datafile").readlines()
lines.sort()
print(lines)
```

```
['AAAAAA\n', 'CCCCCC\n', 'QQQQQQ\n', 'ZZZZZZ\n']
```

You could also use the `sorted()` function, as in `sorted_lines = sorted(lines)`. This function preserves the order of the lines in your original list, which usually is unnecessary. The drawback to using the `sorted()` function is that it creates a new copy of the list. This process takes slightly longer and consumes twice as much memory, which might be a bigger concern.

　　If the dataset is larger than memory and the sort is very simple (just by an easily grabbed field), it may be easier to use an external utility, such as the UNIX `sort` command, to preprocess the data:

```
! sort datafile > datafile.srt
! cat datafile.srt
```

```
AAAAAA
CCCCCC
QQQQQQ
ZZZZZZ
```

In either case, sorting can be done in reverse order and can be keyed by values, not the beginning of the line. For such occasions, you need to study the documentation of the sorting tool you choose to use. A simple example in Python would be to make a sort of lines of text case insensitive. To do this, you give the `sort` method a key function that makes the element lowercase before making a comparison:

```
lines.sort(key=str.lower)
```

This example uses a `lambda` function to ignore the first five characters of each string:

```
lines.sort(key=lambda x: x[5:])
```

Using key functions to determine the behavior of sorts in Python is very handy, but be aware that the key function is called a lot in the process of sorting, so a complex key function could mean a real performance slowdown, particularly with a large dataset.

21.4.3 *Data cleaning problems and pitfalls*

It seems that there are as many types of dirty data as there are sources and use cases for that data. Your data will always have quirks that do everything from making processing less accurate to making it impossible to even load the data. As a result, I can't provide an exhaustive list of the problems you might encounter and how to deal with them, but I can give you some general hints:

- *Beware of whitespace and null characters.* The problem with whitespace characters is that you can't see them, but that doesn't mean that they can't cause trouble. Extra whitespace at the beginning and end of data lines, extra whitespace around individual fields, and tabs instead of spaces (or vice versa) can all make your data loading and processing more troublesome, and these problems aren't always easily apparent. Similarly, text files with null characters (ASCII 0) may seem okay on inspection but break on loading and processing.

- *Beware of punctuation.* Punctuation can also be a problem. Extra commas or periods can mess up CSV files and the processing of numeric fields, and unescaped or unmatched quote characters can also confuse things.

- *Break down and debug the steps.* It's easier to debug a problem if each step is separate, which means putting each operation on a separate line, being more verbose, and using more variables. But the work is worth it. For one thing, it makes any exceptions that are raised easier to understand, and it also makes debugging easier, whether with print statements, logging, or the Python debugger. It may also be helpful to save the data after each step and to cut the file size to just a few lines that cause error.

21.5 *Writing data files*

The last part of the ETL process may involve saving the transformed data to a database (which I discuss in chapter 22), but often it involves writing the data to files. These files may be used as input for other applications and analysis, either by people or by other applications. Usually, you have a particular file specification listing what fields of data should be included, what they should be named, what format and constraints there should be for each, and so on.

21.5.1 *CSV and other delimited files*

Probably the easiest thing of all is to write your data to CSV files. Because you've already loaded, parsed, cleaned, and transformed the data, you're unlikely to hit any unresolved problems with the data itself. And again, using the `csv` module from the Python standard library makes your work much easier.

Writing delimited files with the `csv` module is pretty much the reverse of the read process. Again, you need to specify the delimiter that you want to use, and again, the `csv` module takes care of any situations in which your delimiting character is included in a field:

```
temperature_data = [['State', 'Month Day, Year Code', 'Avg Daily Max Air
Temperature (F)', 'Record Count for Daily Max Air Temp (F)'], ['Illinois',
'1979/01/01', '17.48', '994'], ['Illinois', '1979/01/02', '4.64', '994'],
['Illinois', '1979/01/03', '11.05', '994'], ['Illinois', '1979/01/04',
'9.51', '994'], ['Illinois', '1979/05/15', '68.42', '994'], ['Illinois',
'1979/05/16', '70.29', '994'], ['Illinois', '1979/05/17', '75.34', '994'],
['Illinois', '1979/05/18', '79.13', '994'], ['Illinois', '1979/05/19',
'74.94', '994']]
csv.writer(open("temp_data_03.csv", "w",
                newline='')).writerows(temperature_data)
```

This code results in the following file:

```
State,"Month Day, Year Code",Avg Daily Max Air Temperature (F),Record Coun
➥ for Daily Max Air Temp (F)
Illinois,1979/01/01,17.48,994
Illinois,1979/01/02,4.64,994
Illinois,1979/01/03,11.05,994
Illinois,1979/01/04,9.51,994
Illinois,1979/05/15,68.42,994
Illinois,1979/05/16,70.29,994
Illinois,1979/05/17,75.34,994
Illinois,1979/05/18,79.13,994
Illinois,1979/05/19,74.94,994
```

Just as when reading from a CSV file, it's possible to write dictionaries instead of lists if you use a `DictWriter`. If you do use a `DictWriter`, be aware of a couple of points: you must specify the field names in a list when you create the writer, and you can use the `DictWriter`'s `writeheader` method to write the header at the top of the file. So assume that you have the same data as previously but in dictionary format:

```
data = [{'State': 'Illinois',
 'Month Day, Year Code': '1979/01/01',
 'Avg Daily Max Air Temperature (F)': '17.48',
 'Record Count for Daily Max Air Temp (F)': '994'}]
fields = ['State', 'Month Day, Year Code',
'Avg Daily Max Air Temperature (F)',
'Record Count for Daily Max Air Temp (F)']
```

You can use a `DictWriter` object from the `csv` module to write each row, a dictionary, to the correct fields in the CSV file:

```
fields = ['State', 'Month Day, Year Code',
'Avg Daily Max Air Temperature (F)',
'Record Count for Daily Max Air Temp (F)']
```

```
dict_writer = csv.DictWriter(open("temp_data_04.csv", "w"),
fieldnames=fields)
dict_writer.writeheader()
dict_writer.writerows(data)
del dict_writer
```

21.5.2 Writing Excel files

Writing spreadsheet files is unsurprisingly similar to reading them. You need to create a workbook, or spreadsheet file; then, you need to create a sheet or sheets; and finally, you write the data in the appropriate cells. You could create a new spreadsheet from your CSV data file like this:

```
from openpyxl import Workbook
data_rows = [fields for fields in csv.reader(open("temp_data_01.csv"))]
wb = Workbook()
ws = wb.active
ws.title = "temperature data"
for row in data_rows:
    ws.append(row)

wb.save("temp_data_02.xlsx")
```

It's also possible to add formatting to cells as you write them to the spreadsheet file. For more on how to add formatting, please refer to the `xlswriter` documentation.

21.5.3 Packaging data files

If you have several related data files, or if your files are large, it may make sense to package them in a compressed archive. Although various archive formats are in use, the zip file remains popular and almost universally accessible to users on almost every platform. For hints on how to create `zipfile` packages of your data files, please refer to chapter 20.

21.6 Weather observations

The file of weather observations provided here (Illinois_weather_1979-2011.txt) is by month and then by county for the state of Illinois from 1979 to 2011. Write the code to process this file to extract the data for Chicago (Cook County) into a single CSV or spreadsheet file. This process includes replacing the `'Missing'` strings with empty strings and translating the percentage to a decimal. You may also consider what fields are repetitive (and therefore can be omitted or stored elsewhere). The proof that you've got it right occurs when you load the file into a spreadsheet, or you can also use Colaboratory's file browser (the file icon at the very left) and double-click on it to see the data as a table.

> **NOTE** There is some documentation at the end of the file, so you will need to stop processing the file when the first field of the line is `"---"`.

For reference, it's always a good idea to look at a few lines (at least) of the raw file:

```
['"Notes"\t"Month"\t"Month Code"\t"County"\t"County Code"\tAvg Daily Max
Air Temperature (F)\tRecord Count for Daily Max Air Temp (F)\tMin Temp for
Daily Max Air Temp (F)\tMax Temp for Daily Max Air Temp (F)\tAvg Daily Min
Air Temperature (F)\tRecord Count for Daily Min Air Temp (F)\tMin Temp for
Daily Min Air Temp (F)\tMax Temp for Daily Min Air Temp (F)\tAvg Daily Max
Heat Index (F)\tRecord Count for Daily Max Heat Index (F)\tMin for Daily
Max Heat Index (F)\tMax for Daily Max Heat Index (F)\tDaily Max Heat Index
(F) % Coverage\n',
 '\t"Jan"\t"1"\t"Adams County, IL"\t"17001"\t31.89\t19437\t
10.00\t68.90\t18.01\t19437\t-26.20\t50.30\tMissing\t0\tMissing\tMissing\
t0.00%\n',
 '\t"Jan"\t"1"\t"Alexander County,
IL"\t"17003"\t41.07\t6138\t2.60\t73.20\t26.48\t6138\t
14.00\t60.30\tMissing\t0\tMissing\tMissing\t0.00%\n',
 '\t"Jan"\t"1"\t"Bond County, IL"\t"17005"\t35.71\t6138\t-
2.70\t69.50\t22.18\t6138\t-17.90\t57.20\tMissing\t0\tMissing\tMissing\
t0.00%\n']
```

21.6.1 Solving the problem with AI-generated code

This problem is mostly procedural, with little higher-level design, so it's fairly suitable for an AI solution. As usual, we also need to be sure to include all of the necessary information clearly in the prompt.

21.6.2 Solutions and discussion

This is a much easier problem than those in some of the previous chapters, since we are really just doing some basic data cleaning. The main things to do are load the file, fix/discard some of the data fields, and then write the file as a CSV file.

THE HUMAN SOLUTION

This solution is pretty simple: the input and output files are opened and the raw fields are read in, processed, and saved:

```
import csv                                          Opens both input and
                                                    output files
with (open("Illinois_weather_1979-2011.txt") as infile,
      open("Illinois_weather_1979-2011.csv", "w")   Checks for beginning
                            as outfile):             of documentation
    for row in csv.reader(infile, delimiter="\t"):   section
        if row[0] == '---':
            break
        if "Cook" in row[3]:                    Removes first two
            del row[0:2]                         fields of line
            row = [item.replace("Missing", "")   Replaces "Missing"
                        for item in row]          with an empty string
            row[-1] = row[-1].replace("%", "")
            row[-1] = (float(row[-1])/100 if str.isdigit(row[-1])

                                            Removes % character
                                            from the last field
```

```
                           else row[-1])
          csv.writer(outfile).writerow(row)
```
**Converts percentage
to a decimal value**

As mentioned, the last few lines of this file are documentation, so we end processing when we hit the separator `"---"`. Since we are looking for Chicago (Cook County) data, we will only process a line if the `"County"` field contains `"Cook"`. Alternatively, we could look in the file and see that the county code for Cook County is `"17031"` and only process lines where that is in the `"County Code"` field. As we process the lines, the first thing we do is remove the first two fields—the first field (`"Notes"`) is empty, and second is the month name, which we don't need since we have the month's number in the following field.

The next two operations are changing `"Missing"` to an empty string in any field and then removing the `%` character and converting a text string of the percentage to a decimal number (e.g., `"10"` becomes `0,1`).

The code finishes by writing the newly processed fields to the CVS file.

THE AI SOLUTIONS

Copilot was given the following prompt, which was based closely on the lab assignment:

```
The file of weather observations provided here (Illinois_weather_1979
2011.txt) is by month and then by county for the state of Illinois from
1979 to 2011. Write the code to process this file to extract the data for
Chicago (Cook County) into a single CSV or spreadsheet file. This process
includes replacing the 'Missing' strings with empty strings and translating
the percentage to a decimal. You may also consider what fields are
repetitive (and therefore can be omitted or stored elsewhere). Note: there
is some documentation at the end of the file, so you will need to stop
processing the file when the first field of the line is "---".
```

Copilot offered the following plan, which makes sense:

1 Open the file Illinois_weather_1979-2011.txt for reading.

2 Create a new CSV file for writing the processed data.

3 Iterate through each line of the input file:

 a If the line starts with `"---"`, stop processing.

 b If the line contains data for Cook County (Chicago), process it:

  i. Replace `"Missing"` with an empty string.

  ii. Convert percentage values to decimals.

  iii. Write the processed data to the CSV file.

4 Close both files.

As expected, Copilot did fairly well with this task, offering a solution that *almost* does the job. It generated this code:

```
import csv

input_file = 'Illinois_weather_1979-2011.txt'
```

```
output_file = 'Chicago_weather_1979-2011.csv'

with (open(input_file, 'r') as infile, open(output_file,
        'w', newline='') as outfile):
    reader = csv.reader(infile, delimiter='\t')
    writer = csv.writer(outfile)

    headers = next(reader)
    writer.writerow(headers)  # Write headers to the output file

    for row in reader:
        if row[0].startswith('---'):
            break

        if 'Cook' in row:
            processed_row = [field.replace('Missing', '') for field in row]
            processed_row = [str(float(field.strip('%')) / 100)
                    if '%' in field else field for field in processed_row]
            writer.writerow(processed_row)
```

Checks if a field "Cook" is in the row

This code is quite similar to the human version, with only a few differences. First, it handles headers nicely, copying them to the new file—something that the human version did not do. Second, it does the conversion of the percentages to decimals in one line, rather than two, and checks all fields rather than only the last one. Both of those differences are reasonable—even positive. Finally, all of the fields, even the empty "Notes" field, are preserved. This isn't surprising, since removing/consolidating fields would be a value judgment.

The only problem is that when this code is run, the resulting file, Chicago_weather_1979-2011.csv, only has the header. That's because it checks for "Cook" in the entire row:

```
if 'Cook' in row:
```

For that condition to be true, an *entire field* in the row would have to be exactly "Cook," when in fact the rows we want contain a field "Cook County, IL". The fix for this is to just specify that only row[3] contain "Cook":

```
if 'Cook' in row[3]:
```

With that one change, Copilot's version works perfectly. Here again, we could spend a lot of time experimenting with the prompt to get a complete answer, but the efficient choice is to just make the three-character fix.

The prompt for Colaboratory was a bit different:

```
The file provided here (Illinois_weather_1979-2011.txt) is for the state of
Illinois from 1979 to 2011. Write  code to process this file to extract the
data for Chicago (Cook County) into a single CSV. Replace the 'Missing'
strings with empty strings and translate the percentage to a decimal. Use
the input file headers to decide what fields are repetitive (and therefore
```

can be omitted). Stop processing the file when the first field of the line is "---".

The prompt was edited both since there is a 600-character limit in Colaboratory and because, with the original phrasing, the code generator assigned fields incorrectly. The current wording got around both problems:

```python
import csv

def process_illinois_weather_data():
  """Processes the Illinois weather data file and extracts Chicago data
into a CSV."""

  with open('Illinois_weather_1979-2011.txt', 'r') as infile, \
      open('chicago_weather.csv', 'w', newline='') as outfile:

    reader = csv.reader(infile, delimiter='\t')
    writer = csv.writer(outfile)

    header = next(reader)
    writer.writerow(header)

    for row in reader:
      if row[0] == '---':
        break
      if row[1] == 'Cook':          ◀──── Checks to see if row[1]
        new_row = []                      is equal to "Cook"
        for cell in row:
          if cell == 'Missing':
            new_row.append('')
          elif '%' in cell:
            new_row.append(str(float(cell.replace('%', '')) / 100))
          else:
            new_row.append(cell)

        writer.writerow(new_row)


process_illinois_weather_data()
print("Chicago weather data extracted to chicago_weather.csv")
```

This approach is a bit different. While it preserves all of the fields just as the Copilot version did, it takes a different approach to processing a row. Rather than changing fields in a row, it instead processes each field in a row and then adds that field to a new row, which it writes to the file when the processing for the row is complete. This approach is arguably slightly less efficient since it creates a new list for each row, but in practice, the performance hit is probably slight.

As with the Copilot version, the code as suggested will write a file with only the header row—and for a very similar reason: in checking for Cook County results, it checks to see if row[1] == "Cook". This is wrong both because the value would be "Cook County, IL", as mentioned earlier, and because it checks the Month field, not the County field. The correction would be the same as before. The line should be

```
if 'Cook' in row[3]:
```

Once that change is made, this code produces the correct result.

As mentioned, this task is fairly straightforward, and so it's not as much of a challenge for the AI tools as some more complex tasks. The AI bots' problems came in using the correct technique and field to check the county and in evaluating the fields for possible redundancy. Giving an explicit mapping and instructions in the prompt probably would have helped this, at the expense of making constructing the prompt more laborious.

Summary

- ETL is the process of getting data from one format, making sure that it's consistent, and then putting it in a format you can use. ETL is the basic step in most data processing.
- Encoding can be problematic with text files, but Python lets you deal with some encoding problems when you load files.
- The most common way to handle a wide range of characters in simple text files is to encode them in the Unicode UTF-8 encoding.
- Delimited and CSV files are common, and the best way to handle them is with the csv module.
- Spreadsheet files (in Excel format) can be more complex than CSV files but can be read and written with third-party libraries.
- Currency symbols, punctuation, and null characters are among the most common data cleaning concerns; be on the watch for them.
- Cleaning and presorting your data file can make other steps faster.
- Writing data in the formats discussed is similar to reading them.

22
Data over the network

This chapter covers

- Fetching files via FTP/SFTP, SSH/SCP, and HTTPS
- Getting data via APIs
- Structured data file formats: JSON and XML
- Scraping data

You've seen how to deal with text-based data files. In this chapter, you use Python to move data files over the network. In some cases, those files might be text or spreadsheet files, as discussed in chapter 21, but in other cases, they might be in more structured formats and served from REST or SOAP APIs. Sometimes getting the data may mean scraping it from a website. This chapter discusses all of these situations and shows some common use cases.

22.1 Fetching files

Before you can do anything with data files, you have to get them. Sometimes this process is very easy, such as manually downloading a single zip archive, or maybe the files have been pushed to your machine from somewhere else. Quite often, however, the process is more involved. Maybe a large number of files need to be retrieved from a remote server, files need to be retrieved regularly, or the retrieval process is sufficiently complex to be a pain to do manually. In any of those cases, you might well want to automate fetching the data files with Python.

First, I want to be clear that using a Python script isn't the only way, or always the best way, to retrieve files. The following sidebar offers more explanation of the factors I consider when deciding whether to use a Python script for file retrieval. Assuming that using Python does make sense for your particular use case, however, this section illustrates some common patterns you might employ.

Should I use Python?

Although using Python to retrieve files can work very well, it's not always the best choice. In making a decision, you might want to consider two things:

- *Are simpler options available?* Depending on your operating system and your experience, you may find that simple shell scripts and command-line tools are simpler and easier to configure. If you don't have those tools available or aren't comfortable using them (or the people who will be maintaining them aren't comfortable with them), you may want to consider a Python script.
- *Is the retrieval process complex or tightly coupled with processing?* Although those situations are never desirable, they can occur. My rule these days is that if a shell script requires more than a few lines, or if I have to think hard about how to do something in a shell script, it's probably time to switch to Python.

22.1.1 *Using Python to fetch files from an FTP server*

File transfer protocol (FTP) has been around for a very long time, but it's still a simple and easy way to share files when security isn't a huge concern. To access an FTP server in Python, you can use the `ftplib` module from the standard library. The steps to follow are straightforward: create an FTP object, connect to a server, and then log in with a username and password (or, quite commonly, with a username of "anonymous" and an empty password).

To continue working with weather data, you can connect to the National Oceanic and Atmospheric Administration FTP server, as shown here:

```
import ftplib
ftp = ftplib.FTP('tgftp.nws.noaa.gov')
ftp.login()

'230 Login successful.'
```

When you're connected, you can use the `ftp` object to list and change directories:

```
ftp.cwd('data')

'250 Directory successfully changed.'
```

```
ftp.nlst()
```

```
['climate', 'fnmoc', 'forecasts', 'hurricane_products', 'ls_SS_services',
'marine', 'nsd_bbsss.txt', 'nsd_cccc.txt', 'observations', 'products',
'public_statement', 'raw', 'records', 'summaries', 'tampa',
'watches_warnings', 'zonecatalog.curr', 'zonecatalog.curr.tar']
```

Then you can fetch, for example, the latest METAR report for Chicago O'Hare International Airport:

```
x = ftp.retrbinary('RETR observations/metar/decoded/KORD.TXT',
open('KORD.TXT', 'wb').write)
```

```
'226 Transfer complete.'
```

The `ftp.retrbinary` method takes two parameters—the path to the file on the remote server and a method to handle that file's data when you receive it on your end; in this case, that method is the `write` method of a file opened for binary writing with the same name. When you look at KORD.TXT, you see that it contains the downloaded data:

```
x = ftp.retrbinary('RETR observations/metar/decoded/KORD.TXT', open('KORD.
TXT', 'wb').write)
open('KORD.TXT', 'r').readlines()
```

```
["CHICAGO O'HARE INTERNATIONAL, IL, United States (KORD)
 41-59N 087-55W 200M\n",
 'Aug 19, 2024 - 10:51 PM EDT / 2024.08.20 0251 UTC\n',
 'Wind: from the NNE (030 degrees) at 13 MPH (11 KT):0\n',
 'Visibility: 10 mile(s):0\n',
 'Sky conditions: partly cloudy\n',
 'Temperature: 68.0 F (20.0 C)\n',
 'Dew Point: 55.9 F (13.3 C)\n',
 'Relative Humidity: 65%\n',
 'Pressure (altimeter): 30.17 in. Hg (1021 hPa)\n',
 'Pressure tendency: 0.03 inches (1.0 hPa) higher than three hours ago\n',
 'ob: KORD 200251Z 03011KT 10SM SCT039 SCT050 20/13 A3017
 RMK AO2 SLP212 T02000133 53010\n',
 'cycle: 3\n']
```

You can also use `ftplib` to connect to servers using Transport Layer Security (TLS) encryption by using FTP_TLS instead of FTP:

```
ftp = ftplib.FTPTLS('tgftp.nws.noaa.gov')
```

22.1.2 *Fetching files with SFTP*

If the data requires more security, such as in a corporate context in which business data is being transferred over the network, it's fairly common to use SFTP. SFTP is a full-featured protocol that allows file access, transfer, and management over a Secure Shell (SSH) connection. Even though SFTP stands for SSH file transfer protocol and FTP stands for file transfer protocol, the two aren't related. SFTP isn't a reimplementation of FTP on SSH but a fresh design specifically for SSH.

Using SSH-based transfers is attractive both because SSH is already the de facto standard for accessing remote servers and because enabling support for SFTP on a server is fairly easy (and quite often on by default).

Python doesn't have an SFTP/SCP client module in its standard library, but a community-developed library called `paramiko` manages SFTP operations as well as SSH connections. To use `paramiko`, the easiest thing is to install it via `pip`. If the National Oceanic and Atmospheric Administration site mentioned earlier in this chapter were using SFTP (which it doesn't, so this code won't work!), the SFTP equivalent of the previous code would be

```
import paramiko
t = paramiko.Transport((hostname, port))
t.connect(username, password)
sftp = paramiko.SFTPClient.from_transport(t)
```

It's also worth noting that, although `paramiko` supports running commands on a remote server and receiving its outputs, just like a direct `ssh` session, it doesn't include an `scp` function. This function is rarely something you'll miss; if all you want to do is move a file or two over an `ssh` connection, a command-line `scp` utility usually makes the job easier.

22.1.3 *Retrieving files over HTTP/HTTPS*

The last common option for retrieving data files that I discuss in this chapter is getting files over an HTTP or HTTPS connection. This option is probably the easiest of all the options; you are in effect retrieving your data from a web server, and support for accessing web servers is very widespread. Again, in this case, you may not need to use Python. Various command-line tools retrieve files via HTTP/HTTPS connections and have most of the capabilities you might need. The two most common of these tools are wget and curl. If you have a reason to do the retrieval in your Python code, however, that process isn't much harder. The `requests` library is by far the easiest and most reliable way to access HTTP/HTTPS servers from Python code. Again, `requests` is easiest to install with `pip install requests`. When you have requests installed, fetching a file is straightforward: import `requests` and use the correct HTTP verb (usually, GET) to connect to the server and return your data.

The following example code fetches the monthly temperature data for Heathrow Airport since 1948—a text file that's served via a web server. If you want to, you can put the URL in your browser, load the page, and then save it. If the page is large or you have a lot of pages to get, however, it's easier to use code like the following:

```
import requests
response = requests.get("http://www.metoffice.gov.uk/pub/data/weather/uk/
climate/
stationdata/heathrowdata.txt")
```

The response will have a fair amount of information, including the header returned by the web server, which can be helpful in debugging if things aren't working. The part of the response object you'll most often be interested in, however, is data returned. To retrieve this data, you want to access the response's `text` property, which contains the response body as a string, or the `content` property, which contains the response body as bytes:

```
print(response.text)
```

```
Heathrow (London Airport)
Location 507800E 176700N, Lat 51.479 Lon -0.449, 25m amsl
Estimated data is marked with a * after the value.
Missing data (more than 2 days missing in month) is marked by  ---.
Sunshine data taken from an automatic Kipp & Zonen sensor marked with a #,
otherwise sunshine data taken from a Campbell Stokes recorder.
   yyyy  mm   tmax   tmin     af    rain    sun
              degC   degC   days      mm  hours
   1948   1    8.9    3.3    ---    85.0    ---
   1948   2    7.9    2.2    ---    26.0    ---
   1948   3   14.2    3.8    ---    14.0    ---
   1948   4   15.4    5.1    ---    35.0    ---
   1948   5   18.1    6.9    ---    57.0     -
...
```

Typically, you'd write the response text to a file for later processing, but depending on your needs, you might first do some cleaning or even process it immediately.

Try this: Retrieving a file

If you're working with the example data file and want to break each line into separate fields, how might you do that? What other processing would you expect to do? Try writing some code to retrieve this file and calculate the average annual rainfall or (for more of a challenge) the average maximum and minimum temperature for each year.

22.2 Fetching data via an API

Serving data by way of an API is quite common, following a trend toward decoupling applications into services that communicate via APIs. APIs can work in several ways, but they commonly operate over regular HTTP/HTTPS protocols using the standard HTTP verbs: GET, POST, PUT, and DELETE. Fetching data this way is very similar to retrieving a file, as in section 22.1.3, but the data isn't in a static file. Instead of the application serving static files that contain the data, it queries some other data source and then assembles and serves the data dynamically on request.

Although there's a lot of variation in the ways that an API can be set up, one of the most common is a REpresentational State Transfer (RESTful) interface that operates over the same HTTP/HTTPS protocols as the web. There are endless variations on how an API might work, but commonly, data is fetched by using a GET request, which is what your web browser uses to request a web page. When you're fetching via a GET request, the parameters to select the data you want are often appended to the URL in a query string.

We can test this by getting the current weather in Chicago from Open-Meteo.com, using https://mng.bz/BX9g as your URL. The items after the ? are query string parameters that specify the latitude and longitude of the location and the two fields that we are requesting: temperature and wind speed. For this API, the information will be returned in JSON, which I discuss in section 22.3.1. Notice that the elements of the query string are separated by ampersands (&).

When you know the URL to use, you can use the `requests` library to fetch data from an API and either process it on the fly or save it to a file for later processing. The simplest way to do this is exactly like retrieving a file:

```
response = requests.get("https://api.open-meteo.com/v1/forecast?
    latitude=41.882&longitude=-87.623&current=temperature_2m,
    wind_speed_10m")
weather = response.text
weather
```

```
{"latitude":41.879482,"longitude":-87.64975,"generationtime_ms":0.026941299
438476562,"utc_offset_seconds":0,"timezone":"GMT","timezone_abbreviation":
"GMT","elevation":185.0,"current_units":{"time":"iso8601","interval":
"seconds","temperature_2m":"°C","wind_speed_10m":"km/h"},"current":{"time":
"2024-09-02T02:00","interval":900,"temperature_2m":16.9,
"wind_speed_10m":13.3}}
```

Keep in mind that, ideally, you should escape spaces and most punctuation in your query parameters, because those elements aren't allowed in URLs. It's not absolutely necessary, though, because the `requests` library and many browsers automatically do the escaping on URLs.

For a final example, suppose that you want to grab the crime data for Chicago between noon and 1 P.M. on January 10, 2017. The way that the API works, you specify a date range with the query string parameters of `$where=date between <start datetime>` and `<end datetime>`, where the start and end datetimes are quoted in ISO format. So the URL for getting that 1 hour of Chicago crime data would be https://mng.bz/N1ad:

```
result = requests.get("https://data.cityofchicago.org/resource/
    6zsd-86xi.json?$where=date between '2024-01-10T12:01:00' and
    '2024-01-10T12:10:00'")
result.json()
```

```
[{'id': '13334404',
  'case_number': 'JH111115',
  'date': '2024-01-10T12:01:00.000',
  'block': '009XX W WINONA ST',
  'iucr': '2020',
  'primary_type': 'NARCOTICS',
```

```
        'description': 'POSSESS - AMPHETAMINES',
        'location_description': 'APARTMENT',
        'arrest': True,
        'domestic': False,
        'beat': '2024',
        'district': '020',
        'ward': '48',
        'community_area': '3',
        'fbi_code': '18',
        'x_coordinate': '1169132',
        'y_coordinate': '1934325',
        'year': '2024',
        'updated_on': '2024-01-18T15:41:44.000',
        'latitude': '41.975305734',
        'longitude': '-87.653416364',
        'location': {'type': 'Point', 'coordinates':
                     [-87.653416364, 41.975305734]},
        'location_address': '',
        'location_city': '',
        'location_state': '',
        'location_zip': ''},
 {'id': '13334420',
  'case_number': 'JH111020',
  'date': '2024-01-10T12:01:00.000',
  'block': '009XX W WINONA ST',
  'iucr': '1330',
  'primary_type': 'CRIMINAL TRESPASS',
  'description': 'TO LAND',
  'location_description': 'APARTMENT',
  'arrest': True,
  'domestic': False,
  'beat': '2024',
  'district': '020',
  'ward': '48',
  'community_area': '3',
  'fbi_code': '26',
  'x_coordinate': '1169132',
  'y_coordinate': '1934325',
  'year': '2024',
  'updated_on': '2024-01-18T15:41:44.000',
  'latitude': '41.975305734',
  'longitude': '-87.653416364',
  'location': {'type': 'Point', 'coordinates':
                         [-87.653416364, 41.975305734]},
  'location_address': '',
  'location_city': '',
  'location_state': '',
  'location_zip': ''},
 ...                  ◀─────┘ Several records omitted
]
```

In the example, some characters aren't welcome in URLs, such as the space characters. This is another situation in which the requests library makes good on its aim of making things easier for the user, because, before it sends the URL, it takes care of quoting it properly. The URL that the request actually sends is https://mng.bz/dXvX.

Note that all of the spaces have been quoted with %20 without your even needing to think about it.

> **Try this: Accessing an API**
>
> Write some code to fetch some data from the city of Chicago website. Look at the fields mentioned in the results and see whether you can select records based on another field in combination with the date range.

22.3 Structured data formats

Although APIs sometimes serve plain text, it's much more common for data served from APIs to be served in a structured file format. The two most common file formats are JSON and XML. Both of these formats are built on plain text but structure their contents so that they're more flexible and able to store more complex information.

22.3.1 JSON data

JSON, which stands for JavaScript Object Notation, dates to 1999. It consists of only two structures: key-value pairs, called *structures*, that are very similar to Python dictionaries and ordered lists of values, called *arrays*, that are very much like Python lists.

Keys can be only strings in double quotes, and values can be strings in double quotes, numbers, true, false, null, arrays, or other structures. These elements make JSON a lightweight way to represent most data in a way that's easily transmitted over the network and also fairly easy for humans to read. JSON is so common that most languages have features to translate JSON to and from native data types. In the case of Python, that feature is the `json` module, which became part of the standard library with version 2.6. The original externally maintained version of the module is available as `simplejson`, which is still available. In Python 3, however, it's far more common to use the standard library version, unless you need a feature only supported in `simplejson`, like the decimal number type.

The data you retrieved from the weather and the city of Chicago APIs in section 22.2 is in JSON format. To send JSON across the network, the JSON object needs to be serialized—that is, transformed into a sequence of bytes. So, although the batch of data you retrieved from the weather and Chicago crime APIs looks like JSON, in fact, it's just a byte string representation of a JSON object. To transform that byte string into a real JSON object and translate it into a Python dictionary, you need to use the JSON `loads()` function. If you want to get the weather report, for example, you can do that just as you did previously, but this time you'll convert it to a Python dictionary:

```
import json
import requests
response = requests.get("https://api.open-meteo.com/v1/forecast?latitude
```

```
=41.882&longitude=-87.623&current=temperature_2m,wind_speed_10m")
weather = json.loads(response.text)
weather
```

```
{'latitude': 41.879482,
 'longitude': -87.64975,
 'generationtime_ms': 0.025987625122070312,
 'utc_offset_seconds': 0,
 'timezone': 'GMT',
 'timezone_abbreviation': 'GMT',
 'elevation': 185.0,
 'current_units': {'time': 'iso8601',
  'interval': 'seconds',
  'temperature_2m': '°C',
  'wind_speed_10m': 'km/h'},
 'current': {'time': '2024-09-02T02:15',
  'interval': 900,
  'temperature_2m': 16.9,
  'wind_speed_10m': 13.8}}
```

```
weather['current']['temperature_2m']
```

```
16.9
```

Note that the call to `json.loads()` is what takes the string representation of the JSON object and transforms, or loads, it into a Python dictionary. Also, a `json.load()` function will read from any file-like object that supports a read method.

If you print a dictionary's representation, it can be very hard to make sense of what's going on. Improved formatting, also called *pretty printing*, can make data structures much easier to understand. Use the Python `prettyprint` module to see what's in the example dictionary:

```
from pprint import pprint as pp
pp(weather)
```

```
from pprint import pprint as pp
pp(weather)
{'current': {'interval': 900,
             'temperature_2m': 16.9,
             'time': '2024-09-02T02:15',
             'wind_speed_10m': 13.8},
 'current_units': {'interval': 'seconds',
                   'temperature_2m': '°C',
                   'time': 'iso8601',
                   'wind_speed_10m': 'km/h'},
 'elevation': 185.0,
 'generationtime_ms': 0.025987625122070312,
 'latitude': 41.879482,
 'longitude': -87.64975,
 'timezone': 'GMT',
 'timezone_abbreviation': 'GMT',
 'utc_offset_seconds': 0}
```

Both load functions can be configured to control how to parse and decode the original JSON to Python objects, but the default translation is listed in table 22.1.

Table 22.1   JSON-to-Python default decoding

JSON	Python
object	dict
array	list
string	str
number (int)	int
number (real)	float
true	True
false	False
null	None

Fetching JSON with the requests library

In this section, you used the `requests` library to retrieve the JSON-formatted data and then used the `json.loads()` method to parse it into a Python object. This technique works fine, but because the `requests` library is used so often for exactly this purpose, the library provides a shortcut: the response object actually has a `json()` method that does that conversion for you. So, in the example, instead of

```
weather = json.loads(response.text)
```

you could have used

```
weather = response.json()
```

The result is the same, but the code is simpler, more readable, and more Pythonic.

If you want to write JSON to a file or serialize it to a string, the reverse of `load()` and `loads()` is `dump()` and `dumps()`. `json.dump()` takes a file object with a `write()` method as a parameter, and `json.dumps()` returns a string. In both cases, the encoding to a JSON-formatted string can be highly customized, but the default is still based on table 22.1. So if you want to write your weather report to a JSON file, you could do the following:

```
outfile = open("weather_01.json", "w")
json.dump(weather, outfile)          ◄──┘ Writes the string to outfile
outfile.close()
json.dumps(weather)         ◄──┘ Returns the string
```

{"latitude": 41.879482, "longitude": -87.64975, "generationtime_ms":
0.025987625122070312, "utc_offset_seconds": 0, "timezone": "GMT",
"timezone_abbreviation": "GMT", "elevation": 185.0, "current_units":
{"time": "iso8601", "interval": "seconds", "temperature_2m": "\u00b0C",
"wind_speed_10m": "km/h"}, "current": {"time": "2024-09-02T02:15",
"interval": 900, "temperature_2m": 16.9, "wind_speed_10m": 13.8}}

As you can see, the entire object has been encoded as a single string. With `json.dump` (with no "s" on the end) that string is written to the specified file. With the "s," `json.dumps` returns the serialized string. Here again, it might be handy to format the string in a more readable way, just as you did by using the `pprint` module. To do so easily, use the `indent` parameter with the `dump` or `dumps` function:

```
print(json.dumps(weather, indent=2))
```

```
{
  "latitude": 41.879482,
  "longitude": -87.64975,
  "generationtime_ms": 0.025987625122070312,
  "utc_offset_seconds": 0,
  "timezone": "GMT",
  "timezone_abbreviation": "GMT",
  "elevation": 185.0,
  "current_units": {
    "time": "iso8601",
    "interval": "seconds",
    "temperature_2m": "\u00b0C",
    "wind_speed_10m": "km/h"
  },
  "current": {
    "time": "2024-09-02T02:15",
    "interval": 900,
    "temperature_2m": 16.9,
    "wind_speed_10m": 13.8
  }
}
```

You should be aware, however, that if you use repeated calls to `json.dump()` to write a series of objects to a file, the result is a *series* of legal JSON-formatted strings, but the contents of the file *as a whole* is *not* a legal JSON-formatted object, and attempting to read and parse the entire file by using a single call to `json.load()` will fail. If you have more than one object that you'd like to encode as a single JSON object, you need to put all those objects into a list (or, better yet, an object or structure) and then encode that item to the file.

If you have two or more items of weather data that you want to store in a file as JSON, you have to make a choice. You could use `json.dump()` once for each object, which would result in a file containing JSON-formatted strings. If you assume that `weather_list` is a list of weather-report objects, the code might look like the following:

```
outfile = open("weather_list.json", "w")
for report in weather_list:
    outfile.write(json.dumps(report) + "\n")
outfile.close()
```

If you do this, then you need to load each line as a separate JSON-formatted object:

```
weather_list2 = []
for line in open("weather_list.json"):
    weather_list2.append(json.loads(line))
```

As an alternative, you could put the list into a single JSON object. Because there's a possible vulnerability with top-level arrays in JSON, the recommended way is to put the array in a dictionary:

```
outfile = open("weather_obj.json", "w")
weather_obj = {"reports": weather_list, "count": 2}
json.dump(weather_obj, outfile)
outfile.close()
```

With this approach, you can use one operation to load the JSON-formatted object from the file:

```
with open("weather_obj.json") as infile:
    weather_obj = json.load(infile))
```

The second approach is fine if the size of your JSON files is manageable, but it may be less than ideal for very large files, because handling errors may be a bit harder and you may run out of memory.

> ### Try this: Saving some JSON crime data
>
> Modify the code you wrote in section 22.2 to fetch the Chicago crime data. Then convert the fetched data from a JSON-formatted string to a Python object. Next, see whether you can save the crime events as a series of separate JSON strings in one file and as one JSON object in another file. Then see what code is needed to load each file.

22.3.2 *XML data*

XML has been around since the end of the 20th century. XML uses an angle-bracket tag notation similar to HTML, and elements are nested within other elements to form a tree structure. XML was intended to be readable by both machines and humans, but XML is often so verbose and complex that it's very difficult for people to understand. Nevertheless, because XML is an established standard, it's quite common to find data in XML format. And although XML is machine readable, it's very likely that you'll want to translate it into something a bit easier to deal with.

To take a look at some XML data, let's fetch the XML version of the World Bank's population data for Chile:

```
result = requests.get(
"https://api.worldbank.org/v2/country/CL/indicator/SP.POP.TOTL?format=xml")
pop_data = result.text[3:]
print(pop_data)
```
◄───┐ **Skips extra characters**

```
<?xml version="1.0" encoding="utf-8"?>
<wb:data page="1" pages="2" per_page="50" total="64" sourceid="2"
lastupdated="2024-06-28" xmlns:wb="http://www.worldbank.org">
  <wb:data>
    <wb:indicator id="SP.POP.TOTL">Population, total</wb:indicator>
    <wb:country id="CL">Chile</wb:country>
    <wb:countryiso3code>CHL</wb:countryiso3code>
    <wb:date>2023</wb:date>
    <wb:value>19629590</wb:value>
    <wb:unit />
    <wb:obs_status />
    <wb:decimal>0</wb:decimal>
  </wb:data>
  <wb:data>
    <wb:indicator id="SP.POP.TOTL">Population, total</wb:indicator>
    <wb:country id="CL">Chile</wb:country>
    <wb:countryiso3code>CHL</wb:countryiso3code>
    <wb:date>2022</wb:date>
    <wb:value>19603733</wb:value>
    <wb:unit />
    <wb:obs_status />
    <wb:decimal>0</wb:decimal>
  </wb:data>
    ...                    ◄───┐ **Several records omitted**
</wb:data>
```

This example is just the first section of the document, with most of the data omitted. Even so, it illustrates some of the concerns you typically find in XML data. In particular, you can see the verbose nature of the protocol, with the tags in some cases taking more space than the value contained in them. This sample also shows the nested or tree structure common in XML, as well as the common use of a sizeable header of metadata before the actual data begins. On a spectrum from simple to complex for data files, you could think of CSV or delimited files as being at the simple end and XML at the complex end.

Finally, this file illustrates another feature of XML that makes pulling data a bit more of a challenge. XML supports the use of attributes to store data as well as the text values within the tags. So, if you look at the first `wb:data` element at the top of this sample, you see that this element contains its metadata as tags and then also contains the other data elements. To know which way any given bit of data will be handled, you need to carefully inspect the data or study a specification document.

This kind of complexity can make simple data extraction from XML more of a challenge. You have several ways to handle XML. The Python standard library comes with modules that parse and handle XML data, but none of them are particularly convenient for simple data extraction.

For simple data extraction, the handiest utility I've found is a library called xmltodict, which parses your XML data and returns a dictionary that reflects the tree. In fact, behind the scenes, it uses the standard library's Expat XML parser, parses your XML document into a tree, and uses that tree to create the dictionary. As a result, xmltodict can handle whatever the parser can, and it's also able to take a dictionary and "unparse" it to XML if necessary, making it a very handy tool. Over several years of use, I found this solution to be up to all my XML handling needs. To get xmltodict, you can again use pip install xmltodict.

To convert the XML to a dictionary, you can import xmltodict and use the parse method on an XML-formatted string:

```
import xmltodict
population = xmltodict.parse(pop_data)
population
```

In this case, for compactness, pass the contents of the file directly to the parse method. After being parsed, this data object is an ordered dictionary with the same values it would have if it had been loaded from this JSON:

```
{'wb:data': {'@page': '1',
  '@pages': '2',
  '@per_page': '50',
  '@total': '64',
  '@sourceid': '2',
  '@lastupdated': '2024-06-28',
  '@xmlns:wb': 'http://www.worldbank.org',
  'wb:data': [{'wb:indicator': {'@id': 'SP.POP.TOTL',
      '#text': 'Population, total'},
    'wb:country': {'@id': 'CL', '#text': 'Chile'},
    'wb:countryiso3code': 'CHL',
    'wb:date': '2023',
    'wb:value': '19629590',
    'wb:unit': None,
    'wb:obs_status': None,
    'wb:decimal': '0'},
   {'wb:indicator': {'@id': 'SP.POP.TOTL', '#text': 'Population, total'},
    'wb:country': {'@id': 'CL', '#text': 'Chile'},
    'wb:countryiso3code': 'CHL',
    'wb:date': '2022',
    'wb:value': '19603733',
    'wb:unit': None,
    'wb:obs_status': None,
    'wb:decimal': '0'},
   ...
   ]                          ◄─────┐
 }                                  │  Several records omitted
}
```

Notice that the attributes have been pulled out of the tags but with an @ prepended to indicate that they were originally attributes of their parent tag. If an XML node has both a text value and a nested element in it, notice that the key for the text value is "#text", as in the "wb-indicator" element in each "wb-data" element. If an element is repeated, it becomes a list, as the list of wb-data elements in this sample.

Because dictionaries and lists—even nested dictionaries and lists—are fairly easy to deal with in Python, using xmltodict is an effective way to handle most XML. In fact, I've used it for the past several years in production on a variety of XML documents and never had a problem.

> ### Try this: Fetching and parsing XML
> Write the code to pull the XML data for Chile's population from https://mng.bz/Ea6R. Then use xmltodict to parse the XML into a Python dictionary and report how much Chile's population has changed in the past 25 years.

22.4 Scraping web data

In some cases, the data is on a website but for whatever reason isn't available anywhere else. In those situations, it may make sense to collect the data from the web pages themselves through a process called *crawling* or *scraping*.

Before saying anything more about scraping, let me make a disclaimer: scraping or crawling websites that you don't own or control is at best a legal grey area, with a host of inconclusive and contradictory considerations involving things such as the terms of use of the site, the way in which the site is accessed, and the use to which the scraped data is put. Unless you have control of the site you want to scrape, the answer to the question "Is it legal for me to scrape this site?" usually is "It depends."

If you do decide to scrape a production website, you also need to be sensitive to the load you're putting on the site. Although an established, high-traffic site might well be able to handle anything you can throw at it, a smaller, less active site might be brought to a standstill by a series of continuous requests. At the very least, you need to be careful that your scraping doesn't turn into an inadvertent denial-of-service attack.

Conversely, I've worked in situations in which it was actually easier to scrape our own website to get some needed data than it was to go through corporate channels. Although scraping web data has its place, it's too complex for full treatment here. In this section, I present a very simple example to give you a general idea of the basic method and follow up with suggestions to pursue in more complex cases.

Scraping a website consists of two parts: fetching the web page and extracting the data from it. Fetching the page can be done via requests and is fairly simple. Consider the code of a very simple web page with only a little content and no CSS or JavaScript, as the one shown in the following listing.

> **Listing 22.1   File test.html**

```
<!DOCTYPE HTML PUBLIC "-//IETF//DTD HTML//EN">
<html> <head>
<title>Title</title>
</head>

<body>
<h1>Heading 1</h1>

This is plan text, and is boring
<span class="special">this is special</span>

Here is a <a href="http://bitbucket.dev.null">link</a>

<hr>
<address>Ann Address, Somewhere, AState 00000
</address>
</body> </html>
```

Suppose that you're interested in only a couple of kinds of data from this page: anything in an element with a class name of `"special"` and any links. You can process the file by searching for the strings `'class="special"'` and `"<a href>"` and then write code to pick out the data from there, but even using regular expressions, this process will be tedious, bug prone, and hard to maintain. It's much easier to use a library that knows how to parse HTML, such as Beautiful Soup. If you want to try the following code and experiment with parsing HTML pages, you can use `pip install bs4`.

When you have Beautiful Soup installed, parsing a page of HTML is simple. For this example, assume that you've already retrieved the web page (presumably, using the `requests` library), so you'll just parse the HTML.

The first step is to load the text and create a Beautiful Soup parser:

```
import bs4
html = open("test.html").read()
bs = bs4.BeautifulSoup(html, "html.parser")
```

This code is all it takes to parse the HTML into the parser object `bs`. A Beautiful Soup parser object has a lot of cool tricks, and if you're working with HTML at all, it's really worth your time to experiment a bit and get a feel for what it can do for you. For this example, you look at only two things: extracting content by HTML tag and getting data by class.

First, find the link. The HTML tag for a link is `<a>` (Beautiful Soup by default converts all tags to lowercase), so to find all link tags, you can use the `"a"` as a parameter and call the `bs` object itself:

```
a_list = bs("a")
print(a_list)
```

```
[<a href="http://bitbucket.dev.null">link</a>]
```

Now you have a list of all (one in this case) of the HTML link tags. If that list is all you get, that's not so bad, but in fact, the elements returned in the list are also parser objects and can do the rest of the work of getting the link and text for you:

```
a_item = a_list[0]
a_item.text
```

```
'link'
```

```
a_item["href"]
```

```
'http://bitbucket.dev.null'
```

The other feature you're looking for is anything with a class of `"special"`, which you can extract by using the parser's `select` method as follows:

```
special_list = bs.select(".special")
print(special_list)
```

```
[<span class="special">this is special</span>]
```

```
special_item = special_list[0]
special_item.text
```

```
'this is special'
```

```
special_item["class"]
```

```
['special']
```

Because the items returned by the tag or by the `select` method are themselves parser objects, you can nest them, which allows you to extract just about anything from HTML or even XML.

Try this: Parsing HTML

Given the file forecast.html (which you can create in the notebook for this chapter, also shown bin listing 22.2), write a script using Beautiful Soup that extracts the data and saves it as a CSV file.

Listing 22.2   File forecast.html

```
<html>
  <body>
    <div class="row row-forecast">
        <div class="grid col-25 forecast-label"><b>Tonight</b></div>
        <div class="grid col-75 forecast-text">A slight chance of showers
and thunderstorms before 10pm. Mostly cloudy, with a low around 66. West
southwest wind around 9 mph. Chance of precipitation is 20%. New rainfall
```

```
amounts between a tenth and quarter of an inch possible.</div>
    </div>
    <div class="row row-forecast">
        <div class="grid col-25 forecast-label"><b>Friday</b></div>
        <div class="grid col-75 forecast-text">Partly sunny. High near 77,
with temperatures falling to around 75 in the afternoon. Northwest wind 7
to 12 mph, with gusts as high as 18 mph.</div>
    </div>
    <div class="row row-forecast">
        <div class="grid col-25 forecast-label"><b>Friday Night</b></div>
        <div class="grid col-75 forecast-text">Mostly cloudy, with a low
around 63. North wind 7 to 10 mph.</div>
    </div>
    <div class="row row-forecast">
        <div class="grid col-25 forecast-label"><b>Saturday</b></div>
        <div class="grid col-75 forecast-text">Mostly sunny, with a high
near 73. North wind around 10 mph.</div>
    </div>
    <div class="row row-forecast">
        <div class="grid col-25 forecast-label"><b>Saturday Night</b></div>
        <div class="grid col-75 forecast-text">Partly cloudy, with a low
around 63. North wind 5 to 10 mph.</div>
    </div>
    <div class="row row-forecast">
        <div class="grid col-25 forecast-label"><b>Sunday</b></div>
        <div class="grid col-75 forecast-text">Mostly sunny, with a high
near 73.</div>
    </div>
    <div class="row row-forecast">
        <div class="grid col-25 forecast-label"><b>Sunday Night</b></div>
        <div class="grid col-75 forecast-text">Mostly cloudy, with a low
around 64.</div>
    </div>
    <div class="row row-forecast">
        <div class="grid col-25 forecast-label"><b>Monday</b></div>
        <div class="grid col-75 forecast-text">Mostly sunny, with a high
near 74.</div>
    </div>
    <div class="row row-forecast">
        <div class="grid col-25 forecast-label"><b>Monday Night</b></div>
        <div class="grid col-75 forecast-text">Mostly clear, with a low
around 65.</div>
    </div>
    <div class="row row-forecast">
        <div class="grid col-25 forecast-label"><b>Tuesday</b></div>
        <div class="grid col-75 forecast-text">Sunny, with a high near
75.</div>
    </div>
    <div class="row row-forecast">
        <div class="grid col-25 forecast-label"><b>Tuesday Night</b></div>
        <div class="grid col-75 forecast-text">Mostly clear, with a low
around 65.</div>
    </div>
    <div class="row row-forecast">
        <div class="grid col-25 forecast-label"><b>Wednesday</b></div>
```

```
        <div class="grid col-75 forecast-text">Sunny, with a high near
77.</div>
    </div>
    <div class="row row-forecast">
        <div class="grid col-25 forecast-label"><b>Wednesday
Night</b></div>
        <div class="grid col-75 forecast-text">Mostly clear, with a low
around 67.</div>
    </div>
    <div class="row row-forecast">
        <div class="grid col-25 forecast-label"><b>Thursday</b></div>
        <div class="grid col-75 forecast-text">A chance of rain showers
after 1pm. Mostly sunny, with a high near 81. Chance of precipitation is
30%.</div>
    </div>
  </body>
</html>
```

22.5 *Tracking the weather*

Use the API described in section 22.2 to gather a history of the mean temperatures of
a location (you can use Chicago or supply the latitude and longitude for a different
location) for a month. You will need to use a slightly different URL for the archive API:
`"https://archive-api.open-meteo.com/v1/era5?latitude=<`*latitude*`>&longitude
=<`*longitude*`>&start_date=<`*YYYY-MM-DD*`>&end_date=<`*YYYY-MM-DD*`>&daily=
temperature_2m_mean"` like this:

```
"https://archive-api.open-meteo.com/v1/era5?latitude=41.879&longitude
=-87.64975
　&start_date=2024-07-01&end_date=2024-07-31&daily=temperature_2m_mean"
```

Notice that you will get two lists: a list of the dates and a matching list of the mean temperatures in Celsius for those dates. Transform the data so that you can load it into a
spreadsheet and graph it.

22.5.1 *Solving the problem with AI-generated code*

There is no complex design component in this lab. It requires a good knowledge of
accessing an HTTP API and handling the JSON returned. As such, it's something that
AI should be good at.

22.5.2 *Solutions and discussion*

This problem is a matter of retrieving a file from an HTTP server and then processing
the JSON returned to join two parallel lists.

THE HUMAN SOLUTION

This solution takes a simple way through the problem, using the `requests` library to
fetch and process the data and save the processed data to a file:

```
import requests
import csv
response = requests.get("https://archive-api.open-meteo.com/v1/era5?latitude
=41.879&longitude=-87.64975
  &start_date=2024-07-01&end_date=2024-07-31&daily=temperature_2m_mean")
weather_history = response.json()

weather_data = zip(weather_history["daily"]["time"],
   weather_history["daily"]["temperature_2m_mean"])

with open("weather_history.csv", "w", newline="") as file:
    writer = csv.writer(file)
    writer.writerow(["Date", "Temperature"])
    writer.writerows(weather_data)
```

> **The response object 's json() method returns data as JSON.**

> **The zip() function returns an iterator of the combined lists.**

> **The writerows() method writes all rows the from iterator weather_data.**

This solution takes advantage of the fact that `requests` can return the data as JSON, avoiding the need to parse the text into JSON. The two lists are zipped together, and the resulting data is written as a CSV file. One quirk in using `zip()` is that it returns an iterator, not a list. This isn't a problem for the `writerows()` method, but if you want to look at the results, you need to use the `list()` function to turn it into a list.

THE AI SOLUTIONS

The prompt used for Copliot was really simplified from the lab problem, and the field names were specified:

```
The URL https://archive-api.open-meteo.com/v1/era5?latitude=41.879&longitude
=-87.64975&start_date=2024-07-
  01&end_date=2024-07-31&daily=temperature_2m_mean will return one day's
weather data for Chicago in JSON format. The data will contain a "daily"
field with two lists, "time" and "temperature_2m_mean". Download the data
and save the time and temperature_2m_mean fields into a CSV file that can
later be loaded into a spreadsheet and graphed.
```

This prompt was created to avoid confusion on field names and to remove any nonessential information. The resulting code was quite useful:

```
import requests
import csv

# URL to fetch the weather data
url = "https://archive-api.open-meteo.com/v1/era5?latitude=41.879&longitude=
-87.64975&start_date=2024-07-01
  &end_date=2024-07-31&daily=temperature_2m_mean"

# Fetch the data
response = requests.get(url)
data = response.json()

# Extract the relevant fields
time_data = data['daily']['time']
temperature_data = data['daily']['temperature_2m_mean']
```

```
# Output CSV file
output_file = 'Chicago_weather_July_2024.csv'

# Write the data to the CSV file
with open(output_file, 'w', newline='') as csvfile:
    writer = csv.writer(csvfile)
    writer.writerow(['Date', 'Temperature (°C)'])  # Write the header
    for time, temperature in zip(time_data, temperature_data):
        writer.writerow([time, temperature])
```

This code is fine and works as specified with no changes. It even iterates over the data to write the CSV file, while the human version processes the whole batch of data into a list that is written in one operation. Since the number of elements is known in this case, the memory-saving precaution isn't really needed, but it's interesting to see it. One that is a bit superfluous is the use of the zip() function to combine the two lists. While this is needed in my version to create a list of the data pairs, in this case, the pairs are manually joined into a list as each row is written, so they could have been read from the two lists directly. I would say that zipping them does make the code a bit more natural in Python. Otherwise, it's very much like my version and works well as is.

Colaboratory was given the same prompt:

```
The URL https://archive-api.open-meteo.com/v1/era5?latitude=41.879
⟿ &longitude=-87.64975&start_date=2024-07-01
⟿ &end_date=2024-07-31&daily=temperature_2m_mean will return one day's
weather data for Chicago in JSON format. The data will contain a "daily"
field with two lists, "time" and "temperature_2m_mean". Download the data
and save the time and temperature_2m_mean fields into a CSV file that can
later be loaded into a spreadsheet and graphed.
```

This prompt worked well for Colaboratory as well, although it took a somewhat different approach:

```
import csv
import requests

def download_and_save_chicago_weather():
  """Downloads Chicago weather data and saves it to a CSV file."""

  url = "https://archive-api.open-meteo.com/v1/era5?latitude=41.879&longitude
=-87.64975
⟿ &start_date=2024-07-01&end_date=2024-07-31&daily=temperature_2m_mean"
  response = requests.get(url)
  if response.status_code == 200:
    weather_data = response.json()

    if "daily" in weather_data:
      daily_data = weather_data["daily"]
      if "time" in daily_data and "temperature_2m_mean" in daily_data:
        with open('chicago_weather_july.csv', 'w', newline='') as outfile:
          writer = csv.writer(outfile)
          writer.writerow(['Date', 'Mean Temperature (°C)'])
```

```
# Write header row
        for i in range(len(daily_data["time"])):
            writer.writerow([daily_data["time"][i], daily_
    data["temperature_2m_mean"][i]])
        print("Chicago weather data for July 2024 saved to
chicago_weather_july.csv")
    else:
        print("Error: 'time' or 'temperature_2m_mean' not found
in daily data.")
  else:
    print("Error: 'daily' field not found in weather data.")
  else:
    print("Error downloading data:", response.status_code)


download_and_save_chicago_weather()
```

First, this code has the actual functionality in a function, `download_and_save_chicago_weather()`, which is a nice touch. There isn't much difference in the way the data is retrieved, but there is a fair bit of error checking. This is nice to have, particularly when it's generated with no additional programmer effort, but it's not particularly Pythonic. Instead of using `if` statements and the `print` function, it would have been more idiomatic to use exceptions, most commonly a `KeyError` for the cases where a field didn't exist in the data and possibly some form of `OSError` for a failure to download the data (although probably an error will be raised by the `requests` library before the code gets that far).

Second, this code doesn't `zip()` the two lists together but instead uses a `for` loop based on the length of the lists to get both the data and the mean temperature and write them directly to the CSV file. This is perfectly effective, but it does have a sort of un-Pythonic feel about it, at least to me.

But the bottom line is that with a fairly simple task like this and a very streamlined prompt, Colaboratory as well as Copilot produced code that was usable without changes.

Summary

- Python has the FTP client in the `ftplib` library to fetch data over the network via FTP.
- The `parameiko` library can be used to fetch files via SFTP.
- Using a Python script may not be the best choice for fetching files. Be sure to consider options like curl and wget from the command line.
- Using the `requests` module is your best bet for fetching files by using HTTP/HTTPS and Python.
- Fetching files from an API using `requests` is very similar to fetching static files.
- Parameters for API requests often need to be quoted and added as a query string to the request URL.
- The most common structured format used for serving data is JSON.

- XML is a more complex data format for serving data and is still also used.
- Using a library like Beautiful Soup, you can get data by scraping a website and parsing the HTML.
- Scraping sites that you don't control may not be legal or ethical and requires consideration not to overload the server.

23
Saving data

This chapter covers

- Storing data in relational databases
- Using the Python DB-API
- Accessing databases through an object relational mapper
- Understanding NoSQL databases and how they differ from relational databases

When you have data and have it cleaned, it's likely that you'll want to store it. You'll not only want to store it but also be able to get at it in the future with as little hassle as possible. The need to store and retrieve significant amounts of data usually calls for some sort of database. Relational databases such as PostgreSQL, MySQL, and SQL Server have been established favorites for data storage for decades, and they can still be great options for many use cases. In recent years, NoSQL databases, including MongoDB and Redis (and their various cloud-based relatives), have found favor and can be very useful for a variety of use cases. A detailed discussion of databases would take several books, so in this chapter I look at some scenarios to show how you can access both SQL and NoSQL databases with Python.

23.1 *Relational databases*

Relational databases have long been a standard for storing and manipulating data. They're a mature technology and a ubiquitous one. Python can connect with a number of relational databases, but I don't have the space or the inclination to go through the specifics of each one in this book. Instead, because Python handles databases in a mostly consistent way, I illustrate the basics with one of them—`sqlite3`—and then discuss some differences and considerations in choosing and using a relational database for data storage.

23.1.1 *The Python database API*

As I mentioned, Python handles SQL database access very similarly across several database implementations because of PEP-249 (www.python.org/dev/peps/pep-0249/), which specifies some common practices for connecting to SQL databases. Commonly called the Database API or DB-API, it was created to encourage "code that is generally more portable across databases, and a broader reach of database connectivity." Thanks to the DB-API, the examples of SQLite that you see in this chapter are quite similar to what you'd use for PostgreSQL, MySQL, or several other databases.

23.2 *SQLite: Using the sqlite3 database*

Although Python has modules for many databases, in the following examples I look at `sqlite3`. Although it's not suited for large, high-traffic applications, `sqlite3` has two advantages:

- Because it's part of the standard library, it can be used anywhere you need a database without worrying about adding dependencies.
- `sqlite3` stores all of its records in a local file, so it doesn't need a separate server, which would be the case for PostgreSQL, MySQL, and other larger databases.

These features make `sqlite3` a handy option for both smaller applications and quick prototypes.

To use an `sqlite3` database, the first thing you need is a `Connection` object. Getting a `Connection` object requires calling the `connect` function with the name of the file that will be used to store the data:

```
import sqlite3
conn = sqlite3.connect("datafile.db")
```

It's also possible to hold the data in memory by using `":memory:"` as the filename. For storing Python integers, strings, and floats, nothing more is needed. If you want `sqlite3` to automatically convert query results for some columns into other types, it's useful to include the `detect_types` parameter set to `sqlite3.PARSE_DECLTYPES` `|sqlite3.PARSE_COLNAMES`, which directs the `Connection` object to parse the names and types of columns in queries and attempts to match them with converters you've already defined.

The second step is creating a `Cursor` object from the connection:

```
cursor = conn.cursor()
cursor
```

`<sqlite3.Cursor object at 0xb7a12980>`

At this point, you're able to make queries against the database. In the current situation, because the database has no tables or records yet, you first need to create a table and insert a couple of records:

```
cursor.execute("create table people (id integer primary key, name text,
   count integer)")
cursor.execute("insert into people (name, count) values ('Bob', 1)")
cursor.execute("insert into people (name, count) values (?, ?)",
               ("Jill", 15))
conn.commit()
```

The last `insert` query illustrates the preferred way to make a query with variables. Rather than constructing the query string, it's more secure to use a `?` for each variable and then pass the variables as a tuple parameter to the `execute` method. The advantage is that you don't need to worry about incorrectly escaping a value; `sqlite3` takes care of it for you.

You can also use variable names prefixed with `:` in the query and pass in a corresponding dictionary with the values to be inserted:

```
cursor.execute("insert into people (name, count) values (:username, "
               " :usercount)", {"username": "Joe", "usercount": 10})
```
`<sqlite3.Cursor at 0x7ceda4437ac0>`

After a table is populated, you can query the data by using SQL commands, again using either `?` for variable binding or names and dictionaries:

```
result = cursor.execute("select * from people")
print(result.fetchall())
```

`[(1, 'Bob', 1), (2, 'Jill', 15), (3, 'Joe', 10)]`

```
result = cursor.execute("select * from people where name like :name",
                        {"name": "bob"})
print(result.fetchall())
```

`[(1, 'Bob', 1)]`

```
cursor.execute("update people set count=? where name=?", (20, "Jill"))
result = cursor.execute("select * from people")
print(result.fetchall())
```

`[(1, 'Bob', 1), (2, 'Jill', 20), (3, 'Joe', 10)]`

In addition to the `fetchall` method, the `fetchone` method gets one row of the result, and `fetchmany` returns an arbitrary number of rows. For convenience, it's also possible to iterate over a cursor object's rows similarly to iterating over a file:

```
result = cursor.execute("select * from people")
for row in result:
    print(row)

(1, 'Bob', 1)
(2, 'Jill', 20)
(3, 'Joe', 10)
```

Finally, by default, `sqlite3` doesn't immediately commit transactions. This fact means that you have the option of rolling back a transaction if it fails, but it also means that you need to use the `Connection` object's `commit` method to ensure that any changes made have been saved. Doing so before you close a connection to a database is a particularly good idea because the `close` method doesn't automatically commit any active transactions:

```
cursor.execute("update people set count=? where name=?", (20, "Jill"))
conn.commit()
conn.close()
```

Table 23.1 gives an overview of the most common operations on an `sqlite3` database.

Table 23.1 Common `sqlite3` database operations

Operation	`sqlite3` command
Create a connection to a database	`conn = sqlite3.connect(filename)`
Create a cursor for a connection	`Cursor = conn.cursor()`
Execute a query with the cursor	`cursor.execute(query)`
Return the results of a query	`cursor.fetchall()`, `cursor.fetchmany(num_rows)`, `cursor.fetchone()`
	`for row in cursor:`
	`....`
Commit a transaction to a database	`conn.commit()`
Close a connection	`conn.close()`

These operations usually are all you need to manipulate an `sqlite3` database. Of course, several options let you control their precise behavior; see the Python documentation for more information.

Try this: Creating and modifying tables

Using `sqlite3`, write the code that creates a database table for the Illinois weather data you loaded from a flat file in section 22.2. Suppose that you have similar data for more states and want to store more information about the states themselves. How could you modify your database to use a related table to store the state information?

23.3 Using MySQL, PostgreSQL, and other relational databases

As I mentioned earlier in this chapter, several other SQL databases have client libraries that follow the DB-API. As a result, accessing those databases in Python is quite similar, but there are a couple of differences to look out for:

- Unlike SQLite, those databases require a database server that the client connects to and that may or may not be on a different machine, so the connection requires more parameters—usually including host, account name, and password.

- The way in which parameters are interpolated into queries, such as `"select * from test where name like :name"`, could use a different format—something like `?, %s 5(name)s`.

These changes aren't huge, but they tend to keep code from being completely portable across different databases.

23.4 Making database handling easier with an object relational mapper

There are a few problems with the DB-API database client libraries mentioned earlier in this chapter and their requirement to write raw SQL:

- Different SQL databases have implemented SQL in subtly different ways, so the same SQL statements won't always work if you move from one database to another, as you might want to do if, say, you do local development against `sqlite3` and then want to use MySQL or PostgreSQL in production. Also, as mentioned earlier, the different implementations have different ways of doing things like passing parameters into queries.

- The second drawback is the need to use raw SQL statements. Including SQL statements in your code can make your code more difficult to maintain, particularly if you have a lot of them. In that case, some of the statements will be boilerplate and routine; others will be complex and tricky; and all of them need to be tested, which can get cumbersome.

- The need to write SQL means that you need to think in at least two languages: Python and a specific SQL variant. In plenty of cases, it's worth these hassles to use raw SQL, but in many other cases, it isn't.

Given these factors, people wanted a way to handle databases in Python that was easier to manage and didn't require anything more than writing regular Python code. The solution is an object relational mapper (ORM), which converts, or maps, relational database types and structures to objects in Python. Two of the most common ORMs in the Python world are the Django ORM and SQLAlchemy, although of course there are many others. The Django ORM is rather tightly integrated with the Django web framework and usually isn't used outside it. Because I'm not delving into Django in this book, I won't discuss the Django ORM other than to note that it's the default choice for Django applications and a good one, with fully developed tools and generous community support.

23.4.1 *SQLAlchemy*

SQLAlchemy is the other big-name ORM in the Python space. SQLAlchemy's goal is to automate redundant database tasks and provide Python object-based interfaces to the data while still allowing the developer control of the database and access to the underlying SQL. In this section, I look at some basic examples of storing data into a relational database and then retrieving it with SQLAlchemy.

SQLAchemy is already available in Colaboratory, but if you are using a different environment, you can install SQLAlchemy in your environment with `pip`:

```
pip install sqlalchemy
```

SQLAlchemy offers several ways to interact with the database and its tables. Although an ORM lets you write SQL statements if you want or need to, the strength of an ORM is doing what the name suggests: mapping the relational database tables and columns to Python objects.

We can use SQLAlchemy to replicate what you did in section 23.2: create a table, add three rows, query the table, and update one row. You need to do a bit more setup to use the ORM, but in larger projects, this effort is more than worth it.

First, you import the components you need to connect to the database and map a table to Python objects:

```
from sqlalchemy import (create_engine, select, MetaData, Table, Column,
                        Integer, String)
from sqlalchemy.orm import sessionmaker
```

From the base `sqlalchemy` package, you need the `create_engine` and `select` methods and the `MetaData` and `Table` classes. But because you need to specify the schema information when you create the `table` object, you also need to import the `Column` class and the classes for the data type of each column—in this case, `Integer` and `String`. From the `sqlalchemy.orm` subpackage, you also need the `sessionmaker` function.

Now you can think about connecting to the database:

```
dbPath = 'datafile2.db'
engine = create_engine('sqlite:///%s' % dbPath)          ◀────┘  Creates engine object
metadata = MetaData()
people  = Table('people', metadata,                      ◀────┘  Creates people table object
                Column('id', Integer, primary_key=True),
                Column('name', String),
```

```
                    Column('count', Integer),
                )
Session = sessionmaker(bind=engine)          ◄──── Creates a session
session = Session()
metadata.create_all(engine)                  ◄──── Creates table in database
```

To create and connect, you need to create a database engine appropriate for your database; then you need a `MetaData` object, which is a container for managing tables and their schemas. Create a `Table` object called `people`, giving the table's name in the database, the `MetaData` object you just created, and the column you want to create, as well as their data types. Finally, use the `sessionmaker` function to create a `Session` class for your engine and use that class to instantiate a session object. At this point, you're connected to the database, and the last step is to use the `create_all` method to create the table.

When the table is created, the next step is inserting some records. Again, you have many options for doing this in SQLAlchemy, but you'll be fairly explicit in this example. Create an `insert` object, which you then execute:

```
people_ins = people.insert().values(name='Bob', count=1)
str(people_ins)
```

```
'INSERT INTO people (name, count) VALUES (?, ?)'
```

```
session.execute(people_ins)
```

```
<sqlalchemy.engine.result.ResultProxy object at 0x7f126c6dd438>
```

```
session.commit()
```

Here you use the `insert()` method to create an `insert` query object, also specifying the fields and values you want to insert. `people_ins` is the `insert` object, and you use the `str()` function to show that, behind the scenes, you created the correct SQL `INSERT` command. Then you use the session object's `execute` method to perform the insertion and the `commit` method to commit it to the database (remember that you must call `commit` to have the changes saved to the database):

```
session.execute(people_ins, [
    {'name': 'Jill', 'count':15},
    {'name': 'Joe', 'count':10}
])
```

```
<sqlalchemy.engine.result.ResultProxy object at 0x7f126c6dd908>
```

We could have inserted just one record, but to streamline things a bit we passed in a list of dictionaries of the field names and values for each insert to perform multiple inserts. If we then select the contents of the `people` table, we can see that we added two new records:

```
session.commit()
result = session.execute(select(people))
for row in result:
    print(row)
```

```
(1, 'Bob', 1)
(2, 'Jill', 15)
(3, 'Joe', 10)
```

We can do select operations a bit more directly by instead using the `select()` method with a `where()` method to find a particular record:

```
result = session.execute(select(people).where(people.c.name == 'Jill'))
for row in result:
    print(row)
```

```
(2, 'Jill', 15)
```

In the example, we were looking for any records in which the `name` column equals `'Jill'`. Note that the `where` expression uses `people.c.name`, with the `c` indicating that `name` is a *column* in the `people` table.

Finally, there is also an `update()` method we can use to change a value in the database:

```
result = session.execute(people.update().values(count=20).where
(people.c.name == 'Jill'))
session.commit()
result = session.execute(select(people).where(people.c.name == 'Jill'))
for row in result:
    print(row)
```

```
(2, 'Jill', 20)
```

To perform an update, we need to combine the `update()` method with a `values()` method that specifies what to update and a `where()` method to specify the row that update affects.

MAPPING TABLE OBJECTS TO CLASSES

So far, we've used table objects directly, but it's also possible to use SQLAlchemy to map a table directly to a class. This technique has the advantage that the columns are mapped directly to class attributes; for illustration, to make a class `People`:

```
from sqlalchemy.orm import declarative_base
Base = declarative_base()
class People(Base):
    __tablename__ = "people"
    id = Column(Integer, primary_key=True)
    name = Column(String)
    count = Column(Integer)

results = session.query(People).filter_by(name='Jill')
for person in results:
    print(person.id, person.name, person.count)
```

```
2 Jill 20
```

Inserts can be done just by creating an instance of the mapped class and adding it to the session:

```
new_person = People(name='Jane', count=5)
session.add(new_person)
session.commit()
results = session.query(People).all()
for person in results:
    print(person.id, person.name, person.count)
```

```
1 Bob 1
2 Jill 20
3 Joe 10
4 Jane 5
```

Updates are also fairly straightforward. You retrieve the record you want to update, change the values on the mapped instance, and then add the updated record to the session to be written back to the database:

```
jill = session.query(People).filter_by(name='Jill').first()
jill.name
```

```
'Jill'
```

```
jill.count = 22
session.add(jill)
session.commit()
results = session.query(People).all()
for person in results:
    print(person.id, person.name, person.count)
```

```
1 Bob 1
2 Jill 22
3 Joe 10
4 Jane 5
```

Deleting is similar to updating; you fetch the record to be deleted and then use the session's `delete()` method to delete it:

```
jane = session.query(People).filter_by(name='Jane').first()
session.delete(jane)
session.commit()
jane = session.query(People).filter_by(name='Jane').first()
print(jane)
```

```
None
```

Using SQLAlchemy does take a bit more setup than just using raw SQL, but it also has some real benefits. For one thing, using the ORM means that you don't need to worry about any subtle differences in the SQL supported by different databases. The example works equally well with `sqlite3`, MySQL, and PostgreSQL without making any changes in the code other than giving the string to the `create_engine` and making sure that the correct database driver is available.

Another advantage is that the interaction with the data can happen through Python objects, which may be more accessible to coders who lack SQL experience. Instead of constructing SQL statements, they can use Python objects and methods.

> **Try this: Using an ORM**
>
> Using the database from earlier, write an SQLAlchemy class to map to the data table and use it to read the records from the table.

23.4.2 *Using Alembic for database schema changes*

In the course of developing code that uses a relational database, it's quite common, if not universal, to have to change the structure or schema of the database after you've started work. Fields need to be added, or their types need to be changed, and so on. It's possible, of course, to manually make the changes to both the database tables and to the code for the ORM that accesses them, but that approach has some drawbacks. For one thing, such changes are difficult to roll back if you need to, and it's hard to keep track of the configuration of the database that goes with a particular version of your code.

The solution is to use a database migration tool to help you make the changes and track them. Migrations are written as code and should include code both to apply the needed changes and to reverse them. Then the changes can be tracked and applied or reversed in the correct sequence. As a result, you can reliably upgrade or downgrade your database to any of the states it was in over the course of development.

As an example, this section looks briefly at Alembic, a popular lightweight migration tool for SQLAlchemy. To start, switch to the system command-line window in your project directory, install Alembic, and create a generic environment by using `alemic init`:

```
! pip install alembic
! alembic init alembic
```

This code creates the file structure you need to use Alembic for data migrations. There's an alembic.ini file that you need to edit in at least one place. The `squalchemy .url` line needs to be updated to match your current situation. In the Colaboratory notebook, there is a cell that will do this if you execute it, but in other environments, you can use a text editor and find the following line:

```
sqlalchemy.url = driver://user:pass@localhost/dbname
```

Change the line to

```
sqlalchemy.url = sqlite:///datafile.db
```

Because you're using a local sqlite file, you don't need a username or password.

The next step is creating a revision by using Alembic's revision command:

```
! alembic revision -m "create an address table"
Generating /home/naomi/qpb_testing/alembic/versions/384ead9efdfd_create_a_
test_address
➥_table.py ... done
```

The revision ID in the
filename will be different.

This code creates a revision script, 384ead9efdfd_create_a_test_address_table.py, in the alembic/versions directory. This file looks like this:

```
"""create an address table

Revision ID: 384ead9efdfd
Revises:
Create Date: 2017-07-26 21:03:29.042762

"""
from alembic import op
import sqlalchemy as sa


# revision identifiers, used by Alembic.
revision = '384ead9efdfd'
down_revision = None
branch_labels = None
depends_on = None


def upgrade():
    pass


def downgrade():
    Pass
```

The revision ID in the
filename will be different.

You can see that the file contains the revision ID and date in the header. It also contains a down_revision variable to guide the rollback of each version. If you make a second revision, its down_revision variable should contain this revision's ID.

To perform the revision, we need to update the revision script to supply both the code describing how to perform the revision in the upgrade() method and the code to reverse it in the downgrade() method (this is done in a cell in the notebook):

```
def upgrade():
    op.create_table(
        'address',
        sa.Column('id', sa.Integer, primary_key=True),
        sa.Column('address', sa.String(50), nullable=False),
        sa.Column('city', sa.String(50), nullable=False),
        sa.Column('state', sa.String(20), nullable=False),
```

```
    )

def downgrade():
    op.drop_table('address')
```

When this code is created, you can apply the upgrade. But first, switch back to the Python shell window to see what tables you have in your database:

```
for table in metadata.sorted_tables:
    print(table.name)

people
```

As you might expect, you have only the one table you created earlier. Now you can run Alembic's `upgrade` command to apply the upgrade and add a new table. Switch over to your system command line and run

```
! alembic upgrade head
INFO  [alembic.runtime.migration] Context impl SQLiteImpl.
INFO  [alembic.runtime.migration] Will assume non-transactional DDL.
INFO  [alembic.runtime.migration] Running upgrade  -> 384ead9efdfd,
create an address table
```

If you pop back to Python and check, you see that the database has two additional tables:

```
for table in metadata.sorted_tables:
    print(table.name)

['alembic_version', 'people', 'address'
```

The first new table, `'alembic version'`, is created by Alembic to help track which version your database is currently on (for reference for future upgrades and downgrades). The second new table, `'address'`, is the table you added through your upgrade and is ready to use.

If you want to roll back the state of the database to what it was before, all you need to do is run Alembic's `downgrade` command in the system window. You give the downgrade command `-1` to tell Alembic that you want to downgrade by one version:

```
! alembic downgrade -1
INFO  [alembic.runtime.migration] Context impl SQLiteImpl.
INFO  [alembic.runtime.migration] Will assume non-transactional DDL.
INFO  [alembic.runtime.migration] Running downgrade 384ead9efdfd -> , create
an address table
```

Now if you check in your Python session, you'll be back to where you started:

```
for table in metadata.sorted_tables:
    print(table.name)
people
```

If you want to, of course, you can run the upgrade again to put the table back, add further revisions, make upgrades, and so on.

> **Try this: Modifying a database with Alembic**
>
> Experiment with creating an Alembic upgrade that adds a state table to your database, with columns for ID, state name, and abbreviation. Upgrade and downgrade. What other changes would be needed if you were going to use the state table along with the existing data table?

23.5   *NoSQL databases*

In spite of their longstanding popularity, relational databases aren't the only ways to think about storing data. Although relational databases are all about normalizing data within related tables, other approaches look at data differently. Quite commonly, these types of databases are referred to as *NoSQL* databases, because they usually don't adhere to the row/column/table structure that SQL was created to describe.

Rather than handle data as collections of rows, columns, and tables, NoSQL databases can look at the data they store as key-value pairs, as indexed documents, and even as graphs. Many NoSQL databases are available, all with somewhat different ways of handling data. In general, they're less likely to be strictly normalized, which can make retrieving information faster and easier. As examples, in this chapter I look at using Python to access two common NoSQL databases: Redis and MongoDB. What follows barely scratches the surface of what you can do with NoSQL databases and Python, but it should give you a basic idea of the possibilities. If you're already familiar with Redis or MongoDB, you'll see a little of how the Python client libraries operate, and if you're new to NoSQL databases, you'll at least get an idea of how databases like these work.

Keep in mind that Redis and MongoDB are only two examples of NoSQL databases, chosen to serve as examples. As cloud services have proliferated over the past several years, many other options have arisen, each with particular strengths and weaknesses.

23.6   *Key-value stores with Redis*

Redis is an in-memory networked key-value store. Because the values are in memory, lookups can be quite fast, and the fact that it's designed to be accessed over the network makes it useful in a variety of situations. Redis is commonly used for caching, as a message broker, and for quick lookups of information. In fact, the name (which comes from Remote Dictionary Server) is an excellent way to think of it; it behaves much like a Python dictionary translated to a network service.

The following example gives you an idea of how Redis works with Python. If you're familiar with the Redis command-line interface or have used a Redis client for another language, these short examples should get you well on your way to using Redis with Python. If Redis is new to you, the following gives you an idea of how it works; you can explore more at https://redis.io.

Although several Python clients are available for Redis, at this writing the way to go (according to the Redis website) is one called redis-py. You can install it with `pip install redis`.

> ## Running a Redis server
>
> To experiment, you need to have access to a running Redis server. Depending on how much control you want (and how much work you want to do), you have some options.
>
> Perhaps the easiest option for experimentation is to use a cloud-based Redis server hosted on Redis with a free account. This has the advantage that you don't need to install or maintain a server. A free account is available at https://redis.io/try-free/. This is the recommended option for most readers.
>
> If you have Docker installed, using the Redis Docker instance should also be a quick and easy way to get a server up and running. You should be able to launch a Redis instance from the command line with a command like `docker run -p 6379:6379 redis`.
>
> On Linux systems, you could also install Redis by using the system package manager, and on Mac systems, `brew install redis` should work. On Windows systems, you should check the https://redis.io website or search online for the current options for running Redis on Windows. When Redis is installed, you may need to look online for instructions to make sure that the Redis server is running.

Once you are connected to a server, the following are examples of simple Redis interactions with Python. First, you need to import the Redis library and create a Redis connection object:

```
import redis

r = redis.Redis(
  # set your host address below
  host='',
  port=10032,
  # set your password below
  password='')
```

You can use several connection options when creating a Redis connection, including the host, port, and password or SSH certificate. If the server is running on localhost on the default port of 6379, no options are needed. When you have the connection, you can use it to access the key-value store.

One of the first things you might do is use the `keys()` method to get a list of the keys in the database, which returns a list of keys currently stored (if any). Then you can set some keys of different types and try some ways to retrieve their values:

```
r.keys()
```
                         | Empty because no
[]   ◄────────┘ keys are set yet

```
r.set('a_key', 'my value')
```

True   ◄────┐ **Returns True if**
                 │ **operation successful**

```
r.keys()
```

[b'a_key']

```
v = r.get('a_key')
v
```

b'my value'

```
r.incr('counter')
```

1

```
r.get('counter')
```

b'1'

```
r.incr('counter')
```

2

```
r.get('counter')
```

b'2'

These examples show how you can get a list of the keys in the Redis database, how to set a key with a value, and how to set a key with a `counter` variable and increment it. Note that the first time we list the keys we get an empty list, since no keys have been set. When we set a key, we get a return value of `True` if the operation succeeded. With integer values, we can use the `incr` method to add 1 to the current value of a key (or start with the value of 1, if the key doesn't exist).

The following examples deal with storing arrays or lists:

```
r.rpush("words", "one")
```

1   ◄────┐ **Operation returns**
              │ **new length of array**

```
r.rpush("words", "two")
```

2   ◄────┤

```
r.lrange("words", 0, -1)
```

[b'one', b'two']

```
r.rpush("words", "three")
```

3   ◄────┘

```
r.lrange("words", 0, -1)
```

[b'one', b'two', b'three']

```
r.llen("words")
```

3

```
r.lpush("words", "zero")
```

4

```
r.lrange("words", 0, -1)
```

[b'zero', b'one', b'two', b'three']

```
r.lrange("words", 2, 2)
```

[b'two']

```
r.lindex("words", 1)
```

b'one'

```
r.lindex("words", 2)
```

b'two'

When you start the key, `"words"` isn't in the database, but the act of adding or pushing a value to the end (from the right, the r in rpush) creates the key, makes an empty list as its value, and then appends the value `'one'`. The return value is 1, the new length of the array. Using rpush again adds another word to the end, and returns the new length, 2. To retrieve the values in the list, you can use the lrange() function, giving the key both a starting index and an ending index, with -1 indicating the end of the list.

Also note that you can add to the beginning, or left side, of the list with lpush(). You can use lindex() to retrieve a single value in the same way as lranger(), except that you give it the index of the value you want.

One feature of Redis that makes it particularly useful for caching is the ability to set an expiration for a key-value pair. After that time has elapsed, the key and value are removed. This technique is particularly useful for using Redis as a cache. You can set the timeout value in seconds when you set the value for a key:

```
r.setex("timed", 10,  "10 seconds")
```

True

```
r.pttl("timed")
```

5208

```
r.pttl("timed")
```

```
-2
```

```
r.pttl("timed")
```

```
b"timed" in r.keys()
```

False

In this case, you set the expiration of "timed" by giving the number of seconds (10) as the first parameter after the key. Then, as you use the pttl() method, you can see the time remaining before expiration in milliseconds. When the value expires, the expiration is returned as -2, and both the key and value are automatically removed from the database, shown by checking for b"timed" in r.keys(). This feature and the fine-grained control of it that Redis offers are really useful. For simple caches, you may not need to write much more code to have your problem solved.

It's worth noting that Redis holds its data in memory, so keep in mind that the data isn't persistent; if the server crashes, some data is likely to be lost. To mitigate the possibility of data loss, Redis has options to manage persistence—everything from writing every change to disk as it occurs to making periodic snapshots at predetermined times to not saving to disk at all. You can also use the Python client's save() and bgsave() methods to programmatically force a snapshot to be saved, either blocking until the save is complete with save() or saving in the background in the case of bgsave().

In this chapter, I've only touched on a small part of what Redis can do, as well as its data types and the ways it can manipulate them. If you're interested in finding out more, several sources of documentation are available online, including at https://redislabs .com and https://redis-py.readthedocs.io.

> ### Quick check: Uses of key-value stores
> What sorts of data and applications would benefit most from a key-value store like Redis?

23.7 *Documents in MongoDB*

Another popular NoSQL database is MongoDB, which is sometimes called a document-based database because it isn't organized in rows and columns but instead stores documents. MongoDB is designed to scale across many nodes in multiple clusters while potentially handling billions of documents. In the case of MongoDB, a document is stored in a format called BSON (binary JSON), so a document consists of key-value pairs and looks like a JSON object or Python dictionary. The following examples give you a taste of how you can use Python to interact with MongoDB collections and documents, but a word of warning is appropriate. In situations requiring scale and distribution of data, high insert rates, complex and unstable schemas, and so on, MongoDB is an excellent choice. However, MongoDB isn't the best choice in many situations, so be sure to investigate your needs and options thoroughly before choosing.

Running a MongoDB server

As with Redis, if you want to experiment with MongoDB, you need to have access to a MongoDB server. Again, the simplest and easiest option is to create a free account and instance on MongoDB.com by accessing https://account.mongodb.com/account/register. Once you have created a free account, you can create a free Mongo Atlas cluster for experimentation. Again, this is the recommended option for most readers, but if you don't feel the need to experiment with MongoDB, you can just read the following section.

Hint: Be sure to save the username, password, and the connection string shown when creating your cluster. If you find that your operations are all timing out, you might need to visit the Network Access option in the Security section of the control panel and "Allow Access from Anywhere," if simply allowing your current IP address doesn't work.

As is the case with Redis, if you want to run MongoDB locally, the easiest solution is to run a Docker instance. All you need to do if you have Docker is enter > `docker run -p 27017:27017 mongo` at the command line. On a Linux system, your package manager should also be able to intall MongoDB locally and the Mac's `brew install mongodb` will do it. On Windows systems, check on www.mongodb.com/ for the Windows version and installation instructions. As with Redis, search online for any instructions on how to configure and start the server.

As is the case with Redis, several Python client libraries connect to MongoDB databases. To give you an idea of how they work, look at `pymongo`. The first step in using `pymongo` is installing it, which you can do with `pip`:

```
! pip install pymongo
```

When you have `pymongo` installed, you can connect to a MongoDB server by creating an instance of MongoClient and specifying the usual connection details:

```
from pymongo import MongoClient
client = MongoClient(host='*** connection string here ***')
```

Using the connection string given when you created your instance

When you created your cluster, you had to create a username and password, and you were also shown a connection string that used them. If you saved that connection string, you can use it to connect. If you need to find the connection string, in the cluster control panel click the Connect button, then choose the Drivers option; make sure that the Driver is set to Python, and then under step 3, you will see your connection string with your username, but you will need to add the password manually.

MongoDB is organized in terms of a database that contains collections, each of which can contain documents. Databases and collections don't need to be created before you try to access them, however. If they don't exist, they're created as you insert into them, or they simply return no results if you try to retrieve records from them.

To test the client, make a sample document, which can be a Python dictionary:

```
import datetime
a_document = {'name': 'Jane',
              'age': 34,
              'interests': ['Python', 'databases', 'statistics'],
              'date_added': datetime.datetime.now()
}
db = client.my_data
collection = db.docs
result = collection.find_one()
db.list_collection_names()
[]
```

Selects a database (which hasn't been created yet)

Selects a collection in the database (also not yet created)

Searches for first item; no exception even if neither collection nor database exists yet

Here, you connect to a database called my_data and a collection of documents, docs. In this case, they don't exist, but they'll be created as you access them. Note that no exceptions were raised even though the database and collection didn't exist. When you asked for a list of the collections, however, you got an empty list because nothing has been stored in your collection. To store a document, use the collection's insert() method, which returns the document's unique ObjectId if the operation is successful:

```
collection.insert(a_document)

InsertOneResult(ObjectId('66dfb0c090d33ea950f087e1'),
                acknowledged=True)
db.list_collection_names()

['docs']
```

Unique ObjectId

Now that you've stored a document in the docs collection, it shows up when you ask for the collection names in your database. When the document is stored in the collection, you can query for it, update it, replace it, and delete it:

```
collection.find_one()
{'_id': ObjectId('66dfb0c090d33ea950f087e1'),
 'name': 'Jane',
 'age': 34,
 'interests': ['Python', 'databases', 'statistics'],
 'date_added': datetime.datetime(2024, 9, 10, 2, 36, 48, 617000)}
```

Retrieves first record

The first step is to retrieve the first record with the find_one() method:

```
from bson.objectid import ObjectId
collection.find_one({"_id":
            ObjectId('66dfb0c090d33ea950f087e1')})
```
◄— **Retrieves record matching specification—in this case, ObjectId**

```
{'_id': ObjectId('66dfb0c090d33ea950f087e1'),
 'name': 'Jane',
 'age': 34,
 'interests': ['Python', 'databases', 'statistics'],
 'date_added': datetime.datetime(2024, 9, 10, 2, 36, 48, 617000)}
```

We can also fetch a record by its `ObjectId`, but to do that we first need to import the `ObjectId` class from `bson.objectid`. Using the `ObjectId`, we can also update a specific record:

Updates record according to contents of $set object

```
collection.update_one({"_id":ObjectId('66dfb0c090d33ea950f087e1')},
                {"$set": {"name":"Ann"}})
```
◄—

```
UpdateResult({'n': 1, 'electionId': ObjectId('7fffffff00000000000002b7'),
 'opTime': {'ts': Timestamp(1725936314, 21), 't': 695}, 'nModified': 1,
 'ok': 1.0, '$clusterTime': {'clusterTime': Timestamp(1725936314, 21),
 'signature': {'hash':
b'\xd7F*\xb8?\xa3a\x87\xd9W\x92\xc4\x17\x7f*\xf8\xbe?\x07\xc2\x07', 'keyId':
7368510527980437523}}, 'operationTime': Timestamp(1725936314, 21),
 'updatedExisting': True}, acknowledged=True)
```

```
collection.find_one({"_id":ObjectId('66dfb0c090d33ea950f087e1')})
```

```
{'_id': ObjectId('66dfb0c090d33ea950f087e1'),
 'name': 'Ann',
 'age': 34,
 'interests': ['Python', 'databases', 'statistics'],
 'date_added': datetime.datetime(2024, 9, 10, 2, 36, 48, 617000)}
```

In updating the record, all fields will be updated to match the object passed in. Similarly, we can replace the record with another object:

Replaces record with new object

```
collection.replace_one({"_id":ObjectId('66dfb0c090d33ea950f087e1')},
                {"name":"Maria"})
```
◄—

```
UpdateResult({'n': 1, 'electionId': ObjectId('7fffffff00000000000002b7'),
 'opTime': {'ts': Timestamp(1725936426, 6), 't': 695}, 'nModified': 1, 'ok':
1.0, '$clusterTime': {'clusterTime': Timestamp(1725936426, 6), 'signature':
{'hash': b'=\xef,\x1b\xe5\xd5\xa3`\xf9"\xcb\x1a\xb4X\xec\x96\xa8\xbdJN',
 'keyId': 7368510527980437523}}, 'operationTime': Timestamp(1725936426, 6),
 'updatedExisting': True}, acknowledged=True)
```

```
collection.find_one({"_id":ObjectId('66dfb0c090d33ea950f087e1')})
```

```
{'_id': ObjectId('66dfb0c090d33ea950f087e1'),
                'name': 'Maria'}
```
◄— **The record is replaced with a shorter record.**

In this case, the entire object has been replaced with another. This may be more efficient, depending on how complex the objects are. Finally, we can delete by `ObectId`:

```
collection.delete_one({"_id":ObjectId(                    Deletes record
                '66dfb0c090d33ea950f087e1')})    ◄────── matching specification

DeleteResult({'n': 1, 'electionId': ObjectId('7fffffff00000000000002b7'),
'opTime': {'ts': Timestamp(1725936489, 7), 't': 695}, 'ok': 1.0,
'$clusterTime': {'clusterTime': Timestamp(1725936489, 7), 'signature':
{'hash':
b'\xcd\xf3\x18\xdc\xe7\x86\xba\x81\xbdU\\n\xec\xbe\x8e\xc6\xf3\xe8M\xb6',
'keyId': 7368510527980437523}}, 'operationTime': Timestamp(1725936489, 7)},
acknowledged=True)

collection.find_one()        ◄─────┘ Collection empty, no result
```

First, notice that MongoDB matches according to dictionaries of the fields and their values to match. Dictionaries are also used to indicate operators, such as `$lt` (less than) and `$gt` (greater than), as well as commands such as `$set` for the update. The other thing to notice is that, even though the record has been deleted and the collection is now empty, the collection still exists unless it's specifically dropped:

```
db.collection_names()

['docs']

collection.drop()
db.collection_names()

[]
```

MongoDB can do many other things, of course. In addition to operating on one record, versions of the same commands cover multiple records, such as `find_many` and `update_many`. MongoDB also supports indexing to improve performance and has several methods to group, count, and aggregate data, as well as a built-in map-reduce method.

Quick check: Uses of MongoDB

Think back over the various data samples you've seen so far and other types of data. In your experience, which do you think would be well suited to being stored in a database like MongoDB? Would others clearly not be suited, and if so, why not?

23.8 *Creating a database*

Choose one of the datasets I've discussed in the past few chapters and decide which type of database would be best for storing that data. Create that database and write the code to load the data into it. Then choose the two most common and/or likely types of search criteria and write the code to retrieve both single and multiple matching records. This is an open-ended challenge, so there is no "official" answer. Good luck!

Summary

- Python has a DB-API that provides a generally consistent interface for clients of several relational databases.

- SQLite is a file-based relational database that is part of the Python standard library.

- PostgreSQL and MySQL are popular database servers commonly used with Python.

- Using an ORM can make database code even more standard across databases.

- Using an ORM also lets you access relational databases through Python code and objects rather than SQL queries.

- Tools such as Alembic work with ORMs to use code to make reversible changes to a relational database schema.

- Key-value stores such as Redis provide quick in-memory data access without SQL (NoSQL).

- MongoDB provides scalability and is based on documents, without the strict structure of databases.

Exploring data

Over the past few chapters, I've dealt with some aspects of using Python to get and clean data. Now it's time to look at a few of the things that Python can help you do to manipulate and explore data.

24.1 Python tools for data exploration

In this chapter, we'll look at some common Python tools for data exploration in Jupyter: pandas and Matplotlib. I can only touch briefly on a few features of these tools, but the aim is to give you an idea of what is possible and some initial tools to use in exploring data with Python.

24.1.1 Python's advantages for exploring data

Python has become one of the leading languages for data science and continues to grow in that area. As I've mentioned, however, Python isn't always the fastest language in terms of raw performance. Conversely, some data-crunching libraries, such as NumPy, are largely written in C and heavily optimized to the point that speed isn't a problem. In addition, considerations such as readability and accessibility often outweigh pure speed; minimizing the amount of developer time needed is often more important. Python is readable and accessible, and both on its own and in combination with tools developed in the Python community, it's an enormously powerful tool for manipulating and exploring data.

24.1.2 Python can be better than a spreadsheet

Spreadsheets have been the tools of choice for ad hoc data manipulation for decades. People who are skilled with spreadsheets can make them do truly impressive tricks: spreadsheets can combine different but related datasets, pivot tables, use lookup tables to link datasets, and much more. But although people everywhere get a vast amount of work done with them every day, spreadsheets do have limitations, and Python can help you go beyond those limitations.

One limitation that I've already alluded to is the fact that most spreadsheet software has a row limit—currently, about 1 million rows, which isn't enough for many datasets. Another limitation is the central metaphor of the spreadsheet itself. Spreadsheets are two-dimensional grids, rows, and columns or at best stacks of grids, which limits the ways you can manipulate and think about complex data.

With Python, you can code your way around the limitations of spreadsheets and manipulate data the way you want. You can combine Python data structures, such as lists, tuples, sets, and dictionaries, in endlessly flexible ways, or you can create your own classes to package both data and behavior exactly the way you need.

24.2 Python and pandas

In the course of exploring and manipulating data, you perform quite a few common operations, such as loading data into a list or dictionary, cleaning data, and filtering data. Most of these operations are repeated often, have to be done in standard patterns, and are simple and often tedious. If you think that this combination is a strong reason to automate those tasks, you're not alone. One of the now-standard tools for handling data in Python—pandas—was created to automate the boring heavy lifting of handling datasets.

24.2.1 Why you might want to use pandas

Pandas was created to make manipulating and analyzing tabular or relational data easy by providing a standard framework for holding the data, with convenient tools for frequent operations. As a result, it's almost more of an extension to Python than a library, and it changes the way you can interact with data. The plus side is that after you grok how pandas work, you can do some impressive things and save a lot of time. It does take time to learn how to get the most from pandas, however. As with many tools, if you use pandas for what it was designed for, it excels. The simple examples I show you in the following sections should give you a rough idea whether pandas is a tool that's suited for your use cases.

24.2.2 Installing pandas

If you are using Colaboratory, `pandas`, `matplotlib`, and `numpy` are already installed, but if you don't have `pandas`, it's easy to install with `pip`. It's often used along with `matplotlib` for plotting, so you can install both tools from the command line of your Jupyter virtual environment with this code:

```
> pip install pandas matplotlib
```

From a cell in a Jupyter notebook, you can use

```
!pip install pandas matplotlib
```

If you use pandas, life will be easier if you use the following three lines:

```
%matplotlib inline
import pandas as pd
import numpy as np
```

The first line is a Jupyter "magic" function that enables `matplotlib` to plot data in the cell where your code is (which is very useful). The second line imports `pandas` with the alias of `pd`, which is both easier to type and common among pandas users; the last line also imports `numpy`, which `pip` will install automatically with pandas. Although pandas depends quite a bit on `numpy`, you won't use it explicitly in the following examples, but it's reasonable to get into the habit of importing it anyway.

24.2.3 Data frames

One basic structure that you get with pandas is a data frame. A *data frame* is a two-dimensional grid, rather similar to a relational database table except in memory. Creating a data frame is easy; you give it some data. To keep things absolutely simple, give it a 3×3 grid of numbers as the first example. In Python, such a grid is a list of lists:

```
grid = [[1,2,3], [4,5,6], [7,8,9]]
print(grid)

[[1, 2, 3], [4, 5, 6], [7, 8, 9]]
```

Sadly, in Python, the grid won't look like a grid unless you make some additional effort. See what you can do with the same grid as a pandas data frame:

```
import pandas as pd
df = pd.DataFrame(grid)
```

```
print(df)

   0  1  2
0  1  2  3
1  4  5  6
2  7  8  9
```

That code is fairly straightforward; all you needed to do was turn your grid into a data frame. You've gained a more grid-like display, and now you have both row and column numbers. It's often rather bothersome to keep track of what column number is what, of course, so give your columns names:

```
df = pd.DataFrame(grid, columns=["one", "two", "three"] )
print(df)

   one  two  three
0    1    2      3
1    4    5      6
2    7    8      9
```

You may wonder whether naming the columns has any benefit, but the column names can be put to use with another pandas trick: the ability to select columns by name. If you want the contents only of column "two", for example, you can get it very simply:

```
print(df["two"])

0    2
1    5
2    8
Name: two, dtype: int64
```

Here, you've already saved time in comparison with Python. To get only column 2 of your grid, you'd need to use a list comprehension while also remembering to use a zero-based index (and you still wouldn't get the nice output):

```
print([x[1] for x in grid])

[2, 5, 8]
```

You can loop over data frame column values just as easily as the list you got by using a comprehension:

```
for x in df["two"]:
    print(x)

2
5
8
```

That's not bad for a start, but by using a list of columns in double brackets, you can do better, getting a subset of the data frame that's another data frame. Instead of getting the middle column, get the first and last columns of your data frame as another data frame:

```
edges = df[["one", "three"]]
print(edges)
```

```
   one  three
0    1      3
1    4      6
2    7      9
```

A data frame also has several methods that apply the same operation and argument to every item in the frame. If you want to add 2 to every item in the data frame's edges, you could use the add() method:

```
print(edges.add(2))
```

```
   one  three
0    3      5
1    6      8
2    9     11
```

Here again, it's possible to get the same result by using list comprehensions and/or nested loops, but those techniques aren't as convenient. It's pretty easy to see how such functionality can make life easier, particularly for someone who's more interested in the information that the data contains than in the process of cleaning it.

24.3   *Data cleaning*

In earlier chapters, I discussed a few ways to use Python to clean data. Now that I've added pandas to the mix, I'll show you examples of how to use its functionality to clean data. As I present the following operations, I also refer to ways that the same operation might be done in plain Python, both to illustrate how using pandas is different and to show why pandas isn't right for every use case (or user, for that matter).

24.3.1 *Loading and saving data with pandas*

Pandas has an impressive collection of methods to load data from different sources. It supports several file formats (including fixed-width and delimited text files, spreadsheets, JSON, XML, and HTML), but it's also possible to read from SQL databases, Google BiqQuery, HDF, and even clipboard data. You should be aware that many of these operations aren't actually part of pandas itself; pandas relies on having other libraries installed to handle those operations, such as SQLAlchemy for reading from SQL databases. This distinction matters mostly if something goes wrong; quite often, the problem that needs to be fixed is outside pandas, and you're left to deal with the underlying library.

Reading a JSON file with the read_json() method is simple. For example, mars_data_01.json contains a single day's weather on Mars as reported by the (now sadly defunct) Opportunity rover. To read it, we can use the pandas read_json method:

```
mars = pd.read_json("mars_data_01.json")
```

This code gives you a data frame like the following:

```
                                report
abs_humidity                      None
atmo_opacity                     Sunny
ls                                 296
max_temp                           -1
max_temp_fahrenheit               30.2
min_temp                           -72
min_temp_fahrenheit             -97.6
pressure                           869
pressure_string                 Higher
season                        Month 10
sol                               1576
sunrise           2017-01-11T12:31:00Z
sunset            2017-01-12T00:46:00Z
terrestrial_date            2017-01-11
wind_direction                      --
wind_speed                        None
```

For another example of how simple reading data into pandas is, we can load some data from the CSV file of temperature data from chapter 22. To read a CSV file, we can use the read_csv() method:

> **Note that the \ at the end of the header line is an indication that the table is too long to be printed on one line, and more columns are printed below.**

```
temp = pd.read_csv("temp_data_01.csv")

            4       5     6       7      8       9     10     11
      12       13     14  \
0  1979/01/01  17.48  994     6.0   30.5    2.89   994  -13.6  15.8     NaN    0
1  1979/01/02   4.64  994    -6.4   15.8   -9.03   994  -23.6   6.6     NaN    0
2  1979/01/03  11.05  994    -0.7   24.7   -2.17   994  -18.3  12.9     NaN    0
3  1979/01/04   9.51  994     0.2   27.6   -0.43   994  -16.3  16.3     NaN    0
4  1979/05/15  68.42  994    61.0   75.1   51.30   994   43.3  57.0     NaN    0
5  1979/05/16  70.29  994    63.4   73.5   48.09   994   41.1  53.0     NaN    0
6  1979/05/17  75.34  994    64.0   80.5   50.84   994   44.3  55.7   82.60    2
7  1979/05/18  79.13  994    75.5   82.1   55.68   994   50.0  61.1   81.42  349
8  1979/05/19  74.94  994    66.9   83.1   58.59   994   50.9  63.2   82.87   78

      15    16      17
0    NaN   NaN  0.0000
1    NaN   NaN  0.0000
2    NaN   NaN  0.0000
3    NaN   NaN  0.0000
4    NaN   NaN  0.0000
5    NaN   NaN  0.0000
6   82.4  82.8  0.0020
7   80.2  83.4  0.3511
8   81.6  85.2  0.0785
```

Clearly, loading the file in a single step is appealing, and you can see that pandas had no problems loading the file. You can also see that the empty first column has been translated into NaN (not a number). You do still have the same problem with 'Missing' for some values, and in fact it might make sense to have those 'Missing' values converted to NaN:

```
temp = pd.read_csv("temp_data_01.csv", na_values=['Missing'])
```

The addition of the na_values parameter controls what values will be translated to NaN on load. In this case, you added the string 'Missing' so that the row of the data frame was translated from

```
NaN  Illinois  17  Jan 01, 1979  1979/01/01  17.48  994  6.0  30.5
2.89    994  -13.6  15.8  Missing  0  Missing  Missing  0.00%
```

to

```
NaN  Illinois  17  Jan 01, 1979  1979/01/01  17.48  994  6.0  30.5
2.89    994  -13.6  15.8  NaN    0  NaN  NaN  0.00%
```

This technique can be particularly useful if you have one of those data files in which, for whatever reason, "no data" is indicated in a variety of ways: NA, N/A, ?, -, and so on. To handle a case like that, you can inspect the data to find out what's used and then reload it using the na_values parameter to standardize all those variations as NaN.

SAVING DATA

If you want to save the contents of a data frame, a pandas data frame has a similarly broad collection of methods. If you take your simple grid data frame, you can write it in several ways. The following line

```
df.to_csv("df_out.csv", index=False)
```

◀——┐ **Setting index to False means that the row indexes will not be written.**

writes a file that looks like this:

```
one,two,three
1,2,3
4,5,6
7,8,9
```

Similarly, you can transform a data grid to a JSON object or write it to a file:

┌ **Supplying a file path as an argument writes the JSON to that file rather than returning it.**

```
df.to_json()  ◀——
'{"one":{"0":1,"1":4,"2":7},"two":{"0":2,"1":5,"2":8},
  "three":{"0":3,"1":6,"2":9}}'
```

24.3.2 *Data cleaning with a data frame*

Converting a particular set of values to NaN on load is a very simple bit of data cleaning that pandas makes trivial. Going beyond that, data frames support several operations that can make data cleaning less of a chore. To see how this works, reopen the temperature CSV file, but this time, instead of using the headers to name the columns, use the range() function with the names parameter to give them numbers, which will make referring to them easier. You also may recall from an earlier example that the first field of every line—the "Notes" field—is empty and loaded with NaN values. Although you could ignore this column, it would be even easier if you didn't have it. You can use the range() function again, this time starting from 1, to tell pandas to load all columns except the first one. But if you know that all of your values are from Illinois and you don't care about the long-form date field, you could start from 4 to make things much more manageable:

> Setting header = 0 turns off reading the header for column labels.

```
temp = pd.read_csv("temp_data_01.csv", na_values=['Missing'], header=0,
        names=range(18), usecols=range(4,18))
print(temp)
```

	4	5	6	7	8	9	10	11	12	13	14
0	1979/01/01	17.48	994	6.0	30.5	2.89	994	-13.6	15.8	NaN	0
1	1979/01/02	4.64	994	-6.4	15.8	-9.03	994	-23.6	6.6	NaN	0
2	1979/01/03	11.05	994	-0.7	24.7	-2.17	994	-18.3	12.9	NaN	0
3	1979/01/04	9.51	994	0.2	27.6	-0.43	994	-16.3	16.3	NaN	0
4	1979/05/15	68.42	994	61.0	75.1	51.30	994	43.3	57.0	NaN	0
5	1979/05/16	70.29	994	63.4	73.5	48.09	994	41.1	53.0	NaN	0
6	1979/05/17	75.34	994	64.0	80.5	50.84	994	44.3	55.7	82.60	2
7	1979/05/18	79.13	994	75.5	82.1	55.68	994	50.0	61.1	81.42	349
8	1979/05/19	74.94	994	66.9	83.1	58.59	994	50.9	63.2	82.87	78

	15	16	17
0	NaN	NaN	0.00%
1	NaN	NaN	0.00%
2	NaN	NaN	0.00%
3	NaN	NaN	0.00%
4	NaN	NaN	0.00%
5	NaN	NaN	0.00%
6	82.4	82.8	0.20%
7	80.2	83.4	35.11%
8	81.6	85.2	7.85%

Now you have a data frame that has only the columns you might want to work with. But you still have a problem: the last column, which lists the percentage of coverage for the heat index, is still a string ending with a percentage sign rather than an actual percentage. This problem is apparent if you look at the first row's value for column 17:

```
temp[17][0]
```

```
'0.00%'
```

To fix this problem, you need to do two things: remove the % from the end of the value and then cast the value from a string to a number. Optionally, if you want to represent the resulting percentage as a fraction, divide it by 100. The first bit is simple because pandas lets you use a single command to repeat an operation on a column:

```
temp[17] = temp[17].str.strip("%")
temp[17][0]
```

```
'0.00'
```

This code takes the column and calls a string `strip()` operation on it to remove the trailing %. Now when you look at the first value in the column (or any of the other values), you see that the offending percentage sign is gone. It's also worth noting that you could have used other operations, such as `replace("%", "")`, to achieve the same result.

The second operation is to convert the string to a numeric value. Again, pandas lets you perform this operation with one command:

```
temp[17] = pd.to_numeric(temp[17])
temp[17][0]
0.0
```

Now the values in column 17 are numeric, and if you want to, you can use the `div()` method to finish the job of turning those values into fractions:

```
temp[17] = temp[17].div(100)
temp[17]
```

```
0       0.0000
1       0.0000
2       0.0000
3       0.0000
4       0.0000
5       0.0000
6       0.0020
7       0.3511
8       0.0785
Name: 17, dtype: float64
```

In fact, it would be possible to achieve the same result in a single line by chaining the three operations together:

```
temp[17] = pd.to_numeric(temp[17].str.strip("%")).div(100)
```

This example is very simple, but it gives you an idea of the convenience that pandas can bring to cleaning your data. Pandas has a wide variety of operations for transforming data, as well as the ability to use custom functions, so it would be hard to think of a scenario in which you couldn't streamline data cleaning with pandas.

Although the number of options is almost overwhelming, a wide variety of tutorials and videos is available in the documentation at http://pandas.pydata.org excellent.

> **Try this: Cleaning data with and without pandas**
>
> Experiment with the operations. When the final column has been converted to a fraction, can you think of a way to convert it back to a string with the trailing percentage sign?
>
> By contrast, load the same data into a plain Python list by using the `csv` module, and apply the same changes by using plain Python.

24.4 Data aggregation and manipulation

The preceding examples provide some idea of the many options pandas gives you for performing fairly complex operations on your data with only a few commands. As you might expect, this level of functionality is also available for aggregating data. In this section, I walk through a few simple examples of aggregating data to illustrate some of the many possibilities. Although many options are available, I focus on merging data frames, performing simple data aggregation, and grouping and filtering.

24.4.1 Merging data frames

Quite often in the course of handling data, you need to relate two datasets. Suppose that you have one file containing the number of sales calls made per month by members of a sales team and another file that gives the dollar amounts of the sales in each of their territories:

```
calls = pd.read_csv("sales_calls.csv")
print(calls)
```

	Team member	Territory	Month	Calls
0	Jorge	3	1	107
1	Jorge	3	2	88
2	Jorge	3	3	84
3	Jorge	3	4	113
4	Ana	1	1	91
5	Ana	1	2	129
6	Ana	1	3	96
7	Ana	1	4	128
8	Ali	2	1	120
9	Ali	2	2	85
10	Ali	2	3	87
11	Ali	2	4	87

```
revenue = pd.read_csv("sales_revenue.csv")
print(revenue)
```

	Territory	Month	Amount
0	1	1	54228

```
1          1      2    61640
2          1      3    43491
3          1      4    52173
4          2      1    36061
5          2      2    44957
6          2      3    35058
7          2      4    33855
8          3      1    50876
9          3      2    57682
10         3      3    53689
11         3      4    49173
```

Clearly, it would be very useful to link revenue and team member activity. These two files are very simple, yet merging them with plain Python isn't entirely trivial. Pandas has a function to merge two data frames:

```
calls_revenue = pd.merge(calls, revenue, on=['Territory', 'Month'])
```

The merge function creates a new data frame by joining the two frames on the columns specified in the column field. The merge function works similarly to a relational database join, giving you a table that combines the columns from the two files:

```
print(calls_revenue)
    Team member   Territory   Month   Calls   Amount
0         Jorge           3       1     107    50876
1         Jorge           3       2      88    57682
2         Jorge           3       3      84    53689
3         Jorge           3       4     113    49173
4          Ana            1       1      91    54228
5          Ana            1       2     129    61640
6          Ana            1       3      96    43491
7          Ana            1       4     128    52173
8          Ali            2       1     120    36061
9          Ali            2       2      85    44957
10         Ali            2       3      87    35058
11         Ali            2       4      87    33855
```

In this case, you have a one-to-one correspondence between the rows in the two fields, but the merge function can also do one-to-many and many-to-many joins, as well as right and left joins.

Quick check: Merging datasets

How would you go about merging two datasets like the ones in the Python example?

24.4.2 Selecting data

It can also be useful to select or filter the rows in a data frame based on some condition. In the example sales data, you may want to look only at territory 3, which is also easy:

```
print(calls_revenue[calls_revenue.Territory==3])
```

```
   Team member  Territory  Month  Calls  Amount
0        Jorge          3      1    107   50876
1        Jorge          3      2     88   57682
2        Jorge          3      3     84   53689
3        Jorge          3      4    113   49173
```

In this example, you select only rows in which the territory is equal to 3 but using exactly that expression, `revenue.Territory==3`, as the index for the data frame. From the point of view of plain Python, such use is nonsense and illegal, but for a pandas data frame, it works and makes for a much more concise expression.

More complex expressions are also allowed, of course. If you want to select only rows in which the amount per call is greater than 500, you could use this expression instead:

```
print(calls_revenue[calls_revenue.Amount/calls_revenue.Calls>500])
```

```
   Team member  Territory  Month  Calls  Amount
1        Jorge          3      2     88   57682
2        Jorge          3      3     84   53689
4          Ana          1      1     91   54228
9          Ali          2      2     85   44957
```

Even better, you could calculate and add that column to your data frame by using a similar operation:

```
calls_revenue['Call_Amount'] = calls_revenue.Amount/calls_revenue.Calls
print(calls_revenue)
```

```
    Team member  Territory  Month  Calls  Amount  Call_Amount
0         Jorge          3      1    107   50876   475.476636
1         Jorge          3      2     88   57682   655.477273
2         Jorge          3      3     84   53689   639.154762
3         Jorge          3      4    113   49173   435.159292
4           Ana          1      1     91   54228   595.912088
5           Ana          1      2    129   61640   477.829457
6           Ana          1      3     96   43491   453.031250
7           Ana          1      4    128   52173   407.601562
8           Ali          2      1    120   36061   300.508333
9           Ali          2      2     85   44957   528.905882
10          Ali          2      3     87   35058   402.965517
11          Ali          2      4     87   33855   389.137931
```

Again, note that pandas' built-in logic replaces a more cumbersome structure in plain Python.

Quick check: Selecting in Python

What Python code structure would you use to select only rows meeting certain conditions?

24.4.3 *Grouping and aggregation*

As you might expect, pandas has plenty of tools to summarize and aggregate data as well. In particular, getting the sum, mean, median, minimum, and maximum values from a column uses clearly named column methods:

```
print(calls_revenue.Calls.sum())
print(calls_revenue.Calls.mean())
print(calls_revenue.Calls.median())
print(calls_revenue.Calls.max())
print(calls_revenue.Calls.min())

1215
101.25
93.5
129
84
```

If, for example, you want to get all of the rows in which the amount per call is above the median, you can combine this trick with the selection operation:

```
print(calls_revenue.Call_Amount.median())
print(calls_revenue[calls_revenue.Call_Amount >=
      calls_revenue.Call_Amount.median()])

464.2539427570093
  Team member  Territory  Month  Calls  Amount  Call_Amount
0       Jorge          3      1    107   50876   475.476636
1       Jorge          3      2     88   57682   655.477273
2       Jorge          3      3     84   53689   639.154762
4         Ana          1      1     91   54228   595.912088
5         Ana          1      2    129   61640   477.829457
9         Ali          2      2     85   44957   528.905882
```

In addition to being able to pick out summary values, it's often useful to group the data based on other columns. In this simple example, you can use the groupby method to group your data. You may want to know the total calls and amounts by month or by territory, for example. In those cases, use those fields with the data frame's groupby method:

```
print(calls_revenue[['Month', 'Calls', 'Amount']].groupby(['Month']).sum())

       Calls  Amount
Month
1        318  141165
2        302  164279
3        267  132238
4        328  135201

print(calls_revenue[['Territory', 'Calls', 'Amount']].groupby(['Territory']).
sum())
```

```
        Calls   Amount
Territory
1           444  211532
2           379  149931
3           392  211420
```

In each case, you select the columns that you want to aggregate, group them by the values in one of those columns, and (in this case) sum the values for each group. You could also use any of the other methods mentioned earlier in this chapter.

Again, all these examples are simple, but they illustrate a few of the options you have for manipulating and selecting data with pandas. If these ideas resonate with your needs, you can learn more by studying the pandas documentation: https://pandas .pydata.org/.

> **Try this: Grouping and aggregating**
>
> Experiment with pandas and the data in previous examples. Can you get the calls and amounts by both team member and month?

24.5 Plotting data

Another very attractive feature of pandas is the ability to plot the data in a data frame very easily. Although you have many options for plotting data in Python and Jupyter notebooks, pandas can use `matplotlib` directly from a data frame. (While `matplotlib` has a rich set of plotting and graphics functions that are worth exploration, here we'll just touch on some simple examples. If you are interested in data visualization, you will want to explore `matplotlib` more deeply.) You may recall that when you started your Jupyter session, one of the first commands you gave was the Jupyter "magic" command to enable `matplotlib` for inline plotting:

```
%matplotlib inline
```

Because you have the ability to plot, see how you might plot some data (figure 24.1). To continue with the sales example, if you want to plot the quarter's mean sales by territory, you can get a graph right in your notebook just by adding `.plot.bar()`:

```
calls_revenue[['Territory', 'Calls']].groupby(['Territory']).sum().plot.bar()
```

Other options are available. `plot()` alone and `.plot.line()` create a line graph, `.plot.pie()` creates a pie chart, and so on.

Thanks to the combination of pandas and `matplotlib`, plotting data in a Jupyter notebook is quite easy. I should also note that, although such plotting is easy, there are many things that this combination doesn't do extremely well.

In [147]: `calls_revenue[['Territory', 'Calls']].groupby(['Territory']).sum().plot.bar()`

Out[147]: `<matplotlib.axes._subplots.AxesSubplot at 0x7fdee6c4eeb8>`

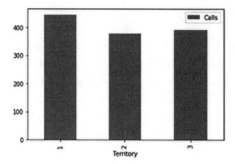

Figure 24.1   Bar plot of a pandas data frame in Jupyter notebook

Try this: Plotting

Plot a line graph of the monthly average amount per call.

24.6 *Why you might not want to use pandas*

The preceding examples illustrate only a tiny fraction of the tools pandas can offer you in cleaning, exploring, and manipulating data. As I mentioned at the beginning of this chapter, pandas is an excellent tool set that shines in what it was designed to do. That doesn't mean, however, that pandas is the tool for all situations or for all people.

There are reasons why you might elect to use plain old Python (or some other tool) instead. For one thing, as I mentioned earlier, learning to fully use pandas is in some ways like learning another language, which may not be something you have the time or inclination to do. Also, pandas may not be ideal in all production situations, particularly with very large datasets that don't require much in the way of math operations or with data that isn't easy to put into the formats that work best with pandas. Munging large collections of product information, for example, probably wouldn't benefit so much from pandas; neither would basic processing of a stream of transactions.

The point is that you should choose your tools thoughtfully based on the problems at hand. In many cases, pandas will truly make your life easier as you work with data, but in other cases, plain old Python may be your best bet.

Summary

- Python offers many benefits for data handling, including the ability to handle very large datasets and the flexibility to handle data in ways that match your needs.

- By allowing you to select, group, and otherwise manipulate data elements, Python often gives you more powerful and flexible data operations than a spreadsheet.
- Pandas is a tool that makes many common data-handling operations much easier.
- A data frame is the structure pandas uses to manipulate data.
- Pandas has methods for loading and saving data from files in several common data formats, including CSV and JSON.
- Pandas operations on columns makes data cleaning easier, operating by column on all rows of the data.
- The `pandas merge` method allows you to combine data frames on a shared field.
- Pandas combined with `matplotlib` also makes simple plotting easy by allowing you to plot data with a single `plot` command.
- In spite of its many advantages, pandas may not always be the best choice, particularly for large datasets that aren't suited to pandas or need near-real-time processing.

Case study

In this case study, you walk through using Python to fetch some data, clean it, and then graph it. This project may be a short one, but it combines several features of the language discussed in this book, and it gives you a chance to see a project worked through from beginning to end. At almost every step, I briefly call out alternatives and enhancements that you can make.

Global temperature change is the topic of much discussion, but those discussions are based on a global scale. Suppose that you want to know what the temperatures have been doing near where you are. One way of finding out is to get historical data for your location, process that data, and plot it to see exactly what's been happening.

Getting the case study code

The following case study was done by using a Jupyter notebook in Colaboratory, the same as the code in the other chapters. You can find the notebook I used (with this text and code) in the source code repository at https://github.com/nceder/qpb4e in the code/Case Study folder as Case_Study.ipynb. You can also execute the code in a standard Python shell, and a version that supports that shell is in the source repository as Case Study.py. Note, however, that you will have to install the packages for `requests`, pandas, and `matplotlib` before running the code.

Fortunately, several sources of historical weather data are freely available. I'm going to walk you through using data from the Global Historical Climatology Network, which has data from around the world. You may find other sources, which may have different data formats, but the steps and the processes I discuss here should be generally applicable to any dataset.

Downloading the data

The first step will be to get the data. An archive of daily historical weather data at https://www1.ncdc.noaa.gov/pub/data/ghcn/daily/ has a wide array of data. The first step is to figure out which files you want and exactly where they are; then you download them. When you have the data, you can move on to processing and ultimately displaying your results.

To download the files, which are accessible via HTTPS, you need the `requests` library, which is already available in Colaboratory. If you are using another environment, you can get `requests` with `pip install requests` at the command prompt. When you have `requests`, your first step is to fetch the readme.txt file, which can guide you as to the formats and location of the data files you want:

```
# import requests
import requests

# get readme.txt file
r = requests.get('https://www1.ncdc.noaa.gov/pub/data/ghcn/daily/readme.txt')
readme = r.text.
```

When you look at the readme file, you should see something like this:

```
print(readme)
README FILE FOR DAILY GLOBAL HISTORICAL CLIMATOLOGY NETWORK (GHCN-DAILY)
Version 3.22


--------------------------------------------------------------------------
How to cite:

Note that the GHCN-Daily dataset itself now has a DOI (Digital Object
    Identifier)
so it may be relevant to cite both the methods/overview journal article as
➥well
as the specific version of the dataset used.

The journal article describing GHCN-Daily is:
Menne, M.J., I. Durre, R.S. Vose, B.E. Gleason, and T.G. Houston, 2012:  An
➥overview
of the Global Historical Climatology Network-Daily Database.  Journal of
➥Atmospheric
and Oceanic Technology, 29, 897-910, doi:10.1175/JTECH-D-11-00103.1.

To acknowledge the specific version of the dataset used, please cite:
Menne, M.J., I. Durre, B. Korzeniewski, S. McNeal, K. Thomas, X. Yin, S.
➥Anthony, R. Ray,
R.S. Vose, B.E.Gleason, and T.G. Houston, 2012: Global Historical
➥Climatology Network -
```

Daily (GHCN-Daily), Version 3. [indicate subset used following decimal,
e.g. Version 3.12].
NOAA National Climatic Data Center. http://doi.org/10.7289/V5D21VHZ [access
➥date].

In particular, you're interested in section II, which lists the contents:

```
II. CONTENTS OF ftp://ftp.ncdc.noaa.gov/pub/data/ghcn/daily

all:               Directory with ".dly" files for all of GHCN-Daily
gsn:               Directory with ".dly" files for the GCOS Surface Network
                   (GSN)
hcn:               Directory with ".dly" files for U.S. HCN
by_year:           Directory with GHCN Daily files parsed into yearly
                   subsets with observation times where available. See the
                /by_year/readme.txt and
                /by_year/ghcn-daily-by_year-format.rtf
                   files for further information
grid:              Directory with the GHCN-Daily gridded dataset known
                   as HadGHCND
papers:            Directory with pdf versions of journal articles relevant
                   to the GHCN-Daily dataset
figures:           Directory containing figures that summarize the inventory
                   of GHCN-Daily station records

ghcnd-all.tar.gz:  TAR file of the GZIP-compressed files in the "all"
➥directory
ghcnd-gsn.tar.gz:  TAR file of the GZIP-compressed "gsn" directory
ghcnd-hcn.tar.gz:  TAR file of the GZIP-compressed "hcn" directory

ghcnd-countries.txt: List of country codes (FIPS) and names
ghcnd-inventory.txt: File listing the periods of record for each station and
                   element
ghcnd-stations.txt: List of stations and their metadata (e.g.,
➥coordinates)
ghcnd-states.txt:  List of U.S. state and Canadian Province codes
                   used in ghcnd-stations.txt
ghcnd-version.txt: File that specifies the current version of GHCN Daily

readme.txt:        This file
status.txt:        Notes on the current status of GHCN-Daily
```

As you look at the files available, you see that ghcnd-inventory.txt has a listing of
the recording periods for each station, which will help you find a good dataset, and
ghcnd-stations.txt lists the stations, which should help you find the station closest to
your location, so you'll grab those two files first:

```
II. CONTENTS OF ftp://ftp.ncdc.noaa.gov/pub/data/ghcn/daily

all:               Directory with ".dly" files for all of GHCN-Daily
gsn:               Directory with ".dly" files for the GCOS Surface
      Network
                   (GSN)
```

```
hcn:                    Directory with ".dly" files for U.S. HCN
by_year:                Directory with GHCN Daily files parsed into yearly
                        subsets with observation times where available.  See
        the
                /by_year/readme.txt and
                /by_year/ghcn-daily-by_year-format.rtf
                files for further information
grid:                   Directory with the GHCN-Daily gridded dataset known
                        as HadGHCND
papers:                 Directory with pdf versions of journal articles relevant
                        to the GHCN-Daily dataset
figures:                Directory containing figures that summarize the inventory
                        of GHCN-Daily station records
ghcnd-all.tar.gz:       TAR file of the GZIP-compressed files in the "all"
                        directory
ghcnd-gsn.tar.gz:       TAR file of the GZIP-compressed "gsn" directory
ghcnd-hcn.tar.gz:       TAR file of the GZIP-compressed "hcn" directory

ghcnd-countries.txt:    List of country codes (FIPS) and names
ghcnd-inventory.txt:    File listing the periods of record for each station and
                        element
ghcnd-stations.txt:     List of stations and their metadata (e.g.,
coordinates)
ghcnd-states.txt:       List of U.S. state and Canadian Province codes
                        used in ghcnd-stations.txt
ghcnd-version.txt:      File that specifies the current version of GHCN Daily

readme.txt:             This file
status.txt:             Notes on the current status of GHCN-Daily
```

```
# get inventory and stations files

r = requests.get('https://www1.ncdc.noaa.gov/pub/data/ghcn/daily/ghcnd-
inventory.txt')
inventory_txt = r.text
r = requests.get('https://www1.ncdc.noaa.gov/pub/data/ghcn/daily/ghcnd-
stations.txt')
stations_txt = r.text
```

When you have those files, you can save them to your local disk so that you won't need to download them again if you need to go back to the original data:

```
# save both the inventory and stations files to disk, in case we need them

with open("inventory.txt", "w") as inventory_file:
    inventory_file.write(inventory_txt)

with open("stations.txt", "w") as stations_file:
    stations_file.write(stations_txt)
```

Start by looking at the inventory file. Here's what the first 137 characters show you:

```
print(inventory_txt[:137])
ACW00011604  17.1167  -61.7833 TMAX 1949 1949
```

```
ACW00011604  17.1167  -61.7833 TMIN 1949 1949
ACW00011604  17.1167  -61.7833 PRCP 1949 1949
```

If we look at section VII of the readme.txt file, we can see that the format of the inventory file is

```
VII. FORMAT OF "ghcnd-inventory.txt"


------------------------------
Variable    Columns   Type
------------------------------
ID             1-11   Character
LATITUDE      13-20   Real
LONGITUDE     22-30   Real
ELEMENT       32-35   Character
FIRSTYEAR     37-40   Integer
LASTYEAR      42-45   Integer
------------------------------
```

These variables have the following definitions:

```
ID          is the station identification code. Please see "ghcnd-
➞stations.txt"
            for a complete list of stations and their metadata.

LATITUDE    is the latitude of the station (in decimal degrees).

LONGITUDE   is the longitude of the station (in decimal degrees).

ELEMENT     is the element type. See section III for a definition of
➞elements.

FIRSTYEAR   is the first year of unflagged data for the given element.

LASTYEAR    is the last year of unflagged data for the given element.
```

From this description, you can tell that the inventory list has most of the information you need to find the station you want to look at. You can use the latitude and longitude to find the stations closest to you; then you can use the FIRSTYEAR and LASTYEAR fields to find a station with records covering a long span of time.

The only question remaining is what the ELEMENT field is; for that, the file suggests that you look at section III. In section III (which I look at in more detail later), you find the following description of the main elements:

```
ELEMENT     is the element type. There are five core elements as well as a
number of addition elements.

        The five core elements are:

            PRCP = Precipitation (tenths of mm)
            SNOW = Snowfall (mm)
```

```
SNWD = Snow depth (mm)
TMAX = Maximum temperature (tenths of degrees C)
TMIN = Minimum temperature (tenths of degrees C)
```

For purposes of this example, you're interested in the TMAX and TMIN elements, which are maximum and minimum temperatures in tenths of degrees Celsius.

Parsing the inventory data

The readme.txt file tells you what you've got in the inventory file so that you can parse the data into a more usable format. You could just store the parsed inventory data as a list of lists or list of tuples, but it takes only a little more effort to use dataclass from the dataclasses library to create a custom class with the attributes named (a named tuple would also be a possibility here):

```
# use dataclass to create a custom Inventory class
from dataclasses import dataclass

@dataclass
class Inventory:
    station:str
    latitude: float
    longitude: float
    element:str
    start:int
    end:int
```

Using the Inventory class you created is very straightforward; you simply create each instance from the appropriate values, which in this case are a parsed row of inventory data.

The parsing involves two steps. First, you need to pick out slices of a line according to the field sizes specified. As you look at the field descriptions in the readme file, it's also clear that there's an extra space between files, which you need to consider in coming up with any approach to parsing. In this case, because you're specifying each slice, the extra spaces are ignored. In addition, because the sizes of the STATION and ELEMENT fields exactly correspond to the values stored in them, you shouldn't need to worry about stripping excess spaces from them.

The second thing that would be nice to do is convert the latitude and longitude values to floats and the start and end years to ints. You could do this at a later stage of data cleaning, and in fact, if the data is inconsistent and doesn't have values that convert correctly in every row, you might want to wait. But in this case, the data lets you handle these conversions in the parsing step, so do it now:

```
# parse inventory lines and convert some values to floats and ints

inventory = [Inventory(x[0:11], float(x[12:20]), float(x[21:30]), x[31:35],
                       int(x[36:40]), int(x[41:45]))
             for x in inventory_txt.split("\n") if x.startswith("US")]
```

```
for line in inventory[:5]:
    print(line)
```

```
Inventory(station='US009052008', latitude=43.7333, longitude=-96.6333,
                element='TMAX', start=2008, end=2016)
Inventory(station='US009052008', latitude=43.7333, longitude=-96.6333,
                element='TMIN', start=2008, end=2016)
Inventory(station='US009052008', latitude=43.7333, longitude=-96.6333,
                element='PRCP', start=2008, end=2016)
Inventory(station='US009052008', latitude=43.7333, longitude=-96.6333,
                element='SNWD', start=2009, end=2016)
Inventory(station='US10RMHS145', latitude=40.5268, longitude=-105.1113,
                element='PRCP', start=2004, end=2004)
```

Selecting a station based on latitude and longitude

Now that the inventory is loaded, you can use the latitude and longitude to find the stations closest to your location and then pick the one with the longest run of temperatures based on start and end years. At even the first line of the data, you can see two things to worry about:

- There are various element types, but you're concerned only with TMIN and TMAX, for minimum and maximum temperature.
- None of the first inventory entries you see covers more than a few years. If you're going to be looking for a historical perspective, you want to find a much longer run of temperature data.

To pick out what you need quickly, you can use a list comprehension to make a sublist of only the station inventory items in which the element is TMIN or TMAX. The other thing that you care about is getting a station with a long run of data, so while you're creating this sublist, also make sure that the start year is before 1920 and that the end year is at least 2024. That way, you're looking only at stations with over 100 years' worth of data:

```
inventory_temps = [x for x in inventory if x.element in ['TMIN', 'TMAX']
                and x.end >= 2015 and x.start < 1920]
inventory_temps[:5]
```

```
[Inventory(station='USC00010583', latitude=30.8839, longitude=-87.7853,
                element='TMAX', start=1915, end=2024),
 Inventory(station='USC00010583', latitude=30.8839, longitude=-87.7853,
                element='TMIN', start=1915, end=2024),
 Inventory(station='USC00011694', latitude=32.8158, longitude=-86.6044,
                element='TMAX', start=1893, end=2024),
 Inventory(station='USC00011694', latitude=32.8158, longitude=-86.6044,
                element='TMIN', start=1893, end=2024),
 Inventory(station='USC00012813', latitude=30.5467, longitude=-87.8808,
                element='TMAX', start=1917, end=2024)]
```

Looking at the first five records in your new list, you see that you're in better shape. Now you have only temperature records, and the start and end years show that you have longer runs.

That leaves the problem of selecting the station nearest your location. To do that, compare the latitude and longitude of the station inventories with those of your location. There are various ways to get the latitude and longitude of any place, but probably the easiest way is to use an online mapping application or online search. (When I do that for the Chicago Loop, I get a latitude of 41.882 and a longitude of -87.629.)

Because you're interested in the stations closest to your location, that interest implies sorting based on how close the latitude and longitude of the stations are to those of your location. Sorting a list is easy enough, and sorting by latitude and longitude isn't too hard. But how do you sort by the distance from your latitude and longitude?

The answer is to define a key function for your sort that gets the difference between your latitude and the station's latitude and the difference between your longitude and the station's longitude and combines them into one number. The only other thing to remember is that you'll want to add the absolute value of the differences before you combine them to avoid having a high negative difference combined with an equally high positive difference that would fool your sort:

```
# Downtown Chicago, obtained via online map
latitude, longitude = 41.882, -87.629

inventory_temps.sort(key=lambda x:  abs(latitude-x.latitude) +
                  abs(longitude-x.longitude))

inventory_temps[:20]
```

```
[Inventory(station='USC00110338', latitude=41.7803, longitude=-88.3092,
element='TMAX', start=1893, end=2024),
 Inventory(station='USC00110338', latitude=41.7803, longitude=-88.3092,
               element='TMIN', start=1893, end=2024),
 Inventory(station='USC00112736', latitude=42.0628, longitude=-88.2861,
               element='TMAX', start=1897, end=2024),
 Inventory(station='USC00112736', latitude=42.0628, longitude=-88.2861,
               element='TMIN', start=1897, end=2024),
 Inventory(station='USC00476922', latitude=42.7028, longitude=-87.7858,
               element='TMAX', start=1896, end=2024),
 Inventory(station='USC00476922', latitude=42.7028, longitude=-87.7858,
               element='TMIN', start=1896, end=2024),
 Inventory(station='USC00124837', latitude=41.6117, longitude=-86.7297,
               element='TMAX', start=1897, end=2024),
 Inventory(station='USC00124837', latitude=41.6117, longitude=-86.7297,
               element='TMIN', start=1897, end=2024),
 Inventory(station='USC00115825', latitude=41.3714, longitude=-88.4333,
               element='TMAX', start=1912, end=2024),
 Inventory(station='USC00115825', latitude=41.3714, longitude=-88.4333,
               element='TMIN', start=1912, end=2024),
 Inventory(station='USC00200710', latitude=42.1244, longitude=-86.4267,
               element='TMAX', start=1893, end=2024),
 Inventory(station='USC00200710', latitude=42.1244, longitude=-86.4267,
               element='TMIN', start=1893, end=2024),
 Inventory(station='USC00114198', latitude=40.4664, longitude=-87.685,
               element='TMAX', start=1902, end=2024),
 Inventory(station='USC00114198', latitude=40.4664, longitude=-87.685,
```

```
                    element='TMIN', start=1902, end=2024),
 Inventory(station='USW00014848', latitude=41.7072, longitude=-86.3164,
                    element='TMAX', start=1893, end=2024),
 Inventory(station='USW00014848', latitude=41.7072, longitude=-86.3164,
                    element='TMIN', start=1893, end=2024),
 Inventory(station='USC00124657', latitude=41.3053, longitude=-86.6286,
                    element='TMAX', start=1897, end=2024),
 Inventory(station='USC00124657', latitude=41.3053, longitude=-86.6286,
                    element='TMIN', start=1897, end=2024),
 Inventory(station='USC00478937', latitude=42.9986, longitude=-88.2525,
                    element='TMAX', start=1894, end=2024),
 Inventory(station='USC00478937', latitude=42.9986, longitude=-88.2525,
                    element='TMIN', start=1894, end=2024)]
```

Selecting a station and getting the station metadata

As you look at the top 20 entries in your newly sorted list, it seems that the first station, USC00110338, is a good fit. It's got both TMIN and TMAX and one of the longer series, starting in 1893 and running up through 2017, for more than 120 years' worth of data. So save that station into your station variable and quickly parse the station data you've already grabbed to pick up a little more information about the station.

Back in the readme file, you find the following information about the station data:

```
IV. FORMAT OF "ghcnd-stations.txt"

------------------------------
Variable   Columns   Type
------------------------------
ID            1-11    Character
LATITUDE     13-20    Real
LONGITUDE    22-30    Real
ELEVATION    32-37    Real
STATE        39-40    Character
NAME         42-71    Character
GSN FLAG     73-75    Character
HCN/CRN FLAG 77-79    Character
WMO ID       81-85    Character
------------------------------

These variables have the following definitions:

ID            is the station identification code.  Note that the first two
              characters denote the FIPS  country code, the third character
              is a network code that identifies the station numbering system
              used, and the remaining eight characters contain the actual
              station ID.

              See "ghcnd-countries.txt" for a complete list of country codes.
              See "ghcnd-states.txt" for a list of state/province/territory
              codes.

              The network code  has the following five values:
```

           0 = unspecified (station identified by up to eight
              alphanumeric characters)
       1 = Community Collaborative Rain, Hail,and Snow (CoCoRaHS)
              based identification number. To ensure consistency with
              with GHCN Daily, all numbers in the original CoCoRaHS IDs
              have been left-filled to make them all four digits long.
              In addition, the characters "-" and "_" have been removed
              to ensure that the IDs do not exceed 11 characters when
              preceded by "US1". For example, the CoCoRaHS ID
              "AZ-MR-156" becomes "US1AZMR0156" in GHCN-Daily
       C = U.S. Cooperative Network identification number (last six
              characters of the GHCN-Daily ID)
       E = Identification number used in the ECA&D non-blended
              dataset
       M = World Meteorological Organization ID (last five
              characters of the GHCN-Daily ID)
       N = Identification number used in data supplied by a
              National Meteorological or Hydrological Center
       R = U.S. Interagency Remote Automatic Weather Station (RAWS)
              identifier
       S = U.S. Natural Resources Conservation Service SNOwpack
              TELemtry (SNOTEL) station identifier
              W = WBAN identification number (last five characters of the
              GHCN-Daily ID)

LATITUDE   is latitude of the station (in decimal degrees).

LONGITUDE   is the longitude of the station (in decimal degrees).

ELEVATION   is the elevation of the station (in meters, missing = -999.9).

STATE   is the U.S. postal code for the state (for U.S. stations only).

NAME   is the name of the station.
GSN FLAG   is a flag that indicates whether the station is part of the GCOS
            Surface Network (GSN). The flag is assigned by cross-referencing
            the number in the WMOID field with the official list of GSN
            stations. There are two possible values:

            Blank = non-GSN station or WMO Station number not available
            GSN   = GSN station

HCN/   is a flag that indicates whether the station is part of the U.S.
CRN FLAG   Historical Climatology Network (HCN). There are three possible
            values:

            Blank = Not a member of the U.S. Historical Climatology
               or U.S. Climate Reference Networks
            HCN = U.S. Historical Climatology Network station
            CRN = U.S. Climate Reference Network or U.S. Regional Climate
               Network Station

WMO ID   is the World Meteorological Organization (WMO) number for the
            station. If the station has no WMO number (or one has not yet
            been matched to this station), then the field is blank.

Although you might care more about the metadata fields for more serious research, right now you want to match the start and end year from the inventory records to the rest of the station metadata in the stations file.

You have several ways to sift through the stations file to find the one station that matches the station ID you selected. You could create a `for` loop to go through each line and break out when you find it; you could split the data into lines and then sort and use a binary search; and so on. Depending on the nature and amount of data you have, one approach or another might be appropriate. In this case, because you have the data loaded already, and it's not too large, use a list comprehension to return a list with its single element being the station you're looking for:

```python
station_id = 'USC00110338'

# parse stations
Station = namedtuple("Station", ['station_id', 'latitude', 'longitude',
                     'elevation', 'state', 'name', 'start', 'end'])

stations = [(x[0:11], float(x[12:20]), float(x[21:30]), float(x[31:37]),
    x[38:40].strip(), x[41:71].strip())
            for x in stations_txt.split("\n") if x.startswith(station_id)]

station = Station(*stations[0] + (inventory_temps[0].start,
                  inventory_temps[0].end))
print(station)

Station(station_id='USC00110338', latitude=41.7803, longitude=-88.3092,
elevation=205.7, state='IL', name='AURORA WATER', start=1915, end=2024)
```

At this point, you've identified that you want weather data from the station at Aurora, Illinois, which is the nearest station to downtown Chicago with more than a century's worth of temperature data.

Fetching and parsing the actual weather data

With the station identified, the next step is fetching the actual weather data for that station and parsing it. The process is quite similar to what you did in the preceding section.

Fetching the data

First, fetch the data file and save it, in case you need to go back to it:

```python
# fetch daily records for selected station

r = requests.get('https://www1.ncdc.noaa.gov/pub/data/ghcn/daily/all/{}.dly'
➥.format(station.station_id))
weather = r.text

# save into a text file, so we won't need to fetch again

with open('weather_{}.txt'.format(station), "w") as weather_file:
```

```
    weather_file.write(weather)

# read from saved daily file if needed (only used if we want to start the
  process over without downloadng the file)

with open('weather_{}.txt'.format(station)) as weather_file:
    weather = weather_file.read()

print(weather[:540])
```

```
USC00110338189301TMAX  -11  6  -44  6 -139  6  -83  6 -100  6  -83  6  -72
    6   -83  6  -33  6 -178  6 -150  6 -128  6 -172  6 -200  6 -189  6 -150
    6  -106  6  -61  6  -94  6  -33  6  -33  6  -33  6  -33  6    6  6  -33
    6   -78  6  -33  6   44  6  -89 I6  -22  6    6  6
USC00110338189301TMIN  -50  6 -139  6 -250  6 -144  6 -178  6 -228  6 -144
    6  -222  6 -178  6 -250  6 -200  6 -206  6 -267  6 -272  6 -294  6 -294
    6  -311  6 -200  6 -233  6 -178  6 -156  6  -89  6 -200  6 -194  6 -194
    6  -178  6 -200  6  -33 I6 -156  6 -139  6 -167  6
```

Parsing the weather data

Again, now that you have the data, you can see it's quite a bit more complex than the
station and inventory data. Clearly, it's time to head back to the readme.txt file and
section III, which is the description of a weather data file. You have a lot of options,
so filter them down to the ones that concern you; leave out the other element types as
well as the whole system of flags specifying the source, quality, and type of the values:

```
III. FORMAT OF DATA FILES (".dly" FILES)

Each ".dly" file contains data for one station.  The name of the file
corresponds to a station's identification code.  For example,
  "USC00026481.dly"
contains the data for the station with the identification code
  USC00026481).

Each record in a file contains one month of daily data.  The variables on each
line include the following:
```

Variable	Columns	Type
ID	1-11	Character
YEAR	12-15	Integer
MONTH	16-17	Integer
ELEMENT	18-21	Character
VALUE1	22-26	Integer
MFLAG1	27-27	Character
QFLAG1	28-28	Character
SFLAG1	29-29	Character
VALUE2	30-34	Integer
MFLAG2	35-35	Character
QFLAG2	36-36	Character
SFLAG2	37-37	Character

```
    .            .              .
    .            .              .
    .            .              .
VALUE31     262-266     Integer
MFLAG31     267-267     Character
QFLAG31     268-268     Character
SFLAG31     269-269     Character
----------------------------
```

These variables have the following definitions:

ID   is the station identification code. Please see "ghcnd-
⮑stations.txt"
            for a complete list of stations and their metadata.
YEAR   is the year of the record.

MONTH   is the month of the record.

ELEMENT   is the element type.   There are five core elements as well as a
            number
 of addition elements.

      The five core elements are:

          PRCP = Precipitation (tenths of mm)
          SNOW = Snowfall (mm)
          SNWD = Snow depth (mm)
          TMAX = Maximum temperature (tenths of degrees C)
          TMIN = Minimum temperature (tenths of degrees C)

...

VALUE1   is the value on the first day of the month (missing = -9999).

MFLAG1   is the measurement flag for the first day of the month.

QFLAG1   is the quality flag for the first day of the month.

SFLAG1   is the source flag for the first day of the month.

VALUE2   is the value on the second day of the month

MFLAG2   is the measurement flag for the second day of the month.

QFLAG2   is the quality flag for the second day of the month.

SFLAG2   is the source flag for the second day of the month.

... and so on through the 31st day of the month. Note: If the month has less
than 31 days, then the remaining variables are set to missing (e.g., for
⮑April,
VALUE31 = -9999, MFLAG31 = blank, QFLAG31 = blank, SFLAG31 = blank).
```

The key points you care about right now are that the station ID is the 11 characters of a row; the year is the next 4, the month the next 2, and the element the next 4 after that.
```

After that, there are 31 slots for daily data, with each slot consisting of 5 characters for the temperature, expressed in tenths of a degree Celsius, and 3 characters of flags. As I mentioned earlier, you can disregard the flags for this exercise. You can also see that missing values for the temperatures are coded with –9999 if that day isn't in the month, so for a typical February, for example, the 29th, 30th, and 31st values would be –9999.

As you process your data in this exercise, you're looking to get overall trends, so you don't need to worry much about individual days. Instead, find average values for the month. You can save the maximum, minimum, and mean values for the entire month and use those.

This means that to process each line of weather data, you need to

1 Split the line into its separate fields and ignore or discard the flags for each daily value.

2 Remove the values with –9999, and convert the year and month into ints and the temperature values into floats, keeping in mind that the temperature readings are in tenths of degrees centigrade.

3 Calculate the average value, and pick out the high and low values.

To accomplish all these tasks, you can take a couple of approaches. You could do several passes over the data, splitting into fields, discarding the placeholders, converting strings to numbers, and, finally, calculating the summary values. Or you can write a function that performs all of these operations on a single line and do everything in one pass. Both approaches can be valid. In this case, take the latter approach and create a `parse_line` function to perform all of your data transformations:

```
def parse_line(line):
    """ parses line of weather data
        removes values of -9999 (missing value)
    """

    # return None if line is empty
    if not line:
        return None

    # split out first 4 fields and string containing temperature values
    record, temperature_string = (line[:11], int(line[11:15]),
                               int(line[15:17]), line[17:21], line[21:]

    # raise exception if the temperature string is too short
    if len(temperature_string) < 248:
        raise ValueError("String not long enough - {} {}".format(temperature_
string, str(line)))

    # use a list comprehension on the temperature_string to extract and
convert the
    values = [float(temperature_string[i:i + 5])/10 for i in range(0, 248, 8)
             if not temperature_string[i:i + 5].startswith("-9999")]

    # get the number of values, the max and min, and calculate average
```

```
    count = len(values)
    tmax = round(max(values), 1)
    tmin = round(min(values), 1)
    mean = round(sum(values)/count, 1)

    # add the temperature summary values to the record fields extracted
earlier and return
    return record + (tmax, tmin, mean, count)
```

If you test this function with the first line of your raw weather data, you get the following result:

```
parse_line(weather[:270])
```

```
('USC00110338', 1893, 1, 'TMAX', 4.4, -20.0, -7.8, 31)
```

So it looks like you have a function that will work to parse your data. If that function works, you can parse the weather data and either store it or continue with your processing:

```
# process all weather data

# list comprehension, will not parse empty lines
weather_data = [parse_line(x) for x in weather.split("\n") if x]
```

```
len(weather_data)
```

```
weather_data[:10]
```

```
[('USC00110338', 1893, 1, 'TMAX', 4.4, -20.0, -7.8, 31),
 ('USC00110338', 1893, 1, 'TMIN', -3.3, -31.1, -19.2, 31),
 ('USC00110338', 1893, 1, 'PRCP', 8.9, 0.0, 1.1, 31),
 ('USC00110338', 1893, 1, 'SNOW', 10.2, 0.0, 1.0, 31),
 ('USC00110338', 1893, 1, 'WT16', 0.1, 0.1, 0.1, 2),
 ('USC00110338', 1893, 1, 'WT18', 0.1, 0.1, 0.1, 11),
 ('USC00110338', 1893, 2, 'TMAX', 5.6, -17.2, -0.9, 27),
 ('USC00110338', 1893, 2, 'TMIN', 0.6, -26.1, -11.7, 27),
 ('USC00110338', 1893, 2, 'PRCP', 15.0, 0.0, 2.0, 28),
 ('USC00110338', 1893, 2, 'SNOW', 12.7, 0.0, 0.6, 28)]
```

Now you have all the weather records, not just the temperature records, parsed and in your list.

Saving the weather data in a database (optional)

At this point, you can save all of the weather records (and the station records and inventory records as well if you want) in a database. Doing so lets you come back in later sessions and use the same data without having to go to the hassle of fetching and parsing the data again.

As an example, the following code is how you could save the weather data in a sqlite3 database:

```
import sqlite3

conn = sqlite3.connect("weather_data.db")
cursor = conn.cursor()

# create weather table

create_weather = """CREATE TABLE "weather" (
    "id" text NOT NULL,
    "year" integer NOT NULL,
    "month" integer NOT NULL,
    "element" text NOT NULL,
    "max" real,
    "min" real,
    "mean" real,
    "count" integer)"""
cursor.execute(create_weather)
conn.commit()

# store parsed weather data in database

for record in weather_data:
    cursor.execute("""insert into weather (id, year, month, element, max,
min, mean, count) values (?,?,?,?,?,?,?,?) """,
                        record)

conn.commit()
```

When you have the data stored, you could retrieve it from the database with code like the following, which fetches only the TMAX records:

```
cursor.execute("""select * from weather where element='TMAX' order by year
    month""")
tmax_data = cursor.fetchall()
tmax_data[:5]

[('USC00110338', 1893, 1, 'TMAX', 4.4, -20.0, -7.8, 31),
 ('USC00110338', 1893, 2, 'TMAX', 5.6, -17.2, -0.9, 27),
 ('USC00110338', 1893, 3, 'TMAX', 20.6, -7.2, 5.6, 30),
 ('USC00110338', 1893, 4, 'TMAX', 28.9, 3.3, 13.5, 30),
 ('USC00110338', 1893, 5, 'TMAX', 30.6, 7.2, 19.2, 31)]
```

Selecting and graphing data

Because you're concerned only with temperature, you need to select just the temperature records. You can do that quickly enough by using a couple of list comprehensions to pick out a list for TMAX and one for TMIN. Or you could use the features of pandas, which you'll be using for graphing the data, to filter out the records you don't want. Because you're more concerned with pure Python than with pandas, take the first approach:

```
tmax_data = [x for x in weather_data if x[3] == 'TMAX']
tmin_data = [x for x in weather_data if x[3] == 'TMIN']
```

```
tmin_data[:5]
```

```
[('USC00110338', 1893, 1, 'TMIN', -3.3, -31.1, -19.2, 31),
 ('USC00110338', 1893, 2, 'TMIN', 0.6, -26.1, -11.7, 27),
 ('USC00110338', 1893, 3, 'TMIN', 3.3, -13.3, -4.6, 31),
 ('USC00110338', 1893, 4, 'TMIN', 12.2, -5.6, 2.2, 30),
 ('USC00110338', 1893, 5, 'TMIN', 14.4, -0.6, 5.7, 31)]
```

Using pandas to graph your data

At this point, you have your data cleaned and ready to graph. To make the graphing easier, you can use pandas and `matplotlib`, as described in chapter 24. If you are using Colaboratory, both are already installed and available. If you are using another environment, you could install them with the following commands at the command line:

```
pip install pandas matplotlib
```

To use pandas, we can import it as usual, but to use `matplotlib` in Colaboratory, we can just use the Jupyter "magic" command to make it available:

```
import pandas as pd
%matplotlib inline        ◄────┘ Magic command to activate matplotib
```

Then you can load pandas and create data frames for your TMAX and TMIN data:

```
tmax_df = pd.DataFrame(tmax_data, columns=['Station', 'Year', 'Month',
'Element', 'Max', 'Min', 'Mean', 'Days'])
tmin_df = pd.DataFrame(tmin_data, columns=['Station', 'Year', 'Month',
'Element', 'Max', 'Min', 'Mean', 'Days'])
```

You could plot the monthly values, but 125 years times 12 months of data is 1,500 data points, and the cycle of seasons also makes picking out patterns difficult.

Instead, it probably makes more sense to average the high, low, and mean monthly values into yearly values and plot those values. You could do this in Python, but because you already have your data loaded in a pandas data frame, you can use that to group by year and get the mean values:

```
# select Year, Min, Max, Mean columns, group by year, average and line plot

tmin_df[['Year','Min', 'Mean', 'Max']].groupby('Year').mean().plot(
                              kind='line', figsize=(16, 8))
```

This result has a fair amount of variation, but it does seem to indicate that the minimum temperature has been on the rise for the past 20 years.

Note that if you wanted to get the same graph without using Jupyter notebook and `matplotlib`, you could use still use pandas, but you'd write to a CSV or Microsoft Excel file, using the data frame's `to_csv` or `to_excel` method. Then you could load the resulting file into a spreadsheet and graph from there.

appendix
A guide to Python's
documentation

The best and most current reference for Python is the documentation that comes with Python itself. With that in mind, it's more useful to explore the ways you can access that documentation than to print pages of edited documentation.

The standard bundle of documentation has several sections, including instructions on documenting, distributing, installing, and extending Python on various platforms, and is the logical starting point when you're looking for answers to questions about Python. The two main areas of the Python documentation that are likely to be the most useful are the "Library Reference" and the "Language Reference." The "Library Reference" is absolutely essential because it has explanations of both the built-in data types and every module included with Python. The "Language Reference" is the explanation of how the core of Python works, and it contains the official word on the core of the language, explaining the workings of data types, statements, and so on. The "What's New" section is also worth reading, particularly when a new version of Python is released, because it summarizes all of the changes in the new version.

A.1   *Accessing Python documentation on the web*

For many people, the most convenient way to access the Python documentation is to go to docs.python.org and browse the documentation collection there. Although doing so requires a connection to the web, it has the advantage that the docs for the most current version are available, as well as the docs for all previous versions. Given that, for many projects, it's often useful to search the web for other documentation and information, having a browser tab permanently open and pointing to the online Python documentation is an easy way to have a Python reference at your fingertips.

If you want the Python documentation saved locally on a computer, tablet, or e-book reader, you can also download the complete documentation from docs.python.org in PDF, HTML plain text. Texinfo, and EPUB formats.

A.2   Best practices: How to become a Pythonista

Every programming language develops its own traditions and culture, and Python is a strong example. Most experienced Python programmers (*Pythonistas*, as they're sometimes called) care a great deal about writing Python in a way that matches the style and best practices of Python. This type of code is commonly called *Pythonic* code and is valued highly, as opposed to Python code that looks like Java, C, or JavaScript.

The challenge that coders new to Python face is how to learn to write Pythonic code. Although getting a feel for the language and its style takes a little time and effort, the rest of this appendix gives you some suggestions on how to start.

A.2.1   Ten tips for becoming a Pythonista

The tips in this section are ones that I share with intermediate Python classes and are my suggestions for leveling up your Python skills. I'm not saying that everyone absolutely agrees with me, but from what I've seen over the years, these tips will put you soundly on the path to being a true Pythonista:

- *Consider The Zen of Python.* "The Zen of Python," or Python Enhancement Proposal (PEP) 20, sums up the design philosophy underlying Python as a language and is commonly invoked in discussions of what makes scripts more Pythonic. In particular, "Beautiful is better than ugly" and "Simple is better than complex" should guide your coding. I've included "The Zen of Python" at the end of this appendix; you can always find it by typing `import this` at a Python shell prompt.

- *Follow PEP 8.* PEP 8 is the official Python style guide, which is also included later in this appendix. PEP 8 offers good advice on everything from code formatting and variable naming to the use of the language. If you want to write Pythonic code, become familiar with PEP 8.

- *Be familiar with the docs.* Python has a rich, well-maintained collection of documentation, and you should refer to it often. The most useful documents probably are the standard library documentation, but the tutorials and how-to files are also rich veins of information on using the language effectively.

- *Write as little code as you can as much as you can.* Although this advice might apply to many languages, it fits Python particularly well. What I mean is that you should strive to make your programs as short and as simple as possible (but no shorter and no simpler) and that you should practice that style of coding as much as you can.

- *Read as much code as you can.* From the beginning, the Python community has been aware that reading code is more important than writing code. Read as much Python code as you can, and if possible, discuss the code that you read with others.

- *Use the built-in data structures over all else.* You should turn first to Python's built-in structures before writing your own classes to hold data. Python's various data types can be combined with nearly unlimited flexibility and have the advantage of years of debugging and optimization. Take advantage of them.

- *Dwell on generators and comprehensions.* Coders who are new to Python almost always fail to appreciate how much list and dictionary comprehensions and generator expressions are a part of Pythonic coding. Look at examples in the Python code that you read, and practice them. You won't be a Pythonista until you can write a list comprehension almost without thinking.

- *Use the standard library.* When the built-ins fail you, look next to the standard library. The elements in the standard library are the famed "batteries included" of Python. They've stood the test of time and have been optimized and documented better than almost any other Python code. Use them if you can.

- *Write as few classes as you can.* Write your own classes only if you must. Experienced Pythonistas tend to be very economical with classes, knowing that designing good classes isn't trivial and that any classes they create are also classes that they have to test and debug.

- *Be wary of frameworks.* Frameworks can be attractive, particularly to coders new to the language, because they offer so many powerful shortcuts. You should use frameworks when they're helpful, of course, but be aware of their downsides. You may spend more time learning the quirks of an un-Pythonic framework than learning Python itself, or you may find yourself adapting what you do to the framework rather than the other way around.

A.3 PEP 8: Style guide for Python code

This section contains a slightly edited excerpt from PEP 8. Written by Guido van Rossum and Barry Warsaw, PEP 8 is the closest thing Python has to a style manual. Some more-specific sections have been omitted, but the main points are covered. You should make your code conform to PEP 8 as much as possible; your Python style will be the better for it.

You can access the full text of PEP 8 and all of the other PEPs put forth in the history of Python by going to the documentation section of peps.python.org and looking at the PEP index. The PEPs are excellent sources for the history and lore of Python as well as explanations of current concerns and future plans.

A.3.1 Introduction

This document gives coding conventions for the Python code comprising the standard library in the main Python distribution. Please see the companion informational PEP describing style guidelines for the C code in the C implementation of Python.[1] This document was adapted from Guido's original "Python Style Guide" essay, with some additions from Barry's style guide.[2] Where there's conflict, Guido's style rules for the purposes of this PEP. This PEP may still be incomplete (in fact, it may never be finished <wink>).

A FOOLISH CONSISTENCY IS THE HOBGOBLIN OF LITTLE MINDS

One of Guido's key insights is that code is read much more often than it's written. The guidelines provided here are intended to improve the readability of code and make it consistent across the wide spectrum of Python code. As PEP 20 says, "Readability counts."[3]

A style guide is about consistency. Consistency with this style guide is important; consistency within a project is more important; consistency within one module or function is even more important.

But the most important thing is to know when to be inconsistent—sometimes the style guide just doesn't apply. When in doubt, use your best judgment. Look at other examples and decide what looks best. And don't hesitate to ask!

The following are two good reasons to break a particular rule:

- When applying the rule would make the code less readable, even for someone who is used to reading code that follows the rules
- To be consistent with surrounding code that also breaks it (maybe for historic reasons), although this is also an opportunity to clean up someone else's mess (in true XP style)

A.3.2   *Code layout*

INDENTATION

Use four spaces per indentation level.

For really old code that you don't want to mess up, you can continue to use eight-space tabs.

TABS OR SPACES?

Never mix tabs and spaces.

The most popular way of indenting Python is with spaces only. The second most popular way is with tabs only. Code indented with a mixture of tabs and spaces should be converted to using spaces exclusively. When you invoke the Python command-line interpreter with the -t option, it puts forth warnings about code that illegally mixes tabs and spaces. When you use -tt, these warnings become errors. These options are highly recommended!

---

[1] PEP 7, "Style Guide for C Code," van Rossum, https://www.python.org/dev/peps/pep-0007/.
[2] Barry Warsaw's "GNU Mailman Coding Style Guide," http://barry.warsaw.us/software/STYLEGUIDE.txt. The URL is empty although it is presented in the PEP 8 style guide.
[3] PEP 20, "The Zen of Python," www.python.org/dev/peps/pep-0020/.

For new projects, spaces only are strongly recommended over tabs. Most editors have features that make this easy to do.

MAXIMUM LINE LENGTH

Limit all lines to a maximum of 79 characters.

Many devices are still around that are limited to 80-character lines; plus, limiting windows to 80 characters makes it possible to have several windows side by side. The default wrapping on such devices disrupts the visual structure of the code, making it more difficult to understand. Therefore, please limit all lines to a maximum of 79 characters. For flowing long blocks of text (docstrings or comments), limiting the length to 72 characters is recommended.

The preferred way of wrapping long lines is by using Python's implied line continuation inside parentheses, brackets, and braces. If necessary, you can add an extra pair of parentheses around an expression, but sometimes using a backslash looks better. Make sure to indent the continued line appropriately. The preferred place to break around a binary operator is *after* the operator, not before it. The following are some examples:

```
class Rectangle(Blob):
    def __init__(self, width, height,
                 color='black', emphasis=None, highlight=0):
        if width == 0 and height == 0 and \
           color == 'red' and emphasis == 'strong' or \
           highlight > 100:
            raise ValueError("sorry, you lose")
        if width == 0 and height == 0 and (color == 'red' or
                                           emphasis is None):
            raise ValueError("I don't think so -- values are %s, %s" %
                             (width, height))
        Blob.__init__(self, width, height,
                      color, emphasis, highlight)
```

BLANK LINES

Separate top-level function and class definitions with two blank lines. Method definitions inside a class are separated by a single blank line. Extra blank lines may be used (sparingly) to separate groups of related functions. Blank lines may be omitted between a bunch of related one-liners (for example, a set of dummy implementations). Use blank lines in functions, sparingly, to indicate logical sections.

Python accepts the Ctrl-L (^L) form feed character as whitespace. Many tools treat these characters as page separators, so you may use them to separate pages of related sections of your file.

IMPORTS

Imports should usually be on separate lines—for example:

```
import os
import sys
```

Don't put them together like this:

```
import sys, os
```

It's okay to say this, though:

```
from subprocess import Popen, PIPE
```

Imports are always put at the top of the file, just after any module comments and doc-strings and before module globals and constants.

Imports should be grouped in the following order:

1 Standard library imports

2 Related third-party imports

3 Local application/library–specific imports

Put a blank line between each group of imports. Put any relevant __all__ specifications after the imports.

Relative imports for intrapackage imports are highly discouraged. Always use the absolute package path for all imports. Even now that PEP 328[4] is fully implemented in Python 2.5, its style of explicit relative imports is actively discouraged; absolute imports are more portable and usually more readable.

When importing a class from a class-containing module, it's usually okay to spell them as follows:

```
from myclass import MyClass
from foo.bar.yourclass import YourClass
```

If this spelling causes local name clashes, then spell them as follows:

```
import myclass
import foo.bar.yourclass
and use myclass.MyClass and foo.bar.yourclass.YourClass.
```

WHITESPACE IN EXPRESSIONS AND STATEMENTS

Here are some of my pet peeves. Avoid extraneous whitespace in the following situations:

- Immediately inside parentheses, brackets, or braces
  Yes:

  ```
  spam(ham[1], {eggs: 2})
  ```

  No:

  ```
  spam( ham[ 1 ], { eggs: 2 } )
  ```

---

[4] PEP 328, "Imports: Multi-Line and Absolute/Relative," www.python.org/dev/peps/pep-0328/.

- Immediately before a comma, semicolon, or colon
  Yes:

```
if x == 4: print x, y; x, y = y, x
```

  No:

```
if x == 4 : print x , y ; x , y = y , x
```

- Immediately before the open parenthesis that starts the argument list of a function call
  Yes:

```
spam(1)
```

  No:

```
spam (1)
```

- Immediately before the open parenthesis that starts an indexing or slicing
  Yes:

```
dict['key'] = list[index]
```

  No:

```
dict ['key'] = list [index]
```

- More than one space around an assignment (or other) operator to align it with another
  Yes:

```
x = 1
y = 2
long_variable = 3
```

  No:

```
x             = 1
y             = 2
long_variable = 3
```

OTHER RECOMMENDATIONS

Always surround these binary operators with a single space on either side: assignment (=), augmented assignment (+=, -=, and so on), comparisons (==, <, >, !=, <>, <=, >=, in, not in, is, is not), and Booleans (and, or, not).

Use spaces around arithmetic operators.
Yes:

```
i = i + 1
submitted += 1

x = x * 2 - 1
hypot2 = x * x + y * y
c = (a + b) * (a - b)
```

No:

```
i=i+1
submitted +=1
x = x*2 - 1
hypot2 = x*x + y*y
c = (a+b) * (a-b)
```

Don't use spaces around the = sign when used to indicate a keyword argument or a default parameter value.
Yes:

```
def complex(real, imag=0.0):
    return magic(r=real, i=imag)
```

No:

```
def complex(real, imag = 0.0):
    return magic(r = real, i = imag)
```

Compound statements (multiple statements on the same line) are generally discouraged.
Yes:

```
if foo == 'blah':
    do_blah_thing()
do_one()
do_two()
do_three()
```

Rather not:

```
if foo == 'blah': do_blah_thing()
do_one(); do_two(); do_three()
```

While sometimes it's okay to put an if/for/while with a small body on the same line, never do this for multiclause statements. Also avoid folding such long lines!
Rather not:

```
if foo == 'blah': do_blah_thing()
for x in lst: total += x
    while t < 10: t = delay()
```

No:

```
if foo == 'blah': do_blah_thing()
else: do_non_blah_thing()
try: something()
finally: cleanup()
do_one(); do_two(); do_three(long, argument,
                            list, like, this)
if foo == 'blah': one(); two(); three()
```

A.4 Comments

Comments that contradict the code are worse than no comments. Always make a priority of keeping the comments up to date when the code changes!

Comments should be complete sentences. If a comment is a phrase or sentence, its first word should be capitalized, unless it's an identifier that begins with a lowercase letter (never alter the case of identifiers!).

If a comment is short, the period at the end can be omitted. Block comments generally consist of one or more paragraphs built out of complete sentences, and each sentence should end in a period. Use two spaces after a sentence-ending period. When writing English, Strunk & White applies.

If you are a Python coder from a non-English-speaking country, you should write your comments in English, unless you are 120% sure that the code will never be read by people who don't speak your language.

BLOCK COMMENTS

Block comments generally apply to some (or all) code that follows them and are indented to the same level as that code. Each line of a block comment starts with a # and a single space (unless it is indented text inside the comment).

Paragraphs inside a block comment are separated by a line containing a single # .

INLINE COMMENTS

Use inline comments sparingly. An inline comment is a comment on the same line as a statement. Inline comments should be separated by at least two spaces from the statement. They should start with a # and a single space.

Inline comments are unnecessary and in fact distracting if they state the obvious. Don't do this:

```
x = x + 1                 # Increment x
```

But sometimes, this is useful:

```
x = x + 1                 # Compensate for border
```

DOCUMENTATION STRINGS

Conventions for writing good documentation strings (docstrings) are immortalized in PEP 257.[5]

Write docstrings for all public modules, functions, classes, and methods. Docstrings are not necessary for nonpublic methods, but you should have a comment that describes what the method does. This comment should appear after the `def` line.

PEP 257 describes good docstring conventions. Note that, most importantly, the `"""` that ends a multiline docstring should be on a line by itself and preferably preceded by a blank line—for example:

```
"""Return a foobang
Optional plotz says to frobnicate the bizbaz first.

"""
```

For one-liner docstrings, it's okay to keep the closing `"""` on the same line.

VERSION BOOKKEEPING

If you have to have Subversion, CVS, or RCS crud in your source file, do it as follows:

```
__version__ = "$Revision: 68852 $"      # $Source$
```

These lines should be included after the module's docstring, before any other code, separated by a blank line above and below.

A.4.1   *Naming conventions*

The naming conventions of Python's library are a bit of a mess, so we'll never get this completely consistent. Nevertheless, the following are the currently recommended naming standards. New modules and packages (including third-party frameworks) should be written to these standards, but where an existing library has a different style, internal consistency is preferred.

DESCRIPTIVE: NAMING STYLES

There are many different naming styles. It helps to be able to recognize what naming style is being used, independent of what it's used for.

The following naming styles are commonly distinguished:

- b (single lowercase letter)
- B (single uppercase letter)
- lowercase
- lower_case_with_underscores
- UPPERCASE
- UPPER_CASE_WITH_UNDERSCORES

---

[5]   PEP 257, "Docstring Conventions," Goodger and van Rossum, www.python.org/dev/peps/pep-0257/.

- CapitalizedWords (or CapWords, or CamelCase—so named because of the bumpy look of its letters). This is also sometimes known as StudlyCaps.
- Note: When using abbreviations in CapWords, capitalize all the letters of the abbreviation. Thus `HTTPServerError` is better than `HttpServerError`.
- mixedCase (differs from CapitalizedWords by initial lowercase character!)
- Capitalized_Words_With_Underscores (ugly!)

There's also the style of using a short unique prefix to group related names together. This is seldom used in Python, but I mention it for completeness. For example, the `os.stat()` function returns a tuple whose items traditionally have names like `st_mode`, `st_size`, `st_mtime`, and so on. (This is done to emphasize the correspondence with the fields of the POSIX system call struct, which helps programmers familiar with that.)

The X11 library uses a leading X for all its public functions. In Python, this style is generally deemed unnecessary because attribute and method names are prefixed with an object, and function names are prefixed with a module name.

In addition, the following special forms using leading or trailing underscores are recognized (these can generally be combined with any case convention):

- _single_leading_underscore

  Weak "internal use" indicator. For example, `from M import *` does not import objects whose name starts with an underscore.

- single_trailing_underscore_

  Used by convention to avoid conflicts with Python keyword—for example:

  ```
  tkinter.Toplevel(master, class_='ClassName').
  ```

- __double_leading_underscore

  When naming a class attribute, it invokes name mangling (inside class `FooBar`, `__boo` becomes `_FooBar__boo`; see later discussion).

- __double_leading_and_trailing_underscore__

  "Magic" objects or attributes that live in user-controlled namespaces. For example, `__init__`, `__import__` or `__file__`. Never invent such names; use them only as documented.

PRESCRIPTIVE: NAMING CONVENTIONS

- Names to avoid

  Never use the characters *l* (lowercase letter el), *O* (uppercase letter oh), or *I* (uppercase letter eye) as single-character variable names.

  In some fonts, these characters are indistinguishable from the numerals 1 (one) and 0 (zero). When tempted to use *l*, use *L* instead.

- Package and module names

Modules should have short, all-lowercase names. Underscores can be used in a module name if it improves readability. Python packages should also have short, all-lowercase names, although the use of underscores is discouraged.

Since module names are mapped to filenames, and some filesystems are case insensitive and truncate long names, it's important that module names be fairly short—this won't be a problem on UNIX, but it may be a problem when the code is transported to older Mac or Windows versions or DOS.

When an extension module written in C or C++ has an accompanying Python module that provides a higher-level (for example, more object-oriented) interface, the C/C++ module has a leading underscore (for example, `_socket`).

- Class names

  Almost without exception, class names use the CapWords convention. Classes for internal use have a leading underscore in addition.

- Exception names

  Because exceptions should be classes, the class-naming convention applies here. However, you should use the suffix `Error` on your exception names (if the exception actually is an error).

- Global variable names

  (Let's hope that these variables are meant for use inside one module only.) The conventions are about the same as those for functions.

  Modules that are designed for use via `from M import *` should use the `__all__` mechanism to prevent exporting globals or use the older convention of prefixing such globals with an underscore (which you might want to do to indicate these globals are module nonpublic).

- Function names

  Function names should be lowercase, with words separated by underscores as necessary to improve readability.

  mixedCase is allowed only in contexts where that's already the prevailing style (for example, threading.py), to retain backward compatibility.

- Function and method arguments

  Always use `self` for the first argument to instance methods.

  Always use `cls` for the first argument to class methods.

  If a function argument's name clashes with a reserved keyword, it's generally better to append a single trailing underscore than to use an abbreviation or spelling corruption. Thus, `print_` is better than `prnt`. (Perhaps better is to avoid such clashes by using a synonym.)

- Method names and instance variables

  Use the function-naming rules: lowercase with words separated by underscores as necessary to improve readability.

  Use one leading underscore only for nonpublic methods and instance variables.

To avoid name clashes with subclasses, use two leading underscores to invoke Python's name-mangling rules.

Python mangles these names with the class name: if class `Foo` has an attribute named `__a`, it cannot be accessed by `Foo.__a`. (An insistent user could still gain access by calling `Foo._Foo__a`.) Generally, double leading underscores should be used only to avoid name conflicts with attributes in classes designed to be subclassed.

Note: There is some controversy about the use of `__names`.

- Constants

  Constants are usually declared on a module level and written in all capital letters with underscores separating words. Examples include `MAX_OVERFLOW` and `TOTAL`.

- Designing for inheritance

  Always decide whether a class's methods and instance variables (collectively called attributes) should be public or nonpublic. If in doubt, choose nonpublic; it's easier to make it public later than to make a public attribute nonpublic.

  Public attributes are those that you expect unrelated clients of your class to use, with your commitment to avoid backward-incompatible changes. Nonpublic attributes are those that are not intended to be used by third parties; you make no guarantees that nonpublic attributes won't change or even be removed.

  We don't use the term *private* here, since no attribute is really private in Python (without a generally unnecessary amount of work).

  Another category of attributes includes those that are part of the subclass API (often called *protected* in other languages). Some classes are designed to be inherited from, either to extend or modify aspects of the class's behavior. When designing such a class, take care to make explicit decisions about which attributes are public, which are part of the subclass API, and which are truly only to be used by your base class.

With this in mind, here are the Pythonic guidelines:

- Public attributes should have no leading underscores.

- If your public attribute name collides with a reserved keyword, append a single trailing underscore to your attribute name. This is preferable to an abbreviation or corrupted spelling. (However, notwithstanding this rule, `cls` is the preferred spelling for any variable or argument that's known to be a class, especially the first argument to a class method.)

  Note 1: See the previous argument name recommendation for class methods.

- For simple public data attributes, it's best to expose just the attribute name, without complicated accessor/mutator methods. Keep in mind that Python provides an easy path to future enhancement should you find that a simple data attribute needs to grow functional behavior. In that case, use properties to hide functional implementation behind simple data attribute access syntax.

Note 1: Properties work only on new-style classes.

Note 2: Try to keep the functional behavior side-effect free, although side effects such as caching are generally fine.

Note 3: Avoid using properties for computationally expensive operations; the attribute notation makes the caller believe that access is (relatively) cheap.

- If your class is intended to be subclassed, and you have attributes that you don't want subclasses to use, consider naming them with double leading underscores and no trailing underscores. This invokes Python's name-mangling algorithm, where the name of the class is mangled into the attribute name. This helps avoid attribute name collisions should subclasses inadvertently contain attributes with the same name.

Note 1: Only the simple class name is used in the mangled name, so if a subclass chooses both the same class name and attribute name, you can still get name collisions.

Note 2: Name mangling can make certain uses, such as debugging and `__getattr__()`, less convenient. However, the name-mangling algorithm is well documented and easy to perform manually.

Note 3: Not everyone likes name mangling. Try to balance the need to avoid accidental name clashes with potential use by advanced callers.

A.4.2   *Programming recommendations*

You should write code in a way that does not disadvantage other implementations of Python (PyPy, Jython, IronPython, Pyrex, Psyco, and such).

For example, don't rely on CPython's efficient implementation of in-place string concatenation for statements in the form `a+=b` or `a=a+b`. Those statements run more slowly in Jython. In performance-sensitive parts of the library, you should use the `''.join()` form instead. This will ensure that concatenation occurs in linear time across various implementations.

Comparisons to singletons like `None` should always be done with `is` or `is not`—never the equality operators.

Also, beware of writing `if x` when you really mean `if x is not None`—for example, when testing whether a variable or argument that defaults to `None` was set to some other value. The other value might have a type (such as a container) that could be false in a Boolean context!

Use class-based exceptions. String exceptions in new code are forbidden, because this language feature was removed in Python 2.6.

Modules or packages should define their own domain-specific base exception class, which should be subclassed from the built-in `Exception` class. Always include a class docstring, for example:

```
class MessageError(Exception):
    """Base class for errors in the email package."""
```

Class-naming conventions apply here, although you should add the suffix `Error` to your exception classes if the exception is an error. Nonerror exceptions need no special suffix.

When raising an exception, use `raise ValueError('message')` instead of the older form `raise ValueError, 'message'`.

The parenthetical form is preferred because, when the exception arguments are long or include string formatting, you don't need to use line continuation characters, thanks to the containing parentheses. The older form was removed in Python 3.

When catching exceptions, mention specific exceptions whenever possible instead of using a bare `except:` clause. For example, use

```
try:
    import platform_specific_module
except ImportError:
    platform_specific_module = None
```

A bare `except:` clause will catch `SystemExit` and `KeyboardInterrupt` exceptions, making it harder to interrupt a program with Ctrl-C, and can disguise other problems. If you want to catch all exceptions that signal program errors, use `except Exception:`.

A good rule of thumb is to limit use of bare `except:` clauses to two cases:

- If the exception handler will be printing out or logging the traceback; at least the user will be aware that an error has occurred.
- If the code needs to do some cleanup work but then lets the exception propagate upward with `raise`; then `try...finally` is a better way to handle this case.

In addition, for all `try/except` clauses, limit the `try` clause to the absolute minimum amount of code necessary. Again, this avoids masking bugs.
Yes:

```
try:
    value = collection[key]
except KeyError:
    return key_not_found(key)
else:
    return handle_value(value)
```

No:

```
try:            # Too broad!
    return handle_value(collection[key])
except KeyError:
    return key_not_found(key)
```
Will also catch KeyError raised by handle_value()

Use string methods instead of the string module.

String methods are always much faster and share the same API with Unicode strings. Override this rule if backward compatibility with Python versions older than 2.0 is required.

Use `''.startswith()` and `''.endswith()` instead of string slicing to check for prefixes or suffixes. `startswith()` and `endswith()` are cleaner and less error-prone.
Yes:

```
if foo.startswith('bar'):
```

No:

```
if foo[:3] == 'bar':
```

The exception is if your code must work with Python 1.5.2 (but let's hope not!).

Object type comparisons should always use `isinstance()` instead of comparing types directly.
Yes:

```
if isinstance(obj, int):
```

No:

```
if type(obj) is type(1):
```

When checking to see if an object is a string, keep in mind that it might be a Unicode string too. In Python 2.3, `str` and `unicode` have a common base class, `basestring`, so you can do the following:

```
if isinstance(obj, basestring):
```

In Python 2.2, the `types` module has the `StringTypes` type defined for that purpose—for example:

```
from types import StringTypes
if isinstance(obj, StringTypes):
```

In Python 2.0 and 2.1, you should do the following:

```
from types import StringType, UnicodeType
if isinstance(obj, StringType) or \
    isinstance(obj, UnicodeType) :
```

For sequences (strings, lists, tuples), use the fact that empty sequences are false.
Yes:

```
if not seq:        if seq:
```

No:

```
if len(seq)        if not len(seq)
```

Don't write string literals that rely on significant trailing whitespace. Such trailing whitespace is visually indistinguishable, and some editors (or more recently, `reindent .py`) will trim them.

Don't compare Boolean values to `True` or `False` using `==`.

Yes:

```
if greeting:
```

No:

```
if greeting == True:
```

Worse:

```
if greeting is True:
```

Regarding copyright, note that this document has been placed in the public domain.

A.4.3   Other guides for Python style

Although PEP 8 remains the most influential style guide for Python, you have other options. In general, these guides don't contradict PEP 8, but they offer wider examples and fuller reasoning about how to make your code Pythonic. One good choice is *The Elements of Python Style*, freely available at https://mng.bz/dXlw. Another useful guide is *The Hitchhiker's Guide to Python*, by Kenneth Reitz and Tanya Schlusser, also freely available at https://docs.python-guide.org.

As the language and programmers' skills continue to evolve, there will certainly be other guides, and I encourage you to take advantage of new guides as they're produced, but only after starting with PEP 8.

A.5   The Zen of Python

The following document is PEP 20, also referred to as "The Zen of Python," a slightly tongue-in-cheek statement of the philosophy of Python. In addition to being included in the Python documentation, "The Zen of Python" is an Easter egg in the Python interpreter. Type `import this` at the interactive prompt to see it.

Longtime Pythoneer Tim Peters succinctly channels the BDFL's (Benevolent Dictator for Life) guiding principles for Python's design into 20 aphorisms, only 19 of which have been written down.

The Zen of Python
Beautiful is better than ugly.
Explicit is better than implicit.
Simple is better than complex.
Complex is better than complicated.
Flat is better than nested.

Sparse is better than dense.
Readability counts.
Special cases aren't special enough to break the rules.
Although practicality beats purity.
Errors should never pass silently.
Unless explicitly silenced.
In the face of ambiguity, refuse the temptation to guess.
There should be one—and preferably only one—obvious way to do it.
Although that way may not be obvious at first unless you're Dutch.
Now is better than never.
Although never is often better than *right* now.
If the implementation is hard to explain, it's a bad idea.
If the implementation is easy to explain, it may be a good idea.
Namespaces are one honking great idea—let's do more of those!

index